THE GUINNESS
NON-LEAGUE FOOTBALL
FACT BOOK

THE GUINNESS NON-LEAGUE FOOTBALL
FACT BOOK

Tony Williams

GUINNESS PUBLISHING

Editor: Charles Richards
Text design and layout: Steve Leaning
Cover design: Ad Vantage Studios

Published in Great Britain by Guinness Publishing Ltd,
33 London Road, Enfield, Middlesex

Typeset in Baskerville and Helvetica by
Interface (0395) 68681

Printed and bound in Great Britain by
The Bath Press, Bath

"Guinness" is a registered trademark of
Guinness Publishing Ltd

British Library Cataloguing in Publication Data
Williams, Tony
    The Guinness non-league football fact book
    1. Great Britain. Association football. Non-league
    clubs
    I. Title
    796.334620941

ISBN 0-85112-970-6

Front Cover: Top *Steve O'Brien saves for Hythe
Town in an FA Vase Semi-Final tie with Yeading at
Beaconsfield Road in 1990.*
Middle *Ken Shearwood (5) and captain Dennis
Saunders defend for Pegasus against Harwich &
Parkeston in the 1953 FA Amateur Cup Final.*
Bottom *The beautifully designed Avenue Stadium
at Dorchester was opened in time for the 1990-91
season.*

CONTENTS

HISTORICAL INTRODUCTION

No-one will ever really know where football began!

There were stories of a form of football being played in China long before the Romans brought us their version known as *harpastrum*. There was evidence that the game was used by the Chinese in the third and fourth centuries BC as a form of military training. Mentions of this activity were recorded in *The History of the Han Dynasty* – which spans the period 206 BC to AD 25!

Japan also had a version of a game which required kicking a ball and this was 'played' in an area of roughly 14 square metres. The Italians had their own *Calcio* which survived for many centuries, and here in Britain we have been kicking a 'football' for over 800 years. Early in the 12th century youngsters chased a ball around in many areas of London and there are paintings to record these scenes. Other towns to develop games of their own were Nottingham, Derby, Kingston-on-Thames, Dorking and Ashburton, where the famous Shrove Tuesday inter-village battles took place – our first 'local derbies'!

Many towns and villages adopted their own versions of 'football' and it wasn't until the 1850s that the game was taken from the streets, where the mobs were playing their barbaric versions, by the public schools and universities who attempted to give the game some consistency of rules and respectability. In 1857 the Sheffield Club became the country's first official football club and six years later, with many schools and clubs still enjoying different versions of the game, the Football Association was formed.

The first 21 years of the Football Association's existence and influence was known as 'The Amateur Era'. The members who joined together at the inaugural meeting were repre-

The famous Corinthians, looking very relaxed during their 1906 tour of Canada and The United States.

sentatives of 11 clubs: Barnes, Blackheath, Blackheath Proprietory School, Crusaders, Crystal Palace, Forest-Leytonstone, Kensington School, N.N. (No Names) Kilburn, Perceval House, Blackheath, Surbiton, W.O. (War Office).

The object of the FA was to bring all footballers under one authority playing to one set of rules, and as the Association grew in strength, other county FAs were born. All introduced their own County Cups but no one at that time could have imagined the success in store for the FA Challenge Cup which was introduced in 1871.

As more and more clubs were formed and the desire to do well in the FA Cup became more intense, money was offered 'under the counter' and 'shamateurism' was rife. It was obvious that professionalism had to be accepted and when it came in 1885 a number of the 'old school' just could not accept its successful development throughout the country.

There were continual disagreements over such innovations as penalty kicks (Corinthians considered that no gentleman would deliberately foul, so was the kick really needed?), over professional clubs gaining affiliation with county associations and scratch clubs not registered with the FA being unable to play.

In 1906 there was an official split, with the counties of Surrey and Middlesex breaking away, and a year later The Amateur Football Defence Federation was formed, with whom many of the true blue amateurs preferred to register. Soon the name was changed to The Amateur Football Association, but in 1913 the hatchet was buried and terms of reconciliation were agreed. These existed until 1934, when the FA asked the AFA to change its name to The Amateur Football Alliance. They have since

lived happily ever after, with the FA recognised as the game's national governing body and the AFA having a delegate on the FA council. With professionalism being introduced in 1885, the international matches played earlier would presumably have been contested by amateurs but the first official Amateur International was not until 1909, while the FA Amateur Cup had started in 1893.

The geographical power swing is discussed in another chapter but amateur football had a big following and like every other level of the game, its attendances reached a peak after the Second World War. Then, as clubs became more and more competitive and one or two paid unofficial match fees and bonuses, the star players 'homed in' on the generous clubs and it was obvious that shamateurism, which had forced the introduction of professionalism originally, would now also force the Football Association to legislate for a more honest approach to players outside the Football League. Official semi-professional leagues such as the Southern League weren't too thrilled with players turning their clubs down in favour of 'amateur' clubs – with whom they would receive more money!

So at the end of the 1973-74 season all footballers became just 'players' and if their clubs wished to pay them they could. In fact a player could receive payment one season and not the next; he could sign a contract with a club as a professional and then once again play for fun when that contract expired. This was an altogether more honest and satisfactory system and no doubt one which will soon be accepted by Rugby Union clubs in England!

With all players outside the Football League being able to play in the same competitions, it

wasn't long before the best semi-professional teams formed a supreme competition, called the Alliance. The Southern Premier and Northern Premier Leagues were invited to feed into it, so the rest of the leagues up and down the country had every incentive to join the 'pyramid' and prepare for the day when the Football League would officially invite the Alliance champions to join them on a 'one up and one down' basis.

The last bastion of old amateur clubs, the Isthmian League, was rocked by the loss of Enfield and Dagenham to the Alliance for season 1981-82, but they soon joined 'the family' and in 1985-86 their champions, Sutton United, were the first Isthmians to 'accept' promotion. The great strength of the pyramid was the fact that clubs who qualified for promotion on the field could only move up if their facilities were acceptable to the senior competition, and conversely if a champion club did not wish to move up, they were quite entitled to stay where they were. In this way it was hoped that all clubs would find their correct 'level' eventually.

Since the abolition of 'the amateur' and the consequent loss of the Amateur Cup and Amateur Internationals, the FA Trophy became the undisputed senior knock-out cup for non-league football. It lacked the glamour and tradition of the FA Amateur Cup, but the clubs and players certainly consider a Wembley appearance in a Trophy Final as one of the greatest honours available to them.

Perhaps the only individual achievement to better it is winning an England semi-professional international cap, now that internationals have been arranged at this level. Hopefully a British or even European tournament can be arranged for the non-league clubs who, after all,

Billericay Town caught the imagination of the Essex footballing public as they reached Wembley on three occasions. Their chairman led community singing before home ties, the little club was bursting at the seams as the crowds streamed in, facilities improved and promotion from the Essex Senior League to the Premier Division of the Isthmian League was achieved. Three FA Vase triumphs certainly put Billericay Town on the footballing map.

represent 95% of the players in our national winter sport and deserve to be busier!

One tremendous success story has been the development of the FA Vase, a knock-out competition for the little clubs below the top layers of the pyramid. Many clubs have been inspired to lift their standards after enjoying a little success in this competition as the Vase has introduced them to a new level of awareness that they would never have understood by playing only local league games. The quality of facilities, programmes, entertainment of visitors and actual play, all prove this point.

The game is in a healthy state, and thanks to the link with the Barclays League and the formation of the pyramid, a huge new family of football lovers can be quite satisfied by enjoying their football involvement within these competitions. The very fact that Guinness Publishing have commissioned this book for their prestigious sports list shows how non-league football is now a very popular and well accepted facet of the modern English sporting scene.

I do hope that this book will indeed portray 'the beautiful game' as it is enjoyed by a 'family of football lovers'. If you are already a 'member', you will understand. And, if you're not, then by the time you have finished this book perhaps you will be ready to join us!

Tony Williams
June 1991

THE GROWTH OF NON-LEAGUE FOOTBALL

The Football Association's birth was not an easy one; there were several meetings and many heated arguments in attempting to frame a set of laws that would embrace all clubs the length and breadth of the country, and at their fifth meeting on 1 December 1863, when a proposal to delete Rules 9 and 10 of the Association which allowed body tackling, scrimmages and 'hacking' was carried, the Blackheath club and others who supported the running, handling and hacking resigned from the Association and in 1871 formed the Rugby Union.

In the 21 years from 1864 to 1885 the FA made steady progress towards becoming the vast organization that we know today that governs all grades of football in this country.

On 20 July 1871, in the offices of a London newspaper, members of the FA met to consider a proposal by the Hon. Secretary to introduce a knock-out Cup competition for members of the Association. The proposal was carried and thus was born the FA Challenge Cup, with the Wanderers defeating the Royal Engineers 1-0 at Kennington Oval before a crowd of 2000 to become the first holders of the trophy.

In 1888 the Football League was founded and the following year saw the first four non-league competitions in operation, the Birmingham and District League, Lancashire League, Midland League and Northern League all coming into being in 1889. The formation of the Northern Alliance and The Combination in 1890 was followed by the Lancashire Combination (1891) with the Birmingham Junior League plus the Western and Wearside Leagues commencing operations in 1892. Two years later the Southern and Kent Leagues made their appearance, the United Counties League followed in 1895, with the Hampshire, London and United League affilia-ting in 1896.

By 1906, professional football had become of major importance. 'Big football' had arrived, and although numerically outnumbered by the amateur clubs and players, it was becoming increasingly obvious that it was playing an ever increasing part in the Council chamber.

Second only to the FA Cup, the FA Amateur Cup was contested for a total of 71 seasons, and in many ways it is sad that this most prestigious competition no longer exists. Ilford, a club no longer in being whose history went back to 1881, took part in the original competition in 1893-94, when it was won by Old Carthusians, and in the very last final at Wembley in 1973-74, when they were beaten 4-1 by Bishops Stortford. By far the most successful of any club in the Amateur Cup were Bishop Auckland who, appearing in the final on 18 occasions, won the trophy a record 10 times.

FORMATION DATES OF COUNTY FOOTBALL ASSOCIATIONS

THE FOOTBALL ASSOCIATION 1863

BEDFORDSHIRE	1894	HAMPSHIRE	1887	NORTHUMBERLAND	1882
BERKS & BUCKS	1878	HERTFORDSHIRE	1886	NOTTINGHAMSHIRE	1882
BIRMINGHAM	1875	HUNTINGDONSHIRE	1886	OXFORDSHIRE	1884
CAMBRIDGESHIRE	1884	KENT	1881	SHEFFIELD & HALLAM	1867
CHESHIRE	1878	LANCASHIRE	1878	SHROPSHIRE	1877
CORNWALL	1889	LEICESTERSHIRE	1887	STAFFORDSHIRE	1877
CUMBERLAND	1885	LINCOLNSHIRE	1881	SUFFOLK	1885
DERBYSHIRE	1883	LIVERPOOL	1882	SURREY	1877
DEVON	1887	LONDON	1882	SUSSEX	1882
DORSET	1887	MANCHESTER	1884	WALSALL	1878
DURHAM	1883	MIDDLESEX	1883	WESTMORELAND	1897
EAST RIDING	1903	NORFOLK	1881	WEST RIDING	1896
ESSEX	1882	NORTHAMPTONSHIRE	1887	WILTSHIRE	1886
GLOUCESTERSHIRE	1886	NORTH RIDING	1881	WORCESTERSHIRE	1893

Crook Town won the cup in each of the five seasons that they reached the final, Clapton were successful in four out of five final appearances, and Dulwich Hamlet were successful four times as well as appearing in 9 semi-finals, a figure equalled by Clapton, Ilford, Leytonstone and Stockton.

The Vauxhall-Opel League, founded in 1905 as the Isthmian League, has a long and proud history, being probably the best known of all the London amateur leagues. Instigators of its formation were TH Kirkup, Secretary of the London FA, George Clarke, Hon. Treasurer of Ilford,

and Frank Evans, Hon. Secretary of Clapton; and on 8 March 1905 the league was formed with Lord Kinnaird as its President. It commenced with just six clubs, London Caledonians being the first winners and Clapton the runners-up. The league's most successful clubs have been Leytonstone, Wimbledon and Wycombe Wanderers, who have each won the championship on eight occasions. Dulwich Hamlet have enjoyed 71 seasons' membership of the Isthmian League, winning the title four times and finishing second seven times.

The Tyneside League was also formed in 1905, with South Shields Adelaide, the forerunners of the South Shields and Gateshead clubs, winning the title for the first two seasons. This league functioned for 30 seasons, the Second World War bringing it to a close at the end of 1938-39.

A league of considerable importance emerged in the form of the North Eastern League in 1906, which continued to operate until 1958 and again briefly between 1962-64. It was a competition mainly dominated by the reserve teams of the North East's Football League clubs.

To further the interests of those amateur clubs in the south who had not been invited to join the Isthmian League, a new competition called the Spartan League was formed in 1907 including amongst its founder members such well known clubs as Bromley, Dulwich Hamlet, Leytonstone and Nunhead. At the same time, the Southern Amateur League run under the auspices of the AFA commenced playing. The championship in the first four seasons was won by New Crusaders, other prominent clubs being Casuals, Cambridge Town, Ipswich Town and Norsemen. This league still operates three divisions, catering in

the main for the Banks and Old Boys clubs.

The last leagues to be formed before the Great War were the Central Alliance (1911), which played a bigger part in the non-league scene after World War Two, and the Athenian League in 1912, which continued to provide a high standard of football right up to the time that its clubs were absorbed into the Isthmian League in 1984.

Although the majority of leagues recommenced activities after the war, new leagues and competitions began to spring up, the first of these in 1919 being the Cheshire County League, a strong semi-professional competition that continued until 1982 when it amalgamated with the Lancashire Combination to form the North-West Counties League.

Next on the scene came another league of considerable substance, the Yorkshire League, a competition that embraced Miners Welfare and Works clubs as well as the reserve and 'A' teams of the local Football League clubs.

In 1922 today's Combined Counties League was founded as the Surrey Senior League and in the same year came the South Midlands League, then known as the Bedfordshire County League, which in its first season had Waterlows (Dunstable) as champions and Arlesey as runners-up.

Although the Birmingham & District AFA first saw the light of day in 1908 when its member clubs competed for their Senior Cup, it was not until 1922 that the Association first organised a league competition. These days they are one of the few Saturday leagues left in the Birmingham area and run eight divisions, whilst it is of interest to note that one of their original members in 1908, Handsworth Grammar

THE GROWTH OF NON-LEAGUE FOOTBALL

FORMATION DATES OF LEAGUES

1888	Football League
1889	Birmingham & District, Lancashire League, Midland League, Northern League
1890	The Combination, Northern Alliance
1891	Lancashire Combination
1892	Birmingham (Combination) Junior League, Western League, Wearside League
1894	Southern League, Kent League
1895	Northants (United Counties) League
1896	Hampshire League, London League, United League, Leicester Senior League
1897	Norfolk & Suffolk (Anglian Combination)
1901	South Eastern League
1904	Great Western Suburban, Midland Amateur Alliance
1905	Isthmian League, Tyneside League
1906	North Eastern League
1907	Spartan League, Southern Amateur League
1908	Birmingham & District AFA
1911	Central Alliance League
1912	Athenian League
1919	Cheshire County League
1920	Sussex County League, Yorkshire League
1921	Cambridgeshire League, Southern Olympian League
1922	Combined Counties League, South Midlands League
1926	Nemean Amateur League
1927	Worcestershire (Midland) Combination
1934	Central Combination
1935	Central Amateur League, Eastern Counties League
1945	Corinthian League
1949	Metropolitan League
1951	Delphinian League, South Western League
1953	Hellenic League, South Warwickshire (Warwickshire Combination) League
1959	Aetolian League, Seanglian League
1964	Greater London League
1968	Gloucestershire County League, Northern Premier (HFS) League
1971	Essex Senior League
1975	London Spartan League
1979	Alliance Premier (GM Conference) League
1982	Northern Counties East League, North West Counties League

Aylesbury United have come through a maze of leagues and have built a fine new ground while establishing a place near the top of the pyramid. This team were the Delphian League Champions in season 1954-55. Back Row, left to right: G Terpilowski, G Halward, F Gearing, R Blake, K Brazier, G Walton. Front Row: Ray Mabbutt (who later played for Bristol Rovers and had a couple of famous sons!), A Comben, I Harper, P Watts, C Brown.

School Old Boys, still runs teams in the league.

The year 1927 saw the birth of the Midland Combination under its original name of Worcestershire Combination and although none of the founder members still have teams in the league, present day clubs like Boldmere St Michael's, Evesham United, Walsall Wood and West Midlands Police have all enjoyed lengthy periods of membership.

In 1934 the ill-fated Central Combination was formed for clubs based in the North Midlands area, but it only survived for three seasons, with Ollerton Colliery the champions in two of these seasons. A year later the Central Amateur League started and included well known Midland amateur clubs Moor Green, Boldmere St Michael's, Coalville Town and RAF Cranwell. With headquarters in Leicester it embraced clubs from eight counties as widespread as Worcestershire and Oxfordshire to Huntingdon and Lincolnshire, but after a brief four post-war seasons it ceased to exist.

First of the new leagues after World War Two was the Corinthian League that was set up in 1945, formed mainly by clubs who had previously been members of the London and Spartan Leagues. Erith & Belvedere, Maidenhead United and Slough Town being members in each of the league's eighteen seasons existence.

The Metropolitan League followed in 1949, operating for 21 seasons in 10 of which the championship was won by either the reserve or 'A' team of a Football League club. At the end of season 1970-71 it amalgamated with the Greater London League.

In 1951 came the Delphian League formed at the instigation of Dagenham and Woodford Town, and at the same time the South Western League entered the non-league arena taking in teams from such places as Bodmin, Falmouth, Launceston and Liskeard.

By this time the Leicestershire Senior League that had originated way back in 1890 as the Leicestershire League was becoming a powerful organization, whilst the formation of the Hellenic League brought a higher standard of football to clubs in the Oxfordshire area, amongst them the town teams of Chipping Norton, Didcot and Witney.

The short lived Aetolian League whose member clubs came mainly from the Kent area, functioned briefly between 1959 and 1964 before merging at the end of that season with the London League to form what is now called the Greater London League.

A major step forward was taken in 1968 when the leading North of England semi-pro clubs formed the Northern Premier League, taking its clubs from the Cheshire County, Lancashire Combination and Midland League. It later become an important part of the 'pyramid' system set up in 1982.

Additional new leagues in the seventies were the Essex Senior and London-Spartan League, formed respectively in seasons 1971 and 1975, then as the eighties came into view so did the Alliance Premier League, now the GM Conference and the most important competition outside the Football League. Non-league football has never been in a healthier state and has come a long way since those early leagues formed in 1889.

ATHENIAN LEAGUE

Founded in 1912, its progress was halted by the Great War. Restarting in 1919 it had amongst its better known clubs at this time Barnet, Kingstonian, Southall and Wimbledon, the latter club resigning in 1921 to join the Isthmian League.

In 1922, Bromley played 14 league matches without dropping a point, going on to win the championship with 40 out of a possible 48 points.

It became one of the leading amateur leagues in the South, with Barking Town in 1927 reaching the final of the FA Amateur Cup, losing 1-3 to Leyton at Millwall. Barnet, who spent 42 seasons in the Athenian League before turning professional and joining the Southern League, defeated Bishop Auckland in the Amateur Cup Final in 1945-46.

BIRMINGHAM & DISTRICT LEAGUE

One of the two oldest leagues still in operation, it was founded in 1889, retaining its title until 1962 when it dropped its parochial title in favour of the more embracing West Midlands (Regional) League. These days, of course, it is known as the Banks's Brewery League.

In its early days the competition was dominated by Aston Villa Reserves who won the title on 12 occasions and were runners-up 6 times, and the non-league clubs were not sorry when, along with other Midland Football League reserve teams, they left to join the Central League.

Kidderminster Harriers (6), Halesowen Town and Tamworth (5), and Alvechurch and Worcester City (4) have been the most successful clubs in terms of championship wins. Sadly the club with the longest membership of the league is now defunct, Brierley Hill Alliance being members for 78 seasons; whilst Stourbridge (63 seasons) are now members of the B & H Southern League.

Identical twins Lee and Paul Joinson celebrate Halesowen Town's first FA Vase triumph at Wembley.   Photo: Martin Dalton

BIRMINGHAM COMBINATION

Established in 1892 as the Birmingham Junior League, it remained in operation for 36 seasons, until 1954 when its few remaining clubs were absorbed into the Birmingham & District League.

Cradley St Luke's, Darlaston, Nuneaton Town and Redditch Town each won the championship on four occasions. Bromsgrove Rovers (35) and Atherstone Town (33) held the longest continual membership, whilst other well-known clubs with lengthy associations included Bournville Athletic and Birmingham Trams.

Evesham Town, who spent 12 seasons in the Combination, reached the final of the FA Amateur Cup in 1923, being beaten 1-2 by London Caledonians at Crystal Palace.

CHESHIRE COUNTY LEAGUE

Was late arriving on the scene, being formed at a meeting in Manchester in 1919. Among the founder members were current GM Conference clubs Altrincham, Macclesfield Town, Northwich Victoria and Runcorn. At various times the league has included the reserve sides of Chester, Crewe Alexandra, Oldham Athletic, Port Vale, Stockport County, Tranmere Rovers and Wrexham.

Macclesfield Town (6) have won the most championships, whilst Stalybridge Celtic (57 seasons), Winsford United (56) and Witton Albion (55) were long time members. In 1982, with the Lancashire Combination, it formed the NW Counties League.

CENTRAL ALLIANCE LEAGUE

Commenced in 1911 and in its early days included, at different times, the reserves of Chesterfield, Derby County, Leicester (Fosse) City, Nottingham Forest, Notts County and Walsall. Resuming activities in 1919, it began to lose clubs each season to other leagues, causing it to close down at the end of the 1924-25 season. In 1947-48 a new league under the same title was formed with 14 clubs; that had risen to 22 by 1963-64.

One of its most successful clubs was Ilkeston Town, champions in four successive seasons (1951-55). Other prominent sides included Alfreton Town, Belper Town, Clay Cross MW, Gresley Rovers, Heanor Town, Matlock Town and Ransome & Marles. Several of these clubs graduated to the Midland League in the early sixties.

CORINTHIAN LEAGUE

Came into being in 1945 through member clubs of the London and Spartan Leagues seeking a higher grade of amateur football, having been unsuccessful in gaining admittance to either the Isthmian or Athenian Leagues. The competition commenced with nine clubs, Grays Athletic being the first champions, and continued until 1963 when its clubs were taken into an extended Athenian League.

Three clubs, Erith & Belvedere, Maidenhead United and Slough Town played in each of the league's 18 seasons. Hounslow Town, Maidenhead United and Walton & Hersham were amongst this league's most successful clubs.

EASTERN COUNTIES LEAGUE

Founded in 1935, it has throughout its history had both amateur and professional clubs amongst its members. The initial season produced joint-champions in Lowestoft Town and Harwich & Parkeston, both finishing with 36 points and drawing 3-3 in a championship deciding match. Lowestoft Town have been outright winners on 9 occasions, while Harwich & Parkeston reached the final of the FA Amateur Cup in 1952-53, in which they were outplayed (0-6) by Pegasus. Tottenham Hotspur's 'A' team have won the title 5 times and in recent seasons the most successful club has been Sudbury Town, who have won the championship four times in the last five seasons, as well as being FA Vase finalists.

HELLENIC LEAGUE

Came on the scene in 1953 bringing senior non-league football to the Oxfordshire area. The league, which now has two divisions, commenced with 16 clubs, with Didcot Town finishing six points clear of Witney Town, who with 8 championship titles became the most successful club prior to moving into the Southern League in 1973. Abingdon Town come next with 4 wins.

Wallingford Town are the only club to have taken part in every one of the league's 37 seasons although Bicester Town (34), Abingdon Town (33), Thame United (29) and Didcot Town and Newbury Town (28) have all enjoyed a lengthy period of membership. In 1953-54, Princes Risborough Town created an unwanted Hellenic League record by losing every one of their 30 league matches.

ISTHMIAN LEAGUE

Formed in 1906, it will always be associated with top class amateur football. Before the Football Association decided to end the distinction between amateur and professional football, the league had provided several FA Amateur Cup winners and many amateur international players; and although Athenian League officials might dispute the fact, they were the premier amateur

This team gave Maidstone United one of its most successful seasons when, in 1955-56, The Corinthian League Memorial Shield, The Kent Amateur Cup and the Corinthian League Championship were all won. The following season they were elected to The Athenian League. Back row, left to right: F Baker, R Reynolds, D Fillery (whose son has enjoyed a long Football League career with Chelsea, QPR and Portsmouth), J Harris. Front Row: D Cutbush, J Fletcher, D Wiltshire, A Wallis, F James, R Burnett.

league in the South.

Many are the famous clubs associated with this league, like founder members Clapton and Ilford, Oxford City, Walthamstow Avenue and Dulwich Hamlet, who have partaken of 71 out of 74 Isthmian League seasons, winning the championship four times and being runners-up on seven occasions. Three clubs, Leytonstone, Wimbledon and Wycombe Wanderers have each won the title eight times, with Enfield gaining seven successes.

In recent seasons Sutton United (as former members) and Woking have brought further distinction to the league by their exploits in the FA Cup.

KENT LEAGUE

Was one of the first semi-professional leagues to be formed in the South in 1894, ambitiously commencing with two divisions, the Second Division only lasting for four seasons, although being re-introduced in 1909.

Maidstone United were the early pace-setters, gaining three successive championships between 1898 and 1901, a feat equalled by Northfleet United (1907-1910) and Millwall Reserves (1910-1913). Between 1934 and 1939, at a time when they were a 'nursery' club for Tottenham Hotspur, Northfleet United took the title four times.

In 1959 the Kent League disbanded, which brought about the formation of the Aetolian and Seanglian Leagues, but it was re-formed in 1968 and is once more a flourishing competition. No one club has dominated the post-war period, but Chatham Town, Ramsgate Athletic, Sheppey United and Sittingbourne have all had their periods of success in winning the championship.

LANCASHIRE COMBINATION

The old established Lancashire Combination, which ceased to exist in 1982 when it merged with the Cheshire County League, was one of the strongest and most respected competitions in the North of England. Prior to the formation of the Central League in 1911, the league was dominated by the reserve sides of the Lancashire Football League clubs, Everton Reserves being champions six times.

Of the non-league clubs, Chorley have been by far the most successful, with 10 titles to their name, added to which they were runners-up six times. Morecambe come next with five wins, and the championship trophy has been won four times by Darwen, Lancaster City, South Liverpool and Wigan Athletic.

Rossendale United played in the league for 55 seasons, and well known names to grace the competition include Accrington Stanley, Bacup Borough, Colne Dynamoes, Fleetwood, Horwich RMI, Nelson and Prescot Cables.

LANCASHIRE LEAGUE

Formed in 1889, it was one of the first leagues to cater for non-league clubs and for a time it rivalled the Lancashire Combination, before being absorbed into that competition in 1904.

Higher Walton were the first champions, with Bury taking the title in the next two seasons before their election to the Football League.

Southport Central were the only club to take part in all 14 of the league's seasons, with Nelson (10) and Chorley (9) being other long time members.

LEICESTER SENIOR LEAGUE

Was formed in 1896 with clubs from the short-lived Leicestershire League (1890-91) and the Leicestershire & Northants League (1891-96). Leicester Fosse Reserves were the initial champions and they later won the title in three successive seasons (1904-07), while Hinckley United won a trio of titles before the First World War.

Resuming in 1919, the league continued until 1930 when a shortage of clubs caused it to suspend activities for four seasons,

re-emerging in 1934 much greater both in quality and quantity. In the post-war period, Leicester City's 'A' team dominated the fifties, with the sixties belonging to Enderby Town (now Leicester United).

Friar Lane Old Boys, joining in 1969, won the Second Division

that season, gaining 62 out of a possible 64 points. Promoted at the end of the season, they then won the title seven times in the next eight seasons. Holwell Works have been members of the league for 45 seasons, whilst nine other clubs have been in membership for over 30 seasons.

MIDLAND LEAGUE

The Midland League, or to give it its correct title, the Midland Counties League, was in at the very beginning in 1889 and for many years was considered to be the strongest competition outside the Football League. This has certainly been borne out by the fact that clubs such as Barnsley, Chesterfield, Doncaster Rovers, Lincoln City and Rotherham County all competed in the Midland League be-

fore being accepted into the Football League. In post-war seasons, Peterborough United, Scunthorpe United and Shrewsbury all took the same route before gaining league status.

In its embryonic stages, the championship was shared around, but between 1902 and 1908 the title was won by the reserves of either Sheffield United or Sheffield Wednesday. In the mid-thirties, Barnsley

Reserves had a run of three successive championships.

After the war, Peterborough United and Nottingham Forest Reserves were two of the most successful sides. Doncaster Rovers, Gainsborough Trinity, Lincoln City and Worksop Town all were members for 50 seasons or more. In March 1982, the Midland League amalgamated with the Yorkshire League to form the Northern Counties East League.

MIDLAND COMBINATION

Originated as the Worcestershire Combination in 1927, with a modest complement of ten clubs, it has grown to become, today, one of the strongest leagues in the Midlands.

In pre-war days, Catshill Village Hall were the most successful club, gaining the championship four times in the period

1934-39. In the immediate post-war period, Evesham United, Jack Mould's Athletic and Smethwick Highfield were successful clubs. Evesham (5) have won the championship most times, with Alvechurch and Paget Rangers four times winners. Alvechurch, Highgate United and Paget Rangers have

twice completed the 'league and cup' double.

Boldmere St Michael's, who can claim 41 years' membership of the Combination, reached the semi-finals of the FA Amateur Cup in 1947-48, as did Highgate United in 1972-73 when they were beaten by the eventual winners, Walton & Hersham.

METROPOLITAN LEAGUE

With a life-span covering the years 1949 to 1971, this was another league that embraced both amateur and professional clubs, for whom it organised separate cup competitions in addition to the Challenge Cup that was open to all clubs. Chelsea 'A', Tonbridge Reserves and West Ham

United 'A' were the most successful professional cup winners, each having their names engraved on the trophy 3 times, with Newbury Town creating a record by winning the league's amateur trophy in 1954-55 and retaining it for the next five seasons. The league championship

was dominated by the professional clubs, with the 'A' teams of Arsenal and Chelsea gaining the most success.

NORTH EASTERN LEAGUE

Was founded in 1906 as the professional counterpart of the all-amateur Northern League, and from then until the formation of the North Regional League in 1958 it provided a high standard of non-league football in the North East.

Few clubs could match the strength of the reserve sides of Middlesbrough (12) and Sunderland (9) who between them won the championship 21 times; in fact out of the first 44 seasons, only on 17 occasions was the championship won by a non-league club, with South Shields (5) and Spennymoor United (4) the most successful.

In 1926-27 a second division was added, with clubs from the Northern Alliance. This lasted for nine seasons, before most of them reverted to the reformed Alliance. Well known clubs associated with the North Eastern League included Ashington, Blyth Spartans, Consett, Shildon and Walker Celtic.

In 1962-63 an attempt was made to revive the competition, but it survived for only two seasons, with Horden Colliery Welfare the last ever North Eastern League champions.

NORTHERN ALLIANCE

As its formation goes back to 1890, the league are at present in their centenary season, and it is to their credit that they have a thriving competition today whilst others have fallen by the wayside, for they have had a chequered career, having been absorbed into the North Eastern League in 1926 and closing down for one season (1964-65).

Although from time to time Durham clubs have been members, the majority of the league's clubs are Northumberland based. In terms of championships, Alnwick Town (9) and Amble (5) have had most success, whilst the Northern Alliance Cup has been won four times by Marine Park.

NORTHERN LEAGUE

From its formation in 1889 to the dissolution of amateur status in 1974, the Northern League had been a bastion of the amateur game and a whole chapter could be written about its clubs and players, but to feature a few highlights will have to suffice.

South Bank, one of the ten founder members, will be playing in their 90th campaign in the 1991-92 season, whilst Bishop Auckland, that most famous of all North Eastern clubs, spent 84 seasons in the league before in an attempt to climb the ladder they joined the HFS Loans League in 1988. Tow Law

Action from the all-Durham 1954 FA Amateur Cup Final, won eventually 1-0 by Crook Town who took three games to eliminate Bishop Auckland. The ties attracted nearly 200,000 spectators.

Town are in their 71st season, whilst Ferryhill Athletic and Willington have both been members for over 60 seasons.

No club can match the feats of Bishop Auckland, winners of the league championship on 19 occasions and runners-up 15 times, seven times winners of the League Challenge Cup and holders of the FA Amateur Cup a record 10 times.

Blyth Spartans, who joined from the North Eastern League in 1964, have 10 championship successes to their name, Spennymoor United have 6 and Shildon and Stockton have both won the title 5 times. In the FA Amateur Cup, Crook Town were successful on all their five final appearances, which included wins over Barnet, Bishop Auckland and Enfield. Other Northern League clubs to win this coveted trophy include Middlesbrough, South Bank, Stockton, West Hartlepool and Willington.

NORTHERN PREMIER LEAGUE

The founding of the NPL in 1968 might well be said to have laid the foundation stone for what later became known as the 'pyramid' system, for by bringing together the top clubs in the North and Midlands it raised the standard of non-league football and set clubs looking for higher goals to attain.

It is interesting to note that out of the 20 founder members, Altrincham, Boston United, Gateshead, Northwich Victoria and Runcorn are all members of today's GM Conference League, whilst Scarborough and Wigan Athletic have been elevated to the Football League, testimony to the strength of this competition.

The most championship wins have been gained by Boston United (4), whilst Runcorn won the League Challenge Cup 3 times.

SOUTHERN LEAGUE

When the Football League commenced in 1888, it did not include any Southern clubs, so it became obvious that a professional competition was needed in the South. When the league began it included Clapton Orient, Luton Town, Millwall, Reading, Southampton St Mary's and Swindon Town, and up to the time that its clubs were elected to form the Third Division of the Football League, it could hold its own with any other competition.

Inter-league matches were regularly played up until 1914 against the Football, Irish and Scottish Leagues, and such was the strength of the Southern League in its early days that one of its members, Tottenham Hotspur, defeated Sheffield United of the Football League in the 1901 FA Cup Final.

During the thirties the league continued with ever decreasing numbers, until the season before the war when numerically the league shot up to 23 clubs. Since the war it has been one of the strongest semi-professional competitions in the country, producing future Football League clubs in Cambridge United, Colchester United, Gillingham, Hereford United, Oxford United and of course Wimbledon.

Other clubs to make their mark in the Southern League include Bath City, Bedford Town, Chelmsford City, Kettering Town, Merthyr Tydfil, Weymouth and Yeovil Town. Today, the Southern League is one of the most important leagues in the 'pyramid' structure.

SOUTH MIDLANDS LEAGUE

For clubs in the Bedfordshire, Hertfordshire and Huntingdonshire area, the formation of the Bedfordshire County League brought a higher grade of football to the Home Counties. In 1929 the title of the league was changed to its present South Midlands League, with Vauxhall Motors one of the most successful pre-war clubs.

Although no club has enjoyed continuous membership of the league, Leighton United (now Town) and Letchworth Town (now Garden City) are present-day participants who were original founder members. Barton Rovers, who reached the final of the FA Vase in 1978, can lay claim to eight Premier Division championships, and Baldock Town, who first won the title in 1927-28, have been four times champions.

SOUTH WESTERN LEAGUE

Senior football came to the southernmost part of the country with the formation of the South Western League in 1951. Of the 12 founder-members, Newquay, Penzance, St Austell and St Blazey have had continuous membership.

Having won the championship on 10 occasions, Falmouth Town have been the most successful club. They won the title in four consecutive seasons (1974-78) and, moving on to the Western League, repeated the feat with four more successive championships, a remarkable run of eight league titles. St Blazey have been champions on six occasions.

At various times, Exeter City, Plymouth Argyle and Torquay United have benefited by running teams in the league. In St Luke's College, who were members from 1963 to 1977, the league had in their number the fourth oldest club in the country, the club having been founded in 1866.

SPARTAN LEAGUE

Formed two years after the Isthmian League, the Spartan League provided London with a second competition for top class amateur clubs and amongst its founder-members were such famous clubs as Bromley, Dulwich Hamlet, Leytonstone and Nunhead. The league continued until 1975 when it joined forces with the Metropolitan League to form the London-Spartan League.

Metropolitan Police had an especially fine record with seven championships to their name, Briggs Sports had four successive league and three cup wins between 1955 and 1959, while Farnborough Town were champions in each of the league's last three seasons.

Berkhamstead Town, Cambridge Town, Finchley, Hayes, St Albans City, Walthamstow Avenue and Wood Green Town are just a few of the other well-known clubs who have enjoyed membership of the Spartan League.

TYNESIDE LEAGUE

Formed way back in 1905, excluding the years 1915-1919 the league had a continuous run of 30 seasons, but did not re-form after the Second World War.

In the league's first six seasons, the championship was won by either South Shields Adelaide (2) or Windy Nook (4) at a time when, along with the Northern Alliance, the competition was second only to the North Eastern League. Windy Nook, who played on a ground owned by the Windy Nook Co-operative Society, were a village club who were known as the 'Nobblers' and in 1911 they attracted a crowd of 3000 to their ground for a Durham Senior Cup tie against Sunderland Reserves.

When the league resumed activities in 1919, St Peter's Albion won five successive titles (1919-1924). Well-known North Eastern clubs who featured in this league included Bolden Villa, Crawcrook Albion, Fatfield Albion, Usworth Colliery and Washington Colliery.

UNITED COUNTIES LEAGUE

Founded way back in 1895 as the Northamptonshire League, it was not until 1934 that the title was changed to the United Counties League. In the early days, Northampton Town entered their first team, winning the title in 1898-99, a feat which was emulated by their reserves five times between 1903 and 1929. Rushden Town have ten titles to their credit and have five times won the league's knockout Cup competition, whilst Stamford, winners of the Cup on four occasions, have a singularly impressive record in the FA Vase, being winners of the trophy in 1980 and losing finalists in 1976 and 1984. Irthingborough Diamonds reached the semi-final of the Vase in 1980-81. Just a few of the clubs to have lengthy membership of the league include Bedford Avenue, Biggleswade Town, Desborough Town, Kettering Town, Rothwell Town and founder members Wellingborough Town.

WEARSIDE LEAGUE

The Wearside League entered its 94th season in 1991, as it continued to operate throughout the Great War, though not during World War Two.

Founded with 10 member clubs in 1892 – one of them, Ryhope Colliery Welfare, in their third spell in the league, having continuous membership from 1956 until 1988 – the league in the main catered for the many colliery teams within the area, amongst the most successful up to 1939 being Seaham, Easington and Blackhall Collieries.

Since the war, Beldon CW, Ryhope CW and Shotton CW have between them won 17 championships. Blue Star (Newcastle) won the title in 1983, 1984 and 1985, to add to previous successes in 1974 and 1976 as well as an FA Vase win in 1978, with Whickham becoming the second Wearside League club to win the Vase in 1981.

WESTERN LEAGUE

Founded in 1892, the Western League is fast approaching its Centenary Year. The league quickly expanded to two divisions, with clubs like Brentford, Millwall and Tottenham Hotspur, who also had sides playing in the Southern League, forming the First Division and the local clubs competing in Division Two. Over the years the league has been noted for its high standard of football for clubs in the West country.

With such a long history, it is surprising to find that no one team has won the championship more than five times, which has been achieved by Bideford, also runners-up on six occasions. Four championships have been won by Bristol City Reserves, Bristol Rovers Reserves, Falmouth Town, Warmley, Welton Rovers and Yeovil & Petters United. The longest period of membership belongs to Welton Rovers (76 seasons), with Paulton Rovers (69), Glastonbury (57), Frome Town (55) and Radstock Town (54) also prominent.

Western League clubs successes in both the FA Trophy and FA Vase have been limited, with Exmouth Town reaching the semi-finals of the Vase in 1985.

YORKSHIRE LEAGUE

The Yorkshire League was one of those to lose its identity with the setting up of the 'pyramid' system, merging as it did with the Midland League to form the Northern Counties East League. One of the late starters – the league was not formed until 1920, its first champions being Bradford (Park Avenue) Reserves – it provided the opportunity for village and colliery teams to compete against the reserve and 'A' teams of the Yorkshire Football League clubs, who found the league a tough but valuable competition in which to groom their young professionals. After 1945 the league went from strength to strength, with a Second Division being formed in 1949 and a Third Division in 1961.

Stocksbridge Works have been one of the league's most successful clubs, winning the championship in four successive seasons (1954-58) and a total of seven times in all, but in recent seasons they have plumbed the depths of the Third Division, as have Selby Town, league winners on five occasions and the only club to have enjoyed 62 years continuous membership of the Yorkshire League.

The final seasons saw the First Division being dominated by Emley, who were three times winners and three times runners-up during this period and in 1988 reached the final of the FA Vase, losing to Colne Dynamoes at Wembley. Amongst clubs with a lengthy membership of the league will be found Denaby United, Farsley Celtic, Frickley Colliery, Goole Town, Norton Woodseats (now Dronfield), Scarborough and Yorkshire Amateurs.

This section features the clubs who played in the four main pyramid leagues in the 1990-91 season, i.e. the GM Vauxhall Conference (formerly the Alliance Premier League), and its three feeder leagues: the Isthmian League (to be sponsored by Diadora from the 1991-92 season), the Beazer Homes League (formerly the Southern League) and the HFS Loans League (formerly the Northern Premier League).

DIRECTORY OF NON-LEAGUE CLUBS 1991

Club	Ground	League for 1991-92	Best FA Trophy performance	Best FA Cup performance	Best league position
ALTRINCHAM (1891) *'The Robins'* Red and white stripes, black shorts	Moss Lane	Conference	Winners 1977-78 1985-86	4th round 1985-86	Champions 1979-80 1980-81
ATHERSTONE UNITED (1979) *'The Adders'* Red and white stripes, red shorts	Sheepy Road Ground	Beazer	1st round	2nd round replay 1990-91	6th 1989-90
AYLESBURY UNITED (1879) *'The Ducks'* Green and white hoops, green or white shorts	The Stadium, Buckingham Road	Isthmian	4th round replay 1980-81	2nd round 1989	20th (Conference) 1988-89

One of the real giants of non-league football in the eighties was Altrincham Football Club. This squad had just beaten near neighbours Runcorn 1-0 to win the FA Trophy in 1986. The club contained some of the "greats" at their level of the game and none was more respected than their captain John Davison (with Trophy), who also captained the England Semi-Professional side and won just about every honour available to him.
Photo: Martin Dalton

Barrow's Tony Chilton, voted the best left back in the Conference, shields the ball from Bolton Wanderers' Stuart Storer in their FA Cup Third Round clash at Burnden Park in 1991.
Photo: John Hudson

BARNET (1888)
'The Bees'
Orange shirts, black shorts
| Underhill Stadium | Barclays Division 4 | Finalists 1971-72 | 3rd round replay 1981-82 | Champions (Conference) 1990-91 |

BARROW (1901)
'Bluebirds'
White shirts, navy blue shorts
| Holker Street | Conference | Winners 1989-90 | 3rd round 1990-91 | 8th 1981-82 |

BANGOR CITY (1876)
'Citizens'
All royal blue
| The Stadium, Farrar Road | HFS | Finalists 1983-84 | 2nd round replay 1960-61, 1969-70, 1983-84 | 9th (Conference) 1979-80 |

BARKING (1880)
'The Blues'
Royal blue shirts, white shorts
| Mayesbrook Park | Isthmian | 2nd round 1979-80 | 2nd round 1978-79, 1979-80, 1981-82, 1983-84 | Champions 1978-79 |

BASHLEY (1947)
'The Bash'
Yellow and black shirts, black shorts
| Bashley Road, New Milton | Beazer | 1st qualifying round 1990-91 | 4th qualifying round 1990-91 | 10th 1990-91 |

BASINGSTOKE TOWN (1896) *'Stoke'*
All royal blue
| Camrose Ground | Isthmian | 1st round 1988-89 | 2nd round 1989-90 | 8th 1988-89 |

BATH CITY (1889)
'City'
Black and white shirts, black shorts
| Twerton Park | Conference | Quarter-finals 1989-90 | 3rd round replay 1963-64 | 4th 1984-85 |

BISHOP AUCKLAND (1886)
'Bishops'
Navy and light blue halved shirts, navy blue shorts
| Kingsway | HFS | Quarter-finals 1978-79 | 4th round 1954-55 | 11th 1989-90 |

BISHOPS STORTFORD (1874) *'Blues' or Bishops'*
Blue and white shirts, white shorts
| George Wilson Stadium | Isthmian | Winners 1980-81 | 3rd round replay 1982-83 | 3rd 1973-74 |

BOGNOR REGIS TOWN (1883) *'The Rocks'*
White shirts, green shorts
| Nyewood Lane | Isthmian | 1st round 1980-81 1990-91 | 2nd round 1984-85, 1985-86, 1988-89 | 2nd (Southern) |

CLUB DIRECTORY

Club	Ground	League for 1991-92	Best FA Trophy performance	Best FA Cup performance	Best league position
BOSTON UNITED (1934) *'The Pilgrims'* Gold shirts, black shorts	York Street	Conference	Finalists 1984-85	3rd round 1955-56, 1973-74	3rd 1988-89
BROMSGROVE ROVERS (1885) *'The Rovers'* Red shirts, black shorts	Victoria Ground	Beazer	Quarter-final replay 1975-76	1st round (6)	2nd 1986-87
BURTON ALBION (1950) *'The Brewers'* Gold shirts, black shorts	Eton Park	Beazer	Finalists 1986-87	3rd round 1984-85	3rd (NPL) 1982-83
BUXTON (1877) *'The Bucks'* All white	Silverlands	HFS	Quarter-final replay 1970-71, 1971-72	3rd round 1951-52	4th 1980-81
CAMBRIDGE CITY (1908) *'City Devils'* White shirts, black shorts	City Ground	Beazer	2nd round 1987-88	1st round 1946, 1948, 1966	Champions 1962-63
CARSHALTON ATHLETIC (1905) *'The Robins'* Maroon shirts, white shorts	War Memorial Sports Ground	Isthmian	3rd round 1980-81	2nd round 1982-83	4th 1988-89
CHELMSFORD CITY (1938) *'City'* Claret shirts, white shorts	The Stadium, New Whittle Street	Beazer	Semi-finals 1969-70	4th round 1938-39	Champions 1945-46, 1967-68, 1971-72
CHELTENHAM TOWN (1892) *'The Robins'* Red shirts with white sleeves, white shorts	Whaddon Road	Conference	4th round 1985-86	3rd round 1933-34	11th 1985-86, 1986-87, 1989-90
CHORLEY (1883) *'The Magpies'* Black and white stripes, black shorts	Victory Park	HFS	Quarter-finals 1976-77	2nd round replay 1986-87	17th (Conference) 1988-89
COLCHESTER UNITED (1937) *'United'* Blue and white stripes, white shorts	Layer Road	Conference	Quarter finals 1990-91	Quarter finals 1970-71	5th (Div 3) 1979-80
CRAWLEY TOWN (1896) *'The Reds'* All red	Town Mead	Beazer	2nd round 1985-86, 1987-88	1st round replay 1971-72	3rd 1984-85
DAGENHAM (1949) *'Daggers'* All red	Victoria Road	Isthmian	Winners 1979-80	3rd round 1983-84	5th (Conference) 1981-82
DARTFORD (1888) *'The Darts'* Black and white hoops, black shorts	Watling Street	Beazer	Finalists 1973-74	3rd round 1935-36, 1936-37	Champions 1983-84
DORCHESTER TOWN (1880) *'The Magpies'* Black and white shirts, black shorts	Avenue Stadium	Beazer	3rd round 1971-72	2nd round 1954-55, 1957-58, 1981-82	Champions (Southern) 1979-80
DOVER ATHLETIC (1983) *'The Lillywhites'* White shirts, black shorts	Crabble Athletic Ground	Beazer	3rd round 1989-90	4th Qualifying replay 1990-91	Champions 1989-90

Club	Ground	League for 1991-92	Best FA Trophy performance	Best FA Cup performance	Best league position
DROYLSDEN (1866) *'The Bloods'* All red	Butchers Arms	HFS	3rd Qualifying round 1973-74, 1976-77, 1979-80	1st round 1976	13th 1990-91
ENFIELD (1893) *'The 'E's'* White shirts, navy blue shorts	Southbury Road	Isthmian	Winners 1981-82, 1987-88	4th round replay 1980-81	Champions (Conference) 1982-83, 1985-86
FARNBOROUGH TOWN (1967) *'Boro'* All yellow with blue trim	Cherrywood Road	Conference	3rd round 1987-88	1st round (7) All since 1980	21st 1989-90
FISHER ATHLETIC (1908) *'The Fish'* Black and white shirts, black shorts	Surrey Docks Stadium	Beazer	3rd round 3rd replay 1987-88	1st round 1984-85, 1988-89	15th 1987-88 (Conference)
FLEETWOOD TOWN (1977) *'Fishermen'* Red shirts with white sleeves, white shorts	Highbury Stadium	HFS	1st round 1988-89, 1990-91	1st round 1980-81, 1990-91	4th 1990-91
FRICKLEY ATHLETIC (1976) *'The Blues'* Blue and white shirts, white shorts	Westfield Lane, South Elmsall	HFS	Quarter-finals 1984-85	3rd round 1985-86	2nd (Conference) 1985-86
GATESHEAD (1977) *'Tynesiders'* Red shirts, white shorts	International Stadium	Conference	3rd round 1983-84	1st round 1980-81	16th 1983-84
GAINSBOROUGH TRINITY (1873) *'Blues'* Royal blue shirts, white shorts	The Northolme	HFS	2nd round 2nd replay 1986-87	2nd round (10)	4th 1968-69, 1985-86
GLOUCESTER CITY (1889) *'The Tigers'* All yellow	Meadow Park	Beazer	3rd round 1990-91	2nd round replay 1989-90	2nd 1990-91
GOOLE TOWN (1900) *'Town' or 'Vickers'* Yellow shirts, black shorts	Victoria Pleasure Ground	HFS	Quarter finals 1974-75	3rd round 1956-57	6th 1976-77, 1988-89
GRAVESEND & NORTHFLEET (1946) *'The Fleet'* Red shirts, white shorts	Stourbridge Road, Northfleet	Beazer	3rd round 1988-89	4th round replay 1962-63	5th (Conference) 1979-80
GRAYS ATHLETIC (1890) *'The Blues'* Royal blue shirts, white shorts	Recreation Ground	Isthmian	2nd round replay 1985-86	1st round 1988-89	4th 1989-90
HALESOWEN TOWN (1873) *'The Yeltz'* Blue shirts, white shorts	Grove Recreation Ground	Beazer	3rd Qualifying round 1969-70	1st round 1954-55, 1988-89, 1990-91	8th 1990-91
HARROW BOROUGH (1933) *'Boro'* All red	Earlsmead	Isthmian	Semi-finals 1982-83	2nd round 1983-84	Champions 1983-84
HAYES (1909) *'The Missioners'* Red and white halves, white shorts	Church Road	Isthmian	Quarter-finals 1978-79	2nd round replay 1972-73	8th 1990-91

Hendon had a memorable side in the sixties, including such Non-League stars as John Swannell, Rod Haider and Tony Jennings. In this cup tie at Newcastle, the Isthmian club held Newcastle United 1-1 with a great goal from Rod Haider on front. Here Iam McFaul saves brilliantly as John Baker moves in for a possible rebound.

HENDON (1908) *'Dons' or 'Greens'* Green shirts, white shorts	Claremont Road	Isthmian	3rd round replay 1976-77, 1977-78	3rd round 1973-74	Champions 1964-65, 1972-73
HORWICH RMI (1896) *'Railwaymen'* Royal blue shirts, white shorts	Victoria Road	HFS	Quarter-finals 1990-91	1st round 1928-29, 1982-83	8th 1983-84
HYDE UNITED (1909) *'The Tigers'* Red shirts with black trim, white shorts	Ewen Fields (all weather pitch)	HFS	Semi-finals 1988-89	1st round (3) 1887-88 1954-55 1983-84	2nd 1987-88, 1988-89
KETTERING TOWN (1881) *'Poppies'* All red	Rockingham Road	Conference	Finalists 1978-79	4th round 1988-89	2nd 1980-81, 1988-89
KIDDERMINSTER HARRIERS (1880) *'Harriers'* Red and white halved shirts, white shorts	Aggborough Stadium	Conference	Winners 1986-87	Last 32, 1890	3rd 1985-86
KINGSTONIAN (1885) *'The 'K's'* Red and white hoops, white shorts	Kingsmead Stadium	Isthmian	4th round 1989-90	1st round replay 1932-33	Champions 1933-34, 1936-37
LEEK TOWN (1946) *'Bluebirds'* Royal blue shirts, white shorts	Harrison Park	HFS	Finalists 1989-90	2nd round 1990-91	9th 1990-91
MACCLESFIELD TOWN (1873) *'The Silkman'* Royal blue shirts, white shorts	Moss Rose	Conference	Winners 1969-70 (First winners)	3rd round 1968-69, 1987-88	4th 1989-90

Club	Ground	League for 1991-92	Best FA Trophy performance	Best FA Cup performance	Best league position
MARINE (1894) *'Lillywhites'* White shirts, black shorts	Rosset Park, Crosby	HFS	Semi-finals 1983-84	2nd round 1975-76	2nd 1985-86
MARLOW (1870) *'The Blues'* Royal blue shirts, white shorts	Alfred Davis Memorial Ground	Isthmian	1st round 1987-88	Semi-finals 1881-82	7th 1990-91
MATLOCK TOWN (1885) *'The Gladiators'* Royal blue shirts, white shorts	Causeway Lane	HFS	Winners 1974-75	3rd round 1976-77	2nd 1983-84
MERTHYR TYDFIL (1945) *'Martyrs'* White shirts, black shorts	Pennydarren Park	Conference	Quarter-final replay 1977-78	2nd round (3)	9th 1989-90, 1990-91
MOOR GREEN (1901) *'The Moors'* All blue	Sherwood Road, Hall Green	Beazer	1st round 1990-91	1st round 1979-80	11th 1989-90
MORECAMBE (1920) *'Shrimps'* Red shirts, white shorts	Christie Park	HFS	Winners 1974	3rd round 1961-62	3rd 1968-69, 1985-86, 1990-91
MOSSLEY (1909) *'Lillywhites'* All white	Seel Park	HFS	Finalists 1979-80	2nd round 1949-50, 1981-82	Champions 1978-79, 1979-80
NORTHWICH VICTORIA (1874) *'Vics'* Green and white shirts, white shorts	Drill Field	Conference	Winners 1983-84	4th round 1976-77, Quarter-finals 1883-84	4th 1980-81
POOLE TOWN (1880) *'Dolphins'* All blue	The Stadium, Wimborne Road	Beazer	1st round replay 1969-70	3rd round 1936-37	17th 1990-91
RUNCORN (1918) *'Linnets'* Yellow shirts, green shorts	Canal Street	Conference	Finalists 1985-86	3rd round 1938-39	Champions 1981-82
RUSHDEN (1889) *'Russians'* All red	Hayden Road	Beazer	3rd Qualifying round 1969-70	4th Qualifying round 1924-25	14th 1990-91
ST ALBANS CITY (1908) *'Saints'* Yellow shirts, blue shorts	Clarence Park	Isthmian	2nd round 1981-82	2nd round replay 1968-69, 1980-81	Champions 1922-23, 1926-27, 1927-28
REDBRIDGE FOREST (1989) *'Stones' or 'Fords'* Red and blue stripes, blue shorts	Dagenham FC	Conference	3rd round 1989-90, 1990-91	1st round 1979-80, 1981-82	Champions 1988-89, 1990-91
SLOUGH TOWN (1890) *'The Rebels'* Amber shirts, navy blue shorts	Wexham Park	Conference	Semi-finals 1979-80	2nd round 1978-79, 1982-83, 1985-86, 1986-87	19th 1990-91
SHEPSHED CHARTERHOUSE (1891) *'The Raiders'* Red and blue stripes, red shorts	The Dovecote	HFS	1st round replay 1985-86 1989-90	1st round 1981-82	7th (Southern) 1985-86

Club	Ground	League for 1991-92	Best FA Trophy performance	Best FA Cup performance	Best league position
SOUTH LIVERPOOL *'South'* White shirts, black shorts	Bootle FC	HFS	3rd round 1974-75	2nd round 1936-37, 1937-38, 1954-55	3rd 1983-84
SOUTHPORT (1881) *'The Sandgrounders'* Amber shirts, black shorts	Haig Avenue	HFS	3rd round 1985-86	2nd round 1935-36	2nd 1987-88
STAFFORD RANGERS (1876) *'Boro'* White and black stripes, black shorts	Marston Road	Conference	Winners 1971-72, 1978-79	4th round 1974-75	6th 1987-88
STAINES TOWN (1892) *'Swans'* Old gold and blue	Wheatsheaf Park	Isthmian	2nd round 2nd replay 1976-77	1st round 1984-85	4th 1981-82
STALYBRIDGE CELTIC (1911) *'Celtic'* All royal blue	Bower Ford	HFS	2nd round 1973-74, 1979-80, 1982-83	2nd round 1935-36	2nd 1990-91
SUTTON UNITED (1898) *'The 'U's'* All amber with chocolate trim	Gander Green Lane	Isthmian	Finalists 1980-81	4th round 1988-89	7th (Conference) 1986-87
TELFORD UNITED (1876) *'Bucks'* White shirts, blue shorts	Bucks Head	Conference	Winners 1970-71, 1982-83, 1988-89	5th round 1984-85	3rd 1981-82
V.S. RUGBY (1956) *'The Valley'* Navy and sky blue shirts, white shorts	Butlin Road	Beazer	3rd Qualifying replay 1989-90	2nd round replay 1984-85	3rd 1988-89
WALTHAM FOREST (1975) *'The Blues'* Royal blue shirts, white shorts	Lea Bridge Road	Isthmian	3rd round 1987-88	1st round 1986-87	7th 1989-90 (As Leyton-Wingate)
WATERLOOVILLE (1910) *'The Ville'* White with blue trim	Jubilee Park	Beazer	2nd round 1976-77	1st round replay (2)	5th (Southern) 1980-81
WEALDSTONE (1889) *'Stones'* White shirts, blue shorts	Lower Mead	Beazer	Winners 1984-85	3rd round 1977-78	Champions (Conference) 1984-85
WELLING UNITED (1963) *'Wings'* All red	Park View Road	Conference	4th round 1988-89	3rd round 1988-89	6th 1989-90
WEYMOUTH (1890) *'Terras'* Terra cotta shirts, sky blue shorts	Wessex Stadium	Beazer	4th round replay 1976-77	4th round 1961-62	2nd (Conference) 1979-80
WINDSOR & ETON (1891) *'Royalists'* All red with green piping	Stag Meadow	Isthmian	3rd round replay 1988-89	2nd round replay 1983-84	5th 1984-85
WITTON ALBION (1890) *'Albion'* Red and white stripes, black shorts	Wincham Park	Conference	Semi-final 1990-91	2nd round 1951-52	Champions 1990-91 (HFS)

Club	Ground	League for 1991-92	Best FA Trophy performance	Best FA Cup performance	Best league position
WIVENHOE TOWN (1974) *'The Dragons'* Royal blue shirts, white shorts	Broad Lane	Isthmian	3rd round 1990-91	4th Qualifying round 1989-90	10th 1990-91
WOKING (1889) *'Cardinals'* Red shirts, white shorts	Kingfield	Isthmian	3rd round 1989-90	4th round 1990-91	2nd 1990-91
WOKINGHAM TOWN (1875) *'The Town'* Amber shirts, black shorts	Finchamp-stead Road	Isthmian	2nd round replay 1989-90	1st round replay 1982-83	2nd 1989-90
WORCESTER CITY (1908) *'City'* Blue and white stripes, blue shorts	St Georges Lane	Beazer	4th round replay 1980-81, 1981-82	4th round 1958-59	4th (Conference) 1981-82
WYCOMBE WANDERERS (1884) *'Choirboys'* Sky and navy blue quarters	Adams Park	Conference	Winners 1990-91	3rd round replay 1974-75	4th 1988-89
YEOVIL TOWN (1895) *'Glovers'* White shirts, green shorts	Huish Park	Conference	Semi-finals 1970-71, 1971-72	5th round 1948-49	7th 1989-90

The most famous of all non-league cup fighters are Yeovil Town, thanks to their 2-1 victory over First Division Sunderland in 1949. This was followed by a visit to Manchester to take on United (at Maine Road because of ground repairs at Old Trafford) where they lost 0-8 but attracted a record crowd for a competitive match outside Wembley of 81,565. The gate receipts were £7,141! This squad led by Brian Hall, one of the most successful managers in modern non-league football, played in the GM Vauxhall Conference and won their League Cup (The Bob Lord Trophy). Back row, left to right: Paul Thorpe, Steve Rutter, Mark Shail, Richard Thompson, Simon Gowans, Barry Blackman, Jimmy Quinn. Centre row: Paul Rogers (Coach), Peter Conning, Len Bond, Micky Spencer, Neil Cordice, Andy Wallace, Davbid Fry, Phil Ferns, Duncan Russell (Physio). Front row: Paul Wilson, Robbie Carroll, Gary Donnellan, Brian Hall (Manager), Tiv Lowe, Gerry Pearson, Jeff Sherwood. Photo: Nigel Andrews

CLUB PROFILES

ALTRINCHAM

Formed in 1891, Altrincham commenced playing in the Manchester League of which they became champions in 1904-05 and 1906-07. In 1912 they moved to the Lancashire Combination where they stayed until joining the newly formed Cheshire County League in 1919. Forty-three seasons were spent with this competition during which time the championship was won in successive seasons (1965-66 and 1966-67) and the League Cup three times.

In 1968 the club became founder-members of the Northern Premier League, enjoying their best season as runners-up to Mossley in 1978-79. Following this, they joined the Alliance Premier League (referred to hereafter as the GM Conference), winning the title in each of the first two seasons and going very close to the Championship and promotion in 1990-91.

Altrincham have a good record of success in cup competitions, being winners of the FA Trophy in 1978 and 1986, and finalists in 1982. They have also had several good results in the FA Cup, including a 2-1 win over First Division Birmingham City at St Andrews in 1986.

BARNET

A club whose beginnings date back to 1888, they first came into prominence when they left the London League to join the Athenian League in 1912. There they spent 42 seasons which saw them champions seven times and runners-up on six occasions. In 1966 the club turned professional and joining the Southern League, they won the League Cup in 1971-72, the season that they were beaten by Stafford Rangers in the FA Trophy final.

In 1979 they became founder-members of the GM Conference, finishing as runners-up three times in four seasons before clinching a thrilling championship race in 1990-91.

In 1945-46 Barnet defeated Bishop Auckland 3-2 in the final of the FA Amateur Cup at Stamford Bridge, and were losing finalists in both 1948 and 1959. In their amateur days the club produced several internationals, the best known being Lester Finch (England) and Denis Kelleher and J J McCarthy (Ireland).

BISHOP AUCKLAND

In their Northern League days Bishop Auckland could claim to be FA Amateur Cup specialists, with the cup ending up in the Kingsway trophy room a record 10 times; they also unsuccessfully contested the final on another eight occasions.

Only Blyth Spartans with 10 championships come anywhere near the 'Bishop's' 19 titles and 15 runners-up spots, gained in 84 seasons spent in the Northern League, whilst the club has had its name inscribed on both the Durham Challenge and Durham Benevolent cups on several occasions.

Over 20 of their players have gained England Amateur International caps, amongst them Max Woosnam, Ernest Proud, Bob Hardisty, Harry Sharratt, Corbett Cresswell (son of Warney), Warren Bradley and Seamus O'Connell,

Despite their success in the Amateur Cup, the club has yet to make its mark in the FA Trophy.

BROMLEY

Although in recent seasons the club has struggled to maintain its place in the Premier Division of the Vauxhall-Opel League, Bromley was a very successful Athenian and Isthmian League club. After spending 27 seasons with the Athenians, which brought them three championships, they joined the Isthmian League in 1952, winning the league title in 1953-54 and 1960-61 to add to those won in 1908-09 and 1909-10 when they were previously members of the competition.

The FA Amateur Cup was won three times, in 1910-11, 1937-38, and 1948-49 when their beaten opponents were Bishop Auckland, Erith & Belvedere and Romford respectively. Outstanding Bromley players include Bobby Noble, George Brown, Tommy

Cornthwaite, Eric Fright and Charlie and Tommy Fuller. Three former Bromley players, Harold Hobbis (Charlton Ath-

letic), George Mills (Chelsea) and Frank Osborne (Fulham) all gained full international caps after turning professional.

Bromley have great traditions and are one of the best known clubs in Kent. Here they are seen with The Kent Senior Cup which they won in 1949-50.

CASUALS

Founded in 1883, membership in those days was restricted to Old Boys of Charterhouse, Eton and Westminster, playing in colours of chocolate and pink. Founder-members of the Isthmian League in 1905, they were still members in 1939 when they amalgamated with the Corinthians.

Although the club had many distinguished players, honours were few and far between, the club's best season being 1935-36 when they finished runners-up in the league and were winners, for the only time, of the Amateur Cup.

They had outstanding forwards that season in E Donald, R Shearer, who captained Ireland at cricket, Howard Fabian, who played for Derby County and WH 'Tagge' Webster, opening batsman for Middlesex CCC. Other well-known Casuals were Bernard Joy (Arsenal), Ken Tewkesbury (Aston Villa) and Tommy Whewell.

CORINTHIANS

Probably the most famous of all amateur clubs, they were early pioneers of dribbling and the short passing game, and no greater tribute could be paid them than to say that others who followed were often referred to as playing 'Corinthian style'.

Although the club regularly entered the FA Cup it was not until the amalgamation with the Casuals that the club first played in a league competition. They invariably gave a good account of themselves against Football League sides and in 1928-29, in the Third Round of the FA Cup, they defeated Norwich City 5-0 at

The Nest, despite losing the services of their outside-right, RGC Jenkins, who was injured as early as the 11th minute of the game. The following season they took Millwall to three matches in the same competition.

There is a multitude of famous Corinthians, many equally well known as cricketers such as CB Fry, the brothers CT, G and H Ashton, AG Doggart, SH Day,

HM Garland-Wells, RS Grant and Sir C Aubrey Smith. Other talented Corinthians include Rev. KRG Hunt, GO Smith, KE Hegan and NFS Smith.

In 1956, as Corinthian-Casuals, they held Bishop Auckland to a 1-1 draw at Wembley in the Amateur Cup final, only to lose the replay 1-4 at Middlesbrough.

CROOK TOWN

An impressive and varied history commenced in 1889 in the Auckland District League, the club then joining the Northern League in 1896. They won the FA Amateur Cup for the first time in 1901, and between 1954 and 1964 made four further appearances in the final, winning the trophy on each occasion.

In January 1928, the Durham County Football Association suspended the club for an alleged infringement of the rules regarding payment to amateur players, and in 1930 the club turned semi-professional, joining the North Eastern League. In 1936 they reverted back to amateur status, rejoining the Northern League whose championship has been won five times.

After the war they played for some seasons as Crook Colliery Welfare, before changing back to their original title in 1949. Eleven Crook players received international calls, amongst them Frank Clark (later Newcastle United), Ron Fryer, Arnold Coates, Jimmy McMillan, Ken Harrison and Peter Garbutt.

DULWICH HAMLET

Another former amateur club whose best days were between the two wars, they have spent 71 seasons in the Vauxhall-Opel (Isthmian) League and have been four times champions and seven times runners-up. The FA Amateur Cup has been bedecked with their famous navy and pink colours and brought to Champion Hill in 1920, 1932, 1936 and 1937.

Sixteen Dulwich players between the wars have won English amateur international caps, whilst four others gained Welsh caps. Amongst those internationals have been Edgar Kail, Bill Caesar, HHC Hill, a goalkeeper who played for several professional clubs, Laurie Fishlock, a cricketer for Surrey and England, and WW Parr, a winger who played as an amateur for both Arsenal and Blackpool, and lost his life in the last war. Dick Jonas and Jack Hugo were two Hamlet defenders unlucky not to have been chosen by their country.

ENFIELD

Formed in 1893, they graduated to the London League in 1903-04 and in 1912-13 became founder-members of the Athenian League, where 38 seasons of meagre success brought them only the championship in 1961-62 and 1962-63, a period when the club was at its strongest, leading to Amateur Cup wins in 1967 and 1970.

In 1963 Enfield accepted an invitation to join the Isthmian League, and between 1967 and 1970 they completed a 'hat-trick' of championship wins. After

David Howell proved a very popular and successful captain of the England Semi-Professional International squad. Here he is seen with the Scottish captain before a Four Nations Tournament match.

gaining their seventh Isthmian League title in 1980 they were accepted into the GM Conference, winning the title at the second attempt and repeating the feat in 1985-86. In recent years, Enfield have provided England with 8 England semi-professional internationals, with skipper David Howell gaining 15 caps.

ILFORD

.One of three London clubs who, famous in their amateur days, no longer grace non-league football. Founded in 1881 they entered the very first FA Amateur Cup competition, when after beating Ipswich Town, West Herts and Whitby FC, they went out 2-4 at Bishop Auckland; so it was with a sense of occasion that they took part in the very last Amateur Cup final in 1974.

After playing in the Southern and London Leagues they became founder-members of the Isthmian League in 1905, staying there for 61 seasons. Their finest period was between 1928 and 1930 when they won both the FA Amateur Cup and London Senior Cup two seasons running, as well as the Essex Senior and London Charity cups. The Isthmian championship was won in sea-sons 1906-07, 1920-21 and 1921-22, and the club also finished second on five occasions. In 1979 they sold their ground and amalgamated with Leytonstone.

Long serving left-half Harry Dodkins captained the England amateur international side several times. Other well-known Ilford players were Eric Cross, Gus Simmons, Vic Welsh, Reg Dellow and Guy Holmes, who played for England in the 1936 Olympic Games.

KETTERING TOWN

A club who today are hopeful of eventually attaining Football League status, they have for many years been the leading Northamptonshire non-league side.

Kettering have featured in several leagues, including the Birmingham & District, Central Alliance, Midland and United Counties, but over 30 seasons were spent in the Southern League, with title wins in 1956-57 and 1972-73, several divisional titles, and a Southern League cup triumph in 1974-75 a measure of the success brought to Rockingham Road. The Birmingham League championship was won in 1947-48, whilst both their first and reserve teams have gained the title in the United Counties League.

In 1989 the club reached the Fourth Round of the FA Cup, losing 1-2 to Charlton Athletic at Selhurst Park, and in 1979 they had been losing finalists in the FA Trophy, the 'Poppies' losing 2-0 to Stafford Rangers at Wembley.

KIDDERMINSTER HARRIERS

Another club whose ambitions go higher than the GM Conference, which they entered in 1983. The Harriers spent 81 seasons playing in either the Birmingham & District or the Southern League, with two years (1945-1947) in the Birmingham Combination.

From 1892 to 1939 they played in the Birmingham League, winning the title in 1937-38 and 1938-39. In 1948 they joined the Southern League for 11 seasons before returning to the Birmingham League in 1960, winning four championships before rejoining the Southern League in 1972. In 1982-83 they were runners-up to the now defunct AP Leamington and the following season were admitted to the GM Conference, invariably finishing in the top half of the table and were FA Trophy winners in 1987 and runners-up in 1991.

Over the years many outstanding players have worn the Harriers colours, including ex-Football League players such as Tom Galley and Alex McIntosh (Wolves), Johnny Dent (Nottm Forest), Dennis Jennings (Birmingham), and the greatest of all Kidderminster characters, centre-forward Billy Boswell. Once called 'the Dixie Dean of non-league football', he scored a record 64 goals in 1935-36 and a total of 125 in three seasons. In more recent times, there have been the brothers Brendan and Peter Wassall, Kim Casey, Paul Davies and Graham MacKenzie.

KINGSTONIAN

Although the history of Old Kingstonians goes back to 1885, the present Kingstonian club was formed in 1919 by an amalgamation of Old Kingstonians and Kingston Town FC. For many years they have been one of the most respected clubs in the South and their Kingsmeadow Stadium is the envy of visiting teams.

Kingstonian began playing in the Athenian League in the year of their formation, twice gaining the championship during their ten years as members of that competition. 1929 found the club competing in the Isthmian League and it was during the thirties that the club enjoyed its greatest success. The FA Amateur Cup was won in 1933, while the following season, and again in 1936-37, the Isthmian League championship was won; they also enjoyed considerable success in both the Surrey Senior and London Charity Cup competitions.

In 1959-60 the 'K's' were losing finalists in the Amateur Cup, when they dominated for most of the game only for Hendon to score twice in the last three minutes. Internationals associated with the club include Frank Macey, W Whittaker and Lionel Thornton, who lost his life in Burma in World War Two.

LEYTON

There is some doubt as to the actual formation date of the club, some sources claiming it was as early as 1868; what *is* known is that the club was playing in 1889 as Matlock Swifts and changed their name to Leyton in 1893. Early days were spent in the South Essex League in which they won two championships.

In 1921 they were accepted into the London League and in 1923-24 won the first of three successive championships. In 1926-27, the year the club joined the Athenian League, they defeated East London rivals Barking Town 3-1 in the Amateur Cup final, and retained the trophy the following year with a 3-2 win over Cockfield at Middlesbrough. In 1928-29 they made their third consecutive appearance in the final, only to lose 1-3 to Ilford.

In 1976 the club amalgamated with Wingate; three Athenian titles had been won as Leyton and two more have followed as Leyton-Wingate. The club now plays in the Premier Division of the Vauxhall-Opel League. Outstanding players in Leyton's cup-winning days included H Terris, T Cable, H Graves, G Smith and H Hall.

LEYTONSTONE

Another famous London club, whose identity was lost with the sale of their Cranleigh Road ground. They are hidden under the name of Redbridge Forest.

Originally founded as Cedars FC in 1886 and renamed Leytonstone in 1882, they became founder members of the Spartan League in 1907-08, but after that initial season they transferred to the Isthmian League, where they have remained ever since. For many years, they met with little success other than in local cup competitions, before winning the Isthmian League title in both 1937-38 and 1938-39.

The club's greatest achievements came in the immediate post-war years; they were league champions five times between 1946 and 1952, and again in 1965-66, as well as being FA Amateur Cup winners in 1946-47, 1947-48 and 1967-68. In 1979, upon amalgamation, they became known as Leytonstone/Ilford, winning the championship in 1981-82 and 1988-89.

No fewer than seven Leytonstone players, Doug Jarvis, Ernie Childs, Jim Paviour, Jack Kavanagh, George Bunce, Alf Noble and Leon Joseph, were selected to play for England after the war, whilst Vic Groves, one of three brothers to play for 'The Stones', turned professional with Arsenal.

MERTHYR TYDFIL

The successors to Merthyr Town, the 'Martyrs' were formed in 1945, and after a season in the Welsh League when they finished as runners-up to Lovells Athletic, they were admitted into the Southern League in 1946, remaining there until their promotion to the GM Conference in

1988-89.

Their early days in the Southern League were halcyon ones; third in 1946-47, they were then champions in 1947-48, 1949-50, 1950-51, 1951-52 and 1953-54, scoring over a century of goals for five consecutive seasons, and in a period of nine years amassing a total of 1059 goals, an average of 118 goals a season.

These were indeed glory days at Pennydarren Park, and two of their star forwards, Bill Hullett (who later returned as player-manager) and Sid Howarth, were transferred to Cardiff City and Aston Villa respectively.

Other sharp-shooting forwards in those days were Bill Jarman, Jenkin Powell, Trevor Reynolds and Stan Davies. Of today's side, Dave Webley has scored over 200 goals whilst nine players have made over 200 appearances for the club.

MOOR GREEN

Paradoxically it could be said that Moor Green were more famous in their amateur days, when they kept the flag flying in the Amateur Cup as the foremost amateur club in the Midlands, than they are today.

Formed in 1901, for some years the club engaged only in friendly matches before joining the Birmingham & District AFA, but during the thirties they fielded as many as five teams. As members of the Amateur Football Alliance, they were Senior Cup winners in 1938-39, beating the London based club Norsemen 5-2. In 1932-33 they entered the Midland Mid-Week League, playing each week against the Midland professional clubs. In 1936 they left the Birmingham AFA for the Central Amateur League, winning the championship in each of the next three seasons, during which period they lost only 8 out of 62 matches.

Tommy Leek gained five England caps playing for the 'Moors' before moving to Barnet, while other outstanding players at The Moorlands in those days were Tommy Stanley, HR 'Bert' Bull, Norman Love and George Dance. In 1939, after beating Boldmere St Michael's and Yorkshire Amateurs in the Amateur Cup, they eventually went out in the Third Round to the Northern League club Willington, losing finalists that season.

After the war they joined the semi-professional Birmingham Combination and produced two first-class goalkeepers in Peter Horne and Mick Taylor. Other more than useful players at that time were Arthur McKenzie, Jack Redford, Stan Tibbins, Fred Dooley and Herbie Smith, who was transferred to Aston Villa. In 1958 they became the first amateur club to win the Birmingham Senior Cup when they defeated Lockheed-Leamington 1-0.

After leaving the Birmingham League, where they spent 11 seasons after the closure of the Combination, in 1965 they replaced their reserve side in the Worcestershire Combination, where after three near misses as runners-up they became champions in 1980-81.

NORTHWICH VICTORIA

One of the two oldest clubs playing in the GM Conference, they have the distinction of having been founder-members of no less than five different competitions. After playing friendly matches in their early days, they were one of the clubs that founded The Combination in 1890, the Football League (Division 2) in 1892, the Cheshire County League in 1919, the Northern Premier League in 1968 and the Alliance Premier League in 1979.

After their brief sojourn in the Football League, they in fact returned to The Combination, later joining the Manchester League (champions in 1902-03) and the Lancashire Combination (1912-15). It is surprising to find that the 'Vics' only won the Cheshire League championship once in 49 seasons' membership and the League Challenge Cup twice.

It is in outside cup competitions that the club has met with most success, with the Cheshire Senior Cup residing at the Drill Field on 15 occasions whilst in the FA Trophy, after losing to Telford United in the 1983 final, they returned the following season to defeat Bangor City 2-1 after a replay.

STAFFORD RANGERS

Began playing in the Birmingham & District League in 1893 and after a brief flirtation with the Shropshire League returned to the B & D League for the next 12 seasons, competing against the reserves sides of Aston Villa, WBA and Wolves among others.

In 1912 they moved to the Birmingham Combination, winning the league in their first season, two points ahead of local rivals Hednesford Town. They were then runners-up the following season and again in 1919-20. From 1921 to 1939 they reverted back to the Birmingham League, but could do no more than twice finish runners-up.

After the Second World War they moved back to the Birmingham Combination for six seasons, but no honours were gained and in fact they had to wait until 1967-68 for their next piece of silverware, when as members of the Cheshire County League they won that competition's League Challenge Cup. In 1969 they were elected to the Northern Premier League, of which they were champions in 1984-85 and twice runners-up, and in 1979 they became members of the GM Conference.

Six times winners of the Staffordshire Senior Cup, they were FA Trophy winners in 1971-72 and again in 1978-79, as well as being losing finalists in 1975-76.

TELFORD UNITED

The name is a relatively recent one and is associated with a very fine record of success in both the FA Cup and FA Trophy, but one has to go right back to 1951-52 for the club's last championship success, when as Wellington Town they were winners of the Cheshire County League.

Founded in 1876, they joined the Birmingham & District League in 1898 and except for a break of three seasons, they were to spend 33 years there, winning three league titles and gaining three runners-up spots before moving to the Cheshire League in 1938. In 13 seasons in that competition, only three times did the club finish lower than sixth, with the championship being won in 1945-46, 1946-47 and 1951-52.

A move was made to the Southern League in 1958, and in 1969 their name was changed to Telford United, although their very fine Bucks Head ground is in Wellington. Ten years later they became founder-members of the GM Conference, and if league honours have been conspicuous by their absence, the 'Lillywhites' have certainly made their mark in the FA Trophy, with three wins and two losing appearances in the final, and with their numerous victories over Football League clubs.

WALTHAMSTOW AVENUE

One very famous name missing these days is Walthamstow Avenue, who became just a memory when they sold their ground in Green Pond Lane.

Founded in the late 1890s as Walthamstow Grange, they played in local leagues until 1921-22 when they were accepted into the Spartan League. They then transferred to the Athenian League in 1929 and proceeded to win the league title five times before the war. Joining the Isthmian League in 1945-46, they spent 42 seasons there, winning the championship in 1945-46, 1952-53 and 1953-54.

In 1951 the Avenue reached the final of the FA Amateur Cup for the first time, beating Leyton 2-1 with a side that included the Essex and England cricketer Trevor Bailey. The following season they reached the Fourth Round of the FA Cup with wins over Wimbledon (3-0), Watford (2-1), Stockport County (2-1). Then after holding Manchester United 1-1 at Old Trafford, they lost the replay (2-5). In 1960-61 the FA Amateur Cup was won a second time, West Auckland Town being beaten 2-1.

For 15 seasons the club was skippered by one of the greatest amateur players, Jim W Lewis, who won 13 amateur and 2 full England international caps before the war; his son Jim also gained amateur international honours as well as making 95 league and cup appearances as an amateur for Chelsea. S Gerula (Leyton Orient), L Julians (Arsenal) and D Saunders (Chelsea) all turned professional after playing for Walthamstow.

WIMBLEDON

The club that has risen from the relative obscurity of the Spartan and Athenian Leagues to the heights of an FA Cup win against Liverpool and a place in the First Division of the Football League.

Originally formed as Wimbledon Old Centrals in 1889 and renamed Wimbledon in 1905, after brief spells in the Spartan and Athenian Leagues they become the first of many clubs to receive an invitation to join the Isthmian League. This they accepted in 1921, and although at first they struggled to get out of the bottom of the Isthmian table, the thirties saw them champions four times between 1930 and 1936. In 1934-35 they reached the final of the Amateur Cup, when after a goalless draw at Middlesbrough, they lost the replay 1-2 to Bishop Auckland at Stamford Bridge.

Reaching the final again in 1946-47, they lost by the odd goal of three to Leytonstone, but it was third time lucky in 1962-63 when Eddie Reyolds scored all four goals in the 4-2 defeat of Sutton United. After winning the Isthmian League championship for three consecutive seasons, giving them a total of eight league titles, they opted to turn professional, joining the Southern League in 1964.

Following championship wins in this competition in 1974-75, 1975-76 and 1976-77, they were justifiably elected into the Football League, where their recent exploits are far too well known to need repeating. Certainly the Plough Lane story has been one of 'rags to riches'.

WYCOMBE WANDERERS

Founded in 1884, their early days (1896-1908) were spent in the Second Division of the Southern League. Then after a spell in the Great Western Suburban League they had two seasons in the Spartan League, winning the championship in both seasons. In 1921 they began a run of 59 seasons in the Isthmian League that brought them seven league titles.

The 'Blues' have made two appearances in the final of the FA Amateur Cup, the first time in 1930-31 when a goal from their inside-left Britnell was sufficient to defeat Hayes at Highbury, then in 1956-57 at Wembley when they were beaten 1-3 by Bishop Auckland, but in 1990-91 they won the FA Trophy. The Berks and Bucks Senior Cup has been won no less than 23 times.

Reg Boreham, who played for England against Ireland and Wales in 1922, signed for Arsenal, and other players who made their mark at Loakes Park include Dennis Syrett, Michael Wicks and Cliff Trott.

YORKSHIRE AMATEURS

Founded in 1919, they regularly competed against professional clubs in the Yorkshire League. First entering as founder-members in 1920, they resigned in 1924 but returned in 1930, retaining their membership thereafter until the Yorkshire League ceased to exist in 1982.

Although few honours have come the club's way, they have always maintained the highest traditional amateur standards. In 1931-32 they won one of the two league competitions organised by the Yorkshire League. The following season they defeated Huddersfield Town 'A' in the final of the League Cup, and in the same season reached the semi-final of the FA Amateur Cup where they were beaten 1-2 by Marine (Liverpool) at Filbert Street, Leicester. This was the most successful season in the Amateurs' history, for they also reached the First Round (Proper) of the FA Cup, losing 1-3 to Carlisle United at their well-appointed ground at Bracken End, Leeds. Other successes include the winning of the West Riding County Cup three times.

Many are the well-known amateurs who have assisted the club from time to time, including Harry McIlvenny, Peter Kippax, Harry Sharrett, Bill Slater, Dennis Saunders and John Tanner.

AMATEUR INTERNATIONALS

INTRODUCTION

The England amateur international side never enjoyed as full a fixture list as its professional big brother, but there were occasions when their matches rose into double figures for a single season – how our present day semi-professional squad would relish that!

Friendly games between England and the other 'home' countries had been played since 1926 but Wales showed a reluctance to play Northern Ireland, so the first amateur Home International Championship wasn't played until 1954, and then ironically, Northern Ireland were the first champions with Wales finishing at the foot of the table!

The Irish picked their team from their own league clubs, Welsh players were spread through their own clubs and the London Leagues, while Scotland relied heavily on players from Queens Park (the only amateur club in senior Scottish football). England, with a massive pulling power in the major amateur leagues, should always have been favourites but it didn't always work out like that as every game offered the chance of giant-killing and this has always inspired the underdog, especially with a national shirt on his back.

The years just after the Second World War saw a number of talented players keeping their amateur status even though they were turning out for Football League clubs. These included Bill Slater (Blackpool and Wolves), George Robb (Finchley and Spurs), and a little later, Seamus O'Connell (Bishop Auckland and Chelsea) and Charlie Mortimore (Aldershot and Woking).

As 'shamateurism' was taking its grip of senior 'amateur' football in the fifties and sixties, players became fitter and certainly more dedicated. To receive their 'expenses' they had to train twice a week and play on Saturdays. Then as floodlights were introduced on most grounds, it would be two games a week and a training day, so the international squads were made up of highly dedicated athletes, similar to the International Rugby Union players of today.

The carefree days of amateur internationals as social occasions supported by good attendances gave way to more serious affairs, considered by the public to be games only for second-rate professionals. Sadly the team suffered, reaching the lowest ever level of quality and entertainment in 1967-68 when Charles Hughes's tactics (of five midfield players – obviously ahead of his time!) produced an England team and then a Great Britain squad that finished the season with a record of P3 W1 D1 L1 F1 A1 for England and P4 W1 D0 L3 F2 A4 for Britain (failing to score in five out of eight games).

Happily, regular weekend get-togethers (which sadly ruled out the chances of many Northern players, as they couldn't get to the meetings) and sometimes as many as 16 internationals in a season, produced a side that was well-drilled, scored consistently and achieved a good ratio of 'results'. This team played many League clubs in 'friendlies' and were considered of at least Third Division standard.

Having come through a difficult time, it was a shame for the players that this regime came to an end, but the game as a whole benefited from the abolition of 'the amateur'.

Hendon have produced some brilliant teams and outstanding players. Lawrie Topp and Dexter Adams made up two thirds of England's half back line with Bill Slater (Wolves) in 1952-53.

RESULTS SUMMARY

ENGLAND v IRELAND*

Year		Venue	
1906	Dec 15	Dublin	2-1
1907	Dec 7	Tottenham	6-1
1908	Nov 21	Dublin	5-1
1909	Nov 20	Leeds	4-4
1910	Nov 19	Belfast	2-3
1911	Nov 18	Huddersfield	2-0
1912	Oct 5	Belfast	2-3
1913	Nov 8	Belfast	2-0
1919	Nov 18	Derby	5-0
1920	Nov 13	Belfast	4-0
1921	Nov 14	Leicester	4-1
1922	Nov 11	Preston	4-0
1923	Nov 10	Crystal Palace	3-0
1924	Nov 8	Belfast	3-2
1925	Nov 7	Maidstone	7-4
1926	Nov 6	Belfast	3-0
1927	Nov 12	Blackpool	1-1
1928	Nov 10	Belfast	2-0
1929	Nov 16	Crystal Palace	7-2
1930	Nov 15	Belfast	1-3
1931	Nov 14	York	3-2
1933	Feb 18	Belfast	3-4
1934	Feb 17	Ilford	4-0
1935	Feb 16	Belfast	4-2
1936	Feb 15	Blackpool	5-0
1937	Feb 13	Belfast	1-5
1938	Feb 19	Leicester	1-1
1939	Feb 18	Belfast	1-0
1947	Feb 8	Southport	3-1
1948	Feb 7	Belfast	5-0
1949	Feb 5	Norwich	0-1
1950	Feb 4	Belfast	3-1
1951	Feb 3	Coventry	6-3
1952	Feb 2	Belfast	3-1
1953	Jan 31	Lincoln	4-1
1953	Sep 12	Coleraine	1-2
1954	Sep 18	Crystal Palace	5-0
1955	Sep 17	Belfast	4-1
1956	Sep 15	Bromley	5-2
1957	Sep 28	Belfast	3-0
1958	Sep 27	Bournemouth	6-2
1959	Sep 26	Belfast	1-1
1960	Sep 24	High Wycombe	3-2
1961	Sep 30	Coleraine	3-0
1962	Sep 29	Dulwich	3-2
1963	Sep 28	Belfast	1-2
1964	Sep 26	Romford	2-1
1965	Sep 25	Ballymena	1-0
1966	Sep 24	Watford	2-0
1967	Sep 23	Ballymena	2-0
1968	Sep 28	Charlton	5-0
1969	Sep 27	Portadown	4-1
1970	Oct 2	Woking	4-1
1972	May 15	Hendon	1-2
1972	Oct 6	Norwich	2-1
1973	Oct 12	Watford	2-0

*IRELAND – Northern Ireland after 1922

ENGLAND v WALES

1908	Feb 22	Stockport	1-0
1909	Feb 20	Aberdare	5-2
1910	Feb 19	Huddersfield	6-0
1911	Feb 18	Newtown	5-1
1912	Feb 17	Bishop Auckland	3-0
1913	Feb 8	Llandudno	3-1
1914	Feb 7	Plymouth	9-1
1920	Jan 24	Merthyr	9-0
1921	Jan 22	Wolverhampton	0-2
1922	Jan 21	Swansea	7-0
1923	Jan 27	Middlesbrough	4-4
1924	Mar 22	Llandudno	2-1
1925	Mar 21	Plymouth	2-1
1926	Mar 20	Wrexham	2-1
1927	Mar 19	Reading	4-0
1928	Mar 17	Cardiff	2-1
1929	Feb 16	Brighton	1-1
1930	Feb 15	Aberystwyth	2-1
1931	Feb 14	Bournemouth	5-0
1932	Feb 27	Swansea	3-1
1933	Jan 21	Torquay	1-0
1934	Jan 27	Bangor	5-3
1935	Jan 19	Wimbledon	6-1
1936	Feb 29	Portmadoc	7-3
1937	Jan 23	Portsmouth	9-1
1938	Jan 29	Rhyl	8-2
1939	Jan 28	Cheltenham	5-2
1947	Jan 25	Dulwich	2-2
1947	Mar 29	Newport	4-1
1948	Jan 24	Bangor	7-2
1948	Mar 6	Shrewsbury	3-4
1949	Jan 22	Swindon	4-1
1949	Mar 12	Llanelly	3-1
1950	Jan 21	Bangor	1-0
1951	Jan 20	Leicester	4-1
1952	Feb 16	Bangor	4-3
1953	Feb 14	Highbury	3-3
1954	Apr 24	Newport	2-0
1955	Apr 23	Bournemouth	3-1
1956	Feb 11	Swansea	1-2
1957	Feb 16	Peterborough	5-0
1957	Nov 9	Bangor	5-2
1958	Nov 8	Shrewsbury	0-0
1959	Nov 7	Bangor	2-0
1960	Nov 5	Brighton	6-1
1961	Nov 18	Ton Pentre	2-2
1962	Nov 17	Shrewsbury	3-2
1963	Nov 23	Bangor	3-3
1964	Nov 21	Shrewsbury	7-0
1965	Nov 20	Aberystwyth	2-1
1966	Dec 3	Kingston	4-1
1967	Nov 18	Portmadoc	0-1
1968	Nov 9	Watford	1-1
1969	Nov 29	Cardiff	1-0
1970	Dec 5	Hendon	3-0
1971	Dec 4	Llanidlog	1-1
1972	Dec 2	Hereford	3-1
1973	Dec 8	Merthyr Tydfil	1-1

ENGLAND v SCOTLAND

Year		Venue		Year		Venue	
1926	Dec 18	Leicester	1-4	1954	Mar 27	Wembley	1-4
1928	Apr 28	Glasgow	2-3	1955	Apr 9	Glasgow	3-3
1929	Mar 16	Leeds	3-1	1956	Mar 24	Wembley	4-2
1930	Mar 15	Glasgow	0-1	1957	Mar 30	Glasgow	0-0
1931	Mar 21	Chelsea	2-1	1958	Mar 29	Wembley	2-3
1932	Mar 19	Glasgow	1-3	1959	Mar 14	Dumfries	1-1
1933	Mar 25	Dulwich	1-0	1960	Mar 26	Southend	2-1
1934	Mar 24	Glasgow	2-3	1961	Mar 18	Glasgow	2-2
1935	Mar 23	Dulwich	2-1	1962	Mar 16	Crystal Palace	3-4
1936	Mar 14	Inverness	0-1	1963	Mar 15	Glasgow	4-2
1937	Mar 13	Dulwich	0-1	1964	Mar 20	Crystal Palace	1-0
1938	Mar 12	Glasgow	5-2	1965	Mar 20	Aberdeen	1-2
1939	Mar 11	Dulwich	8-3	1966	Mar 25	Southend	3-3
1949	Apr 16	Glasgow	2-3	1967	Mar 31	Dundee	2-2
1950	Mar 4	Hull	0-0	1968	Apr 5	White City	0-0
1951	Mar 17	Glasgow	3-2	1969	Mar 28	Glasgow	5-1
1952	Mar 15	Wembley	1-2	1970	Mar 20	Dulwich	1-0
1953	Mar 21	Glasgow	1-0	1971	Mar 17	Falkirk	2-0
				1972	Mar 24	Wigan	4-0

England v Scotland at Wembley, in front of a huge crowd. It was certainly a great occasion and Field-Marshall Viscount Montgomery is introduced to the famous George Robb by the equally well known skipper, Jim Lewis.

| 1973 | Mar 2 | Clyde | 3-0 |
| 1974 | April 5 | Coventry | 1-1 |

ENGLAND v SOUTH AFRICA

1924	Oct 11	Southampton	3-2
1924	Nov 26	Tottenham	3-2
1953	Sep 19	Crystal Palace	0-4
1958	Oct 25	High Wycombe	2-2

ENGLAND v AUSTRIA

1966	Oct 1	Salzburg (ENAC)	0-3
1966	Oct 26	Hendon (ENAC)	2-0
1973	Sep 25	Watford	6-1

ENGLAND v BAHAMAS

| 1969 | July 20 | Nassau | 4-0 |

ENGLAND v BAHRAIN

| 1968 | Nov 14 | Isa Town | 4-0 |

ENGLAND v BELGIUM

1908	Apr 18	Brussels	8-2
1909	Apr 19	Tottenham	11-2
1910	Mar 26	Brussels	2-2
1911	Mar 4	Crystal Palace	4-0
1912	Apr 8	Brussels	2-1
1912	Nov 9	Swindon	4-0
1914	Feb 24	Brussels	8-1
1920	Feb 17	Brussels	1-3
1923	May 5	Brussels	0-3

ENGLAND v DENMARK

1910	May 5	Copenhagen	1-2
1911	Oct 21	Park Royal	3-0
1914	Jun 5	Copenhagen	0-3
1972	May 3	Copenhagen	2-1

ENGLAND v FINLAND

1951	May 10	Swindon	3-2
1957	Sep 15	Helsinki	3-4
1958	Oct 11	Dulwich	3-2
1970	Sep 23	Helsinki	3-1

ENGLAND v FRANCE

1906	Nov 1	Paris	15-0
1908	Mar 23	Park Royal	12-0
1909	May 22	Paris	11-0
1910	Apr 16	Brighton	10-1
1911	Mar 23	Paris	3-1
1913	Feb 27	Paris	4-1
1920	Apr 5	Rouen	5-0
1921	May 5	Paris	1-2
1947	May 17	Lille	4-1
1948	Apr 3	Ilford	0-2
1949	May 22	Grenoble	2-1
1950	Apr 8	Southampton	0-0
1951	May 20	Cherbourg	3-3

1952	Apr 5	Norwich	3-0
1953	May 3	Boulogne	1-0
1953	Nov 14	Luton	4-2
1955	May 8	Brest	1-1
1956	Apr 21	Dulwich	3-1
1957	May 12	Mulhouse	1-3
1958	Apr 26	Leeds	1-1
1959	Apr 5	Bayonne	0-1
1961	Apr 29	Dulwich	2-0
1962	Apr 8	Brest	0-3
1963	May 15	Hartlepool	3-1
1964	May 28	Santa Margherita (ENAC)	3-4
1965	May 16	Annecy	0-1
1969	Oct 8	Enfield (ENAC)	1-2
1970	May 13	Brest (ENAC)	2-3
1971	Feb 17	Dulwich	1-1
1972	Feb 16	Brest	1-1

ENGLAND v GERMANY

1908	Apr 30	Berlin	5-1
1909	May 13	Oxford	9-0
1911	Apr 14	Berlin	2-2
1913	Mar 21	Berlin	3-0
1955	Nov 12	Tottenham	2-3
1957	May 19	Offenburg	1-1
1957	Oct 12	Ilford	2-3
1959	May 27	Siegen	0-2
1960	Mar 5	Dulwich	1-1
1963	May 18	Middlesbrough	0-1
1964	May 30	Finale Ligure (ENAC)	0-1
1973	Oct 31	Wembley (ENAC)	1-0
1974	Mar 13	Bielefeld (ENAC)	1-3

ENGLAND v GUYANA

| 1969 | Jul 29 | Georgetown | 8-0 |
| 1969 | July 31 | Georgetown | 8-0 |

ENGLAND v ICELAND

1956	Aug 7	Reykjavik	3-2
1961	Sep 16	High Wycombe	1-0
1970	Feb 2	Slough	1-0
1970	May 10	Reykjavik	1-1

ENGLAND v REPUBLIC OF IRELAND

1951	Jan 6	Dublin	1-0
1952	Mar 8	Shrewsbury	8-3
1961	Feb 25	Dublin	1-1
1962	Sep 16	Dublin	2-2
1965	Feb 27	Dublin	3-2
1966	Mar 11	Brentford	4-0
1967	Mar 11	Dublin	2-0
1969	Mar 8	Dublin	1-1
1970	Feb 28	Wycombe	3-1
1971	Mar 6	Dublin	1-0
1972	Feb 25	Wycombe	2-0

ENAC — European Nations Amateur Cup

ENGLAND v ITALY

1962	May 12	Ascoli Piceno	0-1
1968	May 23	Enfield	0-0
1969	May 1	Montecatini	0-0
1972	May 10	Plymouth	4-0

ENGLAND v LUXEMBOURG

1948	Mar 26	Ilford	2-1
1959	May 24	Luxembourg	1-3

ENGLAND v MALTA

1973	Dec 5	Gzira (ENAC)	3-0
1974	Mar 6	Reading (ENAC)	2-0

ENGLAND v NETHERLANDS

1907	Apr 1	The Hague	8-1
1907	Dec 21	Darlington	12-2
1909	Apr 12	Amsterdam	4-0
1909	Dec 11	Chelsea	9-1
1911	Apr 17	Amsterdam	1-0
1912	Mar 16	Hull	4-0
1913	Mar 24	The Hague	1-2
1913	Nov 15	Hull	2-1
1948	Mar 29	Dulwich	2-5
1952	Nov 15	Hull	2-2
1953	Mar 7	Rotterdam	0-1
1959	May 20	The Hague	3-1
1962	May 16	Zwolle	0-0
1963	May 20	Gateshead	3-1
1966	May 21	Deventer (ENAC)	0-0
1966	Nov 19	Dulwich (ENAC)	1-0

ENGLAND v NETHERLANDS ANTILLES

1969	Aug 2	Willenstad	2-0

ENGLAND v NEW ZEALAND

1964	Apr 16	Dulwich	4-1

ENGLAND v NORWAY

1951	May 15	Middlesbrough	2-1
1953	May 15	Oslo	1-1
1971	Jul 21	Stavanger	1-2

ENGLAND v SOUTH AFRICA

1924	Oct 11	Southampton	3-2
1924	Nov 26	Tottenham	3-2

ENGLAND v SPAIN

1969	Oct 22	Dulwich (ENAC)	1-2
1969	Nov 20	Tenerife (ENAC)	0-2

ENGLAND v SWEDEN

1908	Sep 8	Gothenburg	6-1
1909	Nov 6	Hull	7-0
1914	Jun 10	Stockholm	5-1
1914	Jun 12	Stockholm	5-0

ENGLAND v SWITZERLAND

1909	May 20	Basle	9-0
1910	Apr 9	Park Royal	6-1
1911	May 25	Berne	4-1

ENGLAND v TRINIDAD

1969	Jul 23	Port of Spain	0-0
1969	Jul 26	San Fernando	3-0

SCOTLAND v GERMANY

1956	Munich	1-4
1957	Glasgow	1-1
1963	Sunderland	5-2

SCOTLAND v HOLLAND

1956	The Hague	2-2
1957	Glasgow	0-1

SCOTLAND v ICELAND

1964	Reykjavik	1-0

SCOTLAND v IRELAND

1930	Londonderry	3-0
1931	Aberdeen	2-0
1932	Belfast	0-4
1933	Glasgow	6-0
1934	Belfast	1-4
1935	Glasgow	2-3
1936	Belfast	5-3
1937	Glasgow	3-0
1938	Belfast	1-2
1939	Glasgow	1-1
1949	Belfast	2-2
1950	Aberdeen	2-5
1951	Londonderry	1-0
1952	Glasgow	2-1
1953	Belfast	0-1
1954	Kilmarnock	0-0
1955	Cliftonville	1-2
1956	Kilmarnock	1-3
1957	Newtownards	1-4
1958	Airdrie	1-3
1959	Coleraine	0-0
1960	Glasgow	2-0
1961	Coleraine	3-3
1962	Falkirk	0-0
1963	Belfast	2-5
1964	Glasgow	2-2
1965	Ballymena	1-1
1966	Kilmarnock	2-3
1967	Newtownards	2-1
1968	Greenock	0-2
1969	Portadown	2-1
1970	Stranraer	3-1
1971	Belfast	1-1
1972	Paisley	0-1
1973	Falkirk	1-0

SCOTLAND v ITALY

1963	Darlington	3-1

SCOTLAND v SWITZERLAND

1963	Crook	1-1

SCOTLAND v WALES

1930	Glasgow	1-0
1931	Swansea	2-1
1932	Edinburgh	1-5
1933	Bangor	0-0
1934	Greenock	4-0
1935	Aberystwyth	5-2
1936	Dumfries	1-1
1937	Bangor	2-0
1950	Dumfries	1-0
1951	Ebbw Vale	1-0
1952	Inverness	3-2
1953	Wrexham	1-0
1954	Ayr	0-0
1955	Bangor	5-0
1956	Glasgow	2-2
1957	Newtown	1-1
1958	Dumfries	3-0
1959	Aberystwyth	3-1
1960	Kilmarnock	3-3
1961	Ton Pentre	3-3
1962	Perth	3-3
1963	Wrexham	1-1
1964	Paisley	1-0
1965	Rhyl	1-1
1966	Perth (ENAC)	2-0
1967	Llanelli (ENAC)	1-1
1968	Glasgow	1-1
1969	Wrexham	1-1
1970	Berwick	0-3
1971	Rhyl	1-3
1972	Hawick	0-2
1973	Barry	2-1
1874	Dumfries	1-1

SCOTLAND v REPUBLIC OF IRELAND

1966	Dublin (ENAC)	4-0
1966	Glasgow (ENAC)	4-0

IRELAND v WALES

Year	Venue	
1954	Belfast	3-2
1955	Llanidloes	2-1
1956	Cliftonville	2-1
1957	Ebbw Vale	1-3
1958	Coleraine	3-1
1959	Llandudno	4-3
1960	Ballymena	3-2
1961	Portmadoc	1-4
1962	Ballymena	3-1
1963	Wrexham	2-0
1964	Belfast	2-2

1965	Newtown	1-1
1966	Portadown	0-0
1967	Newtown	3-3
1968	Portadown	0-1
1969	Ton Pentre	0-1
1970	Ballymena	3-1
1971	Llanelli	1-0
1972	Welshpool	3-0
1973	Rhyll	1-2
1974	Denbigh	3-0

IRELAND v FRANCE

1921	Paris	2-1
1928	Paris	0-4

IRELAND v SOUTH AFRICA

1925	Belfast	2-1
1954	Belfast	2-5

WALES v SOUTH AFRICA

1924	Colwyn Bay	1-0
1954	Bangor	1-0
1959	Bangor	1-3

WALES v NORWAY

1932	Bergen	2-1

WALES v REPUBLIC OF IRELAND

1966	Bangor ENAC	0-1
1966	Dublin ENAC	2-1

WALES v HOLLAND

1969	Bangor	0-2
1970	Otterhousen	1-3

BRITAIN v ICELAND

*1963	Reykjavik	6-0
*1963	Wimbledon	4-0

BRITAIN v GREECE

*1964	Chelsea	2-1
*1964	Athens	1-4

BRITAIN v WEST GERMANY

*1967	Augsburg	2-0
*1967	Hendon	0-1

BRITAIN v SPAIN

*1968	Sabadell	0-1
*1968	White City	0-0

*Olympic Tournament

HOME CHAMPIONSHIPS

FINAL POSITIONS 1953-1974

1953-54	P	W	D	L	F	A	Pts
N IRELAND	3	2	1	0	5	3	5
SCOTLAND	3	1	2	0	4	1	4
ENGLAND	3	1	0	2	4	6	2
WALES	3	0	1	2	2	5	1
1954-55							
ENGLAND	3	2	1	0	11	4	5
N IRELAND	3	2	0	1	4	7	4
SCOTLAND	3	1	1	1	9	5	3
WALES	3	0	0	3	2	10	0
1955-56							
ENGLAND	3	2	0	1	9	5	4
N IRELAND	3	2	0	1	6	6	4
WALES	3	1	1	1	5	5	3
SCOTLAND	3	0	1	2	5	9	1
1956-57							
ENGLAND	3	2	1	0	10	2	5
WALES	3	1	1	1	4	7	3
N IRELAND	3	1	0	2	7	9	2
SCOTLAND	3	0	2	1	2	5	2
1957-58							
ENGLAND	3	2	0	1	10	5	4
SCOTLAND	3	2	0	1	7	5	4
N IRELAND	3	2	0	1	6	5	4
WALES	3	0	0	3	3	11	0
1958-59							
ENGLAND	3	1	2	0	7	3	4
SCOTLAND	3	1	2	0	4	2	4
N IRELAND	3	1	1	1	6	9	2
WALES	3	0	1	2	4	7	1
1959-60							
ENGLAND	3	2	1	0	5	2	5
SCOTLAND	3	1	1	1	6	5	3
N IRELAND	3	1	1	1	4	5	3
WALES	3	0	1	2	5	8	1
1960-61							
ENGLAND	3	2	1	0	11	5	5
SCOTLAND	3	0	3	0	8	8	3
WALES	3	1	1	1	8	10	3
N IRELAND	3	0	1	2	6	10	1
1961-62							
SCOTLAND	3	2	1	0	7	4	5
ENGLAND	3	1	1	1	8	6	3
IRELAND	3	1	1	1	3	4	3
WALES	3	0	1	2	4	8	1
1962-63							
ENGLAND	3	3	0	0	10	6	6
N IRELAND	3	2	0	1	9	5	4
WALES	3	1	0	2	5	6	2
SCOTLAND	3	0	0	3	5	12	0
1963-64							
N IRELAND	3	1	2	0	6	5	4
ENGLAND	3	1	1	1	5	5	3
SCOTLAND	3	1	1	1	3	3	3
WALES	3	0	2	1	5	6	2

1964-65	P	W	D	L	F	A	Pts
ENGLAND	3	2	0	1	10	3	4
SCOTLAND	3	1	2	0	4	2	4
IRELAND	3	0	2	1	3	4	2
WALES	3	0	2	1	2	9	2
1965-66							
ENGLAND	3	2	1	0	7	4	5
SCOTLAND	3	1	1	1	7	6	3
N IRELAND	3	1	1	1	3	4	3
WALES	3	0	1	2	1	4	1
1966-67							
ENGLAND	3	2	1	0	8	3	5
SCOTLAND	3	1	2	0	5	4	4
WALES	3	0	2	1	5	8	2
N IRELAND	3	0	1	2	4	7	1
1967-68							
WALES	3	2	1	0	3	1	5
IRELAND	3	1	1	1	2	2	3
ENGLAND	3	1	1	1	1	1	3
SCOTLAND	3	0	1	2	1	3	1
1968-69							
ENGLAND	3	2	1	0	11	2	5
WALES	3	1	2	0	3	2	4
SCOTLAND	3	1	1	1	4	7	3
N IRELAND	3	0	0	3	1	8	0
1969-70							
ENGLAND	3	3	0	0	6	1	6
WALES	3	1	0	2	4	4	2
SCOTLAND	3	1	0	2	3	5	2
N IRELAND	3	1	0	2	5	8	2
1970-71							
ENGLAND	3	3	0	0	9	1	6
WALES	3	2	0	1	4	4	4
N IRELAND	3	0	1	2	2	6	1
SCOTLAND	3	0	1	2	2	6	1
1971-72							
N IRELAND	3	3	0	0	6	1	6
ENGLAND	3	1	1	1	6	3	3
WALES	3	1	1	1	3	4	3
SCOTLAND	3	0	0	3	0	7	0
1972-73							
ENGLAND	3	3	0	0	8	2	6
SCOTLAND	3	2	0	1	3	4	4
WALES	3	1	0	2	4	6	2
N IRELAND	3	0	0	3	2	5	0
1973-74							
ENGLAND	3	1	2	0	4	2	4
WALES	3	1	2	0	3	2	4
SCOTLAND	2	0	2	0	2	2	2
N IRELAND	2	0	0	2	0	3	0

The Scotland v N Ireland match was not played.

POST-WAR ENGLAND AMATEUR INTERNATIONALS

PLAYERS A-Z

Adams, DW, 19, Hendon

Adams, J, 17, Enfield (7), Slough T (4), Enfield (6)

Agar, R, 5, Walthamstow Ave (2), Tooting and Mitcham U (3)

Alexander, FC, 7, Cambridge Univ (2), Pegasus (3), Corinthian Casuals (2)

Amor, W, 1, Huntley and Palmer's, Reading

Amos, A, 3, Slough T

Andrews, D, 5, Leytonstone

Ardrey, R, 12, Wimbledon

Ashworth, J, 6, Royal Navy (2), Wealdstone (4)

Aston, P, 3, Measham Imperial

Banks, K, 3, Spennymoor U

Barker C, 1, Army

Barker, M, 6, Bishop Auckland

Bass, A, 10, Dagenham (3), Hendon (4), Bishop's Stortford (3)

Bassett, D, 10, Walton and Hersham

Bates, P, 2, Wycombe W

Beardsley, E, 4, Eastbourne (1), Hendon (3)

Bell, R, 1, Ferryhill Athletic

Bennett, E, 8, Southall

Biggs, A, 2, Hounslow T

Bladon, T, 6, Sutton U

Bradley, W, 11, Bishop Auckland

Bridges, AJ, 2, Royal Navy

Bromilow, GJ, 5, Northern Nomads (2), Southport (3)

Brooks, J, 5, Enfield

Broomfield, W, 5, West Auckland T

Brown, BR, 7, Pegasus

Brown, G, 1, West Auckland T

Brown, GR, 1, Bromley

Brown, L, 3, Bishop Auckland

Brown, LG, 8, Dulwich H (4), Wimbledon (4)

Brown, RH, 14, Barnet (11), Fulham (3)

Browning, M, 2, Tooting and Mitcham U

Bumpstead, D, 1, Tooting and Mitcham U

Bunce, G, 4, Leytonstone

Bunker, E, 3, Barnet

Burchell, GS, 4, Walthamstow Ave

Burns, M, 1, Skelmersdale U

Butterfield, J, 19, Enfield (17), Ilford (2)

Candey, M, 9, Maidstone U

Carr, RB, 1, Sutton U

Champelovier, L, 3, Hayes

Charles, J, 3, Leytonstone

Charlton, S, 4, Bromley

Childs, AR, 1, Northern Nomads

Childs, E, 6, Leytonstone

Clark, F, 1, Crook T

Clarke, D, 1, Walthamstow Ave

Clements, P, 8, West Ham U (3), Skelmersdale U (5)

Coates, A, 3, Evenwood T (2), Crook T (1)

Coates J, 3, Royal Navy

Cobb, D, 1, Tooting and Mitcham U

Connell, R, 2, Slough T (1), Walton and Hersham (1)

Cooper, M, 3, Hendon

Cowan, R, 4, Cambridge Univ (1), Pegasus (3)

Creasey W, 5, Hounslow T

Cresswell, C, 10, Bishop Auckland

Crosbie, T, 3, Skelmersdale U

Cross, E, 2, Ilford

Cruse, P, 2, Slough T

Cutbush, D, 5, Royal Navy

D'Arcy, A, 26, Barnet (11), Enfield (15)

D'Arcy, D, 1, Barnet

Darey, J, 4, Wimbledon

Davison, R, 1, Shildon

Day, R, 43, Enfield (23), Slough T (14), Enfield (3), Ilford (3)

Deadman, P, 40, Barking (14), Hendon (26)

Delaney, J, 17, Wycombe W

Dickin, E, 3, Skelmersdale U

Diwell, P, 2, Leytonstone

Dodkins, HE, 26, Ilford

Dougall, J, 6, Pegasus

Doyle, M, 1, Wealdstone

Duggan, C, 1, Bishop's Stortford

Dutchman, J, 2, Corinthian Casuals

Eason, L, 7, Finchley (1), Barnet (6)

Eaton, R, 17, Slough T (14), Enfield (3)

Edelston, M, 3, Reading

Edwards, D, 2, Wycombe W

Evans, D, 1, Hounslow T

Farrer, LT, 20, Bishop Auckland (8), Walthamstow Ave (12)

Feely, P, 2, Enfield

Figg, R, 9, Barnet

Flanagan, D, 3, Loughborough Coll (1) Walthamstow Ave (2)

Fletcher, J, 4, Maidstone U

Frankish, P, 1, Skelmersdale U

Friend, B, 6, Leatherhead

Fright, EG, 18, Bromley (13), Leytonstone (4), Bromley (1)

Fry, P, 12, Enfield

Fryer, R, 2, Crook T

Fuller, CE, 16, Bromley

Fuschillo, P, 1, Wycombe W

Gadsden, RF, 1, Hayes

Gamblin, D, 29, Sutton U (16), Slough T (3), Leatherhead (4), Winchester C (1), Wycombe W (5)

Garbutt, P, 1, Crook T

Gardener, D, 7, Crook T

Goodwin, H, 1, Royal Navy

Gradi, D, 1, Sutton U

Gray, K, 43, Leytonstone (28), Enfield (15)

Greene, P, 1, Dagenham

Greenwood, MM, 7, Bishop Auckland

Griffin, DJ, 3, Leytonstone

Groves, V, 4, Leytonstone (2), Walthamstow Ave (2)

Haider, R, 65, Kingstonian (10), Hendon (55)

Hamm, G, 19, Woking (9), Wimbledon (10)

Hammond, P, 1, Hitchin T

Hardcastle, P, 4, Skelmersdale U

Harding, A, 10, Barnet (6), Enfield (4)

Harding, J, 4, Pegasus (2), Army (1), Kettering T (1)

Hardisty JRE, 16, Bishop Auckland

Harlow, J, 3, Tooting and Mitcham U

Harris, J, 5, Hendon (4), Enfield (1)

Harrison, K, 1, Crook T

Harvey, B, 22, Walthamstow Ave (10), Leytonstone (12)

Heckman, R, 5, Bromley

Hodges, P, 3, Wycombe W

Hogwood, D, 7, Hendon

Holden, G, 1, Tooting and Mitcham U

Holmes, W, 4, Wolverhampton W (3), Blackburn R (1)
Hopper, AH, 7, Bromley
Howard, T, 6, Hendon (2), Enfield (4)
Hunt, L, 5, Marine Liverpool
Hyde, D, 6, Hendon
Ives, A, 1, Tooting and Mitcham U
Jackson, RF, 2, Oxford Univ
Jarvis, DH, 12, Leytonstone
Jeffrey, A, 3, Doncaster R
Jelly, K, 1, Tooting and Mitcham U
Joseph, L, 12, Leytonstone
Kavanagh, JJM, 2, Leytonstone
Kelly, C, 1, Leatherhead
Kelly, M, 1, Wimbledon
King, A, 1, Hounslow T
King, R, 7, St Albans C (5), Hitchin T (2)
Kippax, FP, 1, Yorkshire Amateurs and Liverpool
Knox, A, 2, Whitley Bay
Lailey, J, 7, Oxford C (3), Cheltenham T (4)
Law, RK, 19, Wimbledon
Lawrence, T, 12, Enfield
Laybourne, JS, 4, Corinthian Casuals
Lee, EG, 3, Chester
Lewin, DJ, 5, Bishop Auckland
Lewis, JL, 49, Walthamstow Ave (21), Chelsea (14), Walthamstow Ave (14)
Lindsay, HM, 29, Kingstonian (11), Wealdstone (18)
Littlejohn, R, 2, Bournemouth and Boscombe (1), Woking (1)
Lunn, RG, 3, Pegasus
McGhee, T, 3, Royal Navy
McIlvenny, HJ, 7, Yorkshire Amateurs and Bradford PA
McKenna, F, 3, Bishop Auckland
McKinna, GH, 4, Pegasus
McMillan, J, 1, Crook T
Mahon, M, 3, Newcastle U (1), Loughborough Coll (2)
Major, J, 3, Romford (1) Bishop Auckland (2)
Marshall, D, 2, Bishop Auckland
Martin, B, 8, Wimbledon
Martin, CL, 4, Bromley
Martin, J, 22, Wimbledon
Mason, J, 1, Alvechurch
Mead, K, 2, Slough T
Mellows, M, 16, Sutton U (15), Winchester C (1)
Mendum, A, 1, West Auckland T
Merritt, R, 1, Dulwich H
Mills, DJ, 1, Royal Navy
Moffatt, B, 9, Leytonstone (7), Enfield (2)
Moore, D, 14, Dagenham

Mortimore, CT, 17, Aldershot (5), Woking (12)
Mortimore, J, 4, Woking
Moxon, H, 11, Enfield (9), Wealdstone (2)
Neale, CR, 11, Walton and Hersham
Neale, M, 1, Enfield
Neil, PT, 10, Portsmouth (2), Corinthian Casuals (6), Cambridge Univ (2)
Noble, AW, 18, Leytonstone
O'Connell, S, 4, Bishop Auckland
Oliver, R, 2, Bishop Auckland
Page, R, 5, Barking
Parr, H, 1, Lincoln C
Paviour, JS, 9, Romford (4), Leytonstone (5)
Pawson, HA, 8, Pegasus
Payne, J, 18, Enfield
Peel, AM, 1, Sheffield Univ
Phillips, P, 2, Bishop's Stortford
Phipps, RW, 2, Barnet
Picking, L, 3, Barnet
Pinner, MJ, 52, Cambridge Univ (9), Pegasus (19), Queen's Park Rangers and RAF (5), RAF (2), Manchester U and RAF (2), Hendon (9), Leyton Orient (6)
Potts, HJ, 8, Oxford Univ (4), Pegasus (4)
Powell, E, 51, Sutton U (19), Wycombe W (15), Kingstonian (3), Sutton U (14)
Pragg, M, 3, Shrewsbury T
Preston, M, 13, Kingstonian
Prince, ST, 9, Walthamstow Ave
Pritchard L, 48, Sutton U (22), Wycombe W (26)
Randall, D, 1, Hitchin T
Rawlings, JW, 12, Enfield (11), Hayes (1)
Reardon, T, 1, Wycombe W
Reid, I, 28, Crook T (2), Enfield (8), Hitchin T (18)
Ritchie, J, 2, Slough T
Ritchie, J, 1, Whitley Bay
Robb, G, 17, Finchley
Robertson, JD, 26, Corinthian Casuals (3), Tooting and Mitcham U (23)
Robinson, TH, 10, Brentford (6), Northampton T (4)
Robinson, W, 1, Sutton U
Rosethorn, A, 5, Tow Law T (3), North Shields (2)
Roughley, W, 1, Crook T
Rowe, RG, 3, Royal Navy
Rowlands, LC, 6, Workington (1), Wrexham (4), Ashton U (1)
Russell, W, 4, Bishop Auckland

Rutherford, D, 5, South Shields (1), North Shields (4)
Rutherford, S, 1, Willington
Sadler, D, 2, Maidstone U
Saunders, DF, 1, Pegasus
Saunders, DW, 6, Walthamstow Ave
Sharratt, H, 4, Blackpool (2), Bishop Auckland (2)
Shaw, M, 1, Walthamstow Ave
Shepherd, W, 2, Goslings, Manchester
Shewring, D, 1, Sutton U
Shippey, J, 3, Oxford C
Shuttleworth, GM, 1, Pegasus
Slater, WJ, 20, Blackpool (5), Carnegie Coll (4), Brentford (5), Wolverhampton W (6)
Sleap, RW, 16, Barnet (6), Hendon (10)
Smith, AC, 3, Royal Navy
Smith, D, 1, Prestwich Heys
Smith, NL, 1, Bishop Auckland
Smith, P, 1, Leatherhead
Smith, W, 14, Sutton U (3), Walton and Hersham (11)
Spector, M, 1, Chelsea
Stacey, T, 6, Carshalton Athletic
Stewart, MJ, 1, Corinthian Casuals
Stoker, D, 2, Kingstonians (1), Sutton U (1)
Stratton, L, 5, Walthamstow Ave
Stratton, R, 2, Woking
Streten, B, 4, Shrewsbury T and RAF (2), Luton T and RAF (2)
Stroud, RW, 9, Hendon
Studley, D, 1, Bromley
Suddaby, P, 3, Oxford Univ (1), Wycombe W (2)
Sutcliffe, R, 1, Pegasus
Swannell, J, 61, Hendon
Tanner, JDP, 3, Oxford Univ (2), Yorkshire Amateurs (1)
Taylor, JR, 2, Crook T
Teasdale, H, 3, Bishop Auckland
Terry, P, 2, Enfield
Thompson, P, 4, RAF
Thompson, T, 4, Stockton
Thursby, R, 17, Bishop Auckland (11), Crook T (5), Bishop Auckland (1)
Tilley, L, 19, Leytonstone (11), Enfield (8)
Topp, L, 32, Hendon
Townsend, C, 32, Wealdstone
Tracey, M, 3, Crook T
Trimby, RW, 3, Pegasus (1), Corinthian Casuals (2)
Turley, A, 6, Barnet (2), Enfield (4)
Turner, J, 2, Skelmersdale U
Twissell, C, 5, Royal Navy and Plymouth Argyle (3), Plymouth Argyle (2)

Unsworth, J, 1, Skelmersdale U
Valentine, JH, 5, Loughborough
  Coll
Vaughan, C, 1, Sutton U
Veart, R, 1, Whitby Town
Venables, T, 1, Chelsea
Vowells, RC, 1, Corinthian Casuals
Waiters, AK, 1, Loughborough Coll
Walby, M, 2, Dunstable Town
Wallis, LJ, 4, Leytonstone
Walton, D, 2, Finchley
Walton, JA, 18, Army (3), Bury (9),
  Manchester U (3), Bury (3)
Ward, G, 1, Arsenal
Ward, JR, 3, Scunthorpe Grammar
  School (1), Northampton T (2)
West, L, 1, Enfield
Whittall, A, 1, Ilford
Williams, A, 3, Enfield
Wilson, JJ, 5, Barking
Wilson, P, 3, Whitley Bay
Windsor, A, 1, Skelmersdale U
Wolstenholme, I, 2, Slough Town
Wood, P, 1, Enfield
Woods, D, 2, Northampton Town
Worley, L, 7, Wycombe W (3),
  Tottenham H (1), Wycombe W
  (3)
Worswick, M, 1, Skelmersdale U
Wright, D, 2, Barnsley Grammar
  School
Yenson, K, 1, Leyton
Young, D, 4, Walthamstow Ave

*England Amateurs most capped
goalkeeper, John Swannell, one of
the game's "all time greats" who
played for Corinthian Casuals,
Hendon and Leatherhead and won
all the honours available to him.*

CLUBS WHO PRODUCED MOST AMATEUR INTERNATIONALS

Enfield	24
Bishop Auckland	18
Leytonstone	18
Hendon	15
Pegasus	13
Sutton United	13
Walthamstow Avenue	13
Barnet	11
Crook Town	11
Wycombe Wanderers	11
Tooting & Mitcham United	10

Leytonstone amalgamated with Ilford, then joined
forces with Walthamstow Avenue and are now sharing
Dagenham's ground and playing under the name of
Redbridge Forest.

Pegasus, the club formed for Oxford and Cambridge
University players, was disbanded in the sixties.

Barnet have now won promotion to the Fourth Division
of The Football League. Wycombe Wanderers are a
powerful Conference club and Sutton United were relegated from The Conference to the Isthmian League at
the end of the 1990-91 season where they will renew
rivalry with Enfield and Hendon. Tooting and Mitcham
now play one level lower in Division One.

In the north, Bishop Auckland made a brave move
from the Northern League (after 99 years) to the HFS
Loans League where they have gained promotion to
the Premier Division and are now one of the leading
clubs. Unfortunately the fortunes of their great rivals,
Crook Town, have taken an opposite turn and they are
battling for survival in the Northern League Division Two.

MOST AMATEUR CAPS FOR ENGLAND 1947-1974

Player	Clubs	Total
Ron Haider	Kingstonian (10), Hendon (55)	65
John Swannell	Hendon	61
Mike Pinner	Cambridge University (9), Pegasus (19), QPR & RAF (5), RAF (2), Manchester Utd & RAF (2), Hendon (9), Leyton Orient (6)	52
Ted Powell	Sutton United (19), Wycombe W (15), Kingstonian (3), Sutton United (14)	51
Jim Lewis	Walthamstow Ave (21), Chelsea (14), Walthamstow Ave (14)	49
Larry Pritchard	Sutton United (22), Wycombe W (26)	48
Roger Day	Enfield (23), Slough Town (14), Enfield (3), Ilford (3)	43
Kenny Gray	Leytonstone (28), Enfield (15)	43
Peter Deadman	Barking (14), Hendon (26)	40
Laurie Topp	Hendon	32
Charlie Townsend	Wealdstone	32
Derek Gamblin	Sutton Utd (16), Slough Town (3), Leatherhead (4), Winchester City (1), Wycombe W (5)	29
Ian Reid	Crook Town (2), Enfield (8), Hitchin Town (18)	28

Player	Clubs	Total
Alf D'Arcy	Barnet (11), Enfield (15)	26
Henry Dodkins	Ilford	26
John Robertson	Corinthian Casuals (3), Tooting & Mitcham (23)	26
Brian Harvey	Walthamstow Avenue (10), Leytonstone (12)	22
John Martin	Wimbledon	22
Bill Slater	Blackpool (5), Carnegie College (4), Brentford (5), Wolves (6)	20
Dexter Adams	Hendon	19
Roy Law	Wimbledon	19
Les Tilley	Leytonstone (11), Enfield (8)	19
Eric Fright	Bromley (13), Leytonstone (4), Bromley (1)	18
Alf Noble	Leytonstone	18
John Payne	Enfield	18
Jimmy Walton	Army (3), Bury (9), Man Utd (3), Bury (3)	18
John Adams	Enfield (7), Slough T (4), Enfield (6)	17
John Delaney	Wycombe Wanderers	17
Ray Eaton	Slough Town (14), Enfield (3)	17
Charlie Mortimore	Aldershot (5), Woking (12)	17
George Robb	Finchley	17
Bob Thursby	Bishop Auckland (11), Crook Town (5), Bishop Auckland (1)	17
Charlie Fuller	Bromley	16
Bob Hardisty	Bishop Auckland	16
Mickey Mellows	Sutton Utd (15), Winchester City (1)	16
Roy Sleap	Barnet (6), Hendon (10)	16
Bobby Brown	Barnet (11), Fulham (3)	14
Hugh Lindsay	Kingstonian (11), Wealdstone (3)	14
Denis Moore	Dagenham	14
Willie Smith	Sutton United (3), Walton & Hersham (11)	14
Mickey Preston	Kingstonian	13
Bobby Ardrey	Wimbledon	12
Les Farrer	Bishop Auckland (8), Walthamstow Avenue (4)	12
Paul Fry	Enfield	12
Dennis Jarvis	Leytonstone	12
Leon Joseph	Leytonstone	12
Tommy Lawrence	Enfield	12
Jim Rawlings	Enfield (11), Hayes (1)	12
Warren Bradley	Bishop Auckland	11
Howard Moxon	Enfield (9), Wealdstone (2)	11
Tony Bass	Dagenham (3), Hendon (4), Bishop's Stortford (3)	10
Corbett Cresswall	Bishop Auckland	10
Tony Harding	Barnet (6), Enfield (4)	10
Pat Neil	Portsmouth (2), Corinthian Casuals (6), Cambridge University (2)	10
Tommy Robinson	Brentford (6), Northampton Town (4)	10

Rod Haider has just scored another goal for Hendon. He captained his club and England and was the most capped England Amateur International with 65 caps.

FA AMATEUR CUP

INTRODUCTION

In 1892 Sheffield Football Club offered to donate a Cup to the Football Association so that amateur clubs might enjoy their own knock-out competition. As the professionals were dominating the FA Cup they set up the FA Amateur Cup along the same lines and 81 clubs entered the first competition in 1893-94. (However, the FA did supply the trophy).

In the early competitions the public school old boys teams did very well but soon they launched The Arthur Dunn Cup so they stepped down as the North East Clubs became stronger. Another loss to the competition occurred when a number of clubs formed the Amateur Football Association (now Alliance) and were unable to match the growing Northern dominance. As the

First World War threatened a challenge emerged from Clapton but it was Dulwich Hamlet, whose ground at Champion Hill could hold an impressive 40 000, who won the first final against Tufnell Park at Millwall.

Bishop Auckland hit back with two consecutive successes as did Clapton, Leyton and Ilford. The famous Isthmian giants took a fair grip of the competition in the thirties, when Wycombe Wanderers, Dulwich Hamlet, Kingstonian, Casuals and Bromley all got their names on the famous trophy.

The rivalry between the Isthmian League and the Northern League gave the competition extra spice and attendances rose. The 1948-49 Final was played at Wembley Stadium and attendances immediately rose to over

90 000. Bishop Auckland players became household names and the fairytale rise of Pegasus, the team of Oxford and Cambridge students, also caught the public's imagination. So when Pegasus met Bishop Auckland at Wembley in 1951 there was a capacity 100 000 to see the students win a thrilling match 2-1. The Amateur Cup Final was often featured live on television and all non-league football enjoyed a well earned popularity.

The famous Bishop Auckland team grew old together and despite a number of northern representatives reaching Wembley, Crook Town being the most consistent, it was the might of North London that took up the challenge.

Leytonstone, Enfield, Wealdstone and perhaps the most talented of all Hendon, took their share of Wembley glory but as shamateurism was suspected the Football Association decided to abolish the term amateur so that all players could receive money if clubs offered incentives.

So it was the end of the amateurs. The last northern teams to take the Cup away from London were North Shields in 1969 and Skelmersdale United who achieved a rare North Western success in 1971.

The last holders of the FA Amateur Cup were the Bishops, not from Auckland, whose hat-trick of successes will always be remembered, but from Bishops Stortford, for Hertfordshire.

The captain that day was John Still who hit the headlines again in 1990-91 as manager of the successful Redbridge Forest.

To win the Amateur Cup in 1954, Crook Town beat Bishop Auckland 1-0 in the second replay at Middlesborough. Left to right, back row: J Harvey (coach), T Riley, W Jeffs, RW Davison, F Jarrie, ARJ Steward, JWR Taylor, CW Peart (trainer). Front row: E Appleby, R Thompson, K Harrison, K Williamson, J Coxon, JL McMillan.

FA AMATEUR CUP

FINALS AT A GLANCE

Year	Winners	Runners-up	Score	Venue
1894	Old Carthusians	Casuals	2-1	Richmond
1895	Middlesbrough	Old Carthusians	2-1	Leeds
1896	Bishop Auckland	RA (Portsmouth)	1-0	Leicester
1897	Old Carthusians	Stockton	4-1 aet	Darlington
	(After 1-1 draw at Tufnell Park)			
1898	Middlesbrough	Uxbridge	2-1	Crystal Palace
1899	Stockton	Harwich & Parkeston	1-0	Middlesbrough
1900	Bishop Auckland	Lowestoft Town	5-1	Leicester
1901	Crook Town	King's Lynn	3-0	Ipswich
	(After 1-1 draw at Harwich)			
1902	Old Malvernians	Bishop Auckland	5-1	Leeds
1903	Stockton	Oxford City	1-0	Darlington
	(After 0-0 draw at Reading)			
1904	Sheffield	Ealing	3-1	Bradford
1905	West Hartlepool	Clapton	3-2	Shepherds Bush
1906	Oxford City	Bishop Auckland	3-0	Stockton
1907	Clapton	Stockton	2-1	Chelsea
1908	Depot Bn RE	Stockton	2-1	Bishop Auckland
1909	Clapton	Eston United	6-0	Ilford
1910	RMLI (Gosport)	South Bank	2-1	Bishop Auckland
1911	Bromley	Bishop Auckland	1-0	Herne Hill
1912	Stockton	Eston United	1-0	Middlesbrough
	(After 0-0 draw at Middlesbrough)			
1913	South Bank	Oxford City	1-0	Bishop Auckland
	(After 1-1 draw at Reading)			
1914	Bishop Auckland	Northern Nomads	1-0	Leeds
1915	Clapton	Bishop Auckland	1-0	Millwall
1920	Dulwich Hamlet	Tufnell Park	1-0 aet	Millwall
1921	Bishop Auckland	Swindon Victoria	4-2	Middlesbrough
1922	Bishop Auckland	South Bank	5-2 aet	Middlesbrough
1923	London Caledonians	Evesham Town	2-1 aet	Crystal Palace
1924	Clapton	Erith & Belvedere	3-0	Millwall
1925	Clapton	Southall	2-1	Millwall
1926	Northern Nomads	Stockton	7-1	Sunderland
1927	Leyton	Barking Town	3-1	Millwall
1928	Leyton	Cockfield	3-2	Middlesbrough
1929	Ilford	Leyton	3-1	Arsenal
1930	Ilford	Bournemouth Gasworks	5-1	West Ham
1931	Wycombe Wanderers	Hayes	1-0	Arsenal
1932	Dulwich Hamlet	Marine	7-1	West Ham
1933	Kingstonian	Stockton	4-1	Darlington
	(After 1-1 draw at Dulwich)			
1934	Dulwich Hamlet	Leyton	2-1	West Ham
1935	Bishop Auckland	Wimbledon	2-1	Chelsea
	(After 0-0 draw at Middlesbrough)			
1936	Casuals	Ilford	2-0	West Ham
	(After 1-1 draw at Selhurst Park)			
1937	Dulwich Hamlet	Leyton	2-0	West Ham
1938	Bromley	Erith & Belvedere	1-0	Millwall
1939	Bishop Auckland	Willington	3-0 aet	Sunderland
1946	Barnet	Bishop Auckland	3-2	Chelsea
1947	Leytonstone	Wimbledon	2-1	Arsenal
1948	Leytonstone	Barnet	1-0	Chelsea
1949	Bromley	Romford	1-0	Wembley
1950	Willington	Bishop Auckland	4-0	Wembley
1951	Pegasus	Bishop Auckland	2-1	Wembley
1952	Walthamstow Avenue	Leyton	2-1 aet	Wembley
1953	Pegasus	Harwich & Parkeston	6-0	Wembley
1954	Crook Town	Bishop Auckland	1-0	Middlesbrough
	(After two draws; at Wembley (2-2) and at Newcastle (2-2))			

Corinthian Casuals (white shirts) were one of the last truly amateur clubs in senior non-league football and they have stuck to their principles, although they are now a little further down "The Pyramid". This was one of the club's great days as they held the mighty Bishop Auckland to an Amateur Cup Final draw at Wembley before losing the replay in 1956.

1955	Bishop Auckland	Hendon	2-0	Wembley
1956	Bishop Auckland	Corinthian Casuals	4-1	Middlesbrough
	(After 1-1 draw at Wembley)			
1957	Bishop Auckland	Wycombe Wanderers	3-1	Wembley
1958	Woking	Ilford	3-0	Wembley
1959	Crook Town	Barnet	3-2	Wembley
1960	Hendon	Kingstonian	2-1	Wembley
1961	Walthamstow Avenue	West Auckland Town	2-1	Wembley
1962	Crook Town	Hounslow Town	4-0	Middlesbrough
	(After 1-1 draw at Wembley)			
1963	Wimbledon	Sutton United	4-2	Wembley
1964	Crook Town	Enfield	2-1	Wembley
1965	Hendon	Whitby Town	3-1	Wembley
1966	Wealdstone	Hendon	3-1	Wembley
1967	Enfield	Skelmersdale United	3-0	Manchester City
	(After 0-0 draw at Wembley)			
1968	Leytonstone	Chesham United	1-0	Wembley
1969	North Shields	Sutton United	2-1	Wembley
1970	Enfield	Dagenham	5-1	Wembley
1971	Skelmersdale United	Dagenham	4-1	Wembley
1972	Hendon	Enfield	2-0	Wembley
1973	Walton & Hersham	Slough Town	1-0	Wembley
1974	Bishop's Stortford	Ilford	4-1	Wembley

FA AMATEUR CUP STATISTICS

Most Wins: 10 Bishop Auckland,
5 Clapton, Crook Town
Most Semi-Final appearances: 27 Bishop Auckland
9 Clapton, Dulwich Hamlet, Ilford, Leytonstone, Stockton
Most consecutive appearances in Final
4 Bishop Auckland 1953-57, Leyton 1926-29
Most appearances in Final as a player
6 J Nimmins and R Hardisty, both Bishop Auckland
Cup Doubles
FA Amateur Cup and FA Cup: Old Carthusians

FA Amateur Cup and FA Trophy: Bishops Stortford, Enfield
Walton & Hersham won the Amateur Cup without conceding a goal in 1972-73
Stockton (1902-03), R M L I (Gosport) (1909-10), Bishop Auckland (1920-21) and Pegasus (1950-51) all won the Amateur Cup without playing at home.
The most Amateur Cup ties played by one club in one season was 17 by Chesham United in 1967-68.

FINALS 1893-1964

1893-94 Played at Richmond
Old Carthusians 2, Casuals 1 (*Goals:* Buzzard, Stanborough/ R Topham)   Attendance 3500
Carthusians: Wilkinson, Walters, Bray, Bliss, Wreford Brown, Streatfield, Hewitt, Richardson, Buzzard, Wilson, Stanborough.
Casuals: Harrison, Lodge, Hatton, Barker, Topham A, Grierson, Topham R, Carlton, Perkins, Rhodes T, Rhodes W.

1894-95 Played at Leeds
Middlesbrough 2, Old Carthusians 1 (*Goals:* Mullen, Nelmes/ Smith)   Attendance 4000
Middlesbrough: Cooper, Piercey, Wilson, Allport, Morren, Bache, Johnson, Gittens, Mullen, Nelmes, Murphy.
Carthusians: Wilkinson, Walters A, Walters P, Buzzard, Kite, Streatfield, Hewitt, Broadbent, Smith, Wilson, Stanborough.

1895-96 Played at Leicester
Bishop Auckland 1, Royal Artillery (Portsmouth) 0 (Goal: Lodge)
Bishop Auckland: Ward, Pennington, Tuson, Marshall, Lunson, Adams, Lewin, Lodge, Foster, Wilson, Manners.
RA: Reilly, Phillips, Harris, Patterson, Hill, Kinian, Jardine, Hanna, Cook, Walsh, Meggs.

1896-97 Played at Tufnell Park
Stockton 1, Old Carthusians 1 (*Goals:* Sanderson/ Smith)   Attendance 9000
Stockton: Hamilton, Brannen, Wilson, Shaw, Murray, Monteith, Robson, Daniel, Addison, Sanderson, Lakey.
Carthusians: Wilkinson, Bray, Timmins, Bliss, Wreford Brown, Darvell, Wilson, Buzzard, Smith, Stanborough, Hewitt.
REPLAY. Played at Darlington
Old Carthusians 4, Stockton 1 (*Goals:* Hewitt, Stanborough, Buzzard, Smith/ Halfpenny)   Attendance 10 000
Carthusians: Wilkinson, Bray, Timmins, Darvell, Wreford Brown, Bliss, Hewitt, Buzzard, Smith, Stanborough, Jameson.
Stockton: Hamilton, Brannen, Wilson, Shaw, Murray, Monteith, Robson, Lee, Halfpenny, Sanderson, Lakey.

1897-98 Played at Crystal Palace
Middlesbrough 2, Uxbridge 0 (*Goals:* Kempley, Bishop)   Attendance 1500
Middlesbrough: Smith, Moore, Piercey, Allport, Jackson, Nelmes, Frost, Bishop, Kempley, Longstaff, Wanless.
Uxbridge: Gumbrell, Gayland, Skinner, Brown, Benstead, Jacobs, Woodbridge A, Hickman, Browning, Knight, Woodbridge E.

1898-99 Played at Middlesbrough
Stockton 1, Harwich & Parkeston 0 (*Goal:* Fairburn)   Attendance 7000
Stockton: Fall, Shaw W, Wilson, Brannen, Baker, Monteith, Shaw R, Chatt, Byron, Fairbairn, Lakey.
Harwich: Keith, Bacon, Howard, Ingham, Garton, Whitehead, Garland, Eley, Harwood, Taylor, Snodgrass.

1899-1900 Played at Leicester
Bishop Auckland 5, Lowestoft Town 1 (*Goals:* Allen, Marshall T 2, Marshall J, Ord/ Baker)
Bishop Auckland: Proud, Bousfield, Condon, Ord, Thomas, Pennington, Marshall J, Marshall T, Allan, Marshall L, Crawford.
Lowestoft: Ayres, Timoney, Mewis, Marr, Royal, Beatton, Crews, Cole, Allen, Baker, Wilkins.

1900-1901 Played at Harwich
Crook Town 1, King's Lynn 1 (*Goals:* Iley/ McDonald)   Attendance 4000
Crook Town: Nattrass, Ward, Rule, Law, Rippon, Hammill, Lear, Creasor, Iley, Dargue, Harwood.
King's Lynn: Gay, Haylock, Girton, Reed, Stevens, Sporne, Orviss, Holroyd, McDonald, Horsley, Smith.
REPLAY. Played at Ipswich
Crook Town 3, King's Lynn 0 (*Goals:* Harwood, Rippon, Hammill)   Attendance 1500
Crook Town: Nattrass, Ward, Rule, Law, Rippon, Hammill, Lear, Creasor, Iley, Dargue, Harwood.
King's Lynn: Gay, Sporne, Girton, Reed, Stevens, Haylock, Orviss, Holroyd, McDonald, Horsley, Smith.

1901-02 Played at Leeds
Old Malvernians 5, Bishop Auckland 1 (*Goals:* Corbett, Foster R 2, Graeme, Day/ Wood)   Attendance 1000
Malvernians: Tuff, Simpson-Hayward, Ransome, Todd, Canny, Simpson, Day, Foster B, Graeme, Foster R, Corbett.
Bishop Auckland: Proud, Harwood, Condon, Marshall Jim, Thomas, Marshall T, Marshall Joe, Allan, Newton, Wood, Crawford.

1902-03 Played at Reading
Stockton 0, Oxford City 0
Stockton: Lowe, Starling, King, Rutter, Bell, Hassett, Dunn, Payne, Morgan, Freeland, Blake.
Oxford City: Selby, Witherington, Smith H, Craddock, Ashworth, Dickinson, Draper, Foster, Blackburn, Smith W, Arnett.
REPLAY. Played at Darlington
Stockton 1, Oxford City 0 (*Goal:* Morgan)   Attendance 7000
Stockton: Lowe, Starling, King, Rutter, Bell, Hassett, Dunn, Payne, Morgan, Freeland, Blake.
Oxford City: Selby, Witherington, Smith H, Craddock, Ashworth, Egley, Draper, Foster, Blackburn, Smith W, Arnett.

1903-04 Played at Bradford
Sheffield 3, Ealing 1 (*Goals:* Hoyland J, Bedford, Milne pen/ Hebden)   Attendance 4000
Sheffield: Bolsover, Chambers, Milne, Green, Potts, Frost, Silvester, Bedford, Hoyland G, Hoyland J, Forsdyke.
Ealing: Findlay, Blackburn, Fox, Wood, Mitchell, Pryce, Grice, Hebden, Doll, Powell, Rogers.

1904-05 Played at Shepherds Bush
West Hartlepool 3, Clapton 2 (*Goals:* Trechmann 2, Hegarty T/ Purnell 2)   Attendance 4000
Hartlepool: Bainbridge, Hegarty T, Hegarty R, Black, Hyslop, Stokes, Larkin, Fairweather, Robinson, Trechmann, Hodgson.
Clapton: Wilding, Bayley, Langhorne, Milton, Farnfield P, Hollis, Folks, Brown, Purnell, Farnfield H, Farnfield A.

1905-06 Played at Leicester
Bishop Auckland 0, Oxford City 3 (*Goals:* Hodges, Tabernacle 2)   Attendance 5000
Bishop Auckland: Proud, Ord, Campbell, Kirby, Robinson, Parker, Crawford, Douglas, Hopper, Charnock, Blaylock.
Oxford: Keates, Scothorn, Blackburn, Organ, Smith, Bumpus, Draper, Dickinson, Tabernacle, Hodges, Davis.

1906-07 Played at Stamford Bridge
Clapton 2, Stockton 1 (*Goals:* Russell, Dance/ Chambers)   Attendance 6000
Clapton: Wilding, Bayley, Ewan, Parkinson, Randall, Olley, Eastwood, Russell, Rance, Purnell, Harvey.
Stockton: Gray, Charlton, Chapman, Prosser, Bell, Hassett, Williamson, Featherstone, Chambers, Freeland, Marwood.

1907-08 Played at Bishop Auckland
Depot Battalion Royal Engineers 2, Stockton 1 (*Goals:* Keir, Pearson/ Lowther)   Attendance 8000
RE: Aston, Stanton, May, Shallcross, Webber, Daffern, Lowe, Keir, Pearson, Shepherd, Hawthorne.
Stockton: Gray, Bell, Chapman, Prosser, Charlton, Hassett, Williamson, Chambers, Henderson, Freeland, Lowther.

1908-09 Played at Ilford
Clapton 6, Eston United 0 (*Goals:* Attwood, Purnell 2, Rance 3)   Attendance 5000
Clapton: Jackson, Bayley, Duce, Parkinson, Rist, Olley, Attwood, Purnell, Rance, Tull, Harvey.
Eston: Harrison, Vintner, Bell, Callaghan, Housham, Bunn, Smith, Cail, Best, Ellis, Hollis.

1909-10 Played at Bishop Auckland
RMLI (Gosport) 2, South Bank 1 (*Goals:* Jack, Holmes/ Biggs)   Attendance 8000
RMLI: Turner, Wilkinson, Hirst, Revill, Yates, Wiseman, Exford, White, Holmes, Jack, Smith.
South Bank: Howling, Rand, Oakley, Biggs, Prest, Carr W, Thompson, Carr J, Carr H, Cartwright, Jones.

1910-11 Played at Herne Hill
Bishop Auckland 0, Bromley 1 (*Goal:* Dilley)   Attendance 3000
Bishop Auckland: Walton, Rudd, Ansell, Kirby, Hedley, Robinson, Wanless, Healey, Hopper, Kent, Sowerby.
Bromley: Wood, Peacock, Watson, McWhirter, Noall, Smith, Dilley, Noble, Kennard, Laundrey, Grayer.

1911-12 Played at Middlesbrough
Stockton 1, Eston United 1 (*Goals:* Sutherland/ Parsons)   Attendance 20 000
Stockton: Callaghan, Loney, Chapman, Evans, Stamper, Veitch, Bradford, Dobinson, Sutherland, Davis, Callender.
Eston: Hill, Roddam, Davidson, Smith J, Housham, O'Hara, Allan, Parsons, Smith W, Morris, Hollis.
REPLAY. Played at Middlesbrough
Stockton 1, Eston United 0 (*Goal:* Sutherland)   Attendance 12 000
Stockton: Callaghan, Loney, Chapman, Evans, Stamper, Veitch, Bradford, Dobinson, Sutherland, Davis, Callender.
Eston: Hill, Roddam, Davidson, Smith J, Housham, O'Hara, Allan, Parsons, Smith W, Morris, Hollis.

1912-13 Played at Reading
South Bank 1, Oxford City 1 (*Goals:* Borrie/ Buckingham)   Attendance 6000
South Bank: Howling, Urwin, Oakley, Henry, Prest, Anderson, Carr, Clarke, Borrie, Heron, Evans.
Oxford: Harley, Cadwell, Ansell, Padnage, Hunt, Slatter, Draper, McKinnon, Buckingham, Jakeman, Smith.
REPLAY. Played at Bishop Auckland
South Bank, 1 Oxford City 0 (*Goal:* Carr)   Attendance 7000
South Bank: Howling, Urwin, Oakley, Henry, Prest, Anderson, Carr, Clarke, Borrie, Heron, Evans.
Oxford: Harley, Cadwell, Ansell, Radnage, Hunt, Slatter, Draper, Berry, Buckingham, Jakeman, Smith.

1913-14 Played at Leeds
Bishop Auckland 1, Northern Nomads 0 (*Goal:* Kirby)   Attendance 5000
Bishop Auckland: North, Roe, Rudd, Hopper, Spence, Maddison, Appleby, Douglas, Kirby, Spence, Lunson.
Nomads: Peever, Barlow, Cunliffe, Gotobed, Porter, McKinnon, Davies, Douglas, Cruse, Boardman, Salt.

1914-15 Played at Millwall (New Cross)
Clapton 1, Bishop Auckland 0 (*Goal:* Sherwood)   Attendance 6000
Clapton: Wood, Sharpley, Bartleman, Ward, Prescott, Millars, Walden, Cox, Lloyd, Sherwood, Cordell.
Bishop Auckland: North, Roe, Rudd, Kasher, Green, Maddison, Brown, Gardner, Hopper, Fleming, Lunson.

1919-20 Played at Millwall (The Den)
Dulwich Hamlet 1, Tufnell Park 0 (*Goal:* Kail)   Attendance 25 000
Dulwich: Coleman, Pilkington, Bowker, Jonas, Sweeting, Shipway, Kail, Davis, Nicol, Fuller.
Tufnell: Leese, Butcher, Evans, Goodman, Read, Swayne, Fricker, Lloyd, Hannaford, Williams, Elkington.

1920-21 Played at Middlesbrough
Bishop Auckland 4, Swindon Victoria 2 (*Goals:* Cook, Ward 2, Binks/ Roberts, Poole)   Attendance 25 000
Bishop Auckland: North, Wilson, Garbutt, Nattrass, Atkinson, Kasher, Brown, Cook, Binks, Ward, Wemsley.
Swindon: Weston, Saunders, Poole, Roberts, Cooper, Summers, Rees, Blumsdon, Eggleton, Dawson, Chivers.

1921-22 Played at Middlesbrough
Bishop Auckland 5, South Bank 2 (*Goals:* Cook, Mullen, Binks 2, Nattrass/ Peacock 2)   Attendance 20 000
Bishop Auckland: Potts, Wilson, Taylor, Nattrass, Atkinson, Maddison, Burrows, Cook, Binks, Mullen, Goldsborough.
South Bank: Burns, Thompson, Thomas, Lloyd, Brighton, Tubb, Spencer, Peacock, Towse, Hepworth, Robinson.

1922-23 Played at Crystal Palace
London Caledonians 2, Evesham Town 1 (*Goals:* May, McGubbin/ Jones S0)   Attendance 14 132
Caledonians: Dawson, Gates B, Gates E, Blyth, Barr, Finn, McGubbin, Noble, Sloan, May, Hamilton.
Evesham: Jones R, Stokes, Bridges, Gould, Ratcliff, Pennell, Hampton, Busby, Meaking, Jones S, Osborne.

1923-24 Played at Millwall
Clapton 3, Erith & Belvedere 0 (*Goals:* Potter 2, Barnard)   Attendance 32 000
Clapton: Moore, Penstone, Blake, Williams, Bryant, Cable, Riley, Earle, Gibbins, Potter, Barnard.
Erith: Evans C, Evans R, Wilson, Marks, Duffy, Swayne, Gooch, McKee, Yates, Hillier, Beckford.

1924-25 Played at Millwall
Clapton 2, Southall 1 (*Goals:* Gibbins 2/ Hawkins)   Attendance 25 000
Clapton: Moore, Penstone, Blake, Williams, Bryant, Cable, Riley, Potter, Gibbins, Miller, Barnard.
Southall: Holding, Buttery, Gower, Johnson, Harvey, Wenham, Jance, Jackson, Clark, Corban, Hawkins.

1925-26 Played at Sunderland
Northern Nomads 7, Stockton 1 (*Goals:* Beswick 3, Randle 3, Robertson/ Thompson)   Attendance 13 300
Nomads: Menham, Blair, Abbott, Jones, Fairweather, Waker, Loxham, Robertson, Beswick, Randle, Fairclough.
Stockton: Murray, Longstaff, Shanks, Lowther, Scaife, Pritchard, Evans, Clare, Thompson, Pass, McGiffen.

1926-27 Played at Millwall
Leyton 3, Barking Town 1 (Goals: Cable 2, Salmons/ Hawkins)   Attendance 12 864
Leyton: Grainger, Preston, Terris, Graves, Cable, Goldsmith, Salmons, Hall, Bowyer, Smith, Hawkins.
Barking: McCracken, Carmen, Norrington, Kemp, Jango, Young, Evans, Hawkins, Scarborough, Guyton, Lucas.

1927-28 Played at Middlesbrough
Leyton 3, Cockfield 2 (*Goals:* McKinley, Smith, Cable/ Rutter 2)   Attendance 12 200
Leyton: Burr, Preston, Goldsmith, Graves, Cable, Margetts, McKinley, Hall, Avey, Smith, Hawkins.
Cockfield: Wedge, Dixon, Coates, Barker, Harrison, Oldfield, Longstaff, Pearson, Rutter, Thompson, Kirby.

1928-29 Played at Arsenal
Ilford 3, Leyton 1 (*Goals:* Drane, Peploe, Potter/ Smith)   Attendance 35 000
Ilford: Norman, Banks, Wade, Gilderson, Craymer, Barron, Potter, Welsh, Dellow, Drane, Peploe.
Leyton: Jones, Preston, Goldsmith, Graves, Wright, Margetts, Collins, Hall, Avey, Smith, Hawkins.

1929-30 Played at West Ham
Ilford 5, Bournemouth Gasworks 1 (*Goals:* Dellow, Peploe 2, Welsh, Potter/ Pettey)　　　Attendance 21 800
Ilford: Watson, Triesman, Winterburn, Shappard, Craymer, Webb, Potter, Welsh, Dellow, Drane, Peploe.
Bournemouth: Joyce, Saunders, Cobb, Turner, Phillips, Gillingham, Smith, Pettey, Lavell, Cornbeer, Tapper.

1930-31 Played at Arsenal
Wycombe Wanderers 1, Hayes 0 (*Goal:* Britnell)　　　Attendance 32 000
Wycombe: Kipping, Crump, Cox, Rance, Badrick, Greenwell, Simmons, Brown, Vernon, Braisher, Britnell.
Hayes: Holding, Maskell, Gower, Caesar E, Wainwright, Caesar W, Knight, Rowe, Morgan, Welsh, Lloyd.

1931-32 Played at West Ham
Dulwich Hamlet 7, Marine 1 (*Goals:* Moseley 4, Kail 2, Goodliffe/ O'Donnell)　　　Attendance 22 000
Dulwich: Miles, Hugo, Osmond, Murray, Hamer, Aitken, Morrish, Kail, Goodliffe, Moseley, Robbins.
Marine: Druey, Jackson, Rankin, Crilley, Kelly, Halsall, Keir, Garvey, O'Donnell, King, Bamford.

1932-33 Played at Dulwich
Kingstonian 1, Stockton 1 (*Goals:* Whitehead/ Anderson　　　Attendance 20 448
Kingstonian: Brodrick, Rassell, Urpeth, Lee, Daley, Keen, McCarthy, Gibson, Whitehead, Macey, O'Kin.
Stockton: Newton, Thompson, Little, Foster, Butler, Edwards, Stephenson, Smith, Coulthard, Prest, Anderson.
REPLAY. Played at Darlington
Kingstonian 4, Stockton 1 (*Goals:* Gibson, Urpeth pen, Whitehead 2/ Coulthard)　　　Attendance 16 492
Kingstonian: Brodrick, Rassell, Urpeth, Lee, Daley, Keen, McCarthy, Gibson, Whitehead, Macey, O'Kin.
Stockton: Newton, Thompson, Little, Foster, Pass, Edwards, Stephenson, Smith, Coulthard, Prest, Anderson.

1933-34 Played at West Ham
Dulwich Hamlet 2, Leyton 1 (*Goals:* Robbins, Court/ Davis)　　　Attendance 33 000
Dulwich: Cummings, Hugo, Robbins, Murray, Hamer, Toser, Morrish, Miller, Goodliffe, Benka, Court.
Leyton: Holding, Loveday, Caesar E, Richardson, Mercer, Collins, Gibbins, Skeels, Coates, Davis.

1934-35 Played at Middlesbrough
Bishop Auckland 0, Wimbledon 0　　　Attendance 20 000
Bishop Auckland; Hopps, Minton, Scott, Birbeck, Straughton, Shield, Dodds, Bryan, Wilson, Stephenson, Hogg.
Wimbledon: Irish, Goodchild, Balkwill, Wright, Bridge, Reeves, Batchelor, Barnes, Dowden, Turner, Smith.
REPLAY. Played at Chelsea
Bishop Auckland 2, Wimbledon 1 (*Goals:* Wilson, Bryan/ Dowden)　　　Attendance 30 000
Bishop Auckland; Hopps, Minton, Scott, Birbeck, Straughton, Shield, Dodds, Bryan, Wilson, Stephenson, Hogg.
Wimbledon: Irish, Goodchild, Balkwill, Wright, Bridge, Reeves, Smith, Barnes, Dowden, Turner, Zenthon.

1935-36 Played at Crystal Palace
Casuals 1, Ilford 1 (*Goals:* Riley/ Braund)　　　Attendance 26 064
Casuals: Huddle, Whewell, Evans, Allen, Joy, Couchman, Shearer, Fabian, Clements, Webster, Riley.
Ilford: Tietjon, Holmes, Hayes, Male, Myers, Craymer, Gilderson, Mamley, Watts, Halcrow, Braund.
REPLAY. Played at West Ham
Casuals 2, Ilford 0 (*Goals:* Shearer, Webster)　　　Attendance 27 000
Casuals: Huddle, Whewell, Evans, Allen, Joy, Couchman, Shearer, Fabian, Clements, Webster, Riley.
Ilford: Tietjon, Holmes, Hayes, Male, Myers, Craymer, Gilderson, Mamley, Watts, Halcrow, Braund.

1936-37 Played at West Ham
Dulwich Hamlet 2, Leyton 0 (*Goals:* Morrish 2)　　　Attendance 33 516
Dulwich: Hill, Weymouth, Robbins, Murray, Hugo, Toser, Morrish, Anderson, Wright, Ingleton, Ball.
Leyton: Self, Gentry, Clark, Hunt, Preston, Burns, Smith, Leek, Avery, Boatwright, Camerson.

Four members of the Dulwich Hamlet team who won the FA Amateur Cup in 1937. Left to Right: C Murray,
H Robbins, L Morrish, A Hugo.

1937-38 Played at Millwall
Bromley 1, Erith & Belvedere 0 (*Goal:* Stroud)　　　　　　　　Attendance 33 000
Bromley: Bartaby, Gray, Clark, Wade, Weeks, Barnes, Thomas, Stroud, Brown, Holbrook, Reece.
Erith: Gibbs, Little, O'Hara, Smee, Fuller, Bennett, Young, Scott, Southcombe, Beale, Sanders.

1938-39 Played at Sunderland
Bishop Auckland 3, Willington 0 (*Goals:* Wensley 3)　　　　　　Attendance 20 200
Bishop Auckland: Washiungton, Kirtley, Humble, Wanless, Straughton, Paisley, Twigg, Wensley, Slee, Evans, Young.
Willington: Coe, Cooper, Etheridge, Hardy, Lumby, Hindmarsh, Mitchell, Pratt, McLean, Davidson, Elliott.

1945-46 Played at Chelsea
Barnet 3, Bishop Auckland 2 (*Goals:* Reilly, Phipps, Kelleher/ Teasdale 2)　　　Attendance 53 832
Barnet: Powell, Wheeler, Bunker, Gerrans, Pullen, Weightman, Jordan, Kelleher, Phipps, Finch, Reilly.
Bishop Auckland: Washington, Humble, Farrer, Longstaff, Hadfield, Fairs, Shergold, Richardson, Teasdale, Tait, Anderson.

1946-47 Played at Arsenal
Leytonstone 2, Wimbledon 1 (*Goals:* Noble, Smith/ Stannard)　　　　Attendance 47 000
Leytonstone: Jarvis, Nicholls, Childs, Banham, Lister, Kavanagh, Smith, Noble, Groves, Bunce, Crowe.
Wimbledon: Haydock, Wallis, Cousins, Magill, Clark, Lemmer, Nash, Stannard, Edelson, Head, Laker.

1947-48 Played at Chelsea
Leytonstone 1, Barnet 0 (*Goal:* Groves)　　　　　　　　　Attendance 59 605
Leytonstone: Jarvis, Nicholls, Childs, Wilson, Paviour, Kavanagh, Smith, Noble, Groves, Bunce, Joseph.
Barnet: Powell, Wheeler, Hawkins, Gerrans, Leek, Hawkes, Hsakow, Kelleher, Phipp, Mott, Finch.

1948-49 Played at Wembley
Bromley 1, Romford 0 (*Goal:* Hopper)　　　　　　　　　Attendance 93 000
Bromley: Cornthwaite, Cameron, Yenson, Fuller T, Fuller C, Fright, Martin, Hopper, Brown, Dunmall, Ruddy.
Romford: Ivey, Collier, Fryatt, McKenzie, Barton, Regan, Brooks, Maddick, Bridge, Jennings, Patterson.

1949-50 Played at Wembley
Willington 4, Bishop Auckland 0 (*Goals:* Taylor, Rutherford, Larmouth, Armstrong)　　Attendance 88 000
Willington: Snowdon, Craggs, Howe, Leuthwaite, Yeardley, Dodd, Robinson, Taylor, Larmouth, Armstrong, Rutherford.
Bishop Auckland: Washington, Coxon, Farrer, Taylor, Davison, Nimmins, Major, Hardisty, McIlvenny, Gilholme, Palmer.

1950-51 Played at Wembley
Pegasus 2, Bishop Auckland 1 (*Goals:* Potts, Tanner/ Nimmins)　　　Attendance 100 000
Pegasus: Brown, Cowen, Maugham, Platt, Shearwood, Saunders, Pawson, Dutchman, Tanner, Carr, Potts.
Bishop Auckland: White, Marshall, Farrer, Hardisty, Davison, Nimmins, Taylor, McIlvenny, Williamson, Edwards.

1951-52 Played at Wembley
Walthamstow Avenue 2, Leyton 1 (*Goals:* Lewis, Hall/ Skipp)　　　Attendance 100 000
Walthamstow: Gerula, Young, Stratton, Lucas, Braham, Saunders, Rossiter, Bailey, Lewis, Hall, Camis.
Leyton: Sullivan, Dixon, Pullinger, Gardiner, Yenson, Casey, Fitch, Facey, McIntree, Goddard, Skipp.

1952-53 See Feature pages 57-61

1953-54 Played at Wembley
Bishop Auckland 2, Crook Town 2 (*Goals:* Dixon, Oliver/ Thompson, Appleby)　　Attendance 100 000
Bishop Auckland: Sharratt, Marshall, Fryer, Hardisty, Cresswell, Nimmins, Major, Dixon, Oliver, O'Connell, Watson.
Crook: Jarrie, Riley, Steward, Jeffs, Davison, Taylor, Appleby, Thompson, Harrison, Williamson, McMillan.
REPLAY. Played at Newcastle
Bishop Auckland 2, Crook Town 2 (*Goals:* Oliver 2/ Harrison 2)　　　Attendance 56 008
Bishop Auckland: Sharratt, Marshall, Stewart, Hardisty, Cresswell, Wilkinson, Major, Dixon, Oliver, O'Connell, Watson.
Crook: Jarrie, Riley, Steward, Jeffs, Davison, Taylor, Appleby, Thompson, Harrison, Coxon, McMillan.
SECOND REPLAY. Played at Middlesbrough
Crook Town 1, Bishop Auckland 0 (*Goal:* Harrison)　　　　　Attendance 36 727
Crook: Jarrie, Riley, Steward, Jeffs, Davison, Taylor, Apleby, Thompson, Harrison, Williamson, McMillan.
Bishop Auckland: Sharratt, Marshall, Stewart, Hardisty, Cresswell, Nimmins, Major, Dixon, Oliver, O'Connell, Watson.

Pegasus' Finest Hour

John Tanner (third from left) scores the decisive second goal in the 1950-51 Final against Bishop Auckland. The whole country were looking out for the result of the 'college boys' v the north-eastern 'legends'.

Pegasus Football Club was formed to give the students of Oxford and Cambridge Universities the chance to play senior competitive football and their success really caught the imagination of the football public throughout Great Britain. Undergraduates were older in the fifties as many had already been in the services. Their average age was around 23 and they were fit, experienced and intelligent footballers so their success wasn't surprising, although it was still an inspiration to young players who were enjoying secondary education. Pegasus, led by David Saunders who played in every competitive game in the club's history, enjoyed wonderful seasons including two Amateur Cup victories at Wembley. Sadly as undergraduates became younger and 'amateur' football became more of a business, the club disbanded leaving great memories. Surely if 'Chariots of Fire' made a good film so too would 'The Pegasus Story'.

AMATEUR CUP 1952-53

Extra Preliminary Round

Ashmore Recreation v Stockton Amateur	4-0
Heanor Town v Dunscroft Welfare	3-2
Kents Athletic v Shefford Town	2-2,5-2
Ampthill Town v Kempston Rovers	1-0
Farnham Town v Eastbourne United	3-2
Chertsey Town v Horley	4-3
Finchley v Grays Athletic	5-2
Yiewsley v Aveley	2-4
Wembley v Willesden	3-2
Rainham Town v Twickenham	5-0
Hawker Athletic v Storey Athletic	0-2
Edgware Town v Pinner	5-0
Eton Manor v Hornchurch & Upminster	3-2
Maidenhead United v Buckingham Town	14-1
Wallingford Town v Abingdon Town	5-0
Windsor & Eton v Morris Motors	4-2
Cranfield United v Pressed Steel	2-7
Chesham United v Marlow	5-2
NAC Athletic v Hemel Hempstead	1-2
St Frideswide v Henley Town	3-2
Bicester Town v Slough Centre	1-6
Wolverton & British Railways v Woodstock Town	8-1
Huntley & Palmer v Kidlington	4-1
Osberton Radiator v Aylesbury United	1-5
Didcot Town v Chipping Norton Town	3-2
Berkhamsted Town v Amersham Town	4-0
Thame United v Witney Town	1-3
East Cowes Victoria Athletic v Winchester City	0-3
Thornycroft Athletic v HMS Daedalus	1-3

RAMC Aldershot v Ryde Sports	2-2,1-0
Bournemouth v Bournemouth Gasworks Ath	1-1,3-2
Wootton Bassett Town v Radstock Town	1-2
Coleford Athletic v Devizes Town	0-3
Calne & Harris United v Warminster Town	0-1
Corsham Town v Shepton Mallet Town	0-0,1-4
Melksham v Swindon Victoria	1-2
Westbury United v Roundway Hospital	7-4
Spencer Moulton v Paulton Rovers	3-4
Soundwell v High Littleton (Bristol)	3-1
Chard Town v Worle Old Boys	2-2,3-2
Roche v St Just	4-3

Preliminary Round

Washington Welfare v Seaton Delaval Amateurs	4-5
Cleator Moor Celtic v Hearts of Liddesdale	5-0
Seaton Holy Trinity v Cockfield	1-5
Durham City v West Auckland Town	3-2
Witton Park Institute v Stanley United	1-3
Howden-le-Wear v Ashmore Recreation	2-2,2-0
Stanhope v Durham University	0-4
Eldon Albion v Chilton Athletic	3-0
Bearpark Coll WF v Langley Park Coll WF	2-2,2-0
Hartlepool Railway v Tow Law Town	0-8
Smith's Dock v Whitby Albion Rangers	6-1
Head Wrightsons v Cargo Fleet Works	3-4
Skinningrove Works v Furness Athletic	5-2
Portrack Shamrocks v Pickering Town	3-1
Filey Town v Bridlington Central United	3-2
Cochrane's Sports v South Bank St Peters	0-6
Winterton Hospital v Redcar United	0-3
Eastham Athletic v Earle	2-8
Port Sunlight v Stoneycroft	0-1
Harrowby v ICI (Alkali)	0-6
St Annes Athletic v Atherton Colliery	5-1
Blackpool Rangers v Manchester University	1-3
Stork v Southport Layland Road	10-0
Northern Nomads v Lancs Steel Recreation	6-2
Old Blackburnians v Runcorn Athletic	6-0
Thornhill Edge v Brunswick Institute	2-3
Harrogate Town v Liversedge	2-2,1-3
Ossett Albion v Hull Old Grammarians	2-0
Gedling Colliery v Stanton Ironworks	8-0
Players Athletic v Boots Athletic	1-0
Thurcroft Main v Basford United	2-3
Raleigh Athletic v Heanor Town	2-2,2-5
Lincoln City SOB v Parliament St Methodists	0-1
Penistone Church v Netherfield Albion	2-2,5-3
Hallam v Hampton Sports	2-1
RAF (Cranwell) v Cinderhill Colliery	1-0
Syston St Peters v Cosby United	0-0,4-0
Enderby Town v Anstey Nomads	1-2
Birmingham City Transport v Shepshed Albion	4-1
Loughborough College v Sheldon Town	2-0
Ibstock Peniston Rovers v Paget Rangers	1-3
Knowle *(withdrew)* v Rootes Athletic	1-1
East Shildon Institute v Morris Sports (L'borough)	8-0
Richard Thomas & Baldwin W/O Badsey Rangers	
Lakenheath v Ipswich Electricity	6-1
Whitton United v Beccles	2-2,4-3
Bungay Town v Felixstowe Town	7-3
Eastern Coachworks v Long Melford	0-4
Exning United v Churchman Sports	4-3

Newmarket Town W/O Woodbridge Town *(withdrew)*	
Achilles (Ipswich) v Waterside Works (Ipswich)	4-1
Lowestoft Town v Leiston	4-1
Luton Amateur v Potton United	2-1
Baldock Town v Arlesey Town	3-1
Letchworth Town v AC Sphinx	3-0
Leighton United v Kents Athletic	2-1
Ampthill Town v Wootton Blue Cross	3-1
Vauxhall Motors v Bedford Corinthians	14-2
Stevenage Town v Dunstable Town	4-0
Royston Town v Bedford Avenue	6-5
Maidestone United v Aylesford Paper Mill	0-2
Crockenhill v Bexleyheath & Welling	2-6
Callenders Athletic v Whitstable	1-4
Cray Wanderers v Faversham Town	2-6
Thameside Amateur v Woolwich Polytechnic	1-2
Bexley v Footscray	2-3
Wigmore Ath v Whitehawk & Manor Farm OB	3-2
Hove White Rovers v Southwick	2-0
Chichester City v Littlehampton Town	4-2
Worthing v Arundel	4-0
Newhaven Town v Dorking	2-1
Crawley v Banstead Athletic	2-3
Haywards Heath v Leatherhead	0-2
Bexhill Town v Farnham Town	2-0
Chertsey Town v Camberley Town	2-2,1-4
Cobham v East Grinstead	0-3
Metropolitan Police v Lewes	3-0
Guildford v Hersham	0-8
Stansted v Peartree Old Boys	2-5
Leavesden Hospital v Ware	2-6
Enfield v Welwyn Garden City	5-1
Rickmansworth Town v Hertford Town	2-5
Bishop's Stortford v Tufnell Park Edmonton	1-0
Sawbridgeworth Town v Hoddesdon Town	0-5
Epping Town v Kings Langley	3-0
Harlow Town v Hatfield Town	2-5
Uxbridge v Harrow Town	5-2
Vickers Armstrong (Weybridge) v Storey Athletic	3-1
Ford Sports v McLaren Sports	2-2,2-0
Wood Green Town v Finchley	0-6
Aveley v Eton Manor	2-0
Ruislip Manor v Rainham Town	2-2,0-1
Wembley v Downshall Athletic	2-0
Edgware Town v Polytechnic	2-0
Worcester Park v Surbiton Town	1-2
Carshalton Athletic v Dagenham British Legion	9-1
ROF (SA) v West Thurrock Athletic	1-2
Dagenham Cables v Lathol Athletic	2-2,4-2
Epsom v Devas Institute	3-0
Malden Town v Civil Service	1-1,3-0
Dageham v PO Engineers (Wellington)	4-0
Wingate v Woodford Town	2-1
Bletchley Town v Berkhamsted Town	1-2
Slough Centre v Chesham United	2-2,2-1
Wolverton Town & BR v Aylesbury United	1-1,4-2
Tring Town v Maidenhead United	1-3
Wallingford Town v St Frideswide	0-0,2-1
Didcot Town v Pressed Steel	2-2,0-4
Windsor & Eton v Witney Town	1-1,1-4
Hemel Hempstead Town v Huntley & Palmer	1-2
Swanage v Hamworthy	0-3
Pirelli General Cables v RAMC (Aldershot)	0-1

HMS Excellent v Lymington	2-4
Longfleet St Marys v Winchester City	2-1
HMS Daedalus v Totton	4-2
Blandford United v Alton Town	3-3,1-3
Fareham Town v Shaftesbury	10-0
Bournemouth v Wimborne	3-1
Farnborough v Clandown	0-5
Swindon British Railways v Swindon Victoria	2-2,2-1
Purton v Bulford United	4-2
Peasedown Miners Welfare v Radstock Town	2-1
Devizes Town v Paulton Rovers	5-0
Welton Rovers v Shepton Mallet Town	2-2,0-1
Warminster Town v Odd Down	4-2
Westbury United v Pewsey Vale	9-0
Clevedon v Ilminster Town	4-0
Charlton Kings v Watchet Town	0-2
St Philips Adult School v Burnham United	3-0
Mount Hill Enterprise v Soundwell	4-2
Chard Town v Hanham Athletic	4-1
Highbridge Town v Weston-Super-Mare St Johns	6-0
Taunton British Railways v Douglas (Kingswood)	6-3
Cinderford Town v Bristol St George	4-1
Liskeard Athletic v Mullion	1-5
Oak Villa v Mousehole	2-5
Tavistock v Bugle	0-2
Looe v Roche	5-2
Camelford v Tamerton	3-2
Nanpean Rovers v Helston Athletic	5-1
Dartmouth United v Bodmin Town	8-0
Heavitree United v St Dennis	6-1

First Qualifying Round

Cleator Moor Celtic v Salterbeck	2-1
Holmehead Works v Wallsend St Lukes	5-6
Seaton Delaval Amateurs v Heaton Stannington	3-1
Appleby v Whitley Bay	0-5
Durham C v Tow Law T 2-2,3-5,*after protest*	2-6
Eldon Albion v Howden-le-Wear	2-5
Cockfield v Stanley United	2-0
Bearpark Colliery Welfare v Durham University	0-4
North Skelton Athletic v Cargo Fleet Works	5-0
South Bank St Peters v Portrack Shamrocks	0-4
Smith's Dock v Skinningrove Works	4-2
Redcar Albion v Filey Town	5-3
Stoneycroft v Old Blackburnians	1-3
Stork v St Annes Athletic	1-2
Earle v ICI (Alkali)	1-4
Northern Nomads v Manchester University	4-0
Liversedge v North Ferriby United	1-1,2-1
Leeds University YMI v Bradford Rovers	0-4
Brunswick Institute v Ossett Albion	3-3,1-3
Harrogate & District Railway v Guiseley	3-2
Players Athletic v RAF (Cranwell)	5-3
Penistone Church v Heanor Town	1-4
Gedling Colliery v Basford United	4-2
Hallam v Parliament St Methodists	6-2
Anstey Nomads v Coventry Amateur	7-0
Rootes Ath (Birmingham) v L'borough College	2-6
Syston St Peters v Birmingham City Transport	4-1
Earl Shilton Institute v Paget Rangers	2-1
Jack Moulds Athletic v Fernhill Heath	2-3
Bourneville Athletic v Old Wulfrunians	2-4

Richard Thomas & Baldwin v Walsall Wood	1-3
Staffordshire Casuals v Walsall Trinity	6-3
St Neots St Mary v Atlas Sporta	2-2,2-7
Ely City v Raunds Town	1-6
Cromer v Holt United	2-4
Thetford Town v Fakenham Town	2-2,3-1
Boulton & Paul v Dereham Town	3-0
Sheringham v Wymondham Town	0-1
Lowestoft Town v Whitton United	0-2
Woodbridge Athletic v Long Melford	1-6
Lakenheath v Bungay Town	4-0
Waterside Works (Ipswich) v Exning United	11-1
Baldock Town v Royston Town	3-0
Vauxhall Motors v Leighton United	4-1
Luton Amateur v AC Sphinx	1-2
Stevenage Town v Ampthill Town	8-1
Crittall Athletic v Brentham Athletic	2-2,3-1
Brighlingsea United v Colchester Casuals	2-4
Bexleyheath & Welling v Beckenham	2-0
Footscray v Faversham Town	1-7
Aylesford Paper Mills v Whitstable	1-0
Bowaters Lloyd v Woolwich Polytechnic	7-1
Hove White Rovers v Shoreham	2-2,1-6
Worthing v Brighton Old Grammarians	2-3
Wigmore Athletic v Chichester City	5-3
Lancing Athletic v Bognor Regis Town	1-0
Banstead Athletic v Horsham	3-3,3-2
East Grinstead v Bexhill Town	4-1
Newhaven Town v Leatherhead	1-5
Metropolitan Police v Camberley	2-1
Ware v Hatfield Town	5-3
Hoddesdon Town v Hertford Town	5-2
Peartree Old Boys v Enfield	1-5
Epping Town v Bishop's Stortford	1-4
Vickers (Weybridge) v Edgware Town	2-3
Rainham Town v Finchley	3-3,0-2
Uxbridge v Ford Sports	4-1
Wembley v Aveley	2-1
Carshalton Athletic v Wingate	5-2
Malden Town v Dunstable Cables	0-1
Surbiton Town v West Thurrock United	5-2
Dagenham v Epsom	4-3
Slough Centre v Huntley & Palmers	5-2
Pressed Steel v Maidenhead United	2-4
Berkhamsted Town v Wolverton & British Rail	4-2
Witney Town v Wallingford Town	3-2
RAMC (Aldershot) v Bournemouth	4-1
Alton Town v Longfleet St Marys	6-1
Hamworthy v Lymington	4-4,0-2
Fareham Town v HMS Daedalus	2-2,1-5
Swindon British Railways v Westbury United	0-6
Shepton Mallet T v Peasedown Miners Welfare	3-0
Clandown v Purton	2-1
Warminster Town v Devizes Town	2-4
Watchet Town v Cinderford Town	2-4
Highbridge Town v Mount Hill Enterprise	2-3
Clevedon v St Philips Adult School	4-1
Taunton British Railways v Chard Town	1-1,1-6
Mousehole v Heavitree United	7-1
Nanpean Rovers v Looe	4-0
Dartmouth United v Camelford	5-0

Second Qualifying Round

Cleator Moor Celtic v Wallsend St Lukes	4-2
Seaton Delaval Amateurs v Whitley Bay	1-2
Tow Law Town v Howden-le-Wear	5-0
Cockfield v Durham University	4-0
North Skelton Athletic v Portrack Shamrocks	3-4
Smith's Dock v Redcar Albion	1-1
Old Blackburnians v St Annes Athletic	1-3
ICI Athletic v Northern Nomads	4-2
Liversedge v Bradford Rovers	2-5
Ossett Albion v Harrogate & District Railway	0-1
Players Athletic v Heanor Town	3-1
Gedling Colliery v Hallam	1-4
Anstey Nomads v Loughborough College	3-2
Syston St Peters v Earl Shilton Institute	3-0
Fernhill Heath v Bourneville Athletic	2-1
Walsall Wood v Staffordshire Casuals	2-0
Atlas Sports v Higham Ferrers Town	2-5
Ramsay Town v Raunds Town	4-0
Holt United v Wymondham Town	2-1
Boulton & Paul v Thetford Town	2-0
Whitton United v Waterside Works (Ipswich)	5-1
Lakenheath v Long Melford	2-1
Baldock Town v Stevenage Town	0-7
AC Sphinx v Vauxhall Motors	3-5
Crittall Athletic v Halstead Town	3-0
Saffron Walden Town v Colchester Casuals	3-5
Bexleyheath & Welling v Bowaters Lloyd	6-0
Aylesford Paper Mills v Faversham Town	1-6
Shoreham & Lancing Athletic	2-2,0-4
Wigmore Athletic v Worthing	0-1
Banstead Athletic v Metropolitan Police	3-2
Leatherhead v East Grinstead	2-3
Ware v Bishop's Stortford	1-1,4-2
Enfield v Hoddesdon Town	1-5
Edgware Town v Wembley	3-2
Uxbridge v Finchley	1-3
Carshalton Athletic v Dagenham	1-1,4-2
Surbiton Town v Dagenham Cables	1-3
Slough Centre v Witney Town	6-0
Berkhamsted Town v Maidenhead United	
RAMC (Aldershot) v HMS Daedalus	1-2
Lymington v Alton Town	1-1,1-5
Westbury United v Devizes Town	5-2
Clandown v Shepton Mallet Town	1-4
Cinderford Town v Chard Town	3-2
Clevedon v Mount Hill Enterprise	6-0
Mousehole v Dartmouth United	0-5
Bugle v Nanpean Rovers	2-1

Third Qualifying Round

Cleator Moor Celtic v Whitley Bay	1-4
Tow Law Town v Cockfield	1-3
Portrack Shamrocks v Redcar Albion	3-1
St Annes Athletic v ICI (Alkali)	1-3
Liversedge v Harrogate & District Railway	0-8
Players Athletic v Hallam	0-2
Anstey Nomads v Syston St Peters	5-2
Fernhill Athletic v Walsall Wood	2-5
Higham Ferrers Town v Ramsey Town	6-1
Holt United v Boulton & Paul	0-2
Whitton United v Lakenheath	3-3,3-2
Stevenage Town v Vauxhall Motors	2-3

Crittall Athletic v Colchester Casuals	5-1
Bexleyheath & Welling v Faversham Town	4-1
Lancing Athletic v Worthing	1-6
Banstead Athletic v East Grinstead	2-2,0-2
Ware v Hoddesdon Town	
Edgware Town v Finchley	3-4
Carshalton Athletic v Dagenham Cables	3-0
Slough Centre v Berkhamsted Town	2-1
HMS Daedalus v Alton Town	2-2
Westbury United v Shepton Mallet Town	3-0
Cinderford Town v Clevedon	2-3
Dartmouth United v Bugle	3-2

Fourth Qualifying Round

Evenwood Town v Wolsingham Welfare	5-1
Portrack Shamrocks v Whitley Bay	1-2
Harrogate & District Railway v Penrith	2-1
South Bank v Cockfield	2-6
Salts (Saltaire) v Rawmarsh Colliery Welfare	2-1
Norton Woodseats v ICI (Alkali)	3-3,0-2
Anstey Nomads v Smethwick Town	4-0
Walsall Wood v Hallam	1-1,1-6
Histon Institute v Boulton & Paul	4-1
Whitton United v Stowmarket	2-1
Cambridge City v Higham Ferrers Town	4-0
Harwich & Parkeston v Crittalls Athletic	2-2,2-0
Finchley v Cheshunt	8-0
Hitchin Town v Slough Centre	3-1
Ware v Vauxhall Motors	2-1
Clapton v Hayes	0-5
Tooting & Mitcham United v Worthing	5-1
East Grinstead v Sutton United	1-2
Woking v Bexleyheath & Welling	5-0
Carshalton Athletic v Sheppey United	4-1
Frome Town v Westbury United	2-2,2-1
Clevedon v Salisbury	2-1
Dartmouth United v HMS Daedalus	4-2
Saltash United v Keynsham Town	6-2

First Round Proper

Shildon v Bishop Auckland	2-7
Cockfield v Sheffield	0-3
Salts (Saltaire) v Willington	0-3
Whitby Town v Evenwood Town	2-3
Yorkshire Amateur v Whitley Bay	0-0,2-0
Ferryhill Athletic v ICI (Alkali)	1-2
Harrogate Railway v Billingham Synthonian Rec	2-1
Marine v Crook Town	1-0
Hayes v Pegasus	2-4
Barking v Kingstonian	3-1
Tooting & Mitcham United v Oxford City	5-0
Whitton United v Harwich & Parkeston	1-1,2-4
Walton & Hersham v Tilbury	1-0
Redhill v Hallam	2-2,1-1,0-2
Dulwich Hamlet v Ware	3-2
Wealdstone v Moor Green	1-1,6-1
St Albans City v Romford	4-4,0-4
Wimbledon v Walthamstow Avenue	1-3
Saltash United v Southall	2-2,1-2
Sutton United v Hounslow Town	3-5
Histon Institute v Dartmouth United	3-3,2-3
Leytonstone v Frome Town	6-1
Eastbourne v Slough Town	1-4
Finchley v Erith & Belvedere	2-0

Hendon v Boldmere St Michaels	4-0
Hitchin Town v Wycombe Wanderers	0-0,0-2
Woking v Barnet	3-3,0-2
Cambridge City v Anstey Nomads	2-1
Carshalton Athletic v Ilford	1-0
Clevedon v Briggs Sports	4-0
Leyton v Bromley	1-2
Brentwood & Warley v Corinthian Casuals	0-5

Second Round Proper

Corinthian Casuals v Finchley	4-1
Marine v Evenwood Town	1-3
Carshalton Athletic v Romford	2-3
Slough Town v Barking	2-1
Wycombe Wanderers v Barnet	2-1
ICI (Alkali) v Leytonstone	2-3
Clevedon v Dartmouth United	5-0
Yorkshire Amateur v Walton & Hersham	1-2
Harwich & Parkeston v Harrogate & Dist Rly	3-2
Pegasus v Cockfield	5-0
Tooting & Mitcham United v Cambridge City	4-2
Hendon v Hounslow Town	1-2
Walthamstow Avenue v Wealdstone	0-0,0-1

Southall v Bishop Auckland	2-0
Willington v Bromley	2-1
Hallam v Dulwich Hamlet	1-0

Third Round Proper

Southall v Wealdstone	3-0
Leytonstone v Hallam	3-1
Clevedon v Harwich & Parkeston	1-2
Corinthian Casuals v Pegasus	0-1
Walton & Hersham v Evenwood Town	3-1
Wycombe Wanderers v Romford	0-5
Hounslow Town v Tooting & Mitcham United	1-1,1-2
Willington v Slough Town	1-1,2-3

Fourth Round Proper

Tooting & Mitcham v Walton & Hersham	0-0,0-0
(at Kingstonian)	1-2
Southall v Romford	1-1,2-1
Slough Town v Pegasus	0-2
Leytonstone v Harwich & Parkeston	3-4

Semi Finals

Southall v Pegasus (*at Highbury & Fulham*)	1-1,1-2
Walton & Hersham v Harwich (*at Brentford*)	1-3

Final Played at Wembley

Pegasus 6, Harwich & Parkeston 0 (*Goals:* Saunders, Sutcliffe 2, Carr 2, Laybourne)   Attendance 100 000

Pegasus: Brown, Alexander, McKenna, Vowels, Shearwood, Saunders, Pawson, Carr, Laybourne, Lunn, Sutcliffe.

Harwich: King, Nighingale, Tyrell, Christie, Bloss, Haugh, Stremp, Pearson, Davies, Cooper, Jennings.

Their second triumph at Wembley is celebrated by Pegasus in 1953 with captain Dennis Saunders, who played in every one of the club's competitive matches in its short history, up on the shoulders of Reg Vowels and Ray Sutcliffe. The other players are DB Carr, JS Laybourne, G Lunn, AH Pawson and GH McKinna; kneeling, KA Shearwood, FCM Alexander, BR Brown.

FA AMATEUR CUP

1954-55 Played at Wembley
Bishop Auckland 2, Hendon 0 (*Goals:* Lewin 2)   Attendance 100 000
Bishop Auckland: Sharratt, Marshall, Stewart, Hardisty, Cresswell, Nimmins, Major, Lewin, Oliver, O'Connell, Edwards.
Hendon: Ivey, Fisher, Beardsley, Topp, Adams, Austin, Saffery, Hvidsten, Bahler, Cunningham, Parker.

1955-56 Played at Wembley
Bishop Auckland 1, Corinthian Casuals 1 (*Goals:* McKenna, Kerruish)   Attendance 80 000
Bishop Auckland: Sharratt, Fryer, Stewart, Hardisty, Cresswell, Nimmins, McKenna, Lewin, Oliver, O'Connell, Edwards.
Casuals: Ahm, Alexander, Newton, Shuttleworth, Cowan, Vowels, Insole, Sanders, Laybourne, Citron, Kerruish.
REPLAY. Played at Middlesbrough
Bishop Auckland 4, Corinthian Casuals 1 (*Goals:* Lewin 2, Hardisty, Stewart/ Citron)   Attendance 30 200
Bishop Auckland: Sharratt, Marshall, Stewart, Hardisty, Cresswell, O'Connell, McKenna, Lewin, Oliver, Bradley, Edwards.
Casuals: Ahm, Alexander, Newton, Shuttleworth, Cowan, Vowels, Insole, Sanders, Laybourne, Citron, Kerruish.

1956-57 Played at Wembley
Bishop Auckland 3, Wycombe Wanderers 1 (*Goals:* Russell, Lewin, Bradley/ Smith)   Attendance 90 000
Bishop Auckland: Sharratt, Marshall, Childs, Thursby, Cresswell, Nimmins, Bradley, Lewin, Russell, Hardisty, Edwards.
Wycombe: Syrett, Lawson, Westley, Truett G, Wicks, Truett J, Worley, Trott, Bates, Tomlin, Smith.

1957-58 Played at Wembley   Attendance 71 000
Woking 3, Ilford 0 (*Goals:* Hebdon 2, Stratton)
Woking: Burley, Ellerby, Parsons, Collingwood, Turner, Clacey, Littlejohn, Hebdon, Mortimore, Hamm, Stratton.
Ilford: Gibbins, Simmons, Cross, Sharod, Whittall, Dodkins, Durston, Winch, Taylor, Butler, Castle.

1958-59 Played at Wembley
Crook Town 3, Barnet 2 (*Goals:* Tracey 2, Keating/ Brown 2)   Attendance 60 000
Crook Town: Snowball, Gardener, Steward, Carr, Bainbridge, Wilkie, Coates, O'Connell, Keating, Tracey, McMillan.
Barnet: Goymer, Duncan, Cooper, Sleap, D'Arcy A, Cantwell, Welch, D'Arcy A, Brown, Harding, Drake.

1959-60 Played at Wembley
Hendon 2, Kingstonian 1 (*Goals:* Topp, Howard/ Whing)   Attendance 60 000
Hendon: Shearing, Widdowfield, Harris, Topp, Fisher, Murphy, Candey, Figg, Spector, Quail, Howard.
Kingstonian: Groves, Davies, Bird, Richards, Ashworth, Gilson, Harris K, Coates, Whing, Lindsay, Oakes.

1960-61 Played at Wembley
Walthamstow Avenue 2, West Auckland Town 1 (*Goals:* Groves, Lewis/ Douglass)   Attendance 45 000
Walthamstow: McGuire, Edwards, Bambridge, Andrews, Prine, Keenes, Groves, Minall, Lewis, Saggers, Harvey.
West Auckland: Bowmaker, Siddle, Stafford, Mendum, Summerson, Carter, Briggs, Bromfield, Curtis, Skelton, Douglass.

Action in the West Auckland goalmouth as Walthamstow Avenue strikers Brian Harvey and Alan Minall put pressure on keeper Bowmaker in front of 45,000 at Wembley in 1961.

1961-62 Played at Wembley
Crook Town 1, Hounslow Town 1 (*Goals:* McMillan/ Patterson)   Attendance 43 000
Crook: Snowball, Gardener, Clark, Storey, Heatherington, Brown, Sparks, Garbutt, Coates, Peary, McMillan.
Hounslow: Rhodes, McDonald, Creasey, Evans, Taylor, Digweed, Somers, Fennell, McHattie, Dipper, Patterson.
REPLAY. Played at Middlesbrough
Crook Town 4, Hounslow Town 0 (*Goals:* Coates 2, Sparks, McMillan)
Crook: Snowball, Gardener, Clark, Storey, Heatherington, Brown, Sparks, Garbutt, Coates, Peary, McMillan.
Hounslow: Rhodes, McDonald, Creasey, Evans, Taylor, Digweed, Alder, Somers, McHattie, Dipper, Patterson.

1962-63 Played at Wembley
Wimbledon 4, Sutton United 2 (*Goals:* Reynolds 4/ Goodall, Bladon)   Attendance 45 000
Wimbledon: Kelly, Martin J, Willis, Ardrey, Law, Murphy, Brown, Martin B, Reynolds, Hamm, Williams.
Sutton: Roffey, Gamblin, Shears, Shepherd, Price, Clack, Bladon, Osborne, Bates, Hermitage, Goodall.

1963-64 Played at Wembley
Enfield 1, Crook Town 2 (*Goals:* Day/ Goodfellow, Brown)   Attendance 37 000
Enfield: Mitchell, Neale, Harris, D'Arcy, Kingsland, Cantwell, Thomas, Broomfield, Edwards, Day, Howard.
Crook: Snowball, McCourt, Reid, Storey, Garbutt, Brown, Weir, Goodfellow, Lumsdon, Roughley, McMillan.

THE LAST TEN

AMATEUR CUP 1964-65

First Round

Sutton United v Hendon	1-2
Leytonstone v Wycombe Wanderers	2-2,2-0
Fareham Town v Carshalton Athletic	1-2
Hounslow v Alton Town	10-0
Croydon Amateurs v Clapton	1-1,1-0
Stowmarket v St Albans City	0-1
Aveley v Dulwich Hamlet	0-1
Whitley Bay v West Auckland Town	4-3
Crook Town v Willington	0-1
Woking v Bromley	2-2,1-2
Callenders Athletic v Kingstonian	0-10
Spennymoor United v Skelmerdale United	3-0
Thackley v Penrith	0-2
Tow Law Town v Ferryhill Athletic	1-2
Windsor & Eton v Finchley	1-1,1-5
Hayes v Harrow Town	3-1
Alvechurch v Norton Woodseats	2-0
Tooting & Mitcham v Walthamstow Avenue	1-1,1-0
Bishop Auckland v Loughborough College	2-1
Wealdstone v Grays Athletic	3-0
Eastwood Town v Evenwood Town	2-1
Yorkshire Amateurs v Prestwich Heys	2-3
Enfield v Dagenham	3-2
Maidstone United v Barnet	1-4
Walton & Hersham v Torpoint Athletic	1-1,2-4
Corinthian Casuals v Harwich & Parkeston	0-1
Ilford v Bishop's Stortford	0-2
Ford United v Maidenhead United	2-2,1-3
Hitchin Town v Devizes Town	5-0
Oxford City v Southall	6-0
Eastbourne v Leatherhead	2-1
Whitby Town v Moor Green	3-2

Second Round

Hendon v Leytonstone	5-1
Carshalton Athletic v Hounslow	4-1
Croydon Amateurs v St Albans City	1-2
Dulwich Hamlet v Whitley Bay	1-2
Willington v Bromley	2-4
Kingstonian v Spennymoor United	11-2
Penrith v Ferryhill Athletic	1-3
Finchley v Hayes	4-0
Alvechurch v Walthamstow Avenue	2-1
Bishop Auckland v Wealdstone	2-4
Eastwood Town v Prestwich Heys	5-3
Enfield v Barnet	1-1,3-2
Torpoint Athletic v Harwich & Parkeston	0-4
Bishop's Stortford v Maidenhead United	4-1
Hitchin Town v Oxford City	2-2,1-3
Eastbourne v Whitby Town	0-2

Third Round

Hendon v Carshalton Athletic	5-1
St Albans City v Whitley Bay	0-1
Bromley v Kingstonian	0-0,2-4
Ferryhill Athletic v Finchley	1-2
Alvechurch v Wealdstone	4-1
Eastwood Town v Enfield	2-3
Harwich & Parkeston v Bishop's Stortford	0-0,2-1
Oxford City v Whitby Town	1-2

Fourth Round

Whitley Bay v Hendon	1-3
Kingstonian v Finchley	0-2
Alvechurch v Enfield	1-3
Harwich & Parkeston v Whitby Town	0-0,2-3

FA AMATEUR CUP

Semi Finals

Hendon v Finchley	4-1	Enfield v Whitby Town	1-2
(At Arsenal)		*(At Sunderland)*	

Final at Wembley

Whitby Town 1, Hendon 3 *(Goals:* Mulvaney/ Hyde 2, Quail) Attendance 45 000

Whitby: Pybus, Durnall, Hobbs, Kennerley, Barker, Moody, Geldart, Edwards, Mulvaney, McHale, Crosthwaite
Hendon: Swannell, Hogwood, Sleap, Evans, Riddy, Cantwell, Drake, Slade, Hyde, Quail, Lakey.

AMATEUR CUP 1965-66

First Round

Wealdstone v Hitchin Town	4-1
Willington v Tow Law Town	1-3
Maidstone United v Barking	1-2
Ferryhill Athletic v Evenwood Town	2-2,2-0
Maidenhead United v Windsor & Eton	3-0
Oxford City v Leatherhead	2-3
Corinthian Casuals v Torpoint Athletic	3-0
Hayes v Grays Athletic	3-3,2-1
Loughborough College v Norton Woodseats	3-0
Bromley v Walthamstow Avenue	2-1
Moor Green v Crook Town	1-2
West Auckland Town v Prestwich Heys	4-2
Gosport Borough Athletic v Eastbourne	1-2
Enfield v Walton & Hersham	5-1
Stowmarket v Woking	3-2
Skelmersdale United v Alvechurch	0-2
Spennymoor v Eastwood Town	1-1,3-2
Leyton v Hemel Hempstead	2-2,1-0
Yorkshire Amateurs v Whitley Bay	1-2
Lancing v Kingstonian	0-3
Sutton United v Clapton	7-0
Dagenham v Harlow Town	1-0
Finchley v Dulwich Hamlet	2-0
Whitby Town v Bishop Auckland	1-3
Wycombe Wanderers v Aveley	2-1
Stanley United v Penrith	0-2
Witney Town v Hounslow	2-1
Fareham Town v St Albans City	1-2
Leytonstone v Tooting & Mitcham United	4-2
Bishop's Stortford v Herne Bay	1-0
Ferndale YC v Carshalton Athletic	0-7
Hendon v Harwich & Parkeston	3-1

Second Round

Wealdstone v Tow Law Town	2-1
Barking v Ferryhill Athletic	1-0
Maidenhead United v Leatherhead	0-2
Corinthian Casuals v Hayes	1-2
Loughborough Colleges v Bromley	4-1
Crook Town v West Auckland Town	0-5
Eastbourne v Enfield	0-5
Stowmarket v Alvechurch	2-2,2-3
Spennymoor United v Leyton	1-3
Whitley Bay v Kingstonian	3-0
Sutton United v Dagenham	5-0
Finchley v Bishop Auckland	1-3
Wycombe Wanderers v Penrith	1-0
Witney Town v St Albans City	2-2,1-4
Leytonstone v Bishop's Stortford	3-1
Hendon v Carshalton Athletic	4-0

Third Round

Barking v Wealdstone	1-3
Leatherhead v Hayes	2-2,1-0
Loughborough Colleges v Crook Town	1-2
Enfield v Alvechurch	2-3
Leyton v Whitley Bay	0-5
Sutton United v Bishop Auckland	2-1
Wycombe Wanderers v St Albans City	1-1,3-0
Hendon v Leytonstone	2-1

Fourth Round

Wealdstone v Leatherhead	2-1
Crook Town v Alvechurch	0-2
Whitley Bay v Sutton United	2-0
Hendon v Wycombe Wanderers	2-1

Semi Finals

Wealdstone v Alvechurch	1-0	Hendon v Whitley Bay	2-1
(At Chelsea)		*(At Sunderland)*	

Final at Wembley

Wealdstone 3, Hendon 1 *(Goals:* Childs 2, Bremer/ Riddy) Attendance 45 000

Wealdstone: Goymer, Doyle, Sedgley, Townsend, Ashworth, Dillsworth, Allen, Childs, Coolley, Lindsay, Bremer.
Hendon: Swannell, Hogwood, Cooper, Shacklock, Riddy, Cantwell, Churchill, Evans, Swain, Sleap, Hyde.

AMATEUR CUP 1966-67

First Round

Enfield v Sutton United	3-0
Cambridge University v Wembley	1-1,2-5
Leytonstone v Wycombe Wanderers	4-2
Grays Athletic v Dulwich Hamlet	2-2,2-0
Ferryhill Athletic v Prestwich Heys	1-1,0-4
Vauxhall Motors v Finchley	1-3

Evenwood Town v Highgate United	0-2
Penrith v Eastwood Town	1-3
Hallam v Whitley Bay	0-3
Crook Town v Loughborough Colleges	1-2
Addlestone v Windsor & Eton	2-2,2-3
Walthamstow Avenue v St Albans City	2-0
Bromley v Corinthian Casuals	2-1

Kingstonian v Carshalton Athletic	2-0
Spennymoor United v Consett	1-1,0-2
Hayes v Gosport Borough	0-4
Hoddesdon v Clapton	0-0,1-3
West Thurrock v Fareham Town	1-4
Tow Law Town v West Auckland Town	1-0
Leatherhead v Bishop's Stortford	1-1,2-1
Bristol St George v Dagenham	1-0
Ilford v Hendon	0-3
Eastbourne v Oxford City	0-3
North Shields v Alvechurch	3-0
Southall v Maidenhead United	6-1
Barking v Woking	1-2
Hounslow v Harwich & Parkeston	2-3
Slough Town v Hitchin Town	1-1,3-1
Brook Sports v Whitby Town	1-0
Wealdstone v Stowmarket	1-1,1-1,5-2
Leyton v Torpoint Athletic	1-1,4-2
Skelmersdale United v Bishop Auckland	3-0

Second Round

Wembley v Enfield	1-2
Leytonstone v Grays Athletic	5-1
Prestwich Heys v Finchley	1-3
Highgate United v Eastwood Town	2-1
Whitley Bay v Loughborough Colleges	4-1
Windsor & Eton v Walthamstow Avenue	3-3,0-5

Semi Finals

Enfield v Walthamstow Avenue	1-0
(At Crystal Palace)	

Final at Wembley

Enfield 0, Skelmersdale United 0 Attendance 75 000

Enfield: Wolstenholme, Sedgley, Reid, Payne, D'Arcy, Moxon, Churchill, Connell, Hill, Day, Howard. Sub: Adams.
Skelmersdale: Crosbie, Bermingham, Bridge, Unsworth, Wade, Moorcroft, Whitehead, Worswick, Bennett, Burns, Mansley. Sub: McDermott.

Replay at Manchester City

Enfield 3, Skelmersdale United 0 *(Goals:* Connell, Hill 2) Attendance 55 388

Enfield: Wolstenholme, Sedgley, Reid, Payne, D'Arcy, Moxon, Churchill, Connell, Hill, Day, Adams. Sub: Howard.
Skelmersdale: Crosbie, Bermingham, McDermott, Unsworth, Wade, Moorcroft, Whitehead, Worswick, Bennett, Burns, Mansley. Sub: Felmingham.

Bromley v Kingstonian	1-4
Consett v Gosport Borough	1-5
Clapton v Fareham Town	2-0
Tow Law Town v Leatherhead	0-1
Bristol St George v Hendon	0-0,0-5
Oxford City v North Shields	0-0,1-1,4-3
Southall v Woking	2-1
Harwich & Parkeston v Slough Town	0-2
Brook Sports v Wealdstone	0-3
Skelmersdale United v Leyton	3-0

Third Round

Leytonstone v Enfield	1-1,1-0
Prestwich Heys v Highgate United	1-2
Whitley Bay v Walthamstow Avenue	0-2
Kingstonian v Gosport Borough	4-0
Clapton v Leatherhead	2-3
Hendon v Oxford City	4-3
Southall v Slough Town	0-1
Wealdstone v Skelmersdale United	0-1

Fourth Round

Highgate United v Enfield	0-0,0-0,0-1
Walthamstow Avenue v Kingstonian	5-0
Leatherhead v Hendon	0-3
Slough Town v Skelmersdale United	2-2,0-1

Hendon v Skelmersdale United	0-0,2-2,1-3
(At Derby, replays at Birmingham City and West Bromwich)	

AMATEUR CUP 1967-68

First Round

Penrith v Prestwich Heys	1-2	Sharpness v Dulwich Hamlet	1-2
Eastwood Town v Bishop Auckland	1-0	Cray Wanderers v Eastbourne	4-1
North Shields v Ossett Albion	3-0	Bristol St George v Leyton	3-1
Coventry Amateurs v Hallam	2-1	Barking v Hendon	1-0
Crook Town v Evenwood Town	1-2	Southall v Woking	2-0
West Auckland Town v Loughborough Coll	2-2,1-0	Harwich & Parkeston v Fareham Town	1-2
Alvechurch v Tow Law Town	1-2	Hitchin Town v Sutton United	1-0
Skelmersdale United v Spennymoor United	0-1	City of Norwich OBU v Wycombe Wanderers	1-0
Norton Woodseats Amateurs v Whitley Bay	0-2	Tilbury v Gosport Borough Athletic	2-0
Marine v Ferryhill Athletic	3-1	Bromley v Walton & Hersham	0-0,1-3
Carshalton Athletic v Kingstonian	2-2,3-4	Slough Town v Finchley	3-2
Bishop's Stortford v Walthamstow Avenue	5-3	Torpoint Athletic v Wealdstone	2-4
Corinthian Casuals v Hounslow	4-1	Clapton v Leytonstone	0-2
St Albans City v Oxford City	1-2	Ilford v Lewes	1-2
Windsor & Eton v Enfield	1-3	Hayes v Grays Athletic	3-0
Leatherhead v Dagenham	1-2	Chesham United v Maidenhead United	2-2,2-2,3-1

FA AMATEUR CUP

Second Round

Leystonstone v Southall	1-0
Bishop's Stortford v Bristol St George	3-1
Lewes v Tilbury	3-4
North Shields v Enfield	2-3
West Auckland Town v Slough Town	1-3
Evenwood Town v Sutton United	0-0,0-3
Walton & Hersham v Dagenham	1-2
Marine v City of Norwich OBU	2-0
Hayes v Cray Wanderers	0-0,0-1
Barking v Coventry Amateurs	3-1
Eastwood Town v Whitley Bay	1-0
Wealdstone v Kingstonian	2-0
Oxford City v Tow Law Town	2-1
Prestwich Heys v Spennymoor United	1-1,2-1
Harwich & Parkeston v Corinthian Casuals	0-1
Dulwich Hamlet v Chesham United	1-1,2-4

Third Round

Leytonstone v Bishop's Stortford	7-2
Tilbury v Enfield	0-2
Slough v Sutton United	1-1,0-1
Dagenham v Marine	0-0,4-3
Cray Wanderers v Barking	0-0,0-2
Eastwood Town v Wealdstone	1-1,1-4
Oxford City v Prestwich Heys	4-2
Corinthian Casuals v Chesham United	0-0,0-1

Fourth Round

Enfield v Leytonstone	0-0,0-0,0-1
Sutton United v Dagenham	2-1
Wealdstone v Barking	3-1
Oxford City v Chesham United	0-0,0-2

Semi Finals

Sutton United v Leytonstone	0-0,1-3
(At Crystal Palace, replay at Brentford)	
Wealdstone v Chesham United	0-2
(At Fulham)	

Final at Wembley

Leytonstone 1, Chesham United 0 *(Goal:* Gray) Attendance 52 000

Leytonstone: Hadlow, Tilley, Hames, Andrews, Thomson, Walker, Charles, Gray, Diwell, Minall, Harvey. Sub: Albon.

Chesham: Wells, Thackray, Smith, Caterer, Burgess, McCaffrey, Ellis, Black, Fruen, Harper, Kent. Sub: Frost.

AMATEUR CUP 1968-69

First Round

Sutton United v Bromley	9-0
Leeds & Carnegie College v Billingham SR	2-1
Marine v West Auckland Town	2-2,2-0
Chesham United v Walthamstow Avenue	0-2
Torpoint Athletic v Cray Wanderers	1-3
Leytonstone v Woking	1-0
Kingstonian v Southall	1-1,4-0
Lincoln United v Crook Town	2-1
Alton Town v Croydon Amateurs	3-0
Whitley Bay v Prestwich Heys	1-0
Walton & Hersham v Slough Town	2-2,1-2
Hitchin Town v Stowmarket	2-0
Emley v Evenwood Town	2-1
Dulwich Hamlet v Corinthian Casuals	1-1,2-1
Grays Athletic v Barking	1-1,0-5
Wembley v Leyton	1-0
Dagenham v Windsor & Eton	4-0
Melksham Town v Harwich & Parkeston	2-3
Ilford v Cheshunt	0-1
Enfield v Leatherhead	0-0,1-1,1-0
Skelmersdale United v Hallam	3-0
Oxford City v Wycombe Wanderers	3-2
Carshalton Athletic v Finchley	2-1
Whitby Town v Guinness Exports	1-0
Hertford Town v Wealdstone	0-0,3-3,1-1,1-1,0-1
Fareham Town v Cirencester Town	1-1,1-3
Hayes v Bristol St George	2-1
Tow Law Town v Alvechurch	3-1
St Albans City v Bishop's Stortford	3-0
Hendon v Hornchurch	2-0
Coventry Amateurs v Eastwood Town	1-1,3-1
North Shields v Spennymoor United	4-1

Second Round

Leeds & Carnegie College v Sutton United	2-5
Marine v Walthamstow Avenue	2-0
Cray Wanderers v Leytonstone	2-2,0-2
Kingstonian v Lincoln United	2-0
Alton Town v Whitley Bay	0-2
Slough Town v Hitchin Town	4-0
Emley v Dulwich Hamlet	1-0
Barking v Wembley	4-1
Dagenham v Harwich & Parkeston	0-1
Cheshunt v Enfield	0-0,1-2
Skelmersdale United v Oxford City	1-1,3-1
Carshalton Athletic v Whitby Town	2-2,0-1
Wealdstone v Cirencester Town	3-1
Hayes v Tow Law Town	2-0
St Albans City v Hendon	0-2
North Shields v Coventry Amateurs	3-0

Third Round

Sutton United v Marine	2-0
Leytonstone v Kingstonian	1-0
Whitley Bay v Slough Town	3-2
Emley v Barking	0-1
Harwich & Parkeston v Enfield	1-1,0-4
Skelmersdale United v Whitby Town	3-1
Wealdstone v Hayes	1-0
North Shields v Hendon	1-1,2-0

Fourth Round

Sutton United v Leytonstone	3-1
Whitley Bay v Barking	5-1
Enfield v Skelmersdale United	1-2
Wealdstone v North Shields	0-1

Semi Finals

Sutton United v Whitley Bay   4-2   Skelmersdale United v North Shields   1-1,1-2

(At Birmingham City)   *(At Middlesbrough, replay at Southport)*

Final at Wembley

North Shields 2, Sutton United 1 *(Goals:* Hall, Joicey/ Mellows)   Attendance 47 500

North Shields: Morgan, Driver, Twaddle, Hall, Tatum, Thompson, Wrightson, Lister, Joicey, Cassidy, Rutherford (Orrick).

Sutton: Roffey, Garfield, Grose, Brookes, Clarke, Gradi, Bladon, Mellows, Drabwell, Pritchard, Howard (Gane).

AMATEUR CUP 1969-70

First Round

Wealdstone v Vauxhall Motors	3-2
Bromley v Oxford City	3-2
Croydon Amateurs v Wycombe Wanderers	0-1
Tooting & Mitcham United v Leytonstone	0-0,1-0
Harwich & Parkeston v Leyton	9-0
St Albans City v Wembley	0-0,1-1,2-1
Tow Law Town v Spennymoor United	1-0
Evesham United v Cray Wanderers	1-0
North Shields v Evenwood Town	0-0,0-0,1-3
Hendon v St Austell	5-0
Eastwood Town v Leeds & Carnegie College	0-2
Woking v Walton & Hersham	0-0,1-2
Coventry Amateurs v West Auckland Town	1-2
Guinness Exports v Emley	0-3
Hoddesdon Town v Dagenham	1-2
Hayes v Barking	0-2
Alton Town v Walthamstow Avenue	5-0
Carshalton Athletic v Hitchin Town	0-0,0-3
St Johns College York v Whitley Bay	0-1
Enfield v Redhill	3-2
Prestwich Heys v Marine	1-0
Sutton United v Leatherhead	2-0
Gorleston v Southall	1-4
Bristol St George v Fareham Town	4-2
Paget Rangers v Alvechurch	1-1,2-2,1-3
Whitby Town v Loughborough Colleges	1-1,2-0
Chesham United v Slough Town	2-3
Aveley v Kingstonian	1-0
Bishop's Stortford v Dulwich Hamlet	5-2
Durham City v Skelmersdale United	1-1,2-3
Cheshunt v Windsor & Eton	3-1
Ilford v Witney Town	1-0

Semi Finals

Dagenham v St Albans City	1-1,1-0

(At Millwall, replay at Luton)

Second Round

Wealdstone v Bromley	2-0
Wycombe Wanderers v Tooting & Mitcham	0-0,2-1
Harwich & Parkeston v St Albans City	1-3
Tow Law Town v Evesham United	0-3
Evenwood Town v Hendon	1-1,2-4
Leeds & Carnegie College v Walton & Hersham	0-4
West Auckland Town v Emley	0-1
Dagenham v Barking	1-1,3-1
Alton Town v Hitchin Town	2-1
Whitley Bay v Enfield	1-4
Prestwich Heys v Sutton United	3-1
Southall v Bristol St George	2-2,5-2
Alvechurch v Whitby Town	3-0
Slough Town v Aveley	2-0
Bishop's Stortford v Skelmersdale United	0-4
Cheshunt v Ilford	3-2

Third Round

Wealdstone v Wycombe Wanderers	0-1
St Albans City v Tow Law Town	4-0
Hendon v Walton & Hersham	1-1,0-1
Emley v Dagenham	0-0,0-5
Alton Town v Enfield	2-5
Prestwich Heys v Southall	1-0
Alvechurch v Slough Town	2-2,0-2
Skelmersdale United v Cheshunt	1-0

Fourth Round

Wycombe Wanderers v St Albans City	0-2
Walton & Hersham v Dagenham	0-1
Enfield v Prestwich Heys	2-0
Slough Town v Skelmersdale United	0-0,0-3

Skelmersdale United v Enfield	0-1

(At Derby)

Final at Wembley

Enfield 5, Dagenham 1 *(Goals:* Connell 2, Feely, Adams, own goal/ Brookes)   Attendance 33 000

Enfield: Wolstenholme, Clayton, Fry, Payne, Betson, Day, Adams, Connell, Feely, (D'Arcy), Gray, Hill.

Dagenham: Huttley, Robertson, (Scarfe), Dudley, Daniels, Still, Moore, Leakey, Drake, Smith M, Smith B, Brookes.

FA AMATEUR CUP

AMATEUR CUP 1970-71

First Round
Alton Town v Hendon	1-1,0-6
Alvechurch v Ormskirk	0-1
Barking v Paulton Rovers	4-1
Bracknell Town v Newquay	0-2
Bristol St George v Boreham Wood	0-3
Bromley v St Albans City	3-3,0-4
Carshalton Athletic v Cheshunt	2-1
Cray Wanderers v Kingstonian	1-2
Croydon Amateurs v Harwich & Parkeston	1-4
Dagenham v Leyton	5-0
Durham City v Whitley Bay	2-3
Fareham Town v Tooting & Mitcham United	1-3
Finchley v Woking	2-1
Irlam Town v Oldbury United	1-2
Leeds & Carnegie Coll v Loughborough College	0-2
Marine v Prestwich Heys	2-1
Oxford City v Bishop's Stortford	1-3
Slough Town v Redhill	1-1,3-1
Southall v Dulwich Hamlet	2-3
South Bank v North Shields	1-3
Spennymoor United v Skelmersdale United	1-1,1-5
Stowmarket v Leatherhead	2-2,2-2,2-3
Sutton Coldfield Town v Emley	4-0
Sutton United v Leytonstone	0-0,0-4
Tilbury v Aveley	0-1
Tow Law Town v West Auckland Town	2-1
Vauxhall Motors v Hayes	0-3
Walthamstow Avenue v Ilford	2-0
Walton & Hersham v Enfield	0-2
Whitby Town v Evenwood Town	2-3
Witney Town v Hitchin Town	2-1
Wycombe Wanderers v Wealdstone	1-0

Second Round
Bishop's Stortford v Dagenham	0-1
Boreham Wood v St Albans City	2-1
Carshalton Athletic v Aveley	2-3
Harwich & Parkeston v Slough Town	0-3
Hayes v Witney Town	2-1
Hendon v Barking	4-1
Leatherhead v Dulwich Hamlet	0-0,1-0
Leytonstone v Kingstonian	4-1
Loughborough Colleges v Evenwood Town	1-0
Marine v Ormskirk	3-1
Newquay v Oldbury United	1-7
North Shields v Tow Law Town	0-0,0-6
Skelmersdale United v Sutton Coldfield Town	3-0
Tooting & Mitcham Utd v Walthamstow Avenue	3-1
Whitley Bay v Finchley	2-0
Wycombe Wanderers v Enfield	2-1

Third Round
Boreham Wood v Leatherhead	1-1,1-2
Hendon v Slough Town	1-1,1-3
Leytonstone v Dagenham	0-1
Loughborough Colleges v Hayes	0-3
Marine v Aveley	0-1
Tooting & Mitcham United v Whitley Bay	2-3
Tow Law Town v Skelmersdale United	1-1,0-1
Wycombe Wanderers v Oldbury United	4-0

Fourth Round
Aveley v Slough Town	0-2
Dagenham v Whitley Bay	1-0
Hayes v Leatherhead	1-1,0-1
Wycombe Wanderers v Skelmersdale United	0-3

Semi Finals
Dagenham v Slough Town	3-3,2-1
(At Charlton, replay at Fulham)	
Skelmersdale United v Leatherhead	2-0
(At Bolton)	

Final at Wembley
Skelmersdale United 4, Dagenham 1 *(Goals:* Dickin 3, Windsor/ Bass) Attendance 45 000
Skelmersdale: Frankish, Allen, Poole, Turner, Bennett, McDermott, Swift, Wolfe, Dickin, Hardcastle, Clements.
Sub: Windsor.
Dagenham: Huttley, Ford, Dudley, Davidson, Still, Moore, Leakey, Fry, Bass, Baker, Dear. Sub: Smith.

AMATEUR CUP 1971-72

First Round
Evenwood Town v Oldbury United	3-3,1-1,1-2
Evesham Town v Prestwich Heys	2-1
Spennymoor United v Emley	5-0
Marine v Whitley Bay	4-1
Loughborough College v Whitby Town	4-0
West Auckland Town v Highgate United	1-4
Hallam v North Shields	0-1
Tow Law Town v Leeds & Carnegie College	1-1,3-0
Shildon v Ormskirk	1-1,3-1
Alvechurch v Blyth Spartans	0-1
Leytonstone v Carshalton Athletic	1-0
Hitchin Town v Erith & Belvedere	0-3
Corinthian Casuals v Maidenhead United	0-1
Tooting & Mitcham United v Barking	1-2
Cheshunt v Tilbury	1-1,2-3
Hayes v City of Norwich OBU	5-1
Wokingham Town v Sutton United	0-2
Witney Town v Dulwich Hamlet	2-1
Hendon v Horsham	1-0
Bromley v Oxford City	1-2
Letchworth Town v Cadbury Heath	1-1,1-2
Walton & Hersham v Southall	1-1,1-0
Leatherhead v Dagenham	2-1
Aveley v Wycombe Wanderers	2-2,1-5
Ruislip Manor v Bishop's Stortford	2-2,0-1
Croydon Amateurs v Wantage Town	4-0
Slough Town v Kingstonian	2-0
Bristol St George v Finchley	1-2

Walthamstow Avenue v Enfield	1-3
Harwich & Parkeston v St Albans City	1-1,0-4
Woking v Alton Town	3-1
Ilford v Bognor Regis Town	4-0

Second Round

Slough Town v St Albans City	3-2
Enfield v Evesham United	3-1
Highgate United v Hendon	1-1,1-2
Oxford City v Leatherhead	0-3
Finchley v Bishop's Stortford	0-0,0-2
Cadbury Heath v Walton & Hersham	0-1
Wycombe Wanderers v Spennymoor United	2-1
Tilbury v Croydon Amateurs	1-1,2-3
Tow Law Town v Blyth Spartans	0-4
Ilford v Maidenhead United	1-2
Woking v North Shields	1-0
Barking v Hayes	1-2
Sutton United v Oldbury United	3-1

Semi Finals

Blyth Spartans v Enfield	0-2
(At Newcastle)	

Leytonstone v Loughborough College	1-1,4-1
Witney Town v Marine	2-2,0-2
Hitchin Town v Shildon	1-0

Third Round

Bishop's Stortford v Hitchin Town	1-1,2-2,2-2,0-1
Hayes v Croydon Amateurs	3-1
Hendon v Maidenhead United	0-0,1-0
Leytonstone v Leatherhead	2-2,0-3
Marine v Enfield	0-3
Slough Town v Sutton United	1-0
Walton & Hersham v Wycombe Wanderers	1-2
Woking v Blyth Spartans	0-3

Fourth Round

Blyth Spartans v Leatherhead	1-1,1-0
Enfield v Slough Town	5-1
Hendon v Hitchin Town	2-0
Wycombe Wanderers v Hayes	1-0

Wycombe Wanderers v Hendon	1-2
(At Brentford)	

Final at Wembley

Hendon 2 Enfield 0 *(Goals:* Smith own goal, Bass) Attendance 38 000

Hendon: Swannell, Jennings, Hand, Deadman, Phillips, Haider, Childs, Connell, Bass, Baker, Jameson.
Enfield: Williams, Gibson, Hill, Payne, Betson, Smith, Albom (Brooks), Adams, Butterfield, Gray, Turley.

Not many North West clubs won the Amateur Cup but Skelmersdale United enjoyed some great performances and won the Cup in 1971. Here Ted Dickin, their hat-trick hero, celebrates with his skipper, John Turner, and overjoyed team mates after their 4-1 defeat of Dagenham in front of 45,000 at Wembley.

FA AMATEUR CUP

AMATEUR CUP 1972-73

First Round

Shildon v Spennymoor United	0-1
Marine v Blyth Spartans	0-1
Ormskirk v Loughborough Colleges	2-2,2-1
Prestwich Heys v Leeds & Carnegie College	1-1,0-3
Ossett Albion v Oldbury United	1-1,0-1
Bishop Auckland v Sutton Coldfield Town	0-0,2-0
Whitley Bay v North Shields	1-2
Evenwood Town v Tow Law Town	3-0
Highgate United v Prescot Town	1-0
Ashington v Alvechurch	0-1
Hounslow v Eastbourne United	2-2,0-4
St Albans City v Finchley	2-1
Carshalton Athletic v Harlow Town	0-2
Harwich & Parkeston v Leatherhead	3-1
Witney Town v Witham Town	5-0
Enfield v Leytonstone	1-1,2-3
Paulton Rovers v Croydon Amateurs	0-1
Stowmarket v Kingstonian	0-2
Barking v Shillington	3-0
Aveley v Wembley	3-1
Dagenham v Walthamstow Avenue	2-1
Slough Town v Cadbury Heath School	2-1
Sutton United v Waltham & Hersham	0-3
Devizes Town v Hitchin Town	1-4
Hayes v Tilbury	2-0
Ilford v Fareham Town	2-0
Dulwich Hamlet v Tooting & Mitcham United	1-4
Wycombe Wanderers v Cheshunt	0-1
Hendon v Chichester City	7-0
Bishop's Stortford v Boreham Wood	1-0
Oxford City v Woking	2-1
Maidenhead United v Leyton	1-1,1-2

Second Round

Croydon Amateurs v Alvechurch	1-4
Blyth Spartans v Hendon	1-1,1-0
Leytonstone v Oldbury United	1-1,0-0,1-0
Ilford v Kingstonian	2-1
Leeds & Carnegie Colleges v Walton & Hersham	0-3
Dagenham v Harwich & Parkeston	5-0
Cheshunt v Ormskirk	0-1
Highgate United v Tooting & Mitcham United	3-0
Bishop's Stortford v Bishop Auckland	3-0
St Albans City v Harlow Town	2-0
Aveley v Witney Town	0-0,3-1
Eastbourne United v Slough Town	0-2
Leyton v Spennymoor United	0-3
Barking v Evenwood Town	0-1
Hitchin Town v Hayes	3-4
North Shields v Oxford City	1-0

Third Round

Ormskirk v Dagenham	1-4
Highgate United v Ilford	3-0
Bishop's Stortford v Aveley	1-0
Walton & Hersham v St Albans City	5-0
Spennymoor United v Hayes	2-1
North Shields v Blyth Spartans	0-1
Evenwood Town v Alvechurch	3-1
Slough Town v Leytonstone	2-1

Fourth Round

Dagenham v Bishop's Stortford	1-1,1-2
Walton & Hersham v Spennymoor United	0-0,1-0
Evenwood Town v Highgate United	1-1,0-2
Slough Town v Blyth Spartans	2-1

Semi Finals

Bishop's Stortford v Slough Town	0-1
Walton & Hersham v Highgate United	0-0,4-0

Final at Wembley

Walton & Hersham 1 Slough Town 0 *(Goal:* Connell) Attendance 41 000

Walton: Teale, Thomas, Edwards, Bassett, Donaldson, Lambert, Woffinden, Connell, Smith, Morris, Somers.
Slough: Wolstenholme, Reid, Eaton, Mead, D'Arcy (Jamieson), Reardon, Chatterton, Day, O'Sullivan, Gaine, Anthony.

AMATEUR CUP 1973-74

First Round

Bishop's Stortford v Hayes	2-0
Boreham Wood v Hitchin Town	1-1,2-4
Hampton v Leytonstone	2-4
Dagenham v Walton & Hersham	1-3
Blyth Spartans v Sutton Coldfield Town	3-0
Fareham Town v Cheshunt	1-1,1-1,2-0
Ormskirk v Evenwood Town	1-2
Wycombe Wanderers v Hornchurch	5-0
Oxford City v Slough Town	1-1,0-1
Marine v Ashington	1-2
North Shields v Alvechurch	2-0
Bishop Auckland v Shildon	0-3
Aveley v Alton Town	5-0
Croydon v Leyton	0-1
Horsham v Clacton Town	2-1
Walthamstow Avenue v Woking	1-2

Southall v Carshalton Athletic	2-2,2-1
Spennymoor United v Emley	4-0
Faversham Town v Barking	1-6
Sutton United v Tooting & Mitcham United	3-1
Cadbury Heath School v Tilbury	1-3
Hendon v Harwich & Parkeston	0-0,1-1,2-2,2-0
Middlewich Athletic v Oldbury United	4-0
Leatherhead v Enfield	4-0
Leeds & Carnegie College v Prestwich Heys	4-0
Dulwich Hamlet v Newquay	3-0
Loughborough College v Friar Lane OB	2-2,0-1
Chesham United v Maidenhead United	3-2
Tow Law Town v Highgate United	1-2
Hertford Town v Finchley	2-0
St Albans City v Brockenhurst	1-1,0-2
Kingstonian v Ilford	0-0,1-2

The last Amateur Cup winners were Bishop's Stortford. Skipper Lawrence holds the cup in triumph as Manager Ted Hardy is about to be hoisted in celebration and centre half John Still with the plinth is surrounded by happy faces.

Second Round

Bishop's Stortford v Hitchin Town	2-1
Leytonstone v Walton & Hersham	0-1
Blyth Spartans v Fareham Town	2-0
Evenwood Town v Wycombe Wanderers	0-3
Slough Town v Ashington	1-1,0-1
North Shields v Shildon	2-0
Aveley v Leyton	0-0,1-0
Horsham v Woking	2-2,2-3
Southall v Spennymoor United	1-1,1-4
Barking v Sutton United	1-3
Tilbury v Hendon	0-0,0-2
Middlewich Athletic v Leatherhead	0-9
Leeds & Carnegie College v Dulwich Hamlet	0-2
Friar Lane Old Boys v Chesham United	4-1
Highgate United v Hertford Town	1-0
Ilford v Brockenhurst	3-0

Third Round

Walton & Hersham v Bishop's Stortford	0-0,0-1
Blyth Spartans v Wycombe Wanderers	2-1
Ashington v North Shields	1-1,2-0
Aveley v Woking	1-1,0-2
Spennymoor United v Sutton United	0-2
Hendon v Leatherhead	1-1,1-1,0-2
Dulwich Hamlet v Friar Lane Old Boys	4-1
Ilford v Highgate United	2-1

Fourth Round

Bishop's Stortford v Blyth Spartans	3-1
Ashington v Woking	2-0
Sutton United v Leatherhead	0-1
Ilford v Dulwich Hamlet	1-1,1-0

Semi Finals

Bishop's Stortford v Ashington	0-0,3-0
(At Sunderland, replay at Brentford)	
Ilford v Leatherhead	1-0
At Millwall)	

Final at Wembley

Bishop's Stortford 4 Ilford 1 *(Goals:* Lawrence, Murphy, Leakey, Smith pen/Drabwell)   Attendance 30 500
Bishop's Stortford: Moore, Gibson, Coombes, Lawrence, Still, Payne, Leakey, Dear, Bass, Smith, Murphy.
Ilford: James, Bowhill, Bennett, Betson, Anderson, Day (Guiver), Bookman, Butterfield, Drabwell, McDermid, Turley.

FA CHALLENGE TROPHY

INTRODUCTION

Goalkeeper Terry Moore achieved a great "double" by playing for Bishops Stortford in their successful Amateur Cup and FA Trophy sides at Wembley. Here he is seen celebrating with his captain Dave Blackman after their Trophy success against Sutton United. The only other player to achieve this double is Stan Allen (Skelmersdale United and Altrincham).

The FA Trophy was introduced as a national knock-out competition for the senior semi-professional clubs in the 1969-70 season. It was played alongside the Amateur Cup and in its first year the final attracted 28 000 compared with 45 000 for the amateurs. However, the last Amateur Cup Final was only watched by 30 500 and in 1991 Wycombe Wanderers beat Kidderminster Harriers in front of a record 34 842 for a Trophy Final.

Scarborough's three wins in four visits to Wembley in the seventies gave the North East the privilege of providing the competition's first giants, but they are now in The Football League and Telford United, having reached five finals and won four of them, have the most consistent Trophy record.

The balance of power has swung between the North and South with particularly strong club sides from Altrincham and Enfield making their mark in 1978 and 1988 respectively.

The lowest placed club in the Pyramid to reach Wembley was Leek Town from the H F S Division One in 1990 and of course the most impressive "double" in non-league football was achieved by Wealdstone who won the Gola League (now Conference) and FA Trophy in 1985.

FA TROPHY STATISTICS

Most wins: 3 Scarborough and Telford United
Most Finals: 5 Telford United
Most appearances in Semi-Finals: 6 Altrincham and Telford United
Best attendance: 34 842 Wycombe Wanderers v Kidderminster Harriers, 1991

Lowest attendance: 14 200 Northwich Victoria v Bangor City, 1984
Average attendance: 22 000
Most consecutive appearances in Final: 3 Scarborough, 1975-78
Most individual appearances in Finals: 4 Antone Joseph (Telford United and Kidderminster Harriers).

FINALS AT A GLANCE

Year	Winners	Score	Runners-up	Venue
1970	Macclesfield Town	2-0	Telford United	Wembley
1971	Telford United	3-2	Hillingdon	Wembley
1972	Stafford Rangers	3-0	Barnet	Wembley
1973	Scarborough	2-1	Wigan Athletic	Wembley
1974	Morecambe	2-1	Dartford	Wembley
1975	Matlock Town	4-0	Scarborough	Wembley
1976	Scarborough	3-2	Stafford Rangers	Wembley
1977	Scarborough	2-1	Dagenham	Wembley
1978	Altrincham	3-1	Leatherhead	Wembley
1979	Stafford Rangers	2-0	Kettering Town	Wembley
1980	Dagenham	2-1	Mossley	Wembley
1981	Bishop's Stortford	1-0	Sutton United	Wembley
1982	Enfield	1-0	Altrincham	Wembley
1983	Telford United	2-1	Northwich Victoria	Wembley
1984	Northwich Victoria	2-1	Bangor	Stoke City
(After 1-1 draw at Wembley)				
1985	Wealdstone	2-1	Boston United	Wembley
1986	Altrincham	1-0	Runcorn	Wembley
1987	Kidderminster Harriers	2-1	Burton Albion	West Bromwich Albion
(After 0-0 draw at Wembley)				
1988	Enfield	3-2	Telford United	West Bromwich Albion
(After 0-0 draw at Wembley)				
1989	Telford United	1-0	Macclesfield Town	Wembley
1990	Barrow	3-0	Leek Town	Wembley
1991	Wycombe Wanderers	2-1	Kidderminster Harriers	Wembley

The most consistent Trophy club – Telford United celebrate their 1983 victory over Northwich Victoria. This was Antone Joseph's first Trophy Final (he came on as substitute) but he has now played in a record four Finals.

THE FIRST TROPHY

FA TROPHY 1969-70

First Round Qualifying

Wombwell Sporting v Boldon CW	3-2
Scarborough v Mexborough Town	3-1
Denaby United v Annfield Plain	6-3
Worksop Town v Frickley CW	3-1
Ashby Institute v Hull Brunswick	0-1
Selby Town v Bridlington Trinity	1-2
Skegness Town v Barton Town	2-0
Retford Town v Horden CW	1-2
Stockton v Louth United	3-2
*Prestatyn v Congleton Town	3-3,3-2
Gresley Rovers v Ilkeston Town	0-1
Oswestry Town v Netherfield	2-0
*Portmadoc v Droylesden	1-1,2-1
*Winsford United v Heanor Town	3-3,2-0
Belper Town v Sutton Town	0-3
Rossendale United v Horwich RMI	2-1
Ashton United v Prescot Town	5-1
*Alfreton Town v Chorley	0-0,0-1
Ellesmere Port Town v Bacup Borough	3-0
Sandbach Ramblers v Loughborough United	2-0
Nantwich v Holyhead Town	3-1
Arnold v Leyland Motors	2-0
Clitheroe v Rhyl	1-3
Sittingbourne v Bedford Town	0-4
Stamford v Cambridge City	1-2
Chatham Town v Newmarket Town	0-4
Hastings United v Wellingborough Town	2-0
Soham Town Rangers v Basingstoke Town	1-2
St Neots Town v Clacton Town	2-1
Wisbech Town v Corby Town	0-2
March Town U v Gravesend & Northfleet	0-4
Biggleswade Town v Ramsgate Athletic	0-1
*Boston v Ely City	2-2,2-1
Bexley United v Fleet	2-1
*Potton United v Banbury United	1-1,0-4
*Stevenage Athletic v Folkestone	1-1,0-2
*Dunstable Town v Rushden Town	1-1,0-3
Guildford City v Ashford Town	2-0
Deal Town v Haverhill Rovers	0-3
*Crawley Town v Lowestoft Town	2-2,3-1
*Holbeach U v Hinckley Athletic	0-0,0-0,2-2,3-1
*Tonbridge v Sheppey United	2-2,1-4
Spalding United v Desborough Town	3-1
*Bedworth v Weston-super-Mare	0-0,2-0
Ton Pentre v Lye Town	4-1
*Darlaston v Merthyr Tydfil	1-1,3-4
Salisbury v Lower Gornal Athletic	4-2
Brierley Hill Alliance v Dorchester Town	2-1
*Rugby Town† v Thorneycroft Athletic	2-2,5-4
Barnstaple Town v Wadebridge Town	1-2
Trowbridge Town v Cowes (IOW)	5-0
Abergavenny Thursday v Bath City	2-3

* Home team in first match.

† Rugby Town expelled from competition for playing an ineligible player.

*Portland United v Redditch	1-1,1-4
Stonehouse v Barry Town	3-1
Dudley Town v Stourbridge	1-2
Gloucester City v Chippenham Town	4-0
*Cinderford Town v Lockheed Leamington	0-0, 0-2
Welton Rovers v Pembroke Borough	5-3
Cheltenham Town v St Blazey	8-0
Minehead v Bridport	3-2
Street v Bilston	1-4

Second Round Qualifying

*Wombwell Sporting v Bridlington Trinity	1-1,0-4
Horden Colliery Welfare v Worksop Town	1-2
Denaby United v Hull Brunswick	4-0
Stockton v Scarborough	0-3
*Ilkeston Town v Prestatyn	2-2,1-1,3-1
*Ellesmere Port Town v Portmadoc	3-3,3-3
Sandbach Ramblers v Rossendale United	2-0
Sutton Town v Chorley	2-0
Nantwich v Ashton United	1-2
Arnold v Oswestry Town	3-2
Winsford United v Rhyl	5-0
Corby Town v Holbeach United	5-0
*Ramsgate Athletic v Crawley Town	0-0,3-1
*Canterbury City v Hastings United	1-1,1-2
Sheppey United v Haverhill Rovers	5-2
Skegness Town v Bexley United	1-2
*Thorneycroft Athletic v St Neots Town	1-1,2-0
Folkestone v Rushden Town	0-1
*Bletchley v Basingstoke Town	2-2,0-2
Banbury United v Bedford Town	0-1
Boston v Guildford City	0-3
Newmarket Town v Gravesend & Northfleet	1-2
Cambridge City v Spalding United	6-0
Wadebridge Town v Brierley Hill Alliance	0-1
*Trowbridge Town v Gloucester City	0-0,2-3
*Merthyr Tydfil v Minehead	0-0,0-4
Lockheed Leamington v Salisbury	0-4
*Stourbridge v Welton Rovers	1-1,4-1
Stonehouse v Bilston	2-1
Cheltenham Town v Ton Pentre	3-1
Bath City v Bedworth United	3-1
Redditch v Bridgend Town	0-1

Third Round Qualifying

*Worksop v Scarborough	0-0,1-2
Gateshead v Denaby United	0-1
Matlock Town v Darwen	5-1
Bridlington Trinity v Fleetwood	2-1
Stourbridge v Halesowen	3-2
*Bridgend Town v Minehead	1-1,0-4
*Brierley Hill Alliance v Stonehouse	1-1,1-3
Hereford United v Andover	2-0
Frome Town v Bath City	0-3
Gloucester City v Cheltenham Town	0-1
*Salisbury v Poole Town	1-1,0-1
Atherstone Town v Winsford United	0-1

Sandbach Ramblers v Ilkeston Town	0-2
Arnold v Ashton United	3-2
*Runcorn v Northwich Victoria	0-0,0-3
South Liverpool v Sutton Town	3-0
*Altrincham v Buxton	1-1,2-3
Nuneaton Borough v Ellesmere Port Town	7-0
Telford United v Witton Albion	5-0
*Burton Albion v St Helens Town	1-1,2-0
Dover v Sheppey United	1-0
Grantham v Bury Town	2-1
Corby Town v Basingstoke Town	2-1
Kettering Town v Boston United	2-1
Rushden Town v Barnet	0-5
Bexley United v Hastings United	1-2
Bourne Town v Chelmsford City	2-5
Bedford Town v Ramsgate Athletic	5-1
Brentwood Town v Cambridge City	3-1
*Great Yarmouth Town v Dartford	1-1,0-3
Thorneycroft Athletic v Margate	2-0
Gravesend & Northfleet v Guildford City	2-0

First Round

Arnold v Wigan Athletic	2-5
Nuneaton Borough v Stonehouse	3-0
South Shields v Matlock Town	2-3
Burton Albion v New Brighton	5-0
*Buxton v Lancaster City	1-1,3-2
Hednesford v Kidderminster Harriers	1-4
Macclesfield Town v Burscough	1-0
*Denaby United v Great Harwood	2-2,2-3
*Scarborough v Tamworth	1-1,3-0
Ilkeston Town v Telford United	0-2
Bangor City v Morecambe	4-2
Gainsborough Trinity v Hyde United	3-1
Stourbridge v Northwich Victoria	5-1
*Winsford United v Kirkby Town	2-2,0-1
Stafford Rangers v South Liverpool	5-2
Stalybridge Celtic v Bromsgrove Rovers	2-3
Mossley v Goole Town	4-0
*Bridlington Trinity v Worcester City	0-0,0-3
Gravesend & Northfleet v Hastings United	1-0
*Brentwood Town v Hereford United	1-1,1-2
Bridgwater Town v Taunton Town	2-1
Weymouth v Thorneycroft Athletic	5-0
Corby Town v Yeovil Town	4-3
Cambridge United v Minehead	2-1
Bedford Town v Chelmsford City	3-4
Bath City v Barnet	3-4
*Poole Town v Kettering Town	1-1,0-4
King's Lynn v Grantham	0-2
Hillingdon Borough v Dover	1-0
Dartford v Wimbledon	3-2
Glastonbury v Bideford	1-2
Romford v Cheltenham Town	3-0

Second Round

Telford United v Wigan Athletic	1-0
Bangor City v Kidderminster Harriers	2-0
*Mossley v Scarborough	1-1,3-2
Burton Albion v Stafford Rangers	4-0
Buxton v Matlock Town	1-2
Worcester City v Kirkby Town	3-2
Great Harwood v Grantham	1-3

Macclesfield Town v Gainsborough Trinity	2-0
Chelmsford City v Nuneaton Borough	3-2
Corby Town v Hillingdon Borough	1-2
Barnet v Hereford United	2-0
Weymouth v Bideford	3-0
Gravesend & Northfleet v Romford	2-3
*Stourbridge v Kettering Town	1-1,1-2
Bridgwater Town v Dartford	2-1
Bromsgrove Rovers v Cambridge United	2-1

Third Round

Burton Albion v Bridgwater Town	2-1
*Bangor City v Macclesfield Town	1-1,0-1
*Matlock Town v Mossley	2-2,3-3,1-2
*Grantham v Worcester City	1-1,1-3
*Hillingdon Borough v Weymouth	0-0,1-0
Barnet v Bromsgrove Rovers	2-1
Kettering Town v Chelmsford City	0-3
*Romford v Telford United	1-1,1-2

Quarter Finals

Barnet (2) 8	v Mossley (0) 1	
George 2, Eason 3,	Roberts	
Powell 2, Meadows		
	(*Attendance:* 2989)	

Burton Albion (0) 1	v Macclesfield (0) 1	
Ainger	Fidler	
	(*Attendance:* 4904)	

Hillingdon B (0) 0	v Chelmsford (0) 0	
	(*Attendance:* 2500)	

Worcester C (0) 1	v Telford U (2) 3	
Gould	Madley (og), Bentley,	
	Cotton	
	(*Attendance:* 6703)	

Replays

Chelmsford (0) 2	v Hillingdon (0) 1	
Price, Moffatt	Smith	
	(*Attendance:* 5800)	

Macclesfield (3) 4	v Burton Albion (0) 2	
Lyon, Fidler, Young,	Bostock, Ainger	
Butlin (og)		
	(*Attendance:* 4600)	

Semi Finals

Barnet (0) 0	v Macclesfield (1) 1	
	Young	
	(*Attendance:* 7855)	

Telford U (0) 2	v Chelmsford (0) 0	
Fudge 2 (1 pen)		
	(*Attendance:* 3793)	

Final   At Wembley, (*Attendance:* 28 000)
Macclesfield Town 2 Telford United 0
Scorers: Lyons, Fidler B.
Macclesfield Town: Cooke; Sievwright, Bennett; Beaumont, Collins, Roberts; Lyons, Fidler B, Young, Corfield, Fidler D.
Telford United: Irvine; Harris, Croft; Flowers, Cotor, Ray; Fudge, Hart, Bentley, Murray, Jagger.

FINALS IN DETAIL 1971-1980

1971 (*Attendance:* 29 500)
Telford United 3 (Owen, Bentley, Fudge) **Hillingdon 2** (Reeve, Bishop)   Referee: D Smith
Telford United: Irvine, Harris, Croft, Ray, Coton, Carr, Fudge, Owen, Bentley, Jagger, Murray.
Hillingdon: Lowe, Batt, Langley, Higginson, Newcombe, Moore, Fairchild, Bishop, Reeve, Carter, Knox.

1972 (*Attendance:* 24 000)
Stafford Rangers 3 (Williams 2, Cullerton) **Barnet 0**   Referee: P Partridge
Stafford Rangers: Aleksic, Chadwick, Clayton, Sargeant, Aston, Machin, Cullerton, Chapman, Williams, Bayley, Jones.
Barnet: McClelland, Lye, Jenkins, Ward, Embrey, King, Powell, Rerry, Flatt, Easton, Plume.

1973 (*Attendance:* 23 000)
Scarborough 2 (Leask, Thompson) **Wigan Athletic 1** (Rogers) aet   Referee: H Hackney
Scarborough: Garrow, Appleton, Shoulder, Dunn, Siddle, Fagan, Donoghue, Franks, Leask (Barmby), Thompson, Hewitt.
Wigan Athletic: Reeves, Morris, Sutherland, Taylor, Jackson, Gillibrand, Clements, Oats (McCunnell), Rogers, King, Worswick.

1974 (*Attendance:* 19 000)
Morecambe 2 (Richmond, Sutton) **Dartford 1** (Cunningham)   Referee: B Homewood
Morecambe: Coates, Pearson, Bennett, Sutton, Street, Baldwin, Done, Webber, Roberts (Galley), Kershaw, Richmond.
Dartford: Morton, Read, Payne, Carr, Burns, Binks, Light, Glazier, Robinson (Hearne), Cunningham, Halleday.

1975 (*Attendance:* 21 000)
Matlock Town 4 (Oxley, Dawson, Fenoughty T, Fenoughty N) **Scarborough 0**   Referee: K Styles
Matlock Town: Fell, McKay, Smith, Stuart, Dawson, Swan, Oxley, Fenoughty N, Scott, Fenoughty T, Fenoughty M.
Scarborough: Williams, Hewitt, Rettit, Dunn, Marshall, Todd, Houghton, Woodall, Davidson, Barmby, Aveyard.

1976 (*Attendance:* 21 000)
Scarborough 3 (Woodall, Abbey, Marshall pen) **Stafford Rangers 2** (Jones 2) aet   Referee: R Challis
Scarborough: Barnard, Jackson, Marshall, Dunn H, Ayre, Donoghue, Dunn HA, Dale, Barmby, Woodall, Abbey, Hilley.
Stafford Rangers: Arnold, Ritchie, Richards, Sargeant, Seddon, Morris, Chapman, Lowe, Jones, Hutchinson, Chadwick.

1977 (*Attendance:* 20 500)
Scarborough 2 (Dunn pen, Abbey) **Dagenham 1** (Harris)   Referee: G Courtney
Scarborough: Chapman, Smith, Marshall (Barmby), Dunn, Ayres, Deere, Aveyard, Donoghue, Woodall, Abbey, Dunn
Dagenham: Huttley, Wellman, Currie P, Dunwell, Moore, Currie W, Harkins, Saul, Fox, Harris, Holder.

1978 (*Attendance:* 20 000)
Altrincham 3 (King, Johnson, Rogers) **Leatherhead 1** (Cook)   Referee: A Grey
Altrincham: Eales, Allan, Crossley, Bailey, Owens, King, Morris, Heathcote, Johnson, Rogers, Davidson (Flaherty).
Leatherhead: Swannell, Cooper, Eaton, Davies, Reid, Malley, Cook, Salkeld, Kelly, Baker, Boyle (Bailey).

1979 (*Attendance:* 32 000)
Stafford Rangers 2 (Wood A 2) **Kettering Town 0**   Referee: D Richardson
Stafford Rangers: Arnold, Wood F, Willis, Sargeant, Seddon, Ritchie, Secker, Chapman, Wood A, Cullerton, Chadwick (Jones).
Kettering Town: Lane, Ashby, Lee, Eastall, Dixey, Suddards, Flannagan, Kellock, Phipps, Clayton, Evans (Hughes).

1980 (*Attendance:* 26 000)
Dagenham 2 (Duck, Maycock) **Mossley 1** (Smith)   Referee: K Baker
Dagenham: Huttley, Willman, Scales, Dunwell, Moore, Durrell, Maycock, Horan, Duck, Kidd, Jones (Holder).
Mossley: Fitton, Brown, Vaughan, FGorman, Salter, Polliot, Smith, Moore, Skeefe, O'Connor, Keelan (Wilson).

THE LAST TEN

FA CHALLENGE TROPHY 1980-81

First Round

Bishop's Stortford v Bridgend	1-1,2-1
Dagenham v Bath City	4-0
Alvechurch v Penrith	4-2
Kidderminster Harriers v Bedworth U	2-2,0-1
Frome Town v Yeovil	1-1,1-2
Hastings U v Maidstone U	1-1,2-1
Goole Town v Morecambe	2-0
Minehead v Worcester	1-3
Dartford v Slough Town	4-1
Nuneaton B v Ashington	1-2
Burton A v Blyth Spartans	0-2
Runcorn v Stafford Rangers	0-1
Leytonstone & I v Gloucester	7-0
Leatherhead v Weymouth	1-3
Lancaster C v Winsford U	2-2,2-5
Altrincham v Spennymoor	3-2
Marine v Matlock T	2-0
Witton A v Bangor City	0-3
Boston U v Gateshead	4-0
Hitchin T v Tooting & Mitcham	2-1
Stalybridge v Bootle	2-3
Carshalton v Barking	3-0
Gravesend & N v Kettering T	2-3
Mossley v Scarborough	2-2,0-1
Aylesbury v Enfield	2-2,0-0,1-0
Chorley v Netherfield	1-2
Harlow v Bognor Regis	2-0
Northwich Vic v Barrow	3-0
Dorchester v Walthamstow	0-1
Bedford v Dulwich Hamlet	3-1
Cheltenham v Wycombe	0-1
Woking v Sutton Utd	0-1

Second Round

Bishop's Stortford v Dagenham	1-1,3-2
Alvechurch v Bedworth U	4-1
Yeovil Town v Hastings Utd	1-1,1-2
Goole Town v Worcester	1-4
Dartford v Ashington	1-0
Blyth Spartans v Stafford R	1-0
Leytonstone & I v Weymouth	1-1,4-3(aet)
Winsford Utd v Altrincham	0-2
Marine v Bangor City	0-1
Boston U v Hitchin T	0-1
Bootle v Carshalton	0-0,1-2
Kettering T v Mossley	0-1
Aylesbury v Netherfield	2-0
Harlow v Northwich Vic	0-1
Walthamstow v Bedford	0-0,0-1
Sutton U v Wycombe	5-1

Third Round

Bishop's Stortford v Alvechurch	3-2
Hastings U v Worcester	0-0,1-2
Dartford v Blyth Spartans	1-0

One of the great FA Trophy photos taken by Mick Eason. Terry Sullivan scores the winning goal for Bishops Stortford against Sutton United in 1981.

Leytonstone & I v Altrincham	0-1
Bangor City v Hitchin Town	1-0
Carshalton A v Mossley	0-3
Aylesbury v Northwich Vic	0-0,1-1,1-0
Sutton U v Bedford T	2-0

Fourth Round

Bishop's Stortford v Worcester C	4-0
Dartford v Altrincham	3-1
Bangor City v Mossley	5-3
Sutton U v Aylesbury U	0-0,1-0

Semi-finals (2 legs)

Dartford v Bishop's Stortford	1-1
Bishop's Stortford v Dartford	2-1
Bangor City v Sutton United	2-2
Sutton United v Bangor City	4-1

Final At Wembley, *(Attendance:* 22 578)
Bishop's Stortford 1 (Sullivan) **Sutton United 0**
Referee: J Worrell
Bishop's Stortford: Moore, Blackman, Brame, Smith (Worrell), Bradford, Abery, Sullivan, Knapman, Radford, Simmonds, Mitchell.
Sutton United: Collyer, Rogers, Green, Rains J, Rains T, Stephens (Sunnucks), Waldon, Pritchard, Cornwell, Parsons, Dennis.

FA TROPHY

FA CHALLENGE TROPHY 1981-82

First Round

Altrincham v Nuneaton	1-0
Cheltenham v Epsom & Ewell	2-3
Kettering T v Mossley	0-1
Woking v Barking	2-1
Witton Albion v Horden CW	1-1,2-2,2-1
Hendon v Taunton	5-1
Yeovil v Bishop's Stortford	2-3
Maidstone U v Hastings U	1-1,2-0
Wycombe v Walthamstow	1-1,1-1,5-1
Boston U v Hyde U	0-1
Stalybridge C v Chorley	0-1
Frickley Ath v Bishop Auckland	0-1
Dagenham v Hitchin T	1-0
Wealdstone v Gloucester C	3-1
Kidderminster Harriers v Barrow	0-0,2-2,2-1
Ashington v Blyth Spartans	1-2
Dartford v Leatherhead	2-1
Northwich Vic v Bangor C	3-2
Runcorn v Stafford R	2-0
Lancaster C v Spennymoor U	2-0
Alvechurch v Croydon	1-3
Minehead v Worcester C	1-1,2-5
Tooting & Mitcham v Harlow T	0-0,1-2
Aylesbury U v Sutton U	2-4
Dulwich Hamlet v St Albans C	1-1,3-4
Marine v Scarborough	0-1
Buxton v Rossendale U	1-2
Slough T v Bath C	4-2
Bedford T v Staines T	1-1,2-3
Telford U v Burton A	1-0
Merthyr Tydfil v Dorchester T	2-1
Weymouth v Enfield	0-1

Second Round

Epsom & Ewell v Altrincham	0-1
Woking v Mossley	0-0,0-5
Witton Albion v Hendon	1-0
Bishop's Stortford v Maidstone U	3-0
Hyde U v Wycombe	0-0,2-3
Chorley v Bishop Auckland	0-1
Wealdstone v Dagenham	0-1
Kidderminster Harriers v Blyth Spartans	2-1
Dartford v Northwich Vic	0-2
Runcorn v Lancaster City	4-0
Croydon v Worcester C	1-4
Harlow T v Sutton U	0-1
St Albans C v Scarborough	0-1
Slough T v Rossendale U	1-0
Telford U v Bedford T	0-0,3-0
Merthyr Tydfil v Enfield	0-6

Third Round

Altrincham v Mossley	2-0
Bishop's Stortford v Witton Albion	6-1
Wycombe W v Bishop Auckland	4-1
Kidderminster H v Dagenham	4-3
Northwich V c Runcorn	3-0
Sutton U v Worcester C	1-1,2-5
Scarborough v Slough T	1-1,2-1
Telford U v Enfield	0-1

Fourth Round

Altrincham v Bishop's Stortford	2-2,3-1
Kidderminster H v Wycombe W	0-1
Northwich V v Worcester C	2-1
Enfield v Scarborough	4-2

Semi Finals (2 legs)

Altrincham v Wycombe Wanderers	1-1
Wycombe Wanderers v Altrincham	0-3
Northwich Victoria v Enfield	0-0
Enfield v Northwich Victoria	1-0

Final At Wembley, *(Attendance:* 18 678)
Enfield 1 (Taylor) **Altrincham 0**
Referee: B Stevens
Enfield: Jacobs, Barrett, Tone, Jennings, Waite, Ironton, Ashford, Taylor, Holmes, Oliver (Flint), King.
Altrincham: Connaughton, Crossley, Davison, Bailey, Cuddy, King (Whitbread), Allan, Heathcote, Johnson, Rogers, Howard.

FA CHALLENGE TROPHY 1982-83

First Round

Kidderminster H v Northwich Vic	0-3
Hastings U v Croydon	0-2
Bangor C v Kings Lynn	1-1,2-0
Mossley v Goole Town	1-1,2-0
Whitby T v Blyth Spartans	2-3
Bishop Auckland v Nuneaton B	1-3
Matlock v Tow Law Town	0-1
Corby T v Altrincham	1-1,0-6
Bath C v Worcester C	1-2
Slough T v Dagenham	0-1
Weston-super-Mare v Weymouth	0-0,0-1
Hayes v Leyton/Ilford	0-1
Wycombe v Wealdstone	2-1
Boston U v Marine	3-0
Maidstone U v Aylesbury U	1-0
Dulwich Hamlet v Kettering T	4-2
Ashington v Burscough	1-0
Barrow v Rhyl	2-1
Harrow B v Bromley	2-0
Yeovil T v Sutton U	2-4
Woking v Barnet	0-2
Stafford R v Ilkeston T	2-2,2-3
Dorchester T v Gloucester C	3-2
Enfield v Bishop's Stortford	2-1
Colwyn Bay v Chorley	1-5
Lewes v Dartford	0-2
Waterlooville v Charlton A	0-2
Tilbury v Cheltenham T	2-1
Penrith v Stalybridge C	1-2
Runcorn v Scarborough	0-1
Spennymoor U v Bilston	2-1
Burton A v Telford U	0-1

Second Round

Northwich Vic v Croydon	1-0
Bangor C v Mossley	1-0
Blyth Spartans v Nuneaton B	3-2
Tow Law Town v Altrincham	2-2,0-3
Worcester C v Dagenham	0-3
Weymouth v Leyton/Ilford	1-0
Wycombe v Boston U	0-0,1-1,0-2

78

Maidstone U v Dulwich Hamlet	2-2,3-0
Ashington v Barrow	1-1,0-1
Harrow B v Sutton U	4-1
Barnet v Ilkeston T	1-2
Dorchester T v Enfield	2-3
Chorley v Dartford	0-0,0-3
Carshalton A v Tilbury	2-3
Stalybridge C v Scarborough	1-3
Spennymoor v Telford U	0-0,1-2

Third Round

Northwich Vic v Bangor C	1-1,2-2,1-0
(second replay at Wrexham)	
Blyth Spartans v Altrincham	2-0
Dagenham v Weymouth	3-0
Boston U v Maidstone	2-1
Barrow v Harrow B	1-1,1-1,0-2
(second replay at Stafford)	
Ilkeston T v Enfield	1-5
(match abandoned, tie awarded to Enfield)	
Dartford v Tilbury	2-0
Scarborough v Telford U	0-3

Fourth Round

Northwich Vic v Blyth Spartans	1-1,3-2
Dagenham v Boston U	2-1
Harrow B v Enfield	5-1
Telford U v Dartmouth	4-1

Semi-finals (2 legs)

Northwich Vic v Dagenham	3-2
Dagenham v Northwich Vic	0-1
Telford U v Harrow B	0-2
Harrow B v Telford U	(aet) 1-5

Final At Wembley, *(Attendance: 22 071)*
Telford 2 (Mather 2) **Northwich Victoria 1** (Bennett)
Referee: B Hill
Telford United: Charlton, Lewis, Turner, Mayman (Joseph), Walker, Easton, Barnett, Williams, Mather, Hogan, Alcock.
Northwich Victoria: Ryan, Fretwell, Murphy, Jones, Forshaw, Ward, Anderson, Abel (Bennett), Reid, Chesters, Wilson.

FA CHALLENGE TROPHY 1983-84

First Round

Bangor City v Spennymoor U	3-1
Croydon v Bath City	0-0,0-6
Carshalton A v Harrow B	2-2,2-0
Gateshead v Horden CW	1-1,3-1(aet)
Witton A v AP Leamington	3-4
Welling U v Hastings U	2-1
Sutton U v Chelmsford U	0-3
Weymouth v Hendon	2-3
Hampton v Maidstone U	0-2
Worcester C v Nuneaton B	0-0,0-2
Dagenham v Fareham T	0-0,3-2
Yeovil T v Wealdstone	4-3
Leytonstone/Ilford v Trowbridge T	0-0,1-0
Whitby T v Blyth Spartans	1-1,2-1
Sutton T v Frickley Ath	1-4
Arnold v Barrow	0-1
Mossley v Telford U	1-2
Runcorn v Matlock T	2-1
Bromsgrove R v S Liverpool	2-1

Wycombe W v Dorchester T	4-0
Windsor & Eton v Bishop's Stortford	2-1
Gloucester C v Fisher A	3-3,1-2
Bishop Auckland v Grantham	1-1,0-1
Marine v Scarborough	2-1
Barnet v Dartford	3-0
Durham C v N Shields	1-3
Merthyr Tydfil v Enfield	2-0
Altrincham v Kidderminster H	0-2
Slough T v Dulwich Hamlet	3-4
Chorley v Rhyl	2-1
Barking v Aylesbury	0-1
Boston U v Northwich Vic	1-1,1-5

Second Round

Bangor City v Bath City	1-0
Carshalton Ath v Gateshead	1-2
AP Leamington v Welling U	4-1
Chelmsford C v Hendon	2-1
Maidstone U v Nuneaton B	2-2,0-1
Dagenham v Yeovil T	1-1,4-1
Leytonstone/Ilford v Whitby T	0-1
Frickley Ath v Barrow	5-2
Telford U v Runcorn	2-1
Bromsgrove R v Wycombe W	2-0
Windsor & Eton v Fisher Ath	1-1,0-4
Grantham v Marine	0-3
Barnet v North Shields	4-1
Merthyr Tydfil v Kidderminster H	0-1
Dulwich Hamlet v Chorley	1-1,2-2,2-0
Aylesbury U v Northwich Vic	0-1

Third Round

Gateshead v Bangor C	2-2,0-2
AP Leamington v Chelmsford	4-0
Nuneaton B v Dagenham	2-2,0-1
Whitby T v Frickley Ath	2-0
Telford U v Bromsgrove R	2-0
Fisher Ath v Marine	0-1
Barnet v Kidderminster H	2-1
Dulwich Hamlet v Northwich Vic	0-0,0-0,0-1

Fourth Round

AP Leamington v Bangor C	1-6
Dagenham v Whitby T	2-2,3-0
Telford U v Marine	3-3,0-2
Northwich Vic v Barnet	1-0

Semi-final (2 legs)

Bangor C v Dagenham	1-0
Dagenham v Bangor C	2-2
Northwich Vic v Marine	1-1
Marine v Northwich Vic	0-2

Final At Wembley *(Attendance: 14 200)*
Northwich Victoria 1 (Chesters) **Bangor City 1** (Whelan)
Replay (At Stoke, *(Attendance: 5805)*
Northwich Victoria 2 (Chesters pen, Anderson)
Bangor City 1 (Lunn)
Referee: John Martin
Northwich Victoria: Ryan, Fretwell, Dean, Jones, Forshaw (Power 65 mins), Bennett, Anderson, Abel, Reid, Chesters, Wilson.
Bangor City: Letheren, Cavanagh, Gray, Whelan, Banks, Lunn, Urquart, Morris, Carter), Howat, Sutcliffe (Westwood 105 mins).
(Teams the same for both games).

Wealdstone's Double

To win your Championship Title and the best Cup competition open to you is a tremendous feat in whatever standard of football you play. Wealdstone won the Gola League and FA Trophy "Double" in the 1984-85 season and it was an achievement that rewarded a great deal of planning and hard work. Brian Hall is a meticulous manager who has set ideas about the style of play that his teams should use and the type of players he wants in his sides. This Wealdstone side was the culmination of much team building and with his coach, Les Reed, he drilled his squad so well that they knew their responsibilities for every situation they could expect to face. Apart from their disciplined tactics they also possessed players with flair. Robin Wainwright was a wonderful passer of the ball and in the Cordice brothers the team possessed blistering pace and skill. The driving force came from Paul Bowgett and Dennis Byatt but when you look at the excellent photo in the colour section of this book, the names will remind you what strength in depth Brian Hall had collected. Just look at those trophies and you realise what a great season Wealdstone enjoyed – it's a memory that nobody can take away from them and a feat that very few will equal.

FA CHALLENGE TROPHY 1984-85

Preliminary Round

Netherfield v Bridlington Trinity	1-1,2-1
Radcliffe Borough v Accrington Stanley	3-1
Caernarfon Town v Prescot Cables	3-1
Congleton Town v Ashton United	2-1
Colwyn Bay v St Helens Town	2-1
Glossop v Belper Town	3-0
Banbury United v Cambridge City	2-3
Wellingborough Town v Redditch United	1-3
Highgate United v Milton Keynes City	1-1,2-1
Dunstable v Lewes	2-3
Tonbridge AFC v Hornchurch	2-3
Chatham Town v Hounslow	5-1
Metropolitan Police v Dover Athletic	4-2
Llanelli v Bideford	0-2
Clandown v Maesteg Park	2-1

First Round Qualifying

Lancaster City v Goole Town	1-3
Leyland Motors v Tow Law Town	2-4
Workington v Crook Town	3-0
Burscough v Peterlee Newton	0-1
Ferryhill Athletic v Worksop Town	2-2, 1-4
Shildon v Morecambe	3-5
Consett v Durham City	1-0
Netherfield v Gretna	0-4
Billingham Synthonia v Penrith	0-2
Whitley Bay v Ashington	3-0
Mexborough Town Athletic v Southport	1-4
Evenwood Town v South Bank	1-4
Macclesfield Town v Leek Town	3-0
Hyde United v Oswestry Town	1-0
Caernarfon Town v Bootle	2-4
Winsford United v Radcliffe Borough	1-2
Curzon Ashton v Glossop	2-0
Stalybridge Celtic v Formby	3-1
Colwyn Bay v Stafford Rangers	0-1
Buxton v Horwich RMI	0-0,2-2,4-2
Willenhall Town v Congleton Town	1-1,1-2
Hednesford Town v Highgate United	3-1
Heanor Town v Shepshed Charterhouse	0-1
Bedworth United v Leicester United	0-1
Sutton Coldfield Town v Redditch United	1-2
Ilkeston Town v Dudley Town	2-2,1-5
Stourbridge v Sutton Town	2-1
Tamworth v Lye Town	1-0
Alfreton Town v Gainsborough Trinity	2-2,3-3,0-4

Oldbury United v Arnold	3-1
Moor Green v Alvechurch	0-1
Eastwood Town v Corby Town	3-3,0-2
Hitchin Town v Hampton	1-4
Hillingdon v Tilbury	2-2,2-1
Boreham Wood v Maidenhead United	3-1
Wembley v Hornchurch	0-1
King's Lynn v Clapton	4-2
Walthamstow Avenue v Witney Town	1-2
Cambridge City v Oxford City (at Cambridge Utd)	2-1
Aveley v Hertford Town	0-0,2-0
Spalding United v Billericay Town	1-2
St Albans City v Basildon United	2-1
Harlow Town v Chesham United	2-1
Andover v Epsom & Ewell	0-0,1-2
Folkestone v Thanet United	6-2
Canterbury City v Waterlooville	1-0
Bromley v Fareham Town	1-0
Wokingham Town v Sheppey United	2-0
Kingstonian v Staines Town	1-2
Farnborough Town v Sittingbourne	1-1,2-2,0-2
Addlestone & Weybridge Town v Crawley Town	2-1
Basingstoke Town v Leatherhead	3-1
Bognor Regis Town v Ashford Town	5-0
Chatham Town v Tooting & Mitcham United	0-2
Woking v Lewes	1-1,3-1
Walton & Hersham v Metropolitan Police	1-5
Forest Green Rovers v Poole Town	2-2,4-0
Shepton Mallet Town v Frome Town	1-3
Melksham Town v Clandown	2-1
Taunton Town v RS Southampton	2-0
Bideford v Bridgend Town	3-1
Barnstaple Town v Minehead	1-3
Weston-super-Mare v Salisbury	1-1,0-3
Bye: Cheltenham Town	

Second Round Qualifying

Consett v Tow Law Town	2-1
Morecambe v Goole Town	1-0
Worksop Town v Southport	6-1
Gretna v Whitley Bay	3-0
Bootle v Curzon Ashton	2-0
Stalybridge Celtic v Penrith	3-1
Peterlee Newton v South Bank	0-2
Radcliffe Borough v Workington	0-0,1-0
Buxton v Alfreton Town	0-0,3-1 aet

(Match awarded to Alfreton Town as Buxton played an ineligible player)

Hyde United v King's Lynn	1-2
Hednesford Town v Tamworth	1-2
Cambridge City v Stourbridge (at Soham Town)	2-5
Oldbury United v Shepshed Charterhouse	3-1
Macclesfield Town v Congleton Town	2-1
Leicester United v Dudley Town	1-2
Stafford Rangers v Corby Town	1-1,1-0
Alvechurch v Redditch United	3-2
Boreham Wood v Folkestone	0-2
Hillingdon v St Albans City	1-1,2-1
Hampton v Hornchurch	2-1
Wokingham Town v Addlestone & Weybridge T	5-0
Metropolitan Police v Basingstoke Town	1-3
Aveley v Bognor Regis Town	1-0
Bromley v Farnborough Town	1-1,1-0
Staines Town v Witney Town	4-1
Tooting & Mitcham United v Billericay Town	2-2,1-4
Epsom & Ewell v Woking	1-2
Harlow Town v Canterbury City	5-1
Melksham Town v Forest Green Rovers	0-1
Salisbury v Taunton Town	7-0
Frome Town v Minehead	1-0
Bideford v Cheltenham Town	1-3

Third Round Qualifying

Bishop Auckland v Mossley	3-1
South Liverpool v Bootle	1-1,0-0,0-0,2-1
Stalybridge Celtic v Consett	7-1
Morecambe v South Bank	2-0
Gretna v Spennymoor United	2-0
Horden CW v Radcliffe Borough	1-0
Tamworth v Grantham	1-2
Oldbury United v Stafford Rangers	0-2
Macclesfield Town v Kettering Town	0-2
King's Lynn v Rhyl	1-0
Witton Albion v Bromsgrove Rovers	1-1,2-3
Alvechurch v Boston United	1-2
Worksop Town v Dudley Town	1-2
Burton Albion v Alfreton Town	3-2
Harlow Town v Hendon	1-0
Basingstoke Town v Croydon	0-2
Slough Town v Aylesbury United	2-1
Barking v Gravesend & Northfleet	2-1
Aveley v Woking	2-2,1-2
Staines Town v Hampton	2-1
Chelmsford City v Wokingham Town	1-5
Billericay Town v Bishop's Stortford	1-2
Bromley v Stourbridge	1-1,0-2
Hayes v Sutton United	3-3,1-2
Welling United v Hillingdon	1-1,3-1
Windsor & Eton v Hastings United	3-0
Folkestone v Carshalton Athletic	1-2
Gloucester City v Yeovil Town	2-0
Weymouth v Forest Green Rovers	6-1
Dorchester Town v Cheltenham Town	1-5
Trowbridge Town v Merthyr Tydfil	1-2
Frome Town v Salisbury	7-1

First Round Proper

Dudley Town v AP Leamington	4-0
Morecambe v Altrincham	0-2
Scarborough v Chorley	1-0
Horden CW v Matlock Town	0-0,0-3
Bishop Auckland v North Shields	3-2
Bromsgrove Rovers v Whitby Town	7-1
Gateshead v Stalybridge Celtic	2-1
Frickley Athletic v Barrow	5-1
King's Lynn v Marine	1-2
Burton Albion v Kettering Town	2-1
Boston United v Blyth Spartans	5-4

Gretna v Kidderminster Harriers	3-2
Grantham v Runcorn	0-0,2-3
Northwich Victoria v Telford United	0-4
Stafford Rangers v Nuneaton Borough	2-0
Bootle v Bangor City	1-1,1-2
Wycombe Wanderers v Dartford	6-1
Worthing v Worcester City	3-2
Dulwich Hamlet v Woking	0-0,3-3,2-1
Enfield v Stourbridge	5-1
Frome Town v Windsor & Eton	2-0
Bath City v Bishop's Stortford	0-0,2-2,2,1
Slough Town v Harrow Borough	1-1,0-2
Barking v Staines Town	3-3
Dagenham v Barnet	3-3,2,3
Merthyr Tydfil v Croydon	3-3,5-3 aet
Weymouth v Cheltenham Town	2-3
Harlow Town v Wealdstone	0-0,0-5
Leytonstone/Ilford v Fisher Athletic	0-4
Welling United v Sutton United	2-0
Carshalton Athletic v Wokingham Town	1-2
Gloucester City v Maidstone United	0-2

Second Round Proper

Bromsgrove Rovers v Matlock Town	0-0,3-2 aet
Dulwich Hamlet v Wokingham Town	0-1
Marine v Enfield	0-3
Maidstone United v Worthing	0-0,2-0
Runcorn v Scarborough	1-0
Barnet v Gretna	1-0
Bath City v Cheltenham Town	2-1
Boston United v Frome Town	4-0
Harrow Borough v Staines Town	4-1
Telford United v Fisher Athletic	1-2
Wealdstone v Wycombe Wanderers	2-1
Stafford Rangers v Bangor City	1-1,2-0
Welling United v Merthyr Tydfil	0-0,2-0
Burton Albion v Altrincham	1-2
Bishop Auckland v Dudley Town	4-0
Frickley Athletic v Gateshead	4-1

Third Round Proper

Runcorn v Barnet	0-0,1-1,0-0,0-4
Fisher Athletic v Frickley Athletic	0-3
Boston United v Wokingham Town	1-0
Stafford Rangers v Bromsgrove Rovers	3-1
Harrow Borough v Enfield	1-6
Maidstone United v Bath City	1-1,1-0
Wealdstone v Welling United	3-1
Altrincham v Bishop Auckland	2-1

Fourth Round Proper

Boston United v Runcorn	3-0
Maidston United v Enfield	0-1
Altrincham v Stafford Rangers	4-1
Wealdstone v Frickley Athletic	3-1

Semi Final — First Leg

Enfield v Wealdstone	0-2
Altrincham v Boston United	0-0

Semi Final — Second Leg

Wealdstone v Enfield	0-1
Wealdstone won 2-1 on aggregate	
Boston United v Altrincham	3-2
Boston United won 3-2 on aggregate	

Final at Wembley Stadium (*Attendance:* 20 775)
Wealdstone 2 (Graham, Holmes) **Boston United 1** (Cook)
Referee: J Bray
Wealdstone: Iles, Perkins, Bowgett, Byatt, Davies, Greenaway, Holmes, Wainwright, Donnellan, Graham (Cordice N), Cordice A.
Boston United: Blackwell, Casey, Ladd, Creane, O'Brien, Thomson, Laverick (Mallender), Simpson, Gilbert, Lee, Cook.

FA CHALLENGE TROPHY 1985-86

First Round

Ryhope CA v Altrincham	3-1
Bangor City v Willenhall	1-0
Stafford R v Nuneaton B	1-0
Bishop Auckland v Blyth Spartans	2-0
Dagenham v Sheppey U	3-0
Cheltenham T v Fisher Ath	3-0
Bishop's Stortford v Wokingham	2-0
Northwich Vic v Workington	1-0
Wealdstone v Welling Utd	1-0
Bedworth Utd v Frickley Ath	1-1,0-5
Saltash Utd v Dartford	1-2
South Bank v Whitby T	1-1,2-1
Enfield v Waterlooville	3-0
Maidstone Utd v Weymouth	3-0
Grays Ath v Uxbridge T	2-1
Chelmsford C v Bath City	2-1
Worthing v Salisbury	1-0
Bridgend T v Harrow B	2-2,2-1
Slough Town v Tilbury	1-0
Sutton Utd v Kettering T	0-1
Crawley Town v Worcester C	5-2

Barnet v Wycombe W	0-1
Rhyl v Leek Town	1-1,2-3
Kings Lynn v Macclesfield T	1-1,0-3
Scarborough v Barrow	2-1
Telford Utd v Southport	2-4
Hyde Utd v Corby Town	0-2
Kidderminster H v Boston Utd	5-2
Morecambe v Burton Albion	0-2
Bromsgrove R v Shedshed Charterhouse	1-1,4-1
Dulwich v Windsor & Eton	1-1,1-2
Marine v Runcorn	0-2

Second Round

Altrincham v Bangor City	6-1
Stafford R v Bishop Auckland	0-1
Dagenham v Cheltenham T	0-1
Bishop's Stortford v Northwich Vic	2-0
Wealdstone v Frickley Ath	2-1
Dartford v South Bank	1-3
Enfield v Maidstone Utd	3-2
Grays Ath v Chelmsford C	1-1,1-3
Worthing v Bridgend T	1-0
Slough Town v Kettering Town	1-2
Crawley Town v Wycombe W	0-2

Another single goal win at Wembley. Altrincham's Mick Farrelly watches as his shot hits the roof of the Runcorn net.
Photo: John Rooney

Leek Town v Macclesfield T	2-1
Scarborough v Southport	0-0,1-1,0-1
Corby Town v Kidderminster H	0-4
Burton Albion v Bromsgrove R	1-0
Windsor & Eton v Runcorn	0-1

Third Round

Altrincham v Bishop Auckland	1-0
Cheltenham T v Bishop Stortford	0-0,3-1
Wealdstone v South Bank	0-0,1-2
Enfield v Chelmsford C	5-3
Worthing v Kettering T	0-0,1-2
Wycombe W v Leek Town	2-2,5-5,1-1,1-0
(2nd and 3rd replays at St George's Lane, Worcester)	
Southport v Kidderminster H	1-1,1-6
Burton Albion v Runcorn	0-2

Fourth Round

Cheltenham T v Altrincham	0-2
South Bank v Enfield	0-2
Kettering T v Wycombe W	2-1
Kidderminster H v Runcorn	1-2

Semi-final (2 legs)

Enfield v Altrincham	1-1
Altrincham v Enfield	2-0
Runcorn v Kettering T	0-0
Kettering T v Runcorn	0-2

Final At Wembley *(Attendance:* 15 700)
Altrincham 1 (Farrelly) **Runcorn 0**
Referee: T Ward
Altrincham: Wealands, Gardner, Densmore, Johnson, Farrelly, Conning, Cuddy, Davison, Reid, Ellis, Anderson. Sub: Newton.
Runcorn: McBride, Lee, Roberts, Jones, Fraser, Smith, Crompton S (Crompton A), Imrie, Carter, Mather, Carrodus.

FA CHALLENGE TROPHY 1986-87

First Round

Grantham v Blyth Spartans	1-3
Marine v Leek Town	2-1
Northwich Vic v Burton Albion	0-2
South Bank v Gainsborough Trinity	1-1,1-2
Bromsgrove Rovers v Rhyl	3-0
Telford Utd v Nuneaton Bor	1-4
Newcastle Blue Star v Stafford Rangers	2-1
Southport v Gateshead	1-2
Scarborough v Morecambe	1-0
Bishop Auckland v Runcorn	2-3
Mossley v Kidderminster H	0-0,0-1
Whitley Bay v Barrow	1-1,1-0
Altrincham v Crook Town	1-0
Boston Utd v Frickley Ath	4-3
Dartford v Merthyr Tydfil	1-1,4-2
Crawley Town v Bath City	1-2
Barnet v Wokingham T	6-0
Boreham Wood v Hitchin T	1-1,2-4
Trowbridge Town v Bishop's Stortford	0-1
Maidstone Utd v Wealdstone	1-1,2-1*
Weston-super-Mare v Worthing	0-5
Weymouth v Barking	2-2,3-1
Enfield v Aylesbury Utd	0-2

Cheltenham Town v Dulwich Hamlet	1-0
Saltash Utd v Fareham T	0-2
Chelmsford City v Sutton Utd	1-2
Ashford Town v Corby Town	0-0,1-3
Cambridge City v Tooting & Mitcham Utd	3-1
Kettering Town v Yeovil Town	2-3
Welling Utd v St Albans City	6-0
Leatherhead v Wycombe Wanderers	0-0,1-0
Dagenham v Harrow Borough	2-0

Second Round

Fareham Town v Bromsgrove Rovers	3-3,1-0*
Bath City v Blyth Spartans	2-2,0-1*
Hitchin Town v Barnet	1-1,0-5
Nuneaton Borough v Gateshead	3-2
Kidderminster H v Worthing	2-0
Leatherhead v Aylesbury Utd	0-1
Gainsborough Trinity v Whitley Bay	1-1,1-1,1-3
Dagenham v Marine	2-1
Maidstone Utd v Altrincham	2-0
Sutton Utd v Scarborough	2-2,0-2
Corby Town v Welling Utd	3-0
Dartford v Newcastle Blue Star	1-1,5-1
Runcorn v Yeovil Town	0-0,2-1
Cambridge City v Boston Utd	0-1
Bishop's Stortford v Cheltenham Town	0-1
Burton Albion v Weymouth	3-0

Third Round

Dartford v Runcorn	1-1,2-1
Scarborough v Fareham Town	0-2
Cheltenham Town v Kidderminster H	2-3
Burton Albion v Whitley Bay	1-0
Corby Town v Maidstone	0-3
Aylesbury Utd v Dagenham	0-0,1-2
Barnet v Boston Utd	1-1,3-3(aet),3-0
Nuneaton Boro v Blyth Spa	2-2,2-2(aet),2-2(aet),1-0

Fourth Round

Burton Albion v Maidstone Utd	1-1,1-0
Nuneaton Borough v Dartford	1-3
Dagenham v Kidderminster Harriers	1-3
Barnet v Fareham Town	0-1

Semi-final (2 legs)

Burton Albion v Dartford	2-1
Dartford v Burton Albion	0-2
Kidderminster Harriers v Fareham Town	0-0
Fareham Town v Kidderminster Harriers	0-2

Final At Wembley, *(Attendance:* 23 617)
Kidderminster Harriers 0, Burton Albion 0
Replay At The Hawthorns, West Bromwich,
(Attendance: 15 685)
Kidderminster 2 (Davies 2) **Burton 1** (Groves)
Referee: D Shaw
Kidderminster Harriers: Arnold, Barton, Boxall, Brazier, Collins (Pearson), Woodall, MacKenzie, O'Dowd, Tuohy, Casey, Davies. Subs: Jones, Hazlewood.
Burton Albion: New, Essex, Kamara, Vaughan, Simms, Groves, Bancroft, Land, Dorsett, Redfern, Gauden. Subs: Wood, Patterson.
(Teams same for both games).
Replay Subs: Brazier (Hazlewood), Redfern (Wood).

FA CHALLENGE TROPHY 1987-88

First Round
Frickley Ath v Kidderminster H	1-1,1-3
Bromsgrove Rovers v Blyth Spartans	2-2,2-2,3-2
Newcastle Blue Star v Rhyl	0-3
Lincoln city v South Liverpool	1-1,2-2,3-1
Corby Town v Gateshead	0-0,0-2
Barrow v Burton Albion	0-0,3-0
Marine v Nuneaton Bor	1-1,2-1
Boston Utd v Bangor City	2-2,0-0,2-1
Stafford Rangers v Caernarfon Town	1-1,1-0
Hyde Utd v Altrincham	0-1
Buxton v Telford Utd	2-4
Witton Albion v Whitby Town	2-1
Runcorn v Northwich Vic	2-0
Spennymoor Utd v South Bank	0-0,1-0
Macclesfield Town v Bishop Auckland	2-1
Welling utd v Leyton-Wingate	1-6
Fareham Town v Hendon	0-2
Fish Ath v Marlow	2-0
Enfield v Worthing	4-2
Slough Town v Dagenham	3-1
Barnet v Windsor & Eton	1-1,2-1
Gloucester C v Yeovil T	1-3
Farnborough T v Crawley T	0-2
Sutton Utd v Bishop's Stortford	0-2
Cambridge C v Poole T	2-1
Kettering T v Aylesbury Utd	1-1,5-1
Wealdstone v Banbury Utd	2-2,1-0
Wokingham T v Tooting & Mitcham Utd	4-0
Bath City v Merthyr Tydfil	2-1
Weymouth v Harrow Borough	1-1,1-2
Maidstone Utd v Dartford	5-1
Wycombe W c Cheltenham T	2-3

Second Round
Kidderminster H v Runcorn	0-2
Lincoln C v Cambridge C	2-1
Rhyl v Macclesfield T	0-2
Cheltenham T v Crawley T	2-0
Barrow v Hendon	1-1,2-1
Fisher Ath v Slough T	2-1
Spennymoor Utd v Harrow Bor	1-0
Gateshead v Wokingham T	0-4
Enfield v Bishop's Stortford	3-1
Leyton-Wingate v Boston Utd	5-2
Witton Albion v Yeovil T	3-1
Bath City v Stafford Rangers	0-2
Marine v Maidstone Utd	0-4
Wealdstone v Telford Utd	0-3
Bromsgrove Rovers v Barnet	0-0,3-1
Kettering Town v Altrincham	1-1,2-3

Third Round
Wokingham v Spennymoor United	3-0
Altrincham v Fisher Ath	1-1,0-0,1-1,1-0
Runcorn v Barrow	0-1
Cheltenham T v Bromsgrove Rovers	2-1
Leyton-Wingate v Macclesfield T	1-2
Lincoln City v Maidstone Utd	2-1
Witton Albion v Enfield	1-2
Stafford Rangers v Telford Utd	1-1,2-3

Fourth Round
Enfield v Lincoln City	1-0
Wokingham T v Macclesfield T	2-0
Cheltenham T v Telford Utd	2-4
Barrow v Altrincham	0-0,2-1

Semi-final (2 legs)
Barrow v Enfield	1-2
Enfield v Barrow	0-1,1-1,1-0
(first replay at Kidderminster, second replay at Stafford)	
Telford Utd v Wokingham T	2-0
Wokingham T v Telford Utd	0-1

Final At Wembley, *(Attendance: 20 161)*
Enfield 0, Telford 0
Replay at The Hawthorns, West Bromwich,
(Attendance: 6912)
Enfield 3 (Furlong 2, Howell) **Telford 2** (Biggins,
Norris pen)
Referee: L Dilkes
Enfield: Pape, Cottington, Howell, Keen, Sparrow
(Hayzleden), Lewis (Edmonds), Harding, Cooper,
King, Furlong, Francis.
Replay: Pape, Cottington, Howell, Keen (Edmonds),
Sparrow, Lewis, Harding, Cooper, King, Francis,
Furlong.
Telford: Charlton, McGinty, Storton, Nelson,
Wiggins, Mayman, Sankey, Joseph, Stringer
(Griffiths), Biggins, Norris.
Replay: Charlton, McGinty, Nelson, Storton,
Wiggins, Mayman (Cunningham, Hancock), Sankey,
Joseph, Griffiths, Biggins, Norris.

FA CHALLENGE TROPHY 1988-89

First Round
Atherstone v Barrow	1-4
Bangor City v South Bank	2-3
Gravesend & Northfleet v Barnet	1-1,2-1
Kettering v Basingstoke	1-1,5-3
Wycombe W v Bath City	0-0,4-0
Boston v Stafford	2-0
Bromley v Wealdstone	1-2
Bromsgrove v Woking	2-3
Burton Albion v Chorley	4-1
Buxton v Altrincham	0-2
Frickley Ath v Colwyn Bay	1-1,3-0
Aylesbury v Dagenham	2-2,4-0
Dartford v Dorchester	4-0
Dover v Worcester C	3-1
Enfield v Hendon	4-1
Fareham v Yeovil	1-2
Fisher v Cheltenham	0-1
Bishop Auckland v Fleetwood	0-0,5-1
Kidderminster v Maidstone	2-1
Leicester Utd v Blyth Spartans	3-0
Macclesfield v Marine	2-2,4-1
Matlock v Northwich Vic	2-6
Newcastle Blue Star v South Liverpool	1-0
Runcorn v Gretna	2-3
Stockton v Hyde	1-4
Sutton Utd v Kingstonian	1-0
Telford v Witton	3-0

What a feeling! Having scored the winning goal in the FA Vase Final in 1983 when VS Rugby beat Halesowen Town, Ian Crawley has just done it again for Telford United against Macclesfield Town in the 1989 Trophy Final.

Carshalton v Uxbridge	1-1,5-2
Welling v Slough	4-0
Weymouth v Newport	2-1
Windsor & Eton v Gosport	2-0
Merthyr Tydfil v Wokingham	2-2,1-0

Second Round
Boston Utd v Northwich Vic	3-2
Kettering T v Gravesend & Northfleet	1-1,1-2
Burton Albion v Kidderminster H	1-1,0-1
Aylesbury Utd v Merthyr Tydfil	1-3
Bishop Auckland v Sutton Utd	1-1,2-1
Wealdstone v Wycombe W	0-1
Barrow v Cheltenham T	0-0,0-0,1-0
Altrincham v Carshalton Ath	2-0
Windsor & Eton v Enfield	1-0
Woking v Weymouth	2-1
South Bank v Macclesfield T	0-3
Gretna v Hyde Utd	1-1,2-3
Newcastle Blue Star v Frickley Ath	3-1
Dartford v Dover Ath	0-0,2-0
Yeovil T v Telford Utd	1-4
Leicester Utd v Welling Utd	1-3

Third Round
Dartford v Bishop Auckland	2-0
Newcastle Blue Star v Woking	2-0
Hyde Utd v Windsor & Eton	2-2,2-0

Telford Utd v Kidderminster H	1-1,2-0
Boston Utd v Welling Utd	0-0,0-1
Wycombe W v Merthyr Tydfil	2-0
Altrincham v Barrow	5-3
Macclesfield T v Gravesend & Northfleet	2-0

Fourth Round
Macclesfield T v Welling Utd	1-0
Newcastle Blue Star v Telford Utd	1-4
Hyde United v Wycombe Wanderers	1-0
Dartford v Altrincham	1-0

Semi-final (2 legs)
Dartford v Macclesfield T	0-0
Macclesfield T v Dartford	4-1
Hyde Utd v Telford Utd	0-1
Telford Utd v Hyde Utd	3-0

Final At Wembley (*Attendance:* 18 102)
Telford 1 (Crawley) Macclesfield 0
Referee: T Holbrook
Telford: Charlton, Lee, Brindley, Hancock, Wiggins, Mayman, Grainger, Joseph, Nelson, Lloyd, Stringer. Subs: Crawley, Griffiths.
Macclesfield: Zelem, Roberts, Tobin, Edwards, Hardman, Askey, Lake, Hanion, Imrie, Burr, Timmons. Subs: Derbyshire, Kendall.

FA TROPHY

FA CHALLENGE TROPHY 1989-90

First Round

Colne Dynamoes v Altrincham	5-0
Spennymoor Utd v Leek Town	1-2
Nuneaton Boro v Shepshed Charterhouse	1-1,1-0
Darlington v Billingham Synthonia	2-2,3-1
Stafford Rangers v Billingham Town	2-1
Telford Utd v Burton Albion	2-1
Hyde Utd v Gretna	2-2,1-1,2-1
Bishop Auckland v Northwich Vic	1-1,2-3
Tow Law Town v Sutton Coldfield	2-2,3-1
Barrow v Bangor City	1-0
Witton Albion v Blyth Spartans	2-0
Seaham Red Star v Marine	2-0
Runcorn v Newcastle Blue Star	0-0,4-1
Macclesfield Town v Boston Utd	0-0,3-0
Welling Utd v Fisher Ath	2-0
Wivenhoe Town v Hendon	2-1
Kettering Town v Wokingham Town	0-2
Redbridge Forest v Slough Town	1-1,3-0
Wycombe W v Met Police	1-3
Leyton-Wingate v Kidderminster H	0-3
Weston-super-Mare v Windsor & Eton	2-3
Enfield v Merthyr Tydfil	3-2
Sutton Utd v Dover Ath	0-1
Dartford v Yeovil Town	1-2
Farnborough Town v Staines Town	1-0
Ashford Town v Bath City	0-4
Weymouth v Barnet	2-0
Worcester City v Aylesbury Utd	2-2,0-1
Cheltenham T v Gravesend & Northfleet	5-1
Harrow Boro v Wealdstone	1-1,1-0
Dagenham v Kingstonian	2-5
Woking v Bromsgrove Rovers	3-0

Second Round

Woking v Seaham Red Star	3-1
Nuneaton Boro v Leek Town	1-1,0-1
Kingstonian v Hyde Utd	2-1
Stafford R v Wokingham T	0-0,3-1
Darlington v Macclesfield T	1-0
Barrow v Met Police	1-0
Redbridge Forest v Harrow Boro	0-0,2-0
Kidderminster H v Witton Albion	0-0,2-1
Bath City v Tow Law Town	2-0
Cheltenham Town v Enfield	3-1
Farnborough Town v Windsor & Eton	2-1
Dover Ath v Weymouth	2-1
Runcorn v Wivenhoe Town	1-1,3-2
Welling Utd v Telford Utd	0-0,0-2
Colne Dynamoes v Northwich Vic	1-0
Yeovil Town v Aylesbury Utd	2-0

Little Leek Town had beaten Telford United, Darlington and Stafford Rangers on the way to Wembley but the little H F S Loans League, Division One side lost to Barrow at Wembley and here their keeper Robin Simpson safely plucks the ball off the head of Ken Gordon.
Photo: Dave West

The heroes of Barrow! Long serving Ken Gordon (left) who scored two goals in his last game before emigrating and the club's record goal scorer Colin Cowperthwaite, the other scorer in Barrow's 3-0 success. All the goals were headers and the result was the highlight of the Cumbrian club's years in non-league football since losing their Football League place.
Photo: Dave West

Third Round

Colne Dynamoes v Farnborough Town	2-1
Darlington v Runcorn	1-0
Kidderminster Harriers v Dover Ath	3-0
Cheltenham v Kingstonian	3-3,0-3
Redbridge Forest v Stafford Rangers	1-1,1-2
Leek Town v Telford Utd	0-0,3-0
Bath City v Woking	1-1,2-1
Barrow v Yeovil Town	1-1,2-1

Fourth Round

Bath City v Stafford Rangers	0-2
Colne Dynamoes v Kidderminster H	0-0,2-1
Barrow v Kingstonian	2-2,1-0
Leek Town v Darlington	1-0

Semi Final (2 legs)

Colne Dynamoes v Barrow	0-1
Barrow v Colne Dynamoes	1-1
Stafford Rangers v Leek Town	0-0
Leek Town v Stafford Rangers	1-0

Final At Wembley, *Attendance:* 19 011)
Barrow 3 (Gordon 2, Cowperthwaite) **Leek Town 0**
Barrow: McDonnell, Higgins, Chilton, Skivington, Gordon, Proctor, Doherty (Burgess), Farrell (Gilmore), Cowperthwaite, Lowe, Ferris.
Leek Town: Simpson, Elsby (Smith), Pearce, McMullen, Clowes, Coleman (Russell), Mellor, Somerville, Sutton, Millington, Norris.

FA TROPHY

FA CHALLENGE TROPHY 1990-91

First Round

Northwich Vic v Tow Law Town	2-1
South Bank v Bishop Auckland	?-?
Horwich RMI v Bedworth United	2-1
Guisborough Town v Witton Albion	2-2
Runcorn v Boston United	2-0
Droylsden v Fleetwood Town	2-1
Hyde United v Stafford Rangers	1-2
Burton Albion v Moor Green	3-0
Barrow v Chorley	2-0
Macclesfield Town v Gretna	0-2
Gateshead v Billingham Synthonia	?-?
Leek Town v Altrincham	0-4
Telford United v Emley	0-0
Barnet v Farnborough Town	2-3
Slough Town v Bath City	2-4
Wokingham Town v Wivenhoe Town	1-2
Kidderminster Harriers v Sutton United	4-2
Carshalton Athletic v Dartford	0-0,1-1

Antone Joseph joined Kidderminster Harriers after enjoying three FA Trophy finals with Telford United. In his first two seasons this English Semi-Professional International took his new club to a semi-final and then the next year skippered them at Wembley against Wycombe Wanderers. He is seen here in action against Emley.
Photo: Bob Hill

Enfield v Chesham United	1-0
Dover Athletic v Dorking	1-0
Gloucester v Yeovil Town	1-0
Gravesend & Northfleet v Cheltenham Town	2-2,1-5
Fisher Athletic v Redbridge Forest	1-2
Salisbury v VS Rugby	1-4
Wycombe Wanderers v Wealdstone	1-0
Windsor & Eton v Colchester United	0-1
Bognor Regis Town v Aylesbury United	2-4
Molesey v Merthyr Tydfil	1-1
Welling United v Hayes	3-1
Kettering Town v Woking	2-0
Stroud v Metropolitan Police	2-2,2-0
Bye for Frickley Athletic	

Second Round

Kidderminster Harriers v Dover Athletic	1-0
Farnborough Town v Bath City	1-3
Hyde United v Emley	0-0,2-3(aet)
Barrow v Kettering Town	0-0,1-2(aet)
Colchester United v Runcorn	2-0
Enfield v Wivenhoe Town	0-2
Witton Albion v South Bank	3-2
Merthyr Tydfil v Gloucester City	1-3
Welling United v Aylesbury United	2-1
Altrincham v Gateshead	3-1
Horwich RMI v Gretna	2-1
Redbridge Forest v Frickley Athletic	2-1
Northwich Victoria v Droylsden	4-1
Strouf v Burton Albion	3-2
Dartford v Cheltenham Town	0-2
VS Rugby v Wycombe Wanderers	0-1

Third Round

Kidderminster Harriers v Bath City	3-1
Emley v Kettering Town	3-2
Colchester United v Wivenhoe Town	3-0
Witton Albion v Gloucester City	3-0
Welling United v Altrincham	1-2
Horwich RMI v Redbridge Forest	2-1
Northwich Victoria v Stroud	2-0
Cheltenham Town v Wycombe Wanderers	1-2

Fourth Round

Kidderminster Harriers v Emley	3-0
Colchester United v Witton Albion	0-2
Altrincham v Horwich RMI	5-0
Northwich Victoria v Wycombe Wanderers	2-3

Semi-finals (2 legs)

Kidderminster v Witton Albion	0-1
Witton Albion v Kidderminster	4-3(aet),1-2
(Replay at Stafford Rangers)	
Wycombe Wanderers v Altrincham	2-1
Altrincham v Wycombe Wanderers	0-2

Final At Wembley *(Attendance:* 34 842)
Kidderminster Harriers 1 (Hadley) **Wycombe Wanderers 2** (Scott, West)
Kidderminster Harriers: Jones, Kurila, McGrath, Weir, Barnett, Forsyth, Joseph (Wilcox), Howell (Whitehouse), Hadley, Lilwall, Humphreys.
Wycombe Wanderers: Granville, Crossley, Cash, Kerr, Creaser, Carrol, Ryan, Stapleton, West, Scott, Guppy (Hutchinson).

FA CHALLENGE VASE

INTRODUCTION

When English footballers lost the professional/amateur categories and became just 'players', the FA Amateur Cup was withdrawn. The senior amateur clubs who had competed in the Northern and Isthmian Leagues entered the FA Trophy but the smaller clubs were given a brand new knock-out tournament with a Wembley Final.

After little Hoddesdon Town had won the first FA Vase competition in 1974, Billericay Town dominated the competition with three wins in four years. They created tremendous interest in Essex and they were the first club from the real grass roots of the game to use the inspiration of Vase success to move through the 'Pyramid', while improving facilities and learning about presentation of big matches, entertaining visitors and the media and generally adapting to senior football. The North East, with memories of Bishop Auckland becoming faint, were encouraged by the successes of Whickham and Newcastle Blue Star and one of the very best performances in any of the Wembley

FA official Adrian Titcombe, who has done so much for non-league football, leads the Sudbury Town and Tamworth teams out in front of a record FA Vase attendance of 26 487.

VS Rugby skipper Mick Preston with the FA Vase and their mascot, after their 1-0 defeat of Halesowen Town in 1983.
Photo: Martin Dalton

Cup Finals came from little Forest Green Rovers of the Hellenic League who produced a brilliant performance to beat Rainworth Miners Welfare 3-0.

Following Billericay came Halesowen Town who deservedly pulled great support from the West Midlands for their three finals at Wembley. They included the Joinson twins, the identical Paul and Lee, and one of their successes came against Southall managed by Gordon Bartlett, who four years later took Yeading to the final where they beat Bridlington Town.

The most colourful day for the competition was provided in 1989 when Tamworth and Sudbury Town both brought about 12 000 supporters and in brilliant sunshine, the red and black competed with yellow and red, within a record crowd of 26 487.

VASE WINNERS' LEAGUES

ESSEX SENIOR	4	NORTHERN COUNTIES	1
WEST MIDLANDS	3	SOUTHERN (MIDLAND)	1
NORTH WEST COUNTIES	2	SPARTAN	1
WEARSIDE	2	UNITED COUNTIES	1
HELLENIC	1	ISTHMIAN	1

VASE STATISTICS

Most Wins: 3 Billericay Town.
Most Finals: 3 Billericay Town, Halesowen Town, Stamford.
Best Attendance: 26 487 Tamworth v Sudbury Town, 1989.
Lowest Attendance: 4254 St Helens v Warrington, 1987.

Average Attendance: 13 126.
Most Consecutive Appearances in Final: 2 Billericay Town and Halesowen Town.
Top Individual Scorer at Wembley: 3 Douggie Young (Billericay Town), 1979

FINALS AT A GLANCE

Year	Winners	Score	Runners-up	Venue
1975	Hoddesdon Town	2-1	Epsom & Ewell	Wembley
1976	Billericay Town	1-0	Stamford	Wembley
1977	Billericay Town	2-1	Sheffield	Nottm Forest
	(After 1-1 draw at Wembley)			
1978	Newcastle Blue Star	2-0	Barton Rovers	Wembley
1979	Billericay Town	4-1	Almondsbury Greenway	Wembley
1980	Stamford	2-0	Guisborough Town	Wembley
1981	Whickham	3-2	Willenhall Town	Wembley
1982	Forest Green Rovers	3-0	Rainworth MW	Wembley
1983	VS Rugby	1-0	Halesowen Town	Wembley
1984	Stansted	3-2	Stamford	Wembley
1985	Halesowen Town	3-1	Fleetwood Town	Wembley
1986	Halesowen Town	3-0	Southall	Wembley
1987	St Helens Town	3-2	Warrington Town	Wembley
1988	Colne Dynamoes	1-0	Emley	Wembley
1989	Tamworth	3-0	Sudbury Town	Peterborough
	(After 1-1 draw at Wembley)			
1990	Yeading	1-0	Bridlington Town	Leeds
	(After 0-0 draw at Wembley)			
1991	Guisley	3-1	Gresley Rovers	Sheffield
	(After 4-4 draw at Wembley)			

THE FIRST VASE

FA CHALLENGE VASE 1974-75

First Round

Annan Athletic v Norton Cricket Club	3-1
Lostock Gralam v Stork	2-0
Warrington Town v Molton	1-1,0-5
Prescot Town v Middlewich Athletic	0-2
Chadderton v Wigan Rovers	3-0
Wythenshawe v Old Altrincham	1-5
Old Blackburnians v Irlam Town Amateur	1-2
Curzon Ashton v Manchester YMCA	5-0
Northern Nomads v Glossop	1-2
Liversedge v East Chorlton Amateur	1-0
Brook Sports v Whitkirk Wanderers	3-0
Worsborough Bridge Miners' Welfare v Leeds Ashley Road	2-2,4-4,0-2
Sheffield v Frecheville Com	5-0
Brigg Town v Sheffield University	1-0
Swallownest Miners' Welfare v North Ferriby Utd	1-4
Norton Woodseats Amateur v Lincoln United	0-4
Clipstone Welfare v Midland Athletic	0-0,4-1
Players Athletic v Hinckley Athletic	1-1,2-0
Loughborough Colleges v Friar Lane OB	1-2
Boldmere St Michaels v Mile Oak Rovers & Youth	5-0
Walsall Wood v Donnington Wood	0-1
Gresley Rovers v Bridgnorth Town	2-0
Knowle v Solihull Borough	1-2
Stratford Town v Paget Rangers	0-0,3-0
Astwood Bank Rovers v Northfield Town	1-3
Desborough Town v Valley Sports	2-2,0-5
Wolverton Town & BR v Litterworth Town	4-1
Northampton Spencer v Kempston Rovers	0-0,3-0
City of Norwich School OBU v Warboys Town	3-1
Watton United v Peterborough Rovers	2-4
Stamford Town v Holbeach United	4-2
Brightlingsea Utd v Tiptree United	2-1
Witham Town v Clacton Town	1-1,0-1
Coggeshall Town v Bungay Town	1-0
Billericay Town v Saffron Walden Town	3-0
Stansted v Heybridge Swifts	0-0,0-2
Hoddesdon Town v Epping Town	2-1
Badock Town v Stotfold	2-2,2-2,1-0
Wootton Blue Cross v Shefford Town	3-2
Shillington v Leighton Town	2-1
Crown & Manor v Welwyn Garden	0-2
Wingate v Hemel Hempstead Town	3-0
Vauxhall Motors v Hatfield Town	3-0
Aylesbury United v Thame United	3-1
Tring Town v Hazels	3-2
Marlow v Chalfont St Peter	2-1
Chingford v Rayners Lane	1-3
Willesden v Harefield United	0-0,0-1
Kingsbury Town v Edmonton & Haringey	2-1
East Thurrock Utd v Rainham Town	2-4
Royal Arsenal Sports v Ford United	0-3
Hornchurch v Eton Manor	3-0
Cray Wanderers v Swanley	0-1
Thames Polytechnic v Dartford Amateur	1-3

Slade Green Ath v Crockenhill	0-0,1-2
Epsom & Ewell v Reigate Priory	4-0
Whyteleaf v Malden Town	3-0
Merstham v Horley Town	1-1,0-3
Chessington United v Molesey	0-1
Ulysses v Cobham	2-2,1-1,3-2
Lion Sports v Civil Service	3-1
Chertsey Town v Westfield	2-2,3-2
Windsor & Eton v Egham Town	0-0,2-3
Virginia Water v Chobham	0-2
Farnham Town v Camberley Town	3-1
Bracknell Town v Frimley Green	6-1
Eastbourne Town v Sidley United	5-0
Tunbridge Wells v Herne Bay	3-2
Ringmer v Eastbourne United	3-0
East Grinstead v Whitehawk	2-0
Wigmore Athletic v Lancing	2-2,4-0
Shoreham v Horsham YMCA	0-0,4-0
Chichester City v Selsey	4-0
Worthing v Pagham	3-2
Portfield v Moneyfield Sports	4-5
Brockenhurst v Newbury Town	1-0
Portsmouth Royal Navy v Gosport Borough	0-2
Hungerford Town v Cowes	2-2,1-2
Bicester Town v Moreton Town	0-4
Wallingford Town v Chipping Norton Town	1-3
Didcot Town v Clanfield	2-3
Longlevens Star v Sharpness	2-3
Viney St Swithins v Pegasus Juniors	1-1,4-2
Pershore United v Malvern Town	1-1,0-3
Bristol St George v Hanham Athletic	3-2
Yate Town v Forest Green Rovers	0-1
Glenside Hospital v Cadbury Heath	0-6
Swindon Victoria v Cirencester Town	3-2
Calne Town v Westbury United	4-1
Newquay v Wellington	3-0
Wells City v Paulton Rovers	1-6
Radstock Town v Ottery St Mary	2-3

Second Round

Wallsend Town v Annan Athletic	2-0
Wingate v Heaton Stannington	0-1
Middlewich Athletic v Lostock Gralam	1-0
Hoylake Athletic v Moulton	1-2
Irlam Town Amateur v Chadderton	2-1
Anson Villa v Old Altrinchamians	2-1
Liversedge v Curzon Ashton	2-2,0-4
Chloride Recreation v Glossop	0-0,0-1
Sheffield v Brook Sports	5-1
Birkenshaw Rovers v Leeds Ashley Road	0-3
Lincoln United v Brigg Town	2-0
Ashby Institute v North Ferriby Utd	3-2
Friar Lane OB v Clipstone Welfare	4-1
Anstey Nomads v Players Athletic	4-3
Gresley Rovers v Boldmere St Michaels	2-2,0-1
Blakenall v Donnington Wood	1-0
Northfield Town v Solihull Borough	2-2,0-1

Coventry Sporting v Stratford Town	1-0
Kempston Rovers v Valley Sports (Rugby)	2-0
Burton Park Wanderers v Wolverton Town	0-1
Stamford Town v City of Norwich School OBU	3-0
Bourne Town v Peterborough Rovers	3-0
Coggershall Town v Brightlingsea United	4-2
Braintree & Crittall Athletic v Clacton Town	0-0,0-2
Hoddesdon Town v Billericay Town	1-0
Basildon United v Heybridge Swifts	3-0
Shillington v Baldock Town	0-2
Arlesey Town v Wootton Blue Cross	1-2
Vauxhall Motors v Welwyn Garden	1-1,1-1,3-0
Berkhamsted Town v Wingate	0-1
Marlow v Aylesbury United	3-2
Amersham Town v Tring Town	1-1,1-4
Kingsbury Town v Rayners Lane	2-1
Borough Road College v Harefield United	3-1
Hornchurch v Rainham Town	3-2
Barkingside v Ford United	1-1,1-2
Crockenhill v Swanley	4-0
Bexley v Dartford Amateur	1-3
Horley Town v Epsom & Ewell	0-2
Banstead Athletic v Whyteleaf	2-1
Lion Sports v Molesey	0-1
BAC (Weybridge) v Ulysses	1-0
Chobham v Chertsey Town	1-2
Addlestone v Egham Town	2-2,3-0
Farnborough Town v Farnham Town	3-0
Fleet Town v Bracknell Town	1-1,0-5
Ringmer v Eastbourne Town	2-3
Bexhill Town v Tunbridge Wells	1-3
Shoreham v East Grinstead	0-0,0-3
Burgess Hill Town v Wigmore Athletic	2-1
Moneyfield Sports v Chichester City	3-0
Arundel v Worthing	2-3
Cowes v Brockenhurst	1-3
Bemerton Athletic v Gosport Borough	1-6
Clanfield v Moreton Town	2-0
Abingdon Town v Chipping Norton Town	0-4
Malvern Town v Sharpness	3-0
Evesham United v Viney St Swithin	6-0
Cadbury Heath v Bristol St George	5-0
Avon v Forest Green Rovers	
(walkover for Forest Green Rovers)	
Melksham v Swindon Victoria	4-0
Wantage Town v Calne Town	2-1
Ottery St Mary v Newquay	0-2
Clevedon v Paulton Rovers	0-2

Third Round

Heaton Stannington v Wallsend Town	1-1,0-2
Irlam Town Amateur v Anson Villa	2-2,2-0
Glossop v Middlewich Ath.	2-4
Moulton v Curzon Ashton	3-1
Leeds Ashley Road v Sheffield	1-2
Ashby Institute v Lincoln United	0-0,0-2
Boldmere St Michaels v Blakenhall	1-1,1-2
Bourne Town v Friar Lane OB	4-6
Anstey Nomads v Stamford Town	1-3
Solihull Borough v Coventry Sporting	4-1
Wolverton Town v Kempston Rovers	1-2
Coggeshall Town v Clacton Town	0-3
Basildon United v Hoddesdon Town	1-2

Baldock Town v Wootton Blue Cross	0-0,2-2,2-2,2-1
Wingate v Vauxhall Motors	2-1
Hornchurch v Barkingside	3-0
Dartford Amateurs v Crockenhill	0-0,1-3
Kingsbury Town v Borough Road College	1-0
Bracknell Town v Marlow	0-2
Tring Town v Addlestone	0-3
Banstead Athletic v Molesey	0-1
Chertsey Town v BAC (Weybridge)	3-0
Tunbridge Wells v East Grinstead	1-0
Worthing v Epsom & Ewell	1-4
Eastbourne Town v Burgess Hill Town	2-0
Farnborough Town v Moneyfield Sports	1-0
Gosport v Brockenhurst	1-1,0-3
Malvern Town v Evesham United	1-1,1-0
Wantage Town v Clanfield	0-3
Chipping Norton Town v Forest Green Rovers	3-1
Cadbury Heath v Melksham Town	0-0,4-0
Paulton Rovers v Newquay	3-0

Fourth Round

Lincoln United v Moulton	2-0
Sheffield v Wallsend Town	0-1
Irlam Town Amateur v Middlewich Athletic	0-1
Chipping Norton v Solihull Borough	0-1
Malvern Town v Stamford	2-2,1-6
Blakenall v Friar Lane Old Boys	2-4
Clacton Town v Wingate	0-0,0-4
Kingsbury Town v Kempston Rovers	3-4
Baldock Town v Hoddesdon Town	1-2
Eastbourne Town v Epsom & Ewell	0-2
Tunbridge Wells v Hornchurch	0-5
Crockenhill v Molesey	0-2
Brockenhurst v Cadbury Heath	2-1
Chertsey Town v Marlow	0-1
Clanfield v Farnborough Town	3-4
Addlestone v Paulton Rovers	5-0

Fifth Round

Lincoln United v Wallsend Town	3-0
Friar Lane OB v Middlewich Athletic	3-1
Brockenhurst v Stamford Town	1-4
Marlow v Addlestone	0-0,0-1
Solihull Borough v Wingate	2-2,0-1
Kempston Rovers v Farnborough Town	0-1
Epsom & Ewell v Hornchurch	1-0
Hoddesdon Town v Molesey	1-0

Sixth Round

Lincoln United v Friar Lane OB	0-1
Wingate v Stamford Town	1-3
Hoddesdon Town v Farnborough Town	2-0
Epsom & Ewell v Addlestone	2-0

Semi Finals (2 legs)

Hoddesdon Town v Friar Lane Old Boys	1-1,2-0
Epsom & Ewell v Stamford Town	0-0,2-1

Final at Wembley *(Attendance: 10 000)*
Hoddesdon 2 (Sedgewick 2) **Epsom 1** (Wales)
Epsom: Page; Bennett, Webb, Wales, Worby, Jones, O'Connell, Walker, Tuite, Eales, Lee.
Hoddesdon: Galvin; Green, Hickey, Maybury, Stevenson, Wilson, Bishop, Picking, Sedgewick, Nathan, Schofield.

FA VASE

FINALS IN DETAIL 1976-1986

1976 (*Attendance:* 11 858)
Billericay Town 1 (Aslett) **Stamford 0** aet   Referee: Alan Robinson
Billericay: Griffiths, Payne, Foreman, Pullin, Bone, Coughlan, Geddes, Aslett, Clayden, Scott, Smith (9).
Stamford: Johnson, Kwiatkowski, Marchant, Crawford, Downs, Hird, Barnes, Walpole, Smith, Russell, Broadhurst.

1977 (*Attendance:* 14 000)
Billericay Town 1 (Clayden) **Sheffield 1** (Coughlan OG) aet   Referee: J Worrall
Billericay: Griffiths, Payne, Bone, Coughlan, Pullin, Scott, Wakefield, Aslett, Clayden, Woodhouse, McQueen.
Sub: Whettell.
Sheffield: Wing, Gilbody, Lodge, Hardisty, Watts, Skelton, Kay, Travis, Pugh, Thornhill, Haynes. Sub: Strutt.

Replay at Nottingham Forest (*Attendance:* 3482)
Billericay Town 2 (Aslett, Woodhouse) **Sheffield 1** (Thornhill)   Referee: J Worrall
Billericay: Griffiths, Payne, Pullin, Whettell, Bone, McQueen, Woodhouse, Aslett, Clayden, Scott, Wakefield.
Sheffield: Wing, Gilbody, Lodge, Strutt, Watts, Skelton, Kay, Travis, Pugh, Thornhill, Haines.

1978 (*Attendance:* 16 391)
Blue Star 2 (Dunn, Crumplin) **Barton Rovers 0**   Referee: T Morris
Blue Star: Halbert, Feenan, Thompson, Davidson, Dixon S, Beynon, Storey, Dixon P, Crumplin, Callaghan, Dunn.
Sub: Diamond.
Barton: Blackwell, Stephens, Crossley, Evans, Harris, Dollimore, Dunn, Harnaman, Fossey, Turner, Smith. Sub: Cox.

1979 See feature pages 96-99

1980 (*Attendance:* 11 500)
Stamford 2 (Alexander, McGowan) **Guisborough Town 0**   Referee: N Midgley
Stamford: Johnson, Kwiatowski, Ladd, McGowan, Bliszczak I, Mackin, Broadhurst, Hall, Czarnecki, Potter, Alexander. Sub: Bliszczak S.
Guisborough: Cutter, Scott, Thornton, Angus, Maltby, Percy, Skelton, Coleman, McElvaney, Sills, Dilworth. Sub: Harrison.

1981 (*Attendance:* 12 000)
Whickham 3 (Scott, Williamson, Peck (og)) **Willenhall Town 2** (Smith, Stringer) aet   Referee: R Lewis
Whickham: Thompson, Scott, Knox, Williamson, Cook, Ward, Carroll, Diamond, Cawthra, Robertson, Turnbull.
Sub: Allon.
Willenhall Town: Newton, White, Dams, Woodall, Heath, Fox, Peck, Price, Mathews, Smith, Stringer. Sub: Trevor.

Little Stansted from the Essex Senior League, who had entered the tournament at the Preliminary Round stage, celebrate their third goal against Stamford in their 3-1 success in 1984.   Photo: Eric Marsh

VS Rugby have a message for their supporters after their 1-0 victory in the 1983 Final.
Photo: Martin Dalton

1982 (*Attendance:* 12 500)
Forest Green Rovers 3 (Leitch 2, Norman) **Rainworth Miners Welfare 0** Referee: K Walmsley
Forest Green: Moss, Norman, Day, Turner, Higgins, Jenkins, Burns, Guest, Millard, Leitch, Doughty. Sub: Dangerfield.
Rainworth: Watson, Hallam, Hodgson, Slater, Sterland, Oliver, Knowles, Raine, Radzki, Reah, Comerford. Sub: Robinson.

1983 (*Attendance:* 13 700)
VS Rugby 1 (Crawley) **Halesowen Town 0** Referee: B Daniels
VS Rugby: Burton, McGinty, Harrison, Preston, Knox, Evans, Ingram, Setchell, Owen, Beecham, Crawley. Sub: Haskins.
Halesowen: Coldicott, Penn, Edmonds, Lacey, Randall, Shilvock, Hazelwood, Moss, Woodhouse, Joinson E, Joinson L. Sub: Smith.

1984 (*Attendance:* 8125)
Stansted 3 (Holt, Gillard, Reading) **Stamford 2** (Waddicore, Allen) Referee: T Bune
Stansted: Coe, Williams, Hilton, Simpson, Cooper, Reading, Callanan, Holt, Reeves, Doyle, Gillard. Sub: Williams.
Stamford: Parslow, Smitheringale, Blades, McIlwain, Lyon, Mackin, Genovese, Waddicore, Allen, Robson, Beech. Sub: Chapman.

1985 (*Attendance:* 16 715)
Halesowen 3 (Moss, Joinson L 2) **Fleetwood Town 1** (Moran) Referee: C Downey
Halesowen: Caldicott, Penn, Sherwood, Warner, Randle, Heath, Hazelwood, Moss (Smith), Woodhouse, Joinson P, Joinson L.
Fleetwood: Dobson, Moran, Hadgraft, Strachan, Robinson, Milligan, Hall, Trainor, Taylor (Whitehouse), Cain, Kenneley.

1986 (*Attendance:* 18 340)
Halesowen 3 (Moss 2, Joinson L) **Southall 0** Referee: D Scott
Halesowen: Pemberton, Moore, Lacey, Randle (Rhodes), Sherwood, Heath, Penn, Woodhouse, Joinson P, Joinson L, Moss.
Southall: MacKenzie, James, McGovern, Croad, Holland, Powell (Richmond), Pierre, Richardson, Sweales, Ferdinand, Rowe (12).

Billericay's Triumph

Billericay Town skipper Arthur Coughlin and manager John Newman celebrate with the team after their first Wembley triumph in 1976.

The most successful club in FA Vase history are the Essex side Billericay Town, the only club to have won the competition on three different occasions. Their first success came in 1976 when an extra time goal from Aslett gave them victory over Stamford. The following year Billericay needed a replay at Nottingham Forest to overcome Sheffield and retain the Vase. Although they missed out on the 1978 Final, Billericay were back in 1979 to crush Almondsbury Greenway 4-1 and complete their hat-trick. Billericay set new Vase record attendances on each of their three visits to Wembley.

FA VASE 1978-79

Preliminary Round

Darlington RA v Wallington	3-1	Teesside Polytechnic v Eppleton CW	0-1
Ryhope v Whickham	2-3	Wren R v Little Lever	1-2
Carlisle C v Billingham Social	1-3	Nelson v Old Blackburnians	6-2
Brandon U v Norton CCT	0-1	Leyland Motors v Stork	6-2
Peterlee Newtown v Carlisle Spartans	1-2	Waterloo Dock v Newton	5-0
Heaton Stannington v Boys Welfare	2-1	Salford Amateurs v Blackpool Mechanics	3-1
Boldon CA v Smith's Dock	2-1	Lytham v Whalley Range Amateur	6-2
Wallsend T v Guisborough T	2-1	Wythenshawe Amateurs v North Withington	0-1
Seaham CW Red Star v Appleby	4-2	Prescot BI v Hoylake Ath	1-3
Pickering T v Washington	0-3	East Chorlton Amateur v Kidsgrove Ath	1-3
Wingate v Sunderland Pyrex	1-0	Linotype v Heswall	3-2 aet
		Glossop v Chadderton	2-3

BSC Parkgate v Ossett T	0-6
Thackley v Clitheroe	1-0
Harrogate T v Bradley Rangers	1-0
Fryston Colliery v Normanby PW	1-3
Guiseley v North Ferriby U	1-0
Birkenshaw R v Bentley Vic	2-3
Brook Sports v Hatfield Main	3-0
Yorkshire Amateur v Gainsborough U	1-2
Hall Road Rangers v Ashby Institute	2-1
Immingham T v Retford T	1-4
Ruston Sports v Pilkington Recreation	0-0,1-0
Rawmarsh Welfare v Barton T	4-2
Skegness T v Kiveton Park	2-0
Oakham U v Ruston Bucyrus	0-0,2-0
Thringstone v Newfoundpool WMC	2-3
Norton Woodseats v Staveley Works	3-2 aet
Shepshed Charterhouse v Carrvale U	5-0
Clay Cross Works v Paget Rangers	2-3
Long Eaton Grange v Tividale	2-1 aet
Walsall Sportsco v Oadby T	1-0
Solihull Bor v Hinckley T	0-2 aet
Wednesfield Social v GKN Sankey	5-2
Boldmere St Michaels v Brierley Hill	0-2
Coventry Sporting v Long Buckby (WO for Coventry Sporting as Long Buckby have withdrawn)	
Willenhall T v Desborough T	3-2
Knowle v Coleshill T	3-1
Walsall Wood v Northfield T	0-4
Rothwell T v Valley Sports Rugby	1-0 aet
Ely C v Leverington	3-0
Stowmarket v Holbeach U	2-2,3-2 aet
Holt U v Beccles	0-2
Soham T Rangers v Bungay T	5-1
March Town U v Norwich Union	4-2
Chatteris T v Watton U	0-3
Melton T v Mirrlees Blackstone	2-2,2-3
Royston T v Diss T	4-0
Felixstowe T v Maldon T	2-0 aet
Stratford T v Bicester T	0-2
Eaton Bray U v Northampton Spencer	0-1 aet
Knebworth v Olney T	2-3
Stansted v Langford	2-0
Letchworth GC v Huntingdon U	8-1
Wolverton & BR v Hemel Hempstead	2-1 aet
Sandy Albions v Sun Sports	0-2
Cheshunt v Potton U	4-2
Tiptree U v Haverhill R	0-1
Leggatts OB v Baldock T	1-2
Hatfield T v Thame U	1-6
Wootton Blue Cross v Rolls Royce Engines	3-2 aet
Sawbridgeworth v Arlesey T	1-4
Witham T v Eynesbury R	3-1
Pirton v Saffron Walden T	3-1
Chingford v Selby	0-3
Vauxhall Motors v Edgware	2-0
Heybridge Swifts v Braintree & Crittall	4-1
Wallingford T v Harefield U	2-1
Tansley v Stotfold	2-1
Willesden v Didcot T	3-1
Harpenden T v Shillington	1-2
Woodford T v Kingsbury T	2-1
Norsemen v Swanley T	3-4 aet
Windsor & Eton v Eton Manor	2-0

Ford U v Whyteleafe	0-0,0-1
West Wickham v Darenth Heathside	2-0 aet
At Darenth Heathside FC	
Erith & Belvedere v LB of Greenwich	0-1
Bracknell T v Malden Vale	0-2
Thatcham T v BAC (Weybridge)	0-2
Chalfont St Peter v Banstead Ath	0-1
Civil Service v Frimley Green	3-1
Malden T v Feltham	1-2
Flackwell Heath v Chertsey T	1-4
Ulysses v Egham T	1-3 aet
Kew Association v Marlow	2-2,3-1
Cobham v Shoreham	1-1,0-1
Steyning v Horsham YMCA	1-0
Old Salesians v Camberley T	2-3
Dartford Glentworth v Canvey Island	5-4 aet
Crockenhill v Crown & Manor	6-2
East Grinstead v Whitstable T	2-2,2-3
Faversham T v Sidley U	5-1
Bexley v Welling U	1-4
Herne Bay v Hythe T	3-0
Wigmore Ath v Merstham	2-3
Ringmer v Three Bridges	2-1
Dorking T v Southwick	2-1
Tunbridge Wells v Horley T	1-0
Littlehampton T v Bexhill T	2-1
Worthing v Farnham T	1-0
Newport IOW v Selsey	5-0
Brading T v Swanage & Herston	4-2
Chichester C v Cowes	1-0
Alton T v Swaythling	3-2
First Tower U v Havant T	2-1
Brockenhurst v Sholing Sports	1-3
Fleet T v St Martins	0-1
Amesbury v Wantage T	6-0
Clandown v Larkhall Ath	0-0,0-0,0-2
At Bath C FC	
Ledbury T v Wilton R	6-2
Pegasus Juniors v West Midlands Police	2-5
Worrall Hill v Fairford T	3-1
Malmesbury Vic v Shortwood U	1-3
Calne T v Radstock T	0-1
Sharpness v Chippenham T	3-1
Cirencester T v Bristol St George	0-0,1-2
Ilminster T v Port of Bristol	6-3
Westbury U v Odd Down	4-2
Peasedown Ath v Glenside St Gabriels	1-0 aet
Bristol Manor Farm v Keynsham T	1-1,0-3
Stonehouse v Clanfield	1-2
Forest Green R v Avon Bradfort	12-1
Brixham U v Ottery St Mary	3-1
Exmouth T v Holsworthy	2-1

First Round

Wingate v Wallsend T	1-0
Carlisle Spartans v Washington	2-4 aet
Billingham Social v Boldon CA	1-3
Heaton Stannington v Seaham CW Red Star	1-2
Norton CCT v Annfield Plain	1-3
Whickham v Eppleton CW	4-0
Guiseley v Tadcaster Albion	0-1
Leeds Polytechnic v Darlington RA	0-2

Harrogate T v Thackley	0-5
Irlam T v Leyland Motors	1-1,1-0
Fleetwood T v Little Lever	3-0
Linotype v Hoylake Ath	2-1
Lytham v Warrington T	2-1
Salford Amateurs v Nelson	2-1
Waterloo Dock v Curzon Ashton	3-0
Brook Sports v Chadderton	4-1
Norton Woodseats v Anson Villa	1-0
North Withington v Ossett Albion	1-1,1-2
Appleby FA v Denaby U	2-1 aet
Ossett T v Ruston Sports	2-0
Bentley Vic v Normanby PW	2-1
Hall Road Rangers v Brigg T	5-1
Clipstone Welfare v Gainsborough U	0-1
Rawmarsh Welfare v Retford T	2-3
Bourne T v Oakham U	2-0
Skegness T v Mirrlees Blackstone	5-0
Hinckley T v Paget Rangers	0-1
Rothwell T v Long Eaton Grange	0-0,1-3
Gresley R v Newfoundpool WMC	0-1
Walsall Sportsco v Knowle	1-0
Oldbury U v Shepshed Charterhouse	1-3
Coventry Sporting v Gornal Ath	2-0
Northfield T v Armitage	2-4
Kidsgrove Ath v Bridgnorth T	2-0
Willenhall T v West Midlands Police	3-2
Evesham U v Anstey Nomads	0-2
Racing Club (Warwick) v Brierley Hill A	1-0 aet
Malvern T v Astwood Bank	3-1
Moreton T v Wednesfield Social	2-6
Halesowen T v Ledbury T	4-4,3-1
Felixstowe T v Watton U	3-1
Soham T Rangers v Beccles	2-0
CNSOBU v Stowmarket	2-1
Haverhill R v Royston T	0-2
Vauxhall Motors v March TU	0-1
St Neots T v Shillington	6-1
Pirton v Bicester T	0-2
Northampton Spencer v Berkhamsted T	1-2
Stansted v Baldock T	1-4
Rushden T v Ely C	2-0
Histon v Ampthill T	2-2,2-0
Wootton Blue Cross v Olney T	3-1
Thame U v Letchworth GC	0-1
Arlesey T v Wolverton T & BR	1-0
Kidlington v Amersham T	1-2
Witham T v Basildon U	0-4
Brightlingsea U v Rainham T	1-1,0-1
Leyton-wingate v Heybridge Swifts	2-2,3-1
Coggeshall T v Bowers U	2-1
Faversham T v Ringmer	1-1,4-0
Swanley T v Herne Bay	3-0
Whitstable T v Tunbridge Wells	1-2
West Wickham v Tansley	2-0 aet
Crockenhill v Cheshunt	0-6
Selby v Woodford T	3-1
Banstead Ath v Whyteleafe	2-0
Dartford Glentworth v Grays Ath	0-3
Hoddesdon T v Welling U	3-2
Sun Sports v Kew Association	4-4,0-1
Willesden v Ruislip Manor	1-3

Feltham v Cray W	4-1 aet
Civil Service v Redhill	1-2
Merstham v LB of Greenwich	2-1
Uxbridge v Chessington U	3-0
Arundel v Alton T	1-4
First Town U v Littlehampton T	4-4,2-0
Amesbury v St Martins	1-2 aet
Sholing Sports v Newbury T	0-1
Worthing v Brading T	2-0
Newport IOW v Chichester C	7-0
Malden Vale v Dorking T	2-0
Ash United v Shoreham	4-0
Steyning v Egham T	1-3
Camberley T v Wallingford T	4-3
Windsor & Eton v Chertsey T	2-1
BAC (Weybridge) v Chobham	2-1
Abingdon T v Hazells	1-0
Larkhall Ath v Peasedown Ath	1-2
Worrall Hill v Bristol St George	1-1,2-0
Clanfield v Cadbury Heath	2-0
Westbury U v Shortwood U	3-2 aet
Forest Green R v Yate R	1-1,3-1 aet
Sharpness v Westland-Yeovil	1-2
Radstock T v Keynsham T	1-2
Illogan RBL v Exmouth T	0-1
Ilminster T v Brixham U	3-2

Second Round

Blue Star v Wingate	2-1
Seaham CW Red Star v Annfield Plain	4-1
Washington v Boldon CA	1-3
Whickham v Darlington RA	3-0
Thackley v Fleetwood T	1-1
Prescot T v Hallam	4-3
Lytham v Salford Amateurs	4-0
Ossett Albion v Waterloo Dock	2-1
Leeds Ashley Road v Linotype	2-1
Norton Woodseats v Irlam T	4-2
Ossett T v Tadcaster Albion	2-0
Gainsborough U v Winterton Rangers	0-2
Appleby FA v Hall Road Rangers	3-1
Lincoln U v Brook Sports	6-3
Retford T v Kidsgrove Ath	2-1
Frecheville Community v Bentley Vic	0-1
Sheffield v Congleton T	4-1
Shepshed Charterhouse v Armitage	4-0
Wigston Fields v Skegness T	0-1
Rushden T v Newfoundpool WMC	5-1
Bourne T v Stamford	2-1
Coventry Sporting v Friar Lane OB	0-1
Wednesfield Social v Long Eaton Grange	2-1
Paget Rangers v Hinckley Ath	1-2
Anstey Nomads v Blakenhall	1-0
Racing Club (Warwick) v Irthlingborough	0-0
Willenhall T v Walsall Sportsco	3-1
Halesowen T v Malvern T	5-1
Buckingham T v Bicester T	1-3
CNSOBU v Soham T Rangers	0-7
Felixstowe T v Coggleshall T	2-1
Egham T v Leyton-Wingate	1-4
Barton R v Wootton Blue Cross	3-1 aet
Feltham v Epping T	2-3 aet

Hoddesdon T v Royston T	0-1 aet
St Neots T v Letchworth GC	4-3 aet
Histon v March TU	3-1 aet
Arlesley T v Kempston R	2-1
Selby v Camberley T	0-2
Tring T v Ruislip Manor	2-0
Berkhamsted T v Burnham	2-3
*Billericay T v Rainham T	2-1 aet
Baldock T v Cheshunt	0-5
East Ham U v Basildon U	2-0
Grays Ath v Swanley T	1-0
Windsor & Eton v Banstead Ath	4-1
Kew Association v Haringey Bor	3-5
Molesey v Malden Vale	3-2
Amersham T v Farnborough T	0-1
BAC (Weybridge) v Uxbridge	1-2
Abingdon T v Newbury T	1-3
Eastbourne U v Faversham T	3-1
Merstham v Alma Swanley	1-2
Eastbourne T v Tunbridge Wells	1-2
Redhill v West Wickham	0-2
Newport IOW v Gosport Bor	0-1
Worthing v Ash U	4-2
St Martins v First Tower U	1-0
Hungerford T v Alton T	3-4
Clanfield v Worrall Hill	2-1
Westbury U v Peasedown Ath	0-1
Almondsbury Greenway v Forest Green R	5-0
Exmouth T v Ilminster T	1-4 aet
Westland-Yeovil v Keynsham T	1-0

Replays
Fleetwood T v Thackley	0-3
Irthlingborough D v Racing Club (Warwick)	2-1 aet

Third Round
Seaham CW Red Star v Ossett T	4-0
Leeds Ashley Road v Winterton Rangers	1-1,2-3
Bentley Vic v Bolden CA	3-2
Blue Star v Whickham	2-4
Ossett Albion v Prescot T	0-2
Thackley v Lytham	1-1,2-1 aet
Friar Lane OB v Sheffield	4-2 aet
Skegness T v Bourne T	7-2
Lincoln U v Appleby Frodingham Ath	1-1,3-3,3-0
Willenhall T v Retford T	3-1
Norton Woodseats v Shepshed Charterhouse	1-2
St Neots T v Irthlingborough D	2-4
Anstey Nomads v Halesowen T	7-0
Hinckley Ath v Wednesfield Social	2-1
Rushden T v Bicester T	0-3
Billericay T v Epping T	5-0
Royston T v Histon	2-1
Felixstowe T v Soham T Rangers	4-4,1-3
Haringey Bor v Tring T	3-1
Cheshunt v East Ham U	5-2
Arlesley T v Leyton-Wingate	0-2
Tunbridge Wells v Uxbridge	0-0,2-1 aet
Eastbourne U v Alma Swanley	3-0
Molesey v Grays Ath	1-0
West Wickham v Farnborough T	2-2 aet,2-3
Windsor & Eton v Newbury T	4-2

Clanfield v Camberley T	0-2
Barton R v Burnham	2-1
Alton T v Worthing	1-2
Gosport Bor v St Martins	3-1
Westland-Yeovil v Almondsbury Greenway	0-2
Peasedown Ath v Ilminster T	2-1

Fourth Round
Seaham CW Red Star v Prescot T	1-1,3-1
Thackley v Wickham	2-2,0-2
Bentley Vic v Winterton Rangers	0-2
Irthlingborough D v Anstey Nomads	2-1
Lincoln U v Willenhall T	2-3
Shepshed Charterhouse v Skegness T	1-0
Friar Lane OB v Hickley Ath	1-0
Billericay T v Royston T	2-0
Haringey Bor v Barton R	1-2
Bicester T v Cheshunt	0-2
Soham Town Rangers v Leyton-Wingate	1-2
Windsor & Eton v Almondsbury Greenway	0-2
Camberley T v Eastbourne U	1-2
Molesey v Farnborough T	2-4
Gosport Bor v Tunbridge Wells	4-2
Worthing v Peasedown Ath	5-2

Fifth Round
Shepshed Charterhouse v Winterton R	4-2
Whickham v Seaham CW Red Star	5-2
Friar Lane OB v Barton R	2-4
Willenhall T v Irthlingborough D	2-1
Leyton-Wingate v Eastbourne U	0-0,0-2
Cheshunt v Farnborough T	0-4
Worthing v Billericay T	1-2
Gosport Bor v Almondsbury Greenway	1-1,3-4

Sixth Round
Whickham v Willenhall T	3-2
Barton R v Shepshed Charterhouse	2-3
Eastbourne U v Billericay T	0-1
Almondsbury Greenway v Farnborough T	3-1

Semi Final Ties

First Leg
Billericay T v Shepshed Charterhouse	2-0
Almondsbury Greenway v Whickham	1-0

Second Leg
Shepshed Charterhouse v Billericay	2-0
Whickham v Almondsbury Greenway	1-1

Replay
Billericay T v Shepshed Charterhouse	2-0

At Cambridge CFC

Final at Wembley (*Attendance:* 16 792)
Billericay T 4 (Young 3, Clayden)
Almondsbury Greenway 1 (Price)
Billericay T: Norris; Blackaller, Bingham, Whettell, Bone, Reeves, Pullen, Scott, Clayden, Young, Groom (Carrigan).
Almondsbury Greenway: Hamilton; Bowers Phil, Scarrett, Sullivan, Tudor (Kilbaine), Wookey, Bowers Peter, Shehean, Kerr, Butt, Price.

THE LAST FIVE

FA CHALLENGE VASE 1986-87

Preliminary Round

Shotton Comrades v Esh Winning	5-0
Shildon v Horden Colliery Welfare	3-0
Washington v Nunthorpe Athletic	4-1
West Auckland Town v Langley Park Welfare	2-0
South Shields v Seaton Delaval ST	1-2
Newton Aycliffe v Murton	1-3
Ashington v Evenwood Town	2-1
Northallerton Town v Annfield Plain	0-3
Bridlington Town v Durham City	0-1
Darlington CB v Cleator Moor Celtic	2-3
West Allotment Celtic v Wingate (Durham)	2-1
Norton & Stockton Anc v Harrogate Railway	1-2
Marchon Social v Seaham CW Red Star	3-0
Burscough v Atherton LR	2-1
Flixton v Skelmersdale United	3-3,3-0
St Dominics v Waterloo Dock	3-6
Prescot Cables v Burnley Belvedere	4-0
Irlam Town v Curzon Ashton	3-2
Cheadle Town v Ashton United	0-1
Lancaster City v Chadderton	2-0
Rossendale United v Kirkby Town	1-1,2-1
Maine Road v Linotype	2-3
Wren Rovers v Ford Motors (L'pool)	1-0
Droylsden v Oldham Town	4-1
Poulton Victoria v Heswall	3-0
Atherton Collieries v Maghull	2-1
St Helens Town v General Chemicals	2-1
Ellesmere Port & Neston v Prestwich Heys	5-1
Rylands v Darwen	5-3
Hatfield Main v Louth United	0-1
Stapenhill v Brigg Town	2-1
Armthorpe Welfare v Ossett Town	1-0
Clipstone Welfare v Radford Olympic	1-1,1-0
Garforth Town v Boston	2-1
Graham St Prims v Sheffield	0-1
Oakham United v Maltby Miners Welfare	2-0
Thackley v Grimethorpe Miners Welfare	1-2
Harworth CI v Bentley Victoria	2-0
Bradley Rangers v Long Eaton United	1-0
Bourne Town v Liversedge	2-1
Woolley MW v Pilkington Recreation	2-0
Hall Road Rangers v Kimberley Town	0-1
Arnold Kingswell v Holbeach United	3-1
Farsley Celtic v Immingham Town	2-0
Borrowash Victoria v Denaby United	3-2
Yorkshire Amateurs v Denaby United	0-5
Mickleover RBL v Emley	0-1
Tadcaster Albion v Collingham	0-2
Belper Town v Harrogate Town	3-6
Spalding United v North Ferriby United	3-2
Rowntree Mackintosh v Fryston CW	1-0
Gresley Rovers v Long Buckby	2-1
Chasetown v Walsall Wood	1-0
Wolverton Town v Evesham United	2-0
Malvern Town v Lye Town	3-2

Highgate United v Northampton Spencer	5-1
Mile Oak Rovers v Youth & Olswinford	0-2
Westfields v Desborough Town	4-1
Wednesfield Social v GKN Sankey	3-1
Coventry Sporting v Rushden Town	0-0,3-1
West Midlands Police v Eastwood Hanley	4-6
Brackley Town v Hinckley Town	0-1
Anstey Nomads v Wigston Fields	4-2
Brereton Social v Friar Lane OB	9-1
Tividale v Bridgnorth Town	0-1
Solihull Borough v Northfield	2-3
Rocester v Blakenall	2-0
(at Leek Town)	
Rushall Olympic v Racing Club Warwick	1-1,2-1
Stratford Town v Paget Rangers	1-2
Rothwell Town v Boldmere St Michaels	0-8
Ware v Rainham Town	1-2
Stowmarket Town v Raunds Town	3-1
Brightlingsea United v Newmarket Town	3-2
Witham Town v Baker Perkins	3-1
Thetford Town v RSSC Ransomes	1-0
March Town United v Soham Town Rangers	1-2
Somersham Town v Halstead Town	1-4
Harwich & Parkeston v Saffron Walden Town	2-4
Maldon Town v Haverhill Rovers	0-1
Hadleigh United v Watton United	2-3
Felixstowe Town v Woodford Town	1-3
Ely City v St Ives Town	0-2
Lowestoft Town v Histon	1-1,4-0
Chatteris Town v Beckton United	0-5
Tiptree United v Brantham Athletic	4-1
Downham Town v Bowers United	4-2
Eynesbury Rovers v East Thurrock United	2-2,1-0
Rayners Lane v Stotfold	1-0
Shillington v Leighton Town	4-0
Selby v Feltham	3-2
Hanwell Town v Newport Pagnell Town	1-0
Chalfont St Peter v Flackwell Heath	1-2
Beaconsfield United v Norsemen	1-0
Cockfosters v Milton Keynes Borough	4-2
St Margaretsbury v Potton United	4-1
Winslow United v Hoddesdon Town	1-2
Ruislip v Tring Town	1-2
Hazells (Aylesbury) v Wooton Blue Cross	1-0
Royston Town v Yeading	1-2
Hounslow v Clapton	3-1
Edgware v Vauxhall Motors	0-0,1-2
Maidenhead Town v London Colney	0-6
The 61 FC (Luton) v Hertford Town	0-4
Welwyn Garden City v Letchworth GC	2-0
Leavesden Hospital v Molesey	4-1
Pirton v Brimsdown Rovers	0-1
Berkhamstead Town v Kempston Rovers	2-1
Ruislip Manor v Hemel Hempstead	1-2
Northwood v Haringey Borough	2-2,1-4
Arlesey Town v Amersham Town	2-3
Eaton Bray United v Ampthill Town	2-1
Corinthian v Shoreham	3-0

Ringmer v Herne Bay	2-1
Redhill v Eastbourne Town	0-1
East Grinstead v Hythe Town	1-3
Chobham v Eastbourne United	1-2
Lancing v Burgess Hill Town	2-2,1-3
Petersfield United v Horsham YMCA	6-4
Portfield v Merstham	4-3
Whitehawk v Godalming Town	1-0
Mount Grace (Potters Bar) v Swanley Town	2-1
Farnham Town v Wick	2-1
Metropolitan Police v Whitstable Town	6-2
Hailsham Town v Cobham	1-2
Dorking v West Wickham	2-2,2-0
Horsham v Farleigh Rovers	5-2
Slade Green v Frimley Green	1-2
Greenwich Borough v Horley Town	5-0
Thames Polytechnic v Hastings Town	0-0,4-2
Malden Vale v Chichester City	5-0
Chertsey Town v Portsmouth RN	1-2
Pagham v Faversham Town	0-1
Egham Town v Littlehampton Town	0-2
Banstead Athletic v Arundel	2-1
Darenth Heathside v Ash United	0-3
Warminster Town v Road Sea (Southampton)	0-5
Patchway v Lymington Town	1-1,1-2
Hungerford Town v Wallingford Town	4-0
Bicester Town v Eastleigh	0-2
Didcot Town v Brockenhurst	1-3
Wantage Town v Horndean	1-0
Abingdon United v Calne Town	0-2
Supermarine v Clanfield	2-1
Wotton Rovers v Romsey Town	3-1
Chard Town v Bridport	4-2
Westbury United v Falmouth Town	1-4
Welton Rovers v Wimborne Town	0-2
Bristol Manor Farm v Port of Bristol	2-2,3-1
Larkhall Athletic v Clevedon Town	0-4
Cirencester Town v Almondsbury Greenway	2-0
Odd Down v Cinderford Town	2-1
Mangotsfield United v Radstock Town	5-3
Pegasus Juniors v Ottery St Mary	4-2
Yate Town v Hengrove Athletic	4-1
St Blazey v Flight Refuelling	2-2,2-1
Robinsons DRG v Keynsham Town	3-1
Avon (Bradford) v Paulton Rovers	0-3
Tiverton Town v Dawlish Town	0-3
Glastonbury v Portway Bristol	0-2
Fairford Town v Wellington	3-3,1-1,4-3
(at Forest Green Rovers)	

First Round

Shotton Comrades v West Allotment Celtic	2-3
Seaton Delaval Seaton Terrace v Shildon	2-0
Whickham v Washington	2-0
Durham City v Marchon Social	3-0
West Auckland Town v Coundon TT	3-2
Murton v Harrogate Railway	2-0
Annfield Plain v Ashington	2-3
Cleator Moor Celtic v Eppleton CW	3-3,2-1
Poulton Victoria v Ashton United	3-2
Irlam Town v Rylands	4-0
Prescot Cables v Linotype	1-2*
Clitheroe v Flixton	1-2

Burscough v Guiseley	1-2
Rossendale United v Waterloo Dock	2-0
St Helens Town v Wren Rovers	2-0
Droylsden v Ellesmere Port & Neston	1-0
Atherton Collieries v Lancaster City	0-1
Spalding United v Stapenhill	1-0
Emley v Sheffield	4-2
Farsley Celtic v Grimethorpe MW	4-0
Garforth Town v Armthorpe Welfare	1-0
Louth United v Woolley Miners Welfare	3-1
Bradley Rangers v Clipstone Welfare	2-1
Arnold Kingswell v Rowntree Mackintosh	2-0
Hallam v Frecheville Community	2-0
Borrowash Victoria v Harworth CI	3-0
Bourne Town v Kimberley Town	2-3
Collingham v Harrogate Town	1-2
Ossett Albion v Oakham United	2-3
Wednesfield Social v Wolverton Town	2-1
Highgate United v Malvern Town	0-1
Bridgnorth Town v Brereton Social	2-0
Gresley Rovers v Eastwood Hanley	2-1
Rocester v Hinkley Town	3-1
(at Leek Town)	
Hinckley Athletic v Westfields	1-2
Northfield v Anstey Nomads	2-3
Tamworth v Oldswinford	3-2
Coventry Sporting v Bilston Town	3-0
Rushall Olympic v Chasetown	3-2
Boldmere St Michaels v Paget Rangers	1-1,1-2
Rainham Town v Soham Town Rangers	3-3,5-1
Stowmarket Town v Brightlingsea United	1-1,5-0
St Ives Town v Woodford Town	2-4
Wivenhoe Town v Saffron Walden Town	3-0
Haverhill Rovers v Beckton United	2-2, 2-1
Gorleston v Thetford Town	4-0
Lowestoft Town v Watton United	2-3
Great Yarmouth Town v Witham Town	1-3
Bury Town v Halstead Town	5-5,5-0
Tiptree United v Skegness Town	2-1
Downham Town v Eynesbury Rovers	4-3
Amersham Town v Flackwell Heath	0-3
Hazells (Aylesbury) v Vauxhall Motors	0-1
Tring Town v Haringey Borough	1-2
Shillington v Beaconsfield United	3-2
Welwyn Garden City v Hoddesdon Town	0-1
Hounslow v London Colney	1-0
Barton Rovers v Hanwell Town	4-0
Baldock Town v Hemel Hempstead Town	3-0
Hertford Town v St Margaretsbury	2-2,1-0
Brimsdown Rovers v Leavesden Hospital	1-0
Selby v Rayners Lane	2-0
Eaton Bray United v Cheshunt	5-1
Cockfosters v Marlow	1-2
Berkhamsted Town v Yeading	1-3
Greenwich Borough v Cray Wanderers	4-0
Alma Swanley v Tunbridge Wells	3-1
Thames Polytechnic v Hythe Town	1-4
Dorking v Frimley Green	1-0
Faversham Town v Corinthian Casuals	0-0,2-1
Crockenhill v Eastbourne United	2-0
Horsham v Petersfield United	2-1
Farnham Town v Banstead Athletic	0-0,1-2
Eastbourne Town v Burgess Hill Town	4-1

Corinthian v Ash United	4-1
Three Bridges v Portsmouth RN	1-0
Ringmer v Mount Grace (Potters Bar)	2-3
Portfield v Littlehampton Town	1-3
Cobham v Whitehawk	3-3,0-2
Malden Vale v Metropolitan Police	1-0
Hungerford Town v Brockenhurst	4-0
Totton AFC v Wotton Rovers	2-0
Road Sea (Southampton) v Lymington T	1-1,1-1,0-2
Newbury Town v Supermarine	0-2
Wantage Town v Thatcham Town	2-0
Eastleigh v Calne Town	4-0
Chippenham Town v Moreton Town	3-1
Falmouth Town v Bristol Manor Farm	1-0
Portway Bristol v Cirencester Town	3-1
Robinsons DRG v Clevedon Town	1-1,1-2
Dawlish Town v Yate Town	3-2
Mangotsfield United v Devizes Town	4-1
Fairford Town v Paulton Rovers	0-3
Chard Town v St Blazey	2-8
Shortwood United v Pegasus Juniors	2-1
Odd Down v Wimborne Town	0-1

Second Round

Ashington v Garforth Town	1-5
Murton v Cleator Moor Celtic	1-0
Rossendale United v Durham City	4-2
Farsley Celtic v Seaton Delaval ST	1-2
Guiseley v Lancaster City	4-1
Whickham v Hallam	1-0
West Auckland Town v Emley	0-3
St Helens Town v Guisborough Town	1-0
West Allotment Celtic v Fleetwood Town	2-0
Louth United v Warrington Town	2-4
Rocester v Bradley Rangers	1-0
(at Eastwood Hanley)	
Harrogate Town v Flixton	2-1
Rainworth Miners Welfare v Irlam Town	1-0
Kimberley Town v Hucknall CW	1-2
Linotype v Wythenshawe Amateurs	1-2
Droylsden v Lincoln United	4-1
Oakham United v Borrowash Victoria	0-2
Poulton Victoria v Arnold Kingswell	3-0
Shillington v Atherstone United	1-2
Downham Town v Staveley Works	3-1
Westfields v Spalding United	5-2
Paget Rangers v Rushall Olympic	4-2
Halesowen Town v Malvern Town	2-0
Anstey Nomads v Tamworth	0-4
Stamford v Wisbech Town	0-1
Wednesfield Social v Bridgnorth Town	1-3
Buckingham Town v Irthlingborough Diamonds	2-1
Gresley Rovers v Coventry Sporting	3-0
Baldock Town v Tiptree United	1-0
Vauxhall Motors v Wivenhoe Town	2-1
Watton United v Marlow	4-1
Rainham Town v Collier Row	0-2
Hertford Town v Hoddesdon Town	3-0
Barton Rovers v Stowmarket Town	0-0,1-0
Haringey Borough v Woodford Town	3-5
Witham Town v Bury Town	4-3
Braintree Town v Brimsdown Rovers	3-2
Stansted v Flackwell Heath	1-3

Haverhill Rovers v Gorleston	3-2
Eaton Bray United v Selby	1-2
Sudbury Town v Yeading	1-5
Hounslow v Heybridge Swifts	0-1
Newport IOW v Whyteleafe	3-0
Three Bridges v Whitehawk	1-0
Corinthian v Malden Vale	2-0
Alma Swanley v Southall	3-0
Steyning Town v Eastbourne Town	3-2
Hythe Town v Harefield United	1-2
Littlehampton Town v Faversham Town	5-2
Havant Town v Banstead Athletic	3-0
Crockenhill v Camberley Town	3-1
Dorking v Mount Grace (Potters Bar)	2-1
Horsham v Greenwich Borough	2-1
Torrington v Sholing Sports	3-2
Dawlish Town v St Blazey	1-0
Clevedon Town v Shortwood United	3-0
Totton AFC v Old Georgians	0-2
Sharpness v Portway Bristol	2-3
Lymington Town v Abingdon Town	1-4
Paulton Rovers v Wantage Town	0-1
Exmouth Town v Falmouth Town	1-3
Wimborne Town v Eastleigh	1-1,3-0
Supermarine v Mangotsfield	3-5
Chippenham Town v Hungerford Town	1-2

Third Round

Poulton Victoria v Murton	2-4
Rossendale United v Droylsden	4-3
Emley v Seaton Delaval ST	1-1,2-1
Warrington Town v Borrowash Victoria	2-0
Garforth Town v West Allotment Celtic	3-2
Whickham v Harrogate Town	3-2
St Helens Town v Wythenshawe Amateurs	4-1
Guiseley v Rainworth Miners Welfare	2-4
Wisbech Town v Paget Rangers	1-1,2-0
Bridgnorth Town v Atherstone United	3-4
Halesowen Town v Watton United	2-2,2-0
(at Tividale)	
Rocester v Downham Town	4-0
(at Leek Town)	
Buckingham Town v Westfields	2-3
Gresley Rovers v Hucknall CW	2-1
Tamworth v Baldock Town	1-0
Haverhill Rovers v Littlehampton Town	2-0
Witham Town v Harefield United	2-0
Three Bridges v Yeading	0-2
Woodford Town v Braintree Town	2-1
Barton Rovers v Vauxhall Motors	0-0,1-2
Corinthian v Crockenhill	1-1,1-1,4-1
Selby v Flackwell Heath	2-1
Heybridge Swifts v Steyning Town	1-0
Collier Row v Alma Swanley	2-1
Horsham v Hertford Town	2-1
Havant Town v Dorking	2-0
Portway Bristol v Clevedon Town	1-2
Mangotsfield United v Newport IOW	3-1
Torrington v Falmouth Town	1-1,0-3
Wimborne Town v Abingdon Town	2-3
Wantage Town v Old Georgians	0-2
Hungerford Town v Dawlish Town	0-1

Fourth Round

Garforth Town v Murton	3-2
Warrington Town v Gresley Rovers	4-3
Rainworth Miners Wel v Atherstone Utd	2-1
Wisbech Town v St Helens Town	0-2
Rocester v Halesowen Town	3-1
(at Leek Town FC)	
Rossendale United v Tamworth	1-0
Whickham v Emley 0-2	
Witham Town v Yeading	2-1
Heybridge Swifts v Corinthian	3-0
Vauxhall Motors v Westfields	3-2
Havant Town v Selby	2-0
Collier Row v Horsham	0-0,3-1
Haverhill Rovers v Woodford Town	1-0
Old Georgians v Dawlish Town	2-3
Abingdon Town v Mangotsfield United	1-3
Clevedon Town v Falmouth Town	0-1

Fifth Round

Rocester v Garforth Town	1-3
St Helens Town v Rainworth MW	4-1
Warrington Town v Vauxhall Motors	2-1
Emley v Rossendale United	2-1
Haverhill Rovers v Heybridge Swifts	2-0
Havant Town v Collier Row	2-2,4-5
Witham Town v Falmouth Town	1-2
Mangotsfield United v Dawlish Town	1-2

ixth Round

Falmouth Town v St Helens	1-1,0-1
Haverhill Rovers v Warrington Town	1-3(aet)
Emley v Dawlish Town	3-2
Collier Row v Garforth Town	2-1

Semi-final First Leg

St Helens v Emley	0-1
Warrington Town v Collier Row	2-0

Semi-final Second Leg

Emley v St Helens Town	0-2
Collier Row v Warrington Town	0-1

Final *(Attendance:* 4254)

St Helens 3 (Lay 2, Rigby) **Warrington 2** (Reid, Cook)
Referee: T Mills
St Helens: Johnston, Benson, Lowe, Bendon, Wilson, McComb, Collins (Gledhill), O'Neill, Cummins, Lay, Rigby. Sub: Deakin.
Warrington: O'Brien, Copeland, Hunter, Gratton, Whalley, Reid, Brownville (Woodyer), Cook, Kinsey, Looker (Hill), Hughes.

FA CHALLENGE VASE 1987-88

Preliminary Round

Durham City v Tees Components	4-0	Rylands v Irlam Town	1-3
Prudhoe East End v Marske Utd	3-1	Atherton Collieries v Burnley Belvedere	3-2
Bridlington Trinity v Seaton Delaval ST	0-2	Clitheroe v Ashton Utd	0-2
Harrogate T v Rowntree Mackintosh	1-0	Nelson v Uniasco	1-2
Dormans Ath v Coundon TT	0-2	Newton v Cheadle Town	2-4
Sporting Club Vaux v Langley Pk Welfare	6-3	Fryston CW v Radford	0-2
Ashington v Norton & Stockton Anc	2-1	Immingham Town v Maltby MW	1-1,1-2
Harrogate Railway v Willington	0-1	Clipstone Welfare v Oakham Utd	3-2
Wren Rovers v Gosforth St Nicholas	1-1,1-0	Hatfield Main v Belper Town	0-0,1-1,3-2
Bridlington Town v Washington	3-0	N Ferriby Utd v Denaby Utd	2-1
Marchon Social v Dawdon CW	0-0,1-3	Stapenhill v Hinckley Town	2-3
Esh Winning v Evenwood Town	2-2,1-3	Arnold Kingswell v Liversedge	1-0
W Auckland T v Newton Aycliffe	3-1	Harworth Cl v Skegness Town	4-0
Annfield Plain v Boldon CA	2-1	Hall Road Rangers v Woolley MW	2-3
Darlington CB v Alnwick Town	1-2	Rossington Main v Boston	2-2,1-4
Shotton Comrades v Gt Harwood Town	0-3	Farsley Celtic v Ilkeston Town	3-0
South Shields v Cleator Moors Celtic	1-3	Hallam v Grimethorpe MW	1-0
Daisy Hill v Poulton Victoria	1-0	Sheffield v Kimberley Town	1-0
Leyland Motors v Heswall	0-3	Arnold v Bentley (walkover for Arnold)	
Chadderton v Merseyside Police	1-2	Derby Prims v Armthorpe Welfare	0-1
Ford Motors (L'pool) v Bootle	1-3	Ossett Albion v Thackley	0-3
Maine Road v Christleton	1-2	Ossett Town v Collingham	2-1
Skelmersdale Utd v General Chemicals	0-1	W Mids Police v Mile Oak R & Yth	1-2
Lancaster C v Atherton LR	0-0,3-2	Northampton Spencer v Kirby Muxloe	3-2
Darwen v St Dominics	5-2	Rushall Olympic v Stratford Town	3-1
Ellesmere Pt & Neston v Waterloo Dock	1-3	Friar Lane OB v Rushden Town	2-1
Burscough v Prescot Cables	2-0	Westfields v Spalding Utd	0-1
(at St Helens Town FC)		Boldmere St Michaels v Raunds Town	4-1
Colne Dynamoes v Glossop	5-2	Highgate utd v Desborough Town	0-2
Eastwood Hanley v Droylsden	2-1	Harrisons v Pegasus Juniors	4-2
		Lye Town v Bloxwich	2-0

FA VASE

Hinckley Athletic v Tividale	2-3	
GKN Sankey v Wednesfield Social	0-0,1-5	
Rothwell Town v Wigston Fields	3-0	
Brereton Social v Holbeach Utd	2-2,6-3	
Mirrlees Blackstone v Solihull Borough	2-1	
Chasetown v Bourne Town	5-0	
Racing Club Warwick v Oldbury Utd	3-2	
Long Eaton Utd v Long Buckby	4-0	
Redgate Utd v Hanley Town	0-2	
Brackley Town v Bilston Town	2-0	
Huntingdon Utd v Ely City	1-5	
Gt Yarmouth T v St Neots T	3-1	
St Margaretsbury v Brantham Athletic	5-2	
Coalite Yaxley v St Ives Town	4-2	
Eynesbury R v Royston Town	3-1	
Chatteris Town v Ramsey Town	2-0	
Hertford T v Letchworth GC	1-2	
LBC Ortonians v Eton Manor	3-2	
Harlow Town v Soham T Rangers	1-0	
Halstead T v Lowestoft T	1-2	
Sawbridgeworth T v Watton Utd	3-1	
RSSC Ransomes v Eaton Bray Utd (walkover for RSSC)		
Wivenhoe Town v Somersham Town	6-2	
Canvey Island v Histon	1-1,2-2,3-2	
Thetford Town v Gt Shelford	3-3,2-3	
Waltham Abbey v Saffron Walden T	1-2	
Harwich & Parkeston v Bowers Utd	1-0	
Newmarket T v Pirton	1-3	
March Town Utd v Aveley	4-3	
Tiptree Utd v Purfleet	2-2,2-2,2-4	
Kempston Rovers v Burnham Ramblers	1-1,1-2	
Hounslow v Electrolux	6-1	
Amersham Town v Beaconsfield Utd	0-3	
Barkingside v Totternhoe	1-0	
Newport Pagnell T v Southgate Ath	0-1	
Molesey v Brimsdown Rovers	2-1	
Milton Keynes Borough v Edgware	0-1	
Flackwell Heath v Ruislip Manor	1-1,0-2	
E Thurrock Utd v Welwyn GC	4-0	
Wingate (Herts) v Abingdon Utd	3-3,1-2	
Bicester T v Hoddesdon T	2-3	
Haringey Borough v Hanwell Town	3-1	
Tring Town v Wootton Blue Cross	1-2	
Arlesey Town v Park Street	2-0	
Metropolitan Police v Ware	0-1	
Chalfont St Peter v Norsemen	5-2	
Cockfosters v Shillington	0-1	
Ford Utd (London) v Leighton Town	1-3	
Biggleswade T v Northwood	0-2	
Ruislip v Berkhamsted Town	1-3	
Stotfold v Hornchurch	2-3	
Rainham T v Sandridge R	2-2,2-3	
Portfield v Ramsgate	0-5	
Whitehawk v East Grinstead	1-2	
Darenth Heathside v Eastbourne T	1-5	
Dorking v Thames Polytechnic	2-1	
Corinthian Casuals v West Wickham (at West Wickham)	0-2	
Wick v Hastings Town	0-1	
Greenwich Borough v Farnham Town	4-3	
Old Salesians v Egham Town	1-2	
Slade Green v Godalming Town	0-2	
Littlehampton T v Redhill	1-2	

Hythe Town v Chertsey Town	1-2	
Arundel v Faversham Town	1-3	
Lancing v Horley Town	0-0,1-3	
Bosham v Burgess Hill	1-1,0-4	
Sittingbourne v Shoreham	0-1	
Midland Bank v Cobham	0-1	
Corinthian v Pagham	2-1	
Banstead Ath v Peacehaven & Tels	1-2	
Haywards Heath v Farleigh Rovers	2-3	
Merstham v Southwark Sports	2-0	
Malden Vale v Hersham Town	2-2,2-1	
Bridport v Portsmouth RN	4-0	
Vale Recreation v Brockenhurst	2-2,4-4,9-1	
Bashley v Newbury Town	1-1,5-0	
Supermarine v Flight Refuelling	1-1,1-0	
Calne Town v Didcot Town	2-1	
Horndean v Swanage T & Herston	1-2	
Petersfield Utd v Eastleigh	0-1	
Warminster T v Wantage T	0-0,2-3	
Devizes T v Chichester T	3-2	
Thame Utd v First Tower Utd	5-1	
Sherborne T v Romsey T	1-5	
Westland Sports v Patchway	4-1	
Ilfracombe T v Almondsbury 85	3-2	
Westbury Utd v Tiverton T	5-0	
Bristol Manor Farm v Robinsons DRG	1-0	
Fairford T v Chard T	2-0	
Shortwood Utd v St Blazey	2-0	
Harrow Hill v Cinderford Town	2-3	
Blackwell Utd v Ottery St Mary	2-1	
Wimborne T v Glastonbury	2-1	
Portway Bristol v Keynsham T (walkover Keynsham T)		
Truro City v Yate Town	0-3	
Highworth T v Moreton T	1-2	
Port of Bristol v St Austell	1-2	
Hengrove Ath v Wootton Rovers	3-2	
Larkhall Ath v Paulton Rovers	6-3	
Wellington v Portishead	2-1	

First Round

Murton v Ashington	1-2	
Whickham v Prudhoe East End	1-1,2-3	
Bridlington Town v Annfield Plain	4-0	
Wren Rovers v Evenwood Town	2-0	
W Allotment Celtic v Sporting Club Vaux	2-3	
Durham C v Alnwick T	2-0	
Harrogate T v Coundon TT	2-3	
W Auckland T v Cleator Moor C	3-0	
Willington v Dawton CW	2-1	
Gt Harwood T v Seaton Delaval ST	1-1,2-1	
Rossendale Utd v Lancaster C	2-0	
Heswall v Rochester	2-1	
Burscough v Atherton Collieries	3-2	
Waterloo Dock v Eastwood Hanley	2-3	
Bridgnorth T v General Chemicals	3-0	
Daisy Hill v Ashton Utd	2-0	
Bootle v Christleton	4-3	
Irlam T v Cheadle T	3-0	
Darwen v Colne Dynamoes	1-4	
Merseyside Police v Uniasco	0-2	
Lincoln Utd v Staveley Works	3-2	
Borrowash Victoria v Arnold	2-4	
Harworth Cl v Gresley Rovers	0-1	

Hinckley T v Guiseley	0-2
Radford v Clipstone Welfare	1-2
Arnold Kingswell v Hallam	1-0
Woolley MW v Hatfield Main	2-2,0-0,0-2
(at Ossett Albion FC)	
Armthorpe Welfare v Thackley	2-4
Ossett Town v Maltby MW	2-2,0-1,1-5
(frist replay abandoned after 45 mins)	
Sheffield v N Ferriby Utd	1-3
Farsley Celtic v Boston	4-0
Irthlingborough D v Lye Town	3-0
Friar Lane OB v Northampton Spencer	1-2
Rothwell T v Racing Club Warwick	3-1
Wednesfield Social v Mirrlees Blackstone	3-1
Mile Oak R & Yth v Harrisons	4-1
Rushall Olympic v Long Eaton Utd	3-1
Boldmere St Michaels v Desborough T	1-3
Chasetown v Brackley T	0-1
Tividale v Brereton Social	3-0
Spalding Utd v Hanley Town	2-1
Stamford Utd v Chatteris Town	2-1
Harlow Town v Letchworth GC	0-3
Wivenhoe Town v Bury Town	2-3
Sawbridgeworth T v Harwich & Parkeston	1-2
Gt Shelford v Ely City	4-0
Saffron Walden T v Pirton	3-1
Gt Yarmouth Town v Gorleston	2-2,3-1
Canvey Island v Eynesbury Rovers	2-0
RSSC Ransomes v Purfleet	2-1
Stansted v St Margaretsbury	3-3,2-3
Coalite Yaxley v Lowestoft T	1-2
LBC Ortonians v March Town Utd	0-2
Molesey v Burnham Ramblers	2-0
Vauxhall Motors v Southgate Ath	1-2
Hoddesdon T v Beaconsfield Utd	5-0
Arlesey T v Hounslow	1-2
Sandridge Rovers v Haringey Borough	3-5
Yeading v Edgware	4-1
Hornchurch v Witham Town	0-2
Shillington v Baldock Town	1-0
Woodford T v Leighton T	1-0
Berkhamsted T v Barkingside	3-0
Barton Rovers v Wootton Blue Cross	4-0
Abingdon Utd v Ware	0-2
Ruislip Manor v Chalfont St Peter	0-3
E Thurrock Utd v Northwood	3-1
Faversham T v Shoreham	4-0
Chertsey Town v Merstham	2-2,3-2
Horsham v Crockenhill	4-0
Corinthian v Hastings Town	3-2
Ramsgate v Three Bridges	3-0
Egham T v Dorking	2-4
Thatcham T v Farleigh Rovers	3-0
Eastbourne T v Cobham	4-1
West Wickham v Horley Town	2-0
Peacehaven & Telscombe v Greenwich B	2-3
Burgess Hill T v Alma Swanley	4-0
Malden Vale v Godalming T	1-2
Redhill v East Grinstead	7-4
Vale Recreation v Thame Utd	5-2
Eastleigh v Supermarine	3-3,2-1
Romsey T v Swanage T & Herston	3-4
Bridport v Devizes Town	3-2

Bashley v Totton AFC	1-1,1-0
Wantage Town v Calne Town	2-2,3-1
Chippenham T v Hungerford T	0-1
Yate T v Westland Sports	6-0
Fairford T v Westbury Utd	1-2
Cinderford T v Ilfracombe Town	2-0
Wimborne T v Moreton T	1-3
Hengrove Ath v St Austell	1-1,2-3
Larkhall Ath v Clevedon T	2-3
Bristol Manor Farm v Shortwood Utd	1-2
Backwell Utd v Keynsham T	2-2,1-0
Wellington v Mangotsfield Utd	0-1

Second Round

Wren Rovers v Bridlington T	2-2,3-2
Prudhoe East End v Fleetwood T	1-3
Maltby MW v Willington	6-1
Thackley v Ashington	6-0
Hatfield Main v Gt Harwood T	5-0
Coundon TT v Colne Dynamoes	0-1
Sporting Club Vaux v Garforth T	2-0
Durham C v Rossendale Utd	4-0
W Auckland T v Guiseley	0-1
St Helens T v Rainworth MW	1-1,0-2
N Ferriby Utd v Hucknall T	0-0,2-1
Clipstone Welfare v Eastwood Hanley	0-2
Arnold Kingswell v Emley	2-6
Lincoln Utd v Daisy Hill	2-0
Heswall v Irlam T	2-1
Warrington T v Farsley Celtic	2-3
Wythenshawe Am v Bootle	2-0
Burscough v Uniasco	0-2
Wisbech T v Bridgnorth T	0-1
Tamworth v Arnold	4-0
Gresley R v Mile Oak R & Yth	3-0
Stamford v Atherstone Utd	0-4
Spalding Utd v Rushall Olympic	3-2
Rothwell T v Brackley T	1-1,1-1,0-5
Irthlingborough D v Buckingham T	4-0
Northampton Spen v Desborough T	4-2
Wednesfield Social v Tividale	2-3
Hounslow v March T Utd	3-2
Gt Yarmouth T v Haverhill R	0-1
Gt Shelford v Witham T	2-5
Braintree T v Woodford T	5-1
Chalfont St Peter v Ware	6-0
Letchworth GC v Bury T	1-2
Lowestoft T v Sudbury T	1-3
St Margaretsbury v Harwich & Parkeston	2-3
Hoddesdon T v Canvey Island	3-2
Heybridge Swifts v Berkhamsted T	1-2
RSSC Ransomes v Saffron Walden T	3-2
Shillington v Barton Rovers	1-0
Dorking v Greenwich Borough	2-1
Harefield Utd v Burgess Hill T	2-0
Camberley Town v Chertsey T	3-5
Redhill v Corinthian	1-1,0-4
West Wickham v Godalming T	2-0
Faversham T v Southgate Am	1-3
Ramsgate v Whyteleafe	0-2
E Thurrock Utd v Eastbourne T	1-0
Collier Row v Molesey	0-2
Southall v Horsham	2-3

Haringey B v Yeading	2-0
Vale Recreation v Westbury Utd	4-3
Abingdon T v Newport IOW	1-2
Thatcham T v Eastleigh	3-1
Sholing Sports v Wantage T	3-1
Havant T v Bashley	0-2
Hungerford T v Steyning T	8-1
Shortwood Utd v Moreton T	4-1
Falmouth T v Sharpness	3-2
Cinderford T v Bridport	0-3
St Austell v Swanage T & Herston	4-2
Mangotsfield Utd v Exmouth T	1-0
Yate T v Clevedon T	1-3
Backwell Utd v Old Georgians	1-2
Dawlish T v Torrington	1-1,2-0

Third Round

Fleetwood Town v Rainworth MW	2-0
Guisley v Emley	1-2
Colne Dynamoes v Heswall	2-0
Thackley v Maltby MW	4-1
Sporting Club Vaux v Wren Rovers	2-4
Durham City v Uniasco	2-2,1-1,1-0
Farsley Celtic v Eastwood (Hanley)	5-1
N Ferriby Utd v Wythenshawe Am	3-2
Lincoln Utd v Hatfield Main	0-3
Braintree T v Spalding Utd	1-0
Haringey Borough v Tividale	1-1,2-1
Bury Town v Atherstone Utd	2-3
Hoddesdon T v Harwich & Parkeston	0-2
Northampton Spen v Southgate Ath	4-4,3-1
Chalfont St Peter v E Thurrock Utd	2-1
Irthlingborough D v Brackley T	2-1
Haverhill Rovers v Berkhamsted T	2-1
Gresley R v RSSC Ransomes	0-0,2-1
Sudbury T v Shillington	2-0
Tamworth v Harefield Utd	2-0
Witham T v Bridgnorth T	0-4
Vale Recreation v Sholing Sports	3-1
Hounslow v Molesey	4-2
Hungerford Town v Whyteleafe	0-0,3-2
Newport IOW v Thatcham Town	2-3
Bashley v Dorking	1-0
Chertsey Town v Horsham	3-0
Corinthian v West Wickham	3-1
Bridport v Dawlish Town	2-1
Old Georgians v Clevedon	1-2
Shortwood Utd v St Austell	0-0,3-2
Mangotsfield Utd v Falmouth Town	0-2

Fourth Round

N Ferriby Utd v Wren Rovers	2-1
Hatfield Main v Farsley Celtic	1-1,0-3
Emley v Bridgnorth T	3-3,6-0
Durham City v Thackley	2-2,2-0
Colne Dynamoes v Fleetwood T	2-1
Tamworth v Haringey Borough	3-1
Haverhill Rovers v Atherstone Utd	0-4
Sudbury T v Irthlingborough Diam	5-3
Gresley R v Northampton Spen	2-1
Hungerford T v Braintree T	0-2
Corinthian v Harwich & Parkeston	3-0
Thatcham T v Chertsey T	0-2
Hounslow v Chalfont St Peter	1-0
Shortwood Utd v Falmouth T	2-3
Bashley v Vale Recreation	5-1
Bridport v Clevedon T	1-3

Fifth Round

Gresley Rovers v Emley	0-1
Durham City v Tamworth	4-2
Atherstone Utd v Colne Dynamoes	1-2
North Ferriby Utd v Farsley Celtic	1-2
Clevedon Town v Corinthian	2-1
Falmouth Town v Chertsey Town	0-0,1-2
Bashley v Hounslow	2-0
Sudbury Town v Braintree Town	1-0

Sixth Round

Durham City v Emley	2-4
Colne Dynamoes v Farsley Celtic	2-0
Sudbury Town v Clevedon Town	2-0
Chertsey Town v Bashley	1-3

Semi-final First Leg

Sudbury Town v Colne Dynamoes	1-1
Bashley v Emley	1-1

Semi-final Second Leg

Colne Dynamoes v Sudbury Town	2-0
Emley v Bashley	1-0

Final *(Attendance:* 15 000)
Colne Dynamoes 1 (Anderson) **Emley 0**
Referee: A Seville
Colne: Mason, McFalyen, Westwell, Bentley, Dunn, Roscoe, Rodaway, Whitehead (Burke), Diamond, Anderson, Wood (Coates).
Emley: Dennis, Fielding, Mellor, Codd, Hirst (Burrows), Gartland (Cook), Carmody, Green, Bramald, Devine, Francis.

FA CHALLENGE VASE 1988-89

Preliminary Round

South Shields v Eppleton CW	3-1
ESH Winning v Rowntree Mackintosh	0-4
Peterlee Newton v Harrogate RA	1-3
Alnwich Town v Horden CW	4-3
Darlington CB v Northallerton Town	0-1
Harrogate Town v Durham City	1-0
Dunston FB v Lancaster City	2-0
Norton & Stockton ANC v Seaton Delaval	0-1
Ponteland United v Pickering Town	1-0
Clitheroe v Arlington	3-2
West Auckland v Annfield Plain	0-2
Leyland Motors v Willington	4-1
Wren Rovers v Bridlington Town	0-0,0-3
Darwen v Langley Park Welfare	3-2
Cleator Moor Celtic v Shotton Comrades	2-1
Netherfield v Bedlington Terriers	3-1
Billingham Town v Bridlington Trinity	3-0
Consett v Boldon CA	2-0
Hebburn Reyrolle v Evenwood Town	3-0
Burscough v St Dominics	3-1
Poulton Victoria v Newton	2-0
Heswell v Merseyside Police	3-3,0-1
Droylsden v Prescot Cables	2-1
Bootle v Waterloo Dock	4-1
Daisy Hill v General Chemicals	1-2
Maine Road v Eastwood Hanley	1-2
Chadderton v Maghull	1-3
Meir KA v Curzon Ashton	1-2
Glossop v Newcastle Town	2-2,0-1
Atherton LR v Salford	1-2
Knypersley Vic v Vauxhall GM (Cheshire)	1-3
Irlam Town v Skelmersdale United	4-3
Formby v Ashton United	2-3
Armthorpe Welfare v Stapenhill	0-5
Belper Town v Kimberley Town	1-1,1-1,0-0,3-1
Staveley Works v Long Eaton United	2-0
Gainsborough Town v Radford	3-0
Grimethorpe MW v Melton Town	1-3
Louth United v Sheffield	3-0
Yorkshire Amateur v Heanor Town	1-2
Immingham Town v Oakham United	1-1,1-0
Ilkeston Town v Liversedge	3-2
Boston v Eccleshill United	0-4
Wigston Fields v Ossett Albion	1-2
Derby Prims v Brigg Town	0-4
Maltby MW v Sutton Town	1-0
Rossington Main v Denaby United	1-0
Hallam v Ossett Town	0-3
Kiveton Park v Arnold	1-0
Harworth CI v Collingham	1-0
Baker Perkins v Northfield Town	0-2
Racing Club Warwick v Oldbury United	5-2
Tividale v Harrisons	2-3
Wednesfield Social v Walsall Wood	3-2
Mile Oak Rovers & Yth v Paget Rangers	1-1,1-2
Hinckley Town v Rushall Olympic	2-1
Spalding United v Solihull Borough	1-2
Bilston Town v Anstey Nomads	0-1
Hinckley Athletic v Chasetown	1-2
Desborough Town v Ashtree Highfield	5-4

W Midlands Police v Highgate Utd	3-0
Lye Town v Evesham United	2-1
Long Buckby v Kings Heath	1-0
Malvern Town v Halesowen Harriers	0-1
Rushden Town v Brackley Town	2-2,3-0
Boldmere St Michaels v Rothwell Town	1-0
Eynesbury Rovers v Bourne Town	0-0,2-1
Sawbridgenorth T v Chatteris T	0-2
Norwich United v Harlow Town	0-1
Stansted v Downham Town	2-1
LBC Ortonians v Saffron Walden Town	0-2
Histon v Watton United	0-2
Newmarket Town v Gorleston	1-2
Halstead Town v Holbeach United	2-2,0-3
Great Yarmouth T v Stowmarket T	1-0
Clacton Town v Tiptree United	0-1
Thetford Town v Lowestoft Town	3-2
Burnham Ramblers v Brightlingsea Utd	4-0
St Ives Town v March Town Utd	1-5
Ely City v Brantham Athletic	5-5,4-2
Diss Town v Soham Town Rangers	3-2
Wroxham v Canvey Island	4-2
Felixstowe Town v Bowers Utd	6-2
Hemel Hempstead v Flackwell Heath	0-2
Maidenhead United v Wingate	4-0
Feltham v Wolverton Town (MK)	2-1
London Colney v Baldock Town	0-2
Shillington v Ford United (London)	0-2
Cheshunt v Wootton Blue Cross	2-2,4-1
Edgware Town v Berkhamsted Town	3-3,1-4
Hornchurch v The 61	1-2
Ruislip v Leighton Town	3-2
Aveley v Ruislip Manor	0-3
Hertford Town v Hanwell Town	2-1
Totternhoe v Kempston Rovers	3-1
Milton Keynes Borough v Clapton	1-0
Welwyn Garden City v Beckton United	4-0
Northwood v Letchworth Garden City	2-0
Barkingside v Finchley	0-2
Purfleet v Tring Town	0-1
Hoddesdon Town v Pirton	2-0
Selby v Langford	6-2
Amersham Town v Rainham Town	2-0
Arlesey Town v East Thurrock United	0-1
Stotfold v Potton United	2-1
Tilbury v Stevenage Borough	1-0
Rayners Lane v Royston Town	1-1,0-1
Southgate Athletic v Ware	1-2
Three Bridges v Deal Town	3-1
Bedfont v Faversham Town	3-1
Hythe Town v Sittingbourne	2-0
Egham Town v Eastbourne Town	2-2,1-2
Corinthian Casuals v Horsham YMCA	3-2
Redhill v Darenth Heathside	0-3
Peacehaven & Telscombe v Ringmer	1-2
Molesey v Hastings Town	1-2
Southward Borough v Langney Sports	4-2
Crockenhill v Banstead Athletic	2-3
Lancing v Whitehawk	0-1
Wandsworth & Norwood v Old Salesians	1-1,2-0
Cray Wanderers v Farnham Town	2-1

FA VASE

Chipstead v Whitstable Town	0-2	Belper Town v Ossett Albion	5-2
Chobham v Malden Vale	0-2	Thackley v Guiseley	0-3
Chatham Town v Epsom & Ewell	0-5	Kiveton Park v Hatfield Main	0-1
Oakwood v Haywards Heath	2-1	Lincoln United v Brigg Town	0-0,0-1
Burgess Hill Town v Canterbury City	1-0	Eccleshill United v Rossington Main	0-2
Pagham v Slade Green	4-1	Hucknall Town v Ilkeston Town	1-2
Beckenham Town v Littlehampton Town	1-0	Maltby MW v Borrowash Victoria	3-5
Herne Bay v Eastbourne United	2-7	Gainsborough Town v Stapenhill	2-1
Shoreham v Hailsham Town	0-1	Heanor Town v Harworth Cl	4-3
Ramsgate v Tunbridge Wells	1-0	Staveley Works v Louth United	1-2
West Wickham v Mertsham	2-0	Ossett Town v Immingham Town	2-1
Clanfield v Vale Recreation	7-4	Rushden Town v Wednesfield Social	4-0
Horndean v Portfield	2-1	Buckingham Town v Hinckley Town	0-3
Portsmouth RN v Bournemouth	2-2,2-3	Northampton Spencer v RC Warwick	0-1
Eastleigh v Bosham	3-1	Long Buckby v Boldmere St Michaels	1-2
Thame United v Wick	0-2	Lye Town v Stamford	1-2
Chichester Town v AFC Totton	3-4	Chasetown v W Midlands Police	1-2
East Cowes Victoria v Petersfield Utd	1-0	Desborough Town v Anstey Nomads	5-0
Didcot Town v Arundel	3-0	Harrisons v Paget Rangers	1-4
Newbury Town v Romsey Town	2-3	Solihull Borough v Northfield Town	0-2
Brockenhurst v Abingdon United	2-4	Halesowen Harriers v Irthlingborough D	3-0
Bicester Town v Hartley Wintney	2-0	Wroxham v Saffron Walden Town	2-1
Barnstaple Town v Odd Down	1-0	Eynesbury Rovers v Gorleston	3-1
DRG (FGP) v Calne Town	1-4	Harwich & Parkeston v Harlow Town	0-1
Sherborne Town v Poulton Rovers	1-3	Felixstowe Town v Ely City	3-3,5-2
Moreton Town v Fairford Town	2-1	March Town United v Heybridge Swifts	2-1
Chard Town v Westbury United	1-4	Tiptree United v Burnham Ramblers	0-2
Radstock Town v Penhill	2-1	Thetford Town v Great Yarmouth Town	0-5
Welton Rovers v Glastonbury	3-1	Stansted v Watton United	5-3
St Blazey v Minehead	1-3	Holbeach United v Chatteris Town	1-0
Melksham Town v Wellington	1-3	Diss Town v Bury Town	0-3
Chippenham Town v Pegasus Juniors	2-1	Flackwell Heath v Milton Keynes Bor	4-0
Swanage & Herston v Lawrence WH	1-1,1-2	Amersham Town v Tilbury	0-1
Yate Town v Almondsbury Picksons	2-1	Totternhoe v East Thurrock United	0-1
Larkhall Athletic v Tiverton Town	1-3	Ruislip v Baldock Town	3-3,0-4
Harrow Hill v Clandown	4-1	Selby v Vauxhall Motors	1-1,3-1
Truro City v Wimborne Town	2-1	Hertford Town v Tring Town	1-3
Bishops Cleeve v Bristol Manor Farm	1-0	Welwyn GC v Ford United (London)	0-3
Devizes Town v Brislington	2-1	Maidenhead United v Royston Town	2-5
		Hoddesdon Town v Feltham	2-0
First Round		Berkhamsted Town v Ware	1-1,2-0
Cleator Moor Celtic v Clitheroe	1-2,0-1	Hounslow v Northwood	3-2
(replay ordered due to ineligible Clitheroe player)		Finchley v Stotfold	1-0
Rowntree Mackintosh v Northallerton T	4-1	The 61 v Ruislip Manor	1-0
Annfield Plain v Leyland Motors	1-4	Cheshunt v Barton Rovers	2-0
South Shields v Darwen	4-1	Yeading v Wandsworth & Norwood	2-1
Dunston FB v Ponteland United	1-0	Pagham v Hailsham Town	2-4
Whickham v Seaton Delaval ST	3-0	Whitehawk v Beckenham Town	0-1
Bridlington Town v Alnwick Town	3-1	Hythe Town v Hastings Town	4-3
Billingham Town v West Allotment Celtic	0-2	Steyning Town v Burgess Hill Town	2-3
Harrogate RA v Harrogate Town	3-2	Banstead Athletic v Epsom & Ewell	1-2
Netherfield v Murton	0-2	Eastbourne Town v Cray Wanderers	3-3,3-0
Hebburn Reyrolle v Consett	1-3	Ramsgate v Three Bridges	1-1,0-0,0-2
Irlam Town v Newcastle Town	3-2	Oakwood v Bedfont	0-2
Rocester v Eastwood Hanley	0-0,0-1	West Wickham v Darenth Heathside	0-1
(first game abandoned after 97 mins due to fog)		Dorking v Whitstable Town	0-1
Merseyside Police v Vauxhall GM (Cheshire)	0-1	Malden Vale v Eastbourne United	1-0
Burscough v Rossendale United	1-6	Ringmer v Southwark Borough	2-1
Salford v Droylsden	1-1,1-2	Corinthian Casuals v Camberley Town	1-6
Maghull v Poulton Victoria	2-4	Wick v Eastleigh	2-0
Ashton United v General Chemicals	1-0	Romsey Town v AFC Totton	2-2,3-0
Bootle v Curzon Ashton	0-1	Abingdon United v Clanfield	4-1
North Ferriby Utd v Melton Town	1-0	Horndean v Thatcham Town	0-1

Didcot Town v East Cowes Victoria Ath	0-1
Bournemouth v Bicester Town	0-2
Tiverton Town v Minehead	2-0
Torrington v Poulton Rovers	1-2
Wellington v Chippenham Town	1-2
Shortwood United v Yate Town	0-1
Westbury United v Welton Rovers	0-2
Sharpness v Radstock Town	1-4
Lawrence Weston Hallen v Calne Town	4-1
Truro City v Exmouth Town	0-2
Barnstaple Town v Moreton Town	0-1
Harrow Hill v Bridport	0-2
Devizes Town v Bishops Cleeve	5-0

Second Round

Harrogate RA v Rossington Main	5-1
Garforth Town v Consett	1-0
Rowntree Mackintosh v Dunston FB	0-1
South Shields v Murton	3-4
Leyland Motors v Bridlington Town	0-1
Rossendale United v Farsley Celtic	3-2
West Allotment Celtic v Ossett Town	0-2
Colne Dyamoes v Emley	1-2
Clitheroe v Whickham	2-4
Brigg Town v Droylsden	4-1
Guiseley v Curzon Ashton	2-1
Gainsborough Town v Borrowash Victoria	1-3
Heanor Town v Hatfield Main	3-1
Ilkeston Town v Belper Town	3-1
Eastwood Hanley v St Helens Town	2-0
Irlam Town v North Ferriby United	0-3
Wythenshawe Amateurs v Louth United	2-2,0-2
Poulton Victoria v Ashton United	2-1
Vauxhall GM (Cheshire) v Warrington T	1-0
Hinckley Town v Boldmere St Michaels	0-2
Paget Rangers v Stamford	4-0
Desborough Town v Halesowen Harriers	0-2
W Midlands Police v Gresley Rovers	2-4
Northfield Town v Racing Club Warwick	2-0
Tamworth v Bridgenorth Town	2-1
March Town United v Rainworth MW	5-2
Wisbech Town v Rushden Town	2-1
Hoddesdon Town v Holbeach United	0-2
Braintree Town v Royston Town	3-1
Tring Town v East Thurrock United	2-4
Ford United (London) v Bury Town	0-2
Felixstowe Town v Great Yarmouth Town	1-1,2-4
Burnham Ramblers v Eynesbury Rovers	3-0
Sudbury Town v Baldock Town	2-0
Stansted v Cheshunt	0-1
Berkhamsted Town v Witham Town	3-2
Harefield United v Harlow Town	1-6
Wroxham v Finchley	0-1
Tilbury v The 61	4-1
Selby v Haverhill Rovers	1-1,0-2
Abingdon United v Bedfont	1-0
Horsham v Eastbourne Town	1-4
Ringmer v Hailsham Town	0-3
Hounslow v Sholing Sports	4-0
Bicester Town v Chertsey Town	0-3
Romsey Town v Hythe Town	1-0
Whitstable Town v Corinthian	2-3
Havant Town v Flackwell Heath	1-0

East Cowes Victoria Ath v Thatcham T	2-5
Beckenham Town v Burgess Hill Town	0-3
Whyteleafe v Hungerford Town	0-2
Yeading v Bashley	1-2
Wick v Abingdon Town	2-0
Malden Vale v Darenth Heathside	1-3
Epsom & Ewell v Three Bridges	6-2
Newport IOW v Camberley Town	1-2
Falmouth Town v Bridport	0-3
Tiverton Town v Exmouth Town	2-0
Welton Rovers v Old Georgians	3-2
Chippenham Town v Radstock Town	2-2,2-0
Devizes Town v Clevedon Town	2-2,1-0
Lawrence Weston Hallen v Paulton Rovers	1-4
Yate Town v Mangotsfield United	1-1,3-0
Moreton Town v Dawlish Town	4-2

Third Round

Harrogate RA v Borrowash Victoria	6-3
Whickham v Dunston FB	3-0
Bridlington Town v Ossett Town	2-2,0-1
Emley v Guiseley	4-0
Garforth Town v Rossendale United	1-4
North Ferriby United v Murton	3-0
Ilkeston Town v Northfield Town	4-2
Paget Rangers v Louth United	3-1
Halesowen Harriers v Heanor Town	0-1
Gresley Rovers v Tamworth	1-3
Eastwood Hanley v Poulton Victoria	3-1
Vauxhall GM (Cheshire) v Holbeach United	1-2
Boldmere St Michaels v Brigg Town	2-2,0-1
Finchley v Braintree Town	0-0,0-2
Cheshunt v Bury Town	1-3
Berkhamsted Town v Wisbech Town	2-4
Harlow Town v Tilbury	3-3
(Replay awarded to Tilbury as Harlow failed to fulfil fixture)	
East Thurrock Utd v Great Yarmouth T	3-0
Burnham Ramblers v Haverhill Rovers	6-0
March Town Utd v Sudbury Town	1-2
Hailsham Town v Darenth Heathside	1-0
Chertsey Town v Burgess Hill Town	1-1,3-1
Hungerford Town v Eastbourne Town	5-1
Epsom & Ewell v Wick	1-1,4-2
Hounslow v Corinthian	2-0
Havant Town v Camberley Town	1-7
Abingdon United v Thatcham Town	0-1
Bashley v Moreton Town	4-1
Paulton Rovers v Devizes Town	4-3
Welton Rovers v Yate Town	5-1
Romsey Town v Bridport	1-2
Tiverton Town v Chippenham Town	3-0

Fourth Round

Ossett Town v Whickham	1-0
Rossendale United v Emley	3-1
Eastwood Hanley v Heanor Town	1-1,2-1
Harrogate RA v North Ferriby United	2-2,1-3
Ilkeston Town v Tamworth	1-2
Brigg Town v Holbeach United	3-5
Bury Town v Braintree Town	0-0,2-1
Wisbech Town v Paget Rangers	1-0
East Thurrock United v Chertsey Town	2-0

Hounslow v Sudbury Town 0-1
Epsom & Ewell v Hailsham Town 1-2
Tilbury v Burnham Ramblers 0-1
Camberley Town v Hungerford Town 0-1
Bridport v Welton Rovers 3-0
Tiverton Town v Thatcham Town 1-2
Paulton Rovers v Bashley 1-3

Fifth Round
Ossett Town v North Ferriby United 1-2
Eastwood Hanley v Tamworth 0-1
Holbeach United v Wisbech Town 2-4
Rossendale United v Sudbury Town 0-1
Bury Town v Burnham Ramblers 2-1
Hailsham Town v Hungerford Town 2-3
Bridport v Thatcham Town 0-2
East Thurrock United v Bashley 1-4

Sixth Round
Bury Town v North Ferriby United 1-2
Sudbury Town v Bashley 2-0
Tamworth v Wisbech Town 1-0
Hungerford Town v Thatcham Town 2-0

Semi-final First Leg
Tamworth v North Ferriby Utd 1-2

Hungerford v Sudbury Town 1-0

Semi-final Second Leg
North Ferriby Utd v Tamworth 1-3
Sudbury Town v Hungerford 6-0

Final *(Attendance:* 26 487)
Tamworth 1 (Devaney) **Sudbury 1** (Hubbick) aet
Referee: D Vickers
Tamworth: Belford, Lockett, Atkins, Cartwright,
McCormack, Myers, Finn, Devaney, Moores,
Gordon, Stanton. Subs: Rathbone, Heaton.
Sudbury: Garnham, Henry, Barker G, Boyland,
Thorpe, Klug, Barker D, Barton, Oldfield, Smith,
Hubbick. Subs: Money, Hunt.

Replay at Peterborough *(Attendance:* 11 201)
Tamworth 3 (Stanton 2, Moores) **Sudbury 0**
Tamworth: Belford, Lockett, Atkins, Cartwright, Finn,
Myers, George, Devaney, Moores, Gordon, Stanton.
Sub: Heaton.
Sudbury: Garnham, Henry, Barker G, Boyland,
Thorpe, Klug, Barker D, Barton, Oldfield, Smith,
Hubbick. Subs: Money, Hunt.

A great background for a goal at Wembley. Martin Devaney scores Tamworth's goal against Sudbury Town in front of a record attendance.
Photo: Paul Bowler

FA CHALLENGE VASE 1989-90

Preliminary Round

Esh Winning v Hebburn	1-2
Consett v South Shields	3-1
Washington v Newton Aycliffe	0-1
Norton & Stockton Ancients v Evenwood T	0-0, 2-1
Netherfield v Ryhope CA	4-3
Darlington CB v Chester-le-Street Town	1-2 aet
Coundon TT v Seaton Delaval Amateurs	3-5 aet
Bridlington Trinity v Annfield Plain	5-3
Shotton Comrades v Bedlington Terriers	0-2
Eppleton CW v Crook Town	3-1 aet
Sunderland Roker v Dunston FB	0-3
Northallerton Town v Cleator Moor Celtic	2-0
West Auckland Town v Prudhoe East End	0-1
Alnwick Town v Willington	1-0
Peterlee Newtown v Ashington	3-2
Heswall v Salford	1-0
Lancaster City v Skelmersdale United	3-1
Knowsley United v Vauxhall GM	1-0 aet
Flixton v Merseyside Police	0-2
Prescot Cables v Ashton United	0-1
Great Harwood Town v Curzon Ashton	1-1,0-1
Burscough v Rocester	0-2
Darwen v Knypersley Victoria	2-1
Oldham Town v Atherton LR	0-4
Chadderton v Poulton Victoria	3-2
Leyland Motors v Cheadle Town	1-3
Blackpool Mechanics v Droylsden	0-6
General Chemicals v Maine Road	0-1
St Dominics v Formby	5-2
Blackpool Wren Rovers v Douglas High School Old Boys	1-2
Clitheroe v Bootle	2-1
Glossop v Irlam Town	1-2
Armthorpe Welfare v Sheffield	0-2
Clipstone Welfare v Grimethorpe MW	2-1
Eccleshill United v Staveley Works	
(walkover for Eccleshill United)	
Arnold Town v Bradley Rangers	3-1
Denaby United v Harworth Cl	3-0
Immingham Town v Ossett Albion	4-2
Frecheville Community v Sutton Town	1-4
Pickering Town v Hucknall Town	0-4
Louth United v Thackley	1-2
Lincoln United v Belper Town	1-2
Selby Town v Harrogate Town	1-3
Gainsborough Town v Maltby MW (at Maltby MW)	1-4
Pontefract Collieries v Yorkshire Amateurs	3-1
Walsall Wood v Boldmere St Michaels	0-0,1-3
Westfields v Boston	3-3,0-3
Raunds Town v Wellingborough Town	3-2
Wolverhampton Casuals v Melton Town	2-2,2-0
Anstey Nomads v Racing Club Warwick	2-1
Baker Perkins v Sandwell Borough	2-3 aet
Rushall Olympic v Holwell Sports	2-3
Rushden Town v Chasetown	3-0
Halesowen Harriers v Kings Heath	1-0
Northampton Spencer v Evesham United	2-4
Highgate United v Meir KA	3-2 aet
Harrisons v Stratford Town	3-0
Lye Town v Malvern Town	1-1,1-1,2-1
Oldbury United v Hinckley Athletic	1-2
Spalding United v Knowle	3-0
Wednesfield v Irthlingborough Diamonds	0-1
Northfield Town v Rothwell Town	5-1
Desborough Town v Solihull Borough	1-5
Hinckley Town v Brackley Town	4-0
Bilston Town v Tividale	1-2
RSSC Ransomes v Billericay Town	0-1
Great Shelford v Newmarket Town	1-3
Histon v Long Sutton Athletic	2-1
Felixstowe Town v Lowestoft Town	5-2
Saffron Walden Town v Heybridge Swifts	3-0
Brantham Athletic v Soham Town Rangers	2-3
St Ives Town v Eynesbury Rovers	1-0
Tiptree United v Downham Town	0-0,4-0
Wroxham v Basildon United	1-0
Gorleston v Bowers United	1-2
Norwich United v Kings Lynn	2-1
Halstead Town v Diss Town	1-2
Mirrlees Blackstone v Stowmarket Town	0-3
Royston Town v Canvey Island	1-0
Brightlingsea United v Harwich & Parkeston	2-1
Huntingdon United v Bourne Town	1-9
Edgware Town v Aveley	2-3
Ruislip Manor v Amersham Town	5-1
Rayners Lane v Biggleswade Town	1-0
Rainham Town v Elliott Star	3-3,2-3 aet
Kempston Rovers v Wootton Blue Cross	2-2,2-1
Welwyn Garden City v Beckenham Town	1-2
Flackwell Heath v Northwood	4-3
Woodford Town v Beaconsfield United	2-1
Stotfold v Winslow United	1-0
Tring Town v Arlesey Town	1-0
Letchworth Garden City v Ware	2-0
Sun Sports v Vauxhall Motors	2-0
Eton Manor v Molesey	1-3
Finchley v Hoddesdon Town	3-1
Buckingham Town v Collier Row	3-4 aet
MK Wolverton Town v Hertford Town	4-4,1-1,3-1
Cheshunt v Potton United	0-3
Feltham v Beckton United	2-4
Stevenage Borough v Waltham Abbey	3-1
Brimsdown Rovers v Leighton Town	0-1
Clapton v Shillington	3-0
Hornchurch v Wingate	2-3 aet
Cockfosters v Barton Rovers	0-2
Hemel Hempstead v Walthamstow Pennant	0-1
Cray Wanderers v Ringmer	3-1
Darenth Heathside v Tunbridge Wells	2-1 aet
Hartley Wintney v Banstead Athletic	2-3
Hythe Town v Malden Vale	3-1
Chichester City v Chatham Town	3-1
Danson (Bexley Boro) v Littlehampton Town	0-3
Portfield v Steyning Town	2-3 aet
Oakwood v Egham Town	2-1
Redhill v Midland Bank	1-2
Peacehaven & Telscombe v Farnham Town	3-2 aet
Wandsworth & Norwood v Crockenhill	2-0 aet
Bracknell Town v Ramsgate	2-0
Wick v Lancing	5-0
Langney Sports v Sittingbourne	0-2

A great action shot from photographer Eric Marsh as Yeading striker Paul Sweales clashes with Bridlington Town goalkeeper Ian Taylor.

Horley Town v Deal Town	1-5
Merstham v Pagham	1-0
Maidenhead United v West Wickham	1-0
Eastbourne United v Corinthian Casuals	1-3
Shoreham v Farleigh Rovers	2-1
Haywards Heath v Hastings Town	1-2
Horsham YMCA v Whitstable Town	3-3,0-1
Arundel v Burgess Hill Town	0-2
Alma Swanley v Greenwich Borough	1-2
Three Bridges v Whitehawk	1-0
Chipstead v Bedfont	2-1
Bicester Town v Newbury Town	1-3
Supermarine v Wimborne Town	0-1
Wantage Town v Petersfield United	3-1
Abingdon United v Wallingford Town	0-0,3-1
Brockenhurst v Eastleigh	0-4
Swindon Athletic v Horndean	4-3
Warminster Town v Romsey Town	0-1
AFC Totton v Vale Recreation	2-2,2-6
First Tower United v Swanage Town & Herston	2-1
Westbury United v Bournemouth	0-6
AFC Lymington v Didcot Town	3-1
Thame United v Bishops Cleeve	2-0
East Cowes VA v Headington Amateurs	1-3
Wotton Rovers v Radstock Town	3-1
Clanfield v Yate Town	2-7

Portishead v Clandown	0-2
Sharpness v Trowbridge Town	3-2
Patchway v Bristol Manor Farm	0-2
Port of Bristol v Melksham Town	1-2
DRG (FP) v Fairford Town	1-0 aet
Shortwood United v Devizes Town	4-1
Moreton Town v Backwell United	1-0
Chippenham Town v Almondsbury Picksons	2-1 aet
Highworth Town v Calne Town	2-0
Glastonbury v Brislington	1-4
Barnstaple Town v St Austell	2-1
Torrington v Chard Town	0-3
Wellington v St Blazey	1-0
Minehead v Ilfracombe Town	3-2 aet
Liskeard Athletic v Newquay	1-0

First Round

Seaton Delaval Amateurs v Netherfield	1-5 aet
Northallerton Town v Alnwick Town	2-1
Consett v Murton	1-0
Bridlington Trinity v Dunston FB	0-1
Eppleton CW v Hebburn	4-1
Bedlington Terriers v Whickham *(walkover for Whickham, Bedlington Terriers withdrawn)*	
Prudhoe East End v Peterlee Newtown	1-3

Newton Aycliffe v West Allotment Celtic	5-2
Chester-le-Street Town v Evenwood Town	2-1
Droylsden v Clitheroe	5-0
Warrington Town v Atherton LR	2-0
Cheadle Town v Maine Road	1-2
Wythenshawe Amateurs v Rocester	0-2
Heswall v Merseyside Police	3-1 aet
Ashton United v Knowsley United	3-2
Darwen v Irlam Town	2-1
St Helens Town v Chadderton	4-2
Curzon Ashton v Lancaster City	3-2
St Dominics v Douglas High Sch OB	2-2,4-4,5-5,4-1
Hucknall Town v Maltby MW	3-0
Brigg Town v Denaby United	1-2
Sutton Town v Thackley	1-0
Harrogate RA v Eccleshill United	2-0
Hatfield Main v Rainworth NW	0-2
Sheffield v Ilkeston Town	2-0 aet
Arnold Town v Pontefract Collieries	2-0
Borrowash Victoria v Immingham T	2-2,1-2 aet
Clipstone Welfare v Heanor Town	2-5 aet
Belper Town v Harrogate Town	0-0,2-1
Highgate United v Sandwell Borough	0-0,2-4
Harrisons v Tividale	2-0
Stamford v Spalding United	2-2,0-9
Northfield v Paget Rangers	0-1
Rushden Town v Wolverhampton Casuals	6-1
Raunds Town v Solihull Borough	1-0
Halesowen Harriers v Hinckley Town	1-2
Evesham United v Lye Town	0-2
Hinckley Athletic v Holwell Sports	3-0
Irthlingborough Diamonds v Anstey Nomads	1-0 aet
Boldmere St Michaels v Boston	5-1
Tiptree United v Soham Town Rangers	3-2 aet
Stowmarket Town v Brightlingsea United	0-1
Histon v Witham Town	2-1
Wroxham v Diss Town	0-3
Norwich United v Newmarket Town	3-1
Bowers United v Billericay Town	0-1
Royston Town v Bourne Town	0-1
Felixstowe Town v Tilbury	6-3
St Ives Town v Saffron Walden Town	3-1
Barton Rovers v Beckenham Town	1-1,0-3
Potton United v Finchley	2-1 aet
Stevenage Borough v Flackwell Heath	2-1
Yeading v Beckton United	2-0
Aveley v Rayners Lane	2-1 aet
Walthamstow Pennant v Kempston Rovers	1-0 aet
Collier Row v Woodford Town	2-0 aet
Letchworth Garden City v Molesey	0-1
Elliott Star v Stotfold	1-2 aet
Sun Sports v Harefield United	0-4
Wingate v Ruislip Manor	2-1
Tring Town v Leighton Town	2-1 aet
MK Wolverton Town v Clapton	1-2
Hastings Town v Banstead Athletic	5-1 aet
Merstham v Shoreham	4-3
Wick v Chipstead	2-3 aet
Steyning Town v Corinthian Casuals	0-1
Deal Town v Three Bridges	3-2 aet
Hythe Town v Littlehampton Town	3-1
Epsom & Ewell v Camberley Town	1-3
Chichester City v Maidenhead United	2-5

Oakwood v Horsham	0-1
Greenwich Borough v Cray Wanderers	3-2
Burgess Hill Town v Bracknell Town	1-2 aet
Peacehaven & Telscombe v Whitstable Town	1-3
Wandsworth & Norwood v Darenth Heathside	1-0
Sittingbourne v Midland Bank	3-0
Bournemouth v Sholing Sports	1-3
Eastleigh v AFC Lymington	1-0
Swindon Athletic v Abingdon Town	1-3
Headington Amateurs v Newbury Town	1-1,0-1
Abingdon United v Romsey Town	0-2
Wimborne Town v Newport IOW	2-1 aet
Vale Recreation v First Tower United	2-1
Wantage Town v Thame United	1-2
Moreton Town v Paulton Rovers	1-3
Sharpness v Chippenham Town	4-1
At Gloucester City FC	
Bristol Manor Farm v Mangotsfield United	3-2 aet
Brislington v Welton Rovers	3-0
Clandown v Melksham Town	2-1
Wotton Rovers v Old Georgians	0-4
DRG (FP) v Shortwood United	1-4
Yate Town v Highworth Town	5-0
Dawlish Town v Tiverton Town	3-1
Wellington v Barnstaple Town	4-1
Minehead v Chard Town	1-4
Liskeard Athletic v Exmouth Town	0-2

Second Round

Chester-le-Street v Sheffield	4-2
Bridlington Town v Newton Aycliffe	1-0
Northallerton Town v Consett	1-0
Farsley Celtic v Borrowash Victoria	6-2
Darwen v North Ferriby United	2-1
Emley v Dunston FB	4-1
Eppleton CW v Netherfield	1-2
Guiseley v Whickham	3-1 aet
Harrogate RA v Peterlee Newtown	1-3
Arnold Town v Heanor Town	1-2
Ossett Town v Denaby United	2-4 aet
St Dominics v Curzon Ashton	1-2
Ashton United v Eastwood Hanley	1-2 aet
St Helens Town v Heswall	2-0
Harrogate Town v Rainworth MW	4-2 aet
Warrington Town v Garforth Town	2-0
Rossendale United v Maine Road	6-2
Rocester v Hucknall Town	1-2
Droylsden v Sutton Town	4-0
Hinckley Athletic v Histon	4-1
Bridgnorth Town v Lye Town	0-1
Harrisons v Spalding United	1-3
Holbeach United v Bourne Town	1-2
Irthlingborough Diamonds v Wisbech Town	1-3
Gresley Rovers v Paget Rangers	4-4,2-3
Rushden Town v Sandwell Borough	5-1
March Town United v Raunds Town	1-2
Boldmere St Michaels v Hinckley Town	2-1 aet
Billericay Town v Wingate	2-1
Collier Row v Berkhamsted Town	1-0
Stotfold v Tring Town	3-1
Brightlingsea United v Stevenage Borough	0-2
East Thurrock United v Felixstowe Town	2-1
Braintree Town v Yeading	0-0,2-5

FA VASE

Diss Town v Walthamstow Pennant	0-1
Beckenham Town v Haverhill Rovers (1,45)	0-2
Burnham Ramblers v Aveley	1-2
Clapton v Sudbury Town	1-6
Norwich United v Potton United	0-2
Harefield United v Tiptree United	2-0 aet
Great Yarmouth Town v St Ives Town	3-0
Whitstable Town v Wandsworth & Norwood	3-2 aet
Hailsham Town v Horsham	3-1
Camberley Town v Hythe Town	0-1
Corinthian Casuals v Chertsey Town	2-2,1-4
Deal Town v Chipstead	1-0
Sittingbourne v Bracknell Town	1-2
Molesey v Corinthians	2-0
Havant Town v Hastings Town	1-6
Merstham v Maidenhead United	3-1
Hounslow v Greenwich Borough	1-2
Thame United v Eastleigh	0-1
Vale Recreation v Sholing Sports	1-0
Bashley v Hungerford Town	3-2
Abingdon Town v Romsey Town	2-0
Wimborne Town v Newbury Town	0-2 aet
Bridport v Thatcham Town	2-3 aet
Clevedon Town v Yate Town	0-4
Bristol Manor Farm v Brislington	1-4
Exmouth Town v Wellington	3-2
Chard Town v Sharpness	3-1
Dawlish Town v Old Georgians	2-1
Paulton Rovers v Clandown	1-1,3-0
Falmouth Town v Shortwood United	2-0

Third Round
Droylsden v Rossendale United	3-3
(tie awarded to Rossendale United as Droylsden	
played a suspended player)	
Harrogate Town v Chester-le-Street Town	3-0
Warrington Town v Netherfield	3-1
Guiseley v Northallerton Town	4-2
Emley v Denaby United	3-1
Curzon Ashton v Bridlington Town	1-2
Darwen v St Helens Town	1-2
Peterlee Newtown v Farsley Celtic	0-1 aet
Spalding United v Lye Town	1-0 aet
Heanor Town v Paget Rangers	3-2
Hucknall Town v Boldmere St Michaels	2-1
Bourne Town v Eastwood Hanley	1-0
Raunds Town v Hinckley Athletic	1-0
Rushden Twon v Wisbech Town	3-0
Yeading v East Thurrock United	1-0
Billericay Town v Aveley	3-1
Stotfold v Great Yarmouth Town	0-2
Walthamstow Pennant v Collier Row	1-2
Potton United v Stevenage Borough	2-0
Sudbury Town v Haverhill Rovers	4-1
Whitstable Town v Greenwich Borough	1-2
Bracknell Town v Harefield United	0-2
Eastleigh v Thatcham Town	1-2
Deal Town v Hythe Town	0-1
Hailsham Town v Hastings Town	1-1,2-5
Vale Recreation v Merstham	0-1
Chertsey Town v Molesey	0-2
Chard Town v Dawlish Town	2-1

Exmouth Town v Bashley	0-4
Abingdon Town v Brislington	3-2
Paulton Rovers v Yate Town	2-1
Falmouth Town v Newbury Town	2-1 aet

Fourth Round
Guiseley v Rossendale United	3-1
Harrogate Town v Bridlington Town	1-3
Emley v Warrington Town	2-2,3-0
Farsley Celtic v St Helens Town	1-1,0-0,0-1
Bourne Town v Spalding United	1-1,1-3 aet
Heanor Town v Rushden Town	1-2
Raunds Town v Hucknall Town	1-4
Sudbury Town v Great Yarmouth Town	3-4
Potton United v Hastings Town	2-2,3-1
Harefield United v Greenwich Borough	1-1,5-4 aet
Yeading v Molesey	1-0
Merstham v Billericay Town	2-3
Hythe Town v Collier Row	1-1,3-1
Falmouth Town v Paulton Rovers	0-2
Bashley v Chard Town	1-0
Thatcham Town v Abingdon Town	0-1

Fifth Round
Farsley Celtic v Guiseley	1-3
Rushden Town v Emley	2-0 aet
Great Yarmouth Town v Spalding United	0-2
Bridlington Town v Hucknall Town	5-2
Billericay Town v Potton United	2-1
Paulton Rovers v Yeading	1-1,2-1
Abingdon Town v Hythe Town	1-1,1-3 aet
Harefield United v Bashley	2-1

Sixth Round
Rushden Town v Hythe Town	0-1
Yeading v Harefield United	2-0
Spalding United v Guiseley	1-3
Billericay Town v Bridlington Town	0-1

Semi Finals — First Leg
Hythe Town v Yeading	3-2
Guiseley v Bridlington Town	0-3

Semi Finals — Second Leg
Yeading v Hythe Town	2-0
Bridlington Town v Guiseley	1-0

Final at Wembley Stadium *(Attendance: 5000)*
Bridlington Town 0 Yeading 0
Replay at Leeds United FC *(Attendance: 7932)*
Bridlington Town 0 Yeading 1
Yeading: MacKenzie, Wickens, Turner, Whiskey (McCarthy), Croad, Denton, Matthews, James (Charles), Sweales, Impey, Cordery. (Schwartz replaced Denton, McCarthy substituted for Croad and Welsh substituted for Impey in replay).
Bridlington Town: Taylor, Pugh, Freeman, McNeil, Warburton, Brentano, Wilkes (Hall), Noteman, Gauden, Whiteman, Brattan (Brown). (Brown substituted for Wilkes and Downing substituted for Gauden in replay).
Referee: R Groves (Weston-super-Mare)

FA CHALLENGE VASE 1990-91

Preliminary Round

Chester-le-Street v Marchon	5-3
Langley Park v Washington	2-1
Penrith v Shotton Coms	0-3
N'ton & St'ton A v Horden	0-0,1-2
Peterlee Newtown v Ryhope CA	2-0
Willington v Darlington CB	1-2*
Eppleton CW v W Auckland T	2-2,7-0
W Allotment C v Esh Winning	2-2,5-2
Newton Aycliffe v Annfield Plain	1-1,1-0
(first game abandoned after 90 mins due to high winds)	
Yorkshire Amat v Prudhoe East End	2-3
Netherfield v North'ton Town	1-0
Boldon CA v Hebburn	0-1
Ashington v Cleator Moor C	3-1
Crook Town v Murton	1-3
Billingham Town v South Shields	1-0
Dunston FB v Evenwood Town	3-1
Irlam Town v Lancaster City	0-1
Clitheroe v Bootle	1-1,3-2*
Nantwich Town v Chadderton	2-0
Thackley v Leyland Motors	0-1*
Prescot AFC v Darwen	4-3
Maine Road v Atherton Coll	3-1
Ashton Utd v Formby	6-3
Wythenshawe A v Curzon Ashton	0-1
Merseyside Police v Knypersley Vic	2-3
Blackpool Rovers v Ashville	4-2*
St Dominics v Blackpool Mechanics	1-2
Knowsley United v General Chemicals	3-1
Douglas HS OB v Skelmersdale Utd	0-2
Newcastle Town v Padiham	2-1
Maghull v Vauxhall GM	0-1
Oldham Town v Cammell Laird	0-2
Glossop v Waterloo Dock	2-1*
Gt Harwood T v Burscough	4-0
Liversedge v Maltby MW	1-6
Rossington Main v Priory (Eastwood)	0-2
Denaby United v Louth United	2-0
Arnold Town v Friar Lane OB	2-0
Belper Town v Bradley Rangers	4-4,2-2,2-1
Worsboro Bridge MW v Ilkeston Town	2-0
Armthorpe Welfare v Clipstone Welfare	1-0
Ossett Albion v Long Eaton Utd	2-0
Hatfield Main v Yorkshire Main	0-2
Selby Town v Bacup Borough	2-0
Eccleshill Utd v Stocksbridge P St	2-0*
Winterton Rangers v Brigg Town	2-1
Harworth CI v Sutton Town	4-2*
Pontefract Coll v Sheffield	0-3
Brackley Town v Northampton Spencer	1-0
Wednesfield v Bloxwich Town	2-0
Stratford Town v Wolverhampton Cas	5-0
Melton Town v Stapenhill	2-1
Baker Perkins v Halesowen H	4-3
Mile Oak Rovers v Eccleshall	2-0
Lye Town v Lincoln United	0-1
Lutterworth Town v Desborough Town	3-3,1-1,1-2
Pegasus Juniors v Chasetown	0-3
Heath Hayes v Evesham United	0-3
Northfield Town v Solihull Borough	2-0

Oldbury Utd v Irthlingborough Diamonds	0-2
Holwell Sports v Malvern Town	8-1
Highgate United v Rushall Olympic	0-1
Walsall Wood v Stourport Swifts	2-1
Hinckley Athletic v Bilston Town	1-0
Wellingborough Town v Hinckley Town	1-2
Rothwell Town v West Midlands Police	4-3
Boston v Sandwell Borough	1-0
Coleshill Town v Hamlet S & L	0-2
Racing Club Warwick v Oldswinford	3-1
Princes End Utd v Tividale	2-3
Canvey Island v Thetford Town	0-2
Kings Lynn v Stowmarket Town	2-0
Royston Town v Stamford	3-0
Histon v Rainham Town	4-3
Saffron Walden Town v Soham TR	2-1
Norwich Utd v Felixstowe Town	2-3
Witham Town v Brantham Ath	1-0
Gorleston v Tiptree Utd	3-1
Brightlingsea U v LBC Ortonians	2-1
Ramsey Town v Wroxham	3-1
Newmarket Town v Mirrlees B'stone	1-1,0-2
Clarksteel Yaxley v Harwich & Parkeston	0-3
Barton Rovers v St Ives Town	0-1
Eynesbury Town v Lowestoft Town	1-2
Basildon Utd v Watton United	0-1
Stansted v Halstead Town	1-5
Bracknell Town v Hoddesdon Town	4-0
Vauxhall Motors v Amersham Town	4-2
Southall v Stotfold	1-2
Langford v Brook House	2-0
Arlesey Town v Edgware Town	0-2
Hertford Town v Cockfosters	2-0
Hanwell Town v Ruislip Manor	0-5
Cheshunt v Elliott Star	1-2
Wingate v Buckingham Town	1-4
Mount Grace v Clapton	1-0
Pirton v Brimsdown Rovers	1-2
Hornchurch v Flackwell Heath	0-1
Hemel Hempstead v Wolverton	1-1,6-1
Eton Manor v Northwood	0-1
Walthamstow Pen v Tring Town	0-0,2-0
Feltham v Barkingside	0-5
Finchley v Ware	2-2,2-1
Welwyn GC v Letchworth GC	3-3,1-1,3-5
Cray Wanderers v Purfleet	2-4
Wootton BC v Rayners Lane	1-0
Leighton Town v Haringey Borough	1-0
Kingsbury Town v Stevenage B'gh	0-1
West Wickham v Alma Swanley	1-3*
Littlehampton Town v Corinthian C	3-3,7-2
Sheppey Utd v Croydon Athletic	1-3
Lancing v Langley Sports	0-6
Beckenham Town v Tonbridge AFC	1-1,?-?
Herne Bay v Tunbridge Wells	1-2
Cobham v Faversham Town	1-2
Farnham Town v Steyning Town	3-0
Egham Town v Eastbourne Town	3-1
Ringmer v Chipstead	3-1
Godalming Town v Redhill	3-0
Whitehawk v Peacehaven & Telscombe	1-0

FA VASE

Maidenhead Utd v Sittingbourne	0-1	Garforth Town v Ossett Albion	3-1
Horsham YMCA v Darenth Heathside	1-4	Yorkshire Main v Sheffield	1-2*
Haywards Heath T v Chatham Town	3-0	Denaby United v Worsboro Bridge MW	0-4
Slade Green v Three Bridges	1-0*	Winterton Rangers v Arnold Town	1-0
Eastbourne Utd v Chichester City	2-1	Rainworth MW v Armthorpe Welfare	2-1
Pagham v Leatherhead	2-1	Eccleshill Utd v Priory (Eastwood)	1-2
Ramsgate v Hartley Wintney	2-0	Borrowash Vic v Maltby MW	2-0
Shoreham v Arundel	3-2	Stratford Town v Hamlet S & L	0-3
Banstead Athletic v Horndean	3-1	Boldmere St Michaels v Bridgnorth Town	1-2
Wick v Burgess Hill Town	1-2	Rothwell Town v Wednesfield	2-0
Portfield v Crockenhill	3-4	Racing Club Warwick v Tividale	6-1
Cove v Malden Vale	3-3,2-3	Hinckley Ath v Desborough Town	3-1
AFC Totton v Bicester Town	4-1	Walsall Wood v Chasetown	1-1,1-0
AFC Lymington v First Tower Utd	0-1	Raunds Town v Irthlingborough D	2-0
Kintbury Rangers v Abingdon Utd	1-3	Brackley Town v Northfield	1-2
Newbury Town v Bishops Cleeve	0-1	Hinckley Town v Holwell Sports	0-1
Westbury United v Flight Refuelling	2-1*	Melton Town v Rushall Olympic	0-2
Thame United v East Cowes VA	3-0	Boston v Lincoln United	1-6
Romsey Town v Didcot Town	2-4	Baker Perkins v Evesham Utd	4-3
Vale Recreation v Bournemouth	0-1	Mile Oak Rovers v Gresley Rovers	2-1*
Swanage Tn & H v Newport IOW	4-6	Gorleston v Saffron Walden Town	2-4
Eastleigh v Bemerton H H	2-1	Histon v Bourne Town	5-0
Christchurch v Trowbridge Town	0-2	Halstead Town v St Ives Town	3-1
Warminster Town v Wimborne Town	0-2	Royston Town v Thetford Town	1-2
Shortwood Town v Larkhall Athletic	3-1	Kings Lynn v Mirrlees B'stone	2-0
Bridgwater Town v Frome Town	0-1	Watton United v Felixstowe Town	0-1
Cinderford Town v Bristol Manor Farm	2-0	Tilbury v Harwich & Parkeston	4-6*
Mangotsfield Utd v Fairford Town	3-0	Witham Town v Ramsey Town	2-2,3-2
Highworth Town v Keynsham Town	2-4	Berkhamsted T v Lowestoft T	3-5
Chippenham Town v Radstock Town	3-3,2-0	March Town Utd v Brightlingsea Utd	3-0
Almondsbury Picksons v Minehead	1-1,5-3	Mount Grace v Wootton BC	1-0
Wellington v Calne Town	3-1	Purfleet v Stotfold	2-0
Moreton Town v Melksham Town	1-3	Barkingside v Collier Row	2-1*
Devizes Town v Hallen	2-4*	Edgware Town v Letchworth GC	1-0
Wotton Rovers v Glastonbury	3-1	Hemel Hempstead v Stevenage Boro	1-0
Welton Rovers v Backwell Utd	0-2	Buckingham Town v Bracknell Town	4-1
Ilfracombe Town v Barnstaple Town	0-2	Ruislip Manor v Leighton Town	4-3
Newquay v Ottery St Mary	5-0	Brimsdown Rovers v Hounslow	3-0
Torrington v St Blazey	2-1	Elliott Star v Hertford Town	5-4*
Tiverton Town v Liskeard Athletic	2-1	Vauxhall Motors v Finchley	3-2
* After extra time		Walthamstow Pen v Langford	1-0
		Flackwell Heath v Northwood	0-2
First Round		Epsom & Ewell v Shoreham	2-3
Darlington CB v Horden CW	1-2	Littlehampton Town v Godalming Town	5-0
Billingham Town v Netherfield	2-0	Faversham Town v Ringmer	1-0
Chester-le-Street v Peterlee Newtown	1-0	Alma Swanley v Tunbridge Wells	1-2
Murton v Shotton Coms	2-0	Farnham Town v Egham Town	4-0
Ashington v Hebburn	1-0*	Darenth Heathside v Hailsham Town	1-0
Langley Park v Prudhoe East End	1-0	Sittingbourne v Pagham	1-2
Eppleton CW v W Allotment C	5-1	Horsham v Whitehawk	2-1*
Dunston FB v Newton Aycliffe	3-1	Crockenhill v Haywards Heath	0-3
Blackpool Rovers v Ashton United	3-0	Eastbourne Utd v Burgess Hill Town	1-2
Maine Road v Warrington Town	0-2	Langney Sports v Beckenham	3-1
Gt Harwood Town v Vauxhall GM	2-0	Slade Green v Whitstable Town	2-0
Prescot AFC v Nantwich Town	4-5*	Malden Vale v Camberley Town	1-1,3-0
Leyland Motors v Skelmersdale United	0-2	(First match abandoned 110 mins floodlight failure)	
Glossop v Curzon Ashton	6-1	Greenwich Boro v Croydon Ath	2-1
Clitheroe v Newcastle Town	3-2	Banstead Ath v Corinthian	2-2,?-?
Knowsley United v Knypersley Vic	5-0	Merstham v Ramsgate	1-1,1-1*
St Helens Town v Cammell Laird	1-2	Wimborne Town v Newport IOW	1-0*
Lancaster City v Blackpool Mechanics	1-0	AFC Totton v Trowbridge Town	1-4
Selby Town v Harrogate Town	0-2	Abingdon Utd v Didcot Town	0-3
Belper Town v Harworth CI	3-1	Havant Town v Bishops Cleeve	4-0

Sholing Sports v First Tower Utd	2-1
Thame United v Bournemouth	0-1
Eastleigh v Westbury Utd	1-0
Yate Town v Frome Town	2-2*,3-0
Wotton Rovers v Almondsbury Picksons	0-2
Chard Town v Shortwood Utd	1-2
Hallen v Old Georgians	1-2
Melksham Town v Wellington	0-1
Clevedon Town v Chippenham Town	3-1
Cinderford Town v Mangotsfield Town	1-3*
Welton Rovers v Keynsham Town	2-0
Newquay v Torrington	2-1
Tiverton Town v Dawlish Town	3-4
Barnstaple Town v Exmouth Town	5-1
* after extra time	

Second Round

Bridlington Town v Blackpool rovers	1-0*
Horden CW v Gt Harwood Town	1-2
Harrogate Ra v Chester-le-Street	2-1
Rossendale United v Ossett Town	0-2
Lancaster City v Eppleton CW	1-2
North Ferriby U v Murton	5-3
Langley Park v Ashington	0-1
Farsley Celtic v Clitheroe	1-0
Dunston FB v Billingham Town	2-3
Rainworth MW v Harrogate Town	2-1
Knowsley United v Eastwood Hanley	5-3
Glossop v Winterton Rangers	4-0
Cammell Laird v Sheffield	4-1
Borrowash Vic v Belper Town	5-3*
Warrington Town v Guiseley	2-2,1-1,1-3
Skelmersdale U v Garforth Town	1-4
Lincoln United v Priory (Eastwood)	1-2
Worsboro Bridge MW v Heanor Town	4-1
Nantwich Town v Hucknall Town	2-2,1-2
Raunds Town v Holbeach Utd	2-2,3-0
Hinckley Ath v March Town Utd	3-0
Racing Club Warwick v Gresley Rovers	1-3*
Walsall Wood v Rushall Olympic	1-2
Spalding United v Northfield	1-0
Hamlet S & L v Wisbech Town	1-3
Rothwell Town v Holwell Sports	3-2
Potton United v Paget Rangers	1-3
Baker Perkins v Histon	1-3
Kings Lynn v Bridgnorth Town	4-0
Ruislip Manor v Sudbury Town	0-0,0-2
Harwich & Parkeston v Burnham Ramblers	6-1
Barkingside v Braintree Town	2-2,3-2*
Northwood v Felixstowe Town	2-1
Elliott Star v Mount Grace	1-3
Halstead Town v Gt Yarmouth Town	5-1
Thetford Town v Billericay Town	4-1
Vauxhall Motors v Purfleet	0-1
Walthamstow Penn v Edgware Town	2-1
Saffron Walden Town v Witham Town	5-2
Brismdown Rovers v East Thurrock Utd	0-1
Buckingham Town v Lowestoft Town	2-1
Haverhill Rovers v Hemel Hempstead	1-0
Pagham v Hythe Town	3-4
Slade Green v Faversham Town	1-0
Littlehampton Town v Abingdon Town	2-0
Eastleigh v Langney Sports	1-0

Didcot Town v Banstead Athletic	2-0
Haywards Heath Town v Farnham Town	3-1
Burgess Hill Town v Shoreham	2-0
Havant Town v Merstham	2-0
Hungerford Town v Chertsey Town	1-0
Whitehawk v Malden Vale	1-2
Thatcham Town v Tunbridge Wells	4-5*
Harefield Utd v Greenwich Boro	2-0
Darenth Heathside v Hastings Town	2-3
Old Georgians v Almondsbury Picks	0-2
Bridport v Shortwood Utd	2-0
Paulton Rovers v Clevedon Town	0-0,3-0
Barnstaple Town v Dawlish Town	3-3,0-1
Newquay v Bournemouth	1-0
Mangotsfield United v Wimborne Town	1-4
Sholing Sports v Trowbridge Town	1-2
Wellington v Welton Rovers	3-1
Yate Town v Falmouth Town	2-1

Third Round

Glossop v North Ferriby Utd	1-0
Cammell Laird v Ashington	1-1
Garforth Town v Borrowash Vic	2-6
Farsley Celtic v Guiseley	0-1
Bridlington Town v Eppleton CW	4-0
Knowsley United v Ossett Town	4-2
Billingham Town v Harrogate RA	3-1
Worsboro Bridge MW v Gt Harwood Town	1-2
Kings Lynn v Rushall Olympic	2-1
Paget Rangers v Hinckley Athletic	0-4
Rainworth MW v Hucknall Town	1-2
Gresley Rovers v Raunds Town	2-1
Spalding United v Wisbech Town	1-0
Rothwell Town v Priory (Eastwood)	2-2
East Thurrock Utd v Eastleigh	1-2
Saffron Walden Town v Burgess Hill Town	4-3
Haywards Heath v Thetford Town	1-2
Hythe Town v Haverhill Rovers	4-0
Halstead Town v Histon	0-1
Harefield United v Havant Town	3-1
Hastings Town v Tunbridge Wells	5-0
Buckingham Town v Mount Grace	2-1
Sudbury Town v Harwich & Parkeston	3-3
Walthamstow Penn v Barkingside	5-2
Littlehampton Town v Slade Green	5-0
Malden Vale v Didcot Town	1-1
Northwood v Purfleet	0-1
Almondsbury Picks v Trowbridge Town	1-2
Hungerford Town v Newquay	0-2
Dawlish Town v Wellington	4-1
Paulton Rovers v Bridport	0-1
Yate Town v Wimborne Town	5-3

Fourth Round

Gresley Rovers v Billingham Town	2-1
Knowsley United v Spalding United	3-0
Glossop v Cammell Laird	2-2,1-2
Harwich & Parkeston v Purfleet	2-1
Eastleigh v Littlehampton Town	0-1
Walthamstow Pen v Thetford Town	5-1
Gr Harwood Town v Rothwell Town	1-1,1-0
Bridlington Town v Borrowash Victoria	3-1
Hastings Town v Histon	4-0
Harefield United v Hythe Town	0-5

FA VASE

Trowbridge Town v Yate Town | 5-0
Didcot Town v Dawlish Town | 0-1
Newquay v Saffron Walden | 2-2,0-1
Buckingham Town v Bridport | 0-0,2-0
Hinckley Ath v Hucknall Town | 2-1
Kings Lynn v Guiseley | 1-4

Fifth Round
Knowsley United v Gresley Rovers | 4-5*
Cammell Laird v Harwich & Parkeston | 3-2*
Littlehampton Town v Walthamstow Pen | 3-2
Gt Harwood Town v Bridlington Town | 1-1,1-0*
Hastings Town v Hythe Town | 0-0,1-3
Trowbridge Town v Dawlish Town | 1-0
Saffron Walden v Buckingham Town | 1-2
Hinckley Ath v Guiseley | 1-4*

Sixth Round
Harwich & Parkeston v Gresley Rovers | 0-2
Littlehampton Town v Gt Harwood Town | 2-1
Trowbridge Town v Hythe Town | 0-0,1-1,3-1
Buckingham Town v Guiseley | 0-1

Semi Finals
Gresley Rovers v Littlehampton Town | 3-2,1-1
Trowbridge Town v Guiseley | 1-1,2-1

Final at Wembley Stadium. *(Attendance:* 11 314)
Gresley Rovers (1) 4 (Smith 2, Rathbone, Stokes pen)
v Guiseley (3) 4 (Tennison 2, Walling, Roberts A)
Gresley Rovers: Aston, Barry, Elliot (Adcock),
Denby, Land, Astley, Stokes, Smith, Acklam,
Rathbone, Lovell (Weston).
Guiseley: Maxted, Bottomley, Hogarth, Tetley,
Morgan, McKenzie (Adams), Tennison,
Walling, Roberts A, Roberts W (Annan).
Replay at Sheffield United FC (Attendance: 7505)
Gresley Rovers (1) 1 (Astley) **Guiseley (2) 3**
(Tennison, Walling Atkinson)
Gresley Rovers: Same team as Final with substitutes
Adcock for Lovell and Weston for Stokes.
Guiseley: Maxted, Atkinson, Hogarth, Tetley,
Morgan, McKenzie (Bottomley), Roberts A, Tennison
(Noteman), Walling, Annan, Roberts W.

A superb action photo from the thrilling 4-4 Vase Final contested by Gresley Rovers and Guiseley, whose goalkeeper Paul Maxted saves bravely at the feet of two-goal Kieron Smith.
Photo: Roger Cain

FA CUP GIANT KILLING

INTRODUCTION

Some of the most exciting moments of every season are to be found in the early rounds of the FA Cup Competition Proper.

It is the highlight of the campaign for the semi-professional clubs to get through the Fourth Qualifying Round. They have reached their 'cup final' and the excitement of the draw on the Monday morning when they find out if they have been paired with a 'giant' can send the adrenelin racing round a town, let alone its football club.

Over the years the most famous cup stories are linked with that handful of minnows who actually overturned First Division opposition. This of course should never happen, but however much senior professional players are warned about over-

confidence, it is extremely difficult to motivate players who know they are really in a class above the opposition.

The real highlights have been Yeovil Town's winning goal by Eric Bryant against Sunderland in front of 17 000 on The Huish slope, Radford's 'goal of the season' to give Hereford United victory over Newcastle United, Altrincham's victory at Birmingham City, and Coventry City's amazing elimination at Sutton United only two seasons after winning the FA Cup against Tottenham Hotspur.

Wimbledon also won at First Division Burnley but probably the outstanding memory of their run was the penalty save of Dickie Guy at Leeds United in the next round, when the mighty

Yorkshiremen were taken to a replay and only won with a deflection off Wimbledon's Dave Bassett.

However, the greatest individual goalscoring performance, in as complete a piece of 'giantkilling' as can be imagined, was Tim Buzaglo's hat trick for Woking at Second Division West Bromwich Albion in 1991.

The FA Cup often starts in August but whether you play in the heat of the summer or the mud and snow of mid-winter, the thrill of competing in the greatest knock out club tournament in the world is appreciated by one and all. Whether the 'surprise' is Liskeard Athletic beating Dorchester Town 5-1 or Woking triumphing at The Hawthorns, that FA Cup thrill is just as sweet!

That never to be forgotten moment when the First Division leaders, Middlesborough, and 32 000 supporters salute Wycombe Wanderers after their tremendous display at Ayresome Park in the 1975 3rd Round Replay when a last minute goal knocked the Isthmians out of the FA Cup.

SEASON BY SEASON

Season	Round	Non League Club	League	League Club	Div	Ven	Score
1945/46	1R/1L	Chorley	LC	Accrington Stanley	3N	H	2-1
	1R/1L	Lovells Ath	WH	Bournemouth & Bosc	3S	H	4-1
	1R/1L	Shrewsbury Town	ML	Walsall	3S	H	5-0
	1R/1L	Yorkshire Amateurs	YK	Lincoln City	3N	H	1-0
	1R/2L	Gainsborough Trinity	ML	Mansfield Town	3S	A	4-2
	1R/2L	Newport IOW	HA	Clapton Orient	3S	H	2-0
1946/47	1R	Merthyr Tydfil	SL	Bristol Rovers	3S	H	3-1
	2R	Gillingham	SL	Bristol City	3S	A	2-1
1947/48	1R	Gillingham	SL	Leyton Orient	3S	H	1-0
	2R	Colchester Utd	SL	Wrexham	3N	H	1-0
	2R/r	Gillingham	SL	Rochdale	3N	H	3-0
	3R	Colchester Utd	SL	Huddersfield T	1	H	1-0
	4R	Colchester Utd	SL	Bradford PA	2	H	3-2
1948/49	1R	Leytonstone	IL	Watford	3S	H	2-1
	3R	Yeovil Town	SL	Bury	2	H	3-1
	4R	Yeovil Town	SL	Sunderland	1	H	2-1
1949/50	1R/r	Weymouth	SL	Aldershot	3S	H	3-2
1950/51	4Q	Hereford Utd	SL	Scunthorpe Utd	3N	A	1-0
	1R	Ashington	NE	Halifax Town	3N	A	3-2
1951/52	1R	Leytonstone	IL	Shrewsbury Town	3S	H	2-0
	1R/r	Stockton	NE	Mansfield Town	3N	A	2-0
	2R	Buxton	CC	Aldershot	3S	H	4-3
1952/53	1R	Bath City	SL	Southend Utd	3S	H	3-1
	1R	Peterborough Utd	ML	Torquay Utd	3S	H	2-1
	2R	Finchley	AT	Crystal Palace	3S	H	3-1
	2R/r	Walthamstow Ave	IL	Watford	3S	A	2-1
	3R	Walthamstow Ave	IL	Stockport County	3N	H	2-1
1953/54	1R	Gt Yarmouth Town	EC	Crystal Palace	3S	H	1-0
	1R	Nuneaton Borough	BL	Walford	3S	H	3-0
	1R	Walthamstow Ave	IL	Gillingham	3S	H	1-0
	1R/r	Cambridge Utd	EC	Newport County	3S	A	2-1
	1R/r	Hereford Utd	SL	Exeter City	3S	H	2-0
	1R/r	Rhyl	CC	Halifax Town	3N	H	4-3
	2R	Hastings Utd	SL	Swindon Town	3S	H	4-1
	2R	Peterborough Utd	ML	Aldershot	3S	H	2-1

INDEX OF LEAGUES

AP	Alliance Premier League	KT	Kent League	SL	Southern League
AT	Athenian League	LC	Lancashire Combination	TC	The Combination
BC	Birmingham Combination	LE	Liecestershire League	VC	Vauxhall Conference
BL	Birmingham League	LL	Lancashire League	VO	Vauxhall-Opel League
CA	Central Alliance	MC	Midland Counties League	WE	Western League
CC	Cheshire County League	ML	Midland League	WH	Welsh League (South)
CE	Central Combination	MU	Multipart League	WM	West Midlands League
CL	Central League	NA	Northern Alliance	WN	Welsh League (North)
EC	Eastern Counties League	NC	Northern Counties League	YK	Yorkshire League
FA	Football Alliance	NE	North Eastern League		
GL	Gola League	NL	Northern League		THESE ARE ORIGINAL NAMES
HA	Hampshire League	NP	Northern Premier League		NOT SPONSORS' NAMES
IL	Isthmian League	NR	Northern Regional League		

NOTES

Venue is applicable to Non League Club Rounds:

1Q = 1st Qualifying Round
1N = Intermediate Round
.1R = 1st Round Proper

SF = Semi Final
F = Final
/r = Replay
/2r = 2nd replay

One of the most famous days in FA Cup history. Yeovil beat Sunderland and here home keeper Dyke punches clear during an attack by the First Division club. In the Fourth Round the little Somerset club travelled to Manchester where 81 565, the largest crowd to watch a competitive football match in England outside Wembley, saw them lose to Manchester United 0-8

Photo: The Press Association

Season	Round	Non League Club	League	League Club	Div	Ven	Score
	2R/r	Headington Utd	SL	Millwall	3S	H	1-0
	3R/r	Headington Utd	SL	Stockport County	3N	H	1-0
1954/55	1R	Wigan Athletic	LC	Carlisle Utd	3N	A	6-1
	1R/2r	Walthamstow Ave	IL	QPR	3S	H	4-0
	2R	Bishop Auckland	NL	Crystal Palace	3S	A	4-2
	2R	Wigan Athletic	LC	Torquay Utd	3S	H	3-1
	3R	Bishop Auckland	NL	Ipswich Town	2	H	3-0
1955/56	1R	Peterborough Utd	ML	Ipswich Town	3S	H	3-1
	2R	Bedford Town	SL	Watford	3S	H	3-2
	2R	Boston Utd	ML	Derby County	3N	A	6-1
	2R/r	Burton Albion	BL	Halifax Town	3N	H	1-0
1956/57	1R	Bedford Town	SL	Norwich City	3S	A	4-2
	1R	Bishop Auckland	NL	Tranmere Rovers	3N	H	2-1
	1R	Hereford Utd	SL	Aldershot	3S	H	3-2
	1R	Weymouth	SL	Shrewsbury T	3S	H	1-0
	1R/r	New Brighton	LC	Stockport County	3N	A	3-2
	2R	New Brighton	LC	Derby County	3N	A	3-1
	2R	Peterborough Utd	ML	Bradford PA	3N	H	3-0
	3R/r	Peterborough utd	ML	Lincoln City	2	A	5-4
	2R/r	Goole Town	ML	Workington	3N	A	1-0
	3R	New Brighton	LC	Torquay Utd	3S	H	2-1
	3R	Rhyl	CC	Notts County	2	A	3-1
	3R/r	Peterborough Utd	ML	Lincoln City	2	A	6-4
1957/58	1R	Bath City	SL	Exeter City	3S	A	2-1
	1R	Wigan Athletic	LC	Southport	3N	H	2-1
	1R	Wisbech Town	ML	Colchester Utd	3S	A	1-0
	2R	Hereford Utd	SL	QPR	3S	H	6-1

FA CUP GIANT KILLING

Season	Round	Non League Club	League	League Club	Div	Ven	Score
1958/59	1R	Tooting & Mitcham	IL	Bournemouth & Bosc	3	H	3-1
	1R/r	South Shields	ML	Crewe Alexander	4	H	5-0
	1R/r	Yeovil Town	SL	Southend Utd	3	H	1-0
	2R	Tooting & Mitcham	IL	Northampton Town	4	H	2-1
	2R	Worcester City	SL	Millwall	4	H	5-2
	3R	Worcester City	SL	Liverpool	2	H	2-1

It wasn't the Liverpool we know today, they were in the Second Division, but Worcester City still enjoyed the thrill of putting them out of the Cup in 1959. Tommy Skuse is seen opening their scoring in the 9th minute, in front of 15 000 at St George's Lane.

Photo: Birmingham Post and Mail

Season	Round	Non League Club	League	League Club	Div	Ven	Score
1959/60	1R	Bath City	SL	Millwall	4	H	3-1
	1R	Kings Lynn	SL	Aldershot	4	H	3-1
	1R	Peterborough Utd	ML	Shrewsbury Town	3	H	4-3
	1R	South Shields	ML	Chesterfield	3	H	2-1
	2R	Bath City	SL	Notts County	4	A	1-0
	2R	Peterborough Utd	ML	Walsall	4	A	3-2
	3R	Peterborough Utd	ML	Ipswich Town	2	A	3-2
1960/61	1R	Bangor City	CC	Wrexham	4	H	1-0
	1R	Yeovil Town	SL	Walsall	4	A	1-0
1961/62	1R	Gateshead	NC	Tranmere Rovers	2	A	3-2
	1R	Margate	SL	Bournemouth & Bosc	4	A	3-0
	1R/r	Dartford	SL	Exeter City	3	H	2-1
	1R/r	Kettering Town	SL	Swindon Town	4	H	3-0
	2R	Kings Lynn	SL	Coventry City	3	A	2-1
	2R	Morecambe	LC	Chester	4	A	1-0
	2R	Weymouth	SL	Newport County	3	H	1-0
1962/63	1R	Gravesend & North	SL	Exeter City	3	H	3-2
	1R	Wimbledon	IL	Colchester Utd	4	H	2-1
	3R	Gravesend & North	SL	Carlisle Utd	3	A	1-0
1963/64	1R	Gateshead	NR	Darlington	4	A	4-1
	1R	Yeovil Town	SL	Southend Utd	3	H	1-0
	1R/r	Kettering Town	SL	Millwall	3	A	3-2
	2R	Yeovil Town	SL	Crystal Palace	4	H	3-1
	3R	Bedford Town	SL	Newcastle Utd	3	A	2-1

Season	Round	Non League Club	League	League Club	Div	Ven	Score
1964/65	1R	Crook Town	NL	Carlisle Utd	3	H	1-0
	1R	Scarborough	MC	Bradford City	4	H	1-0
	1R/r	South Liverpool	LC	Halifax Town	4	H	4-2
1965/66	1R	Bedford Town	SL	Exeter City	3	A	2-1
	1R	Bath City	SL	Newport County	3	H	2-0
	1R	South Shields	NR	York City	4	H	3-1
	1R/r	Wigan Athletic	CC	Doncaster Rovers	3	H	3-1
	2R	Altrincham	CC	Rochdale	3	A	3-1
	2R	Hereford Utd	SL	Millwall	4	H	1-0
	2R/r	Bedford Town	SL	Brighton & Hove A	3	H	2-1
	2R/r	Corby Town	SL	Luton Town	3	A	1-0
1966/67	2R	Nuneaton Borough	SL	Swansea Town	3	H	2-0
	2R/r	Bedford Town	SL	Oxford United	3	H	1-0
1967/68	1R	Runcorn	CC	Notts County	3	H	1-0
	1R	Tow Law Town	NL	Mansfield Town	4	H	5-1
	1R/r	Guildford City	SL	Brentford	4	H	2-1
	1R/r	Macclesfield Town	CC	Stockport County	3	H	2-1
	1R/2r	Chelmsford City	SL	Oxford United	3	N	1-0
1968/69	1R	Dartford	SL	Aldershot	4	A	3-1
1969/70	1R	Brentwood Town	SL	Reading	3	H	1-0
	1R	South Shields	NP	Bradford PA	4	H	2-1
	1R	Tamworth	WM	Torquay Utd	3	H	2-1
	2R	Hillingdon Borough	SL	Luton Town	3	H	2-1
	2R/r	South Shields	NP	Oldham Athletic	4	A	2-1
1970/71	1R	Barnet	SL	Newport County	4	H	6-1
	1R	Boston Utd	NP	Southport	4	A	2-0
	1R	Grantham	MC	Stockport County	4	H	2-1
	1R	Rhyl	CC	Hartlepool Utd	4	H	1-0
	1R/r	Hereford Utd	SL	Northampton T	4	A	2-1
	2R	Wigan Athletic	NP	Peterborough Utd	4	H	2-1
	2R	Yeovil Town	SL	Bournemouth & Bosc	4	A	1-0
	2R/2r	Rhyl	CC	Barnsley	3	N	2-0
1971/72	1R	Blyth Spartans	NL	Crewe Alexandra	4	A	1-0
	1R	Wigan Athletic	NP	Halifax Town	3	H	2-1
	1R/r	South Shields	NP	Scunthorpe Utd	4	A	3-2
	2R	Blyth Spartans	NL	Stockport County	4	H	1-0
	2R	Boston Utd	NP	Hartlepool Utd	4	H	2-1
	2R/2r	Hereford Utd	SL	Northampton T	4	N	2-1
	3R/r	Hereford Utd	SL	Newcastle Utd	1	H	2-1
1972/73	1R	Bangor City	NP	Rochdale	3	A	2-1
	1R	Hayes	IL	Bristol Rovers	3	H	1-0
	1R	Margate	SL	Swansea City	3	H	1-0
	1R	Walton & Hersham	IL	Exeter City	4	H	2-1
	1R	Yeovil Town	SL	Brentford	3	H	2-1
	1R/r	Scarborough	NP	Oldham Ath	3	H	2-1
1973/74	1R	Altrincham	NP	Hartlepool	4	H	2-0
	1R	Alvechurhc	WM	Exeter City	4	A	1-0
	1R	Wycombe W	IL	Newport County	4	H	3-1
	1R/r	Scarborough	NP	Crewe Alexandra	4	H	2-1
	1R/r	Walton & Hersham	IL	Brighton & Hove A	3	A	4-0
	2R/r	Grantham	SL	Rochdale	3	A	5-3
1974/75	1R/r	Altrincham	NP	Scunthorpe Utd	4	H	3-1
	1R/r	Gateshead Utd	NP	Crewe Alexandra	4	H	1-0
	1R/r	Kettering T	SL	Swansea City	4	H	3-1
	1R/r	Stafford Rangers	NP	Stockport County	4	H	1-0
	1R/r	Wigan Athletic	NP	Shrewbury Town	4	H	2-1
	2R	Leatherhead	IL	Colchester Utd	3	H	1-0
	2R	Stafford Rangers	NP	Halifax Town	3	H	2-1
	2R/r	Wycombe W	IL	APC Bournemouth	4	A	2-1
	3R	Leatherhead	IL	Brighton & Hove A	3	A	1-0
	3R	Wimbledon	SL	Burnley	1	A	1-0

FA CUP GIANT KILLING

Season	Round	Non League Club	League	League Club	Div	Ven	Score
	3R/r	Stafford Rangers	NP	Rotherham Utd	4	A	2-0
1975/76	1R	Coventry Sporting	WM	Tranmere Rovers	4	N	2-0
	1R	Gateshead Utd	NP	Grimsby Town	3	A	3-1
	1R	Hendon	IL	Reading	4	H	1-0
	1R	Leatherhead	IL	Cambridge Utd	4	H	2-0
	1R	Marine	CC	Barnsley	4	H	3-1
	1R	Spennymoor Utd	NL	Southport	4	H	4-1
	1R/r	Dover	SL	Colchester Utd	3	H	4-1
	2R	Scarborough	NP	Preston North End	3	H	3-2
	3R/r	Tooting & Mitcham	IL	Swindon Town	3	H	2-1
1976/77	1R	Hillingdon B	SL	Torquay Utd	4	A	2-1
	1R	Kettering T	SL	Oxford Utd	3	A	1-0
	1R	Leatherhead	IL	Northampton T	3	H	2-0
	1R	Minehead	SL	Swansea City	4	A	1-0
	1R/2r	Northwich Victoria	NP	Rochdale	4	N	2-1
	2R	Matlock Town	NP	Mansfield Town	3	A	5-2
	2R	Northwich Victoria	NP	Peterborough Utd	3	H	4-0
	3R	Northwich Victoria	NP	Watford	4	H	3-2
1977/78	1R	Enfield	IL	Wimbledon	4	H	3-0
	1R	Nuneaton B	SL	Oxford Utd	3	H	2-0
	1R	Scarborough	NP	Rochdale	4	H	4-2
	1R	Wigan Athletic	NP	York City	4	H	1-0
	R/r	Runcorn	NP	Southport	4	H	1-0
	1R/r	Wealdstone	SL	Hereford Utd	3	A	3-2
	2R	Blyth Spartans	NL	Chesterfield	3	H	1-0
	2R	Enfield	IL	Northampton T	4	A	2-0
	2R	Wigan Athletic	NP	Sheffield Wed	3	H	1-0
	2R	Wealdstone	SL	Reading	4	H	2-1
	2R/r	Scarborough	NP	Crewe Alexandra	4	H	2-0
	4R	Blyth Spartans	NL	Stoke City	2	A	3-2
1978/79	1R	Droylsden	CC	Rochdale	4	A	1-0
	1R	Worcester City	SL	Plymouth Argyle	3	H	2-0
	2R	Maidstone Utd	SL	Exeter City	3	H	1-0
1979/80	1R	Altrincham	AP	Crewe Alexandra	4	H	3-0
	1R	Barking	IL	Oxford Utd	3	H	1-0
	2R/r	Altrincham	AP	Rotherham Utd	3	A	2-0
	2R/r	Harlow Town	IL	Southend Utd	3	H	1-0
	3R/r	Harlow Town	IL	Leicester City	2	H	1-0

Every club has its day! Harlow Town are certainly not one of the regular headline makers, but in 1979-80 season they dumped Southend United and Leicester City out of the Cup and this was the happy dressing room scene as scorer McKenzie is given the star treatment.

Photo: Press Association

Season	Round	Non League Club	League	League Club	Div	Ven	Score
1980/81	1R	Mossley	NP	Crewe Alexandra	4	H	1-0
	2R	Enfield	IL	Hereford Utd	4	H	2-0
	2R/r	Altrincham	AP	Scunthorpe Utd	4	H	1-0
	2R/2r	Maidstone Utd	AP	Gillingham	3	A	2-0
	3R/r	Enfield	IL	Port Vale	4	H	3-0
1981/82	1R	Penrith	NL	Chester	3	H	1-0
	1R/r	Altrincham	AP	Sheffield Utd	4	H	3-0
	2R	Enfield	AP	Wimbledon	3	H	4-1
	2R/r	Altrincham	AP	York City	4	H	4-3
1982/83	1R	Altrincham	AP	Rochdale	4	H	2-1
	1R	Bishop's Stortford	IL	Reading	3	A	2-1
	1R	Boston Utd	AP	Crewe Alexandra	4	H	3-1
	1R	North Shields	NL	Halifax Town	4	A	1-0
	1R	Slough Town	IL	Millwall	3	H	1-0
	1R/r	Northwich Victoria	AP	Chester	4	H	3-1
	1R/r	Telford Utd	AP	Wigan Athletic	3	H	2-1
	2R	Weymouth	AP	Cardiff City	3	A	3-2
	2R	Worcester City	AP	Wrexham	3	H	2-1
1983/84	1R	Telford Utd	AP	Stockport County	4	H	3-2
	1R	Whitby Town	NL	Halifax Town	4	A	2-1
	1R/r	Maidstone Utd	AP	Exeter City	3	H	2-1
	1R/r	Worcester City	AP	Aldershot	4	H	2-1
	2R/r	Telford Utd	AP	Northampton T	4	H	3-2
	3R	Telford Utd	AP	Rochdale	4	A	4-1
1984/85	1R	Altrincham	GL	Blackpool	4	A	1-0
	1R	Northwich Victoria	GL	Crewe Alexandra	4	H	3-1
	1R/r	Bognor Regis T	IL	Swansea City	3	H	3-2
	1R/r	Dagenham	GL	Swindon Town	4	A	2-1
	1R/r	Enfield	GL	Exeter City	4	A	3-0
	1R/r	Telford Utd	GL	Lincoln City	3	H	2-1
	2R	Burton Albion	NP	Aldershot	4	A	2-0
	2R	Dagenham	GL	Peterborough Utd	4	H	1-0
	2R	Telford Utd	GL	Preston North End	3	A	4-1
	3R	Telford Utd	GL	Bradford City	3	H	2-1
	4R/r	Telford Utd	GL	Darlington	4	H	3-0
1985/86	1R	Dagenham	GL	Cambridge Utd	4	H	2-1
	1R	Telford Utd	GL	Stockport County	4	A	1-0
	1R	Wycombe W	GL	Colchester Utd	4	H	2-0
	2R	Altrincham	GL	Blackpool	3	A	2-1
	2R	Frickley Ath	MU	Hartlepool Utd	4	A	1-0
	3R	Altrincham	VC	Birmingham City	1	A	2-1
1986/87	1R	Caernarfon T	MU	Stockport County	4	H	1-0
	1R	Telford Utd	VC	Burnley	4	H	3-0
	1R/2r	Chorley	MU	Wolverhampton W	4	N	3-0
	2R	Maidstone Utd	VC	Cambridge Utd	4	H	1-0
	2R/r	Caernarfon T	MU	York City	3	A	2-1
1987/88	1R	Lincoln City	VC	Crewe Alexandra	4	H	2-1
	1R	Macclesfield T	VC	Carlisle Utd	4	H	4-2
	1R	Runcorn	VC	Chester City	3	A	1-0
	1R	Sutton Utd	VC	Aldershot	3	H	3-0
	2R	Macclesfield T	VC	Rotherham Utd	3	H	4-0
	2R	Sutton Utd	VC	Peterborough Utd	4	A	3-1
	2R	Yeovil Town	VO	Cambridge Utd	4	A	1-0
1988/89	1R	Altrincham	VC	Lincoln City	4	H	3-2
	1R	Runcorn	VC	Wrexham	4	A	3-2
	1R	Bognor Regis Town	IL	Exeter City	4	H	2-1
	1R/r	Enfield	VC	Leyton Orient	4	A	1-0
	2R	Kettering Town	VC	Bristol Rovers	3	H	2-1
	3R	Kettering Town	VC	Halifax Town	4	A	3-2
	3R	Sutton United	VC	Coventry City	1	H	2-1

One of the great winning goals! Robert Hopkins draws his keeper David Seaman out of goal and rolls in a tragic back pass to give Altrincham a 2-1 victory at First Division Birmingham City in 1986. Photo: John Rooney

Robbie Cooke flashes a header at goal against Halifax Town. Kettering drew this home tie but won the replay and went on to visit Charlton Athletic in the Fourth Round in season 1988-89.

Season	Round	Non League Club	League	League Club	Div	Ven	Score
1989/90	1R	Aylesbury Utd	IL	Southend Utd	4	H	1-0
	1R	Whitley Bay	HFS	Scarborough	4	A	1-0
	1R	Welling United	VC	Birmingham City	3	H	1-0
	2R	Darlington	VC	Halifax Town	4	H	3-0
	2R	Whitley Bay	HFS	Preston North End	3	H	2-0
1990/91	1R	Leek Town	HFS	Scarborough	4	A	1-0
	1R	Hayes	IL	Cardiff City	3	H	1-0
	1R	Chorley	HFS	Bury	3	H	2-1
	1R	Colchester Utd	VC	Reading	3	H	2-1
	2R	Barnet	VC	Northampton Town	4	A	1-0
	3R	Woking	IL	West Bromwich A	2	A	4-2

FIRST DIVISION CLUBS DEFEATED BY NON-LEAGUE CLUBS SINCE 1947/48

1947/48	4th Rnd	Colchester United (Southern League)	1	Huddersfield Town	0
1948/49	4th Rnd	Yeovil Town (Southern League)	2	Sunderland	1
1971/72	3rd Rnd	Hereford United (Southern League	2	Newcastle United	1
1974/75	3rd Rnd	Burnley	0	Wimbledon (Southern League)	1
1985/86	3rd Rnd	Birmingham City	1	Altrincham (Vauxhall Conference)	2
1988/89	3rd Rnd	Sutton United (Vauxhall Conference)	2	Coventry City	1

SECOND DIVISION CLUBS DEFEATED BY NON-LEAGUE CLUBS SINCE 1947/48

1947/48	4th Rnd	Colchester United (Southern League)	3	Bradford Park Avenue	2
1948/49	3rd Rnd	Yeovil Town (Southern League)	3	Bury	1
1954/55	3rd Rnd	Bishop Auckland (Northern League)	3	Notts County	0
1956/57	3rd Rnd	Notts County	1	Rhyl (Cheshire Co.)	3
1956/57	3rd Rnd	Lincoln City	4	Peterborough United (Midland League)	5
1958/59	3rd Rnd	Worcester City (Southern League)	2	Liverpool	1
1959/60	3rd Rnd	Ipswich Town	2	Peterborough United (Midland League)	3
1977/78	4th Rnd	Stoke City	2	Blyth spartans (Northern League)	3
1979/80	3rd Rnd	Harlow (Isthmian League)	1	Leicester City	0
1990/91	3rd Rnd	West Bromwich Albion	2	Woking (Isthmian League)	4

HIGHEST WIN BY NON LEAGUE CLUB

7-1   Crystal Palace v Chelsea   1905/06

HIGHEST AWAY WIN BY NON LEAGUE CLUB

6-1   Wigan Athletic v Carlisle Utd   1954/55
6-1   Boston Utd v Derby County   1955/56

BEST FA CUP RECORDS IN NON-LEAGUE FOOTBALL

	First Round	Second Round	Third Round	Fourth Round	Fifth Round	P	W	D	L	F	A
1. YEOVIL TOWN	22	10	9	-	1	92	32	18	42	114	161

(Seasons in Competition Proper: 42)
League Clubs who defeated Yeovil Town
Arsenal, Aldershot, Bournemouth, Bristol City, Brentford, Bury, Brighton, Chester, Colchester Utd (2),
Chesterfield, Shrewsbury T, Fulham (2), Liverpool, Manchester Utd (2), Millwall, Norwich (2), Notts County,
Plymouth (2), Swindon T, Sheff Wed, Southend Utd, Walsall, Torquay Utd (2), Hereford, QPR, Maidstone Utd
League Clubs Beaten
C Palace (2), Southend (2), Bury, Exeter C, Sunderland, Walsall, Brentford, Bournemouth, Brighton & H,
Gillingham, Cambridge Utd

	First Round	Second Round	Third Round	Fourth Round	Fifth Round	P	W	D	L	F	A
2. KETTERING TOWN	23	7	2	1	-	66	14	19	33	83	133

(Seasons in Competition Proper: 33)
League Clubs who defeated Kettering Town
Bristol Rov (2), Coventry C, Charlton Ath (2), C Palace (2), Blackpool, Colchester Utd, Grimsby T, Oxford Utd,
Northampton (2), Millwall, Newport C, Orient, QPR, Reading (2), Swansea, Walsall (2), Bournemouth, Gillingham
League Clubs beaten
Oxford Utd, Millwall, Swansea, Swindon T, Bristol Rovers, Halifax Town

3. WEYMOUTH 21 7 2 1 - 61 14 16 31 67 127
(Seasons in Competition Proper: 31)
League Clubs who defeated Weymouth
Aldershot, Bournemouth, Bristol Rov (2), Cambridge Utd (2), Gillingham, Orient (2), Northampton T (2), Coventry C, Man Utd, Newport C, Peterborough, PNE, Southend (2), Swindon T, Swansea, Torquay Utd, Southampton, Colchester Utd, Millwall
League Clubs beaten
Aldershot, Cardiff C, Newport Co, Shrewsbury

4. BLYTH SPARTANS 14 9 1 - 1 59 15 19 25 77 118
(Seasons in Competition Proper: 25)
League Clubs who defeated Blyth Spartans
Accrington (2), Bournemouth, Carlisle Utd, Chester, Doncaster, Grimsly T, Hull C, Hartlepool, Mansfield (2), PNE, Reading, Stockport C, Walsall, Wrexham (3), Torquay U, York C
League Clubs beaten
Crewe Alex, Chesterfield, Stockport Co, Hartlepool U, Stoke City

5. ALTRINCHAM 9 7 6 1 - 57 22 12 23 72 78
(Seasons in Competition Proper: 23)
League Clubs who defeated Altrincham
Barrow, Burnley, Blackburn R, Crewe A, Darlington, Everton, Huddersfield, Halifax T (2), Liverpool, Notts Co, Orient, Rotherham U, Tottenham H, Wolverhampton W, Wrexham, Doncaster R, Wigan Ath, York C
League Clubs beaten
Rochdale (2), Crewe A, Hartlepool, Scunthorpe U (2), Sheffield U, Rotherham U, York City, Blackpool (2), Birmingham City, Lincoln C

Above *Altrincham beat Blackpool in two consecutive seasons in the eighties. Both games were at Bloomfield Road and here photographer John Rooney catches Paul Reid as he stabs in 'Alty's' first goal in a 2-1 victory in 1985-86*
Right *Enfield's Peter Burton scores a last minute equaliser at Barnsley and sets up a replay at White Hart Lane, which attracted over 35 000.*   Photo: Mick Eason

6. BARNET	20	4	5	-	-	56	14	12	30	79	120

(Seasons in Competition Proper: 29)
League Clubs who defeated Barnet
Brentford, Brighton (2), Colchester U, Exeter C, Peterborough, PNE, Southampton, Southend U, QPR (3), Torquay U (2), Plymouth A, Bristol R, Portsmouth
League Clubs beaten
Newport Co, Northampton T

7. TELFORD UNITED	21	5	1	1	1	56	14	12	30	68	111

(Seasons in Competition Proper: 29)
League Clubs who defeated Telford United
Accrington S, Aldershot, Bristol C, Bristol R (2), Chester, Doncaster R, Gillingham, Norwich C, Mansfield T (2), Port Vale, Swansea, Southend U, Stockport C (2), Walsall (2), Watford, Tranmere R, Everton, Derby Co, Leeds U, Carlisle U, Darlington
League Clubs beaten
Darlington, Wigan Ath, Stockton Co (2), Northampton T, Rochdale, Lincoln, PNE, Burnley, Bradford

8. ENFIELD	11	10	2	1	-	56	17	15	24	85	96

(Seasons in Competition Proper: 24)
League Clubs who defeated Enfield
Bournemouth, Barnsley, Bristol C, Brighton, Cardiff C (3), Cambridge U, C Palace, Peterborough (2), Newport C, Reading, Swansea, Swindon (2), Watford, Millwall
League Clubs beaten
Wimbledon (2), Northampton, Hereford U, Port Vale, Exeter C, Orient

9. BATH CITY   9   10   5   -   -   54 21 8 25 79 90
(Seasons in Competition Proper: 24)
League Clubs who defeated Bath City
Bolton W, Brentford, Brighton (2), Bournemouth, Colchester U, Charlton A, Coventry C, Grimsby T, Norwich C, QPR, Plymouth A, Swindon T, Walsall, Peterborough, Bristol C, Mansfield, Fulham, Hereford
League Clubs beaten
C Palace, Exeter C, Newport C, Notts C, Millwall, Southend

10. BOSTON UNITED   20   5   4   -   -   53 13 11 29 72 113
(Seasons in Competition Proper: 29)
League Clubs who defeated Boston United
Bradford PA, Barnsley, Chester, Crewe A, Darlington (2), Derby Co, Orient, Portsmouth, Oldham A, Northampton, Lincoln C, Chesterfield, Sheff U, Scunthorpe U, Sunderland, Tottenham H, Tranmere R, Rotherham U, York C
League Clubs beaten
Bradford, Crewe A, Derby Co, Hartlepool, Mansfield, Southport

11. WYCOMBE WANDERERS   15   7   2   -   -   50 11 15 24 56 76
(Seasons in Competition Proper: 24)
League Clubs who defeated Wycombe Wanderers
Bournemouth, Bristol R, Cardiff C, Gillingham, Newport C, Northampton, Middlesbrough, Peterborough U, Reading, Watford, York C
League Clubs beaten
Newport C, Bournemouth, Colchester U

12. CHELMSFORD CITY   16   8   1   1   -   49 13 9 27 63 94
(Seasons in Competition Proper: 26)
League Clubs who defeated Chelmsford City
Aldershot, Birmingham, Brentford, Colchester, C Palace, Charlton A, Ipswich T (2), Mansfield T, Northampton, Notts Co, Port Vale, Shrewsbury T, Torquay U, Watford
League Clubs beaten
Darlington, Southampton, Oxford U

13. DARTFORD   17   7   2   -   -   46 11 9 26 64 97
(Seasons in Competition Proper: 26)
League Clubs who defeated Dartford
Aldershot, Bristol C (2), Bristol R, Bournemouth, C Palace, Darlington, Derby Co, Orient, Port Vale, Plymouth A, Reading, Swindon T, Exeter C
League Clubs beaten
Aldershot, Cardiff C, Exeter C

14. BISHOP AUCKLAND   9   9   -   1   -   42 12 9 21 66 86
(Seasons in Competition Proper: 19)
League Clubs who defeated Bishop Auckland
Bury, Chester C, Coventry C, Carlisle U, Halifax T, Tranmere R, PNE, Rochdale, Scunthorpe U, Stockport C, York C (3), Blackpool, Crewe A
League Clubs beaten
C Palace, Ipswich T, Tranmere R

FA CUP NON-LEAGUE TABLE 1925-90

	Club	Round reached					Matches played 1st Round onwards						Last in 1st Rd	Wins against Lge clubs
		1st	2nd	3rd	4th	5th	P	W	D	L	F	A		
1	Yeovil Town	22	10	9	-	1	92	32	18	42	114	161	90/91	13
2	Kettering Town	23	7	2	1	-	66	14	19	33	83	133	89/90	6
3	Weymouth	21	7	2	1	-	61	14	16	31	67	127	85/86	4
4	Blyth Spartans	14	9	1	-	1	59	15	19	25	77	117	81/82	5
5	Altrincham	9	7	6	1	-	57	22	12	23	72	78	90/91	13
6	Barnet	20	4	5	-	-	56	14	12	30	79	120	90/01	2
7	Telford United	21	5	1	1	1	56	14	12	30	68	111	90/91	10
8	Enfield	11	10	2	1	-	56	17	15	24	85	96	88/89	7
9	Bath City	9	10	5	-	-	54	21	8	25	79	90	89/90	6
10	Boston United	20	5	4	-	-	53	13	11	29	72	113	90/91	5
11	Wycombe Wanderers	15	7	2	-	-	50	11	15	24	56	76	90/91	3
12	Chelmsford City	16	8	1	1	-	49	13	9	27	63	94	90/91	3
13	Dartford	17	7	2	-	-	46	11	9	26	64	97	89/90	3
14	Bishop Auckland	9	9	-	1	-	42	12	9	21	66	86	89/90	3

A great moment for Bishops Stortford as Lyndon Lynch crashes home the opening goal of the match during the Isthmian League side's draw with Middlesborough in 1983.

SEASONS REVIEWED 1979-91

INTRODUCTION

The most frustrating time for non-league football used to occur at the end of every season when the bottom clubs in the Fourth Division had to apply for re-election. A few non-league clubs would challenge them for a place in the League but the member clubs would always look after 'their own' (they might need the vote themselves next season) and no non-league club really had a chance.

To create a little more hope just one club was nominated to challenge 'the old pals act', but without much luck. So it was really the frustration caused by this situation that forced the senior semi-professional world to put its house in order and you can see how the pyramid took shape by studying the league structure through the featured seasons in this section of the book.

It is worth stressing here once again that a number of famous competitions of great tradition sacrificed themselves so that the national structure was formed on good foundations. It is a great credit to the league officials who accepted 'redundancy' and it is hoped they will have felt that the success of the new scheme, with which the Football League were happy to link, has made all their efforts worth while.

It will be interesting to check in ten years time and see where the clubs are playing e.g. where were Welling United in the 1979-80 season and where will they be in 1999?

Enfield – one of the success stories of the '80s

1979-80

The 1979-80 season was historic, as it marked the implementation of the Alliance Premier League, now known as the GM Vauxhall Conference. For the first time there was a national semi-professional competition, and the concept of the 'Pyramid' was born.

Of the twenty clubs that contested the first Alliance Premier League championship, thirteen had been supplied by the Southern League, with the remaining seven originating from the Northern League. Altrincham became the first champions holding off the challenge of Weymouth by just two points, but they were to suffer bitter disappointment by missing election to the league by just one vote.

The FA Trophy and Vase competitions saw first Wembley victories for two clubs who had experienced the bitter taste of defeat in previous finals. The Trophy went to Dagenham who in beating Mossley erased the memory of defeat against Scarborough three years earlier. Meanwhile Stamford beat Guisborough Town 2-0 in the FA Vase final; Stamford had lost to Billericay in the final in 1976.

The non-league club who captured the imagination of the country were Harlow Town. They remained undefeated until their fifth match against Football League opposition in the FA Cup. During this run they knocked out Southend United and the Second Division champions to be, Leicester City, both after replays, before finally succumbing at Watford in the Fourth Round, a match that was televised on 'Match of the Day'. Harlow led at half-time, conceded four quick goals at the start of the second period, but battled back wonderfully to lose just 4-3.

SUMMARY

FA VASE

	Winners	Runners-up	Semi-finalists
	Stamford	Guisborough Town	Curzon Ashton, Hungerford Town

FA TROPHY

	Winners	Runners-up	Semi-finalists
	Dagenham	Mossley	Boston United, Woking

FA CUP   Most Successful Team: Harlow

1st Rd: Harlow 2 Leyton/Ilford 1; 2nd Rd: Southend 1 Harlow 1; 2nd Rd Replay: Harlow 1 Southend 0; 3rd Rd: Leicester City 1 Harlow 1; 3rd Rd Replay: Harlow 1 Leicester 0; 4th Rd: Watford 4 Harlow 3

ALLIANCE PREMIER LEAGUE   Champions: Altrincham   Runners-up: Weymouth

ALLIANCE PREMIER LEAGUE TABLE

	P	W	D	L	F	A	Pts
Altrincham	38	24	8	6	79	35	56
Weymouth	38	22	10	6	73	37	54
Worcester City	38	19	11	8	53	36	49
Boston United	38	16	13	9	52	43	45
Gravesend & N'fleet	38	17	10	11	49	44	44
Maidstone United	38	16	11	11	54	37	43
Kettering Town	38	15	13	10	55	50	43
Northwich Victoria	38	16	10	12	50	38	42
Bangor City	38	14	14	10	41	46	42
Nuneaton Borough	38	13	13	12	58	44	39
Scarborough	38	12	15	11	47	38	39
Yeovil Town	38	13	10	15	46	49	36
Telford United	38	13	8	17	52	60	34
Barrow	38	14	6	18	47	55	34
Wealdstone	38	9	15	14	42	54	33
Bath City	38	10	12	16	43	69	32
Barnet	38	10	10	18	32	48	30
AP Leamington	38	7	11	20	32	63	25
Stafford Rangers	38	6	10	22	41	57	22
Redditch United	38	5	8	25	26	69	18

ALLIANCE PREMIER STATISTICS

Top Crowds

4872	Yeovil Town v Weymouth (26.12.79)
3120	Scarborough v Kettering Town (3.11.79)
3025	Scarborough v Northwich Victoria (17.11.79)
2867	Kettering Town v Altrincham (6.10.79)
2812	Scarborough v Barrow (22.8.79)

Top Scorers

29	Graham Smith (Northwich Victoria)
28	Tom Paterson (Weymouth)
24	John Rogers (Altrincham)
22	Iannone (Weymouth)
21	John Daubney (Maidstone Utd)

Manager of the Month Awards

Dec	Tony Sanders (Altrincham)
Jan	S Morgan (Weymouth)
Feb	Ken Payne (Wealdstone)
Mar	M Taylor (Barrow)
Apr	Albert Phelan (Boston Utd)

ISTHMIAN LEAGUE

Premier Division	P	W	D	L	F	A	Pts
Enfield	42	25	9	8	74	32	84
Walthamstow Ave	42	24	9	9	87	48	81
Dulwich Hamlet	42	21	16	5	66	37	79
Sutton United	42	20	13	9	67	40	73
Dagenham	42	20	13	9	82	56	73
Tooting & Mitcham	42	21	6	15	62	59	69
Barking	42	19	10	13	72	51	67
Harrow Borough	42	17	15	10	64	51	66
Woking	42	17	13	12	78	59	64
Wycombe Wnderers	42	17	13	12	72	53	64
Harlow Town	42	14	12	16	54	60	54
Hitchin Town	42	13	15	14	54	68	54
Hendon	42	12	13	17	50	57	49
Slough Town	42	13	10	19	54	71	49
Boreham Wood	42	13	10	19	50	69	49
Staines Town	42	14	6	22	46	67	48
Hayes	42	12	9	21	48	68	45
Leatherhead	42	11	11	20	51	60	44
Carshalton Athletic	42	12	7	23	48	78	43
Croydon	42	12	7	23	48	78	43
Oxford City	42	10	9	23	49	87	39
Tilbury *	42	7	11	24	41	90	30

* 2 points deducted

Division One

	P	W	D	L	F	A	Pts
Leytonstone & Ilford	42	31	6	5	83	35	99
Bromley	42	24	10	8	93	44	82
Maidenhead United	42	24	8	10	81	46	80
Bishop's Stortford	42	24	8	10	74	47	80
Kingstonian	42	22	8	12	59	44	74
Chesham United	42	18	13	11	68	56	67
St Albans City	42	17	13	12	65	47	64
Farnborough Town	42	19	7	16	70	57	64
Epsom & Ewell	42	18	7	17	62	57	61
Camberley Town	42	16	10	16	43	38	58
Walton & Hersham	42	15	12	15	61	50	57
Wembley	42	16	8	18	46	52	56
Wokingham Town	42	14	11	17	45	49	53
Hertford Town	42	13	11	18	71	74	50
Aveley	42	12	13	17	45	55	49
Hampton	42	14	7	21	57	74	49
Finchley	42	13	9	20	44	59	48
Metropolitan Police	42	13	8	21	46	67	47
Ware	42	11	12	19	41	57	45
Clapton	42	14	3	25	48	77	45
Harwich & Prkeston*	42	11	6	25	51	84	38
Horsham	42	6	4	32	29	113	22

* One point deducted

Division Two

	P	W	D	L	F	A	Pts
Billericay Town	36	31	3	2	100	18	96
Lewes	36	24	7	5	82	33	79
Hungerford Town	36	21	8	7	77	35	71
Eastbourne United	36	21	6	9	77	45	69
Letchworth Gdn City	36	21	6	9	63	32	69
Hornchurch	36	21	6	9	66	39	69
Molesey	36	15	9	12	67	60	54
Barton Rovers	36	15	7	14	49	49	52
Worthing	36	14	9	13	58	54	51
Cheshunt	36	13	7	16	47	52	46
Rainham Town	36	12	7	17	54	65	43
Egham Town	36	11	9	16	47	53	42
Southall	36	11	6	19	43	69	39
Feltham	36	8	11	17	23	49	35
Tring Town	36	7	3	16	38	55	34
Epping Town	36	10	4	22	44	69	34
Willesden	36	9	6	21	32	83	33
Hemel Hempstead	36	4	9	23	33	72	21
Corinthian Casuals	36	6	3	27	24	92	21

SOUTHERN LEAGUE

Midland Division	P	W	D	L	F	A	Pts
Bridgend Town	42	28	6	8	85	39	62
Minehead	42	22	15	5	70	42	59
Bedford Town	42	20	12	10	71	42	52
Kidderminster Har	42	23	6	13	81	59	52
Merthyr Tydfil	42	20	11	11	70	47	51
Enderby Town	42	21	8	13	62	50	50
Stourbridge	42	19	11	12	67	49	49
Alvechurch	42	17	14	11	78	60	48
Trowbridge Town	42	19	9	14	62	61	47
Bromsgrove Rovers	42	18	10	14	67	56	46
Barry Town	42	15	12	15	64	58	42
King's Lynn	42	15	11	16	48	55	41
Banbury United	42	13	14	15	56	56	40
Taunton Town	42	16	8	18	55	62	40
Witney Town	42	10	19	13	43	45	39
Bedworth United	42	12	15	15	40	42	39
Milton Keynes City	42	15	7	20	46	59	37
Gloucester City	42	10	14	18	55	68	32*
Cheltenham Town	42	13	5	24	49	70	31
Wellingborough Tn	42	9	7	26	54	106	25
Cambridge City	42	6	9	27	30	73	21
Corby Town	42	5	9	28	40	94	19

* Two points deducted for playing ineligible player

Southern Division	P	W	D	L	F	A	Pts
Dorchester Town	46	25	12	9	81	53	62
Aylesbury United	46	25	11	10	73	40	61
Dover	46	22	13	11	78	48	57
Gosport Borough	46	21	15	10	70	50	57
Dartford	46	21	14	11	66	45	56
Bognor Regis Town	46	20	15	11	66	38	55
Hillingdon Borough	46	19	16	11	64	41	54
Dunstable	46	17	19	10	93	64	53
Addlestone	46	20	13	13	72	57	53
Hastings United	46	19	15	12	74	65	53
Fareham Town	46	16	16	14	61	53	48
Waterlooville	46	17	12	17	67	64	46
Andover	46	16	13	17	65	65	45
Poole Town	46	16	13	17	69	64	45
Canterbury Town	46	15	14	17	56	60	44
Hounslow	46	14	15	17	44	57	43
Margate	46	17	8	21	51	62	42
Folkestone	46	14	11	21	54	62	39
Ashford Town	46	12	14	20	54	71	38
Crawley Town	46	13	11	22	55	72	37
Chelmsford City	46	9	18	19	47	66	36
Basingstoke Town	46	9	15	22	48	69	33
Salisbury	46	10	12	24	47	58	32
Tonbridge AFC	46	3	9	34	31	128	15

NORTHERN PREMIER LEAGUE

	P	W	D	L	F	A	Pts
Mossley	42	28	9	5	96	41	65
Witton Albion	42	28	8	6	89	30	64
Frickley Athletic	42	24	13	5	93	48	61
Burton Albion	42	25	6	11	83	42	56
Matlock Town	42	18	17	7	87	53	53
Buxton	42	21	9	12	61	48	51
Worksop Town	42	20	10	12	65	52	50
Macclesfield Town	42	18	11	13	67	53	47
Grantham	42	18	8	16	71	65	44
Marine	42	16	10	16	65	57	42
Goole Town	42	14	13	15	61	63	41
Lancaster City	42	13	13	16	74	77	39
Oswestry Town	42	12	14	16	44	60	38
Gainsborough Trinity	42	14	8	20	64	75	36
Runcorn	42	11	11	20	46	63	33
Gateshead	42	11	11	20	50	77	33
Morecambe	42	10	12	20	40	59	32
Netherfield	42	7	15	20	37	66	29
Southport	42	8	13	21	30	75	29
South Liverpool	42	7	14	21	51	84	28
Workington	42	8	12	22	50	85	28
Tamworth	42	8	9	25	26	77	25

WEST MIDLANDS (REGIONAL) LEAGUE

Premier Division	P	W	D	L	F	A	Pts
Sutton Coldfield Tn	42	28	11	3	96	39	67
Lye Town	42	30	7	5	73	29	67
Willenhall Town	42	23	11	8	95	45	57
Hednesford Town	42	19	16	7	72	41	54
Brereton Social	42	20	11	11	86	45	51
Brierley Hill Alliance	42	20	11	11	62	49	51
Shifnal Town	42	19	10	13	72	53	48
Dudley Town	42	20	6	16	61	52	46
Coventry Sporting	42	16	10	16	64	67	42
Ledbury Town	42	13	15	14	62	71	41
Malvern Town	42	13	11	18	56	71	37
Halesowen Town	42	13	11	18	52	69	37
Hinckley Athletic	42	12	12	18	40	59	36
Tividale	42	13	9	20	70	75	35
Gresley Rovers	42	10	14	18	49	69	34
Armitage	42	12	9	21	39	55	33
VS Rugby	42	11	11	20	43	60	33
Blakenall	42	11	11	20	45	76	33
Wednesfield Social	42	10	12	20	44	66	32
Darlaston	42	9	13	20	42	86	31
Gornal Athletic	42	7	16	19	52	69	30
Bilston	42	8	13	21	50	79	29

DRYBROUGH'S NORTHERN LEAGUE

	P	W	D	L	F	A	Pts
Blyth Spartans	38	29	5	4	93	28	92
Spennymoor United	38	26	7	5	83	40	85
Horden Colliery Welf	38	24	6	8	73	32	78
Ashington	38	21	8	9	88	53	71
Crook Town	38	21	8	9	77	51	71
Bishop Auckland	38	18	9	11	64	54	63
Consett	38	16	7	15	68	52	55
South Bank	38	16	7	15	70	71	55
Shildon	38	16	7	15	70	71	55
West Auckland Tn	38	16	6	16	57	52	54
Whitby Town	38	14	10	14	72	62	52
Tow Law Town	38	16	4	18	50	56	52
Evenwood Town	38	14	9	15	49	55	51
Penrith	38	13	5	20	54	72	44
Bilingham Synthonia	38	10	12	16	44	72	42
North Shields	38	12	3	23	62	81	39
Ferryhill Athletic	38	9	7	22	38	60	34
Durham City	38	7	9	22	30	63	30
Willington	38	6	5	27	27	105	23
Whitley Bay	38	4	7	27	31	90	16*

* Three points deducted

WESTERN LEAGUE

Premier Division	P	W	D	L	F	A	Pts
Barnstaple Town	38	23	10	5	67	31	56
AFC Bournemouth	38	24	7	7	100	26	55
Weston-super-Mare	38	22	11	5	81	45	55
Frome Town	38	19	10	9	57	38	48
Bridgwater Town	38	17	12	9	64	43	46
Exeter City	38	16	11	11	71	59	43
Clevedon Town	38	16	10	12	74	58	42
Portway-Bristol	38	16	10	12	66	53	42
Saltash United	38	14	14	10	64	51	42
Bideford	38	16	10	12	61	51	42
Keynsham Town	38	16	10	12	56	53	42
Falmouth Town	38	14	10	14	58	53	38
Dawlish	38	10	11	17	39	67	31
Clandown	38	12	6	20	53	76	30
Tiverton Town	38	8	14	16	36	65	30
Welton Rovers	38	10	9	19	59	84	29
Paulton Rovers	38	11	6	21	50	68	28
Mangotsfield United	38	7	10	21	37	80	24
Bridport	38	4	14	20	31	67	21*
Ilminster Town	38	2	11	25	31	87	15

* One point deducted for playing an ineligible player

CHESHIRE COUNTY LEAGUE

First Division

	P	W	D	L	F	A	Pts
Stalybridge Celtic	38	26	7	5	94	46	59
Winsford United	38	23	6	9	72	41	52
Chorley	38	20	11	7	60	35	51
Ashton United	38	15	15	8	71	65	45
Burscough	38	16	11	11	67	54	43
Hyde United	38	16	10	12	60	48	42
Droylsden	38	15	10	13	63	45	40
Horwich RMI	38	13	12	13	53	52	38
Curzon Ashton	38	11	14	13	48	55	36
Darwen	38	12	12	14	41	52	36
Rossendale United	38	12	12	14	48	73	36
St Helens Town	38	10	15	13	59	55	35
Bootle	38	14	7	17	50	53	35
Nantwich Town	38	14	7	17	53	62	35
New Mills	38	11	13	14	44	57	35
Formby	38	13	7	18	50	58	33
Fleetwood Town	38	10	11	17	51	63	31
Leek Town	38	10	9	19	45	66	29
Rhyl	38	10	7	21	54	66	27
Radcliffe Borough	38	6	10	22	45	82	22

Second Division

	P	W	D	L	F	A	Pts
Prescot Town	34	22	7	5	89	25	51
Accrington Stanley	34	20	9	5	67	33	49
Kirkby Town	34	23	3	8	70	40	49
Prescot BI	34	19	7	8	77	54	45
Congleton Town	34	18	8	8	61	42	44
Eastwood (Hanley)	34	15	10	9	65	44	40
Glossop	34	14	7	13	53	45	35
Maghull	34	12	10	12	49	49	34
Ford Motors	34	13	6	15	48	44	32
New Brighton	34	13	6	15	59	63	32
Atherton Collieries	34	9	14	11	44	48	32
Irlam Town	34	12	7	15	48	49	31
Middlewich Athletic	34	12	6	16	55	64	30
Skelmersdale United	34	9	10	15	46	69	28
Warrington Town	34	9	6	19	48	80	24
Prestwich Heys	34	8	6	20	36	71	22
Ashton Town	34	3	12	19	35	83	18
Anson Villa	34	5	6	23	29	76	16

MIDLAND FOOTBALL COMBINATION

Division One

	P	W	D	L	F	A	Pts
Bridgnorth Town	38	26	7	5	78	20	59
Moor Green	38	24	8	6	83	39	56
Oldbury United	38	21	8	9	71	41	50
Walsall Sportsco	38	18	13	7	55	36	49
Highgate United	38	18	8	12	65	56	44
Chipping Norton Tn	38	16	11	11	56	41	43
Mile Oak Rovers	38	13	16	9	46	42	42
Boldmere St Mich'ls	38	14	13	11	51	34	41
Evesham United	38	16	9	13	58	42	41
West Mids Police	38	16	8	14	52	56	40
Cinderford Town	38	12	15	11	41	41	39
Solihull Borough	38	13	10	15	53	63	36
Knowle	38	11	11	16	36	43	33
Coleshill Town	38	12	9	17	42	54	33
Racing Club Wck	38	8	15	15	31	54	31
Walsall Wood	38	7	15	16	36	57	29
Paget Rangers	38	9	9	20	41	64	27
Cradley Town	38	9	8	21	34	57	26
Studley Sporting Clb	38	6	9	23	40	97	21
Northfleet Town	38	5	10	23	31	63	20

Division Two

	P	W	D	L	F	A	Pts
Hurley Daw Mill	38	26	7	5	32	32	59
Smethwick Highfield	38	26	5	7	100	39	57
GEC Witton Social	38	23	7	8	64	34	53
Bedworth Utd Res	38	20	12	6	76	45	52
Mile Oak Rovrs Res	38	20	11	7	70	42	51
Chelmsley Town	38	20	7	11	61	44	47
Stratford Town	38	19	7	12	71	48	45
Stafford FC	38	19	7	12	59	46	45
Moor Green Res	38	15	13	10	78	56	43
Rockwood Albion	38	15	6	17	55	63	36
Kings Heath	38	11	13	14	47	49	35
Polesworth	38	12	10	16	49	49	34
Alcester Town	38	12	10	16	38	51	34
Sutton Coldfld T Res	38	12	8	18	58	59	32
Astwood Bank	38	11	9	18	29	54	31
Tamworth Reserves	38	10	6	22	37	76	26
Ludlow Colts	38	7	10	21	42	79	24
Bournemouth Ath	38	5	10	23	37	82	20
Rowley Regis	38	5	9	24	37	77	19
Highgate United Res	38	5	7	26	41	101	17

KINGSMEAD ATHENIAN LEAGUE

	P	W	D	L	F	A	Pts
Windsor & Eton	38	26	6	6	72	26	58
Burnham	38	24	8	6	73	28	56
Leyton-Wingate	38	22	8	8	86	48	52
Dorking Town	38	20	8	10	61	41	48
Welling United	38	20	7	11	86	46	47
Uxbridge	38	20	7	11	49	41	47
Grays Athletic	38	20	2	16	69	48	42
Ruislip Manor	38	16	10	12	55	46	42
Marlow	38	16	10	12	66	58	42
Edgware	38	15	11	12	62	63	41
Redhill	38	15	9	14	55	46	39
Banstead Athletic	38	15	9	14	57	54	39
Woodford Town	38	13	9	16	57	60	35
Hoddesdon Town	38	12	7	19	56	55	31
Chalfont St Peter	38	10	10	18	50	67	30
Harefield United	38	10	8	20	41	60	28
Fleet Town	38	10	6	22	43	80	26
Haringey Borough	38	9	7	22	41	83	25
Alton Town	38	8	5	25	43	101	21
Chertsey Town	38	4	3	31	33	104	11

MIDLAND COUNTIES LEAGUE

Premier Division	P	W	D	L	F	A	Pts
Belper Town	34	18	11	5	50	25	47
Bridlington Trinity	34	19	9	6	56	34	47
Boston FC	34	18	8	8	60	28	44
Long Eaton United	34	17	9	8	50	32	43
Mexborough Town	34	13	13	8	46	38	39
Eastwood Town	34	16	6	12	57	43	38
Arnold FC	34	13	11	10	54	42	37
Heanor Town	34	14	9	11	53	49	37
Brigg Town	34	13	10	11	45	45	36
Alfreton Town	34	11	13	10	45	46	35
Skegness Town	34	11	11	12	46	45	33
Ashby FC	34	12	7	15	43	52	31
Ilkeston Town	34	9	12	13	36	37	30
Kimberley Town	34	11	8	15	38	53	30
Appleby Frodingham	34	9	10	15	55	61	28
Spalding United	34	5	13	16	32	51	23
Sutton Town	34	6	10	18	33	58	22
Retford Town	34	3	6	25	23	83	12

Division One	P	W	D	L	F	A	Pts
Arnold Kingswell	30	17	11	2	76	37	45
Oakham United	30	19	5	6	63	34	43
Staveley Works	30	15	9	6	51	30	39
Borrowash Victoria	30	14	10	6	53	26	38
Long Eaton Grange	30	13	11	6	55	31	37
Linby Colliery	30	14	8	8	50	51	36
Cresswell Colliery	30	13	8	9	51	42	34
Sutton Trinity	30	14	5	10	60	51	33
Eastwood Town Res	30	11	6	13	49	49	28
Arnold FC Reserves	30	10	8	12	34	39	28
Grantham FC Res	30	11	4	15	31	37	26
Carr Vale United	30	7	8	15	39	60	22
Attenborough FC	30	9	2	19	30	60	20
Long Eaton Utd Res	30	6	7	17	48	95	19
Retford Rail	30	6	5	19	27	65	17
Rolls Royce (Hcknll)	30	5	5	20	52	77	15

YORKSHIRE LEAGUE

Division One	P	W	D	L	F	A	Pts
Emley	30	22	6	2	62	21	50
Guiseley	30	20	7	3	62	23	47
Thackley	30	13	9	8	43	35	35
Scarborough	30	14	6	10	43	37	34
Sheffield	30	11	11	8	34	24	33
Winterton Rangers	30	15	2	13	49	39	32
Hallam	30	13	5	12	42	46	31
North Ferriby	30	9	12	9	32	30	30
Liversedge	30	10	9	11	34	33	29
Leeds Ashley Road	30	10	8	12	39	36	28
Frecheville CA	30	10	7	13	30	37	27
Bridlington Town	30	9	7	14	42	50	25
Thorne Colliery	30	8	7	15	35	52	23
Ossett Town	30	7	8	15	31	47	22
Fryston CW	30	7	6	17	22	49	20
Ossett Albion	30	4	6	20	26	67	14

UNITED COUNTIES LEAGUE

Premier Division	P	W	D	L	F	A	Pts
Stamford AFC	36	26	6	4	76	29	58
Desborough Town	36	23	9	4	71	31	55
Irthlingborough Dia	36	21	8	7	70	36	50
Potton United	36	17	11	8	58	34	45
Rushden Town	36	18	9	9	56	41	45
Rothwell Town	36	14	13	9	52	36	41
Ampthill Town	36	14	11	11	52	48	39
Wootton Blue Cross	36	14	9	13	64	49	37
Stewrt & Llyds (Cby)	36	14	9	13	50	50	37
Long Buckby AFC	36	13	9	14	54	59	35
Buckingham Town	36	13	9	14	50	56	35
St Neots Town	36	12	8	16	45	52	32
Olney Town	36	12	7	17	39	54	31
Holbeach United	36	11	9	16	46	67	31
Wolverton Town	36	11	7	18	42	51	29
Bourne Town	36	8	7	21	38	64	23
Kempston Rovers	36	8	6	22	40	68	22
Eynesbury Rovers	36	8	4	24	26	59	20
Northampton Spencer	36	5	9	22	23	68	19

HELLENIC LEAGUE

Premier Division	P	W	D	L	F	A	Pts
Bicester Town	30	19	8	3	57	25	46
Fairfield Town	30	17	9	4	64	35	43
Moreton Town	30	13	10	7	54	41	36
Flackwell Heath	30	14	7	9	43	33	35
Abingdon Town	30	14	5	11	49	41	33
Forest Green Rvrs	30	11	10	9	56	45	32
Northwood	30	14	4	12	55	54	32
Newbury Town	30	12	7	11	59	47	31
Didcot Town	30	12	5	13	48	41	29
Morris Motors	30	11	7	12	53	59	29
Kidlington	30	11	7	12	36	40	29
Abingdon United	30	11	6	13	38	43	28
Thame United	30	9	10	11	42	48	28
Wallingford Town	30	9	3	18	36	55	21
Clanfield	30	5	5	20	43	82	15
Worrall Hill	30	3	7	20	40	84	13

LONDON SPARTAN LEAGUE

Premier Division	P	W	D	L	F	A	Pts
Berkhamsted Town	30	21	3	6	50	24	45
Amersham Town	30	20	4	6	65	31	44
Merstham	30	18	7	5	55	31	43
Malden Vale	30	15	8	7	60	36	38
Chingford	30	15	5	10	60	39	35
Waltham Abbey	30	15	4	11	48	41	34
Whyteleafe	30	11	10	9	37	35	32
Fisher Athletic	30	9	12	9	46	42	30
Swanley Town	30	11	8	11	46	47	30
Beckton United	30	11	6	13	33	43	28
Kingsbury Town	30	11	5	14	46	49	27
Alma Swanley	30	10	7	13	38	52	26
Horley Town	30	7	8	15	36	52	22
Beckenham Town	30	6	6	18	21	44	18
Frimley Green	30	4	7	19	17	61	15
Farnham Town	30	4	5	21	35	66	13

TOWN & COUNTRY LEAGUE

	P	W	D	L	F	A	Pts
Gorleston	42	25	13	4	86	31	63
Tiptree United	42	27	8	7	69	35	62
Wisbech Town	42	26	5	11	87	53	57
Sudbury Town	42	23	11	8	70	46	57
Bury Town	42	19	13	10	92	65	51
Brantham Athletic	42	17	14	11	52	47	48
Lowestoft Town	42	19	9	14	74	55	47
Newmarket Town	42	17	13	12	72	69	47
Gt Yarmouth Town	42	15	13	14	69	55	43
Soham Town Rng	42	16	10	16	71	72	42
Thetford Town	42	14	14	14	66	68	42
Ely City	42	12	17	13	60	50	41
Histon	42	14	12	16	45	57	40
Clacton Town	42	14	11	17	48	51	39
March Town United	42	13	13	16	70	75	39
Colchester Utd Res	42	13	12	17	80	82	38
Haverhill Rovers	42	13	11	18	60	68	37
Felixstowe Town	42	12	10	20	52	68	34
Stowmarket	42	8	17	17	49	71	33
Saffron Walden Tn	42	7	11	24	41	67	25
Chatteris Town	42	7	9	26	47	98	23
Braintree & Crittall Ath	42	5	6	31	39	107	16

LANCASHIRE COMBINATION

	P	W	D	L	F	A	Pts
Clitheroe	32	17	12	3	55	25	46
Colne Dynamoes	32	18	8	6	54	35	44
Barrow Res	32	16	9	7	56	30	41
Gt Harwood Town	32	15	11	6	53	29	41
Vulcan Newton	32	14	12	6	60	34	40
Bacup Borough	32	16	8	8	63	41	40
Padiham	32	15	8	9	49	34	38
Chorley Reserves	32	11	13	8	42	38	35
Whitworth Valley	32	13	9	10	52	53	35
Leyland Motors	32	10	14	8	50	36	34
Lytham	32	10	9	13	42	63	29
Daisy Hill	32	11	6	15	35	40	28
Wren Rovers	32	9	8	15	38	48	26
Nelson	32	7	8	17	46	67	22
Blackpool Mech	32	5	9	18	27	56	19
Ashton Athletic	32	7	3	22	25	68	17
Wigan Rovers	32	2	5	25	29	79	9

VAUX WEARSIDE LEAGUE

	P	W	D	L	F	A	Pts
Hartlepool Reserves	38	27	5	6	92	36	59
Blue Star	38	26	5	7	102	47	57
Seaham CW Red St	38	25	6	7	101	40	56
Whickham	38	25	4	9	89	44	54
Sunderland Res	38	22	8	8	71	35	50*

* 2 points deducted

ESSEX SENIOR LEAGUE

	P	W	D	L	F	A	Pts
Basildon United	30	25	3	2	65	8	53
Wivenhoe Town	30	16	9	5	53	31	41
Canvey Island	30	17	5	8	57	34	39
Witham Town	30	16	6	8	55	34	38
East Ham United	30	14	9	7	44	30	37

GLOUCESTERSHIRE COUNTY LEAGUE

	P	W	D	L	F	A	Pts
Almondsbury Grnwy	34	24	5	5	123	44	53
Shortwood United	34	19	8	7	89	60	46
Sharpness	34	13	15	6	53	42	41
Matson Athletic	34	14	12	8	67	54	40
Yate Town	34	15	10	9	66	57	40

HAMPSHIRE LEAGUE

Division One	P	W	D	L	F	A	Pts
Newport IOW	30	24	4	2	87	22	52
Brockenhurst	30	22	4	4	62	26	48
Sholing Sports	30	13	12	5	47	24	38
Romsey Town	30	14	9	7	51	44	37
Pirelli General	30	14	8	8	37	32	36

KENT LEAGUE

	P	W	D	L	F	A	Pts
Chatham Town	32	23	7	2	69	22	53
Cray Wanderers	32	20	9	3	80	25	49
Hythe Town	32	19	4	9	57	48	42
Darenth Heathside	32	17	7	8	52	34	41
Sittingbourne	32	15	9	8	49	43	39

LEICESTERSHIRE SENIOR LEAGUE

Division One	P	W	D	L	F	A	Pts
Shepshed Charter	30	22	7	1	82	21	51
Anstey Nomads	30	20	7	3	75	26	47
Oadby Town	30	17	8	5	72	26	42
Birstall United	30	16	9	5	55	37	41
Friar Lane OB	30	15	7	8	49	37	37

SUSSEX COUNTY LEAGUE

Division One	P	W	D	L	F	A	Pts
Chichester City	30	21	5	4	66	30	47
Southwick	30	19	7	4	63	25	45
Burgess Hill Town	30	18	6	6	65	37	42
Pagham	30	15	9	6	52	13	39
Eastbourne Town	30	13	9	8	50	37	35

TEESSIDE FOOTBALL LEAGUE

	P	W	D	L	F	A	Pts
Smiths Dock	34	24	5	5	82	31	53
Stockton Buffs	34	21	5	8	75	33	47
Hartlepool BWOB	34	19	9	6	80	40	47
Marske United	34	19	9	6	70	37	47
Darlington RA	34	20	5	9	68	38	45

WILTSHIRE COUNTY LEAGUE

Division One	P	W	D	L	F	A	Pts
Amesbury	30	21	3	6	78	31	45
Sanford	30	16	10	4	64	33	42
Park	30	17	5	8	66	39	39
Bromham	30	17	4	9	47	39	38
Vickers	30	13	8	9	48	38	34

1980-81

Altrincham were once again crowned 'Non-League Champions' winning their second consecutive Alliance Premier League title, but once again they were to see their Football League ambitions dashed in the end of season ballot. The only serious challenge to Alty's supremacy came from Kettering Town, but despite some superbly consistent runs they just failed to wrest the honours from Moss Lane.

Surprisingly, only one Alliance club made it to the last four of the FA Trophy, and that was basement team Bangor City. The final was an all Isthmian affair with Division One champions Bishop's Stortford, who had to battle right through from the Preliminary Round, surprisingly beating Premier Division Sutton United. Stortford thus became the first former FA Amateur Cup winners to record a victory in the FA Trophy, and it was a personal triumph for manager Trevor Harvey who had led the club to success in the very last FA Amateur Cup.

Enfield were the FA Cup giantkillers this time. They defeated Hereford United and Port Vale before losing in a replay against Barnsley at Tottenham, a match watched by a massive 35 244 crowd.

The FA Vase final proved to be a real thriller. West Midlands League side Willenhall Town took a 2-0 lead against favourites Whickham, but then lost the services of their keeper and eventually lost in extra-time.

To cap an interesting year for this level of the game, the England Semi-Professional side, managed by Keith Wright, lifted the Four Nation Trophy in Italy (competed for against the hosts, Scotland and Holland).

SUMMARY

	Winners	Runners-up	Semi-finalists
FA VASE	Whickham	Willenhall Town	Irthlingborough Diamonds, Windsor & Eton
FA TROPHY	Bishops Stortford	Sutton United	Bangor City, Darford

FA CUP   Most Successful Team: Enfield
1st Rd: Enfield 3 Wembley 0; 2nd Rd: Enfield 2 Hereford 0; 3rd Rd: Port Vale 1 Enfield 1;
3rd Rd Replay: Enfield 3 Port Vale 0; 4th Rd: Barnsley 1 Enfield 1; 4th Rd Replay Enfield 0 Barnsley 3

ALLIANCE PREMIER LEAGUE   Champions: Altrincham   Runners-up: Kettering Town

ALLIANCE PREMIER STATISTICS

Top Crowds
2864	Altrincham v Yeovil Town (4.5.81)
2608	Kettering Town v Boston United (1.1.81)
2530	Northwich Victoria v Altrincham (24.1.81)
2457	Yeovil Town v Weymouth (1.1.81)
2314	Kettering Town v Maidstone United (20.4.81)

Top Scorers
28	Colin Williams (Northwich)
25	Nicky Evans (Kettering)

Manager of the Month Awards
Aug	Clark (Worcester)
Sep	Clarke (Kettering)
Oct	Sanders (Altrincham)
Nov	Watling (Maidstone)
Dec	Storton (Northwich)
Jan	Morgan (Weymouth)
Feb	Sanders (Sltrincham)
Mar	Clarke (Kettering)
Apr	McAnearney (Scarborough)

ALLIANCE PREMIER LEAGUE

			Home				Away				
Southern Division	P	W	D	L	F	A	W	D	L	F	A	Pts
Altrincham	38	14	2	3	40	21	9	6	4	32	20	54
Kettering Town	38	13	4	2	38	12	8	5	6	28	25	51
Scarborough	38	10	7	2	25	11	7	6	6	24	18	47
Northwich Victoria	38	12	4	3	32	13	5	7	7	21	27	45
Weymouth	38	11	4	4	30	18	8	2	9	24	22	44
Bath City	38	9	6	4	23	8	7	4	8	28	24	42
Maidstone United	38	12	4	3	42	18	4	5	10	22	35	41
Boston United	38	10	4	5	39	30	6	5	8	24	28	41
Barrow	38	11	3	6	27	18	4	5	9	23	31	38
Frickley Athletic	38	10	4	5	36	22	5	4	10	25	40	38
Stafford Rangers	38	10	4	5	34	22	1	11	7	22	34	37
Worcester City	38	10	4	5	33	25	4	3	12	14	29	35
Telford United	38	7	6	7	26	25	6	3	9	21	34	35
Yeovil Town	38	9	2	8	37	30	5	4	10	23	34	34
Gravesend & Northfleet	38	8	5	7	26	21	5	3	10	22	34	34
AP Leamington	38	6	7	6	29	26	4	4	11	18	40	31
Barnet	38	8	5	6	27	26	4	2	13	12	38	31
Nuneaton Borough	38	6	5	8	27	31	4	4	11	22	34	29
Wealdstone	38	6	8	5	27	19	3	3	13	10	37	29
Bangor City	38	5	6	8	25	34	1	6	12	10	34	24

SOUTHERN LEAGUE

Southern Division	P	W	D	L	F	A	Pts
Dartford	46	26	14	6	76	39	66
Bognor Regis Town	46	25	13	8	95	43	63
Hastings United	46	24	14	8	89	43	62
Gosport Borough	46	24	12	10	84	52	60
Waterlooville	46	19	21	6	67	50	59
Dorchester Town	46	21	13	12	84	56	55
Dover	46	22	10	14	70	50	54
Poole Town	46	19	14	13	70	56	52
Addlestone & Wey-	46	21	9	16	66	57	51
bridge Town							
Dunstable	46	19	13	14	73	68	51
Aylesbury United	46	20	10	16	67	60	50
Hounslow	46	17	13	16	65	55	47
Hillingdon Borough	46	16	15	15	50	49	47
Basingstoke Town	46	16	14	16	69	58	46
Crawley Town	46	18	4	24	64	78	40
Ashford Town	46	12	15	19	55	76	39
Tonbridge AFC	46	12	15	19	44	68	39
Chelmsford City	46	13	12	21	54	78	38
Canterbury City	46	12	13	21	40	59	37
Salisbury	46	14	8	24	57	76	36
Folkestone	46	11	11	24	47	65	33
Margate	46	11	7	28	65	117	29
Fareham Town	46	5	18	23	31	73	28
Andover	46	6	10	30	41	94	22

Midland Division	P	W	D	L	F	A	Pts
Alvechurch	42	26	9	7	76	40	61
Bedford Town	42	25	11	6	63	32	61
Trowbridge Town	42	24	9	9	69	39	57
Kidderminster H	42	23	9	10	68	42	55
Barry Town	42	21	9	12	60	40	51
Stourbridge	42	17	16	9	75	49	50
Enderby Town	42	21	8	13	71	47	50
Cheltenham Town	42	18	12	12	70	59	48
Bromsgrove Rovers	42	19	9	14	65	50	47
Corby Town	42	19	7	16	69	58	45
Bridgend Town	42	19	7	16	74	64	45
Minehead	42	19	7	16	54	60	45
Gloucester City	42	19	6	17	82	72	44
Merthyr Tydfil	42	15	12	15	59	49	42
Bedworth United	42	14	12	16	50	46	40
Banbury United	42	11	11	20	51	65	33
Taunton Town	42	10	9	23	48	68	29
Cambridge City	42	8	12	22	46	87	28
Witney Town	42	9	9	24	44	65	27
Wellingborough T	42	10	7	25	43	91	27
Redditch United	42	11	4	27	54	92	26
Milton Keynes City	42	3	7	32	28	103	13

NORTHERN PREMIER LEAGUE

	P	Home					Away					Pts
		W	D	L	F	A	W	D	L	F	A	
Runcorn	42	16	3	2	53	8	16	4	1	46	14	71
Mossley	42	10	4	7	43	27	14	2	4	52	28	55
Marine	42	16	4	1	47	15	6	6	9	19	26	54
Buxton	42	10	5	6	38	24	11	2	8	26	26	49
Gainsborough T	42	12	6	3	48	22	5	7	9	32	35	47
Burton Albion	42	11	6	4	38	19	8	2	11	25	35	46
Witton Albion	42	14	2	5	49	24	5	6	10	21	38	46
Goole Town	42	9	6	6	34	25	5	10	6	22	25	44
South Liverpool	42	13	2	6	32	24	6	4	11	27	40	44
Workington	42	9	8	4	34	16	6	5	10	23	32	43
Gateshead	42	7	9	5	27	23	5	9	7	38	38	42
Worksop Town	42	9	4	8	33	24	6	7	8	33	37	41
Macclesfield T	42	5	7	9	29	40	8	6	7	23	29	39
Grantham	42	9	4	8	36	31	5	5	11	21	43	37
Matlock Town	42	6	7	8	30	39	6	5	10	27	41	36
Lancaster City	42	7	5	9	30	32	6	4	11	18	38	35
Netherfield	42	8	5	8	38	32	3	7	11	35	49	34
Oswestry Town	42	9	4	8	32	27	4	4	13	22	40	34
King's Lynn	42	5	10	6	26	27	3	8	10	20	38	34
Southport	42	5	9	7	27	31	6	2	13	15	37	33
Morecambe	42	8	3	10	27	32	3	5	13	15	42	30
Tamworth	42	7	5	9	23	33	2	7	12	15	43	30

ISTHMIAN LEAGUE

Premier Division

	P	W	D	L	F	A	Pts
Slough Town	42	23	13	6	73	34	82
Enfield	42	23	11	8	81	43	80
Wycombe Wand	42	22	9	11	76	49	75
Leytonstone & Ilford	42	19	12	11	78	57	69
Sutton United	42	19	12	11	82	65	69
Hendon	42	18	10	14	66	58	64
Hayes	42	18	8	16	45	50	62
Dagenham	42	17	11	14	79	66	62
Harrow Borough	42	16	11	15	57	52	59
Bromley	42	16	9	17	63	69	57
Staines Town	42	15	9	18	60	61	54
Tooting & Mitcham	42	15	8	19	49	53	53
Hitchin Town	42	14	10	18	64	52	52
Croydon	42	12	15	15	51	51	51
Dulwich Hamlet	42	13	12	17	62	67	51
Leatherhead	42	12	14	16	36	50	50
Carshalton Athletic	42	14	8	20	57	82	50
Barking	42	13	12	17	58	72	49*
Harlow Town	42	11	15	16	54	66	48
Walthamstow Ave	42	13	7	22	51	82	46
Boreham Wood	42	10	13	19	46	69	43
Woking	42	11	7	24	40	70	37+

* 2 points deducted
+ 3 points deducted

Division One

	P	W	D	L	F	A	Pts
Bishop's Stortford	42	30	6	6	84	28	96
Billericay Town	42	29	6	7	67	34	93
Epsom & Ewell	42	24	12	6	80	36	84
Farnborough Town	42	23	11	8	75	39	80
St Albans City	42	24	5	13	85	61	77
Kingstonian	42	20	9	13	63	51	66*
Oxford City	42	18	9	15	71	48	63
Wokingham Town	42	16	15	11	70	56	63
Metropolitan Police	42	18	7	17	61	58	61
Chesham United	42	17	7	18	64	64	58
Lewes	42	17	7	18	72	83	58
Maidenhead United	42	16	7	19	58	62	55
Walton & Hersham	42	12	15	15	46	53	51
Hertford Town	42	13	11	18	46	65	50
Hampton	42	12	13	17	46	53	49
Aveley	42	13	9	20	54	55	48
Wembley	42	13	8	21	47	61	47
Clapton	42	12	8	22	53	86	44
Ware	42	9	13	20	50	69	40
Tilbury	42	10	8	24	42	84	38
Camberley Town	42	8	7	27	42	88	31
Finchley	42	6	11	25	35	77	29

Division Two

	P	W	D	L	F	A	Pts
Feltham	38	24	10	4	65	30	82
Hornchurch	38	25	6	7	74	35	81
Hungerford Town	38	23	10	5	84	29	79
Barton Rovers	38	19	11	8	61	26	68
Worthing	38	19	11	8	74	43	68
Cheshunt	38	19	11	8	57	33	68
Letchworth G'den C	38	18	7	13	49	40	61
Southall	38	14	11	13	48	52	53
Dorking Town	38	13	12	13	47	45	51
Horsham	38	16	3	19	47	47	51
Hemel Hempstead	38	14	7	17	49	55	49
Egham Town	38	13	9	16	45	62	48
Harwich & P'keston	38	12	11	15	57	58	47
Rainham Town	38	11	13	14	44	45	46
Epping Town	38	12	7	19	37	50	43
Eastbourne United	38	11	10	17	59	75	43
Willesden	38	11	8	19	57	68	41
Tring Town	38	11	6	21	40	71	39
Molesey	38	4	9	25	31	83	21
Corinthian Casuals	38	1	8	29	17	95	11

DRYBROUGH'S NORTHERN LEAGUE

	P	W	D	L	F	A	Pts
Blyth Spartans	38	27	5	6	89	35	86
Spennymoor United	38	26	7	5	82	38	85
Bishop Auckland	38	22	7	9	68	36	73
Tow Law town	38	18	13	7	83	54	67
Ashington	38	17	12	9	95	66	63
Ferryhill Athletic	38	17	10	11	71	49	61
Shildon	38	17	8	13	56	54	59
South Bank	38	16	9	13	55	44	57
Billingham Synth	38	13	15	10	52	51	54
Penrith	38	15	8	15	75	66	53
Whitby Town	38	15	7	16	55	59	52
Horden Colliery W	38	12	9	17	48	65	45
Consett	38	12	6	20	49	54	42
North Shields	38	10	10	18	56	71	40
Evenwood Town	38	10	10	18	41	66	40
West Auckland T	38	10	10	18	40	67	40
Durham City	38	9	11	18	46	74	38
Crook Town	38	10	8	20	47	79	38
Whitley Bay	38	9	7	22	53	72	34
Willington	38	6	6	26	41	102	24

WEST MIDLANDS (REGIONAL) LEAGUE

Premier Division

	P	W	D	L	F	A	Pts
Shifnal Town	42	31	7	4	89	33	69
Lye Town	42	27	9	6	80	36	63
Willenhall Town	42	25	11	6	93	41	61
Brereton Social	42	22	8	12	74	51	52
Hednesford Town	42	20	11	11	73	48	51
Coventry Sporting	42	19	12	11	75	54	50
Ledbury Town	42	19	10	13	74	52	48
Dudley Town	42	19	10	13	55	44	48
Sutton Coldfield T	42	18	10	14	71	56	46
Bilston	42	18	10	14	78	65	46
Armitage	42	20	5	17	58	59	45
Rushall Olympic	42	15	13	14	50	52	43
Blakenall	42	14	15	13	55	58	43
Darlaston	42	17	5	20	68	95	39
Gresley Rovers	42	13	10	19	46	62	36
Halesowen Town	42	10	15	17	53	67	35
Wednesfield Social	42	11	11	20	52	67	33
VS Rugby	42	9	10	23	50	80	28
Tividale	42	5	17	20	35	64	27
Malvern Town	42	9	7	26	56	93	25
Brierley Hill Alliance	42	6	8	28	33	85	20
Hinckley Athletic	42	3	10	29	43	99	16

CHESHIRE COUNTY LEAGUE

Division One

	P	W	D	L	F	A	Pts
Nantwich Town	38	26	6	6	87	34	58
Hyde United	38	23	9	6	75	27	55
Winsford United	38	20	10	8	75	38	50
Formby	38	21	7	10	65	39	49
Stalybridge Celtic	38	16	15	7	62	50	47
Chorley	38	17	11	10	65	48	45
Bootle	38	18	7	13	68	53	43
Prescot Cables	38	16	9	13	60	46	41
Horwich RMI	38	15	9	14	53	49	39
Leek Town	38	15	9	14	50	47	39
Ashton United	38	12	12	14	70	73	36
Curzon Ashton	38	14	8	16	48	63	36
St Helens Town	38	14	7	17	63	82	35
Fleetwood Town	38	9	13	16	33	53	31
Rossendale United	38	9	12	17	49	69	30
Burscough	38	11	6	21	52	62	28
Darwen	38	8	10	20	46	74	26
Droylsden	38	9	8	21	49	82	26
Kirkby Town	38	6	11	21	30	65	23
New Mills	38	8	7	23	34	80	23

Division Two

	P	W	D	L	F	A	Pts
Accrington Stanley	38	26	3	9	73	20	55
Glossop	38	23	9	6	76	38	55
Leyland Motors	38	20	10	8	68	42	50
Middlewich Athletic	38	20	10	8	56	32	50
Atherton LR	38	19	11	8	61	39	49
Prescot BI	38	20	5	13	59	40	45
Rhyl	38	20	5	13	69	57	45
Maghull	38	15	12	11	55	41	42
Ford Motors	38	16	9	13	49	52	41
Congleton Town	38	16	8	14	67	55	40
Radcliffe Borough	38	15	10	13	58	48	40
Irlam Town	38	15	6	17	49	51	36
Warrington Town	38	15	5	18	59	78	35
Prestwich Heys	38	15	4	19	66	68	34
Salford	38	9	13	16	50	70	31
Eastwood (Hanley)	38	12	6	20	47	55	30
Skelmersdale United	38	9	10	19	51	68	28
Atherton Collieries	38	8	5	25	39	83	21
Ashton Town	38	6	5	27	40	93	17
New Brighton	38	6	4	28	31	93	16

MIDLAND FOOTBALL COMBINATION

Division One

	P	W	D	L	F	A	Pts
Moor Green	38	28	7	3	109	30	63
Bridgnorth Town	38	22	7	9	76	38	51
Mile Oak Rovers	38	21	8	9	63	43	50
Cinderford Town	38	22	5	11	68	30	49
Boldmere St Mich'ls	38	18	11	9	50	39	47
Oldbury United	38	18	10	10	65	47	46
Chipping Norton T	38	16	11	11	58	45	43
Racing Club W'wick	38	16	10	12	66	46	42
Knowle	38	16	10	12	50	42	42
Hurley Daw Mill	38	14	11	13	54	56	39
Highgate United	38	16	6	16	79	61	38
West Mid's Police	38	11	15	12	62	58	37
Paget Rangers	38	13	11	14	42	41	37
Solihull Borough	38	13	10	15	58	69	36
Evesham United	38	10	10	18	57	81	30
Walsall Sportsco	38	8	12	18	49	69	28
Walsall Wood	38	10	8	20	42	71	28
Smethwick Highfield	38	8	10	20	37	74	26
Cradley Town	38	5	4	29	33	100	14
Coleshill Town	38	5	4	29	27	104	14

ATHENIAN LEAGUE

	P	W	D	L	F	A	Pts
Windsor & Eton	38	27	6	5	100	32	60
Basildon Utd	38	24	11	3	71	24	59
Banstead	38	23	10	5	73	32	56
Grays	38	23	7	8	81	42	53
Edgware	38	20	8	10	77	38	48
Leyton Wingate	38	18	12	8	72	46	48
Welling	38	19	8	11	62	48	46
Woodford	38	18	9	11	84	53	45
Burnham	38	20	4	14	62	45	44
Harefield	38	16	10	12	67	51	42
Ruislip M	38	14	13	11	49	51	41
Uxbridge	38	11	13	14	38	39	35
Fleet	38	8	13	17	50	65	29
Haringey B	38	9	10	19	41	68	28
Redhill	38	8	11	19	45	59	27
Hoddesdon	38	10	6	22	53	80	26
Chertsey	38	9	7	22	30	84	25
Marlow	38	7	10	21	43	85	24
Chalfont St Peter	38	5	5	28	39	89	15
Alton	38	2	5	31	33	139	9

WESTERN LEAGUE

Premier Division

	P	W	D	L	F	A	Pts
Bridgwater Town	38	25	6	2	54	25	56
Barnstaple Town	38	22	6	10	58	40	50
Frome Town	38	21	6	11	74	51	48
Falmouth Town	38	18	9	11	71	53	45
Bideford	38	18	8	12	58	42	44
Saltash United	38	17	9	12	73	47	43
Portway-Bristol	38	16	11	11	55	45	43
Clevedon Town	38	15	11	12	65	52	41
Clandown	38	16	9	13	60	53	41
Devizes Town	38	14	13	11	61	56	41
Bridport	38	12	15	11	56	52	39
Keynsham Town	38	12	15	11	33	34	39
Melksham Town	38	13	11	14	45	49	37
Liskeard Athletic	38	11	11	16	58	70	33
Mangotsfield United	38	8	15	15	43	66	31
Dawlish	38	7	16	15	40	50	30
Welton Rovers	38	9	11	18	50	69	29
Weston-super-Mare	38	11	7	20	42	61	29
Paulton Rovers	38	9	11	18	45	72	29
Tiverton Town	38	1	10	27	23	77	12

MIDLAND COUNTIES LEAGUE

Premier Division	P	W	D	L	F	A	Pts
Boston FC	34	23	9	2	70	18	55
Alfreton Town	34	16	10	8	73	40	42
Eastwood Town	34	16	9	9	63	41	41
Bridlington Trinity	34	15	10	9	62	40	40
Guisborough Town	34	16	7	11	60	48	39
Belper Town	34	15	8	11	44	43	38
Arnold FC	34	14	8	12	55	47	36
Heanor Town	34	13	10	11	57	52	36
Skegness Town	34	12	11	11	49	52	35
Long Eaton United	34	13	8	13	54	51	34
Appleby Frodingham	34	12	10	12	56	56	34
Sutton Town	34	12	10	12	48	51	34
Mexborough Town	34	12	5	17	42	67	29
Spalding United	34	10	7	17	28	47	27
Ashby FC	34	12	3	19	40	60	27
Ilkeston Town	34	7	9	18	44	65	23
Brigg Town	34	6	10	18	42	63	22
Kimberley Town	34	6	8	20	34	81	20

UNITED COUNTIES LEAGUE

Premier Division	P	W	D	L	F	A	Pts
Stamford AFC	34	22	9	3	76	36	53
Wootton Blue Cross	34	23	4	7	81	33	50
Kempston Rovers	34	22	3	9	96	54	47
Holbeach United	34	21	5	8	59	43	47
Desborough Town	34	18	9	7	79	55	45
Long Buckby AFC	34	15	12	7	70	54	42
Rushden Town	34	16	7	11	57	33	39
Potton United	34	15	8	11	48	41	38
Irthlingborough Dia	34	15	5	14	60	54	35
Stewart & Lloyds (Corby)	34	13	9	12	53	51	35
Buckingham Town	34	13	8	13	48	45	34
Wolverton Town	34	11	9	14	49	70	31
St Neots Town	34	9	6	19	35	61	24
Bourne Town	34	7	9	18	41	64	23
Rothwell Town	34	6	10	18	37	58	22
Ampthill Town	34	6	10	18	39	69	22
Eynesbury Rovers	34	7	7	20	37	71	21
Northampton Spencr	34	1	2	31	21	94	4

HELLENIC LEAGUE

Premier Division	P	W	D	L	F	A	Pts
Newbury Town	30	23	4	3	75	27	50
Thame United	30	17	8	5	51	22	42
Hazells	30	16	8	6	53	36	40
Moreton Town	30	15	8	7	72	35	38
Flackwell Heath	30	13	8	9	47	30	34
Abingdon Town	30	13	8	9	48	37	34
Forest Green Rovers	30	14	6	10	57	53	34
Fairford Town	30	15	2	13	47	42	32
Didcot Town	30	9	99	12	36	47	27
Maidenhead Town	30	10	5	15	42	48	25
Bicester Town	30	7	11	12	41	60	25
Northwood	30	6	10	14	37	52	22
Kidlington	30	8	6	16	32	55	22
Wallingford Town	30	8	5	17	43	73	21
Morris Motors	30	7	6	17	36	57	20
Abingdon United	30	5	4	21	31	74	14

LONDON SPARTAN LEAGUE

Premier Division	P	W	D	L	F	A	Pts
Fisher Athletic	30	22	3	5	56	18	47
Malden Vale	30	18	7	5	63	30	43
Whyteleafe	30	14	12	4	59	31	40
Greenwich Borough	30	12	12	6	52	43	36
Kingsbury Town	30	15	5	10	50	39	35
Merstham	30	12	10	8	39	33	34
Waltham Abbey	30	11	10	9	37	29	32
Berkhamstead Town	30	10	11	9	40	42	31
Alma Swanley	30	13	3	14	52	56	29
Horley Town	30	7	12	11	30	39	26
Beckton United	30	8	9	13	36	51	25
Swanley Town	30	9	6	15	57	63	24
Amersham Town	30	8	8	14	32	46	24
Beckenham Town	30	8	6	16	32	48	22
Chingford	30	7	4	19	33	60	18
Chobham	30	4	6	20	23	63	14

YORKSHIRE LEAGUE

Division One	P	W	D	L	F	A	Pts
Leeds Ashley Road	30	18	8	4	58	25	44
Emley	30	17	8	5	61	36	42
North Ferriby	30	16	8	6	40	23	40
Thackley	30	14	7	9	48	39	35
Guiseley	30	10	12	8	48	41	32
Winterton Rangers	30	12	8	10	35	31	32
Scarborough	30	13	5	12	55	49	31
Frecheville CA	30	10	11	9	41	38	31
Hallam	30	11	7	12	42	39	29
Liversedge	30	11	7	12	35	49	29
Barton Town	30	8	10	12	39	41	26
Sheffield	30	9	8	13	24	41	26
Bentley VW	30	9	7	14	47	47	25
Maltby WM	30	9	7	14	37	41	25
Kiveton Park	30	9	7	14	40	50	25
Bridlington Town	30	1	6	23	12	72	8

TOWN & COUNTRY LEAGUE

	P	W	D	L	F	A	Pts
Gorleston	42	32	7	3	98	33	71
Sudbury Town	42	28	8	6	99	37	64
Tiptree United	42	23	10	9	81	52	56
Ely City	42	21	13	8	100	48	55
Gt Yarmouth Town	42	22	9	11	95	59	53
March Town United	42	20	12	10	63	47	52
Saffron Walden T	42	17	14	11	70	56	48
Lowestoft Town	42	15	15	12	69	60	45
Bury Town	42	16	11	15	66	62	43
Newmarket Town	42	17	8	17	64	76	42
Wisbech Town	42	16	9	17	73	74	41
Stowmarket	42	14	11	17	63	79	39
Colchester Utd Res	42	15	8	19	85	72	38
Brantham Ath	42	12	14	16	61	61	38
Clacton Town	42	13	12	17	50	60	38
Felixstowe Town	42	13	8	21	56	81	34
Braintree & Crittall	42	12	10	20	43	74	34
Soham Town Rngrs	42	8	17	17	38	68	33
Thetford Town	42	10	12	20	54	91	32
Haverhill Rovers	42	9	12	21	44	55	30
Chatteris Town	42	7	7	28	50	117	21
Histon	42	3	12	27	36	96	18

LANCASHIRE COMBINATION

	P	W	D	L	F	A	Pts
Wren Rovers	34	24	7	3	75	25	55
Colne Dynamoes	34	21	5	8	57	30	47
Gt Harwood Town	34	18	7	9	68	42	43
Padiham	34	16	11	7	57	40	41*
Chorley Res	34	15	11	8	53	42	41
Caernarfon Town	34	15	7	12	55	37	37
Vulcan Newton	34	15	6	13	53	44	36
Lytham	34	14	8	12	51	45	36
Clitheroe	34	14	7	13	42	36	35
Chadderton	34	14	7	13	58	64	35
Whitworth Valley	34	13	8	13	50	54	34
Wigan Rovers	34	13	8	13	50	60	34
Daisy Hill	34	12	9	13	52	48	33
Bacup Borough	34	9	11	14	47	57	29
Ashton Athletic	34	9	6	19	47	73	24
Blackpool Mech	34	6	11	17	32	57	23
Nelson	34	7	3	24	29	60	17
Manchester Poly	34	2	6	26	24	86	10

VAUX WEARSIDE LEAGUE

	P	W	D	L	F	A	Pts
Chester-le-Street	38	28	9	1	79	13	65
Whickham	38	29	6	3	95	33	64
Blue Star	38	25	8	5	94	40	58
Reyrolles	38	22	7	9	83	49	51
Peterlee Newtown	38	20	10	8	59	34	50
South Shields	38	17	9	12	97	58	43
Hartlepool Res	38	15	13	10	54	45	43
Seaham CW Red Str	38	17	6	15	61	48	40
Heaton Stannington	38	14	8	16	64	64	36
Wallsend Town	38	11	10	17	63	73	32
Ryhope CW	38	12	8	18	47	68	32
Roker Zanussi	38	12	7	19	56	64	31
Annfield Plain	38	13	5	20	53	83	31
Wingate	38	10	10	18	49	73	30
Eppleton CW	38	9	10	19	37	59	28
Stockton FC	38	11	6	21	39	84	28
Murton FC	38	11	5	22	55	79	27
Boldon CA	38	8	11	19	39	65	27
Washington	38	6	13	19	38	86	25
Easington CW	38	8	3	27	41	85	19

ESSEX SENIOR LEAGUE

	P	W	D	L	F	A	Pts
Bowers	32	22	8	2	73	31	52
Heybridge	32	20	7	5	69	27	47
Wivenhoe	32	20	5	7	67	34	45
Canvey Island	32	14	13	5	53	35	41
Witham	32	13	12	7	54	30	38

GLOUCESTERSHIRE COUNTY LEAGUE

	P	W	D	L	F	A	Pts
Almondsbury Grnwy	34	27	4	3	108	45	58
Shortwood United	34	23	3	8	78	37	49
Wilton Rovers	34	22	4	8	72	43	48
Port of Bristol	34	17	9	8	65	45	43
Matson Athletic	34	18	5	11	85	54	41

HAMPSHIRE FOOTBALL ASSOCIATION

Division One	P	W	D	L	F	A	Pts
Newport	38	30	3	5	106	32	63
AFC Totton	38	21	9	8	81	33	51
Sholing Sports	38	20	11	7	56	24	51
Southampton A	38	18	14	6	70	45	50
Eastleigh	38	16	9	13	47	42	41

KENT LEAGUE

Division One	P	W	D	L	F	A	Pts
Cray W	32	24	5	3	92	27	53
Chatham	32	22	6	4	61	23	50
Crockenhill	32	20	5	7	63	37	45
Erith & Belvedere	32	19	5	8	57	30	43
Sittingbouurne	32	18	5	9	74	29	41

LEICESTERSHIRE SENIOR LEAGUE

Division One	P	W	D	L	F	A	Pts
Shepshed Charter	30	23	3	4	77	20	49
Anstey Nomads	30	22	3	5	83	24	47
Wigston Fields	30	21	5	4	66	27	47
Bristall United	30	17	5	8	64	29	39
Oadby Town	30	16	6	8	53	36	38

SUSSEX COUNTY LEAGUE

Division One	P	W	D	L	F	A	Pts
Pagham	30	18	9	3	52	22	45
Peacehaven & Tels	30	16	10	4	53	28	42
Steyning Town	30	15	10	5	61	37	40
Hastings Town	30	14	8	8	64	35	36
Southwick	30	10	13	7	42	35	33

TEESSIDE LEAGUE

	P	W	D	L	F	A	Pts
Marske United	34	24	7	3	85	36	55
Hartlepool BWOB	34	22	4	8	97	46	48
Norton CCT	34	18	11	5	83	37	47
Darlington RA	34	20	7	7	71	37	47
Billingham Social	34	16	12	6	66	34	44

WILTSHIRE COUNTY LEAGUE

Division One	P	W	D	L	F	A	Pts
Park	30	18	9	3	79	29	45
Sanford	30	17	8	7	69	36	40
Vickers	30	19	2	9	67	49	40
Amesbury	30	16	6	8	59	44	38
Melksham T Res	30	16	3	11	63	50	35

1981-82

This season saw another giant step towards the creation of the 'Pyramid' that we know today. Four of the nation's most famous leagues, namely the Cheshire County League, the Lancashire Combination, the Midland Counties League and the Yorkshire League finally chose to lose their identity. The first two would be replaced from 1982-83 by the North West Counties League, with the Northern Counties (East) League being established to cater for the latter two. Both these new leagues hoped to strike a promotion/relegation agreement with the Northern Premier League. Equally significant was the decision that the Isthmian League should feed into the Alliance Premier League alongside the Northern Premier League and the Southern League.

After Runcorn had won a Northern Premier League and Cup double in 1980-81, many suspected that they would make an immediate impact in the Alliance Premier, and this they certainly did. John Williams' team won the title by a clear seven points. Ironically the Alliance Premier League runners-up, Enfield, were also experiencing their first season in the competition. Their disappointment in letting the title slip was tempered by triumph in the FA Trophy; in winning the competition they emulated Bishop's Stortford's achievement of having recorded victories in both the Trophy and the FA Amateur Cup.

Altrincham surprisingly finished in just mid-table in the Alliance, but they did reach Wembley in the Trophy, and recorded victories over York City and Sheffield United in the FA Cup. Perhaps the most dominant Non-League club in the country were Leytonstone-Ilford who cruised to the Isthmian League championship. They also won the Hitachi (Isthmian League) Cup, the London Senior Cup, and the Essex Senior Cup.

SUMMARY

FA VASE	**Winners** Forest Green Rovers	**Runners Up** Rainworth Miners Welfare	**Semi-finalists** Barton Rovers, Blue Star
FA TROPHY	**Winners** Enfield	**Runners-up** Altrincham	**Semi-finalists** Northwich Victoria, Wycombe Wanderers

FA CUP   **Most Successful Team:** Barnet

1st Rd: Harlow 0 Barnet 0; 1st Rd Replay: Barnet 1 Harlow 0; 2nd Rd: Barnet 2 Wycomber Waderers 0;
3rd Rd: Barnet 0 Brighton & HA 0; 3rd Rd Replay: Brighton & HA 3 Barnet 1

ALLIANCE PREMIER LEAGUE   **Champions:** Runcorn   **Runners Up:** Enfield

---

ALLIANCE PREMIER STATISTICS

Top Crowds

2920	Scarborough v Enfield (20.2.82)
2758	Scarborough v Altrincham (19.8.81)
2276	Yeovil Town v Weymouth (1.1.82)
2139	Scarborough v Boston United (9.9.81)
2102	Scarborough v Frickley Athletic (7.4.82)

Top Scorers

27	Colin Williams (Scarborough)
23	Antone Iannone (Weymouth)
20	Nick Ironton (Enfield)

Manager of the Month Awards

Aug	Hardy (Dagenham)
Sep	Williams (Runcorn)
Oct	McCluskey (Enfield)
Nov	Williams (Runcorn)
Dec	No Award
Jan	Fry (Barnet)
Feb	McCluskey (Enfield)
Mar	McCluskey (Enfield)
Apr	Storton (Telford)

ALLIANCE PREMIER LEAGUE

	P	W	D	L	F	A	W	D	L	F	A	Pts
		Home					Home					
Runcorn	42	17	2	1	48	17	11	7	4	27	20	93
Enfield	42	14	4	4	55	22	12	4	5	38	26	86
Telford United	42	13	4	4	38	20	10	4	7	32	31	77
Worcester City	42	12	4	5	38	23	9	4	8	32	37	71
Dagenham	42	10	7	5	34	35	9	5	6	35	26	69
Northwich Victoria	42	12	6	3	35	17	8	3	10	21	29	69
Scarborough	42	11	6	4	34	19	8	5	8	31	32	68
Barrow	42	15	4	2	45	17	3	7	11	14	33	65
Weymouth	42	11	4	6	33	21	7	5	9	23	26	63
Boston United	42	14	4	5	46	23	3	7	11	15	34	62
Altrincham	42	10	6	5	39	22	4	7	10	27	34	55
Bath City	42	7	7	7	30	26	8	3	10	20	31	55
Yeovil Town	42	10	4	7	33	27	4	7	10	23	41	53
Stafford Rangers	42	7	8	6	22	19	5	8	8	26	28	52
Frickley Athletic	42	11	4	6	35	23	3	6	12	12	37	52
Maidstone United	42	8	6	7	33	22	3	9	9	22	37	48
Trowbridge	42	8	7	6	26	33	4	4	13	12	31	47
Barnet	42	5	8	8	17	20	4	6	11	19	32	41
Kettering Town	42	6	7	8	35	32	3	6	12	29	44	40
Gravesend & Northfleet	42	7	6	8	34	31	3	4	14	17	38	40
Dartford	42	7	5	9	23	25	3	4	14	26	42	39
AP Leamington	42	1	7	13	20	44	3	3	15	20	61	22

ISTHMIAN LEAGUE

Premier Division

	P	W	D	L	F	A	Pts
Leytonstone & Ilford	42	26	5	11	91	52	83
Sutton United	42	22	9	11	72	49	75
Wycombe Wandrs	42	21	10	11	63	48	73
Staines Town	42	21	9	12	59	46	72
Walthamstow Ave	42	21	7	14	81	62	70
Harrow Borough	42	18	13	11	77	55	67
Tooting & Mitcham	42	19	10	13	58	47	67
Slough Town	42	17	13	12	64	54	64
Leatherhead	42	16	12	14	57	52	60
Hayes	42	16	10	16	58	52	58
Croydon	42	16	9	17	59	57	57
Barking	42	14	14	14	51	51	56
Hendon	42	13	13	16	56	65	52
Dulwich Hamlet	42	14	10	18	47	59	52
Bishop's Stortford	42	15	5	22	50	70	50
Carshalton Athletic	42	14	8	20	58	86	50
Billericay Town	42	11	16	15	41	50	49
Hitchin Town	42	12	11	19	56	77	47
Bromley	42	13	7	22	63	79	46
Woking	42	11	13	18	57	75	46
Harlow	42	10	11	21	50	73	41
Boreham Wood	42	8	13	21	47	58	37

Division One

	P	W	D	L	F	A	Pts
Wokingham Town	40	29	5	6	86	30	92
Bognor Regis Town	40	23	10	7	65	34	79
Metropolitan Police	40	22	11	7	75	48	77
Oxford City	40	21	11	8	82	47	74
Feltham	40	20	8	12	65	49	68
Lewes	40	19	7	14	73	66	64
Hertford Town	40	16	10	14	62	54	58
Wembley	40	14	15	11	69	55	57
Farnborough Town	40	15	11	14	71	57	56
Epsom & Ewell	40	16	8	16	53	44	56
Kingstonian	40	16	7	17	57	56	55
Hampton	40	15	9	16	52	52	54
Hornchurch	40	13	15	12	42	50	54
Aveley	40	14	10	16	46	58	52
St Albans City	40	14	9	17	55	55	51
Maidenhead United	40	11	10	19	49	70	43
Tilbury	40	9	15	16	49	67	42
Walton & Hersham	40	10	11	19	43	65	41
Chesham United	40	9	9	22	39	71	36
Clapton	40	9	7	24	44	73	34
Ware	40	5	2	33	29	105	17

Division Two

	P	W	D	L	F	A	Pts
Worthing	40	29	6	5	95	25	93
Cheshunt	40	25	7	8	79	33	82
Hungerford Town	40	22	10	8	89	42	74*
Barton Rovers	40	22	8	10	65	32	74
Windsor & Eton	40	22	6	12	69	49	72
Corinthian Casuals	40	19	12	9	67	50	69
Harwich & Parkeston	40	19	12	9	64	47	69
Letchworth Gden C	40	15	11	14	67	55	56
Dorking Town	40	13	17	10	52	44	56
Hemel Hempstead	40	15	9	16	54	49	54
Basildon United	40	16	5	19	64	51	53
Finchley	40	14	9	17	57	68	51
Southall	40	12	14	14	36	42	50
Epping Town	40	12	11	17	48	62	47
Molesey	40	13	7	20	61	73	46
Egham Town	40	11	9	20	56	64	42
Rainham Town	40	11	9	20	53	83	42
Tring Town	40	9	13	18	49	78	40
Eastbourne United	40	9	12	19	51	73	39
Horsham	40	10	9	21	42	79	39
Camberley Town	40	3	2	35	21	140	11

* 2 points deducted

NORTHERN PREMIER LEAGUE

	P	Home W	D	L	F	A	Away W	D	L	F	A	Pts
Bangor City	42	17	4	0	52	22	10	4	7	56	38	62
Mossley	42	15	4	2	52	23	9	7	5	24	20	59
Witton Albion	42	13	5	3	45	18	9	5	7	30	26	54
Gateshead	42	11	8	2	36	17	8	6	7	29	32	52
King's Lynn	42	11	8	2	33	13	8	4	9	28	23	50
Grantham	42	10	8	3	33	21	8	5	8	32	32	49
Burton Albion	42	11	7	3	39	24	8	2	11	32	38	47
Southport	42	10	8	3	31	21	6	6	9	32	34	46
Marine	42	12	6	3	35	20	5	6	10	29	37	46
Macclesfield Town	42	12	4	5	40	24	5	5	11	27	34	43
Workington	42	11	3	5	35	22	5	4	12	27	38	43
Worksop Town	42	10	7	4	33	27	5	6	10	19	33	43
South Liverpool	42	8	7	6	28	20	5	6	10	27	37	39
Goole Town	42	10	5	6	35	26	3	8	10	21	34	39
Oswestry Town	42	10	4	7	37	29	4	7	10	18	30	39
Buxton	42	10	5	6	35	26	4	6	11	13	30	39
Lancaster City	42	9	5	7	25	23	4	7	10	22	27	38
Gainsborough T	42	9	5	7	41	31	1	8	12	19	38	33
Tamworth	42	5	4	12	16	28	5	5	11	15	28	29
Morecambe	42	5	7	9	20	37	4	4	13	23	49	29
Matlock Town	42	5	4	12	20	38	2	8	11	18	34	26
Netherfield	42	2	5	14	18	44	3	4	14	13	47	19

SOUTHERN LEAGUE

Southern Division	P	W	D	L	F	A	Pts
Wealdstone	46	32	8	6	100	32	72
Hastings United	46	31	9	6	79	34	71
Dorchester Town	46	21	18	7	76	41	60
Gosport Borough	46	26	8	12	76	45	60
Fareham Town	46	20	14	12	58	48	54
Poole Town	46	19	15	12	92	63	53
Waterlooville	46	22	9	15	75	53	53
Welling United	46	19	13	14	70	48	51
Addlestone & Weyge	46	17	17	12	71	53	51
Chelmsford City	46	20	11	15	64	53	51
Aylesbury United	46	19	12	15	79	61	50
Basingstoke Town	46	18	12	16	75	61	48
Dover	46	19	8	19	61	63	46
Ashford Town	46	16	14	16	52	56	46
Tonbridge AFC	46	19	7	20	62	70	45
Dunstable	46	18	8	20	63	68	44
Salisbury	46	16	10	20	64	81	42
Hounslow	46	15	11	20	59	83	41
Hillingdon Borough	46	14	10	22	46	58	38
Canterbury City	46	10	16	20	49	78	36
Crawley Town	46	9	12	25	46	81	30
Folkestone	46	10	6	30	49	101	26
Andover	46	4	11	31	39	100	19
Thanet United	46	5	7	34	37	110	17

Midland Division	P	W	D	L	F	A	Pts
Nuneaton Borough	42	27	11	4	88	32	65
Alvechurch	42	26	10	6	79	34	62
Kidderminster Har	42	22	12	8	71	40	56
Stourbridge	42	21	10	11	69	47	52
Gloucester City	42	21	9	12	64	48	51
Bedworth United	42	20	10	12	59	40	50
Enderby Town	42	20	10	12	79	66	50
Witney Town	42	19	8	15	71	49	46
Barry Town	42	16	14	12	59	46	46
Corby Town	42	19	8	15	70	59	46
Merthyr Tydfil	42	16	12	14	63	54	44
Wellingborough T	42	15	12	15	50	45	42
Bridgend Town	42	13	13	16	50	62	39
Bromsgrove Rovers	42	15	8	19	57	63	38
Bedford Town	42	12	13	17	45	54	37
Cheltenham Town	42	11	14	17	65	68	36
Taunton Town	42	12	8	22	46	76	32
Banbury United	42	11	8	23	63	91	30
Minehead	42	12	6	24	38	69	30
Cambridge City	42	10	8	24	38	80	28
Milton Keynes City	42	6	11	25	34	70	23
Redditch United	42	8	5	29	37	103	21

CHESHIRE COUNTY LEAGUE

Division One	P	W	D	L	F	A	Pts
Hyde United	38	27	8	3	91	34	62
Chorley	38	23	9	6	70	34	55
Burscough	38	21	10	7	70	39	52
Winsford United	38	21	9	8	68	43	51
Rossendale United	38	18	10	10	63	44	46
Glossop	38	13	19	6	52	30	45
Darwen	38	16	10	12	63	62	40
Curzon Ashton	38	12	15	11	57	50	39
Prescot Cables	38	16	8	14	51	45	38
Stalybridge Celtic	38	14	9	15	71	66	37
Fleetwood Town	38	12	13	13	42	55	37
Formby	38	12	11	15	42	55	35
Accrington Stanley	38	11	11	16	40	57	33
Nantwich Town	38	10	13	15	48	49	31
Leek Town	38	10	11	17	39	45	31
Horwich RMI	38	12	7	19	58	72	31
Bootle	38	11	12	15	49	47	30
St Helens Town	38	7	11	20	34	71	25
Ashton United	38	8	6	24	38	77	22
Droylsden	38	3	4	31	26	96	10

DRYBROUGH'S NORTHERN LEAGUE

	P	W	D	L	F	A	Pts
Blyth Spartans	38	25	8	5	77	31	83
Whitby Town	38	23	11	4	64	21	80
South Bank	38	20	7	11	72	44	67
Tow Law Town	38	18	8	12	76	58	62
Spennymoor United	38	16	13	9	59	37	61
Billingham Synthonia	38	17	9	12	57	46	60
Bishop Auckland	38	16	8	14	63	51	59
Durham City	38	17	5	16	75	67	56
Shildon	38	16	8	14	57	54	56
North Shields	38	14	13	11	67	51	55
Ferryhill Ath	38	16	6	16	55	59	54
Horden CW	38	15	6	17	55	58	51
Crook Town	38	15	6	17	60	69	51
Evenwood Town	38	13	9	16	57	66	48
Penrith	38	13	10	15	63	66	46
Consett	38	10	10	18	46	64	40
West Auckland	38	9	10	19	42	67	37
Ashington	38	9	8	21	51	87	35
Whitley Bay	38	8	7	23	47	83	31
Willington	38	3	10	25	46	102	19

WEST MIDLANDS LEAGUE

Premier Division	P	W	D	L	F	A	Pts
Shifnal Town	42	24	11	5	82	36	63
Sutton Coldfield Tn	42	26	9	7	80	43	61
Halesowen Town	42	24	8	10	84	45	56
Bilston	42	23	8	11	70	49	54
Ledbury Town	42	19	14	9	83	58	52
Rushall Olympic	42	16	18	8	72	54	50
Willenhall Town	42	18	11	13	64	46	47
VS Rugby	42	20	7	15	67	51	47
Blakenhall	42	20	7	15	59	53	47
Dudley Town	42	17	12	13	61	52	46
Wednesfield Social	42	15	13	14	43	42	43
Lye Town	42	15	12	15	59	49	42
Hednesford Town	42	17	7	17	61	57	42
Coventry Sporting	42	13	11	18	43	54	37
Gresley Rovers	42	13	9	20	50	59	35
Hinckley Athletic	42	12	10	20	43	66	34
Tividale	42	13	6	23	56	82	32
Malvern Town	42	11	10	21	49	78	32
Armitage	42	10	11	21	43	69	31
Oldswinford	42	9	11	22	48	74	29
Brereton Social	42	7	10	25	47	100	24
Darlaston	42	6	8	28	37	84	20

MIDLAND FOOTBALL COMBINATION

Division One	P	W	D	L	F	A	Pts
Chipping Norton T	42	27	9	6	106	43	63
Highgate United	42	27	10	8	78	49	58
Mile Oak Rovers	42	24	10	8	78	49	58
Cinderford Town	42	19	16	7	71	40	54
Oldbury United	42	22	8	12	67	44	52
Bridgnorth Town	42	20	12	10	65	47	52
Moor Green	42	22	7	13	84	59	51
Knowle	42	16	16	10	64	50	48
Walsall Sportsco	42	18	10	14	68	54	46
Racing Club W'wick	42	16	13	13	68	64	45
West Mids Police	42	14	14	14	70	70	42
Boldmere St Mich'ls	42	14	14	14	59	60	42
Coleshill Town	42	16	8	18	57	68	40
Stratford Town	42	12	12	18	37	49	36
Smethwick Highfield	42	13	10	19	49	64	36
Northfield Town	42	15	6	21	56	76	36
Solihull Borough	42	11	13	18	46	68	35
Cradley Town	42	12	10	20	60	80	34
Paget Rangers	42	10	14	18	43	63	34
Walsall Wood	42	9	8	25	40	82	26
Evesham United	42	6	9	27	40	83	21
Hurley Daw Mill	42	3	7	32	42	96	13

ATHENIAN LEAGUE

	P	W	D	L	F	A	Pts
Leyton-Wingate	36	28	8	0	87	19	64
Edgware	36	20	10	6	76	52	50
Uxbridge	36	20	9	7	56	27	49
Burnham	36	19	7	10	64	44	45
Redhill	36	14	13	9	43	38	41
Harefield United	36	14	12	10	52	47	40
Ruislip Manor	36	15	9	12	58	55	39
Banstead Athletic	36	13	12	11	51	39	38
Chertsey Town	36	11	14	11	43	44	36
Woodford Town	36	13	8	15	48	45	34
Marlow	36	12	8	16	40	46	32
Kingsbury Town	36	11	10	15	43	52	32
Whyteleafe	36	8	15	13	30	41	31
Horley Town	36	10	10	16	40	45	30
Hoddesdon Town	36	11	7	18	50	57	29
Grays Athletic	36	10	8	18	41	62	28
Chalfont St Peter	36	8	10	18	42	50	26
Fleet Town	36	7	9	20	38	76	23
Haringey Borough	36	4	9	23	27	90	17

GREAT MILLS WESTERN LEAGUE

Premier Division	P	W	D	L	F	A	Pts
Bideford	38	26	10	2	88	20	62
Barnstaple Town	38	26	8	4	78	31	59*
Bridgwater Town	38	16	16	6	70	46	48
Clandown	38	17	12	9	49	37	46
Melksham Town	38	17	11	10	58	50	45
Frome Town	38	16	9	13	67	58	41
Weston-super-Mare	38	15	11	12	47	42	41
Saltash United	38	15	7	16	47	53	37
Devizes Town	38	14	7	17	53	60	35
Dawlish	38	11	13	14	45	53	35
Liskeard Athletic	38	11	12	15	39	48	34
Bridport	38	12	10	16	43	54	34
Clevedon Town	38	11	12	15	58	60	33*
Chippenham Town	38	12	9	17	33	39	33
Falmouth Town	38	12	9	17	46	55	33
Portway Bristol	38	9	13	16	40	47	31
Wellington	38	10	11	17	50	62	31
Keynsham Town	38	9	13	16	39	55	31
Mangotsfield United	38	11	6	21	30	59	28
Welton Rovers	38	7	7	24	37	88	21

* One point deducted for playing an ineligible player

MIDLAND COUNTIES LEAGUE

Premier Division	P	W	D	L	F	A	Pts
Shepshed Charter	34	22	7	5	78	26	51
Alfreton Town	34	20	7	7	64	24	47
Eastwood Town	34	19	8	7	62	34	46
Spalding United	34	14	14	6	49	34	42
Guisborough Town	34	16	9	9	49	37	41
Appleby Frodingham	34	16	8	10	53	50	40
Heanor Town	34	12	15	7	40	32	39
Mexborough Town	34	14	8	12	45	41	36
Boston	34	12	11	11	45	35	35
Skegness Town	34	12	11	11	32	37	35
Long Eaton United	34	11	12	11	44	50	34
Belper Town	34	10	13	11	47	49	33
Bridlington Trinity	34	10	9	15	48	56	29
Ilkeston Town	34	8	9	17	35	46	25
Brigg Town	34	6	11	17	30	61	23
Arnold	34	9	4	21	46	74	22
Sutton Town	34	5	8	21	27	67	18
Ashby	34	4	8	22	24	65	16

UNITED COUNTIES LEAGUE

Premier Division	P	W	D	L	F	A	Pts
Stamford	36	25	5	6	71	28	55
Irthlingborough	36	23	8	5	73	34	54
Rushden	36	19	7	10	61	32	45
Buckingham	36	19	7	10	63	43	45
Bourne	36	18	7	11	64	44	43
Potton	36	15	11	10	41	30	41
Ampthill	36	14	11	11	73	67	39
Long Buckby	36	14	10	12	57	60	38
Holbeach	36	14	9	13	53	46	37
Wootton	36	14	9	13	57	58	37
Kempston	36	13	10	13	63	62	36
Stevenage	36	12	9	15	50	49	33
Desborough	36	10	13	13	47	55	33
S & L Corby	36	10	12	14	46	57	32
Rothwell	36	12	6	18	58	60	30
Brit Timken Duston	36	11	8	17	46	67	30
Eynesbury	36	8	9	19	35	58	25
Wolverton	36	8	4	24	36	78	20
St Neots	36	2	7	27	25	91	11

HELLENIC LEAGUE

Premier Division	P	W	D	L	F	A	Pts
Forest Green Rovers	30	23	1	6	71	20	47
Moreton Town	30	13	13	4	44	32	39
Wantage Town	30	14	10	6	42	28	38
Newbury Town	30	14	8	8	62	38	36
Maidenhead Town	30	14	6	10	46	34	34
Fairford Town	30	12	10	8	41	29	34
Abingdon Town	30	13	7	10	34	32	33
Flackwell Heath	30	11	10	9	27	30	32
Thame United	30	9	10	11	40	39	28
Bicester Town	30	9	10	11	40	42	28
Wallingford Town	30	11	5	14	40	54	27
Clanfield	30	8	8	14	33	47	24
Northwood	30	9	3	18	35	47	21
Hazells	30	7	7	16	26	51	21
Didcot Town	30	5	10	15	18	40	20
Kidlington	30	6	6	18	26	56	18

LONDON SPARTAN LEAGUE

Premier Division	P	W	D	L	F	A	Pts
Fisher Athletic	26	17	7	2	60	18	41
Bracknell Town	26	15	5	6	47	30	35
Merstham	26	14	4	8	41	28	32
Malden Vale	26	13	6	7	41	30	32
Beckton United	26	10	8	8	39	31	28
Waltham Abbey	26	11	5	10	41	28	27
Alma Swanley	26	10	7	9	47	49	27
Beckenham Town	26	8	8	10	28	24	24
Chingford	26	10	4	12	47	57	24
Swanley Town	26	8	6	12	35	45	22
Amersham Town	26	6	9	11	33	53	21
Berkhamsted Town	26	7	5	14	26	43	19
Greenwich Borough	26	6	5	15	29	49	17
Ambrose Fleming	26	5	5	16	29	55	15

YORKSHIRE LEAGUE

Division One	P	W	D	L	F	A	Pts
Emley	30	16	9	5	57	27	41
Guiseley	30	17	5	8	52	33	39
Leeds Ashley Road	30	15	9	6	44	30	39
Scarborough	30	15	7	8	51	38	37
Bentley VW	30	13	9	8	46	37	35
Lincoln United	30	13	8	9	47	35	34
Winterton Rangers	30	13	8	9	37	30	34
Thackley	30	13	7	10	51	35	33
Ossett Albion	30	10	11	9	28	26	31
North Ferriby	30	10	7	13	46	46	27
Sheffield	30	10	7	13	33	46	27
Hallam	30	10	6	14	46	53	26
Grecheville CA	30	11	3	16	39	48	25
Farsley Celtic	30	10	2	18	38	54	22
Liversedge	30	6	5	19	24	52	17
York RI	30	5	3	22	28	77	13

EASTERN COUNTIES LEAGUE

	P	W	D	L	F	A	Pts
Tiptree United	42	28	9	5	78	32	66
Sudbury Town	42	25	10	7	82	38	60
Gorleston	42	24	8	10	91	44	56
Gt Yarmouth Town	42	22	11	9	84	44	55
Wisbech Town	42	21	9	12	66	40	51
Saffron Walden Tn	42	21	9	12	75	57	51
Newmarket Town	42	19	11	12	72	56	49
Brantham Ath	42	18	13	11	59	50	49
Chatteris Town	42	17	15	10	58	49	49
Colchester Utd Res	42	15	14	13	67	63	44
Haverhill Rovers	42	12	17	13	52	53	41
March Town United	42	13	15	14	58	62	41
Lowestoft Town	42	15	9	18	68	63	39
Felixstowe Town	42	14	10	18	60	81	38
Ely City	42	12	13	17	55	78	37
Histon	42	12	12	18	48	72	36
Thetford Town	42	9	18	15	51	70	36
Bury Town	42	12	10	20	53	77	34
Braintree	42	10	8	24	53	86	28
Clacton Town	42	7	9	26	43	73	23
Soham Town Rngrs	42	6	9	27	47	74	21
Stowmarket	42	5	11	26	42	83	21

LANCASHIRE COMBINATION

	P	W	D	L	F	A	Pts
Caernarfon Town	34	23	8	3	71	27	54
Colne Dynamoes	34	24	4	6	72	33	52
Nelson	34	19	7	8	66	44	45
Wren Rovers	34	18	7	9	67	47	43
Clitheroe	34	13	16	5	67	40	42
Gt Harwood Town	34	16	8	10	61	47	40
Chadderton	34	17	5	12	62	43	39
Blackpool Mech	34	14	9	11	47	34	37
Vulcan Newton	34	13	8	13	61	56	34
Padiham	34	14	6	14	47	47	34
Lytham	34	11	11	12	74	66	33
Oldham Dew	34	12	6	16	48	61	30
Wigan Rovers	34	11	7	16	44	53	29
Bacup Borough	34	9	8	17	47	77	26
Whitworth Valley	34	5	12	17	42	68	22
Daisy Hill	34	5	9	20	31	64	19
Bolton ST	34	7	4	23	40	86	18
Ashton Athletic	34	4	7	23	22	76	15

VAUX WEARSIDE LEAGUE

	P	W	D	L	F	A	Pts
Seaham CW Red Star	38	27	5	6	67	27	59
Peterlee Newtown	38	24	8	6	81	31	56
Chester-le-Street Tn	38	24	7	7	69	34	55
Reyrolles	38	23	7	8	82	50	53
Blue Star	38	21	9	8	88	40	51
Brandon United	38	21	8	9	73	48	50
Whickham	38	19	11	8	81	46	49
South Shields	38	22	7	10	66	48	49
Hartlepool Res	38	18	8	12	69	50	44
Easington	38	17	9	12	66	53	43
Roker	38	13	13	12	63	68	39
Washington	38	12	9	17	50	56	33
Heaton Stannington	38	13	5	20	53	76	31
Eppleton CW	38	8	9	21	42	58	25
Annfield Plain	38	7	9	22	50	84	23
Wingate	38	9	4	25	49	75	22
Murton	38	6	9	23	29	79	21
Stockton	38	8	5	25	46	100	21
Ryhope CW	38	6	7	25	44	89	19
Boldon CA	38	4	9	25	38	94	17

ESSEX SENIOR LEAGUE

	P	W	D	L	F	A	Pts
Heybridge Swifts	32	26	4	2	74	21	56
Wivenhoe Town	32	20	4	8	66	35	44
Brentwood	32	19	5	8	61	32	43
Bowers United	32	16	8	8	56	33	40
Witham Town	32	16	6	10	49	27	38

GLOUCESTERSHIRE COUNTY LEAGUE

	P	W	D	L	F	A	Pts
Shortwood United	32	22	6	4	92	49	50
Almondsbury Grnwy	32	21	7	4	88	32	49
Lydbrook Athletic	32	17	11	4	69	36	45
Wilton Rovers	32	18	6	8	66	44	42
Immediate Br St G	32	19	5	8	75	42	41

HAMPSHIRE LEAGUE

Division One	P	W	D	L	F	A	Pts
AFC Totton	38	24	7	7	67	33	55
Sholing Sports	38	23	6	9	65	28	52
Newport IOW	38	20	9	9	56	40	49
Eastleigh	38	19	8	11	53	29	46
Southampton 'A'	38	18	7	13	57	49	43

KENT LEAGUE

Division One	P	W	D	L	F	A	Pts
Erith & Belvedere	30	17	10	3	45	22	44
Sittingbourne	30	18	5	7	61	34	41
Chatham	30	18	5	7	61	34	41
Sheppey United	30	16	5	9	60	40	37
Crockenhill	30	11	13	6	54	41	35

LEICESTERSHIRE SENIOR LEAGUE

Division One	P	W	D	L	F	A	Pts
Anstey Nomads	30	22	7	1	81	25	49*
Birstall United	30	19	6	5	64	29	44
Enderby Reserves	30	19	4	7	53	36	42
Stapenhill	30	19	2	9	74	43	38*
Wigston Fields	30	16	3	11	56	39	35

SUSSEX COUNTY LEAGUE

Division One	P	W	D	L	F	A	Pts
Peacehaven & T	30	22	6	2	66	20	48
Littlehampton Town	30	17	8	5	67	32	42
Burgess Hill Town	30	14	10	6	58	48	38
Steyning Town	30	16	5	9	65	37	37
Pagham	30	13	9	8	49	36	35

TEESSIDE LEAGUE

	P	W	D	L	F	A	Pts
Billingham Social	30	25	1	4	76	25	51
Smith's Dock	30	20	2	8	61	47	42
Cassel Works	30	17	3	10	61	39	37
Brotton Tees Com	30	12	11	7	50	43	35
Hartlepool BWOB	30	14	6	10	56	53	34

WILTSHIRE COUNTY LEAGUE

Division One	P	W	D	L	F	A	Pts
Park	32	22	7	3	80	28	51
Avebury	32	23	5	4	71	29	51
Warminster Town	32	19	6	7	74	40	44
Amesbury Town	32	18	6	8	66	39	42
Melksham Town Res	32	16	9	7	77	51	41

1982-83

After finishing as runners-up in 1982, Enfield went one better this time and became the first southern club to win the Alliance Premier League championship. Eddie McCluskie decided that after the previous season's success there was no need for changes of personnel. He kept the same squad, and his faith was amply repaid. The power-shift to the south was emphasised by the fact that Maidstone and Wealdstone finished second and third.

The outstanding performance in the FA Trophy was Harrow Borough's incredible run which took them right through to a Semi-Final appearance against Telford United. On the way, they beat 1981 finalists Sutton United, and thrashed holders Enfield 5-1 in the Quarter-Finals. In the Semi-Finals they took a lead from the first leg, went further ahead at Bucks Head, but were eventually overhauled in extra-time, and Telford went on to beat Northwich in the final.

Halesowen Town reached their first FA Vase final (they were to reach three in four seasons), where they lost 0-1 to VS Rugby in an all-Midlands affair. The victors thus became the seventh holders of the Vase, and completed a notable rags-to-riches rise; they had started life as Valley Sports in the Third Division of the Rugby & District League in 1956.

Bishop's Stortford were the most imprssive Non-League side in the FA Cup. They eliminated Reading and Slough Town (who had earlier disposed of Millwall), then recovered from a 0-2 deficit to draw at Middlesborough before narrowly losing a thrilling replay in which they scored first. On the whole it was a good year as, apart from the aforementioned successes of Stortford and Slough, Worcester City, Weymouth, Telford United, Boston United, Northwich Victoria and Altrincham also beat League clubs.

SUMMARY

	Winners	Runners Up	Semi-finalists
FA VASE	VS Rugby	Halesowen	Burnham, Great Yarmouth Town
FA TROPHY	Winners	Runners-up	Semi-finalists
	Telford United	Northwich Victoria	Dagenham, Harrow Borough

FA CUP   **Most Successful Team:** Bishop's Stortford
1st Rd: Reading 1 Bishop's Stortford 2; 2nd Rd: Slough Town 1 Bishop's Stortford 4;
3rd Rd: Middlesbrough 2 Bishop's Stortford 2; 3rd Rd Replay: Bishop's Stortford 1 Middlesbrough 2

ALLIANCE PREMIER LEAGUE   Champions: Enfield   Runners Up: Maidstone United

ALLIANCE PREMIER STATISTICS

Top Crowds
2452	Maidstone United v Wealdstone (2.4.83)
2299	Yeovil Town v Weymouth (27.12.82)
2200	Maidstone United v Dagenham (27.12.82)
2065	Maidstone United v Scarborough (7.4.83)
1824	Maidstone United v Northwich Vic (16.10.82)

Top Scorer
41   John Bartley (Maidstone)

Manager of the Month Awards
Aug	Fry (Barnet)
Sep	Williams (Maidstone)
Oct	Batsford (Wealdstone)
Nov	Morgan (Weymouth)
Dec	Morgan (Weymouth)
Jan	Froggatt (Boston)
Feb	Hardy (Dagenham)
Mar	Cottam (Scarborough)
Apr	McCluskey (Enfield)

ALLIANCE PREMIER LEAGUE

		Home					Away					
	P	W	D	L	F	A	W	D	L	F	A	Pts
Enfield	42	16	3	2	57	21	9	6	6	38	27	84
Maidstone United	42	17	1	3	55	13	8	7	6	28	21	83
Wealdstone	42	13	5	3	45	17	9	8	4	35	24	79
Runcorn	42	15	5	1	50	21	7	3	11	23	32	72
Boston United	42	14	5	2	46	25	6	7	8	31	32	72
Telford United	42	16	3	2	46	17	4	8	9	23	31	71
Weymouth	42	13	6	2	37	14	7	4	10	26	34	70
Northwich Victoria	42	15	5	1	48	22	3	5	13	20	41	64
Scarborough	42	10	6	5	39	23	7	6	8	32	35	63
Bath City	42	12	3	6	41	25	5	6	10	17	30	60
Nuneaton Borough	42	11	6	4	36	20	4	7	10	21	40	58
Altrincham	42	13	5	3	40	17	2	5	14	22	39	55
Bangor City	42	8	9	4	33	29	6	4	11	38	48	55
Dagenham	42	5	9	7	30	26	7	6	8	30	39	51
Barnet	42	9	3	9	37	39	7	0	14	18	39	51
Frickley Athletic	42	11	6	4	41	25	1	7	13	25	52	49
Worcester City	42	10	7	4	43	33	2	3	16	15	54	46
Trowbridge	42	9	5	7	31	30	3	2	16	25	58	43
Kettering Town	42	9	5	7	45	37	2	2	17	24	62	40
Yeovil Town	42	10	4	7	37	36	1	3	17	26	63	40
Barrow	42	7	4	10	26	35	1	8	12	20	39	36
Stafford Rangers	42	4	8	9	22	30	1	6	14	18	45	29

SOUTHERN LEAGUE

Premier Division

	P	W	D	L	F	A	Pts
AP Leamington	38	25	4	9	78	50	79
Kidderminster Harr	38	23	7	8	69	40	76
Welling United	38	21	6	11	63	40	69
Chelmsford City	38	16	11	11	57	40	59
Bedworth United	38	16	11	11	47	39	59
Dartford	38	16	8	14	48	38	56
Gosport Borough	38	14	13	11	47	43	55
Fareham Town	38	16	7	15	73	82	55
Dorchester Town	38	14	12	12	52	50	54
Gravesend & Nthflt	38	14	12	12	49	50	54
Gloucester City	38	13	12	13	61	57	51
Witney Town	38	12	13	13	60	48	47*
Alvechurch	38	13	8	17	60	66	47
Stourbridge	38	12	11	15	48	54	47
Corby Town	38	12	11	15	58	67	47
Hastings United	38	11	11	16	48	61	44
Enderby Town	38	11	9	18	44	62	42
Waterlooville	38	10	9	19	62	83	39
Poole Town	38	9	9	20	57	73	36
Addlestone & Wey	38	5	10	23	24	62	25

* 2 points deducted for ineligible player

Midland Division

	P	W	D	L	F	A	Pts
Cheltenham Town	32	22	5	5	65	29	71
Sutton Coldfield T	32	21	7	4	62	24	70
Forest Green Rovers	32	21	3	8	68	32	66
Merthyr Tydfil	32	17	7	8	64	45	58
Willenhall Town	32	17	6	9	74	49	57
Oldbury Town	32	16	6	10	52	49	54
Banbury United	32	15	3	14	59	55	48
Bridgend Town	32	12	11	9	46	37	47
Wellingborough Tn	32	13	7	12	49	37	46
Bromsgrove Rovers	32	13	5	14	47	47	44
Dudley Town	32	12	7	13	40	45	43
Bridgwater Town	32	12	6	14	42	43	42
Aylesbury United	32	12	5	15	37	51	41
Redditch United	32	8	6	18	51	73	30
Taunton Town	32	5	7	20	30	64	22
Minehead	32	5	7	20	24	62	22
Milton Keynes City	32	0	4	28	22	90	4

Southern Division

	P	W	D	L	F	A	Pts
Fisher Athletic	34	23	5	6	79	34	74
Folkestone	34	22	6	6	79	41	72
RS Southampton	34	19	5	10	57	39	62
Dunstable	34	19	5	10	57	39	62
Hillingdon Borough	34	14	11	9	41	30	53
Salisbury	34	14	10	10	58	49	52
Crawley Town	34	14	9	11	51	43	51
Ashford Town	34	13	10	11	51	41	49
Tonbridge AFC	34	14	5	15	57	57	47
Hounslow	34	11	12	11	46	47	45
Canterbury City	34	12	9	13	52	63	45
Cambridge City	34	12	5	17	56	63	41
Dover	34	11	7	16	35	52	40
Thanet United	34	10	5	19	30	61	35
Basingstoke Town	34	8	10	16	37	56	34
Woodford Town	34	6	9	19	29	57	27
Andover	34	6	8	20	28	53	26
Erith & Belvedere	34	5	9	20	26	62	24

ISTHMIAN LEAGUE

Premier Division

	P	W	D	L	F	A	Pts
Wycombe Wandrs	42	26	7	9	79	47	85
Leytonstone & Ilford	42	24	9	9	71	39	81
Harrow Borough	42	24	7	11	91	58	79
Hayes	42	23	9	10	63	41	78
Sutton United	42	20	8	14	96	71	68
Dulwich Hamlet	42	18	14	10	59	52	68
Slough Town	42	18	13	11	73	36	67
Bognor Regis Town	42	19	8	15	53	48	65
Tooting & Mitcham	42	18	9	15	58	56	63
Billericay Town	42	17	10	15	54	51	61
Croydon	42	17	9	16	68	58	60
Hendon	42	18	6	18	68	61	60
Bishop's Stortford	42	17	9	16	61	58	60
Barking	42	14	14	14	47	55	46
Bromley	42	14	12	16	51	50	54
Carshalton Athletic	42	15	9	18	58	60	54
Wokingham Town	42	13	9	20	37	51	48
Walthamstow Ave	42	12	11	19	48	64	47
Staines Town	42	12	11	19	62	79	47
Hitchin Town	42	11	9	22	49	77	42
Woking	42	6	6	30	30	79	24
Leatherhead	42	4	5	33	36	121	17

Division One

	P	W	D	L	F	A	Pts
Worthing	40	25	6	9	76	39	81
Harlow Town	40	21	11	8	84	55	74
Farnborough Town	40	20	13	7	69	39	73
Hertford Town	40	20	11	9	70	61	71
Oxford City	40	19	13	8	70	49	70
Boreham Wood	40	21	6	13	62	42	69
Metropolitan Police	40	19	9	12	77	57	66
Walton & Hersham	40	17	6	17	65	59	57
Hampton	40	15	10	15	62	60	55
Wembley	40	14	10	16	62	61	52
Aveley	40	15	7	18	52	62	52
Kingstonian	40	13	12	15	53	53	51
Tilbury	40	12	10	18	41	47	46
Feltham	40	11	12	17	45	54	45
Chesham United	40	13	6	21	43	70	45
Epsom & Ewell	40	10	14	16	44	49	44
Lewes	40	12	8	20	47	71	44
Cheshunt	40	10	13	17	41	49	43
Hornchurch	40	11	8	21	45	74	41
Maidenhead United	40	10	10	20	47	87	40
St Albans City	40	10	9	21	52	79	37*

* 2 points deducted

Division Two

	P	W	D	L	F	A	Pts
Clapton	42	30	4	8	96	46	94
Windsor & Eton	42	27	7	8	98	43	88
Barton Rovers	42	26	6	10	86	48	84
Leyton Wingate	42	25	8	9	111	41	83
Basildon United	42	23	13	6	92	42	82
Uxbridge	42	22	12	8	80	42	78
Hungerford Town	42	22	10	10	82	39	76
Corinthian Casuals	42	23	6	13	95	48	75
Egham Town	42	21	8	13	77	67	71
Tring Town	42	20	10	12	86	59	70
Letchworth Gdn C	42	18	13	11	68	53	66*
Southall	42	18	7	17	81	80	61
Molesey	42	17	9	16	73	56	60
Dorking Town	42	15	9	18	56	75	54

	P	W	D	L	F	A	Pts
Hemel Hempstead	42	12	14	16	53	59	50
Rainham Town	42	14	4	24	57	94	46
Eastbourne United	42	10	6	26	54	104	36
Epping Town	42	6	8	28	29	89	26
Ware	42	6	6	30	34	97	24
Finchley	42	4	12	26	28	92	24
Horsham	42	5	7	30	32	106	22
Harwich & Parkeston	42	5	7	30	42	130	22

* 1 point deducted

NORTHERN PREMIER LEAGUE

Premier Division	P	W	D	L	F	A	Pts
Gateshead	42	32	4	6	114	43	100
Mossley	42	25	9	8	77	42	84
Burton Albion	42	24	9	9	81	53	81
Chorley	42	23	11	8	77	49	80
Macclesfield Town	42	24	8	10	71	49	80
Marine	42	17	17	8	81	57	68
Workington	42	19	10	13	71	55	67
Hyde United	42	18	12	12	91	63	66
King's Lynn	42	17	13	12	62	44	64
Matlock Town	42	18	10	14	70	65	64
Witton Albion	42	17	12	13	82	52	63
Buxton	42	17	9	16	60	62	60
Morecambe	42	16	11	15	75	66	59
Grantham	42	15	13	14	49	50	58
Southport	42	11	14	17	58	65	47
Goole Town	42	13	7	22	52	66	46
Gainsborough Trinity	42	11	9	22	60	71	42
Oswestry Town	42	10	8	24	56	99	38
S Liverpool	42	7	15	20	57	91	36
Tamworth	42	7	8	27	44	97	29
Worksop Town	42	5	10	27	50	98	25
Netherfield	42	2	9	31	28	129	15

DRYBROUGHS NORTHERN LEAGUE

First Division	P	W	D	L	F	A	Pts
Blyth Spartans	36	23	11	2	92	31	80
Whitby Town	36	23	9	4	80	34	78
Horden Colliery Welf	36	21	5	10	65	35	68
Bishop Auckland	36	17	13	6	69	34	64
Spennymoor United	36	17	10	9	70	53	61
Billingham Synthonia	36	16	12	8	71	43	60
North Shields	36	17	7	12	73	46	58
Tow Law Town	36	16	10	10	71	63	58
Consett	36	15	10	11	53	37	55
Crook Town	36	16	7	13	54	47	55
South Bank	36	14	12	10	56	32	54
Ferryhill Athletic	36	14	12	10	53	42	54
Whitley Bay	36	13	8	15	56	50	47
Shildon	36	9	11	16	48	71	38
Evenwood Town	36	9	8	19	49	67	35
Ashington	36	9	6	21	36	73	33
Durham City	36	4	8	24	32	83	20
West Auckland Tn	36	5	2	28	37	110	18
Willington	36	2	2	32	26	140	8

NORTH WEST COUNTIES LEAGUE

Division One	P	W	D	L	F	A	Pts
Burscough	38	26	7	5	93	45	59
Rhyl	38	23	11	4	76	30	57
Horwich RMI	38	22	10	6	77	35	54
Stalybridge Celtic	38	17	15	6	60	32	49
Winsford United	38	18	10	10	72	48	46
Darwen	38	17	12	9	68	46	46
Lancaster City	38	17	11	10	69	54	45
Congleton Town	38	13	14	11	52	35	40
Penrith	38	17	6	15	68	51	40
Accrington Stanley	38	13	12	13	56	55	38
Leek Town	38	14	9	15	42	44	37
Curzon Ashton	38	14	8	16	46	47	36
Ashton United	38	13	10	15	55	69	36
Bootle	38	14	6	18	55	79	32*
Prescot Cables	38	9	13	16	50	60	31
Formby	38	10	8	20	48	68	28
Leyland Motors	38	7	10	21	34	74	24
Glossop	38	6	11	21	29	67	23
St Helens Town	38	5	10	23	29	80	20
Nantwich Town	38	6	5	27	43	93	17

Division Two							
Radcliffe Borough	38	33	4	1	110	25	70
Caernarfon Town	38	28	7	3	85	27	63
Wren Rovers	38	23	7	8	84	38	53
Eastwood Hanley	38	23	7	8	81	42	53
Kirkby Town	38	22	3	13	80	60	47
Irlam Town	38	17	8	13	79	52	42
Chadderton	38	18	6	14	55	51	42
Rossendale United	38	15	10	13	75	68	40
Ford Motors	38	18	4	16	61	59	40
Ellesmere Port & Nst	38	17	5	16	56	68	39
Skelmersdale United	38	13	11	14	70	63	37
Fleetwood Town	38	12	8	18	54	80	32
Atherton LR	38	11	9	18	52	70	31
Lytham	38	11	5	22	54	71	27
Great Harwood Tn	38	8	10	20	54	76	26
Salford	38	10	6	22	43	86	26
Droylsden	38	11	5	22	49	71	25*
Prescot Bl	38	10	5	23	46	81	25
Padiham	38	8	6	24	41	74	22
New Mills	38	7	4	27	30	106	18

Division Three							
Colne Dynamoes	34	25	5	4	95	37	55
Warrington Town	34	24	6	4	83	33	54
Clitheroe	34	22	7	5	87	35	51
Prestwich Heys	34	18	11	5	70	37	47
Vulcan Newton	34	13	10	11	70	65	36
Blackpool Mech	34	11	13	10	67	56	35
Bacup Borough	34	14	7	13	53	45	35
Atherton Collieries	34	12	11	11	55	57	35
Whitworth Valley	34	13	9	12	54	65	35
Nelson	34	7	16	11	49	56	30
Daisy Hill	34	10	10	14	47	58	30
Maghull	34	10	9	15	56	61	29
Ashton Town	34	12	5	17	53	73	29
Newton	34	8	12	14	59	62	28
Oldham Dew	34	10	8	16	48	61	28
Bolton ST	34	9	6	19	50	84	24
Wigan Rovers	34	5	7	22	35	72	17
Ashton Athletic	34	3	8	23	18	92	14

* 2 points deducted

NORTHERN COUNTIES EAST LEAGUE

Premier Division		Home					Away					
	P	W	D	L	F	A	W	D	L	F	A	Pts
Shepshed Charterhouse	38	16	2	1	74	11	8	6	5	35	23	56
Eastwood Town	38	12	5	2	37	17	9	6	4	34	24	53
Belper Town	38	11	6	2	42	13	10	4	5	33	19	52
Spalding United	38	12	5	2	44	25	7	9	3	25	19	52
Guiseley	38	12	5	2	41	11	9	4	6	31	24	51
Winterton Rangers	38	13	3	3	31	10	7	6	6	24	22	49
Thackley	38	10	5	4	40	20	8	6	5	22	22	47
Arnold	38	10	6	3	47	24	7	6	6	30	32	46
Heanor Town	38	10	7	2	32	14	7	5	7	18	29	46
Emley	38	11	5	3	56	21	3	6	10	18	37	39
Appleby-Frodingham Ath	38	8	4	7	26	18	7	5	7	33	43	39
Guisborough Town	38	10	2	7	31	29	6	4	9	28	30	38
Alfreton Town	38	10	2	7	32	21	6	1	12	15	34	35
Sutton Town	38	7	6	6	35	32	5	4	10	24	32	34
Ilkeston Town	38	4	7	8	22	31	6	4	9	28	42	31
Boston	38	8	7	4	35	28	2	4	13	18	63	31
Bridlington Trinity	38	6	1	12	22	37	4	2	13	17	52	23
Skegness Town	38	3	5	11	26	36	2	3	14	20	46	18
Bentley Victoria Welfare	38	3	1	15	21	50	3	1	15	23	57	14
Mexborough Town Athletic	38	1	2	16	18	42	1	0	18	14	62	6

EASTERN COUNTIES LEAGUE

	P	W	D	L	F	A	Pts		P	W	D	L	F	A	Pts
Saffron Walden Tn	42	31	6	5	107	40	68	Bury Town	42	16	11	15	68	57	43
Gorleston	42	27	9	6	97	50	63	Tiptree United	42	13	10	19	61	71	36
Yarmouth Town	42	26	9	7	101	52	61	Stowmarket	42	13	10	19	62	84	36
Bramham Athletic	42	25	8	9	96	46	58	Haverhill Rovers	42	13	9	20	64	71	35
Sudbury Town	42	21	15	6	101	57	57	Chatteris Town	42	11	10	21	65	85	32
Colchester Utd Res	42	24	8	10	104	42	42	Soham Town Rngrs	42	11	9	22	54	75	31
Lowestoft Town	42	22	9	11	85	49	53	Braintree	42	9	8	25	48	102	26
Felixstowe Town	42	19	15	8	70	50	53	Histon	42	9	6	27	53	101	24
Wisbech Town	42	22	7	13	83	67	51	Clacton Town	42	8	8	26	44	100	24
Newmarket Town	42	16	14	12	70	60	46	Thetford Town	42	7	6	28	36	109	20
March Town United	42	14	16	12	63	53	44	Ely City	42	2	3	37	21	129	7

MIDLAND FOOTBALL COMBINATION

Division One	P	W	D	L	F	A	Pts
Bridgenorth Town	38	29	6	3	102	30	64
Moor Green	38	27	6	5	106	44	60
Boldmere St Mich'ls	38	25	7	6	60	36	57
Highgate United	38	20	12	6	74	38	52
Cinderford Town	38	21	7	10	76	51	49
Paget Rangers	38	17	9	12	63	40	43
Stratford Town	38	15	11	12	59	62	41
Mile Oak Rovers	38	15	10	13	58	50	40
Hurley Daw Mill	38	13	10	15	60	62	36
Evesham United	38	13	10	15	52	58	36
Cradley Town	38	14	7	17	62	74	36
West Mids Police	38	10	13	15	66	73	33
Racing Club W'wick	38	12	9	17	52	65	33
Coleshill Town	38	13	7	18	45	58	33
Walsall Borough	38	10	9	19	34	67	29
Smethwick Highfield	38	8	12	18	38	58	28
Northfield Town	38	10	6	22	53	81	26
Chipping Norton Tn	38	7	11	20	32	59	25
Solihull Borough	38	6	8	24	43	83	20
Knowle	38	6	8	24	43	89	20

WEST MIDLANDS (REGIONAL) LEAGUE

Premier Division	P	W	D	L	F	A	Pts
Halesowen Town	38	28	6	4	124	37	62
Hinckley Athletic	38	28	6	4	124	32	55
Hednesford Town	38	22	4	12	64	53	48
Shifnal Town	38	19	9	10	78	48	47
Atherstone United	38	21	5	12	73	46	47
Bilston	38	19	7	12	82	50	45
VS Rugby	34	17	10	11	69	36	44
Armitage	38	18	8	12	61	51	44
Gresley Rovers	38	15	11	12	69	52	41
Tividale	38	18	5	15	52	48	41
Wednesfield Social	38	17	7	14	47	47	41
Wolverhampton Utd	38	14	12	12	50	47	40
Lye Town	38	13	10	15	50	49	36
Rushall Olympic	38	12	8	18	59	66	32
Blakenall	38	8	13	17	45	61	29
Coventry Sporting	38	7	14	17	40	64	28
Oldswinford	38	6	11	21	46	78	23
Brereton Soc	38	8	6	24	43	89	22
Ledbury Town	38	6	7	25	45	117	19
Malvern Town	38	6	4	28	40	125	16

GREAT MILLS WESTERN LEAGUE

Premier Division	P	W	D	L	F	A	Pts
Bideford	38	26	9	3	67	32	61
Frome Town	38	23	10	5	75	34	56
Dawlish	38	20	8	10	68	47	48
Clandown	38	19	9	10	54	39	47
Saltash United	38	14	18	6	50	39	46
Falmouth Town	38	16	13	9	63	57	45
Plymouth Argyle	38	15	14	9	67	41	44
Barnstaple Town	38	18	6	14	67	57	42
Liskeard Athletic	38	16	9	13	69	47	41
Weston-super-Mare	38	15	11	12	57	46	41
Shepton Mallet Tn	38	15	4	19	50	55	34
Devizes Town	38	12	9	17	50	58	33
Chippenham Town	38	12	8	18	40	54	32
Clevedon Town	38	9	12	17	36	56	30
Bridport	38	8	13	17	49	60	29
Exmouth Town	38	10	9	19	40	59	29
Melksham Town	38	8	13	17	43	63	29
Wellington	38	8	12	18	46	74	28
Keynsham Town	38	7	11	20	32	68	25
Portway-Bristol	38	8	4	26	35	72	20

HELLENIC LEAGUE

Premier Division	P	W	D	L	F	A	Pts
Moreton Town	30	10	4	1	44	12	10
Almondsbury Grnwy	30	9	1	5	30	15	9
Abingdon Town	30	9	5	1	38	19	6
Wallingford Town	30	6	4	5	27	24	11
Thame United	30	6	4	5	22	22	8
Didcot Town	30	7	3	5	24	20	7
Fairford Town	30	6	3	6	19	21	6
Wantage Town	30	3	10	2	19	14	6
Northwood	30	6	3	6	20	23	5
Bicester Town	30	7	3	5	20	13	5
Clanfield	30	6	3	6	23	19	4
Abingdon United	30	6	1	8	19	19	5
Maidenhead T & Yth	30	7	1	7	19	20	3
Hazells (Aylesbury)	30	4	1	10	20	25	4
Shortwood United	30	3	2	10	14	27	3
Lambourn Sports	30	1	3	11	8	39	1

LONDON SPARTAN LEAGUE

Premier Division	P	W	D	L	F	A	Pts
Bracknell Town	24	18	4	2	76	18	40
Swanley Town	24	16	3	5	44	23	35
Greenwich Borough	24	14	7	3	54	34	35
Malden Vale	24	14	4	6	43	24	32
Beckton United	24	13	3	8	40	26	29
Merstham	24	9	6	9	53	38	24
Highfield	24	9	4	11	42	53	22
Berkhamsted Town	24	5	9	10	26	42	19
BROB Barnet	24	6	6	12	38	56	18
Amersham Town	24	6	4	14	22	53	16
Waltham Abbey	24	5	5	14	25	45	15
Chingford	24	5	4	15	39	68	14
Ambrose Fleming	24	5	3	16	31	53	13

UNITED COUNTIES LEAGUE

Premier Division	P	W	D	L	F	A	Pts
Irthlingborough	34	19	11	4	61	27	49
Rushden	34	19	9	6	65	38	47
Stamford	34	14	13	7	46	40	41
Bourne	34	14	12	8	55	40	40
Potton	34	13	13	8	48	36	39
Desborough	34	16	6	12	58	46	38
Long Buckby	34	13	12	9	56	44	38
Wotton	34	12	13	9	61	55	37
Arlesey	34	14	9	11	49	48	37
Buckingham	34	13	8	13	42	51	34
Newport Pagnell	34	7	7	10	42	41	31
Stevenage	34	10	10	14	51	56	30
Holbeach	34	9	11	14	60	55	29
S & L Corby	34	9	11	14	44	54	29
Ampthill	34	10	7	17	57	66	27
Rothwell	34	10	9	15	40	55	27
Eynesbury	34	7	8	19	28	60	23
Kempston	34	4	7	23	39	90	15

ATHENIAN LEAGUE

	P	W	D	L	F	A	Pts
Newbury Town	38	27	5	6	97	42	59
Grays Athletic	38	25	3	10	79	27	53
Redhill	38	22	9	7	68	38	53
Marlow	38	21	8	9	67	40	50
Chalfont St Peter	38	18	12	8	64	40	48
Burnham	38	17	13	8	80	46	47
Banstead Athletic	38	16	10	12	62	50	42
Whyteleafe	38	15	12	11	46	39	42
Harefield United	38	15	12	11	54	55	42
Kingsbury Town	38	16	10	12	56	40	41*
Hoddesdon Town	38	15	10	13	58	54	40
Flackwell Heath	38	11	13	14	45	50	35
Horley Town	38	10	13	15	45	58	33
Edgware	38	12	7	19	48	62	31
Chertsey Town	38	10	10	18	61	88	30
Ruislip Manor	38	12	4	22	55	70	28
Fleet Town	38	8	10	20	38	65	25*
Thatcham Town	38	8	6	24	30	85	22
Haringey Borough	38	5	9	24	27	82	19
Camberley Town	18	4	10	24	31	80	16**

* 1 point deducted
** 2 points deducted

VAUX WEARSIDE LEAGUE

	P	W	D	L	F	A	Pts
Blue Star	34	27	3	4	100	30	57
Chester-le-Street Tn	34	23	5	6	84	28	51
Brandon United	34	25	0	9	84	45	50
Easington	34	21	5	8	71	38	47
Coundon	34	20	4	10	65	47	44
Stockton	34	14	12	8	67	46	40
Ryhope CW	34	14	8	12	51	41	36
Whickham	34	14	8	12	45	44	36
Seaham CW Red Str	34	14	7	13	57	50	35
South Shields	34	13	8	13	53	58	34
Eppleton CW	34	11	7	16	59	65	29
Murton	34	10	6	18	35	46	26
Washington	34	10	6	18	42	54	26
Boldon CA	34	10	5	19	36	70	25
Annfield Plain	34	7	9	18	48	79	23
Wingate	34	6	7	21	56	95	19
Reyrolles	34	6	7	21	40	82	19
Roker	34	5	5	24	53	127	15

ESSEX SENIOR LEAGUE

	P	W	D	L	F	A	Pts
Heybridge Swifts	31	24	3	4	86	21	51
Stansted	32	22	7	3	64	30	51
Halstead Town	32	24	2	6	87	32	50
Canvey Island	31	17	7	7	61	39	41
Bowers United	30	18	3	9	70	38	39

GLOUCESTERSHIRE COUNTY LEAGUE

	P	W	D	L	F	A	Pts
Old Georgians	32	26	3	3	73	23	55
Port of Bristol	32	20	7	5	64	33	47
Lawrence Weston Hallen	32	18	6	8	52	29	42
Hanham Athletic	32	16	10	6	49	28	42
Sharpness	32	14	8	10	51	48	36

HAMPSHIRE LEAGUE

Division One

	P	W	D	L	F	A	Pts
Sholing Sports	38	32	4	2	93	20	68
AFC Totton	38	25	8	5	73	35	58
Havant Town	38	21	6	11	73	60	48
Newport	38	20	6	12	79	61	46
Pirelli General	38	15	13	10	51	43	43

KENT LEAGUE

Division One

	P	W	D	L	F	A	Pts
Crockenhill	32	19	6	7	55	26	44
Hythe Town	32	18	7	7	66	37	43
Deal Town	32	15	11	6	51	34	41
Sittingbourne	32	15	10	7	70	33	40
Tunbridge Wells	32	14	9	9	52	46	37

LEICESTERSHIRE SENIOR LEAGUE

Division One

	P	W	D	L	F	A	Pts
Anstey Nomads	30	22	3	5	67	38	47
Wigston Fields	30	20	6	4	70	33	46
Friar Lane OB	30	16	6	8	70	43	38
Wigston Town	30	16	6	8	50	40	38
Birstall United	30	14	8	8	50	42	36

SUSSEX COUNTY LEAGUE

Division One

	P	W	D	L	F	A	Pts
Peacehaven & Tels	30	22	6	2	61	19	50
Southwick	30	17	9	4	67	32	43
Hastings Town	30	18	6	6	86	39	42
Steyning Town	30	18	5	7	52	29	41
Whitehawk	30	15	9	6	49	30	39

TEESSIDE LEAGUE

	P	W	D	L	F	A	Pts
Nunthorpe Ath	30	25	5	0	103	25	55
Hartlepool BWOB	30	17	9	4	66	38	43
ICI Cassel Works	30	18	6	6	64	39	42
Wilton ICI	30	18	4	8	63	33	40
Brotton Tees Com	30	15	5	10	67	44	37

WILTSHIRE COUNTY

Division One

	P	W	D	L	F	A	Pts
Penhill	30	21	7	2	69	21	49
Avebury	30	18	8	4	66	34	44
Bemerton Athletic	30	18	8	4	66	34	44
Avon Bardford	30	15	8	7	56	39	38
Amesbury Town	30	15	6	9	63	35	36

1983-84

Maidstone United improved on their runners-up spot of 1983 to claim their first Alliance Premier League title, but access to the Football League was denied them in the end of season ballot. The Kent club were pushed all the way to the line in the title race by Nuneaton Borough whose striker Paul Culpin was unstoppable; he bagged 54 in all.

Stansted created one of the major shocks in the history of Non-League football by winning the FA Vase. The Essex club battled through to the final from the Preliminary Round to beat experienced Vase campaigners Stamford in the final. Stansted had never won more than one game in any previous Vase competition.

Northwich Victoria recovered from their disappointment of the previous year by winning the FA Trophy. They were up against the already relegated Bangor City in the final, and although they could not kill the tie off at Wembley, the Vics emerged victorious from a replay at Stoke City.

Telford United, who had served notice of their intention the previous year by beating Wigan, made their first major FA Cup stir, beating Stockport, Northampton and Rochdale before losing very unluckily at Derby County in the Fourth Round. Telford's gallant run aside, it was not a vintage year for Non-League clubs in the FA Cup; Whitby Town and Maidstone United were the only others to record victories over League opposition.

SUMMARY

	Winners	Runners Up	Semi-finalists
FA VASE	Stansted	Stamford	Irthlingborough Diamonds, Whickham
FA TROPHY	Winners	Runners-up	Semi-finalists
	Northwich Victoria	Bangor City	Dagenham, Marine

FA CUP   Most Successful Team: Telford United

1st Rd: Telford 3 Stockport 0; 2nd Rd: Northampton 1 Telford 1; 2nd Rd Replay: Telford 3 Northampton 2; 3rd Rd: Rochdale 1 Telford 4; 4th Rd Derby County 3 Telford 2

ALLIANCE PREMIER LEAGUE   Champions: Maidstone United   Runners Up: Nuneaton Borough

ALLIANCE PREMIER LEAGUE STATISTICS

Top Crowds

3597	Nuneaton Borough v Maidstone Utd (30.4.84)
2502	Maidstone United v Telford United (5.5.84)
2265	Worcester City v Kidderminster H (26.12.83)
1967	Trowbridge Town v Bath City (26.12.83)
1911	Yeovil Town v Weymouth (2.1.84)

Top Scorers

41	Paul Culpin (Nuneaton)
30	Mark Graves (Wealdstone)
27	John Bartley (Maidstone)

Manager of the Month Awards

Aug	Williams (Runcorn)
Sep	Hall (Wealdstone)
Oct	Marshall (Frickley)
Nov	Cottam (Scarborough)
Dec	Storton (Telford)
Jan	Jones (Bath)
Feb	Hardy (Dagenham)
Mar	Williams (Maidstone)
Apr	King (Northwich)

ALLIANCE PREMIER LEAGUE

	P	W	D	L	F	A	W	D	L	F	A	Pts
			Home						**Away**			
Maidstone United	42	12	8	1	40	15	11	5	5	31	19	70
Nuneaton Borough	42	14	6	1	44	17	10	5	6	24	19	69
Altrincham	42	13	3	5	40	20	10	6	5	24	19	65
Wealdstone	42	15	4	2	48	14	6	10	5	27	22	62
Runcorn	42	11	8	2	34	18	9	5	7	27	27	62
Bath City	42	10	7	4	33	17	7	5	9	27	31	53
Northwich Vic	42	11	8	2	35	18	5	6	10	19	29	51
Worcester C	42	9	7	5	36	22	6	6	9	28	33	49
Barnet	42	9	3	9	27	28	7	7	7	28	30	49
Kidderminster H	42	7	9	5	32	30	7	5	9	22	31	49
Telford United	42	13	3	5	32	19	4	8	9	18	39	49
Frickley Athletic	42	13	3	5	49	25	4	7	10	19	31	48
Scarborough	42	10	10	1	32	16	4	6	11	20	39	48
Enfield	42	8	3	10	27	27	6	6	9	34	31	43
Weymouth	42	5	4	12	28	33	8	4	9	26	32	42
Gateshead	42	7	9	5	35	30	5	4	12	24	43	42
Boston United	42	10	6	5	39	30	3	6	12	27	50	41
Dagenham	42	10	3	8	34	26	4	5	12	23	43	40
Kettering Town	42	8	3	10	31	31	4	6	11	22	36	37
Yeovil Town	42	9	5	7	34	28	3	3	15	21	49	35
Bangor City	42	7	4	10	35	32	3	2	16	19	50	29
Trowbridge Town	42	3	4	14	15	34	2	3	16	18	53	19

ISTHMIAN LEAGUE

Premier Division	P	W	D	L	F	A	Pts
Harrow Borough	42	25	13	4	73	42	88
Worthing	42	20	11	11	89	72	71
Slough Town	42	20	9	13	73	56	69
Sutton United	42	18	12	12	67	45	66
Hayes	42	17	13	12	56	41	64
Hitchin Town	42	16	15	11	58	57	63
Wycombe Wandrs	42	16	14	12	63	52	62
Wokingham Town	42	18	10	14	78	55	61*
Hendon	42	17	10	15	62	51	61
Dulwich Hamlet	42	16	11	15	61	64	59
Bishop's Stortford	42	15	13	14	56	57	58
Harlow Town	42	15	11	16	64	70	56
Bognor Regis Town	42	14	13	15	62	69	55
Staines Town	42	15	9	18	63	72	54
Billericay Town	42	15	8	19	53	73	53
Barking	42	13	13	16	60	64	52
Croydon	42	14	10	18	52	58	52
Walthamstow Ave	42	13	10	19	53	67	49
Leytonstone-Ilford	42	13	9	20	54	67	48
Carshalton Athletic	42	11	10	21	59	72	43
Tooting & Mitcham	42	10	13	19	50	63	43
Bromley	42	7	11	24	33	72	32

Division One	P	W	D	L	F	A	Pts
Windsor & Eaton	42	26	7	9	89	44	85
Epsom & Ewell	42	23	9	10	73	51	78
Wembley	42	21	11	10	65	32	74
Maidenhead United	42	22	8	12	67	42	74
Boreham Wood	42	22	7	13	74	43	73
Farnborough Town	42	18	12	12	78	60	66
Hampton	42	18	12	12	65	49	66
Metropolitan Police	42	20	5	17	79	64	65
Chesham United	42	18	8	16	64	57	62
Tilbury	42	17	10	15	54	64	61
Leatherhead	42	15	10	17	67	56	55

	P	W	D	L	F	A	Pts
Aveley	42	15	10	17	49	53	55
Woking	42	16	7	19	66	73	55
Hertford Town	42	15	9	18	56	73	54
Oxford City	42	14	9	19	57	56	51
Lewes	42	13	12	17	49	65	51
Walton & Hersham	42	13	10	19	52	70	49
Hornchurch	42	13	10	19	43	63	49
Kingstonian	42	13	9	20	47	67	48
Clapton	42	12	11	19	49	67	47
Cheshunt	42	12	8	22	45	64	44
Feltham	42	7	4	31	31	106	25

Division Two	P	W	D	L	F	A	Pts
Basildon United	42	30	7	5	88	27	97
St Albans City	42	29	9	4	100	46	96
Leyton Wingate	42	29	4	9	97	41	91
Tring Town	42	23	11	8	89	44	80
Corinthian Casuals	42	23	11	8	75	47	80
Hungerford Town	42	21	12	9	94	47	75
Uxbridge	42	18	15	9	61	36	69
Grays Athletic	42	20	9	13	72	57	69
Dorking	42	21	5	16	66	54	68
Southall	42	20	8	14	79	60	65*
Egham Town	42	16	15	11	59	49	63
Epping Town	42	15	16	11	61	50	61
Molesey	42	13	14	15	59	68	53
Barton Rovers	42	15	8	19	54	64	53
Letchworth Grden C	42	15	7	20	48	66	52
Newbury Town	42	14	5	23	60	82	47
Hemel Hempstead	42	12	9	21	63	69	45
Rainham Town	42	7	5	30	38	114	26
Finchley	42	5	9	28	28	78	24
Eastbourne United	42	7	3	32	36	98	24
Ware	42	6	6	30	48	114	24
Horsham	42	7	4	31	40	104	24+

* 3 points deducted   + 2 points deducted

SOUTHERN LEAGUE

Premier Division	P	W	D	L	F	A	Pts
Dartford	38	23	9	6	67	32	78
Fisher Athletic	38	22	9	7	80	42	75
Chelmsford City	38	19	9	10	67	45	66
Gravesend & Nthflt	38	18	9	11	50	38	63
Witney Town	38	18	6	14	75	50	60
King's Lynn	38	18	6	14	42	45	60
Folkestone	38	16	9	13	60	56	57
Cheltenham Town	38	16	7	15	63	56	55
Gloucester City	38	13	15	10	55	50	54
Hastings United	38	15	9	14	55	57	54
Bedworth United	38	15	9	14	51	55	54
Welling United	38	15	7	16	61	61	52
AP Leamington	38	14	9	15	73	83	51
Corby Town	38	12	14	12	55	54	50
Fareham Town	38	13	11	14	65	70	50
Alvechurch	38	12	12	14	56	63	48
Sutton Coldfield Tn	38	10	14	14	49	53	44
Gosport Borough	38	6	15	17	31	64	33
Dorchester Town	38	4	8	26	40	69	20
Stourbridge	38	4	7	27	30	82	19

Division One Mid							
Willenhall Town	38	27	4	7	100	44	85
Shepshed Charter	38	25	5	8	88	37	80
Bromsgrove Rovers	38	20	8	10	73	43	68
Dudley Town	38	18	13	7	71	43	67
Aylesbury United	38	17	15	6	62	35	66
Moor Green	38	18	12	8	63	44	66
Rushden Town	38	17	12	9	68	42	63
Merthyr Tydfil	38	18	8	12	63	44	62
Redditch United	38	17	9	12	67	67	60

	P	W	D	L	F	A	Pts
VS Rugby	38	15	12	11	68	51	57
Forest Green Rovers	38	15	12	11	67	51	57
Bridgnorth Town	38	16	9	13	64	52	57
Leicester United	38	12	9	17	58	58	45
Oldbury United	38	10	13	15	53	51	43
Coventry Sporting	38	11	7	20	40	67	40
Bridgwater Town	38	10	8	20	39	65	38
Wellingborough Tn	38	7	9	22	43	80	30
Banbury United	38	6	11	21	37	78	29
Milton Keynes City	38	3	9	26	31	110	18
Tamworth	38	2	7	29	25	118	13

Division One South							
RS Southampton	38	26	6	6	83	35	84
Crawley Town	38	22	9	7	68	28	75
Basingstoke Town	38	20	9	9	54	36	69
Tonbridge AFC	38	20	9	9	61	44	69
Addlestone & Wey	38	19	11	8	58	34	68
Poole Town	38	20	7	11	68	42	67
Hillingdon	38	18	11	9	43	20	65
Ashford Town	38	19	5	14	65	47	62
Salisbury	38	17	8	13	61	48	59
Cambridge City	38	13	9	16	43	53	48
Canterbury City	38	12	9	17	44	52	45
Waterlooville	38	12	9	17	56	69	45
Dover Athletic	38	12	9	17	51	74	45
Chatham Town	38	11	10	17	46	56	43
Andover	38	12	6	20	35	54	42
Erith & Belvedere	38	11	9	18	43	68	42
Dunstable	38	10	8	20	38	65	38
Thanet United	38	9	8	21	40	65	35
Woodford Town	38	7	8	23	30	69	29
Hounslow	38	4	12	22	30	58	24

NORTHERN PREMIER LEAGUE

		Home					Home					
	P	W	D	L	F	A	W	D	L	F	A	Pts
Barrow	42	17	4	0	57	16	12	6	3	35	22	97
Matlock Town	42	13	3	5	38	18	10	5	6	34	30	77
South Liverpool	42	14	5	2	31	16	8	6	7	24	28	77
Grantham	42	12	4	5	40	21	8	4	9	24	30	68
Burton Albion	42	9	4	8	34	24	8	9	4	27	23	64
Macclesfield Town	42	12	4	5	38	26	6	6	9	27	29	64
Rhyl	42	11	2	8	35	23	8	4	9	29	32	63
Horwich RMI	42	11	5	5	35	23	7	4	10	29	36	63
Gainsborough Town	42	9	9	3	48	26	8	2	11	34	40	62
Stafford Rangers	42	9	7	5	37	23	6	10	5	28	29	62
Hyde United	42	9	3	9	29	28	8	5	8	32	35	59
Marine	42	8	6	7	37	32	8	4	9	26	36	58
Witton Albion	42	11	5	5	38	23	3	9	9	26	34	56
Chorley	42	6	6	9	34	36	8	5	8	34	29	53
Workington	42	9	5	7	34	23	5	4	12	20	33	51
Southport	42	9	5	7	32	28	5	3	13	25	46	50
Worksop Town	42	7	4	10	32	37	6	4	11	25	37	47
Goole Town	42	6	7	8	36	38	6	3	12	23	42	46
Morecambe	42	9	6	6	35	25	2	6	13	24	50	45
Oswestry Town	42	7	5	9	38	47	4	3	14	28	50	41
Buxton	42	6	3	12	24	34	5	3	13	28	57	39
*Mossley	42	5	6	10	26	35	4	3	14	21	39	33

* Three points deducted for fielding ineligible player

DRYBROUGH'S NORTHERN LEAGUE

Division One	P	W	D	L	F	A	Pts
Blyth Spartans	34	23	9	2	74	22	78
North Shields	34	21	6	7	81	51	69
Whitby Town	34	20	7	7	79	33	67
Tow Law Town	34	19	8	7	72	44	65
Bishop Auckland	34	19	7	8	80	39	64
South Bank	34	18	7	9	62	35	61
Billingham Synthonia	34	14	8	12	56	54	50
Gretna	34	15	7	12	65	58	49*
Whitley Bay	34	14	5	15	37	60	47
Horden Colliery Welf	34	12	7	15	48	59	43
Spennymoor United	34	10	9	15	41	58	39
Consett	34	10	8	16	43	58	38
Peterlee Newtown	34	11	5	18	50	78	38
Crook Town	34	9	10	15	38	50	37
Shildon	34	10	6	18	50	63	36
Ferryhill Athletic	34	9	6	19	47	61	33
Ashington	34	7	8	19	59	71	26*
Evenwood Town	34	1	5	28	27	95	8

* 3 points deducted

NORTHERN COUNTIES EAST LEAGUE

Premier Division	P	W	D	L	F	A	Pts
Spalding United	34	20	8	6	76	43	48
Arnold	34	22	3	9	82	37	47
Emley	34	20	7	7	59	32	47
Alfreton Town	34	18	6	10	56	32	42
Eastwood Town	34	17	7	10	75	49	41
Ilkeston Town	34	14	11	9	49	38	39
Guiseley	34	14	11	9	54	48	39
Guisborough Town	34	16	6	12	58	54	38
Thackley	34	14	6	14	61	54	34
Winterton Rangers	34	13	7	14	48	42	33
Belper Town	34	12	8	14	47	46	32
Boston	34	10	12	12	46	57	32
Sutton Town	34	10	7	17	36	63	27
Appleby Frodingham	34	8	9	17	51	75	25
Mexborough Town	34	6	12	16	34	68	24
Bridlington Trinity	34	7	9	18	40	60	23
Heanor Town	34	7	9	18	31	68	23
Bentley VW	34	6	6	22	45	82	18

NORTH WEST COUNTIES LEAGUE

First Division	P	W	D	L	F	A	Pts
Stalybridge Celtic	38	26	8	4	81	30	60
Penrith	38	23	9	6	88	39	55
Radcliffe Borough	38	26	3	9	79	41	55
Burscough	38	22	8	8	87	47	52
Curzon Athletic	38	21	5	12	74	51	47
Lancaster City	38	21	3	14	76	56	43*
Accrington Stanley	38	17	8	13	67	60	42
St Helens Town	38	17	7	14	69	55	41
Congleton Town	38	18	5	15	64	50	41
Prescot Cables	38	17	6	15	72	45	40
Leek Town	38	14	10	14	56	64	38
Winsford United	38	12	12	14	49	54	36
Formby	38	14	7	17	48	61	35
Caernarfon Town	38	11	12	15	46	55	34
Glossop	38	11	11	16	38	61	33
Bootle	38	11	7	20	46	69	27*
Leyland Motors	38	9	9	20	44	79	27
Netherfield Motors	38	5	11	22	27	73	21
Ashton United	38	7	9	22	47	86	19**
Darwen	38	2	2	34	29	111	6

Second Division	P	W	D	L	F	A	Pts
Fleetwood Town	34	24	8	2	73	24	56
Eastwood Hanley	34	21	6	7	69	35	48
Irlam Town	34	19	8	7	67	41	46
Warrington Town	34	18	7	9	65	45	41
Droylsden	34	19	5	10	59	42	43
Colne Dynamoes	34	16	9	9	55	37	41
Ellesmere Port & Nst	34	12	10	12	49	38	34
Chadderton	34	14	6	14	56	46	34
Atherton LR	34	11	11	12	37	41	33
Wren Rovers	34	11	10	13	45	47	32
Skelmersdale United	34	13	6	15	60	63	32
Ford Motors	34	9	9	16	38	53	27
Prescot BI	34	9	9	16	50	66	27

	P	W	D	L	F	A	Pts
Lytham	34	13	3	18	56	81	27*
Rossendale United	34	10	6	18	53	84	26
Great Harwood Tn	34	5	12	17	36	60	22
Salford	34	5	11	18	24	60	21
Nantwich Town	34	8	2	24	44	73	18

Third Division	P	W	D	L	F	A	Pts
Clitheroe	34	22	7	5	79	29	51
Padiham	34	19	8	7	58	34	46
Ashton Town	34	19	7	8	54	42	45
Oldham Dew	34	17	9	8	63	37	43
Daisy Hill	34	19	3	12	54	40	41
Maghull	34	16	8	10	60	50	40
Blackpool Mech	34	17	5	12	70	49	39
Atherton Collieries	34	14	9	11	54	50	37
Vulcan Newton	34	15	8	11	64	54	36*
Prestwich Heys	34	15	5	14	61	59	33*
Whitworth Valley	34	11	8	15	45	53	30
Bolton ST	34	10	10	14	49	64	30
Bacup Borough	34	11	9	14	65	60	27**
Nelson	34	8	10	16	49	55	26
Cheadle Town	34	9	8	17	39	67	26
Urmston Town	34	7	9	18	35	67	23
Newton	34	8	4	22	33	63	20
Ashton Athletic	34	4	3	27	30	89	11

Each asterisk denotes the deduction of two points for breach of rule.

A record 34 842 watched Wycombe Wanderers (in blue) defeat Kidderminster Harriers 2–1 in the 1991 FA Trophy Final. Stuart Cash slides in to tackle Delwyn Humphreys (Photo: Barry O'Brady)

A happy return . . . Lincoln City needed to beat Wycombe Wanderers in their last Conference match to return to the Football League at the first attempt. A superb attendance of 9432, the highest at Sincil Bank for 16 years saw their heroes clinch the 1987–88 Conference title with a 2–0 win (**Photo: Martin Wray**)

Match of the Day . . . In the First Round proper of the 1988–89 FA Cup, Enfield drew with Leyton Orient at home then put up a sparkling display at Brisbane Road to thoroughly deserve a 2–2 draw after extra time, in front of the BBC cameras. In the second replay, Enfield travelled across London again and won 1–0 (**Photo: Leo Hoenig**)

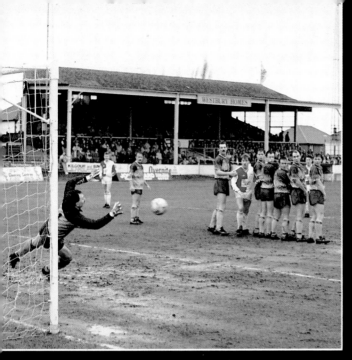

Left *Runcorn's well constructed 'wall' gives their keeper Arthur Williams the opportunity to save this free-kick from Richard Forsyth at Kidderminster. The Harriers ground has recently had new terraces erected behind both goals and the grandstand is soon to be completely refurbished* (Photo: AM Carter)

Below *All cup competitions have their giant-killers and the Surrey Senior Cup saw Dorking from the Vauxhall League's Division One beat Sutton United and Woking 3–0 before taking on Carshalton Athletic at the new Kingstonian home at Kingsmeadow in the Final. Dorking (in hoops) put on early pressure but eventually lost 2–4* (Photo: Dennis Nicholson)

Above *The 1989–90 Conference championship again went 'to the wire' and Darlington won at Welling United to gain a quick return to the Fourth Division. Their gates increased by 55 per cent during their year's exile. Here David Corner and Kevan Smith put pressure on the Welling defence* (Photo: Dennis Nicholson)

Right *Grantham arrive at Newtown in Wales by taxi after the coach taking them to their Trophy match had broken down*

Left *A very smartly turned-out Val Andrews meets the skippers of Farleigh Rovers and Godalming Town before their FA Vase Extra Preliminary Round tie. Women officials are now on most county lists and are well respected for their contribution to the game* (Photo: David Burton)

Below *Dusk comes to Adams Park, Wycombe as the home side lead the Conference pacemakers Kettering Town by 5–1* (Photo: Andy Cussell)

Above *Autumn leaves give a colourful backdrop to the action in front of Eltham Town's little stand, as Beckenham visit in the Kent Senior Trophy* (Photo: Mike Floate)

Below *Another action photo from Kent as the Gravesend goalkeeper Tony Stapley saves confidently under pressure at Margate* (Photo: Francis Short)

Above *Match of the Day (2) . . . Unijet Sussex League club Littlehampton Town entertain Northampton Town in the First Round proper of the FA Cup, so they need a television gantry* (Photo: Roger Turner)

Below *England's Semi-Professional international players don't get many games but Mark Carter, seen here in action against Italy at Kettering, has scored a record 13 goals in 12 games for England* (Photo: Mick Cheney)

Above *One step from the big time . . . Tiverton Town (Great Mills Western League) entertain Peacehaven (Unijet Sussex League) in the Fourth Qualifying Round of the FA Cup – the prize for the winners turned out to be a visit to Aldershot. Here the visitors' Adie Chipper looks for a way past Martyn Rogers but it was the westerners who visited Hampshire in the next round* (Photo: Francis Short)

Left *Non-league carpet . . . Hyde United have an excellent all-weather pitch which brings in a great deal of revenue for the club. Here the home keeper John Platt saves from South Liverpool's Andy Green* (Photo: Rob Ruddock)

Above right *Bedfont entertain Godalming Town in a Dan Air League match. But British Airways seem to want to get in on the act!* (Photo: David Burton)

Above *Get in! Croydon's Carl Roberts thumps home a fine header against Chalfont St Peter in their Vauxhall League Division One match. The smart Croydon stand acts as a suitable background to an excellent action shot* (Photo: David West)

Below *Arsenal would have been proud of their lookalikes' defensive organisation as Cheltenham Town defend against Kettering Town in the GM Vauxhall Conference* (Photo: Martin Wray)

Top *Little did they know . . . Woking's Derek Brown (7) wheels away having scored a vital FA Cup goal against Bath City. Worldwide acclaim was around the corner for this Vauxhall League club* (Photo: Dennis Nicholson)

Above *Ninety minutes later . . . West Bromwich Albion were preparing to look for a new manager and Woking became national heroes. Skippers Graham Roberts (WBA) and Adie Cowler pose before the Vauxhall League club's 4–2 FA Cup victory at The Hawthorns*

Above *A day to remember . . . Matthew Hanlon shoots for goal watched by Sutton United colleagues Nigel Golley, Lenny Dennis and Vernon Pratt. In the second half of this Cup tie he was to gain overnight stardom by scoring the winner against First Division Coventry City. The GM Vauxhall Conference club's 2–1 success was to inspire non-league clubs throughout the country*

Top *Dave Regis was snapped up by Notts County from Barnet, but here he is seen driving a shot past the post having broken through the Clapton defence in an FA Cup tie (Photo: Gavin Ellis)*

Young Andy Hunt was signed from local football by Kettering Town before the 1990–91 season and by halfway through he had joined Newcastle United for £150000. At least the Poppies' bank manager must have been pleased (Photo: Mick Cheney)

Above *Over 27000 fans, a record for the FA Vase, gave Sudbury Town and Tamworth a wonderful atmosphere in which to contest the 1989 Final. Sudbury keeper Dean Graham saves from Mark Stanton* (Photo: Francis Short)

Left *Accrington Stanley are very much alive and enjoying life in the HFS Loans League. Here Martin White saves for them as Chris Beckford leads an attack for Gretna, the only Scottish club in English football. Stanley beat their Northern League opponents 2–1 in this Third Qualifying Round FA Cup tie* (Photo: Alan Watson)

One of the most exciting Wembley Finals of all time saw Gresley Rovers (white) come back from 0–3 to 4–3 and then concede a late goal for a 4–4 draw in the 1991 FA Vase. Guiseley won the replay 3–1 in another excellent game. Here Guiseley striker Dean Walling challenges keeper Bob Aston (Photo: Dave West)

Brian Hall's Wealdstone squad achieved 'the double' that stands as non-league football's greatest achievement in 1984–85 when they won the Gola League (now Conference) and the FA Trophy.
Back row *Steve Tapley, Robin Wainwright, Andy Graham, Vinny Jones, Steve McCargo.* Middle *Les Reed (coach), Brian Greenway, Alan Cordice, Bob Iles, Neil Cordice, Mark Graves, Arnold Reed (physio).* Front *Gary Donnellan, Lee Holmes, Paul Bowgett (captain), Brian Hall (manager), Dennis Byatt, Nigel Johnson, Derek Doyle*

EASTERN COUNTIES LEAGUE

	P	W	D	L	F	A	Pts
Braintree T	42	29	9	4	125	45	67
Wisbech T	42	29	9	4	91	37	67
Colchester U Res	42	26	7	9	94	41	59
Lowestoft T	42	24	7	11	77	46	55
Sudbury T	42	21	11	10	87	56	53
Saffron Walden T	42	22	8	12	88	47	52
Gorleston	42	18	16	8	73	47	52
Tiptree U	42	20	9	13	83	64	49
Gt Yarmouth T	42	19	10	13	75	51	48
Chatteris T	42	17	10	15	57	58	44
Brantham A	42	16	9	17	66	68	41
Newmarket T	42	16	9	17	62	73	41
Bury T	42	16	8	18	69	73	40
Felixstowe T	42	13	13	16	53	57	39
March T United	42	13	11	18	57	63	37
Histon	42	12	11	19	53	60	35
Haverhill R	42	16	3	23	68	91	35
Soham Town R	42	11	7	24	49	90	29
Stowmarket T	42	10	8	24	57	99	28
Ely C	42	7	8	27	45	108	22
Clacton T	42	6	4	32	47	120	16
Thetford T	42	6	3	33	43	125	15

MIDLAND FOOTBALL COMBINATION

Premier Division	P	W	D	L	F	A	Pts
Studley Sporting	38	22	8	8	83	49	52
Coleshill Town	38	22	7	9	77	43	51
West Mids Police	38	20	10	8	82	52	50
Highgate United	38	17	14	7	70	41	48
Racing Club W'wick	38	21	4	13	79	66	46
Paget Rangers	38	15	15	8	55	35	45
Hurley Daw Mill	38	16	11	11	68	55	43
Evesham United	38	16	10	12	55	49	42
Stratford Town	38	16	6	16	58	71	38
Boldmere St Mich'ls	38	14	9	15	46	37	37
Northfield Town	38	14	9	15	63	56	37
Mile Oak Rovers	38	15	7	16	58	53	37
Solihull Borough	38	15	7	16	54	57	37
Chipping Norton Tn	38	13	10	15	49	51	36
Kings Heath	38	11	14	13	50	59	36
Cinderford Town	38	12	9	17	51	63	33
Walsall Borough	38	13	6	19	54	58	32
Smethwick Highfield	38	7	13	18	45	66	27
Southam United	38	7	8	23	35	76	22
Knowle North Star	38	3	5	30	34	129	11

WEST MIDLANDS (REGIONAL) LEAGUE

Premier Division	P	W	D	L	F	A	Pts
Halesowen Town	38	32	3	3	112	36	67
Hednesford Town	38	23	10	5	70	34	56
Atherstone United	38	17	11	10	63	44	45
Gresley Rovers	38	17	9	12	68	61	43
Lye Town	38	15	12	11	55	45	42
Wolverhampton U	38	17	7	14	53	55	41
Oldswinford	38	15	11	12	61	64	41
Armitage	38	17	5	16	67	61	39
Shifnal Town	38	13	12	13	59	56	38
Wednesfield Social	38	15	8	15	52	58	38
Tividale	38	12	12	14	53	48	36
Malvern Town	38	14	7	17	64	61	35
Rushall Olympic	38	11	11	16	55	59	33
Hinckley Athletic	38	12	9	17	51	61	33
GKN Sankey	38	13	7	18	54	74	33
Brereton Social	38	10	12	16	46	62	32
Bilston Town	38	10	11	17	44	58	31
Blakenall	38	11	7	20	39	59	29
Chasetown	38	9	8	21	39	81	26
Bradley Town	38	9	4	25	44	72	22

GREAT MILLS WESTERN LEAGUE

Premier Division	P	W	D	L	F	A	Pts
Exmouth Town	38	21	11	6	59	35	53
Saltash United	38	22	7	9	72	39	51
Barnstaple Town	38	21	9	8	68	40	51
Frome Town	38	20	10	8	78	35	50
Liskeard Athletic	38	18	9	11	64	38	45
Bideford	38	16	10	12	71	49	42
Clevedon Town	38	16	8	14	55	56	40
Bristol Manor Farm	38	14	11	13	54	42	39
Plymouth Argyle	38	16	8	14	68	58	38*
Minehead	38	15	7	16	55	68	37
Shepton Mallet Tn	38	14	9	15	55	74	37
Taunton Town	38	10	15	13	46	52	35
Mangotsfield United	38	12	10	16	47	48	34
Dawlish Town	38	13	8	17	38	43	34
Weston-super-Mare	38	13	8	17	46	54	34
Chippenham Town	38	13	8	17	44	56	34
Clandown	38	12	10	16	34	51	34
Melksham Town	38	9	11	18	49	66	29
Devizes Town	38	4	8	26	29	95	16

* 2 points deducted for playing ineligible players

LONDON SPARTAN LEAGUE

Premier Division	P	W	D	L	F	A	Pts
Collier Row	28	21	4	3	66	26	46
Malden Vale	28	21	1	6	80	25	43
Brimsdown Rovers	28	18	7	3	63	22	43
Bracknell Town	28	17	3	8	69	43	37
Waltham Abbey	28	14	8	6	52	26	36
Beaconsfield United	28	12	9	7	39	29	33
Beckton United	28	14	4	10	46	36	32
Greenwich B	28	14	2	12	58	50	30
Swanley Town	28	12	5	11	45	37	29
Merstham	28	9	9	10	42	45	27
Amersham Town	28	4	10	14	31	66	18
BROB Barnet	28	5	6	17	34	66	16
Highfield	28	4	4	20	34	77	12
Chingford	28	5	2	21	29	78	12
Ambrose Fleming	28	2	2	24	16	78	6

HELLENIC LEAGUE

Premier Division	P	W	D	L	F	A	Pts
Almondsbury Grnwy	32	23	4	5	107	19	73
Moreton Town	32	18	11	3	51	10	65
Thame United	32	19	5	8	53	30	62
Abingdon United	32	16	9	7	68	34	57
Abingdon Town	32	14	9	9	53	38	51
Rayners Lane	32	11	9	10	38	40	48
Supermarine	32	11	12	9	40	34	45
Bicester Town	32	13	6	13	37	32	45
Didcot Town	32	10	10	12	39	49	40
Wallingford Town	32	10	9	13	42	45	39
Clanfield	32	7	16	9	39	43	37
Maidenhead Town & Youth	32	8	12	12	40	44	36
Northwood	32	9	7	16	34	53	34
Fairford Town	32	7	12	13	39	57	33
Wantage Town	32	8	6	18	43	53	30
Avon Bradford	32	7	7	18	36	71	28
Hazells (Aylesbury)	32	3	8	21	30	89	17

UNITED COUNTIES LEAGUE

Premier Division	P	W	D	L	F	A	Pts
Buckingham	36	26	6	4	77	24	58
Baldock	36	21	8	7	75	42	50
Stamford	36	18	11	7	75	42	47
Bourne	36	19	8	9	66	49	46
Potton	36	13	16	7	50	39	42
Stevenage	36	16	9	11	52	46	41
Irthlingborough	36	15	10	11	59	40	40
Long Buckby	36	13	13	10	55	48	39
Wooton	36	13	11	12	56	49	37
Ampthill	36	13	10	13	56	54	36
Arlesey	36	12	12	12	45	56	36
Newport Pagnell	36	11	11	14	40	50	33
rothwell	36	11	10	15	52	58	32
Raunds	36	10	10	16	56	68	30
Holbeach	36	12	6	18	44	68	30
Eynesbury	36	10	9	17	51	74	29
S & L Corby	36	7	7	22	34	63	21
Desborough	36	5	10	21	32	62	20
St Neots	36	3	11	22	28	74	17

No clubs relegated.

VAUX WEARSIDE LEAGUE

	P	W	D	L	F	A	Pts
Blue Star	34	27	3	4	94	24	57
Coundon	34	27	2	5	93	29	56
Easington CW	34	24	7	2	79	34	55
Wingate	34	19	5	10	66	37	43
Whickham	34	18	6	10	66	44	42

COMBINED COUNTIES LEAGUE

Premier Division	P	W	D	L	F	A	Pts
Godalming Town	32	22	4	6	59	24	70
Malden Town	32	20	7	5	81	34	67
Ash United	32	17	9	6	55	32	60
Chobham	32	17	6	9	42	31	57
Hartley Wintney+	32	16	5	11	50	41	55

+ points awarded

ATHENIAN LEAGUE

	P	W	D	L	F	A	Pts
Redhill	40	28	9	3	73	28	93
Chalfont St Peter	40	27	10	1	88	32	91
Burnham	40	27	7	6	80	29	88
Whyteleafe	40	24	8	8	63	32	80
Flackwell Heath	40	21	7	12	57	37	70
Harefield United	40	20	8	12	62	47	68
Banstead Athletic	40	19	10	11	63	48	67
Marlow	40	17	7	16	65	63	58
Hoddesdon Town	40	15	13	12	53	52	58
Ruislip Manor	40	16	9	15	59	44	57
Kingsbury Town	40	15	12	13	58	52	57
Wolverton Town	40	12	12	16	59	65	48
Edgware	40	13	8	19	47	51	47
Harwich & Parkeston	40	13	9	18	54	66	45*
Chertsey Town	40	12	6	22	41	63	42
Berkhamsted Town	40	10	11	19	50	63	41
Thatcham Town	40	8	14	18	65	79	35*
Horley Town	40	9	6	25	34	83	33
Haringey Borough	40	8	8	24	44	80	32
Fleet Town	40	6	8	26	31	82	26
Camberley Town	40	4	10	26	35	85	22

SOUTH MIDLANDS LEAGUE

Premier Division	P	W	D	L	F	A	Pts
Shefford Town	28	17	9	2	55	23	43
Pirton	28	19	4	5	58	25	42
Eaton Bray United	28	16	6	6	51	30	38
Stotfold	28	15	6	7	48	31	36
Hatfield Town	28	14	4	10	48	38	32

ESSEX SENIOR LEAGUE

	P	W	D	L	F	A	Pts
Heybridge	32	27	3	2	65	21	57
Bowers	32	17	10	5	56	25	44
Witham	32	18	6	8	61	32	42
Stansted	31	18	4	9	62	29	40
Chelmsford	32	17	4	11	62	37	38

HAMPSHIRE LEAGUE

Division One	P	W	D	L	F	A	Pts
Sholing Sports	38	28	8	2	81	22	64
AFC Totton	38	28	6	4	93	33	62
Pirelli General	38	19	10	9	49	29	48
Eastleigh	38	16	14	8	51	33	46
Portsmouth RN	38	17	9	12	62	44	43

HERTS COUNTY LEAGUE

Premier Division	P	W	D	L	F	A	Pts
Cokfosters	30	21	6	3	66	25	48
Bedmond Social	30	18	8	4	67	36	44
Leaveden Hospital	30	17	7	6	63	36	41
London Colney	30	15	7	8	59	35	37
Sandridge Rover	30	14	8	8	63	44	36

KENT LEAGUE

Division One	P	W	D	L	F	A	Pts
Sittingbourne	30	24	3	3	87	26	75
Sheppey	30	21	3	6	61	28	66
Hythe	30	17	5	8	63	39	56
Cray Wanderers	30	14	7	9	66	40	49
Tunbridge Wells	30	12	7	11	61	44	43

LEICESTERSHIRE SENIOR LEAGUE

Premier Division	P	W	D	L	F	A	Pts
Melton Town	30	23	4	3	81	28	50
Narboro' & L'thorpe	30	17	7	6	65	35	41
Anstey Nomads	30	16	8	6	58	34	40
Birstall United	30	15	9	6	54	37	39
Wigston Town	30	15	5	10	44	30	35

NOTTS ALLIANCE

Senior Division	P	W	D	L	F	A	Pts
Meadows Albion	30	20	5	5	60	23	45
Rainworth MW	30	21	2	7	79	39	44
Keyworth Utd	30	19	6	5	59	26	44
City Sher Hosp	30	16	5	9	55	37	37
Clipstone MW	30	16	4	10	65	54	36

SUSSEX COUNTY LEAGUE

Division One	P	W	D	L	F	A	Pts
Whitehawk	30	23	5	2	77	19	74
Littlehampton	30	22	5	3	92	32	71
Steyning	30	20	6	4	62	27	66
Southwick	30	18	9	3	67	22	63
Three Bridges	30	16	4	10	59	45	52

1984-85

This year goes down in history as being the first (and as yet only) time that a club won the 'Non-League Double' of Alliance Premier League and FA Trophy in one season. The triumphant club were Wealdstone, who under the guidance of Brian Hall claimed their first successes in the two major national Non-League competitions. Under a new sponsorship deal the Alliance Premier League had become the Gola League at the start of the season.

Telford United, boosted by their achievements of the previous season, became the first Non-League club since Blyth Spartans in 1978 to reach the Fifth Round of the FA Cup. They experienced a momentous day out at Everton where they held the champions-to-be for a half before going down 0-3. On the way to Goodison the Shropshire club had eliminated Lincoln City, Preston North End (4-1 away!), Bradford City (Third Division champions) and Darlington, thus taking their total of Football League scalps to eight in three seasons.

Halesowen Town returned to Wembley just two years after their defeat against VS Rugby, and this time returned to the West Midlands with the FA Vase after an impressive win over Fleetwood Town.

Bishop Auckland are one of the most famous names at this level of the game, holding the record of ten wins in the FA Amateur Cup. They celebrated their centenary, and did so in grand style by winning the Dryborough Northern League and the Durham Senior Cup.

SUMMARY

FA VASE

	Winners	Runners Up	Semi-finalists
	Halesowen Town	Fleetwood Town	Exmouth Town, Wisbech

FA TROPHY

	Winners	Runners-up	Semi-finalists
	Wealdstone	Boston United	Altrincham, Enfield

FA CUP   Most Successful Team: Telford United

1st Rd: Lincoln City 1 Telford 1; 1st Rd Replay: Telford 2 Lincoln 1; 2nd Rd: Preston NE 1 Telford 4;
3rd Rd: Telford 2 Bradford City 1; 4th Rd: Darlington 1 Telford 1; 4th Rd Replay: Telford 2 Darlington 0;
5th Rd: Everton 3 Telford 0

GOLA LEAGUE   Champions: Wealdstone   Runners Up: Nuneaton Borough

GOLA LEAGUE STATISTICS

Top Crowds

2258	Worcester City v Kidderminster H (26.11.84)
2176	Kettering Town v Nuneaton Borough (1.1.85)
2102	Yeovil Town v Weymouth (26.12 84)
2099	Yeovil Town v Northwich Victoria (26.1.85)
1806	Yeovil Town v Runcorn (16.2.85)

Top Scorers

36	Paul Culpin (Nuneaton)
30	Gary Hooley (Frickley)
21	John Powell (Kidderminster)

Manager of the Month Awards

Aug	Mann (Boston United)
Sep	Hall (Wealdstone)
Oct	King (Altrincham)
Nov	King (Altrincham)
Dec	Needham (Kettering)
Jan	Storton (Telford)
Feb	McCluskey (Enfield)
Mar	Carr (Nuneaton)
Apr	Dixey (Nuneaton)

GOLA LEAGUE

		Home					Away					Pts
	P	W	D	L	F	A	W	D	L	F	A	
Wealdstone	42	8	8	5	31	26	12	2	7	33	28	62
Nuneaton Boro	42	13	8	0	55	23	6	6	9	30	30	58
Dartford	42	7	7	7	28	25	10	6	5	29	23	57
Bath City	42	15	1	5	30	22	6	8	7	22	27	57
Altrincham	42	13	2	6	39	21	8	4	9	24	26	56
Scarborough	42	10	7	4	35	20	7	6	8	34	42	54
Enfield	42	11	7	3	48	27	6	6	9	36	34	53
Kidderminster H	42	8	4	9	40	38	9	4	8	39	39	51
Northwich Vic	42	9	4	8	22	19	7	7	7	28	27	50
Telford United	42	10	7	4	36	24	5	7	9	23	30	49
Frickley Athletic	42	12	3	6	38	25	6	4	11	27	46	49
Kettering Town	42	9	6	6	37	22	6	6	9	31	37	48
Maidstone United	42	10	7	4	38	24	5	6	10	20	27	48
Runcorn	42	6	9	6	27	21	7	6	8	21	26	48
Barnet	42	9	7	5	36	20	6	4	11	23	32	47
Weymouth	42	13	1	7	41	32	2	12	7	29	34	45
Boston United	42	10	5	6	43	32	5	5	11	26	37	45
Barrow	42	6	5	9	25	22	5	7	9	22	35	43
Dagenham	42	8	6	7	28	27	5	4	12	19	40	41
Worcester City	42	7	4	10	29	36	5	5	11	26	48	38
Gateshead	42	5	6	10	27	42	4	6	11	24	40	33*
Yeovil Town	42	4	7	10	26	36	2	4	15	18	51	25

* One point deduction

Three points for an away win, two points for a home win.

SOUTHERN LEAGUE

Premier Division

	P	W	D	L	F	A	Pts
Cheltenham Town	38	24	5	9	83	41	77
King's Lynn	38	23	6	9	73	48	75
Crawley Town	38	22	8	8	76	52	74
Willenhall Town	38	20	8	10	57	38	68
RS Southampton	38	21	4	13	76	52	67
Welling United	38	18	11	9	55	38	65
Folkestone	38	19	6	13	70	54	63
Fisher Athletic	38	19	5	14	67	57	62
Chelmsford City	38	17	10	11	52	50	61
Shepshed Charter	38	18	5	15	67	50	59
Corby Town	38	15	6	17	56	54	51
Bedworth United	38	14	8	16	48	52	50
Gravesend & Nthflt	38	12	12	14	46	46	48
Fareham town	38	13	8	17	52	55	47
Alvechurch	38	11	7	20	53	59	40
Hastings United	38	11	7	20	46	71	40
Witney Town	38	9	12	17	51	58	39
Gloucester City	38	10	6	22	49	74	36
Trowbridge	38	10	5	23	45	83	35
AP Leamington	38	2	5	31	22	112	11

Midland Division

Dudley Town	34	21	8	5	70	36	71
Aylesbury United	34	20	7	7	62	30	67
Hednesford Town	34	18	7	9	58	42	61
Moor Green	34	17	9	8	63	43	60
VS Rugby	34	17	9	8	59	41	60
Bromsgrove Rovers	34	16	10	8	53	42	58
Stourbridge	34	15	11	8	52	45	56
Redditch United	34	12	11	11	68	57	47
Sutton Coldfield Tn	34	13	6	15	50	56	45

Bridgnorth Town	34	13	5	16	67	65	44
Coventry Sporting	34	11	9	14	45	52	42
Merthyr Tydfil	34	10	11	13	43	46	41
Rushden Town	34	10	7	17	42	52	37
Forest Green Rovers	34	9	10	15	49	65	37
Wellingborough Tn	34	10	7	17	39	63	37
Oldbury United	34	10	6	18	52	66	36
Banbury United	34	9	5	20	33	59	32
Leicester United	34	3	6	25	17	62	15

Southern Division

Basingstoke Town	38	24	9	5	61	22	81
Gosport Borough	38	22	6	10	78	41	72
Poole Town	38	20	12	6	69	38	72
Hillingdon	38	19	10	9	51	23	67
Thanet United	38	19	9	10	63	47	66
Salisbury	38	19	5	14	55	54	62
Sheppey United	38	18	6	14	49	45	60
Addlestone & Wey	38	16	9	13	68	54	57
Waterlooville	38	15	10	13	71	63	55
Canterbury City	38	15	7	16	61	54	52
Woodford Town	38	13	13	12	46	53	52
Tonbridge AFC	38	16	3	19	59	62	51
Andover	38	15	5	18	42	54	50
Dorchester Town	38	13	7	18	45	60	46
Cambridge City	38	11	11	16	59	71	44
Chatham Town	38	12	8	18	44	66	44
Ashford Town	38	10	9	19	54	69	39
Dunstable	38	8	10	20	35	56	34
Dover Athletic	38	7	7	24	39	78	28
Erith & Belvedere	38	6	8	24	36	65	26

NORTHERN PREMIER LEAGUE

	P	Home					Away					Pts
		W	D	L	F	A	W	D	L	F	A	
Stafford Rangers	42	13	4	4	46	18	13	4	4	35	22	86
Macclesfield Town	42	13	6	2	37	20	10	7	4	30	19	82
Witton Albion	42	14	4	3	34	16	8	4	9	23	23	74
Hyde Albion	42	11	2	8	38	28	10	6	5	30	24	71
Marine	42	10	8	3	33	15	8	7	6	26	19	69
Burton Albion	42	10	10	1	42	19	8	5	8	28	30	69
Worksop Town	42	12	5	4	35	20	7	5	9	33	36	67
Horwich RMI	42	9	7	5	33	21	7	7	7	34	29	62
Bangor City	42	12	3	6	44	25	5	6	10	26	36	60
Gainsborough T	42	10	6	5	47	39	4	8	9	25	34	56
Southport	42	9	3	9	33	30	6	6	9	32	36	54
Matlock Town	42	8	5	8	33	35	6	4	11	23	31	51
Oswestry Town	42	10	2	9	39	32	4	7	10	20	43	51
Mossley	42	12	2	7	27	23	2	7	12	18	42	51
Goole Town	42	6	7	8	31	26	7	4	10	29	39	50
Rhyl	42	7	7	7	29	30	4	7	10	23	33	47
Morecambe	42	6	9	6	32	30	5	5	11	19	37	47
Chorley	42	8	5	8	30	29	4	5	12	17	34	46
South Liverpool	42	6	10	5	22	21	3	5	13	21	50	42
Grantham*	42	5	10	6	23	21	3	3	15	18	48	36
Buxton	42	5	3	13	17	29	3	3	15	21	50	30

* 1 point deducted for fielding ineligible player

VAUXHALL-OPEL LEAGUE

Premier Division	P	W	D	L	F	A	Pts
Sutton United	42	23	15	4	115	55	84
Worthing	42	24	8	10	89	59	80
Wycombe Wandrs	42	24	6	12	68	46	78
Wokingham Town	42	20	13	9	74	52	73
Windsor & Eton	42	19	10	13	67	55	67
Bognor Regis Town	42	20	6	16	67	58	66
Dulwich Hamlet	42	16	17	9	82	57	65
Harrow Borough	42	18	8	16	70	56	62
Hayes	42	17	8	17	60	58	59
Tooting & Mitcham	42	16	11	15	64	66	59
Walthamstow Ave	42	15	11	16	64	65	56
Croydon	42	15	12	15	62	63	54+
Epsom & Ewell	42	13	14	15	63	62	53
Slough Town	42	13	12	17	69	74	51
Carshalton Athletic	42	14	8	20	55	68	50
Bishop's Stortford	42	12	12	18	48	67	48
Hendon	42	9	19	14	62	65	46
Billericay Town	42	11	14	17	53	74	46*
Barking	42	13	7	22	43	75	46
Hitchin Town	42	10	15	17	55	70	45
Leytonstone/Ilford	42	11	10	21	37	72	43
Harlow Town	42	5	12	25	45	95	27

* 1 point deducted
+ 2 points deducted

Division One	P	W	D	L	F	A	Pts
Farnborough Town	42	26	8	8	101	45	86
Kingstonian	42	23	10	9	67	39	79
Leatherhead	42	23	10	9	109	61	76+
Chesham United	42	22	8	12	78	46	74
Wembley	42	20	10	12	59	40	70
St Albans City	42	19	10	13	79	59	67
Tilbury	42	18	13	11	86	68	67
Bromley	42	18	9	15	71	65	63
Hampton	42	17	11	14	75	62	62
Staines Town	42	16	11	15	59	53	59
Maidenhead United	42	17	8	17	65	64	59
Walton & Herhsam	42	16	8	18	60	69	55*
Aveley	42	16	7	19	62	78	55
Oxford City	42	14	12	16	62	53	54
Lewes	42	15	9	18	70	72	54
Basildon United	42	15	8	19	55	61	53
Boreham Wood	42	15	7	20	72	83	52
Hornchurch	42	15	6	21	55	74	51
Woking	42	15	6	21	60	91	51
Metropolitan Police	42	10	12	20	65	92	42
Clapton	42	5	11	26	50	124	26
Hertford Town	42	5	10	27	36	97	25

* 1 point deducted
+ 3 points deducted

VAUXHALL-OPEL LEAGUE

Division Two North	P	W	D	L	F	A	Pts
Leyton-Wingate	38	24	9	5	98	49	81
Finchley	38	24	8	6	66	31	79*
Heybridge Swifts	38	22	9	7	71	33	75
Stevenage Borough	38	23	6	9	79	49	75
Saffron Walden Tn	38	22	8	8	73	31	74
Tring Town	38	19	11	8	76	41	68
Chalfont St Peter	38	17	10	11	72	41	61
Flackwell Heath	38	16	11	11	53	40	59
Berkhamsted Town	38	15	12	11	50	42	57
Letchworth Gden C	38	17	6	15	66	69	57
Royston Town	38	13	9	16	47	77	48
Cheshunt	38	14	5	19	52	57	47
Marlow	38	13	6	19	64	81	45
Hemel Hempstead	38	11	7	20	49	64	40
Barton Rovers	38	9	8	21	40	62	35
Wolverton Town	38	9	8	21	38	77	35
Kingsbury Town	38	9	7	22	53	72	34
Harefield United	38	7	9	22	51	81	30
Haringey Borough	38	6	12	20	38	79	30
Ware	38	7	5	26	40	100	26

* 1 point deducted

Division Two South	P	W	D	L	F	A	Pts
Grays Athletic	36	24	9	3	84	25	81
Uxbridge	36	22	10	4	81	20	76
Molesey	36	20	5	11	62	42	65
Hungerford Town	36	18	9	9	71	49	63
Whyteleafe	36	17	10	9	66	34	61
Egham Town	36	17	7	12	54	42	58
Southall	36	18	3	15	54	57	57
Bracknell town	36	15	7	14	54	48	52
Banstead Athletic	36	14	8	14	63	70	50
Horsham	36	13	10	13	44	39	49
Ruislip Manor	36	13	10	13	48	49	49
Dorking	36	12	11	13	45	50	47
Rainham Town	36	12	8	16	58	61	44
Feltham	36	10	13	13	44	58	43
Camberley Town	36	10	12	14	44	54	42
Eastbourne United	36	10	9	17	66	72	39
Petersfield United	36	9	5	22	41	80	32
Newbury Town	36	8	7	21	35	69	16+
Chersey Town	36	2	3	31	23	118	6*

* 3 points deducted   + 15 points deducted

NORTH WEST COUNTIES LEAGUE

First Division	P	W	D	L	F	A	Pts
Radcliffe Borough	38	24	10	4	67	33	58
Caernarfon Town	38	23	9	6	73	40	55
Burscough	38	23	7	8	81	46	53
Stalybridge Celtic	38	21	10	7	89	40	52
Eastwood Hanley	38	20	12	6	72	42	52
Curzon Ashton	38	21	6	11	85	60	48
Winsford United	38	20	7	11	58	37	47
Fleetwood Town	38	18	8	12	84	57	44
Leek Town	38	16	11	11	52	38	43
Congleton Town	38	13	11	14	43	46	37
Leyland Motors	38	13	8	17	52	67	34
St Helens Town	38	12	9	17	64	75	33
Prescot Cables	38	13	7	18	64	68	31*
Bootle	38	10	11	17	34	48	31
Accrington Stanley	38	11	8	19	45	59	30
Glossop	38	8	11	19	46	70	27
Formby	38	9	9	20	41	79	25*
Netherfield	38	7	9	22	42	80	23
Lancaster City	38	8	5	25	46	90	21
Penrith	38	4	4	30	36	99	12

Second Division	P	W	D	L	F	A	Pts
Clitheroe	34	19	13	2	70	33	51
Irlam Town	34	21	9	4	60	24	51
Warrington Town	34	17	14	3	59	29	48
Ashton United	34	17	7	10	56	55	41
Droylsden	34	15	10	9	51	47	40
Wren Rovers	34	15	9	10	53	41	39
Great Harwood T	34	17	4	13	49	44	38
Chadderton	34	13	9	12	47	46	35
Colne Dynamoes	34	9	14	11	45	40	32
Atherton LR	34	13	6	15	42	43	32
Nantwich Town	34	13	5	16	50	47	31
Ford Motors	34	11	8	15	44	45	30
Skelmersdale United	34	11	8	15	39	56	30
Rossendale United	34	10	9	15	51	53	29
Salford	34	11	5	18	46	64	27
Darwen	34	7	6	21	32	62	20
Padiham	34	8	5	21	42	74	19*
Ellesmere Port & N	34	5	7	22	34	67	15*

Each asterisk denotes the deduction of two points for breach of Rule.

NORTHERN COUNTIES EAST LEAGUE

Premier Division	P	W	D	L	F	A	Pts
Belper Town	36	25	6	5	74	30	81
Eastwood Town	36	23	3	10	98	59	72
Guiseley	36	21	7	8	78	47	70
Alfreton Town	36	20	6	10	69	39	66
Guisborough Town	36	18	8	10	71	49	62
Denaby United	36	18	8	10	71	51	62
Arnold	36	17	9	10	72	49	60
Emley	36	16	7	13	67	52	55
Bridlington Trinity	36	16	5	15	71	67	53
Thackley	36	15	6	15	55	61	51
Spalding United	36	14	8	14	55	48	50
Sutton Town	36	14	5	17	45	69	47
Ilkeston Town	36	14	4	18	49	54	46
Pontefract Colls	36	11	10	15	45	54	43
Bentley VW	36	11	6	19	47	67	39
Appleby Frodingham	36	8	9	19	46	73	33
Boston	36	8	6	22	35	88	30
Heanor Town	36	8	5	23	50	89	29
Mexborough Town	36	2	8	26	32	84	14

DRYBROUGH'S NORTHERN LEAGUE

Division One	P	W	D	L	F	A	Pts
Bishop Auckland	34	26	4	4	92	26	82
Blyth Spartans	34	24	3	7	86	36	75
South Bank	34	19	10	5	62	30	67
Tow Law Town	34	18	10	6	57	45	64
North Shields	34	19	5	10	62	49	62
Gretna	34	17	8	9	56	39	59
Whitby Town	34	17	7	10	61	44	58
Chester-le-Street Tn	34	15	6	13	54	44	51
Peterlee Newtown	34	13	7	14	51	44	46
Ryhope Community	34	13	6	15	49	55	45
Spennymoor United	34	11	8	15	63	56	41
Billingham synthonia	34	11	5	18	39	65	38
Whitley Bay	34	8	11	15	51	55	32*
Ferryhill Athletic	34	8	8	18	39	70	32
Consett	34	8	3	23	42	95	27
Crook Town	34	6	8	20	32	66	26
Horden Colliery Welf	34	5	10	19	36	67	25
Shildon	34	5	7	22	41	87	22

* 3 points deducted

MIDLAND FOOTBALL COMBINATION

Premier Division	P	W	D	L	F	A	Pts
Mile Oak Rovers	38	27	6	5	91	28	60
Solihull Borough	38	22	10	6	68	36	54
Paget Rangers	38	21	10	7	60	35	52
Boldmere St Mich'ls	38	21	8	9	67	40	50
New World	38	21	6	11	71	41	48
Highgate United	38	20	8	10	73	47	48
Poleworth North Wrk	38	20	8	10	58	34	48
West Mids Police	38	17	9	12	80	56	43
Stratford Town	38	15	13	10	53	40	43
Racing Club Wrk	38	13	12	13	69	67	38
Walsall Borough	38	13	10	15	47	44	36
Smethwick Highfield	38	10	13	15	50	58	33
Evesham United	38	13	7	18	57	81	33
Hurley Daw Mill	38	11	9	18	43	56	31
Studley Sporting	38	8	14	16	50	69	30
Northfield Town	38	11	7	20	63	76	29
Coleshill Town	38	10	8	20	44	60	28
Kings Heath	38	7	11	20	31	61	25
Southam United	38	6	5	27	45	102	17
Knowle North Star	38	4	6	28	40	129	14

WEST MIDLANDS (REGIONAL) LEAGUE

Premier Division	P	W	D	L	F	A	Pts
Halesowen Town	38	28	6	4	96	36	62
Bilston Town	38	24	5	9	84	49	53
Atherstone United	38	20	8	10	64	40	48
Wednesfield Social	38	20	8	10	52	34	48
Tipton Town	38	19	10	9	67	52	48
Tividale	38	19	9	10	55	39	47
Tamworth	38	16	14	8	66	38	46
Gresley Rovers	38	16	8	14	62	56	40
Hinckley Athletic	38	14	10	24	63	59	38
Oldswinford	38	14	7	17	61	61	35
GKN Sankey	38	11	13	14	47	50	35
Lye Town	38	11	12	15	47	47	34
Rushall Olympic	38	12	10	16	57	58	34
Breton Social	38	12	10	16	58	83	34
Wolverhampton Utd	38	10	11	17	39	49	31
Chasetown	38	10	11	17	45	65	31
Malvern Town	38	9	12	17	49	57	30
Blakenall	38	7	10	21	40	69	24
Armitage	38	8	7	23	45	95	23
Shifnal Town	38	5	9	24	30	88	19

EASTERN COUNTIES LEAGUE

	P	W	D	L	F	A	Pts
Braintree Town	42	26	10	6	100	45	62
Sudbury Town	42	24	9	9	96	51	57
Great Yarmouth Tn	42	19	14	9	70	39	52
Lowestoft Town	42	23	6	13	73	43	52
Wisbech Town	42	18	15	9	69	42	51
March Town United	42	20	11	11	78	55	51
Colchester Utd Res	42	22	5	15	80	65	49
Histon	42	20	8	14	62	50	48
Bury Town	42	20	7	15	77	59	47
Stowmarket Town	42	20	7	15	71	53	47
Gorleston	42	17	9	16	64	61	43
Soham Town Rngrs	42	18	6	18	55	60	42
Tiptree United	42	16	9	17	69	50	41
Felixstowe Town	42	12	16	14	57	67	40
Chatteris Town	42	12	12	18	51	75	36
Brantham Athletic	42	12	8	22	51	79	32
Clacton Town	42	10	11	21	50	72	31
Ely City	42	9	13	20	34	64	31
Newmarket Town	42	13	5	24	46	84	31
Haverhill Rovers	42	9	12	21	52	87	30
Harwich & Parkeston	42	11	8	23	47	88	30
Thetford Town	42	7	7	28	49	103	21

GREAT MILLS WESTERN LEAGUE

Premier Division	P	W	D	L	F	A	Pts
Saltash United	42	26	12	4	88	43	64
Bideford	42	26	8	8	78	29	60
Bristol City	42	21	14	7	69	49	56
Exmouth Town	42	22	8	12	83	51	52
Paulton Rovers	42	20	11	11	61	45	51
Bristol Manor Farm	42	21	7	14	70	55	49
Chippenham Town	42	16	14	12	62	49	46
Mangotsfield United	42	17	11	14	63	56	45
Melksham Town	42	17	11	14	57	59	45
Liskeard Athletic	42	17	10	15	69	54	44
Chard Town	42	15	13	14	58	57	43
Minehead	42	16	9	17	55	54	41
Barnstaple Town	42	18	5	19	65	65	41
Clandown	42	14	12	16	50	52	40
Plymouth Argyle	42	12	14	16	58	62	38
Dawlish Town	42	12	13	17	44	54	37
Clevedon Town	42	12	12	18	45	56	35*
Frome Town	42	10	14	18	56	63	34
Weston-super-Mare	42	11	11	20	58	78	33
Taunton Town	42	11	11	20	53	74	33
Shepton Mallet Tn	42	4	15	23	35	86	22*
Devizes Town	42	2	9	31	34	121	13

* 1 point deducted for playing an ineligible player

HELLENIC LEAGUE

Premier Division	P	W	D	L	F	A	Pts
Shortwood United	34	22	10	2	73	30	76
Moreton Town	34	19	6	9	64	32	63
Supermarine	34	17	10	7	57	33	61
Sharpness	34	15	10	9	85	54	55
Hounslow	34	14	12	8	59	37	54
Abingdon United	34	15	8	11	59	37	53
Wantage Town	34	15	6	13	45	42	51
Fairford Town	34	13	11	10	47	43	50
Morris Motors	34	15	4	15	36	45	49
Almondsbury Grnwy	34	11	14	9	32	37	47
Abingdon Town	34	12	10	12	43	44	46
Rayners Lane	34	11	10	13	47	44	43
Maidenhead Town	34	10	10	14	50	65	40
Bicester Town	34	9	12	13	42	46	39
Wallingford Town	34	7	12	15	36	48	33
Thame United	34	6	14	14	51	62	32
Didcot Town	34	5	12	17	33	66	27
Clanfield	34	3	3	28	34	128	12

UNITED COUNTIES LEAGUE

Premier Division	P	W	D	L	F	A	Pts
Arlesey	38	22	10	6	86	34	54
Long Buckby	38	22	9	7	93	52	53
Buckingham	38	22	7	9	90	39	51
Irthlingborough	38	18	11	9	78	41	47
Stamford	38	18	9	11	75	56	45
Desborough	38	18	9	11	66	63	45
Potton	38	15	12	11	62	53	42
Baldock	38	15	11	12	51	45	41
Wootton	38	16	7	15	50	49	39
Bourne	38	14	10	14	48	64	38
S & L Corby	38	14	6	18	56	59	34
Newport Pagnell	38	13	8	17	40	54	34
Raunds	38	15	3	20	47	61	33
Stotfold	38	11	10	17	41	54	32
Rothwell	38	12	8	18	49	66	32
Brackley	38	10	11	17	72	78	31
Eynesbury	38	11	9	18	61	89	31
Holbeach	38	12	6	20	55	73	29
St Neots	38	11	5	22	37	77	27
Ampthill	38	7	7	24	41	91	21

LONDON SPARTAN LEAGUE

Premier Division	P	W	D	L	F	A	Pts
Burnham	32	25	3	4	90	20	53
Collier Row	32	21	8	3	59	27	50
Brimsdown R	32	16	8	8	69	45	40
Thatcham T	32	15	8	9	54	34	38
Hanwell T	32	15	8	9	52	38	38
Northwood	32	13	11	8	45	22	37
Redhill	32	14	8	10	46	35	36
Waltham Abbey *	31	14	6	11	45	44	34
Beaconsfield U	32	12	7	13	47	43	31
Pennant	32	11	9	12	47	52	31
Amersham T	32	11	6	15	46	61	28
Danson	32	10	7	15	39	50	27
Swanley T	32	7	11	14	34	48	25
Edgware	32	8	9	15	40	55	25
Beckton U *	31	7	11	13	35	52	25
Corinthian Casuals	32	6	4	22	35	68	16
BROB Barnet	32	1	6	25	20	109	8

* Waltham Abbey v Beckton U (not played)

NORTH WEST COUNTIES

Third Division	P	W	D	L	F	A	Pts
Kirkby Town	34	26	5	3	83	30	57
Colwyn Bay	34	22	10	2	75	32	54
Newton	34	16	10	8	56	33	42
Urmston Town	34	14	10	10	42	39	38
Blackpool Mech	34	15	7	12	61	48	37

VAUX WEARSIDE LEAGUE

	P	W	D	L	F	A	Pts
Blue Star	38	29	7	2	124	28	65
Whickham	38	28	7	3	81	30	63
Coundon	38	27	5	6	105	44	59
South Shields	38	25	7	6	105	36	57
Eppleton	38	19	6	13	70	59	44

COMBINED COUNTIES

Premier Division	P	W	D	L	F	A	Pts
Malden Vale	36	24	10	2	82	33	82
*Southwick	36	25	5	6	103	73	80
Merstham	36	23	6	7	66	32	75
Brit Aero (Wey)	36	20	10	6	82	38	70
Ash United	36	20	6	10	77	42	66

* Promoted to Vauxhall-Opel League and replaced by Chertsey Town.

SOUTH MIDLANDS LEAGUE

Premier Division	P	W	D	L	F	A	Pts
Eaton Bray United	30	20	7	3	71	34	47
Vauxhall Motors	30	18	6	6	46	24	42
Shefford Town	30	17	5	8	56	31	39
Knebworth	30	15	9	6	44	32	39
Winslow United	30	15	6	9	52	32	36

ESSEX SENIOR LEAGUE

	P	W	D	L	F	A	Pts
Maldon Town	30	20	4	6	71	29	64
Witham Town	30	20	4	6	59	27	64
Stansted	30	19	5	6	80	29	62
Wivenhoe Town	30	16	10	4	54	27	58
Brentwood	30	18	3	9	73	46	57

GLOUCESTER COUNTY LEAGUE

	P	W	D	L	F	A	Pts
Old Georgians	36	23	10	3	109	46	56
Port of Bristol	36	20	10	6	78	42	50
Hanham Athletic	36	18	10	8	62	36	46
Lydbrook Athletic	36	19	7	10	80	51	45
Lawrence Weston	36	16	12	8	64	49	44
Hallen							

HAMPSHIRE LEAGUE

Division One	P	W	D	L	F	A	Pts
AFC Totton	38	29	6	3	99	22	64
Sholing Sports	38	26	10	2	86	28	62
Havant Town	38	16	15	7	82	48	47
Eastleigh	38	18	11	9	52	36	47
Pirelli General	38	16	11	11	44	34	43

HERTS COUNTY LEAGUE

Premier Division	P	W	D	L	F	A	Pts
Bedmond	28	19	7	2	63	24	45
Cockfosters	28	17	6	5	49	30	40
London Colney	28	13	11	4	43	27	37
Bovingdon	28	16	4	8	58	38	36
St Margaretsbury	28	13	6	9	57	35	32

KENT LEAGUE

Division One	P	W	D	L	F	A	Pts
Tunbridge Wells	32	22	6	4	83	39	72
Hythe Town	32	22	6	4	70	33	72
Sittingbourne	32	21	4	7	77	43	67
Beckenham Town	32	17	8	7	67	46	59
Cray Wanderers	32	17	2	13	59	51	53

LEICESTERSHIRE SENIOR LEAGUE

Premier Division	P	W	D	L	F	A	Pts
Thringstone	30	24	3	3	83	28	51
Wigston Fields	30	21	6	3	69	25	48
Anstey Nomads	30	16	7	7	63	41	39
Friar Lane Old Boys	30	13	8	9	53	43	34
Wigston Town	30	11	10	9	48	35	32

NOTTS ALLIANCE

Senior Division	P	W	D	L	F	A	Pts
Keyworth Utd	28	22	2	4	72	27	46
Rainworth MW	28	20	3	5	75	23	43
Clipstone MW	28	18	5	5	71	27	41
Meadows Albion	28	16	4	8	52	34	36
Hucknall CW	28	15	4	9	61	21	34

SUSSEX COUNTY LEAGUE

Division One	P	W	D	L	F	A	Pts
Steyning T	30	23	3	4	74	26	72
Littlehampton T	30	21	3	6	65	26	66
Eastbourne T	30	19	6	5	66	26	63
Whitehawk	30	18	7	5	69	34	61
Arundel	30	17	7	6	77	38	58

1985-86

This campaign marked the last of Gola's sponsorship of the Alliance Premier League; it adopted its present title of the GMV Conference at the end of the season. During the year it was announced that the long-awaited one-up-one-down system between the Fourth Division and the Conference would be operational from 1986-87. This decision had an invigorating effect on clubs right through the Pyramid, though it might have taken some of the gloss off Enfield's championship; they won the title knowing that they would be the last champions not to be automatically accepted into the Football League.

Enfield's championship meant that Altrincham were no longer the only side to have won the Alliance Premier League on more than one occasion, but Alty's other achievements during the campaign will have compensated for this; they clinched the FA Trophy for the first time since 1978 by beating local rivals Runcorn at Wembley, and in the FA Cup enjoyed a fabulous win at First Division Birmingham City.

Halesowen Town became only the second side to retain the FA Vase. They returned to Wembley and disposed of Southall 3-0 in front of a Vase record crowd of over 18 000. Another team to sparkle were Halesowen's near neighbours Kidderminster Harriers who found a goalscorer extraordinaire in Kim Casey. He found the net an incredible 73 times in all competitions. The Aggborough side blasted their way to the Welsh Cup final beating four Football League clubs en route.

SUMMARY

FA VASE

	Winners	Runners Up	Semi-finalists
	Halesowen Town	Southall	Warrington Town, Wisbech Town

FA TROPHY

	Winners	Runners-up	Semi-finalists
	Altrincham	Runcorn	Enfield, Kettering Town

FA CUP   **Most Successful Team:** Altrincham

1st Rd: Chorley 1 Altrincham 2; 2nd Rd: Blackpool 1 Altrincham 2; 3rd Rd: Birmingham 1 Altrincham 2; 4th Rd: York 2 Altrincham 0

GOLA LEAGUE   **Champions:** Enfield   **Runners Up:** Frickley Athletic

GOLA LEAGUE STATISTICS

Top Crowds

2067	Boston United v Wealdstone (4.9.85)	
1958	Stafford Rangers v Telford United (7.9.85)	
1952	Kettering Town v Maidstone United (7.9.85)	
1557	Telford United v Enfield (26.4.86)	
1553	Boston United v Kettering Town (26.12.85)	

Top Scorers

36	Kim Casey (Kidderminster)
25	Mick Doherty (Weymouth)
22	Mark Carter (Runcorn)

Manager of the Month Awards

Sep	King (Altrincham)
Oct	McCluskey (Enfield)
Nov	Williams (Runcorn)
Dec	Marshall (Frickley)
Jan	Williams (Runcorn)
Feb	Allner (Kidderminster)
Mar	McCluskey (Enfield)
Apr	Reid (Stafford)

GOLA LEAGUE

			Home				Away					
	P	W	D	L	F	A	W	D	L	F	A	Pts
Enfield	42	15	4	2	48	20	12	6	3	46	27	76
Frickley	42	16	4	1	46	21	9	6	6	32	29	69
Kidderminster	42	12	4	5	51	28	12	3	6	48	34	67
Altrincham	42	14	3	4	42	27	8	8	5	28	22	63
Weymouth	42	11	8	2	43	24	8	7	6	32	36	61
Runcorn	42	11	6	4	40	17	8	8	5	30	27	60
Stafford	42	10	7	4	30	22	9	6	6	31	32	60
Telford	42	13	5	3	42	24	5	5	11	26	42	51
Kettering	42	11	6	4	37	24	4	9	8	18	29	49
Wealdstone	42	10	5	6	35	28	6	4	11	22	28	47
Cheltenham	42	13	4	4	47	27	3	7	11	22	42	46
Bath	42	5	8	8	28	25	8	3	10	25	29	45
Boston	42	11	5	5	41	26	5	2	14	25	50	44
Barnet	42	9	4	8	32	23	4	7	10	24	37	41
Scarborough	42	10	4	7	35	31	3	7	11	19	35	40
Northwich	42	5	6	10	24	25	5	6	10	18	29	37
Maidstone	42	7	9	5	35	29	2	7	12	22	37	36
Nuneaton	42	8	3	10	27	27	5	2	14	31	46	36
Dagenham	42	6	7	8	23	29	4	5	12	25	37	36
Wycombe	42	7	6	8	30	35	3	7	11	25	49	36
Dartford	42	7	6	8	36	33	1	3	17	15	49	26
Barrow	42	5	6	10	26	34	2	2	17	15	52	24

Points scoring: Home win = 2 pts; Away win = 3 pts; Draw = 1 pt.

VAUXHALL-OPEL LEAGUE

Premier Division	P	W	D	L	F	A	Pts
Sutton United	42	29	8	5	109	39	95
Yeovil Town	42	28	7	7	92	48	91
Farnborough Town	42	23	8	11	90	50	77
Croydon	42	23	7	12	70	50	76
Harrow Borough	42	21	8	13	76	66	71
Slough Town	42	18	8	16	66	68	62
Bishop's Stortford	42	17	10	15	55	61	61
Kingstonian	42	15	15	12	57	56	60
Dulwich Hamlet	42	17	9	16	64	79	60
Wokingham Town	42	16	10	16	67	64	58
Windsor & Eaton	42	17	7	18	58	75	58
Tooting & Mitcham U	42	14	11	17	65	76	53
Walthamstow Ave	42	12	14	16	69	70	50
Worthing	42	13	10	19	72	82	49
Bognor Regis Town	42	15	6	21	63	70	48*
Hayes	42	10	17	15	36	42	47
Hitchin Town	42	11	14	17	53	69	47
Barking	42	11	13	18	45	55	46
Hendon	42	10	13	19	59	77	43
Carshalton Athletic	42	9	13	20	56	79	40
Billericay Town	42	9	12	21	59	78	39
Epsom & Ewell	42	8	12	22	63	90	36

* 3 points deducted by league

Division One	P	W	D	L	F	A	Pts
St Albans City	42	23	11	8	92	61	80
Bromley	42	24	8	10	68	41	80
Wembley	42	22	12	8	59	30	78
Oxford City	42	22	11	9	75	51	77
Hampton	42	21	11	10	63	45	74
Leyton Wingate	42	21	10	11	77	56	73
Uxbridge	42	20	8	14	64	49	68
Staines Town	42	18	10	14	69	66	64
Boreham Wood	42	15	16	11	62	54	61
Walton & Hersham	42	16	10	16	68	71	58
Lewes	42	16	8	18	61	75	56
Leytonstone Ilford	42	13	15	14	57	67	54
Finchley	42	12	17	13	61	59	53
Grays Athletic	42	13	11	18	69	75	50
Leatherhead	42	14	8	20	62	68	50
Tilbury	42	13	11	18	60	66	50
Maidenhead United	42	13	7	22	61	67	46
Basildon United	42	12	9	21	52	72	45
Hornchurch	42	11	11	20	44	59	44
Chesham United	42	12	6	24	51	87	42
Harlow Town	42	8	14	20	53	70	38
Aveley	42	8	6	28	59	98	30

Division Two North	P	W	D	L	F	A	Pts
Stevenage Borough	38	26	6	6	71	24	84
Kingsbury Town	38	25	8	5	84	35	83
Heybridge Swifts	38	20	8	10	65	46	68
Cheshunt	38	18	10	10	60	40	64
Hertford Town	37	17	7	14	60	50	58
Chalfont St Peter	38	15	11	12	53	50	56
Tring Town	38	14	13	11	58	46	55
Royston Town	38	13	13	12	59	57	52
Saffron Walden Tn	38	13	12	13	61	65	51
Berkhamsted Town	38	14	8	16	45	52	50
Haringey Borough	38	14	7	17	49	51	49
Letchworth Gdn C	38	13	8	17	46	52	47
Rainham Town	38	14	4	20	54	91	46
Hemel Hempstead	38	12	9	17	50	66	45
Ware	38	11	11	16	56	61	44
Vauxhall Motors	38	11	10	17	58	62	43
Barton Rovers	38	12	7	19	50	60	43
Harefield Utd	38	9	12	17	56	72	39
Clapton	38	10	7	21	51	90	37
Wolverton Town	38	8	11	19	42	58	35

Division Two South	P	W	D	L	F	A	Pts
Southwick	38	25	8	5	86	34	83
Bracknell Town	38	24	9	5	80	23	81
Woking	38	23	9	6	94	45	78
Newbury Town	38	22	7	9	86	53	73
Whyteleafe	38	21	10	7	61	41	73
Molesey	38	21	8	9	59	39	71
Metropolitan Police	38	20	6	12	72	48	66
Southall	38	19	7	12	77	59	64
Dorking	38	18	10	10	70	57	64
Feltham	38	16	7	15	65	60	55
Banstead Athletic	38	15	8	15	60	66	53
Petersfield Utd	38	12	9	17	61	71	45
Hungerford Town	38	11	6	21	57	78	39
Flackwell Heath	38	11	6	21	46	72	39
Eastbourne Utd	38	9	8	21	51	81	35
Camberley Town	38	9	7	22	53	64	34
Egham Town	38	7	8	23	41	83	29
Horsham	38	6	10	22	33	74	28
Ruislip Manor	38	5	12	21	44	87	27
Marlow	38	6	5	27	47	108	23

NORTHERN (MULTIPART) PREMIER LEAGUE

	P	Home					Away					Pts
		W	D	L	F	A	W	D	L	F	A	
Gateshead	42	15	4	2	49	21	9	6	6	36	30	82
Marine	42	13	1	7	40	23	10	10	1	23	12	80
Morecambe	42	10	9	2	32	15	7	8	6	27	24	68
Gainsborough T	42	14	4	3	48	23	4	10	7	18	29	68
Burton Albion	42	11	5	5	32	22	7	7	7	32	25	66
Southport	42	7	7	7	30	29	10	4	7	40	37	62
Worksop Town	42	9	6	6	28	22	8	4	9	23	26	61
*Workington	42	6	10	5	26	23	8	8	5	28	23	59
Macclesfield T	42	8	5	8	38	28	9	3	9	29	37	59
Hyde United	42	9	7	5	32	27	5	8	8	31	35	57
*Witton Albion	42	8	7	6	30	28	7	6	8	26	31	57
Mossley	42	6	10	5	32	30	7	6	8	24	30	55
Bangor City	42	9	6	6	28	22	4	9	8	23	29	54
Rhyl	42	7	5	9	33	34	7	5	9	32	37	52
South Liverpool	42	5	8	8	20	23	6	9	6	23	21	50
*Horwich RMI	42	10	3	8	30	28	5	3	13	23	35	50
Caernarfon T	42	8	10	3	32	31	3	7	11	19	32	50
Oswestry T	42	6	9	6	23	20	6	4	11	28	40	49
Buxton	42	9	5	7	33	33	2	7	12	22	43	45
Chorley	42	6	7	8	23	33	3	8	10	33	31	42
Matlock T	42	7	9	5	34	32	2	6	13	25	43	42
*Goole T	42	4	6	11	19	37	3	5	13	18	41	31

* 1 point deducted for breach of rule.

SOUTHERN LEAGUE

Premier Division

	P	W	D	L	F	A	Pts
Welling United	38	29	6	3	95	31	93
Chelmsford City	38	20	10	8	68	41	70
Fisher Athletic	38	20	7	11	67	45	67
Alvechurch	38	19	9	10	71	56	66
Worcester City	38	19	9	10	64	50	66
Crawley Town	38	18	5	15	76	59	59
Shepshed Charter	58	19	1	18	51	52	58
Aylesbury United	38	14	10	14	52	49	52
Folkestone	38	14	10	14	56	56	52
Bedworth United	38	14	8	16	44	49	50
Willenhall Town	38	12	13	13	51	44	49
Dudley Town	38	15	4	19	58	62	49
Corby Town	38	14	7	17	61	67	49
King's Lynn	38	12	10	16	39	42	46
Basingstoke Town	38	13	4	21	36	67	43
RS Southampton	38	11	9	18	44	61	42
Witney Town	38	11	6	21	44	74	39
Gosport Borough	38	10	8	20	42	66	38
Fareham Town	38	8	13	17	40	62	37
Gravesend & Nthflt	38	9	9	20	29	55	36

Division One Mid

	P	W	D	L	F	A	Pts
Bromsgrove Rovers	40	29	5	6	95	44	92
Redditch United	40	23	6	11	70	42	75
Merthyr Tydfil	40	21	10	9	60	40	75
VS Rugby	40	17	14	9	41	31	65
Stourbridge	40	15	14	11	62	49	59
Rushden Town	40	17	7	16	69	74	58
Bilston Town	40	15	12	13	60	48	57
Bridgnorth Town	40	13	18	9	56	45	57
Gloucester City	40	15	12	13	61	57	57
Grantham	40	16	7	17	46	59	55
Wellingborough Tn	40	15	9	16	56	56	54
Sutton Coldfield Tn	40	13	14	13	60	45	53
Hednesford Town	40	14	9	17	67	70	51
Forest Green Rovers	40	14	9	17	52	56	51
Mile Oak Rovers	40	14	8	18	56	73	50
Leicester United	40	13	10	17	41	48	49
Banbury United	40	13	8	19	38	55	47
Coventry Sporting	40	10	15	15	42	48	45
Moor Green	40	12	6	22	63	91	42
Leamington	40	10	6	24	40	77	36
Oldbury United	40	8	7	25	50	87	31

Division One South

	P	W	D	L	F	A	Pts
Cambridge City	40	23	11	6	87	41	80
Salisbury	40	24	8	8	84	51	80
Hastings Town	40	23	9	8	83	51	78
Dover Athletic	40	23	6	11	89	53	75
Corinthian	40	20	9	11	78	45	69
Tonbridge AFC	40	17	13	10	65	51	64
Dunstable	40	17	11	12	70	61	62
Ruislip	40	17	6	17	67	66	57
Erith & Belvedere	40	14	12	14	35	40	54
Waterlooville	40	16	6	18	52	58	54
Burnham & Hillingdn	40	16	6	18	44	59	54
Canterbury City	40	13	13	14	58	58	52
Trowbridge Town	40	13	13	14	57	63	52
Sheppey United	40	14	10	16	43	53	52
Thanet United	40	13	7	20	58	63	46
Woodford Town	40	12	10	18	49	62	46
Poole Town	40	12	7	21	55	63	43
Ashford Town	40	10	12	18	45	65	42
Chatham Town	40	8	15	17	53	70	39
Andover	40	10	8	22	52	92	38
Dorchester Town	40	5	8	27	35	94	23

NORTHERN COUNTIES EAST LEAGUE

Premier Division	P	W	D	L	F	A	Pts
Arnold	38	24	8	6	83	36	79*
Emley	38	22	11	5	77	47	77
Guiseley	38	22	6	10	81	52	72
Long Eaton United	38	19	11	8	70	39	68
Eastwood Town	38	21	5	12	73	62	67*
Alfreton Town	38	21	2	15	66	47	65
Sutton Town	38	18	6	14	69	57	60
Farsley Celtic	38	14	12	12	71	55	54
Belper Town	38	15	9	14	54	45	54
Thackley	38	14	11	13	52	58	53
Denaby United	38	13	14	11	63	56	52*
Pontefract Colls	38	15	7	16	55	54	52
Armthorpe Welfare	38	15	7	16	57	58	52
Bentley VW	38	12	11	15	61	65	47
Heanor Town	38	11	9	18	61	69	41*
Spalding United	38	9	12	17	41	62	39
Boston	38	10	6	22	42	79	36
Appleby Frodingham	38	6	12	20	40	83	30
Bridlington Trinity	38	4	14	20	34	85	26
Ilkeston Town	38	5	7	26	31	72	22

* 1 point deducted for breach of rule.

DRYBROUGH'S NORTHERN LEAGUE

First Division	P	W	D	L	F	A	Pts
Bishop Auckland	38	21	10	7	79	45	73
Bedlington Terriers	38	19	10	9	65	44	67
South Bank	38	18	12	8	66	36	66
Blyth Spartans	38	19	9	10	79	52	66
Tow Law Town	38	18	10	10	72	47	64
Peterlee Newton	38	19	6	13	66	56	63
Chester-le-Street Tn	38	18	7	13	62	53	61
Brendon United	38	16	10	12	72	68	58
Crook Town	38	15	8	15	73	70	53
Hartlepool Utd Res	38	14	10	14	65	69	52
Gretna	38	13	11	14	70	69	50
North Shields	38	14	8	16	65	72	50
Consett	38	13	9	16	44	58	48
Spennymoor United	38	12	11	15	51	54	47
Ryhope Community	38	13	7	18	50	69	46
Whitby Town	38	12	9	17	50	74	45
Whitley Bay	38	11	8	19	65	73	41
Ferryhill Athletic	38	11	6	21	62	94	39
Billingham Synthonia	38	8	11	19	47	66	35
Billingham Town	38	6	8	24	46	89	26

NORTH WEST COUNTIES LEAGUE

First Division	P	W	D	L	F	A	Pts
Clitheroe	38	20	14	4	61	30	54
Congleton Town	38	22	10	6	51	29	54
Eastwood Hanley	38	22	9	7	68	45	53
Stalybridge Celtic	38	21	10	7	62	39	52
Fleetwood Town	38	21	10	7	70	34	50*
Irlam Town	38	16	14	8	66	45	46
Leek Town	38	20	6	12	64	44	46
Curzon Ashton	38	18	9	11	52	50	45
Burscough	38	15	10	13	45	35	40
St Helens Town	38	15	8	15	65	55	38
Accrington Stanley	38	13	11	14	62	60	37
Leyland Motors	38	13	8	17	62	67	34
Winsford United	38	14	6	18	55	68	34
Radcliffe Borough	38	12	9	17	48	49	33
Bootle	38	11	7	20	46	54	29
Penrith	38	9	8	21	46	63	26
Netherfield	38	8	10	20	38	76	26
Glossop	38	7	10	21	37	69	24
Prescot Cables	38	5	8	25	35	85	18

Second Division	P	W	D	L	F	A	Pts
Kirkby Town	34	24	7	3	85	30	55
Rossendale United	34	20	8	6	81	36	48
Wren Rovers	34	18	8	8	60	46	44
Warrington Town	34	17	9	8	62	48	43
Colwyn Bay	34	17	8	9	74	53	42
Chadderton	34	15	12	7	66	48	42
Colne Dynamoes	34	15	9	10	59	43	39
Great Harwood Tn	34	13	10	11	38	45	36
Skelmersdale United	34	14	5	15	58	53	33
Droylsden	34	13	7	14	48	56	33
Atherton LR	34	12	6	16	49	61	30
Lancaster City	34	10	9	15	57	66	29
Ellesmere Port & N	34	9	9	16	45	61	27
Ashton United	34	11	5	18	46	64	26*
Darwen	34	8	8	18	48	57	24
Salford	34	9	4	21	38	72	22
Ford Motors	34	5	10	19	36	64	20
Nantwich Town	34	5	8	21	31	78	18

EASTERN COUNTIES LEAGUE

	P	W	D	L	F	A	Pts
Sudbury Town	42	30	6	6	107	45	66
Colchester Utd Res	42	29	6	7	109	49	64
Great Yarmouth Tn	42	29	5	8	94	46	63
Bury Town	42	23	10	9	93	54	56
Tiptree United	42	24	7	11	78	54	55
Braintree Town	42	22	11	9	91	53	53*
March Town United	42	22	8	12	74	62	52
Stowmarket Town	42	19	13	10	79	62	51
Wisbech Town	42	22	5	15	79	55	49
Histon	42	20	7	15	75	58	47
Lowestoft Town	42	16	12	14	75	50	44
Felixstowe Town	42	19	6	17	62	54	44
Gorleston	42	15	9	18	74	64	39
Haverhill Rovers	42	16	6	20	61	59	38
Thetford Town	42	10	10	22	48	87	30
Brantham Athletic	42	13	4	25	57	108	30
Harwich & Parkeston	42	10	9	23	52	72	29
Soham Town Rngrs	42	11	7	24	55	92	29
Chatteris Town	42	10	6	26	37	79	26
Ely City	42	8	9	25	46	82	25
Newmarket Town	42	9	5	28	59	119	23
Clacton Town	42	2	5	35	28	130	9

UNITED COUNTIES LEAGUE

Premier Division	P	W	D	L	F	A	Pts
Buckingham Town	40	25	10	5	78	31	16
Stewart & Lloyds Corby	40	24	11	5	85	32	59
Baldock Town	40	26	6	8	91	43	58
Irthlingborough Diam	40	22	8	10	69	45	52
Stamford	40	22	6	12	71	52	50
Long Buckby	40	18	10	12	75	54	46
Potton United	40	20	6	14	69	53	46
Wootton Blue Cross	40	16	11	13	63	58	43
Arlesey Town	40	16	9	15	63	57	41
Holbeach United	40	16	8	16	66	75	40
Northampton Spen	40	17	5	18	60	62	40
Rothwell Town	40	16	7	17	61	74	39
Raunds Town	40	16	7	17	61	74	39
Ampthill Town	40	13	10	17	55	68	36
Desborough Town	40	11	9	20	70	89	31
Brackley Town	40	10	10	20	62	70	30
Bourne Town	40	9	12	19	43	71	30
St Neots Town	40	9	9	22	59	69	27
Stotfold	40	10	7	23	43	77	27
Eynesford Rovers	40	7	12	21	45	86	26
Newport Pagnell T	40	4	12	24	43	77	20

MIDLAND COMBINATION

Premier Division	P	W	D	L	F	A	Pts
Boldmere St Mich'ls	38	25	10	3	72	24	60
Paget Rangers	38	24	9	5	94	31	57
West Mids Police	38	23	8	7	65	41	54
Northfield Town	38	18	12	8	74	50	48
Bloxwich AFC	38	18	11	9	77	50	47
Stratford Town	38	17	12	9	53	32	46
Solihull Borough	38	18	7	13	62	45	43
Walsall Borough	38	15	13	10	52	37	43
Polesworth Nth Wck	38	16	10	12	52	46	42
Racing Cub Warwick	38	13	15	10	52	50	41
Coleshill Town	38	14	13	11	54	54	41
Highgate Utd	38	16	8	14	56	55	40
Evesham Utd	38	12	9	17	62	80	33
Hurley Daw Mill	38	12	8	18	44	59	32
New World	38	9	7	22	46	73	25
Knowle North Star	38	8	9	21	35	63	25
Southam Utd	38	6	12	20	52	90	24
Studley Sporting	38	7	8	23	43	75	22
Smethwick Highfield	38	5	11	22	31	75	21
Kings Heath	38	5	6	27	24	70	16

GREAT MILLS WESTERN LEAGUE

Premier Division	P	W	D	L	F	A	Pts
Exmouth	42	30	9	3	95	31	69
Liskeard	42	31	6	5	103	34	68
Bideford	42	27	8	7	97	27	62
Saltash	42	21	13	8	81	44	55
Chippenham	42	21	10	11	60	44	52
Mangotsfield	42	18	13	11	86	58	49
Taunton	42	19	9	14	59	54	47
*Dawlish	42	19	8	15	53	49	45
Bristol C	42	18	6	18	74	61	42
Clevedon	42	12	18	12	55	47	42
Bristol MF	42	16	9	17	71	72	41
Minehead	42	16	9	17	55	70	41
Frome *	42	14	12	16	49	62	39
Clandown	42	15	8	19	46	57	38
Torrington	42	13	11	18	51	62	37
Melksham	42	11	13	18	50	77	35
Barnstaple	42	13	7	22	46	68	33
Weston	42	12	8	22	69	93	32
Paulton	42	9	12	21	50	82	30
Plymouth	42	9	11	22	60	67	29
Chard	42	8	4	30	33	112	20
Shepton Mill *	42	4	8	30	36	110	15

* 1 point deducted for playing an ineligible player

HELLENIC LEAGUE

Premier Division	P	W	D	L	F	A	Pts
Sharpness	34	24	4	6	88	41	76
Shortwood United	34	23	2	9	79	43	71
Hounslow	34	20	6	8	83	44	66
Abingdon Town	34	19	8	7	60	36	65
Supermarine	34	21	2	11	56	48	65
Rayners Lane	34	18	7	9	65	48	60*
Abingdon United	34	17	8	9	46	33	59
Yate Town	34	15	8	11	57	44	53
Moreton Town	34	15	8	11	51	40	53
Thame United	34	13	8	13	51	54	47
Pegasus Juniors	34	13	5	16	56	64	44
Wallingford Town	34	12	5	17	45	56	41
Fairford Town	34	8	8	18	39	49	32
Morris Motors	34	7	10	17	30	44	31
Bicester Town	34	9	3	22	46	79	30
Wantage Town	34	7	6	21	40	65	27
Almondsbury Grnwy	34	7	3	24	34	82	24
Maidenhead Town	34	5	5	24	34	90	20

* 1 point deducted

WEST MIDLANDS (REGIONAL) LEAGUE

Premier Division	P	W	D	L	F	A	Pts
Halesowen Town	38	31	4	3	108	28	66
Gresley Rovers	38	25	9	4	91	29	59
Atherstone United	38	26	7	5	90	48	59
Harrisons	38	22	9	7	82	40	53
Wednesfield Social	38	21	7	10	88	48	49
Lye Town	38	18	11	9	54	39	47
GKN Sankey	38	15	12	11	59	64	42
Hinckley Athletic	38	15	11	12	60	50	41
Tamworth	38	15	8	15	68	52	38
Brereton Social	38	13	11	14	58	54	37
Rushall Olympic	38	14	8	15	63	65	37
Malvern Town	38	13	10	15	51	61	36
Shifnal Town	38	9	10	19	38	76	28
Oldswinford	38	9	9	20	46	68	27
Blakenall	38	9	8	21	38	61	26
Tividale	38	8	10	20	51	83	26
Chasetown	38	7	10	21	40	74	24
Wolverhampton Utd	38	8	8	22	31	66	24
Tipton Town	38	8	8	22	43	79	24
Armitage	38	7	3	28	44	118	17

LONDON SPARTAN LEAGUE

Premier Division	P	W	D	L	F	A	Pts
Collier Row	30	24	3	3	79	27	51
Yeading	30	24	2	4	80	16	50
Redhill	29	22	3	4	57	19	49*
Thatcham Town	30	18	5	7	57	36	41
Brimsdown Rovers	30	15	6	9	56	38	36
Beaconsfield	30	13	6	11	45	44	32
Edgware	29	11	6	12	40	37	28
Northwood	30	9	10	11	42	44	28
Hanwell Town	30	10	6	14	44	50	26
Waltham Abbey	30	9	7	14	44	44	25
Crown & Manor	30	8	9	13	40	53	25
Danson	30	8	7	15	42	53	23
Beckton United	30	7	7	16	28	52	21
Pennant	30	8	3	19	30	66	19
Amersham town	30	4	7	19	29	85	15
Swanley Town	30	2	7	21	31	90	11

* Two points awarded in unplayed match v Edgware

NORTH WEST COUNTIES

Third Division	P	W	D	L	F	A	Pts
Blackpool Mech	28	22	2	4	77	33	44
Oldham Town	28	14	9	5	56	29	37
Maghull	28	15	6	7	62	36	36
Daisy Hill	28	13	7	8	62	45	33
Atherton Collieries	28	13	7	8	48	37	33

NORTHERN COUNTIES EAST

Division One	P	W	D	L	F	A	Pts
North Ferriby	30	18	5	7	54	31	59
Sheffield	30	16	8	6	54	39	56
Harrogate Town	30	16	6	8	65	42	54
Rowntree Mckintosh	30	16	5	9	67	45	53
Ossett Albion	30	13	11	6	54	39	50

VAUX WEARSIDE LEAGUE

	P	W	D	L	F	A	Pts
Coundon	34	25	7	2	72	24	57
Murton	34	25	4	5	70	18	54
Wickham	34	22	7	5	68	23	51
Annfield Plain	34	17	9	8	71	49	43
Sc Vaux	34	19	4	11	68	49	42

SOUTH MIDLANDS LEAGUE

Premier Division	P	W	D	L	F	A	Pts
Selby	30	18	7	5	59	25	61
Welwyn Garden City	30	16	9	5	47	24	57
Leighton Town	30	16	5	9	39	28	53
The 61 FC (Luton)	30	14	10	6	44	31	52
Shefford Town	30	12	12	6	47	31	48

ESSEX SENIOR LEAGUE

	P	W	D	L	F	A	Pts
Witham Town	32	24	5	3	73	23	77
Wivenhoe Town	32	19	5	8	82	47	62
Ford United	32	19	4	9	65	41	61
Maldon Town	32	17	9	6	48	24	60
East Thurrock Utd	32	16	9	7	64	41	57

HAMPSHIRE LEAGUE

Division One	P	W	D	L	F	A	Pts
East Cowes Vics	38	31	7	0	97	24	60
AFC Totton	38	23	9	6	71	26	55
Horndean	38	29	9	6	90	55	51
Havant Town	38	20	9	9	80	47	49
Eastleigh	38	20	9	9	69	45	49

HERTS COUNTY LEAGUE

Premier Division	P	W	D	L	F	A	Pts
Bedmond Special	30	19	8	3	59	29	46
London Colney	30	19	7	4	57	22	45
Wingate	30	20	2	8	71	39	42
Cockfosters	30	16	5	9	46	32	37
Mt Grace Pottrs Bar	30	13	9	8	45	32	35

WINSTONLEAD KENT LEAGUE

Division One	P	W	D	L	F	A	Pts
Alma Swanley	34	22	9	3	78	39	75
Sittingbourne	34	21	7	6	76	37	70
Crockenhill	34	21	5	8	68	33	68
Darenth Heathside	34	17	11	6	57	32	62
Tunbridge Wells	34	15	13	6	99	58	58

LEICESTERSHIRE SENIOR LEAGUE

Premier Division	P	W	D	L	F	A	Pts
Thringstone	30	21	2	7	62	32	44
Anstey Nomads	30	17	8	5	69	21	42
Narbro' & L'thorpe	30	17	8	5	63	32	42
Birstall United	30	17	6	7	53	35	40
Wigston Town	30	14	10	6	47	29	38

NOTTS ALLIANCE

Senior Division	P	W	D	L	F	A	Pts
John Players FC	30	20	6	4	66	36	46
Plessey FC	30	19	7	4	60	31	45
Keyworth United	30	16	8	6	48	30	40
Rainworth MW	30	16	7	7	51	26	39
Hucknall CW	30	16	5	9	65	30	37

SUSSEX COUNTY LEAGUE

Division One	P	W	D	L	F	A	Pts
Steyning Town	30	22	6	2	61	16	72
Three Bridges	30	19	6	5	58	24	63
Eastbourne Town	30	18	7	5	71	23	61
Whitehawk	30	13	11	6	46	30	50
Peacehaven & Tels	30	15	4	11	55	44	49

1986-87

At last the Conference title was fought out with the winners knowing that they would accede to the Fourth Division with no Football League ballot to deny them. For most of the season it looked as though Barnet would make it, but Scarborough put together a great run to get the nod. When their opening Fourth Division game was subsequently wrecked by morons from Wolves, they must have wondered whether it was all worth it!

Kidderminster Town confirmed their arrival at the pinnacle of the Non-League game by winning the FA Trophy against surprise finalists Burton Albion. The first match at Wembley ended in a disappointing stalemate, but the replay at the Hawthorns was a thriller with the Harriers pulling through 2-1.

Halesowen's stranglehold on the FA Vase was broken at last. Amazingly the side to knock them out were little Rocester of the Staffs Senior League who were competing for the first time. The final was between two sides from the North West Coun-

ties League, and resulted in a surprise 3-2 win for St Helens Town over neighbours Warrington Town. St Helens had started their run in the Extra-Preliminary Round, thus bettering Stansted's run of 1983-84.

In the FA Cup Caernarfon Town were the surprise package with wins over Stockport County and York City before a narrow replay defeat at Barnsley. Telford United thrashed Barnsley 3-0 to claim their tenth Football League scalp of the decade; the win meant that they had beaten League opposition in each of the last five competitions.

SUMMARY

FA VASE	Winners	Runners Up	Semi-finalists
	St Helens Town	Warrington Town	Emley, Collier Row

FA TROPHY	Winners	Runners-up	Semi-finalists
	Kidderminster H	Burton Albion	Fareham Town, Dartford

FA CUP   **Most Successful Team:** Caernarfon Town
1st Rd: Caernarfon 1 Stockport 0; 2nd Rd: Caernarfon 0 York 0; 2nd Rd Replay: York 1 Caernarfon 2;
3rd Rd: Caernarfon 0 Barnsley 0; 3rd Rd Replay: Barnsley 1 Caernarfon 0

GM VAUXHALL CONFERENCE   **Champions:** Scarborough   **Runners Up:** Barnet

GM VAUXHALL CONFERENCE STATISTICS

Top Crowds
5640	Scarborough v Weymouth (2.5.87)	
4130	Barnet v Enfield (26.12.86)	
3764	Scarborough v Runcorn (20.4.87)	
2520	Barnet v Altrincham (31.1.87)	
2453	Altrincham v Cheltenham Town (18.10.86)	

Top Scorers
38	Kim Casey (Kidderminster)
30	Mark Carter (Runcorn)
24	Steve Butler (Maidstone)

Manager of the Month Awards
Sep	Fry (Barnet)
Oct	Storton (Telford)
Nov	Warnock (Scarborough)
Dec	Warnock (Scarborough)
Jan	Fry (Barnet)
Feb	Hobbins (Welling)
Mar	Jones (Bath)
Apr	King (Runcorn)

GM VAUXHALL CONFERENCE

	P	Home					Away					Pts
		W	D	L	F	A	W	D	L	F	A	
Scarborough	42	12	7	2	31	19	15	3	3	33	14	91
Barnet	42	13	4	4	47	22	12	6	3	39	17	85
Maidstone United	42	14	4	3	43	16	7	6	8	28	32	73
Enfield	42	9	5	7	32	21	12	2	7	34	26	70
Altrincham	42	11	7	3	35	18	7	8	6	31	35	69
Boston United	42	11	4	6	40	28	10	2	9	42	46	69
Sutton United	42	12	4	5	52	24	7	7	7	29	27	68
Runcorn	42	12	7	2	45	23	6	6	9	26	35	67

	P	W	D	L	F	A	W	D	L	F	A	Pts
Telford United	42	12	5	4	41	23	6	5	10	28	36	64
Bath City	42	9	5	7	35	31	8	7	6	28	31	63
Cheltenham	42	11	4	6	43	25	5	9	7	21	25	61
Kidderminster H	42	10	4	7	46	34	7	0	14	31	47	55
Stafford Rangers	42	9	5	7	32	25	5	6	10	26	35	53
Weymouth	42	10	5	6	43	33	3	7	11	25	44	51
Dagenham	42	10	4	7	32	29	4	3	14	24	43	49
Kettering Town	42	8	5	8	35	28	4	6	11	19	38	47
Northwich Victoria	42	6	7	8	25	23	4	7	10	28	46	44
Nuneaton Borough	42	6	8	7	23	28	4	6	11	25	45	44
Wealdstone	42	7	5	9	26	34	4	5	12	24	36	43
Welling United	42	8	4	9	39	38	2	6	13	22	46	40
Frickley Athletic	42	5	7	9	28	37	2	4	15	19	45	32
Gateshead	42	3	7	11	26	45	3	6	12	22	50	31

VAUXHALL-OPEL LEAGUE

Premier Division

Premier Division	P	W	D	L	F	A	Pts
Wycombe Wnderers	42	32	5	5	103	32	101
Yeovil Town	42	28	8	6	71	27	92
Slough Town	42	12	8	11	70	44	77
Hendon	42	22	7	13	67	53	73
Bognor Regis Town	42	20	10	12	85	61	70
Harrow Borough	42	20	10	12	68	44	70
Croydon	42	18	19	14	51	48	64
Barking	42	16	14	12	76	56	62
Farnborough Town	42	17	11	14	66	72	62
Bishop's Stortford	42	15	15	12	62	57	60
Bromley	42	16	11	15	63	72	59
Kingstonian	42	16	9	17	58	50	57
Windsor & Eton	42	13	15	14	47	52	54
St Albans City	42	14	9	19	61	70	51
Carshalton Athletic	42	13	9	20	55	68	48
Hayes	42	12	12	18	45	68	48
Wokingham Town	42	14	6	22	47	61	48
Dulwich Hamlet	42	12	10	20	62	71	46
Tooting & Mitcham U	42	12	9	21	41	53	45
Hitchin Town	42	13	5	24	56	69	44
Worthing	42	8	9	25	58	107	53
Walthamstow Ave	42	4	6	32	36	113	18

Division One

Division One							
Leytonstone-Ilford	42	30	5	7	78	29	95
Leyton-Wingate	42	23	13	6	68	31	82
Bracknell Town	42	24	9	9	92	48	81
Southwick	42	23	7	12	80	66	76
Wembley	42	21	9	12	61	47	72
Grays Athletic	42	19	10	13	76	64	67
Kingsbury Town	42	20	7	15	69	67	67
Boreham Wood	42	20	6	16	59	52	66
Uxbridge	42	18	9	15	60	59	63
Leatherhead	42	17	11	14	45	48	62
Hampton	42	18	5	19	57	55	59
Basildon United	42	16	10	16	58	60	58
Billericay	42	14	12	16	57	52	54
Staines Town	42	13	13	16	40	51	52
Lewes	42	15	6	21	55	65	51
Stevenage Borough	42	12	11	19	61	67	47
Oxford City	42	11	10	21	64	72	43
Walton & Hersham	42	11	10	21	53	74	43
Tilbury	42	12	7	23	46	70	43
Epsom & Ewell	42	12	7	23	44	68	43
Maidenhead United	42	11	4	27	44	76	37
Finchley	42	6	11	25	44	90	29

Division Two North

Division Two North	P	W	D	L	F	A	Pts
Chesham United	42	28	6	8	81	48	90
Wolverton Town	42	23	14	5	74	32	83
Haringey Borough	42	22	13	7	86	40	79
Heybridge Swifts	42	21	11	10	81	54	74
Aveley	42	19	13	10	68	50	70
Letchworth Gdn City	42	19	11	12	77	62	68
Barton Rovers	42	18	11	13	49	39	65
Tring Town	42	19	7	16	69	49	64
Collier Row	42	19	5	18	67	65	62
Ware	42	17	8	17	51	50	59
Saffron Walden Tn	42	14	14	14	56	54	56
Wivenhoe Town	42	15	11	16	61	61	56
Vauxhall Motors	42	15	10	17	61	57	55
Hornchurch	42	13	16	12	60	60	55
Hertford Town	42	14	13	15	52	53	55
Berkhamsted Town	42	12	16	14	63	64	52
Harlow Town	42	13	11	18	45	55	50
Rainham Town	42	12	11	19	53	70	47
Clapton	42	10	11	21	45	63	41
Hemel Hempstead	42	9	12	21	48	77	39
Royston Town	42	4	12	26	37	109	24
Cheshunt	42	5	6	32	43	114	21

Division Two South

Division Two South							
Woking	40	27	7	6	110	32	88
Marlow	40	28	4	8	78	36	88
Dorking	40	24	12	4	78	30	84
Feltham	40	24	12	4	78	30	84
Feltham	40	25	3	12	79	34	78
Ruislip Manor	40	22	10	8	85	47	76
Chertsey Town	40	18	11	11	56	44	65
Metropolitan Police	40	16	13	11	70	61	61
Chalfont St Peter	40	17	10	13	60	55	61
Hungerford Town	40	14	14	12	55	48	56
Haresfield United	40	14	14	12	53	47	56
Eastbourne United	40	15	10	15	72	59	55
Whyteleafe	40	12	15	13	52	63	51
Horsham	40	14	8	18	54	61	50
Egham Town	40	14	6	20	45	77	48
Camberley Town	40	13	3	24	62	89	42
Flackwell Heath	40	9	11	20	34	63	38
Banstead Athletic	40	7	15	18	44	61	36
Petersfield United	40	9	8	23	45	84	34
Molesey	40	7	12	21	37	89	33
Newbury	40	6	14	20	51	83	32
Southall	40	6	6	28	28	85	24

NORTHERN PREMIER LEAGUE

		Home					Away					
	P	W	D	L	F	A	W	D	L	F	A	Pts
Macclesfield Town	42	15	4	2	52	27	11	6	4	28	20	88
Bangor City	42	16	3	2	40	8	9	9	3	34	27	87
Caernarfon Town	42	14	5	2	38	14	6	11	4	29	26	76
Marine	42	11	6	4	40	17	10	4	7	30	26	73
South Liverpool	42	11	4	6	32	22	10	6	5	26	18	73
Morecambe	42	11	5	5	32	22	9	7	5	34	27	72
Matlock Town	42	12	6	3	43	26	8	4	9	38	41	70
Southport	42	11	6	4	36	20	8	5	8	31	29	68
Chorley	42	12	5	4	33	20	4	7	10	25	39	60
Mossley	42	10	8	3	35	21	5	4	12	22	31	57
Hyde United	42	8	4	9	50	36	7	6	8	31	34	55
Burton Albion	42	9	1	11	31	34	7	5	9	25	34	54
Buxton	42	5	10	6	35	30	8	4	9	36	38	53
Whitton Albion	42	10	5	6	39	29	5	3	13	29	50	53
Barrow	42	10	3	8	24	21	5	4	12	18	36	52
Goole Town	42	7	4	10	28	28	6	8	7	30	34	51
Oswestry Town	42	7	7	7	35	38	7	1	13	20	45	50
Rhyl	42	7	8	6	36	34	3	7	11	20	40	45
Worksop Town	42	6	9	6	35	33	3	4	14	21	41	40
Gainsborough Trinity	42	5	4	12	25	38	4	6	11	28	39	37
*Workington	42	4	9	8	21	29	1	5	15	17	41	28
*Horwich RMI	42	2	6	13	23	38	1	6	14	13	47	20

* One point deducted for breach of rule.

SOUTHERN LEAGUE

		Home					Away					
Premier Division	P	W	D	L	F	A	W	D	L	F	A	Pts
Fisher Athletic	42	14	5	2	41	15	11	6	4	31	14	86
Bromsgrove Rovers	42	11	6	4	44	22	13	5	3	38	19	83
Aylesbury United	42	15	4	2	46	19	9	7	5	26	21	83
Dartford	42	12	6	3	52	20	7	6	8	24	23	69
Chelmsford City	42	13	4	4	26	14	4	9	8	22	31	64
Cambridge City	42	8	10	3	38	29	6	10	5	30	23	62
Redditch United	42	7	10	4	29	24	9	4	8	30	30	62
Alvechurch	42	13	4	4	40	25	5	4	12	26	37	62
Corby Town	42	10	8	3	36	15	4	9	8	29	36	59
Worcester City	42	9	6	6	38	22	7	5	9	24	33	59
Shepshed Charterhouse	42	9	6	6	36	23	7	4	10	23	36	58
Bedworth United	42	11	4	6	36	23	4	8	9	19	28	57
Crawley Town	42	8	4	9	30	31	6	7	8	29	29	53
Fareham Town	42	7	11	3	41	21	4	6	11	17	28	50
Willenhall Town	42	8	6	7	33	24	5	5	11	15	33	50
Basingstoke Town	42	10	6	5	32	30	2	6	13	21	48	48
Witney Town	42	10	4	7	19	19	2	8	11	10	37	48
Gosport Borough	42	8	4	9	22	23	3	9	9	20	34	36
Salisbury	42	7	5	9	31	36	5	2	14	21	46	43
King's Lynn	42	9	5	7	27	20	0	8	13	21	52	40
Dudley Town	42	5	6	10	19	25	4	3	14	20	51	36
Folkestone	42	5	9	7	24	28	3	2	16	12	51	35

Division One Midland												
VS Rugby	38	15	1	3	47	19	10	4	5	34	24	80
Leicester United	38	17	0	2	54	17	9	1	9	35	32	79
Merthyr Tydfil	38	13	1	5	62	30	10	5	4	33	24	75
Moor Green	38	10	3	6	32	23	12	3	4	41	32	72
Halesowen Town	38	9	9	1	32	18	10	3	6	40	32	69
Hednesford Town	38	12	3	4	51	23	9	2	8	33	33	68
Gloucester City	38	10	3	6	48	31	9	2	8	29	28	62
Coventry Sporting	38	8	4	7	26	27	9	4	6	29	27	59

		Home					Away					
	P	W	D	L	F	A	W	D	L	F	A	Pts
Forest Green Rovers	38	10	5	4	44	24	6	4	9	21	29	57
Stourbridge	38	10	2	7	32	29	6	5	8	24	27	55
Grantham	38	9	4	6	43	23	6	5	8	31	31	54
Banbury United	38	8	3	8	36	28	6	4	9	19	37	49
Buckingham Town	38	7	4	8	31	27	6	5	8	24	32	48
Bridgnorth Town	38	9	2	8	33	24	3	7	9	26	39	45
Wellingborough Town	38	7	5	7	26	26	6	1	12	29	50	45
Mile Oak Rovers	38	6	6	7	28	26	5	4	10	22	37	43
Sutton Coldfield Town	38	4	5	10	29	39	4	5	10	27	39	34
Bilston Town	38	2	5	12	12	31	6	2	11	25	45	31
Leamington	38	3	6	10	22	36	1	7	11	15	44	25
Rushden Town	38	1	6	12	20	58	0	4	15	22	66	13
Division One South												
Dorchester Town	38	12	4	3	40	18	11	4	4	43	24	77
Ashford Town	38	11	5	3	30	11	12	2	5	33	21	76
Woodford Town	38	15	1	3	46	16	7	5	8	26	28	72
Hastings Town	38	12	6	1	41	23	8	4	7	33	31	70
Dover Athletic	38	12	1	6	37	16	8	5	6	29	27	66
Gravesend & Northfleet	38	12	2	5	41	19	6	5	8	26	27	61
Tonbridge AFC	38	10	3	6	42	33	6	7	6	31	34	58
Erith & Belvedere	38	8	6	5	35	27	7	6	6	22	23	57
Chatham Town	38	8	4	7	30	24	8	5	6	23	22	57
Thanet United	38	9	6	4	38	26	5	8	6	18	24	56
Waterlooville	38	10	4	5	39	27	6	4	9	27	38	56
Trowbridge Town	38	8	5	6	44	30	7	4	8	33	35	54
Dunstable	38	5	8	6	30	26	8	1	10	30	31	48
Corinthian	38	7	5	7	33	35	4	7	8	23	30	45
Sheppey United	38	5	8	6	19	21	4	4	11	24	44	39
Andover	38	3	5	11	24	43	6	4	9	27	37	36
Burnham & Hillingdon	38	3	5	11	13	28	4	6	9	19	34	32
Poole Town	38	6	2	11	33	40	2	4	13	17	50	30
Ruislip	38	1	8	10	14	33	5	4	10	21	42	30
Canterbury Town	38	5	3	11	22	33	3	2	14	24	49	29

NORTHERN COUNTIES EAST

Premier Division	P	W	D	L	F	A	Pts
Alfreton Town	36	25	6	5	74	29	81
Farsley Celtic	36	24	6	6	74	41	78
North Ferriby	36	20	10	6	57	26	70
Emley	36	17	10	9	60	41	61
Sutton Town	36	17	10	9	54	45	61
Denaby United	36	15	10	11	59	43	55
Thackley	36	14	13	9	47	45	55
Pontefract Colls	36	16	6	14	54	44	54
Harrogate Town	36	14	10	12	48	48	52
Bridlington Town	36	12	14	10	57	49	50
Long Eaton United	36	12	11	13	41	43	47
Armthorpe Welfare	36	13	6	17	55	60	45
Eastwood Town	36	11	9	16	45	57	42
Bentley VW	36	10	9	17	64	77	39
Belper Town	36	8	12	16	49	47	36
Guiseley	36	9	8	19	46	76	35
Bridlington Trinity	36	6	11	19	46	76	29
Brigg Town	36	6	9	21	35	73	27
Boston	36	6	4	26	23	68	22

NORTH WEST COUNTIES LEAGUE

Division One	P	W	D	L	F	A	Pts
Stalybridge Celtic	38	25	8	5	74	39	58
Accrington Stanley	38	19	15	4	63	32	53
Clitheroe	38	20	12	6	76	47	52
Kirkby Town	38	22	4	12	71	48	48
Bootle	38	19	10	9	52	38	48
St Helens Town	38	19	9	10	65	37	47
Winsford United	38	19	8	11	55	39	46
Fleetwood Town	38	16	13	9	61	49	45
Penrith	38	16	10	12	62	59	42
Rossendale United	38	14	11	13	66	59	39
Congleton Town	38	13	11	14	38	39	37
Burscough	38	11	11	16	58	54	33
Leyland Motors	38	13	7	18	52	56	33
Eastwood Hanley	38	10	11	17	40	50	31
Radcliffe Borough	38	11	8	19	46	57	30
Leek Town	38	9	12	17	42	55	30
Netherfield	38	12	5	21	45	73	29
Irlam Town	38	4	13	21	36	74	21
Curzon Ashton	38	4	12	22	35	78	20
Glossop	38	5	8	25	33	87	18

NORTHERN COUNTIES EAST

Division One

	P	W	D	L	F	A	Pts
Ossett Albion	34	22	4	8	65	43	70
Rowntree Mckintosh	34	20	4	10	101	54	64
Hatfield Main	34	19	7	8	69	47	64
Harrogate Railway	34	19	7	8	65	44	64
Bradley Rangers	34	17	8	9	64	51	59
Hallam	34	16	8	10	49	37	56
Staveley	34	14	9	11	51	46	51
York RI	34	15	5	14	49	56	50
Maltby MW	34	13	7	14	53	57	46
Pilkington Recs	34	13	6	15	51	49	45
Garforth Town	34	11	10	13	44	48	43
Grimthorpe MW	34	13	4	17	60	65	43
Woolley MW	34	11	9	14	57	61	42
Kiveton Park	34	11	6	17	41	64	39
Parkgate	34	10	8	16	51	57	38
Mexborough Town	34	8	10	16	38	64	34
Sheffield	34	9	6	19	41	55	33
Dronfield United	34	4	4	26	33	84	16

Division Two

	P	W	D	L	F	A	Pts
Frecheville CA	34	24	7	3	57	27	79
Eccleshill United	34	22	6	6	75	36	72
Immingham Town	34	18	4	12	53	43	58
Hall Road Rangers	34	16	9	9	72	48	57
Collingham	34	14	13	7	67	34	55
Worsbro Bridge MW	34	15	7	12	61	48	52
Stockbridge PS	34	12	15	7	50	38	51
Selby Town	34	14	8	12	47	42	50

NORTH WEST COUNTIES LEAGUE

Division Two

	P	W	D	L	F	A	Pts
Droylsden	34	20	8	6	79	42	48
Warrington Town	34	16	13	5	48	34	45
Ashton United	34	19	6	9	73	45	44
Wren Rovers	34	18	8	8	65	39	44
Colwyn Bay	34	17	9	8	61	43	43
Darwen	34	15	8	11	45	47	38
Chadderton	34	14	9	11	52	47	37
Colne Dynamoes	34	14	8	12	57	44	36
Skelmersdale United	34	13	10	11	52	53	36
Ellesmere Port & N	34	15	5	14	68	54	35
Formby	34	13	7	14	54	55	33
Blackpool Mech	34	12	8	14	56	64	32
Lancaster City	32	12	7	15	55	53	31
Prescot Cables	34	12	6	16	46	48	28*
Great Harwood Tn	34	9	8	17	36	59	24*
Oldham Town	34	7	9	18	38	57	23
Atherton LR	34	8	5	21	32	61	21
Salford	34	1	8	25	17	89	10

Division Three

	P	W	D	L	F	A	Pts
Atherton Collieries	24	16	4	4	46	22	36
Flixton	24	15	5	4	58	29	35
Maghull	24	14	2	8	44	29	30
Nelson	24	12	6	6	37	29	30
Newton	24	11	5	8	42	36	27
Ford Motors	24	9	8	7	38	27	26
Bacup Borough	24	10	6	8	27	27	26
Cheadle Town	24	9	5	10	33	44	23

GREAT MILLS FOOTBALL LEAGUE

Premier Division

	P	W	D	L	F	A	Pts
Saltash United	42	31	8	3	101	40	70
Exmouth Town	42	22	10	10	82	63	54
Bristol City	42	23	5	14	94	57	51
Liskeard Athletic	42	20	9	13	68	46	49
Bristol Manor Farm	42	19	10	13	58	46	48
Bideford	42	21	4	17	59	57	46
Plymouth Argyle*	42	21	4	17	92	56	45
Taunton Town	42	17	9	16	61	64	43
Chippenham Town	42	14	14	14	53	50	42
Mangotsfield United	42	17	8	17	71	71	42
Barnstaple Town	42	15	12	15	56	66	42
Clevedon Town	42	14	13	15	58	60	41
Weston-super-Mare	42	13	13	13	66	69	39
Dawlish Town	42	14	10	18	63	62	38
Torrington	42	14	10	18	61	69	38
Paulton Rovers	42	14	8	20	56	72	36
Radstock Town	42	11	13	18	55	73	35
Melksham Town	41	10	15	16	39	62	35
Frome Town	42	12	10	20	50	65	34
Clandon	42	12	10	20	40	59	34
Minehead	42	10	12	20	54	87	32
Chard Town	42	11	7	24	49	89	29

NENE GROUP UNITED COUNTIES LEAGUE

Premier Division

	P	W	D	L	F	A	Pts
Potton United	40	16	2	2	65	17	15
Baldock Town	40	14	2	4	44	17	14
Stotfield	40	14	2	4	35	20	10
Irthlingborough	40	9	4	7	35	38	12
Stewart & Lloyds C	40	11	4	5	44	24	11
Raunds Town	40	12	3	5	48	25	9
Spalding T	40	9	7	4	33	21	10
Holbeach U	40	12	3	5	40	19	6
Long Buckby	40	11	4	5	46	31	9
Stamford	40	5	8	6	18	21	9
Brackley T	40	9	5	6	41	25	6
Northampton S	40	9	5	6	41	28	6
Desborough T	40	8	5	7	32	34	8
Wootton B C	40	7	4	9	31	41	7
Arlesey T	40	7	3	10	27	36	5
Kempston R	40	3	8	9	19	23	7
Eynesbury R	40	4	2	14	22	43	6
Rothwell T	40	4	4	12	29	42	4
St Neots T	40	1	8	11	13	32	3
Bourne Town	40	5	3	12	24	43	3
Ampthill T	40	1	1	18	17	68	0

MIDLAND FOOTBALL COMBINATION

Premier Division	P	W	D	L	F	A	Pts
Stratford Town	38	23	13	2	81	29	59
Paget Rangers	38	24	9	5	98	30	57
Racing Club Wck	38	24	8	6	93	29	56
Boldmere St Mich'ls	38	22	11	5	73	32	55
West Mids Police	38	14	16	8	65	51	44
Northfield Town	38	15	10	13	57	46	40
Solihull Borough	38	13	13	12	58	69	39
Walsall Wood	38	16	6	16	54	62	38
Highgate United	38	15	7	16	50	49	37
Ashtre Highfield	38	15	6	17	47	59	36
Polesworth Nth Wck	38	13	10	15	51	64	36
Princes End United	38	14	8	16	51	69	36
Evesham United	38	10	11	17	62	75	31
Knowle	38	11	8	19	51	66	30
Kings Heath	38	9	12	17	36	52	30
Bloxwich	38	12	5	21	56	73	29
Southam United	38	9	11	18	42	75	29
Coleshill Town	38	11	5	22	49	81	27
Studley Sporting	38	9	8	21	43	78	26
Bolehall Swifts	38	7	11	21	46	84	25

BANK'S BREWERY WEST MIDLANDS LEAGUE

Premier Division	P	W	D	L	F	A	Pts
Atherstone United	38	29	4	5	115	30	62
Oldbury United	38	28	5	5	89	28	61
Wednesfield Social	38	26	5	7	80	32	57
Gresley Rovers	38	23	11	4	73	39	57
Tamworth	38	21	4	13	103	47	46
Malvern Town	38	20	6	12	74	51	46
Halesowen Harriers	38	19	6	13	75	51	44
Hinckley Athletic	38	18	6	14	70	67	42
Chasetown	38	12	15	11	64	63	39
Harrisons	38	15	8	15	60	56	38
GKN Sankey	38	13	12	13	73	69	38
Rushall Olympic	38	13	8	17	60	63	34
Lye Town	38	12	9	17	41	56	33
Brereton Social	38	14	5	19	61	80	33
Tividale	38	12	8	18	54	71	32
Wolverhampton Utd	38	11	8	19	44	63	30
Oldswinford	38	7	8	23	49	93	22
Tipton Town	38	5	8	25	37	109	18
Armitage	38	5	5	28	37	113	15
Blakenall	38	4	5	29	38	116	13

GREENE KING SPARTAN LEAGUE

Premier Division	P	W	D	L	F	A	Pts
Yeading	32	26	6	0	102	20	84
Redhill	32	22	5	5	60	23	71
Brimsdown Rov	32	17	8	7	53	26	59
Edgware	32	17	5	10	56	37	56
Southgate Ath	32	14	11	7	62	36	53
Waltham Abbey	32	14	8	10	48	40	50
Northwood	32	14	7	11	35	32	46
Pennant	32	11	10	11	50	43	43

HALL'S BREWERY HELLENIC LEAGUE

Premier Division	P	W	D	L	F	A	Pts
Abingdon Town	34	26	6	2	85	27	84
Hounslow	34	25	2	7	73	42	77
Shortwood United	34	20	6	8	79	38	66
Viking Sports	34	17	4	13	67	51	55
Sharpness	34	15	6	13	72	52	51
Abingdon United	34	14	9	11	49	37	51
Morris Motors	34	11	14	9	43	40	47
Moreton Town	34	13	8	13	47	49	47
Penhill	34	12	10	12	50	49	46
Yate Town	34	11	12	11	53	46	45
Supermarine	34	12	5	17	37	51	41
Pegasus Juniors	34	10	10	14	53	56	40
Rayners Lane	34	9	12	13	35	45	39
Bicester Town	34	8	11	15	31	50	35
Fairford Town	34	9	8	17	39	77	35
Wallingford Town	34	10	4	20	42	64	34
Thame United	34	9	7	18	50	84	34
Wantage Town	34	5	6	23	26	73	21

BUILDING SCENE EASTERN COUNTIES

	P	W	D	L	F	A	Pts
Sudbury Town	44	29	9	6	113	43	67
Braintree Town	44	28	9	7	106	49	65
Bury Town	44	26	10	8	114	52	62
March Town United	44	28	6	10	80	45	62
Tiptree United	44	24	12	8	82	50	60
Great Yarmouth Tn	44	22	13	9	70	33	57
Colchester United R	44	19	11	14	82	58	49
Watton United	44	18	12	14	77	71	48
Lowestoft Town	44	15	17	12	53	53	47
Stowmarket Town	44	18	10	16	84	66	46
Wisbech Town	44	17	12	15	72	60	46
Clacton Town	44	14	18	12	60	61	46
Haverhill Rovers	44	13	15	16	60	57	41
Harwich & Parkeston	44	15	9	20	70	76	39
Chatteris Town	44	16	7	21	62	82	39
Newmarket Town	44	12	13	19	43	62	37
Felixstowe Town	44	12	11	21	56	92	35
Gorleston	44	11	11	22	73	101	33
Brantham Athletic	44	10	10	24	59	92	30
Soham Town Rngrs	44	11	7	26	62	112	29
Histon	44	8	11	25	47	88	27
Ely City	44	11	4	29	44	102	26
Thetford Town	44	4	13	27	33	97	21

SOUTH MIDLANDS LEAGUE

Premier Division	P	W	D	L	F	A	Pts
Selby	30	21	4	5	67	29	67
Shillington	30	19	6	5	53	25	63
Hoddesdon Town	30	18	5	7	61	39	59
Milton Keynes Bor	30	14	8	8	55	40	50
Winslow United	30	13	10	7	56	38	49
Totternhoe	30	15	4	11	45	36	49
The 61 FC (Luton)	30	13	8	9	49	35	47
Pirton	30	12	8	10	50	43	44

ESSEX LEAGUE

Senior Division	P	W	D	L	F	A	Pts
Canvey Island	32	22	4	6	62	32	70
Witham Town	32	19	6	7	58	22	63
Purfleet	32	18	7	7	83	40	61
Bowers United	32	17	7	8	62	33	58
East Thurrock Utd	32	15	10	7	62	45	55
Burnham Ramblers	32	14	9	9	49	36	51
Woodford	32	14	9	9	50	38	51
Sawbridgeworth Tn	32	14	5	13	53	57	47

DAN AIR COMBINED COUNTIES LEAGUE

Premier Division	P	W	D	L	F	A	Pts
Ash United	34	24	6	4	72	26	78
Farnham Town	34	23	3	8	80	37	72
Malden Vale	34	21	6	7	76	41	69
Chipstead	34	18	9	7	59	37	63
B Aerospace (Wey)	34	17	7	10	55	41	58
Merstham	34	17	6	11	63	37	57
Godalming Town	34	16	9	9	55	37	57
Hartley Wintney	34	16	8	10	63	43	56

HERTS SENIOR COUNTY LEAGUE

Premier Division	P	W	D	L	F	A	Pts
London Colney	30	21	8	1	92	34	71
J & M Sports	30	17	7	6	59	38	58
Bedmond Social	30	16	9	5	57	28	57
St Margaretsbury	30	14	7	9	74	48	49
Mount Grace P B	30	15	4	11	56	50	49
Cockfosters	30	14	6	10	60	48	48
Park Street	30	14	5	11	51	44	47
Sandridge Rovers	30	15	1	14	63	61	46

WESSEX LEAGUE

	P	W	D	L	F	A	Pts
Bashley	32	24	3	5	71	30	75
Road Sea	32	22	7	3	70	26	73
AFC Totton	32	20	7	5	62	21	67
Newport	32	15	8	9	51	36	53
Havant Town	32	15	7	10	57	48	52
Thatcham Town	32	15	6	11	53	33	51
Wellworthy Athletic	32	14	6	12	48	50	48
Eastleigh	32	14	6	12	40	42	48

WINSTONLEAD KENT LEAGUE

Division One	P	W	D	L	F	A	Pts
Greenwich Boro	34	24	6	4	113	36	78
Crockenhill	34	22	9	3	63	31	75
Alma Swanley	34	20	7	7	69	34	67
Ramsgate	34	18	8	8	59	42	62
Herne Bay	34	17	9	8	76	58	60
Sittingbourne	34	17	8	9	60	43	59
Tunbridge Wells	34	14	8	12	56	45	50
Whitstable Town	34	14	8	12	45	47	50

SUSSEX COUNTY LEAGUE

Division One	P	W	D	L	F	A	Pts
Arundel	30	20	5	5	83	39	65
Whitehawk	30	19	6	5	56	24	63
Haywards Heath	30	18	5	7	63	39	59
Three Bridges	30	18	4	8	67	41	58
Eastbourne Town	30	15	11	4	56	23	56
Littlehampton Town	30	14	7	9	49	33	49
Peacehaven & Tels	30	13	7	10	49	61	46
Shoreham	30	12	8	10	41	42	44

DRYBROUGH'S NORTHERN LEAGUE

First Division	P	W	D	L	F	A	Pts
Blyth Spartans	38	29	7	2	87	36	94
Bishop Auckland	38	26	2	10	96	42	80
Spennymoor United	38	20	13	5	89	41	73
Newcastle Blue Star	38	20	11	7	74	34	71
Whitley Bay	38	19	9	10	74	53	66
North Shields	38	18	10	10	65	47	64
Gretna	38	17	10	11	73	57	61
South Bank	38	16	12	10	59	36	60

VAUXHALL WEARSIDE LEAGUE

	P	W	D	L	F	A	Pts
Annfield Plain	38	27	5	6	104	38	86
Murton	38	27	4	7	71	35	85
Sporting Club Vaux	38	24	6	8	82	39	78
Whickham	38	22	7	9	76	39	73
Hartlepool BWOB	38	21	9	8	75	42	72
Eppleton CW	38	21	5	12	79	47	68
Marske United	38	18	9	11	67	47	63
Coundon TT	38	15	14	9	67	46	59

1987-88

The newly introduced promotion/relegation system between the Conference and the Football League received its ultimate vindication when Lincoln City won an immediate return to the Fourth Division. No longer would League clubs need to dread losing their status; Lincoln's attendances swelled considerably during their year's exile, and their title-clinching victory over Wycombe Wanderers was watched by a Conference record crowd of over 9,000. For a second consecutive season Barnet were the unlucky side to miss out on the title and promotion by just one place.

The FA Vase heralded the emergence of two major forces. First Colne Dynamoes, who won the competition in only their second season of entry. In the final they beat Emley, semi-finalists the previous year, in extra-time. The Dynamoes, still managed by their original founder Graham White, were rapidly proving the effectiveness of the Pyramid in North West England; winning the North West Counties League earned them promotion to the newly formed First Division of the Northern Premier League, a Division they were to win at the first attempt. The other surprise package were Bashley, a club from a tiny village in the New Forest. They encapsulated the real spirit of the Vase by battling through to the Semi-Finals where they lost to Emley.

Just as in 1986-87 the FA Trophy burst to life in a replay at West Bromwich after a dull first game at Wembley. Enfield claimed their second success in the competition by beating Telford United by the odd goal in five.

SUMMARY

FA VASE	**Winners**	**Runners Up**	**Semi-finalists**
	Colne Dynamoes	Emley	Sudbury Town, Bashley
FA TROPHY	**Winners**	**Runners-up**	**Semi-finalists**
	Enfield	Telford United	Barrow, Wokingham Town

FA CUP   **Most Successful Team: Sutton United**
1st Rd: Sutton 3 Aldershot 0; 2nd Rd: Peterborough 1 Sutton 3; 3rd Rd: Sutton 1 Middlesbrough 1; 3rd Rd Replay: Middlesbrough 1 Sutton 0 (AET)

GM VAUXHALL CONFERENCE   Champions: Lincoln City   Runners Up: Barnet

GM VAUXHALL CONFERENCE STATISTICS

Top Crowds
9432	Lincoln City v Wycombe Wanderers (2.5.88)
7542	Lincoln City v Boston United (4.4.88)
5822	Boston United v Lincoln City (26.12.87)
5143	Barnet v Runcorn (30.4.88)
4892	Lincoln City v Maidstone United (27.4.88)

Top Scorers
24	Paul Davies (Kidderminster)
24	Steve Norris (Telford)
24	Phil Derbyshire (Stafford)

Manager of the Month Awards
Sep	Fry (Barnet)
Oct	Murphy (Lincoln) & Buckley (Kettering)
Nov	King (Runcorn)
Dec	Wragg (Macclesfield)
Jan	Murphy (Lincoln)
Feb	McCluskey (Enfield)
Mar	Buckley (Kettering
Apr	King (Runcorn)

GM VAUXHALL CONFERENCE

		Home					Away					
	P	W	D	L	F	A	W	D	L	F	A	Pts
Lincoln C	42	16	4	1	53	13	8	6	7	33	35	82
Barnet	42	15	4	2	57	23	8	7	6	36	22	80
Kettering T	42	13	5	3	37	20	9	4	8	31	28	75
Runcorn	42	14	4	3	42	20	7	7	7	26	27	74
Telford United	42	11	5	5	33	23	9	5	7	32	27	70
Stafford Rangers	42	12	4	5	43	25	8	5	8	36	33	69
Kidderminster H	42	11	8	2	42	28	7	7	7	33	38	69
Sutton United	42	9	8	4	41	25	7	10	4	36	29	66
Maidstone United	42	8	5	8	38	33	10	4	7	41	31	63
Weymouth	42	13	7	1	33	13	5	2	14	20	30	63
Macclesfield T	42	10	5	6	36	27	8	4	9	28	35	63
Enfield	42	8	5	8	35	34	7	5	9	33	44	55
Cheltenham T	42	6	11	4	36	32	5	9	7	28	35	53
Altrincham	42	11	5	5	41	21	3	5	13	18	38	52
Fisher Athletic	42	8	7	6	28	23	5	6	10	30	38	52
Boston United	42	9	5	7	33	25	5	2	14	27	50	49
Northwich Vic	42	8	6	7	30	25	2	11	8	16	32	47
Wycombe Wanderers	42	8	5	8	32	43	3	8	10	18	33	46
Welling United	42	8	4	9	33	32	3	5	13	17	40	42
Bath C	42	7	5	9	27	32	2	5	14	21	44	37
Wealdstone	42	3	11	7	20	33	2	6	13	19	43	32
Dagenham	42	4	3	14	20	46	1	3	17	17	58	21

BEAZER HOMES (SOUTHERN) LEAGUE

Premier Division	P	W	D	L	F	A	Pts
Aylesbury United	42	27	8	7	79	35	89
Dartford	42	27	8	7	79	39	89
Cambridge City	42	24	8	10	84	43	80
Bromsgrove Rovers	42	22	11	9	65	39	77
Worcester City	42	22	6	14	58	48	72
Crawley Town	42	17	14	11	73	63	65
Alvechurch	42	17	13	12	54	52	64
Leicester United	42	15	14	13	68	59	59
Fareham Town	42	16	11	15	51	59	59
Corby Town	42	16	8	18	61	64	56
Dorchester Town	42	14	14	14	51	57	56
Ashford Town	42	12	16	14	45	54	52
Shepshed Charter	42	13	11	18	53	62	50
Bedworth United	42	12	14	16	49	64	50
Gosport Borough	42	10	17	15	39	49	47
Burton Albion	42	11	14	17	62	74	47
VS Rugby	42	10	16	16	52	57	46
Redditch United	42	10	13	19	55	63	43
Chelmsford City	42	11	10	21	60	75	43
Willenhall Town	42	9	12	21	39	76	39
Nuneaton Borough	42	8	13	21	58	77	37
Witney Town	42	8	11	23	45	71	35

Division One Mid	P	W	D	L	F	A	Pts
Merthyr Tydfil	42	30	4	8	102	40	94
Moor Green	42	26	8	8	91	49	86
Grantham Town	42	27	4	11	97	53	85
Atherstone United	42	22	10	10	93	56	76
Sutton Coldfield Tn	42	22	6	14	71	47	72
Halesowen Town	42	18	15	9	75	59	69
Gloucester City	42	18	14	10	86	62	68
Dudley Town	42	20	5	17	64	55	65
Forest Green Rovers	42	14	16	12	67	54	58
Banbury United	42	17	7	18	48	46	58
Buckingham Town	42	16	7	19	59	75	55
Bridgnorth Town	42	15	9	18	74	75	54
Kings Lynn	42	16	6	20	53	63	54
Wellingborough Tn	42	14	10	18	67	70	52
Rushden Town	42	14	9	19	69	85	51
Trowbridge Town	42	14	3	25	53	82	45
Bilston Town	42	12	8	22	52	87	44
Hednesford Town	42	11	10	21	50	81	43
Mile Oak Rovers	42	9	14	19	43	65	41
Coventry Sporting	42	11	8	23	46	83	41
Stourbridge	42	10	10	22	46	79	40
Paget Rangers	42	10	9	23	49	89	39

BEAZER HOMES (SOUTHERN) LEAGUE

Division One South	P	W	D	L	F	A	Pts
Dover Athletic	40	28	10	2	81	28	94
Waterlooville	40	27	10	3	88	33	91
Salisbury	40	24	11	5	71	33	83
Gravesend & Nthflt	40	20	12	8	60	32	72
Thanet United	40	17	13	10	60	38	64
Andover	40	17	13	10	64	58	64
Dunstable	40	17	12	11	78	56	63
Burnham	40	17	10	13	61	45	61
Bury Town	40	17	7	16	80	67	58
Erith & Belvedere	40	16	9	15	52	56	57
Sheppey United	40	14	10	16	58	52	52

	P	W	D	L	F	A	Pts
Hastings Town	40	14	10	16	62	70	52
Tonbridge AFC	40	14	8	18	51	56	50
Poole Town	40	13	10	17	69	70	49
Baldock Town	40	12	12	16	44	53	48
Hounslow	40	11	8	21	41	76	41
Folkestone	40	9	11	20	47	76	38
Corinthian	40	9	10	21	49	67	37
Ruislip	40	5	13	22	33	80	28
Canterbury Town	40	7	6	27	33	87	27
Chatham Town	40	7	5	28	39	88	26

VAUXHALL-OPEL LEAGUE

Premier Division	P	W	D	L	F	A	Pts
Yeovil Town	42	24	9	9	66	34	81
Bromley	42	23	7	12	68	40	76
Slough Town	42	21	9	12	67	41	72
Leytonstone Ilford	42	20	11	11	59	43	71
Wokingham Town	42	21	7	14	62	52	70
Hayes	42	20	9	13	62	48	69
Windsor & Eton	42	16	17	9	59	43	65
Farnborough Town	42	17	11	14	63	60	62
Carshalton Athletic	42	16	13	13	49	41	61
Hendon	42	16	12	14	62	58	60
Tooting & Mitcham	42	15	14	13	57	59	59
Harrow Borough	42	15	11	16	53	58	56
Bishop's Stortford	42	15	10	17	55	58	55
Kingstonian	42	14	12	16	47	53	54
St Albans City	42	15	6	21	60	69	51
Bognor Regis Town	42	14	9	19	41	57	51
Leyton-Wingate	42	14	8	20	58	64	50
Croydon	42	11	13	18	40	52	46
Barking	42	11	12	19	44	57	45
Dulwich Hamlet	42	10	11	21	46	64	41
Hitchin Town	42	10	8	24	46	79	38
Basingstoke Town	42	6	17	19	37	71	35

Division One	P	W	D	L	F	A	Pts
Marlow	42	32	5	5	100	44	101
Grays Athletic	42	30	10	2	74	25	100
Woking	42	25	7	10	91	52	82
Boreham Wood	42	21	9	12	65	45	72
Staines Town	42	19	11	12	71	48	68
Wembley	42	18	11	13	54	46	65
Basildon United	42	18	9	15	65	58	63
Walton & Hersham	42	15	16	11	53	44	61
Hampton	42	17	10	15	59	54	61
Leatherhead	42	16	11	15	64	53	59
Southwick	42	13	12	17	59	63	51
Oxford City	42	13	12	17	70	77	51
Worthing	42	14	8	20	67	73	50
Kingsbury Town	42	11	17	14	62	69	50
Walthamstow Ave	42	13	11	18	53	63	50
Lewes	42	12	13	17	83	77	49
Uxbridge	42	11	18	15	41	47	49
Chesham United	42	12	10	20	69	77	46
Bracknell Town	42	12	9	21	54	80	45
Billericay Town	42	11	11	20	58	88	44
Stevenage Borough	42	11	9	22	36	64	42
Wolverton Tn (MK)	42	3	3	36	23	124	12

Division Two North	P	W	D	L	F	A	Pts
Wivenhoe Town	42	26	10	6	105	42	88
Collier Row	42	22	13	7	71	39	79
Tilbury	42	18	15	9	61	40	69
Berkhamsted Town	42	19	12	11	71	53	69
Harlow Town	42	17	16	9	67	36	67
Ware	42	17	15	10	63	58.	66
Witham Town	42	17	14	11	69	47	65
Vauxhall Motors	42	16	17	9	56	42	65
Heybridge Swifts	42	17	13	12	56	50	64
Tring Town	42	18	6	18	69	67	60
Letchworth Gdn City	42	18	5	19	59	64	59
Finchley	42	16	10	16	67	54	58
Clapton	42	14	15	13	50	62	57
Hornchurch	42	13	15	14	56	65	54
Barton Rovers	42	13	10	19	43	60	49
Rainham Town	42	12	12	18	63	66	48
Royston	42	13	8	21	49	70	47
Saffron Walden Tn	42	13	7	22	34	67	46
Hemel Hempstead	42	11	12	19	38	71	45
Haringey Borough	42	11	8	23	54	78	41
Aveley	42	8	13	21	42	65	37
Hertford Town	42	8	4	30	45	92	28

Division Two South	P	W	D	L	F	A	Pts
Chalfont St Peter	42	26	9	7	81	35	87
Metropolitan Police	42	23	17	2	80	32	86
Dorking	42	25	11	6	86	39	86
Feltham	42	21	12	9	74	41	75
Epsom & Ewell	42	21	11	10	71	49	74
Chertsey Town	42	22	7	13	63	47	73
Whyteleafe	42	20	11	11	84	55	71
Hungerford Town	42	21	7	14	66	54	70
Ruislip Manor	42	21	5	16	74	57	68
Yeading	42	19	10	13	83	56	67
Maidenhead	42	18	12	12	69	54	66
Eastbourne United	42	18	10	14	67	57	64
Harefield United	42	18	6	18	59	60	60
Egham Town	42	12	12	18	45	45	48
Horsham	42	12	10	20	45	66	46
Suthall	42	13	7	22	45	72	46
Molesey	42	11	11	20	42	63	44
Newbury Town	42	8	13	21	40	81	37
Camberley Town	42	9	9	24	51	94	36
Flackwell Heath	42	6	8	28	42	96	26
Banstead Athletic	42	6	7	29	34	81	25
Petersfield United	42	6	7	29	45	102	25

NORTHERN PREMIER LEAGUE

Premier Division	P	Home					Away					Pts
		W	D	L	F	A	W	D	L	F	A	
Chorley	42	14	5	2	44	17	12	5	4	34	18	88
Hyde United	42	16	4	1	50	17	9	6	6	41	35	85
Caernarfon Town	42	14	4	3	34	18	8	6	7	22	16	76
Morecambe	42	11	7	3	33	17	8	8	5	28	24	72
Barrow	42	13	2	6	45	21	8	6	7	25	20	71
Worksop Town	42	12	4	5	43	24	8	7	6	31	31	71
Bangor City	42	10	6	5	40	25	10	4	7	32	30	70
Rhyl	42	10	5	6	35	18	8	8	5	35	24	67
Marine	42	12	5	4	36	18	7	5	9	31	27	67
Frickley Athletic	42	11	4	6	34	27	7	7	7	27	28	65
Witton Albion	42	9	5	7	34	24	7	7	7	27	23	60
Goole Town	42	11	4	6	42	26	6	5	10	29	35	60
Horwich	42	10	4	7	22	19	7	5	9	24	23	60
Southport	42	8	7	6	25	22	7	5	9	18	26	57
South Liverpool	42	5	9	7	31	35	5	10	6	25	29	49
Buxton	42	6	8	7	33	34	5	6	10	39	42	47
Mossley	42	6	8	7	24	29	5	3	13	30	46	44
Gateshead	42	9	4	8	31	25	2	3	16	21	46	40
Matlock Town	42	5	6	10	40	47	5	2	14	18	42	38
Gainsborough Trinity	42	5	6	10	20	36	3	4	14	18	45	34
Oswestry Town	42	5	6	10	25	44	1	4	16	19	57	28
Workington	42	4	3	14	15	44	2	0	19	13	69	21

First Division	P	W	D	L	F	A	W	D	L	F	A	Pts
Fleetwood Town	36	10	3	5	39	25	12	4	2	46	20	73
Stalybridge Celtic	36	12	3	3	41	16	10	3	5	31	26	72
Leek Town	36	11	4	3	27	16	9	6	3	36	22	70
Accrington Stanley	36	11	4	3	42	16	10	2	6	29	23	69
Farsley Celtic	36	11	3	4	34	24	7	6	5	30	24	63
Droylsden	36	10	3	5	39	29	6	7	5	24	19	58
Eastwood Hanley	36	6	6	6	27	20	8	6	4	23	17	54
Winsford United	36	6	3	9	28	26	9	3	6	31	21	51
*Congleton Town	36	5	8	5	20	20	7	8	3	23	19	51
Harrogate Town	36	7	4	7	28	26	6	5	7	23	24	48
Alfreton Town	36	7	6	5	28	24	6	2	10	25	30	47
Radcliffe Borough	36	7	7	4	43	32	4	6	8	23	30	46
Irlam Town	36	7	6	5	24	21	5	4	9	15	24	46
Penrith	36	8	3	7	32	22	3	8	7	14	29	44
Sutton Town	36	6	3	9	27	38	5	2	11	24	58	38
Lancaster City	36	4	5	9	22	33	6	1	11	23	39	36
Eastwood Town	36	2	6	10	19	30	6	4	8	26	35	34
Curzon Ashton	36	3	2	13	19	37	5	2	11	24	36	28
Netherfield	36	2	2	14	12	38	2	2	14	23	55	16

* 1 point deducted for breach of rules

BASS NORTH WEST COUNTIES LEAGUE

Division One	P	W	D	L	F	A	Pts
Colne Dynamoes	34	24	7	3	71	14	55
Rossendale United	34	24	7	3	68	23	55
Clitheroe	34	18	10	6	51	20	46
Colwyn Bay	34	20	7	7	60	42	45*
St Helens Town	34	18	6	10	61	36	42
Ellesmere Port	34	17	5	12	55	48	39
Darwen	34	14	10	10	55	45	38
Warrington Town	34	16	5	13	68	47	37
Kirkby Town	34	11	13	10	57	54	35
Burscough	34	14	7	13	45	51	35
Leyland Motors	34	10	11	13	53	53	31

	P	W	D	L	F	A	Pts
Prescot Cables	34	10	11	13	34	45	29*
Bootle	34	12	5	17	43	61	29
Formby	34	6	10	18	32	63	22
Salford	34	8	6	20	33	66	22
Skelmersdale	34	4	11	19	34	64	19
Atherton LR	34	4	7	23	31	78	15
Glossop	34	5	4	25	30	71	14

* points deducted for breach of rules

NORTHERN COUNTIES EAST LEAGUE

Premier Division	P	W	D	L	F	A	Pts
Emley	32	20	8	4	57	21	68
Armthorpe Welfare	32	21	5	6	56	36	68
Denaby United	32	19	4	9	61	46	61
Bridlington Town	32	18	5	9	63	25	59
Thackley	32	16	8	8	50	37	56
North Ferriby	32	12	11	9	49	41	47
Guiseley	32	14	5	13	52	51	47
Pontefract Colls	32	11	10	11	42	42	43
Grimethorpe MW	32	11	9	12	46	49	42
Hallam	32	11	6	15	48	53	39
Hatfield Main	32	11	6	15	52	59	39
Harrogate Railway	32	9	9	14	40	56	36
Bridlington Trinity	32	8	9	15	52	68	33
Long Eaton United	32	9	6	17	24	44	33
Brigg Town	32	8	8	16	40	57	32
Belper Town	32	5	12	15	32	52	27
Ossett Albion	32	4	9	19	31	58	21

BANKS'S BREWERY WEST MIDLANDS LEAGUE

Premier Division	P	W	D	L	F	A	Pts
Tamworth	34	27	3	4	98	31	57
Oldbury United	34	25	6	3	91	39	56
Lye Town	34	22	8	4	65	27	52
Gresley Rovers	34	20	10	4	74	36	50
Chasetown	34	22	4	8	74	40	48
Halesowen H	34	18	6	10	66	40	42
Malvern Town	34	15	6	13	59	47	36
Wednesfield Social	34	14	7	13	43	43	35
Rushall Olympic	34	13	7	14	43	44	33
Hinckley Athletic	34	11	9	14	58	58	31
Harrisons	34	13	5	16	54	61	31
Blakenhall	34	11	7	16	42	49	29
Tividale	34	11	5	18	40	68	27
Westfields	34	10	6	18	60	64	26
Tipton Town	34	7	9	18	38	56	23
GKN Sankey	34	7	7	20	46	73	21
Wolverhampton U	34	4	4	26	25	88	12
Oldswinford	34	1	1	32	16	128	3

JEWSON EASTERN COUNTIES LEAGUE

	P	W	D	L	F	A	Pts
March Town United	42	28	11	3	92	33	67
Braintree Town	42	27	110	5	96	34	64
Sudbury Town	42	26	11	5	94	44	63
Great Yarmouth Tn	42	22	10	10	53	31	54
Histon	42	21	9	12	63	52	51
Wisbech Town	42	18	13	11	62	41	49
Chatteris Town	42	18	9	15	64	60	45
Lowestoft Town	42	16	12	14	72	68	44
Watton United	42	18	7	17	51	62	43
Haverhill Rovers	42	16	10	16	58	51	42
Tiptree United	42	13	15	14	50	49	39*
Clacton Town	42	15	8	19	54	66	38
Harwich & Parkeston	42	14	10	18	47	61	38
Colchester Utd Res	42	12	13	17	61	52	37
Newmarket Town	42	12	13	17	49	58	37
Thetford Town	42	14	7	21	70	82	35
Felixstowe Town	42	12	11	19	64	76	35
Gorleston	42	13	7	22	56	95	31*
Stowmarket Town	42	10	10	22	44	66	30
Brantham Athletic	42	11	6	25	50	93	28
Soham Town Rngrs	42	8	10	24	42	78	26
Ely City	42	7	10	25	34	74	24

* Two points deducted for playing an unregistered player.

MIDLAND FOOTBALL COMBINATION

Premier Division	P	W	D	L	F	A	Pts
Racing Club Wck	36	22	12	2	74	23	56
Boldmere St Mich'ls	36	22	6	8	69	30	50
Ashtree Highfield	36	20	10	6	70	44	50
Stratford Town	36	20	8	8	65	40	48
Evesham United	36	20	6	10	81	47	46
West Mids Police	36	20	3	13	77	57	43
Coleshill Town	36	16	10	10	61	41	42
Princes End United	36	16	9	11	55	55	41
Northfield Town	36	14	12	10	48	40	40
Kings Heath	36	12	12	12	45	50	36
Solihull Borough	36	14	6	16	62	65	34
Bolehall Swifts	36	11	8	17	40	53	30
Walsall Wood	36	10	9	17	51	61	29
Knowle	36	10	8	18	40	60	28
Leamington	36	8	11	17	37	59	27
Polesworth Nth Wck	36	8	8	20	53	85	24
Highgate United	36	9	6	21	44	80	24
Wilmcote	36	5	8	23	28	65	18
Bloxwich AFC	36	7	4	25	45	90	18

GREAT MILLS WESTERN LEAGUE

Premier Division	P	W	D	L	F	A	Pts
Liskeard Athletic	42	29	10	3	96	33	68
Saltash United	42	27	6	9	116	41	60
Mangotsfield United	42	25	10	7	99	38	60
Plymouth Argyle Res	42	26	8	8	105	46	60
Weston-super-Mare	42	21	8	13	81	62	50
Exmouth Town	42	19	10	13	61	55	48
Bristol City	42	16	15	11	76	53	47
Bristol Manor Farm	42	17	14	11	66	52	47*
Taunton Town	42	15	15	12	49	48	45
Bideford	42	17	9	16	60	61	43
Swanage & Herston	42	16	10	16	73	63	42
Barnstaple Town	42	17	6	19	62	72	40
Clevedon Town	42	13	12	17	42	56	38
Paulton Rovers	42	13	10	19	46	72	36
Dawlish Town	42	14	6	22	49	77	34
Radstock Town	42	13	9	20	44	57	33*
Torrington	42	12	7	23	49	83	31
Frome Town	42	9	13	20	36	69	30
Minehead	42	10	10	22	47	87	30
Chippenham Town	42	10	8	24	35	62	28
Melksham Town	42	7	14	21	45	84	28
Clandown	42	5	12	25	33	102	22

NENE GROUP UNITED COUNTIES LEAGUE

Premier Division	P	Home					Away					Pts
		W	D	L	F	A	W	D	L	F	A	
Spalding United	40	17	2	1	57	14	11	4	5	40	21	90
Rothwell Town	40	13	3	4	47	29	10	4	6	34	27	76
Raunds Town	40	11	5	4	43	24	10	3	7	29	22	71
Potton United	40	10	6	4	39	15	9	6	5	37	23	69
Stotfold	40	12	3	5	39	22	8	6	6	33	27	69
Stewart & Lloyds Corby	40	12	4	4	56	30	6	9	5	40	30	67
Desborough Town	40	10	5	5	37	23	8	4	8	34	32	63
Northampton Spencer	40	12	2	6	37	21	7	3	10	28	32	62
Arlesey Town	40	11	5	4	33	22	6	4	10	27	43	60
Long Buckby	40	9	4	7	36	34	8	4	8	34	31	59
Cogenhoe United	40	10	6	4	32	23	5	4	11	26	41	55
Stamford	40	9	6	5	32	30	4	8	8	27	36	53
Irthlingborough Diamonds	40	7	8	5	27	23	5	6	9	26	29	50
Brackley Town	40	8	4	8	29	25	6	3	11	23	32	49
Baker Perkins	40	7	7	6	44	37	5	5	10	24	33	48
Eynesbury Rovers	40	8	7	5	35	33	4	5	11	21	39	48
Wootton Blue Cross	40	7	6	7	25	26	3	5	12	16	40	41
St Neots Town	40	8	2	10	20	33	1	6	13	15	51	35
Kempston Rovers	40	5	10	5	31	34	1	5	14	15	48	33
Holbeach United	40	5	2	13	25	52	3	5	12	22	66	31
Bourne Town	40	4	6	10	22	29	2	4	14	18	42	28

FEDERATED HOMES HELLENIC LEAGUE

Premier Division	P	W	D	L	F	A	Pts
Yate Town	34	25	7	2	73	20	82
Abingdon Town	34	22	8	4	76	31	74
Shortwood United	34	20	8	6	78	45	68
Abingdon United	34	17	11	6	58	36	62
Didcot Town	34	13	12	9	55	47	51
Penhill	34	14	9	11	47	44	51
Sharpness	34	13	11	10	63	48	50
Fairford Town	34	12	10	12	44	38	46
Thame United	34	11	13	10	54	54	46
Bicester Town	34	12	8	14	42	43	44
Viking Sports	34	11	8	15	44	64	41
Moreton Town	34	11	5	18	41	57	38
Rayners Lane	34	9	8	17	42	64	35
Morris Motors	34	8	11	15	36	63	35
Supermarine	34	8	9	17	46	58	33
Bishops Cleeve	34	7	11	16	42	70	32
Pegasus Juniors	34	9	3	22	46	61	30
Wallingford T	34	5	6	23	26	69	21

WESSEX LEAGUE

	P	W	D	L	F	A	Pts
Bashley	36	26	6	4	91	26	84
Havant Town	36	24	8	4	91	31	80
Romsey Town	36	22	3	11	69	46	69
Newport	36	19	8	9	71	37	65
Christchurch	36	17	11	8	50	40	62
Wimborne Town	36	17	8	11	68	53	59
Sholing Sports	36	15	12	9	50	45	57
AFC Totton	36	16	8	12	52	37	56
E Cowes Vics	36	15	10	11	49	32	55
Bournemouth	36	14	8	14	55	38	50
Thatcham T	36	14	7	15	50	53	49
Eastleigh	36	13	8	15	36	39	47
Folland Sports	36	13	7	16	42	48	46
Horndean	36	12	9	15	52	58	45
Wellworthy Ath	36	12	8	16	46	53	44
Portsmouth RN	36	11	4	21	39	72	37
Steyning T	36	6	8	22	24	81	26
Brockenhurst	36	2	8	26	23	93	14
Lymington	36	0	7	29	27	103	7

NORTHERN COUNTIES EAST

Division One	P	W	D	L	F	A	Pts
York RI	30	22	2	6	66	29	68
Rowntree Mckintosh	30	20	5	5	74	35	65
Maltby MW	30	18	6	6	61	32	60
Parkgate	30	18	4	8	52	34	58
Bradley Rangers	30	15	9	6	64	45	54
Woolley MW	30	14	8	8	69	39	50
Eccleshill United	30	13	8	9	49	50	47
Sheffield	30	13	4	13	38	34	43

Division Two	P	W	D	L	F	A	Pts
Pickering Town	28	18	6	4	66	33	60
Collingham	28	16	9	3	63	26	57
Yorkshire Amateurs	28	16	9	3	44	23	57
Ossett Town	28	16	7	5	78	37	55
Worsborough Bridge	28	14	4	10	54	43	46
Liversedge	28	13	5	10	51	40	44
Yorkshire Main	28	11	8	9	53	58	41
Stocksbridge PS	28	11	7	10	50	37	40

SUSSEX COUNTY LEAGUE

Division One	P	W	D	L	F	A	Pts
Pagham	30	20	7	3	60	22	67
Three Bridges	30	18	7	5	59	26	61
Wick	30	18	4	8	52	40	58
Eastbourne Town	30	17	4	9	63	41	55
Whitehawk	30	15	3	12	47	31	48
Hailsham Town	30	14	6	10	46	33	48
Haywards Heath	30	11	6	13	53	51	39
Peacehaven & Tel	30	10	8	12	49	55	38

NORTH WEST COUNTIES LEAGUE

Division Two	P	W	D	L	F	A	Pts
Ashton United	42	32	6	4	107	30	70
Flixton	42	27	10	5	94	38	64
Wren Rovers	42	26	9	7	92	51	61
Newcastle Town	42	26	7	9	81	39	59
Maine Road	42	23	4	15	74	48	50
Maghull	42	18	11	13	73	66	47
Vauxhall GM	42	15	16	11	58	50	46
Atherton Collieries	42	20	6	16	63	63	46

GREENE KING SPARTAN LEAGUE

Premier Division	P	W	D	L	F	A	Pts
Edgware Town	32	20	8	4	69	32	68
Southgate Athletic	32	19	9	4	66	29	66
Southwark Sports	32	18	7	7	53	29	58+
Cheshunt	32	15	10	7	56	38	55
Brimsdown Rovers	32	16	6	10	51	38	54
Hanwell Town	32	15	6	11	38	30	51
Redhill	32	15	8	9	53	41	50+
Pennant	32	12	10	10	51	43	46

+ Three points deducted for breach of League rules.

SOUTH MIDLANDS LEAGUE

Premier Division	P	W	D	L	F	A	Pts
Shillington	32	21	7	4	48	17	70
Selby	32	21	6	5	74	35	69
Langford	32	21	3	8	58	26	66
Totternhoe	32	18	7	7	58	34	61
Hoddesdon Town	32	17	8	7	63	38	59
Leighton Town	32	16	5	11	58	38	53
The 61 FC (Luton)	32	13	9	10	54	40	48
Electrolux	32	13	6	13	42	37	45

ESSEX SENIOR LEAGUE

	P	W	D	L	F	A	Pts
Purfleet	32	23	4	5	76	24	73
Brentwood	32	22	5	5	84	36	71
Halstead Town	32	19	6	7	79	38	63
Woodford Town	32	19	6	7	61	27	63
East Thurrock Utd	32	17	7	8	73	39	58
Ford United	32	16	4	12	45	42	52
Stansted	32	15	6	11	58	45	51
Sawbridgeworth T	32	14	7	11	67	51	49

DAN AIR COMBINED COUNTIES LEAGUE

Premier Division	P	W	D	L	F	A	Pts
B Aerospace Weybr	34	22	6	6	83	43	72
Merstham	34	22	3	9	85	34	69
Farnham Town	34	20	9	5	73	33	69
Cobham	34	20	3	11	68	45	63
Godalming Town	34	16	12	6	59	32	60
Malden Town	34	18	6	10	73	50	60
Chipstead	34	14	12	8	64	40	54
Malden Vale	34	14	11	9	87	53	53

WINSTONLEAD KENT LEAGUE

Division One	P	W	D	L	F	A	Pts
Greenwich Boro	36	26	5	5	111	50	83
Faversham	36	23	7	6	92	36	76
Whitstable	36	20	8	8	57	37	68
Sittingbourne	36	17	11	8	68	53	62
Hythe Town	36	19	4	13	70	58	61
Kent Police	36	16	8	12	69	66	56
Cray Wanderers	36	16	7	13	72	51	55
Beckenham	36	16	5	15	61	55	53

HAMPSHIRE LEAGUE

Division One	P	W	D	L	F	A	Pts
B A T	34	24	7	3	88	26	55
Basing Rovers	34	22	5	7	69	29	49
Blackf'd & Langley	34	20	7	7	77	26	47
Overton United	34	17	9	8	54	36	43
Alton Town	34	16	9	9	59	41	41
Locksheath	34	17	7	10	58	41	41
Colden Common	34	14	10	10	55	40	38
ISL Midanbury	34	12	13	9	53	52	37

SKOL NORTHERN LEAGUE

Division One	P	W	D	L	F	A	Pts
Blyth Spartans	38	28	8	2	106	36	92
Newcastle Blue Star	38	28	3	7	79	33	87
Billingham Synthonia	38	23	8	7	76	41	77
Whitley Bay	38	22	9	7	60	27	75
Guisborough Town	38	18	12	8	63	41	66
Bishop Auckland	38	19	7	12	70	48	64
Gretna	38	17	6	15	69	46	57
Tow Law Town	38	16	6	16	65	72	54

VAUX WEARSIDE LEAGUE

	P	W	D	L	F	A	Pts
Whickham	38	26	9	3	82	30	87
Coundon TT	38	22	5	11	71	46	71
Eppleton CW	38	19	13	6	79	47	70
Murton	38	17	14	7	63	36	65
South Shields	38	17	11	10	78	57	62
Marske Utd	38	18	8	12	72	62	62
Reyrolles	38	18	7	13	77	49	61
Dawdon CW	38	18	6	14	85	61	60

1988-89

The GMV Conference race turned out to be a strange affair. In complete contrast to the sparkling form shown by Lincoln City in 1987-88, the relegated club this time round, Newport County, completely flopped and were already bottom by the time they folded in mid-season. Champions with surprising ease were Maidstone United who were in their first season playing at Dartford, having sold their own ground to developers. The Stones therefore gained the promotion that had been cruelly denied them four years earlier. Exile from their spiritual home, however, slightly marred the achievement.

Telford United returned to Wembley for a record fifth FA Trophy final, and made up for their disappointment of the previous season by beating Macclesfield Town. This was a repeat of the first ever Trophy final, but this time the result was reversed. The competition was enhanced by exciting giantkilling runs from semi-finalists Hyde United and Dartford.

The FA Vase produced perhaps its most glamorous final to date. The supporters of Sudbury Town and Tamworth, over 26 000 in total, created a carnival atmosphere at Wembley. The trophy eventually went to the Midlands club after a replay.

One event that will stand out for ever in the memories of Non-League supporters will be Sutton United's elimination of First Division Coventry City in the Third Round of the FA Cup. Only two years earlier, Coventry had won the competition. In the following round Sutton lost 0-8 in front of the TV cameras at Norwich City, but by then they had captured the imagination of the country.

SUMMARY

FA VASE	**Winners**	**Runners Up**	**Semi-finalists**
	Tamworth	Sudbury Town	North Ferriby United, Hungerford Town
FA TROPHY	**Winners**	**Runners-up**	**Semi-finalists**
	Telford United	Macclesfield Town	Hyde United, Dartford

FA CUP   Most Successful Teams: Kettering Town & Sutton United
1st Rd: Kettering 2 Dartford 1; 2nd Rd: Kettering 2 Bristol Rovers 1; 3rd Rd: Kettering 1 Halifax 1;
3rd Rd Replay: Halifax 2 Kettering 2; 4th Rd: Charlton Ath 2 Kettering 1
1st Rd: Dagenham 0 Sutton 4; 2nd Rd: Aylesbury 0 Sutton 1; 3rd Rd: Sutton 2 Coventry City 1;
4th Rd: Norwich 8 Sutton 0

GM VAUXHALL CONFERENCE   Champions: Maidstone United   Runners Up: Kettering Town

GM VAUXHALL CONFERENCE STATISTICS

Top Crowds
4890   Wycombe v Kettering (8.4.89)
4450   Kettering v Welling (1.4.89)
4377   Kettering v Kidderminster (25.3.89)
4247   Barnet v Enfield (2.1.89)
4239   Wycombe v Kidderminster (18.2.89)

Top Scorers
26   Steve Butler (Maidstone)
26   Mark Gall (Maidstone)
23   Chris Camden (Stafford)
23   Mark Carter (Runcorn)

Manager of the Month Awards
Sep   Wragg (Macclesfield)
Oct   Williams (Sutton)
Nov   Allner (Kidderminster)
Dec   Brigden (Welling)
Jan   Roberts (Northwich)
Feb   Kelman (Wycombe) &
          Wragg (Macclesfield)
Mar   Whitbread (Runcorn)
Apr   Still (Maidstone)

GM VAUXHALL CONFERENCE

	P	Home					Away					Pts
		W	D	L	F	A	W	D	L	F	A	
Maidstone United	40	12	5	3	48	22	13	4	3	44	24	84
Kettering Town	40	16	1	3	35	15	7	6	7	21	24	76
Boston United	40	12	3	5	36	28	10	5	5	25	23	74
Wycombe Wanderers	40	9	7	4	34	25	11	4	5	34	27	71
Kidderminster Harriers	40	10	4	6	32	32	11	2	7	36	25	69
Runcorn	40	11	3	6	39	22	8	5	7	38	31	65
Macclesfield Town	40	9	5	6	31	26	8	5	7	32	31	61
Barnet	40	11	2	7	36	30	7	5	8	28	39	61
Yeovil Town	40	8	5	7	34	30	7	6	7	34	37	56
Northwich Victoria	40	8	5	7	31	30	6	6	8	33	35	53
Welling United	40	8	6	6	27	16	6	5	9	18	30	53
Sutton United	40	10	5	5	43	26	2	10	8	21	28	51
Enfield	40	7	4	9	33	32	7	4	9	29	35	50
Altrincham	40	6	8	6	24	23	7	2	11	27	38	49
Cheltenham Town	40	7	7	6	32	29	5	5	10	23	29	48
Telford United	40	5	5	10	17	24	8	4	8	20	19	48
Chorley	40	6	4	10	26	32	7	2	11	31	39	45
Fisher Athletic	40	6	4	10	31	32	4	7	9	24	33	41
Stafford Rangers	40	7	4	9	27	32	4	3	13	22	42	40
Aylesbury United	40	7	4	9	27	30	2	5	13	16	41	36
Weymouth	40	6	7	7	27	30	1	5	16	10	40	31

BEAZER HOMES (SOUTHERN) LEAGUE

Premier Division	P	W	D	L	F	A	Pts
Merthyr Tydfil	42	26	7	9	104	58	85
Dartford	42	24	9	10	79	33	82
VS Rugby	42	24	7	11	64	43	79
Worcester City	42	20	13	9	72	49	73
Cambridge city	42	20	16	12	72	51	70
Dover Athletic	42	19	12	11	65	47	69
Gosport Borough	42	18	12	12	73	57	66
Burton Albion	42	18	10	14	79	68	64
Bath City	42	15	13	12	66	56	58
Bromsgrove Rovers	42	14	16	16	68	56	58
Wealdstone	42	16	10	12	60	53	58
Crawley Town	42	14	16	12	58	56	58
Dorchester Town	42	14	16	12	56	61	58
Alvechurch	42	16	8	17	56	61	56
Moor Green	42	14	13	15	58	70	55
Corby Town	42	14	11	17	55	59	53
Waterlooville	42	13	13	16	61	63	52
Ashford Town	42	13	13	16	59	76	52
Fareham Town	42	15	16	21	43	68	51
Leicester United	42	6	11	25	46	84	29
Redditch United	42	5	7	30	36	105	22
Bedworth United	42	4	7	31	36	102	19

Division One Mid	P	W	D	L	F	A	Pts
Gloucester City	42	28	8	6	95	37	92
Atherstone United	42	26	9	7	85	38	87
Tamworth	42	26	9	7	85	45	87
Halesowen Town	42	25	10	7	85	42	85
Grantham Town	42	23	11	8	66	37	80
Nuneaton Borough	42	19	9	14	71	58	66
Rushden Town	42	19	8	15	71	50	65
Spalding United	42	17	15	13	72	64	64
Dudley Town	42	16	13	13	73	62	61
Sutton Coldfield Tn	42	18	7	17	56	56	61
Willenhall Town	42	16	11	14	55	71	60
Forest Green Rovers	42	12	16	14	64	67	52
Bilston Town	42	15	7	20	63	72	52
Ashtree Highfield	42	12	15	15	57	62	51
Hednesford Town	42	12	15	15	49	57	51
Banbury United	42	10	14	18	53	74	44
Bridgnorth Town	42	12	7	23	59	77	43
Stourbridge	42	11	10	21	37	65	43
Kings Lynn	42	7	13	22	31	67	34
Coventry Sporting	42	6	13	23	37	91	31
Wellingborough Tn	42	5	15	22	39	72	30
Mile Oak Rovers	42	5	10	27	46	98	25

Division One South	P	W	D	L	F	A	Pts
Chelmsford City	42	30	5	7	106	38	95
Gravesend & Nthflt	42	27	6	9	70	40	87
Poole Town	42	24	11	7	96	48	83
Bury Town	42	25	7	10	75	34	82
Burnham	42	22	13	7	78	47	79
Baldock Town	42	23	5	14	69	40	74
Hastings Town	42	21	11	10	75	48	74
Hounslow	42	21	6	15	75	60	69
Salisbury	42	20	5	17	79	58	65
Trowbridge Town	42	19	7	16	59	52	64
Folkestone	42	17	8	17	62	65	59
Corinthian	42	13	13	16	59	69	52
Canterbury City	42	14	8	20	52	60	50
Witney Town	42	13	11	18	61	71	50
Dunstable	42	11	15	17	42	57	47
Buckingham Town	42	12	10	20	56	79	46
Erith & Belvedere	42	11	10	21	48	63	43
Andover	42	11	9	22	56	90	42
Sheppey United	42	10	8	24	50	90	38
Thanet United	42	7	15	20	47	95	36
Tonbridge AFC	42	7	6	29	50	98	27
Ruislip	42	6	8	28	47	112	26

VAUXHALL-OPEL LEAGUE

Premier Division	P	W	D	L	F	A	Pts
Leytonstone-Ilford	42	26	11	5	76	36	89
Farnborough Town	42	24	9	9	85	61	81
Slough Town	42	24	6	12	72	42	78
Carshalton Athletic	42	19	15	8	59	36	72
Grays Athletic	42	19	13	10	62	47	70
Kingstonian	42	19	11	12	54	37	68
Bishop's Stortford	42	20	6	18	70	56	66
Hayes	42	18	12	12	61	47	66
Bognor Regis Town	42	17	11	14	38	49	62
Barking	42	18	13	13	49	45	61
Wokingham Town	42	15	11	16	60	54	56
Hendon	42	13	17	12	51	68	56
Windsor & Eton	42	14	13	15	52	50	55
Bromley	42	13	15	14	61	48	54
Leyton-Wingate	42	13	15	14	55	56	54
Dulwich Hamlet	42	12	12	18	58	57	48
St Albans City	42	12	9	21	51	59	45
Dagenham	42	11	12	19	53	68	45
Harrow Borough	42	9	13	20	53	75	40
Marlow	42	9	11	22	48	83	38
Tooting & Mitcham U	42	10	6	26	41	81	36
Croydon	42	4	9	29	27	81	21

Division One	P	W	D	L	F	A	Pts
Staines Town	40	26	9	5	79	29	87
Basingstoke Town	40	25	8	7	65	36	83
Woking	40	24	10	6	72	30	82
Hitchin Town	40	21	11	8	60	32	74
Wivenhoe Town	40	22	6	12	62	44	72
Lewes	40	21	8	11	72	54	71
Walton & Hersham	40	21	7	12	56	36	70
Kingsbury Town	40	20	7	13	65	41	67
Uxbridge	40	19	7	14	60	54	64
Wembley	40	18	6	16	45	58	60
Boreham Wood	40	16	9	15	57	52	57
Leatherhead	40	14	8	18	56	58	50
Metropolitan Police	40	13	9	18	52	68	48
Chesham United	40	12	9	19	54	67	45
Southwick	40	9	15	16	44	58	42
Chalfont St Peter	40	11	9	20	56	82	42
Hampton	40	7	14	19	37	62	35
Worthing	40	8	10	22	49	80	32
Collier Rown	40	8	7	25	37	82	31
Bracknell Town	40	8	6	26	38	70	30
Basildon United	40	6	7	27	34	77	25

Division Two North	P	W	D	L	F	A	Pts
Harlow Town	42	27	9	6	83	38	90
Purfleet	42	22	12	8	60	42	78
Tring Town	42	22	10	10	65	44	78
Stevenage Borough	42	20	13	9	84	55	73
Heybridge Swifts	42	21	9	12	64	43	72
Billericay Town	42	19	11	12	65	52	68
Clapton	42	18	11	13	65	56	65
Barton Rovers	42	18	11	13	58	50	65
Aveley	42	18	10	14	54	52	64
Hertford Town	42	16	13	13	62	49	59
Ware	42	17	8	17	60	65	59
Hemel Hempstead	42	16	10	16	55	58	58
Witham Town	42	16	7	19	69	67	55
Vauxhall Motors	42	15	9	18	53	57	54
Berkhamsted Town	42	14	10	18	57	70	52
Hornchurch	42	11	16	15	59	61	49
Tilbury	42	13	10	19	53	60	49
Royston Town	42	12	7	23	46	72	43
Rainham Town	42	9	15	18	49	62	42
Saffron Walden Tn	42	8	16	18	54	72	40
Letchworth Gdn City	42	4	18	20	34	71	30
Wolverton Town	42	5	7	30	42	95	13

Division Two South	P	W	D	L	F	A	Pts
Dorking	40	32	4	4	109	35	100
Whyteleafe	40	25	9	6	88	41	84
Finchley	40	21	9	10	70	45	72
Molesey	40	19	13	8	58	42	70
Harefield	40	19	7	14	56	45	64
Hungerford Town	40	17	13	10	55	45	64
Ruislip	40	16	9	15	56	43	57
Feltham	40	16	9	15	58	53	57
Epsom & Ewell	40	16	8	16	55	55	56
Egham Town	40	16	7	17	54	58	55
Eastbourne Utd	40	15	9	16	68	61	54
Chertsey Town	40	13	14	13	55	58	53
Flackwell Heath	40	13	11	16	51	49	50
Camberley Town	40	15	5	20	51	71	50
Yeading	40	13	9	18	47	63	46
Banstead Athletic	40	12	8	20	50	65	44
Maidenhead Utd	40	10	13	17	44	61	43
Southall	40	11	10	19	41	73	43
Newbury Town	40	11	8	21	47	65	41
Horsham	40	7	14	19	36	68	35
Petersfield Utd	40	5	7	28	36	87	22

BANKS'S BREWERY WEST MIDLANDS LEAGUE

Premier Division	P	W	D	L	F	A	Pts
Blakenhall	40	25	11	4	81	31	86
Gresley Rovers	40	24	13	3	100	30	85
Halesowen Harriers	40	23	9	8	74	43	78
Paget Rangers	40	23	8	9	91	41	77
Rushall Olympic	40	22	11	7	73	39	77
Oldbury United	40	22	10	8	89	49	76
Hinckley Town	40	23	6	11	96	38	75
Lye Town	40	20	7	13	61	42	67
Chasetown	40	19	9	12	54	48	66
Malvern Town	40	17	12	11	81	47	63
Rochester	40	14	15	11	67	49	57
Harrisons	40	12	10	18	50	71	46
Tividale	40	10	9	21	65	84	39
Hinckley Athletic	40	9	12	19	50	76	39
Wolverhampton Cas	40	8	13	19	49	86	37
Wednesfield Social	40	9	8	23	33	82	35
Westfields	40	8	9	23	43	97	33
Millfields	40	9	5	26	42	85	32
Oldswinford	40	8	8	24	42	98	32
Tipton Town	40	8	6	26	30	86	30
Stourport Swifts	40	6	11	23	45	94	29

HFS LOANS NORTHERN PREMIER LEAGUE

Premier Division	P	Home					Away					Pts
		W	D	L	F	A	W	D	L	F	A	
Barrow	42	15	2	4	38	17	11	7	3	31	18	87
Hyde United	42	14	4	3	49	17	10	4	7	28	27	80
Witton Albion	42	13	5	3	40	16	9	8	4	27	23	79
Bangor City	42	12	4	5	40	24	10	6	5	37	24	76
Marine	42	12	5	4	39	21	11	2	8	30	27	76
Goole Town	42	14	2	5	49	31	8	5	8	26	29	73
Fleetwood Town	42	12	6	3	28	16	7	10	4	30	28	73
Rhyl	42	10	6	5	43	30	8	4	9	32	35	64
Frickley Athletic	42	11	5	5	38	25	6	5	10	26	28	61
Mossley	42	9	6	6	24	19	8	3	10	32	39	60
South Liverpool	42	8	7	6	36	29	7	6	8	29	28	58
Caernarfon Town	42	8	6	7	21	20	7	4	10	28	43	55
Matlock Town	42	12	4	5	47	32	4	1	16	18	41	53
Southport	42	7	6	8	36	22	6	6	9	30	30	51
Buxton	42	6	9	6	35	30	6	5	10	26	33	50
Morecambe *1	42	9	6	6	35	25	4	3	14	20	35	47
Gainsborough	42	7	5	9	33	35	5	6	10	23	38	47
Shepshed Ch *6	42	8	5	8	27	21	6	3	12	22	39	44
Stalybridge C	42	3	8	10	20	35	6	5	10	26	46	40
Horwich	42	4	6	11	19	35	3	8	10	23	35	35
Gateshead	42	6	5	10	18	24	1	8	12	18	46	34
Worksop Town	42	4	1	16	22	58	2	4	15	20	45	23

* points deducted for breach of rules

Division One	P	Home					Away					Pts
		W	D	L	F	A	W	D	L	F	A	
Colne Dynamoes *3	42	18	3	0	61	5	12	8	1	41	16	98
Bishop Auckland	42	16	2	3	42	11	12	3	6	36	17	89
Leek Town *1	42	12	6	3	36	17	13	5	3	38	24	85
Droylsden	42	14	5	2	49	23	11	4	6	35	25	84
Whitley Bay	42	12	4	5	39	22	11	2	8	38	27	75
Accrington Stanley	42	11	6	4	55	33	10	4	7	26	27	73
Lancaster City	42	13	3	5	39	24	8	5	8	37	30	71
Harrogate Town	42	13	3	5	47	22	6	4	11	21	39	64
Newtown	42	9	8	4	39	24	6	4	11	26	35	57
Congleton Town	42	11	5	5	32	21	4	6	11	30	45	56
Workington	42	13	1	7	41	27	4	2	15	18	47	54
Eastwood Town	42	8	5	8	31	31	6	5	10	24	30	52
Curzon Ashton	42	8	4	9	44	37	5	7	9	30	35	50
Farsley Celtic	42	9	9	3	34	27	3	4	14	18	46	49
Irlam Town	42	7	7	7	30	29	4	7	10	23	34	47
Penrith	42	11	3	7	33	35	3	2	16	28	56	47
Radcliffe Bor	42	10	4	7	38	35	2	6	13	24	51	46
Eastwood Hanley	42	7	7	7	28	28	4	5	12	18	39	45
Winsford United	42	11	4	6	33	23	2	2	17	25	70	45
Alfreton Town	42	5	6	10	25	42	3	5	13	19	50	35
Netherfield *1	42	5	2	14	34	47	3	7	11	23	43	32
Sutton Town	*4 42	6	3	12	40	45	1	3	17	30	64	

* Points deducted for breach of rules

NORTHERN COUNTIES EAST LEAGUE

Premier Division	P	Home					Away					Pts
		W	D	L	F	A	W	D	L	F	A	
Emley	32	14	1	1	51	7	11	4	1	29	11	80
Hatfield Main	32	13	3	0	45	10	8	6	2	22	14	72
Bridlington Town	32	13	1	2	41	9	8	4	4	26	17	68
North Ferriby Utd	32	10	5	1	38	13	7	4	5	25	18	60
Guiseley	32	9	6	1	30	13	7	4	5	20	14	58
Denaby Utd	32	7	4	5	28	19	6	3	7	24	31	46
Pontefract Collieries	32	7	6	3	18	10	3	5	8	19	24	41
Harrogate Railway Ath	32	7	4	5	21	16	3	7	6	20	27	41
Thackley	32	7	2	7	26	28	4	4	8	17	31	39
Belper Town	32	6	5	5	33	27	3	5	8	12	24	37
Armthorpe Welfare	32	5	7	4	23	25	4	2	10	21	35	36
Hallam	32	7	2	7	28	30	2	3	11	19	47	32
Long Eaton Utd	32	6	5	5	17	15	2	2	12	15	39	31
Brigg Town	32	6	4	6	27	25	2	3	11	16	41	31
Grimethorpe Welfare	32	6	4	6	20	19	2	1	13	18	40	29
Bridlington Trinity	32	4	3	9	27	35	2	4	10	13	37	25
Ossett Albion	32	4	4	8	19	29	1	5	10	14	42	24

BASS NORTH WEST COUNTIES LEAGUE

Division One	P	W	D	L	F	A	Pts
Rossendale	34	24	8	2	84	27	56
Knowsley United	34	21	8	5	85	43	50
St Helens Town	34	20	8	6	60	25	48
Colwyn Bay	34	19	9	6	77	45	47
Darwen	34	19	9	6	64	36	47
Warrington Town	34	16	10	8	47	37	42
Flixton	34	15	8	11	61	44	38
Leyland Motors	34	15	8	11	53	44	38
Bootle	34	14	4	16	49	54	32
Burscough	34	11	10	13	40	51	32
Ellesmere Port	34	9	12	13	36	42	30
Clitheroe	34	8	12	14	38	41	28
Skelmersdale	34	8	9	17	39	68	25
Atherton LR	34	9	6	19	47	74	24
Prescot Cables	34	7	9	18	36	60	23
Salford	34	7	8	19	33	70	22
Ashton United	34	7	6	21	37	72	18*
Formby	34	3	4	27	24	77	10

* points deducted for breach of rule

NENE GROUP UNITED COUNTIES LEAGUE

Premier Division	P	Home					Away					Pts
		W	D	L	F	A	W	D	L	F	A	
Potton United	38	13	2	4	35	15	11	4	4	35	22	78
Brackley Town	38	10	5	4	34	15	10	3	6	37	18	68
Holbeach United	38	8	5	6	35	24	10	5	4	35	22	64
Irthlingborough Diamonds	38	11	6	2	28	12	6	7	6	28	25	64
Rothwell Town	38	9	5	5	35	28	9	3	7	28	27	62
Raunds Town	38	11	4	4	26	17	7	4	8	28	30	62
Stamford	38	7	5	7	27	26	10	5	4	28	25	61
Wootton Blue Cross	38	10	4	5	29	21	7	4	8	21	25	59
Long Buckby	38	9	4	6	39	27	6	4	9	21	28	53
Stotfold	38	7	8	4	29	22	7	2	10	30	33	52
Desborough Town	38	8	4	7	28	28	5	6	8	30	37	49
Eynesbury Rovers	38	6	7	6	21	18	6	5	8	26	26	48
Northampton Spencer	38	8	2	9	32	28	5	6	8	24	27	47
Arlesey Town	38	6	2	11	16	36	8	3	8	24	30	47
Stewart & Lloyds (Corby)	36	7	4	8	34	35	5	4	10	23	33	44
Cogenhoe United	38	7	4	8	30	36	5	4	10	23	35	44
Baker Perkins	38	8	3	8	24	27	2	8	9	19	35	41
Mirrlees Blackstone	38	3	4	12	25	35	7	4	8	18	23	38
Kempston Rovers	38	5	5	9	25	34	3	6	10	21	33	35
Bourne Town	38	5	7	7	21	33	3	3	13	18	39	34

FEDERATED HOMES HELLENIC LEAGUE

Premier Division	P	W	D	L	F	A	Pts
Yate Town	32	26	5	1	75	16	83
Sharpness	32	21	8	3	77	31	71
Abingdon Utd	32	18	6	8	54	26	60
Fairford Town	32	15	7	10	45	40	52
Pegasus Juniors	32	15	6	11	60	55	51
Bicester Town	32	12	8	10	70	40	50
Moreton Town	32	12	10	10	51	47	46
Didcot Town	32	12	10	10	38	36	46
Penhill	32	13	4	15	41	36	43
Bishops Cleeve	32	12	5	15	32	54	41
Shortwood Utd	32	11	7	14	40	47	40
Wantage Town	32	9	9	14	42	57	36
Rayners Lane	32	8	7	17	41	60	31
Supermarine	32	8	5	19	29	57	29
Kintbury Rangers	32	6	8	18	24	51	26
Wallingford Town	32	6	8	18	31	64	26
Viking Sports	32	6	7	19	28	61	25

MEDISPORT WESSEX LEAGUE

	P	W	D	L	F	A	Pts
Bashley	32	26	4	2	87	24	82
Havant Town	32	21	8	3	67	26	71
Newport	32	20	6	6	67	32	66
Thatcham Town	32	17	7	8	60	26	58
AFC Lymington	32	16	9	7	51	32	57
Wimborne Town	32	14	6	12	59	55	48
Romsey Town	32	9	16	7	47	39	43
East Cowes Vics	32	11	8	13	44	48	41
Eastleigh	32	10	10	12	39	34	40
Folland Sports	32	10	10	12	46	42	40
Horndean	32	11	5	16	45	70	38
Bournemouth	32	10	6	16	49	64	36
Christchurch	32	9	7	16	40	71	34
AFC Totton	32	8	9	15	39	58	33
Sholing Sports	32	6	6	20	29	65	24
Brockenhurst	32	3	11	18	17	52	20
Portsmouth RN	32	5	4	23	25	73	19

SCORELINE MIDLAND FOOTBALL COMBINATION

Premier Division	P	W	D	L	F	A	Pts
Boldmere St Mich'ls	34	23	9	2	76	22	55
Racing Club Wck	34	22	8	4	77	31	52
Evesham United	34	21	7	6	82	30	49
Princes End United	34	17	9	8	58	37	43
West Mids Police	34	18	6	10	66	41	42
Northfield Town	34	15	10	9	55	43	40
Stratford Town	34	14	10	10	60	44	38
Walsall Wood	34	13	10	11	49	52	36
Hinckley FC	34	12	11	11	49	55	35
Highgate United	34	9	15	10	60	61	33
Bolehall Swifts	34	12	8	14	44	55	32
Kings Heath	34	9	11	14	42	52	29
Chelmsley Town	34	10	7	17	37	65	27
Knowle	34	8	10	16	34	58	26
Polesworth Nth Wck	34	4	14	16	37	62	22
Coleshill Town	34	8	6	20	46	73	22
Solihull Borough	34	7	6	21	41	72	20
Shirley Town	34	4	3	27	20	80	11

JEWSON EASTERN COUNTIES LEAGUE

Premier Division	P	W	D	L	F	A	Pts
Sudbury Town	40	29	6	5	117	46	93
Braintree Town	40	26	7	7	106	41	85
Wisbech Town	40	24	12	4	84	40	84
March Town Utd	40	22	9	9	76	49	72
Gt Yarmouth Town	40	21	9	10	75	50	72
Histon	40	19	7	14	87	57	64
Haverhill Rovers	40	18	8	14	63	63	62
Stowmarket Town	40	17	9	14	69	51	60
Thetford Town	40	17	8	14	79	74	59
Gorleston	40	15	10	15	58	69	55
Felixstowe Town	40	15	11	14	82	67	53
Lowestoft Town	40	15	8	17	68	71	53
Watton United	40	14	7	19	70	82	49
Harwich & Parkeston	40	12	11	17	60	64	47
Tiptree United	40	13	6	20	60	70	45
Newmarket Town	40	10	12	18	39	63	42
Brantham Athletic	40	11	8	21	57	90	41
Clacton Town	40	9	13	18	42	65	40
Chatteris Town	40	9	9	22	44	75	36
Ely City	40	8	6	26	48	108	30
Soham Rangers	40	6	4	30	36	125	22

GREAT MILLS WESTERN LEAGUE

Premier Division	P	W	D	L	F	A	Pts
Saltash United	40	26	10	4	90	35	62
Exmouth Town	40	29	4	7	79	43	62
Taunton Town	40	23	10	7	95	41	56
Liskeard Ath	40	20	12	8	46	25	52
Plymouth Argyle	40	19	13	8	84	39	51
Bristol Mr Farm	40	20	7	13	72	49	47
Weston S Mare	40	17	8	15	73	52	42
Paulton Rovers	40	14	14	12	60	53	42
Barnstaple T	40	17	7	16	61	54	41
Swanage & Hers	40	15	10	15	71	73	40
Clevedon T	40	16	7	17	63	70	39
Chippenham T	40	11	14	15	48	52	36
Welton Rovers	40	13	10	17	50	57	36
Radstock T	40	9	18	13	38	65	36
Chard T	40	12	11	17	49	78	35
Bideford	40	12	9	19	49	72	33
Frome T	40	11	10	19	54	80	32
Mangotsfield Utd	40	10	9	21	53	74	29
Dawlish T	40	11	7	22	48	69	29
Torrington	40	7	12	21	46	84	26
Minehead	40	5	4	31	30	94	14

SUSSEX COUNTY LEAGUE

Division One	P	W	D	L	F	A	Pts
Pagham	34	25	6	3	83	33	81
Three Bridges	34	19	9	6	70	29	66
Whitehawk	34	19	8	7	55	32	65
Hailsham	34	16	10	8	55	33	58
Burgess Hill	34	17	5	12	54	41	56
Wick	34	13	11	10	50	40	50
Littlehampton	34	14	8	12	43	33	50
Peacehaven	34	14	8	12	48	41	50

NORTH WESTERN COUNTIES LEAGUE

Division Two	P	W	D	L	F	A	Pts
Vauxhall GM	34	25	8	1	68	17	58
Maine Road	34	22	7	5	96	40	51
Chadderton	34	20	9	5	71	29	49
Wren Rovers	34	19	10	5	77	45	48
Nantwich Town	34	20	4	10	66	28	44
Newcastle Town	34	15	10	9	53	37	40
Great Harwood	34	16	6	12	52	40	38
Maghull	34	12	13	9	46	44	37

NORTHERN COUNTIES EAST LEAGUE

Division One	P	W	D	L	F	A	Pts
Sheffield	30	21	5	4	76	25	68
Rowntree Mackin-tosh	30	18	6	6	68	36	60
Woolley MW	30	16	11	3	49	28	59
Maltby MW	30	17	5	8	68	38	56
Pickering Town	30	16	4	10	58	54	52
Garforth Town	30	16	5	10	56	34	50
Eccleshill United	30	15	4	11	47	39	49
Collingham	30	14	5	11	38	30	47

GREENE KING SPARTAN LEAGUE

Premier Division	P	W	D	L	F	A	Pts
Abingdon T	38	25	9	4	95	26	84
Wandsworth & Nor	38	25	9	4	83	34	84
Northwood	38	25	4	9	84	40	79
Edgware T	38	22	9	7	88	55	75
Barkingside	38	21	11	6	73	41	74
Cheshunt	38	20	11	7	78	44	71
Brimsdown R	38	21	7	10	77	44	70
Southgate Ath	38	19	11	8	83	37	68

KEY CONSULTANTS SOUTH MIDLANDS LEAGUE

Premier Division	P	W	D	L	F	A	Pts
Langford	34	26	4	4	73	24	82
Thame United	34	23	6	5	81	32	75
Selby	34	19	9	6	70	38	66
Shillington	34	19	8	7	62	40	65
Hoddesdon T	34	17	10	7	53	33	61
Welwyn Garden City	34	15	9	10	64	50	54
The 61 FC (Luton)	34	15	8	11	50	48	53
Pitstone & I	34	13	10	11	53	49	49

ESSEX SENIOR LEAGUE

	P	W	D	L	F	A	Pts
Brightlingsea U	32	21	5	6	68	28	68
East Thurrock U	32	19	8	5	70	38	65
Ford U	32	18	7	7	56	31	61
Burnham R	32	17	8	7	65	43	59
Stansted	32	15	5	12	53	52	50
Canvey Island	32	14	7	11	62	52	49
Southend Manor	32	13	10	9	48	39	49
Eton Manor	32	12	9	11	48	43	45

DAN AIR COMBINED COUNTIES LEAGUE

Premier Division	P	W	D	L	F	A	Pts
B Ae (Weyb)	36	23	8	5	85	34	77
Malden Vale	36	20	10	6	68	32	70
Merstham	36	18	12	6	71	38	66
Chipstead	36	18	10	8	75	40	64
Farnham T	36	19	7	10	73	43	64
Steyning T	36	16	12	8	69	49	60
Hartley Wit	36	18	6	12	56	47	60
Farleigh R	36	16	9	11	62	47	57

WINSTONLEAD KENT LEAGUE

Division One	P	W	D	L	F	A	Pts
Hythe T	38	29	3	6	133	41	90
Deal T	38	24	4	10	80	35	76
Faversham	38	22	7	9	68	36	73
Darenth Heath	38	20	8	10	69	44	68
Sittingbourne	38	18	12	8	59	43	66
Alma Swanley	38	18	10	10	66	46	64
Cray Wanderers	38	19	7	12	67	53	64
Whitstable T	38	18	9	11	75	42	63

LEADING AGENCIES HAMPSHIRE LEAGUE

Division One	P	W	D	L	F	A	Pts
BAT	32	24	5	3	73	17	53
Blackfield & Langley	32	19	9	4	70	29	47
Pirelli General	32	18	10	4	58	33	48
Locksheath	32	18	9	5	82	48	45
Alton Town	32	18	8	6	74	30	44
Awbridge	32	14	6	12	48	42	34
Brading Town	32	14	5	13	49	53	33
SR Basingstoke	32	13	6	13	54	52	32

NORTHERN LEAGUE

Division One	P	W	D	L	F	A	Pts
Billingham Synthonia	38	26	6	6	83	34	84
Tow Law Town	38	23	8	7	74	45	77
Gretna	38	22	7	9	80	37	73
Guisborough	38	21	9	8	74	37	72
Billingham Town	38	20	4	14	59	47	64
Newcastle Blue Star	38	17	10	11	61	38	61
Brandon United	38	15	8	15	50	60	53
Ferryhill Athletic	38	15	7	16	72	65	52

VAUX WEARSIDE LEAGUE

Division One	P	W	D	L	F	A	Pts
Dunstan FB	32	23	7	2	70	23	76
Eppleton CW	32	24	3	5	76	25	75
Vaux Ryhope	32	22	2	8	74	33	68
South Shields	32	19	5	8	67	46	62
Hebburn	32	18	6	8	68	44	60
Marske United	32	15	7	10	60	49	52
Newton Aycliffe	32	14	4	14	49	60	46
Boldon CA	32	12	7	13	47	47	43

1989-90

Just as Lincoln City had done two years earlier, Darlington took a positive attitude to their relegation from the Fourth Division. They retained a full time playing squad and were rewarded with increased gates and ultimately the Conference title. The Quakers did have to wait until the final day to secure the championship with a win at Welling, and once again the unlucky side to miss out by just one place were Barnet.

The FA Trophy was not short of fascinating stories. Leek Town created the biggest by going all the way to Wembley. On the way they beat holders Telford, Conference leaders Darlington, and local rivals Stafford Rangers. In the final they were beaten by Barrow, a famous old club beset by worries, that had been magnificently managed to success by Ray Wilde.

Colne Dynamoes continued to create a stir. With a full time professional staff, Graham White's side cruised to the HFS Loans League title, and in their first season in the FA Trophy they reached the semi-finals, beating four Conference sides on the way. However, promotion to the Conference was not granted due to the inadequacy of their ground. Beazer Homes League champions Dover Athletic were also denied promotion for the same reason; right across the Pyramid each senior and feeder league were starting to implement very strict ground-grading criteria.

The season ended with Pyramid football saying farewell to two of its most famous venues, Wycombe Wanderers' Loakes Park and Yeovil Town's Huish. Both clubs moved to luxurious out-of-town grounds.

SUMMARY

	Winners	Runners Up	Semi-finalists
FA VASE	Yeading	Bridlington Town	Hythe Town, Guisley
FA TROPHY	Barrow	Leek Town	Colne Dynamoes, Stafford Rangers

FA CUP   Most Successful Team: Darlington
1st Rd: Darlington 6 Northwich Victoria 2; 2nd Rd: Darlington 3 Halifax 0; 3rd Rd: Cambridge Utd 0 Darlington 0;
3rd Rd Replay: Darlington 1 Cambridge 3

GM VAUXHALL CONFERENCE   Champions: Darlington   Runners Up: Barnet

GM VAUXHALL CONFERENCE STATISTICS

Top Crowds
5880	Barnet v Darlington (31.3.90)
5525	Darlington v Cheltenham Town (28.4.90)
4741	Darlington v Barrow (26.12.89)
4546	Darlington v Macclesfield Town (3.4.90)
4481	Barnet v Enfield (26.12.89)

Top Scorers
28	Rob Cooke (Kettering)
25	Efan Ekoku (Sutton)
23	Simon Read (Farnborough)

Manager of the Month Awards
Sep	Little (Darlington)
Oct	Little (Darlington)
Nov	Brigden (Welling)
Dec	Brigden (Welling)
Jan	Brigden (Welling)
Feb	Little (Darlington)
Mar	O'Neill (Wycombe)
Apr	Blunt (Sutton)

GM VAUXHALL CONFERENCE

	P	Home					Away					Pts
		W	D	L	F	A	W	D	L	F	A	
Darlington	42	13	6	2	43	12	13	3	5	33	13	87
Barnet	42	15	4	2	46	14	11	3	7	35	27	85
Runcorn	42	16	3	2	52	20	3	10	8	27	42	70
Macclesfield Town	42	11	6	4	35	16	6	9	6	21	25	66
Kettering Town	42	13	5	3	35	15	5	7	9	31	38	66
Welling United	42	11	6	4	36	16	7	4	10	26	34	65
Yeovil Town	42	9	8	4	32	25	8	4	9	30	29	63
Sutton United	42	14	2	5	42	24	5	4	12	26	40	63
Merthyr Tydfil	42	9	9	3	41	30	7	5	9	26	33	62
Wycombe Wanderers	42	11	6	4	42	24	6	4	11	22	32	61
Cheltenham Town	42	9	6	6	30	22	7	5	9	28	38	59
Telford United	42	8	7	6	31	29	7	6	8	25	34	58
Kidderminster H	42	7	6	8	37	33	8	3	10	27	34	54
Barrow	42	11	8	2	33	25	1	8	12	18	42	52
Northwich Victoria	42	9	3	9	29	30	6	2	13	22	37	50
Altrincham	42	8	5	8	31	20	4	8	9	18	28	49
Stafford Rangers	42	9	6	6	25	23	3	6	12	25	39	48
Boston United	42	10	3	8	36	30	3	5	13	12	37	47
Fisher Athletic	42	9	1	11	34	34	4	6	11	21	44	46
Chorley	42	9	5	7	26	26	4	1	16	16	41	45
Farnborough Town	42	7	5	9	33	30	3	7	11	27	43	42
Enfield	42	9	3	9	36	34	1	3	17	16	55	36

HFS LOANS NORTHERN PREMIER LEAGUE

Premier Division	P	Home					Away					Pts
		W	D	L	F	A	W	D	L	F	A	
Colne Dynamoes	42	17	2	2	46	24	15	4	2	40	16	102
Gateshead	42	13	4	4	41	28	9	6	6	37	30	76
Witton Albion	42	14	3	4	39	10	8	4	9	29	29	73
Hyde United	42	13	2	6	43	24	8	6	7	30	26	71
South Liverpool	42	11	4	6	43	32	9	5	7	46	47	69
Matlock Town	42	13	3	5	39	17	5	9	7	22	25	66
Southport	42	10	7	4	27	17	7	7	7	27	31	65
Fleetwood Town	42	10	5	6	39	35	7	7	7	34	31	63
Marine	42	8	9	4	31	27	8	5	8	28	28	62
Bangor City	42	11	7	3	38	22	4	8	9	26	36	60
Bishop Auckland	42	9	4	9	46	34	8	4	9	26	30	59
Gainsborough T	42	11	4	6	34	20	5	4	12	25	35	56
Frickley Ath	42	10	4	7	32	29	6	4	11	24	32	56
Horwich (-3)	42	8	7	6	38	33	7	6	8	28	36	55
Morecambe	42	11	5	5	39	30	4	4	13	19	40	54
Buxton	42	9	6	6	31	28	6	2	13	28	44	53
Stalybridge C	42	8	4	9	31	30	4	5	12	17	31	45
Mossley	42	3	8	10	27	42	8	2	11	34	40	43
Goole Town	42	5	1	15	26	46	7	4	10	28	31	41
Shepshed Chart	42	5	4	12	26	38	6	3	12	29	44	40
Caernarfon Town	42	5	6	10	25	30	5	2	14	31	56	38
Rhyl (-1)	42	4	6	11	21	33	3	4	14	22	44	30

HFS LOANS NORTHERN PREMIER LEAGUE

First Division	P	Home					Away					Pts
		W	D	L	F	A	W	D	L	F	A	
Leek Town	42	14	6	1	45	13	12	2	7	25	18	86
Droylsden (-7)	42	19	1	1	57	23	8	5	8	24	23	80
Accrington Stanley	42	14	4	3	46	19	8	6	7	34	34	75
Whitley Bay	42	10	4	7	46	32	11	7	3	47	27	74
Emley	42	14	3	4	45	17	6	6	9	25	25	69
Congleton (-3)	42	12	4	5	34	19	8	8	5	31	34	69
Winsford Utd	42	12	5	4	39	20	6	5	10	26	33	64
Curzon Ashton	42	9	5	7	30	24	8	6	7	36	36	62
Harrogate Town	42	10	4	7	40	29	7	5	9	28	33	60
Lancaster City	42	11	8	2	39	17	4	6	11	34	37	59
Eastwood Town	42	8	7	6	37	35	8	4	9	24	29	59
Farsley Celtic	42	10	4	7	33	29	7	2	12	38	47	57
Rossendale Utd	42	10	5	6	43	28	5	4	12	30	41	54
Newtown	42	7	7	7	25	26	7	5	9	24	36	54
Irlam Town	42	9	5	7	31	24	5	6	10	30	42	53
Workington	42	7	6	8	32	31	7	2	12	24	33	50
Radcliffe Bor	42	9	5	8	27	27	6	2	13	20	35	49
Alfreton Town	42	9	5	7	38	39	4	3	14	21	46	47
Worksop Town	42	9	3	9	37	33	4	2	15	19	62	44
Netherfield	42	9	1	11	32	34	2	5	14	24	55	39
Eastwood Hanley	42	6	3	12	26	45	3	6	12	18	43	36

VAUXHALL LEAGUE

Premier Division	P	W	D	L	F	A	Pts
Slough	42	27	11	4	85	38	92
Wokingham	42	26	11	5	67	34	89
Aylesbury United	42	25	9	8	86	30	84
Kingstonian	42	24	9	9	87	51	81
Grays Athletic	42	19	13	10	59	44	70
Dagenham	42	17	15	10	54	43	66
Leyton-Wingate	42	20	6	16	54	48	66
Basingstoke Town	42	18	9	15	65	55	63
Bishop's Stortford	42	19	6	17	60	59	63
Carshalton Athletic	42	19	5	18	63	59	59
Redbridge Forest	42	16	11	15	65	62	59
Hendon	42	15	10	17	54	63	55
Windsor & Eton	42	13	15	14	51	47	54
Hayes	42	14	11	17	61	59	53
St Albans	42	13	10	19	49	59	49
Staines Town	42	14	6	22	53	69	48
Marlow	42	11	13	18	42	59	46
Harrow Borough	42	11	10	21	51	79	43
Bognor Regis Town	42	9	14	19	37	87	41
Barking	42	7	11	24	53	86	32
Bromley	42	7	11	24	32	69	32
Dulwich Hamlet	42	6	8	28	32	80	26

Division One	P	W	D	L	F	A	Pts
Wivenhoe Town	42	31	7	4	94	36	100
Woking	42	30	8	4	102	28	98
Southwick	42	23	15	4	68	30	84
Hitchin Town	42	22	13	7	60	30	70
Walton & Hersham	42	20	10	12	68	50	70
Dorking	42	19	12	11	66	41	69
Boreham Wood	42	17	13	12	60	59	64
Harlow Town	42	16	13	13	60	53	61
Met Police	42	16	11	15	64	59	59
Chesham United	42	15	12	15	46	49	67
Chalfont St Peter	42	14	13	15	50	59	55
Tooting & Mitcham	42	14	13	15	42	51	55
Worthing	42	15	8	19	56	63	53
Whyteleafe	42	11	16	15	50	65	49
Lewes	42	12	11	19	55	65	47
Wembley	42	11	10	21	57	68	43
Croydon	42	9	16	17	43	57	43
Uxbridge	42	11	10	21	52	76	43
Hampton	42	8	13	21	28	51	37
Leatherhead	42	7	10	25	34	77	31
Purfleet	42	7	8	27	33	78	29
Kingsbury *	42	8	10	24	45	78	25

* Kingsbury 9 points deducted by order of the League

VAUXHALL-OPEL LEAGUE

Division Two North	P	W	D	L	W	D	L	F	A	GD	Pts
Heybridge Swifts	42	12	5	4	14	4	3	79	29	50	87
Aveley	42	9	11	1	14	5	2	68	24	44	85
Hertford Town	42	14	4	3	10	7	4	92	51	41	83
Stevenage Boro	42	11	8	2	10	8	3	70	31	39	79
Barton Rovers	42	12	4	5	10	2	9	60	45	15	72
Tilbury	42	10	5	6	10	4	7	68	54	14	69
Basildon Utd	42	4	11	6	9	9	3	50	44	6	59
Collier Row	42	6	6	9	9	7	5	43	45	-2	58
Royston Town	42	3	8	10	12	3	6	63	72	-9	56
Saffron Walden	42	11	3	7	4	8	9	60	73	-13	56
Vauxhall Motors	42	7	4	10	7	9	5	55	54	1	55
Clapton *	42	9	7	5	4	11	6	50	46	4	54
Ware	42	3	9	9	11	2	8	53	59	-6	53
Hemel Hempstead	42	8	7	6	4	8	9	58	70	-12	51
Billericay	42	7	5	9	6	6	9	49	58	-9	50
Hornchurch	42	5	6	10	7	6	8	49	64	-15	48
Berkhamsted	42	5	7	9	4	9	8	44	68	-24	43
Finchley	42	7	3	11	4	7	10	50	75	-25	43
Tring Town	42	3	6	12	7	3	11	48	70	-22	39
Witham Town	42	6	7	8	2	7	12	44	56	-12	38
Rainham Town	42	5	6	10	4	5	12	48	75	-27	38
Letchworth G C	42	3	6	12	4	6	11	30	68	-38	33

* Clapton one point deducted by order of the League

Division Two South	P	W	D	L	W	D	L	F	A	GD	Pts
Yeading	40	14	3	3	15	1	4	86	37	49	91
Molesey	40	13	6	1	11	5	4	76	30	46	83
Abingdon Town	40	14	4	2	8	5	7	64	39	25	75
Ruislip Manor	40	11	6	3	9	6	5	60	32	28	72
Maidenhead Utd	40	9	9	2	11	3	6	66	39	27	72
Southall	40	12	1	7	10	4	6	56	33	23	71
Newbury	40	12	3	5	9	4	7	50	36	14	70
Flackwell Heath	40	10	6	4	6	5	9	69	65	4	59
Hungerford	40	10	7	3	4	9	7	54	51	3	58
Egham Town	40	7	7	6	5	7	8	39	38	1	50
Banstead Athletic	40	7	4	9	7	4	9	46	47	-1	50
Harefield	40	6	6	8	7	3	10	44	46	-2	48
Chertsey Town	40	7	5	8	6	4	10	53	58	-5	48
Epsom & Ewell	40	6	4	10	7	5	8	49	54	-5	48
Malden Vale	40	6	3	11	7	4	9	36	67	-31	46
Eastbourne Utd	40	7	5	8	4	5	11	47	65	-18	43
Camberley	40	8	4	8	3	5	12	44	66	-22	42
Feltham	40	8	3	9	3	4	13	47	80	-33	40
Bracknell	40	5	3	12	5	6	9	40	57	-17	39
Petersfield	40	6	5	9	4	3	13	48	93	-45	38
Horsham	40	1	3	16	3	5	12	29	70	-14	20

WEEKLY WYNNER NORTHERN COUNTIES EAST LEAGUE

Premier Division	P	W	D	L	F	A	Pts
Bridlington Town	34	22	9	3	72	24	75
North Shields	34	21	6	7	63	31	69
Denaby United	34	19	5	10	55	40	62
Bridlington Trinity	34	18	6	10	82	44	60
Harrogate Railway	34	17	9	8	59	50	60
North Ferriby United	34	18	5	11	66	43	59
Armthorpe Welfare	34	18	4	12	53	39	58
Sutton Town	34	16	9	9	52	38	57
Sheffield	34	15	10	9	44	33	55
Brigg Town	34	13	7	14	57	50	46
Guiseley	34	12	7	15	54	46	43
Belper Town	34	11	6	17	39	50	39
Pontefract Colls	34	10	7	17	43	67	37
Hallam	34	9	8	17	45	64	35
Thackley	34	7	9	18	43	64	30
Ossett Albion	34	6	7	21	27	69	25
Grimethorpe MW	34	7	3	24	40	90	24
Hatfield Main	34	6	5	23	27	79	23

BASS NORTH WEST COUNTIES LEAGUE

Division One	P	W	D	L	F	A	Pts
Warrington Town	34	22	6	6	69	31	72
Knowsley United	34	21	6	7	68	45	69
Colwyn Bay	34	16	12	6	79	50	60
Vauxhall GM	34	16	9	9	50	42	57
Clitheroe	34	17	6	11	48	47	57
Darwen	34	15	9	10	40	34	54
Nantwich Town	34	13	5	16	50	52	44
St Helens Town	34	10	13	11	50	48	43
Ashton United	34	11	10	13	39	45	43
Prescot Cables	34	10	11	13	49	54	41
Bootle	34	11	8	15	44	58	41
Flixton	34	11	7	16	37	47	40
Leyland Motors	34	10	7	17	55	64	37
Atherton LR	34	8	13	13	43	58	37
Skelmersdale United	34	8	11	15	48	59	35
Salford	34	8	11	15	31	47	35
Burscough *	34	8	12	14	38	41	33
Chadderton	34	7	12	15	39	55	33

* Burscough had points deducted for breach of rule

BEAZER (SOUTHERN) LEAGUE

Premier Division	P	W	D	L	F	A	Pts
Dover Athletic	42	32	6	4	87	27	102
Bath City	42	30	8	4	81	28	98
Dartford	42	26	9	7	80	35	87
Burton Albion	42	20	12	10	64	40	72
VS Rugby	42	19	12	11	51	35	69
Atherstone United	42	19	10	13	60	52	67
Gravesend & Nthflt	42	18	12	12	44	50	66
Cambridge City	42	17	11	14	76	56	62
Gloucester City	42	17	11	14	80	68	62
Bromsgrove Rovers	42	17	10	15	56	48	61
Moor Green	42	18	7	17	62	59	61
Wealdstone	42	16	9	17	55	54	57
Dorchester Town	42	16	7	19	52	67	55
Worcester City *	42	15	10	17	62	63	54
Crawley Town	42	13	12	17	53	57	51
Waterlooville	42	13	10	19	63	81	49
Weymouth	42	11	13	18	50	70	46
Chelmsford City	42	11	10	21	52	72	43
Ashford Town	42	10	7	25	43	75	37
Corby Town	42	10	6	26	57	77	36
Alvechurch	42	7	5	30	46	95	26
Gosport Borough	42	6	5	31	28	93	23

* 1 point deducted

BEAZER (SOUTHERN) LEAGUE

Division One Mid	P	W	D	L	F	A	Pts
Halesowen Town	42	28	8	6	100	49	92
Rushden Town	42	28	5	9	82	39	89
Nuneaton Boro	42	26	7	9	81	47	85
Tamworth	42	22	8	12	82	70	74
Barry Town	42	21	8	13	67	53	71
Spalding United	42	20	7	15	73	63	67
Sutton Coldfield T	42	18	10	14	72	69	64
Stourbridge	42	17	12	13	73	61	63
Dudley Town	42	18	9	15	69	64	63
Stroud	42	16	13	13	75	62	61
Leicester Utd	42	17	5	20	66	77	56
Bridgnorth Town	42	13	14	15	68	73	53
King's Lynn	42	16	5	21	57	69	53
Grantham Town	42	14	10	18	57	63	52
Bedworth United	42	14	9	19	50	60	51
Hednesford T	42	11	14	17	50	62	47
Bilston Town	42	11	14	17	40	54	47
Redditch United	42	11	13	18	57	64	46
Racing Club Wck	42	11	11	20	45	66	44
Wilenhall Town	42	9	9	24	37	66	36
Banbury United *	42	9	9	24	46	83	34
Sandwell Borough	42	6	12	24	46	79	30

* 2 points deducted

Division One South	P	W	D	L	F	A	Pts
Bashley	42	25	7	10	80	47	82
Poole Town	42	23	8	11	85	60	77
Buckingham Town	42	22	10	10	67	46	76
Dunstable	42	20	14	8	56	38	74
Salisbury	42	21	9	12	72	50	72
Hythe Town	42	20	12	10	69	48	72
Trowbridge Town	42	20	9	13	79	64	69
Hastings Town	42	20	9	13	64	54	69
Bury Town	42	18	12	12	76	62	66
Baldock Town	42	18	11	13	69	52	65
Burnham	42	17	11	14	77	52	62
Fareham Town	42	14	14	14	49	53	56
Yate Town	42	16	6	20	53	52	54
Witney Town	42	16	6	20	54	56	54
Canterbury City	42	14	10	18	52	52	52
Margate	42	12	15	15	46	45	51
Folkestone	42	14	9	19	61	83	51
Andover	42	13	11	18	54	70	50
Hounslow	42	11	5	26	39	82	38
Erith & Belvedere	42	8	11	23	34	73	35
Corinthian	42	6	10	26	44	93	28
Sheppey United	42	6	7	29	35	83	25

BANKS'S BREWERY WEST MIDLANDS LEAGUE

Premier Division	P	W	D	L	F	A	Pts
Hinckley Town	40	24	10	6	87	30	82
Rocester	40	25	7	8	85	44	82
Gresley Rovers	40	24	8	8	89	42	80
Blakenhall	40	24	5	11	78	52	77
Lye Town	40	22	10	8	68	35	76
Hinckley Ath	40	18	10	12	58	47	64
Wednesfield	40	16	14	10	60	44	62
Oldbury United	40	18	8	14	62	60	62
Halesowen Harr	40	17	10	13	79	55	61
Chasetown	40	16	12	12	57	36	60
Paget Rangers	40	18	6	16	74	63	60
Harrisons STS	40	15	11	14	55	54	56
Malvern Town	40	15	10	15	62	62	55
Rushall Olympic	40	15	5	20	65	56	50
Stourport Swifts	40	12	10	18	40	59	46
Wolverhampton Cas	40	10	9	21	41	80	39
Westfields	40	10	7	23	44	84	37
Oldswinford	40	10	5	25	39	82	35
Tividale	40	8	8	24	42	80	32
Millfields	40	6	9	25	39	90	27
Tipton Town	40	4	12	24	30	99	24

GREAT MILLS WESTERN LEAGUE

Premier Division	P	W	D	L	F	A	Pts
Taunton Town	40	28	8	4	80	41	92
Liskeard Athletic	40	28	7	5	91	30	91
Mangotsfield Utd	40	27	7	6	96	42	88
Tiverton Town	40	26	6	8	92	51	84
Exmouth Town	40	24	5	11	74	37	77
Weston-super-Mare	40	20	8	12	86	56	68
Plymouth Argyle	40	19	10	11	75	47	67
Saltash United	40	19	9	12	62	41	66
Swanage & H'ton	40	18	7	15	77	67	61
Clevedon Town	40	16	8	16	58	60	56
Paulton Rovers	40	16	7	17	51	52	55
Bristol Manor F	40	13	12	15	49	59	51
Chippenham Town	40	14	7	19	36	46	49
Dawlish Town	40	12	7	21	55	78	43
Chard Town	40	8	14	18	50	74	38
Bideford	40	8	14	18	37	76	38
Torrington	40	8	11	21	48	74	35
Barnstaple Town	40	8	10	22	38	75	34
Radstock Town	40	7	12	21	43	82	33
Frome Town	40	4	14	22	43	77	26
Welton Rovers	40	3	5	32	30	106	14

JEWSON EASTERN COUNTIES LEAGUE

Premier Division	P	W	D	L	F	A	Pts
Sudbury	40	28	4	8	130	52	88
Thetford Town	40	23	7	10	86	56	76
Braintree Town	40	22	9	9	94	49	75
Harwich & Parkeston	40	20	13	7	77	42	73
Gorleston	40	20	9	11	61	46	69
Great Yarmouth Tn	40	19	10	11	80	62	67
Histon	40	19	8	13	85	60	65
Brantham Athletic	40	19	8	13	78	63	65
March Town United	40	18	11	11	68	58	65
Wisbech Town	40	18	9	13	73	46	63
Stowmarket Town	40	17	9	14	54	51	60
Wroxham	40	16	9	15	71	76	57
Felixstowe Town	40	13	12	15	59	61	51
Halstead Town	40	14	7	19	82	99	49
Haverhill Rovers	40	12	8	20	64	69	44
Watton United	40	8	19	13	62	61	43
Newmarket Town	40	10	13	17	42	54	43
Lowestoft Town	40	11	8	21	65	77	41
Tiptree United	40	9	10	21	46	68	37
Clacton Town	40	7	8	25	48	89	29
Chatteris Town	40	0	3	37	22	208	3

THE HELLENIC LEAGUE

Premier Division	P	W	D	L	F	A	Pts
Newport AFC	34	23	6	5	71	28	75
Shortwood United	34	20	7	7	81	39	67
Abingdon United	34	20	7	7	66	33	67
Sharpness	34	16	9	9	76	59	57
Fairford Town	34	17	6	11	59	42	57
Bicester Town	34	15	11	8	43	30	56
Almondsbury Pcksns	34	15	9	10	60	41	54
Kintbury Rangers	34	14	8	12	37	45	50
Pegasus Juniors	34	14	6	14	47	62	48
Swindon Athletic	34	12	11	11	48	36	47
Rayners Lane	34	12	6	16	43	45	42
Headington Amatrs	34	9	14	11	43	44	41
Moreton Town	34	11	8	15	55	65	41
Wantage Town	34	10	10	14	52	58	40
Didcot Town	34	11	6	17	54	48	39
Bishops Cleeve	34	7	9	18	33	61	30
Supermarine	34	6	5	23	25	72	23
Ruislip Park	34	2	6	26	32	117	12

SCORELINE MIDLAND FOOTBALL COMBINATION

Premier Division	P	W	D	L	F	A	Pts
Boldmere St Michael	38	24	9	5	72	24	81
Northfield Town	38	22	8	8	79	32	74
Evesham United	38	22	7	9	79	44	73
Stapenhill	38	21	7	10	77	35	70
Stratford Town	38	18	9	11	77	50	63
West Mids Police	38	18	8	12	80	66	62
Bloxwich Town	38	17	9	12	65	62	60
Bolehall Swifts	38	16	6	16	70	58	54
Princes End United	38	14	11	13	68	55	53
Solihull Boro	38	16	3	19	53	52	51
Highgate United	38	12	13	13	46	50	49
Hinckley FC	38	13	9	16	39	69	48
Chelmsley Town	38	13	6	19	46	66	45
Polesworth NW	38	11	10	17	51	72	43
Kings Heath	38	10	12	16	55	74	42
Coleshill Town	38	11	8	19	38	54	41
Walsall Wood	38	9	12	17	50	73	39
Knowle	38	10	9	19	50	81	39
Mile Oak Rovers	38	8	14	16	47	74	38
Streetly Celtic	38	7	6	25	38	89	27

HEREWARD SPORTS UNITED COUNTIES LEAGUE

Premier Division	P	Home					Away					Pts
		W	D	L	F	A	W	D	L	F	A	
Holbeach United	42	15	3	3	56	22	14	2	5	38	24	92
Rothwell Town	42	15	3	3	46	19	12	5	4	26	19	89
Raunds Town	42	10	5	6	32	20	10	5	6	35	22	70
Bourne Town	42	12	5	4	46	25	7	8	6	25	22	70
Cogenhoe United	42	8	6	7	20	28	12	4	5	37	18	70
Stotfold	42	9	6	6	29	27	10	3	8	37	25	66
Northampton Spencer	42	11	4	6	40	28	8	5	8	23	23	66
Mirrlees Blackstone	42	9	6	6	43	34	9	6	6	30	29	66
Arlesey Town	42	11	5	5	30	25	6	5	10	25	35	61
Long Buckby	42	10	3	8	34	30	6	6	9	24	31	57
Hamlet S & L	42	8	9	4	24	16	4	8	9	22	26	53
Irthlingborough Diamonds	42	7	1	13	30	32	7	9	5	34	34	52
Baker Perkins	42	9	4	8	26	27	5	5	11	24	36	51
Potton United	42	5	8	8	28	28	7	6	8	26	22	50
Stamford	42	7	7	7	32	27	6	4	11	23	36	50
Desborough Town	42	6	6	9	32	34	7	5	9	33	43	50
Burton Park Wanderers	42	6	7	8	19	28	6	5	10	29	39	48
Wootton Blue Cross	42	8	6	7	30	31	4	5	12	22	40	47
Wellingborough Town	42	9	4	8	33	25	4	3	14	26	45	46
Brackley Town	42	7	5	9	22	26	5	5	11	24	41	46
Eynesbury Rovers	42	4	7	10	15	34	4	7	10	15	34	38
Kempston Rovers	42	2	5	14	13	42	6	4	11	28	36	33

JEWSON WESSEX LEAGUE

	P	W	D	L	F	A	Pts
Romsey Town	36	25	6	5	84	31	81
Newport IOW	36	24	7	5	92	29	79
B A T	36	21	7	8	74	35	70
Wimborne Town	36	20	8	8	83	48	68
AFC Lymington	36	19	8	9	68	44	65
AFC Totton	36	17	8	11	58	45	59
Thatcham Town	36	15	12	9	56	45	57
Bemerton H H	36	16	8	12	61	47	56
Sholing Sports	36	16	8	12	57	51	56
Bournemouth	36	15	9	12	69	70	54
Havant Town	36	13	8	15	49	50	47
Folland Town	36	13	6	17	42	47	45
East Cowes Vics	36	11	10	15	47	54	43
Eastleigh	36	10	11	15	60	66	41
Christchurch	36	10	9	17	47	59	39
Horndean	36	10	6	20	56	75	36
Brockenhurst	36	5	8	23	35	98	23
Fleet Town	36	5	5	26	22	86	20
Portsmouth RN	36	4	2	30	38	108	14

UNIJET SUSSEX COUNTY LEAGUE

Division One	P	W	D	L	F	A	Pts
Wick	34	25	4	5	88	30	79
Littlehampton	34	24	4	6	65	22	76
Langney Sports	34	20	6	8	63	33	66
Burgess Hill T	34	18	8	8	68	38	62
Peacehaven & Tels	34	15	8	11	44	33	53
Whitehawk	34	16	4	14	45	41	52
Three Bridges	34	13	12	9	61	38	51
Pagham	34	15	6	13	53	46	51

BASS NORTH WEST COUNTIES LEAGUE

Division Two	P	W	D	L	F	A	Pts
Maine Road	30	22	4	4	84	35	70
Bacup Borough	30	21	5	4	76	30	68
Blackpool Mech	30	17	6	7	59	30	57
Wren Rovers	30	16	7	7	72	38	55
Great Harwood Tn	30	16	6	8	52	29	54
Cheadle Town	30	13	8	9	54	45	47
Maghull	30	13	6	11	40	43	45
Atherton Collieries	30	12	7	11	34	38	43

WEEKLY WYNNER NORTHERN COUNTIES EAST LEAGUE

Division One	P	W	D	L	F	A	Pts
Rowntree Mckintosh	28	18	7	3	63	23	61
Liversedge	28	17	3	8	57	29	54
Ossett Town	28	15	9	4	49	22	54
Woolley MW	28	15	5	8	51	33	50
Maltby MW	28	12	11	5	51	29	47
Garforth Town	28	13	7	8	42	23	46
Eccleshill Utd	28	11	9	8	50	45	42
Kiveton Park	28	13	2	13	35	31	41

Division Two	P	W	D	L	F	A	Pts
Winterton Rangers	26	15	6	5	46	28	51
Selby Town	26	13	8	5	51	29	47
Bradley Rangers	26	12	9	5	48	34	45
Fryston CW	26	12	8	6	39	29	44
Yorkshire Main	26	13	3	10	41	46	42
Glasshouse Welfare	26	10	7	9	40	35	37
Stocksbridge PS	26	9	9	8	36	28	36
Yorkshire Amateurs	26	8	9	9	41	34	33

GREENE KING SPARTAN LEAGUE

Premier Division	P	W	D	L	F	A	Pts
Edgware Town	36	27	5	4	96	29	86
Northwood	36	26	6	4	97	36	84
Southgate Athletic	36	20	10	6	72	40	70
Cheshunt	36	20	8	8	83	41	68
Corinthian Casuals	36	20	8	8	76	39	68
Haringey Borough	36	20	6	10	65	53	66
Walthamstow Pnt	36	17	11	8	56	34	62
Barkingside	36	16	10	10	74	51	58

KEY CONSULTANTS SOUTH MIDLANDS LEAGUE

Premier Division	P	W	D	L	F	A	Pts
Pitstone & IV	36	22	8	6	72	33	74
Thame United	36	20	8	8	70	43	68
Leighton Town	36	19	9	8	67	34	66
Hoddesdon T	36	18	10	8	74	41	64
Biggleswade T	36	20	4	12	64	42	64
Totternhoe	36	18	9	9	72	47	63
Shillington	36	17	7	12	59	43	58
Electrolux	36	16	9	11	72	49	57

ESSEX SENIOR LEAGUE

Division One	P	W	D	L	F	A	Pts
Brightingsea Utd	30	21	5	4	70	22	68
Woodford Town	30	19	7	4	64	35	64
East Thurrock Utd	30	16	8	6	64	29	56
Canvey Island	30	15	10	5	76	34	55
Sawbridgeworth T	30	15	7	8	67	46	52
Stambridge	30	14	8	8	66	37	50
Brentwood	30	14	7	9	55	40	49
Burnham R	30	12	8	10	62	45	44

DAN AIR COMBINED COUNTIES LEAGUE

Premier Division	P	W	D	L	F	A	Pts
Chipstead	34	24	7	3	83	32	79
Merstham	34	24	6	4	79	28	78
Cove	34	21	4	9	70	43	67
Ash United	34	20	7	7	67	48	67
Malden Town	34	19	7	8	69	42	64
Farnham Town	34	16	7	11	66	44	55
Steyning Town	34	16	4	14	45	49	52
Cobham	34	14	9	11	45	48	51

WINSTONLEAD KENT LEAGUE

Division One	P	W	D	L	F	A	Pts
Faversham	38	28	4	6	101	30	88
Sittingbourne	38	27	5	6	85	39	86
Tonbridge AFC	38	26	6	6	87	42	84
Deal Town	38	21	11	6	88	48	74
Alma Swanley	38	22	8	8	80	41	74
Greenwich Boro *	38	20	6	12	66	55	65
Tunbridge Wells	38	17	9	12	85	66	60
Whitstable Town	38	17	5	16	51	57	56

* Record amended for irregularities

CHARRINGTON CHILTONIAN LEAGUE

Premier Division	P	W	D	L	F	A	Pts
Cooper Payen (SI)	28	21	4	3	77	31	67
Sonning Common P	28	19	4	5	75	26	61
ITS Reading	28	15	7	6	62	34	52
Mill End Sports	28	16	4	8	58	35	52
Chinnor	28	14	3	11	50	44	45
Holmer Green	28	12	5	11	44	42	41
Chalfont Wasps	28	11	5	12	37	44	38
Finchampstead	28	10	7	11	44	41	37

NORTHERN LEAGUE

First Division	P	W	D	L	F	A	Pts
Billingham Synthonia	38	29	4	5	87	35	91
Gretna	38	23	6	9	79	44	75
Tow Law Town	38	22	7	9	78	57	73
Newcastle Blue Star	38	19	10	9	77	48	67
Stockton	38	18	8	12	73	64	62
Consett	38	16	9	13	57	61	57
Guisborough Town	38	16	8	14	59	46	56
Alnwick Town	38	16	6	16	59	54	54

VAUX WEARSIDE LEAGUE

Division One	P	W	D	L	F	A	Pts
Dunston FB	28	21	5	2	60	14	68
Eppleton CW	28	18	8	2	77	25	62
Newton Aycliffe	28	14	9	5	59	32	51
Boldon CA	28	13	9	6	46	38	45*
South Shields	28	11	10	7	68	46	43
Coundon TT	28	12	4	12	61	60	40
Annfield Plain	28	12	4	12	42	51	40
Marske United	28	11	5	12	50	57	38

* 3 points deducted

1990-91

The startling news to rock the game during the pre-season period was the disbandment of Colne Dynamoes. Six Colne players promptly signed for Witton Albion who went on to emulate the Dynamoes' achievements of 1989-90; they won the HFS Loans League by a distance and progressed to the FA Trophy semi-finals. During the season the most significant development was perhaps the assimilation into the Pyramid of the Northern and Central Midlands League. With the inclusion of these competitions and their relevant feeders, the Pyramid is now, arguably, complete.

Most neutrals were happy to see Barnet claim the Conference title and promotion to the Barclays League after three near misses. Manager Barry Fry had raked in well over £1 million in transfer fees by selling his best players, but was still able to put together a title winning squad, a quite superlative feat. In the most thrilling title race yet, Barnet nosed ahead by winning against relegated Fisher Athletic on the final day.

The FA Vase produced an eight goal classic for its final. Gresley Rovers pulled back to lead after trailing Guiseley by three goals, but lost the replay at Sheffield United. The FA Trophy final also produced some outstanding football, and Wycombe Wanderers capped a fine season by beating Kidderminster 2-1 to carry off the Trophy for the first time.

After a couple of disappointing FA Cup years, Non-League fans again had something to celebrate. Vauxhall League Woking put in a tremendous second half display to demolish West Bromwich Albion 4-2 in the Third Round. Then they went to Everton and lost just 0-1.

SUMMARY

FA VASE	Winners	Runners Up	Semi-finalists
	Guiseley	Gresley Rovers	Littlehampton Town, Trowbridge Town

FA TROPHY	Winners	Runners-up	Semi-finalists
	Wycombe Wanderers	Kidderminster	Altrincham, Witton Albion

FA CUP   Most Successful Team: Woking

1st Rd: Woking 0 Kidderminster 0; 1st Replay: Kidderminster 1 Woking 1 (AET); 2nd Replay: Kidderminster 1 Woking 2; 2nd Rd: Woking 5 Merthyr Tydfil 1; 3rd Rd: West Bromwich Albion 2 Woking 4; 4th Rd: Everton 1 Woking 0

GM VAUXHALL CONFERENCE   Champions: Barnet   Runners Up: Colchester United

GM VAUXHALL CONFERENCE STATISTICS

Top Crowds
7221	Colchester United v Altrincham (20.4.91)
5105	Barnet v Colchester United (1.1.91)
5048	Colchester United v Kettering Town (17.4.91)
5020	Kettering Town v Colchester United (10.11.90)
4579	Barnet v Wycombe Wanderers (18.9.90)

Top Scorers
30	Gary Bull (Barnet)
24	Mark West (Wycombe)
22	Ken McKenna (Altrincham)

Manager of the Month Awards
Sep	Peter Morris (Kettering)
Oct	Barry Fry (Barnet)
Nov	Peter Wragg (Macclesfield)
Dec	John King (Altrincham)
Jan	Ian Atkins (Colchester)
Feb	John King (Altrincham)
Mar	John King (Altrincham)
Apr	Martin O'Neill (Wycombe)

GM VAUXHALL CONFERENCE

	P	W	D	L	F	A	Pts
Barnet	42	26	9	7	103	52	87
Colchester United	42	25	10	7	68	35	85
Altrincham	42	23	13	6	87	46	82
Kettering Town	42	23	11	8	67	45	80
Wycombe Wdrs	42	21	11	10	75	46	74
Telford United	42	20	7	15	62	52	67
Macclesfield Town	42	17	12	13	63	52	63
Runcorn	42	16	10	16	69	67	58
Merthyr Tydfil	42	16	9	17	62	61	57
Barrow	42	15	12	15	59	65	57
Welling United	42	13	15	14	55	57	54
Northwich Victoria	42	13	13	16	65	75	52
Kidderminster H	42	14	10	18	56	67	52
Yeovil Town	42	13	11	18	58	58	50
Stafford Rangers	42	12	14	16	48	51	50
Cheltenham Town	42	12	12	18	54	72	48
Gateshead	42	14	6	22	52	92	48
Boston United	42	12	11	19	55	69	47
Slough Town	42	13	6	23	51	80	45
Bath City	42	10	12	20	55	61	42
Sutton United	42	10	9	23	62	82	39
Fisher Athletic	42	5	15	22	38	79	30

VAUXHALL LEAGUE

Premier Division	P	W	D	L	F	A	Pts
Redbridge Forest	42	20	6	7	74	43	93
Enfield	42	26	11	5	83	30	89
Aylesbury Utd	42	24	11	7	90	47	83
Woking	42	24	10	8	84	39	82
Kingstonian	42	21	12	9	86	57	75
Grays Athletic	42	20	8	14	66	53	68
Marlow	42	18	13	11	72	49	67
Hayes	42	20	5	17	60	57	65
Carshalton Ath	42	19	7	16	80	67	64
Wivenhoe Town	42	16	11	15	69	66	59
Wokingham Town	42	15	13	14	58	54	58
Windsor & Eton	42	15	10	17	48	63	55
Bishop's Stortford	42	14	12	16	54	49	54
Dagenham	42	13	11	18	62	68	50
Hendon	42	12	10	20	48	62	46
St Albans City	42	11	12	19	60	74	45
Bognor Regis T	42	12	8	22	44	71	44
Basingstoke Town	42	12	7	23	57	95	43
Staines Town *	42	10	10	22	46	79	39
Harrow Borough	42	10	8	24	57	84	38
Barking	42	8	10	24	41	85	34
Leyton-Wingate	42	7	7	28	44	91	28

* 1 point deducted by Vauxhall League

Division One	P	W	D	L	F	A	Pts
Chesham United	42	27	8	7	102	37	89
Bromley	42	22	14	6	62	37	80
Yeading	42	23	8	11	75	45	77
Aveley	42	21	9	12	76	43	72
Hitchin Town	42	21	9	12	78	50	72
Tooting & Mitcham	42	20	12	10	71	48	72
Walton & Hersham	42	21	8	13	73	48	71
Molesey	42	22	5	15	65	46	71
Whyteleafe	42	21	6	15	62	53	69
Dorking	42	20	5	17	78	67	65
Chalfont St Peter	42	19	5	18	56	63	62
Dulwich Hamlet	42	16	11	15	67	54	59
Harlow Town	42	17	8	17	73	64	59
Boreham Wood	42	15	8	19	46	53	53
Wembley	42	13	12	17	62	59	51
Uxbridge	42	15	5	22	45	61	50
Croydon	42	15	5	22	44	85	50
Heybridge Swifts	42	13	10	19	46	59	49
Southwick	42	13	8	21	49	75	47
Lewes	42	10	8	24	49	82	38
Met Police	42	9	6	27	55	76	33
Worthing	42	2	4	36	28	157	10

Division Two North	P	W	D	L	F	A	Pts
Stevenage Boro	42	34	5	3	122	29	107
Vauxhall Motors	42	24	10	8	82	50	82
Billericay Town	42	22	8	12	70	41	74
Ware	42	22	8	12	78	51	74
Berkhamstead Tn	42	19	11	12	60	51	68
Witham Town	42	19	10	13	70	59	67
Purfleet	42	17	14	11	68	57	65
Rainham Town	42	19	7	16	57	46	64
Hemel Hempstead	42	16	14	12	62	56	62
Barton Rovers	42	17	10	15	61	58	61
Saffron Walden T	42	16	13	13	72	77	61
Collier Row	42	16	11	15	63	63	59
Kingsbury Town	42	17	8	17	64	72	59
Edgware Town	42	17	7	18	73	65	58
Hertford Town	42	16	10	16	69	70	58
Royston Town	42	14	15	13	78	62	57
Tilbury	42	14	6	22	70	79	48
Basildon United	42	11	10	21	61	90	43
Hornchurch	42	10	9	23	53	87	39
Clapton *	42	9	10	23	54	93	34
Finchley	42	6	7	29	50	112	25
Tring Town	42	1	9	32	30	99	12

Division Two South	P	W	D	L	F	A	Pts
Abingdon Town	42	29	7	6	95	28	94
Maidenhead Utd	42	28	8	6	85	33	92
Egham Town	42	27	6	9	100	46	87
Malden Vale	42	26	5	11	72	44	83
Ruislip Manor	42	25	5	12	93	44	80
Southall	42	23	10	9	84	43	79
Harefield Utd	42	23	10	9	81	56	79
Newbury Town	42	23	8	11	71	45	77
Hungerford Town	42	16	13	13	84	69	61
Leatherhead	42	17	9	16	82	55	60
Banstead Ath	42	15	13	14	58	62	58
Hampton	42	14	15	13	62	43	57
Epsom & Ewell	42	15	12	15	49	50	57
Chertsey Town	42	15	9	18	76	72	54
Horsham	42	14	7	21	58	67	49
Flackwell Heath	42	11	11	20	56	78	44
Bracknell Town	42	11	7	24	60	97	40
Feltham	42	10	8	24	45	80	38
Cove	42	10	7	25	51	94	37
Eastbourne Town	42	10	7	25	53	109	37
Petersfield Utd	42	6	3	33	35	119	21
Camberley Town	42	1	6	35	27	143	9

HFS LOANS LEAGUE

Premier Division	P	W	D	L	F	A	Pts
Witton Albion	40	28	9	3	81	31	93
Stalybridge Celtic	40	22	11	7	44	26	77
Morecambe	40	19	16	5	72	44	73
Fleetwood Town	40	20	9	11	69	44	69
Southport	40	18	14	8	66	48	68
Marine	40	18	11	11	56	39	65
Bishop Auckland	40	17	10	13	62	56	61
Buxton	40	17	11	12	66	61	59
Leek Town	40	15	11	14	48	44	56
Frickley Athletic	40	16	6	18	64	62	54
Hyde United	40	14	11	15	73	63	53
Goole Town	40	14	10	16	68	74	52
Droylsden	40	12	11	17	67	70	47
Chorley	40	12	10	18	55	55	46
Mossley	40	13	10	17	55	68	45
Horwich	40	13	6	21	62	81	45
Matlock Town	40	12	7	21	52	70	43
Bangor City	40	9	12	19	52	70	39
South Liverpool	40	10	9	21	58	92	39
Gainsborough Trin	40	9	11	20	57	84	38
Shepshed Ch'se	40	6	7	27	38	83	25

First Division	P	W	D	L	F	A	Pts
Whitley Bay	42	25	10	7	95	38	85
Emley	42	24	12	6	78	37	84
Worksop Town	42	25	7	10	85	56	82
Accrington Stanley	42	21	13	8	83	57	76
Rhyl	42	21	7	14	62	63	70
Eastwood Town	42	17	11	14	70	60	62
Warrington Town	42	17	10	15	68	52	61
Lancaster City	42	19	8	15	58	56	61
Bridlington Town	42	15	15	12	72	52	60
Curzon Ashton	42	14	14	14	49	57	56
Congleton Town	42	14	12	16	57	71	54
Netherfield	42	14	11	17	67	66	53
Newtown	42	13	12	17	68	75	51
Caernarfon Town	42	13	10	19	51	64	49
Rossendale United	42	12	13	17	66	67	48
Radcliffe Borough	42	12	12	18	50	69	48
Irlam Town	42	12	11	19	55	76	47
Winsford United	42	11	13	18	51	66	46
Harrogate Town	42	11	13	18	55	73	46
Workington	42	11	11	20	54	67	41
Farsley Celtic	42	11	9	22	49	78	39
Alfreton Town	42	7	12	23	41	84	33

BEAZER HOMES LEAGUE

Premier Division	P	W	D	L	F	A	Pts
Farnborough T	42	26	7	9	79	43	85
Gloucester City	42	23	14	5	86	49	83
Cambridge City	42	21	14	7	63	43	77
Dover Athletic	42	21	11	10	56	37	74
Bromsgrove R	42	20	11	11	68	49	71
Worcester City	42	18	12	12	55	42	66
Burton Albion	42	15	15	12	59	48	60
Halesowen Town	42	17	9	16	73	67	60
V S Rugby	46	16	11	15	56	46	59
Bashley	42	15	12	15	56	52	57
Dorchester Town	42	15	12	15	47	54	57
Wealdstone	42	16	8	18	57	58	56
Dartford	42	15	9	18	61	6	54
Rushden Town	42	14	11	17	64	66	53
Atherstone Utd	42	14	10	18	55	58	52
Moor Green	42	15	6	21	64	75	51
Poole Town	42	12	13	17	56	69	49
Chelmsford City	42	11	15	16	57	68	48
Crawley Town	42	12	12	18	45	67	48
Waterlooville	42	11	13	18	51	70	46
Gravesend & N'fleet	42	9	7	26	46	91	34
Weymouth	42	4	12	26	50	88	24

Midland Division	P	W	D	L	F	A	Pts
Stourbridge	42	28	6	8	80	48	90
Corby Town	42	27	4	11	99	48	85
Hednesford Town	42	25	7	10	79	47	82
Tamworth	42	25	5	12	84	45	80
Nuneaton Boro' ***	42	21	11	10	74	51	70
Barry Town	42	20	7	15	61	48	67
Newport AFC	42	19	6	17	54	46	63
King's Lynn	42	17	9	16	53	62	60
Grantham Town	42	17	7	18	62	56	58
Redditch United	42	16	10	16	66	75	58
Hinckley Town	42	16	9	17	72	68	57
Sutton Coldfield	42	15	11	16	56	65	56
Bedworth United	42	15	9	18	57	73	54
Bilston Town	42	14	9	19	69	79	51
Leicester Utd *	42	14	10	18	65	77	51
R C Warwick	42	12	13	17	56	65	49
Bridgnorth Town	42	13	9	20	62	74	48
Stroud	42	11	14	17	51	64	47
Dudley Town	42	11	13	18	48	73	46
Alvechurch	42	10	8	24	54	92	38
Willenhall T **	42	10	10	22	58	69	37
Spalding United	42	8	9	25	35	70	33

Southern Division	P	W	D	L	F	A	Pts
Buckingham Town	40	25	8	7	73	38	83
Trowbridge Town	40	22	12	6	67	31	78
Salisbury	40	22	11	7	63	39	77
Baldock Town	40	21	9	10	66	52	72
Ashford Town	40	23	5	13	82	52	71
Yate Town	40	21	8	11	76	48	71
Hastings Town	40	18	11	11	66	46	65
Hythe Town *	40	17	9	14	55	44	59
Andover	40	16	6	18	60	76	54
Margate	40	14	11	15	52	55	53
Burnham	40	12	16	12	57	49	52
Bury Town	40	15	5	20	58	74	50
Sudbury Town	40	13	10	17	60	68	49
Newport IOW	40	13	9	18	56	62	48
Gosport Boro'	40	12	11	17	47	58	47
Witney Town	40	12	11	17	57	75	47
Dunstable	40	9	15	16	48	63	42
Canterbury City	40	12	6	22	60	83	42
Erith & Belvedere	40	10	6	24	46	73	36
Fareham Town	40	9	9	23	46	74	36
Corinthian	40	5	12	23	34	78	27

* 1 point deducted
** Three points deducted
*** Four points deducted
Records of Folkestone Town (1990) expunged

BANKS BREWERY LEAGUE

Premier Division	P	W	D	L	F	A	Pts
Gresley Rovers	42	32	5	5	104	36	101
Chasetown	42	24	13	5	79	32	85
Oldbury United	42	23	14	5	75	37	83
Darlaston	42	20	11	11	89	67	71
Hinckley Athletic	42	20	10	12	75	51	70
Wednesfield	42	21	7	14	76	59	70
Ilkeston Town	42	19	12	11	75	49	69
West Bromwich T	42	19	11	12	76	51	68
Lye Town	42	19	19	13	53	41	67
Halesowen H	42	19	9	14	84	54	66
Rocester	42	18	12	12	72	44	66
Rushall Olympic	42	17	12	13	67	51	63
Stourport Swifts	42	15	13	14	74	56	58
Blakenall	42	14	16	12	56	59	58
Pelsall Villa	42	10	14	18	49	64	44
Wolverhampton C	42	11	10	21	50	98	43
Paget Rangers	42	10	8	24	50	94	38
Oldwinsford	42	9	10	23	60	89	37
Tividale	42	9	15	28	45	100	32
Westfields *	42	9	11	22	49	87	32
Malvern Town	42	6	7	29	36	106	25
Tipton Town	42	4	8	30	27	97	20

* 6 points deducted

GREAT MILLS LEAGUE

Premier Division	P	W	D	L	F	A	Pts
Mangotsfield Utd	40	28	8	4	113	39	92
Torrington	40	25	7	8	91	41	82
Plymouth Arg Res	40	25	6	7	100	28	79
Tiverton Town	40	22	11	7	85	45	77
Weston-s-Mare	40	20	10	10	74	57	70
Saltash United	40	20	6	14	67	46	66
Taunton Town	40	18	9	13	49	33	52
Liskeard Ath	40	18	7	15	85	69	61
Dawlish Town	40	15	16	9	58	49	61
Paulton Rovers	40	16	11	13	74	60	59
Clevedon Town	40	16	10	14	52	55	58
Bideford	40	13	10	17	61	76	49
Frome Town	40	14	6	20	58	78	48
Bristol Manor F	40	12	9	19	52	66	45
Welton Rovers	40	11	11	18	40	61	44
Chard Town	40	11	10	19	46	86	43
Chippenham T	40	10	12	19	42	64	42
Ottery St Mary	40	11	4	25	43	88	37
Exmouth Town	40	9	8	23	59	93	35
Barnstaple Town	40	8	10	22	44	86	34
Radstock Town	40	4	5	31	46	116	17

UNITED COUNTIES LEAGUE

Premier Division	P	W	D	L	F	A	Pts
Bourne Town	42	29	6	7	83	45	93
Rothwell Town	42	25	10	7	75	37	85
Eynesbury Rov	42	24	9	9	68	42	81
Potton United	42	23	7	12	64	46	76
Northampton SP	42	22	8	12	84	59	74
Raunds Town	42	21	8	13	72	43	71
Desborough T	42	19	13	20	62	40	70
Cogenhoe United	42	17	12	13	68	58	63
Long Buckby	42	18	8	16	60	64	62
Stotfold	42	18	5	19	71	59	59
Baker Perkins	42	17	8	17	56	59	59
Mirrlees B	42	16	10	16	61	59	58
Holbeach United	42	17	6	19	75	77	57
Irthlingborough D	42	13	10	19	80	82	49
Kempston Rov	42	11	16	15	56	52	49
Wellingborough T	42	11	16	15	54	65	49
Hamlet S & L	42	11	14	17	49	54	47
Arlesey Town	42	11	13	18	57	75	46
Wootton Blue C	42	11	7	21	42	82	40
Brackley Town	42	9	10	23	51	83	37
Stamford	42	9	6	27	54	106	33
Burton Park W	42	5	8	29	38	86	23

HELLENIC LEAGUE

Premier Division	P	W	D	L	F	A	Pts
Milton United	34	20	11	3	66	26	71
Fairford Town	34	22	5	7	69	38	71
Bicester Town	34	19	6	9	70	37	63
Didcot Town	34	18	8	8	65	30	62
Headington AM	34	18	8	8	54	34	62
Shortwood United	34	18	5	11	77	60	59
Abingdon United	34	17	6	11	57	37	57
Banbury United	34	17	4	13	58	51	55
Hounslow	34	16	5	13	63	47	53
Almondsbury P	34	13	9	12	57	58	48
Kintbury Rangers	34	12	8	14	54	57	44
Carterton Town	34	10	7	17	49	62	37
Rayners Lane	34	10	6	18	34	63	36
Bishops Cleeve	34	9	8	17	43	79	35
Pegasus Juniors	34	8	7	19	46	68	31
Swindon Athletic	34	6	10	18	31	64	28
Moreton Town	34	5	7	22	30	73	22
Wantage Town	34	4	8	22	31	70	20

BASS NORTH WEST COUNTIES LEAGUE

First Division	P	W	D	L	F	A	Pts
Knowsley United	36	25	8	3	95	37	83
Colwyn Bay	36	22	10	4	85	32	76
Ashton United	36	20	7	9	80	45	67
Eastwood Hanley	36	16	12	8	42	29	60
Vauxhall GM	36	15	10	11	42	36	55
Prescot Cables	36	13	12	11	57	55	51
Flixton	36	14	7	15	48	72	49
St Helens Town	36	13	9	14	52	47	48
Maine Road	36	13	9	14	58	61	48
Skelmersdale Utd	36	12	11	13	56	49	47
Nantwich Town	36	13	8	15	43	56	47
Leyland Daf-Sgl	36	12	10	14	51	53	46
Bootle	36	10	9	17	55	64	39
Bacup Borough	36	9	12	15	38	47	39
Clitheroe	36	10	8	18	50	63	38
Darwen	36	9	11	16	44	62	38
Penrith	36	10	8	18	41	65	38
Atherton L R	36	9	11	16	42	68	38
Salford City	36	6	10	20	30	68	28

NORTHERN LEAGUE

First Division	P	W	D	L	F	A	Pts
Gretna	38	30	5	3	86	23	95
Guisborough T	38	21	12	5	79	43	75
Blyth Spartans	38	20	8	10	80	50	68
Billingham Syn	38	20	8	10	72	43	68
Consett	38	19	11	8	67	43	68
Whitby Town	38	16	13	9	66	49	61
Tow Law Town	38	16	10	12	65	64	58
Ferryhill Ath *	38	16	9	11	55	50	54
Northallerton	38	14	11	13	50	46	53
Newcastle B S	38	13	13	12	59	48	52
Seaham Red Star	38	12	12	14	44	46	48
South Bank	38	9	16	13	40	43	43
Murton	38	10	11	17	47	59	41
Shildon	38	10	9	19	49	75	39
Whickham	38	10	9	19	44	71	39
Peterlee Newtown	38	7	17	14	57	65	38
Brandon United	38	9	11	18	44	70	38
Stockton	38	10	6	22	40	79	36
Alnwick Town	38	7	10	21	40	78	31
Durham City	38	6	9	23	47	86	27

JEWSON (EASTERN) LEAGUE

Premier Division	P	W	D	L	F	A	Pts
Wisbech Town	40	27	10	3	97	39	91
Braintree Town	40	25	10	5	85	38	85
Halstead Town	40	26	4	10	105	52	82
Haverhill Rovers	40	24	8	8	82	45	80
Harwich & Parke	40	23	4	13	85	51	73
Watton United	40	20	10	10	62	50	70
Wroxham	40	17	13	10	63	64	64
Cornard United	40	16	12	12	73	59	60
Lowestoft Town	40	16	12	12	56	51	60
Histon	40	17	7	16	55	53	58
Stowmarket Town	40	15	11	14	51	52	56
Clacton Town	40	15	9	16	64	56	54
Felixstowe Town	40	14	11	15	59	58	53
Thetford Town	40	14	10	16	65	81	52
March Town United	40	12	9	19	48	62	45
Tiptree United	40	12	6	22	45	65	42
Gorleston	40	11	5	24	53	74	38
Gt Yarmouth T *	40	9	6	25	43	90	32
Brantham Athletic	40	6	9	25	41	74	27
Newmarket Town	40	6	8	26	32	87	26
Chatteris Town	40	5	6	29	29	92	21
* 1 point deducted							

JEWSON (WESSEX) LEAGUE

	P	W	D	L	F	A	Pts
Havant Town	38	24	8	6	76	30	80
Swanage & Herston	38	24	6	8	88	41	78
Bournemouth	38	24	4	10	69	33	76
Romsey Town	38	20	11	7	59	35	71
Wimborne Town	38	22	4	12	80	45	70
Thatcham Town	38	19	11	8	68	32	68
Brockenhurst	38	17	8	13	56	51	59
B A T	38	16	10	12	54	48	58
AFC Lymington	38	16	9	13	60	50	57
Fleet Town	38	17	6	15	64	57	57
Ryde Sports	38	17	6	15	52	45	57
Eastleigh	38	13	8	17	40	62	47
East Cowes Vics	38	12	10	16	45	49	46
AFC Totton	38	13	6	19	54	70	45
Christchurch	38	11	10	17	37	55	43
Aerostructures	38	11	6	21	32	62	39
Portsmouth RN	38	10	5	33	51	102	35
Bemerton Hth Har	38	7	11	20	41	59	32
Sholing Sports	38	6	8	24	30	84	26
Horndean	38	5	5	28	39	92	20

KENT COUNTY LEAGUE

Division One	P	W	D	L	F	A	Pts
Sittingbourne	40	32	8	0	87	19	104
Cray Wanderers	40	27	11	2	91	33	92
Herne Bay	40	24	11	5	83	28	83
Tonbridge AFC	40	24	8	8	72	34	79
Deal Town	40	23	8	9	88	43	77
Faversham Town	40	20	10	10	62	33	70
Whitstable Town	40	20	8	12	67	44	68
Alma Swanley	40	18	9	13	59	53	63
Slade Green	40	16	10	14	65	49	58
Ramsgate	40	16	9	15	60	63	57
Tunbridge Wells	40	16	6	18	71	79	54
Chatham Town	40	13	9	18	61	71	48
Darenth Heathside	40	12	9	19	44	68	45
Beckenham Town	40	12	7	21	37	54	43
Crockenhill	40	10	11	19	47	89	40
Thames Poly	40	10	7	23	49	76	37
Greenwich Boro'	40	10	5	25	49	77	35
Danson (Bex Boro)	40	7	13	20	41	80	34
Kent Police	40	8	9	23	51	77	33
Met Police	40	5	10	25	37	89	25
Sheppey United	40	6	4	30	39	105	22

NORTHERN COUNTIES (EAST) LEAGUE

Premier Division	P	W	D	L	F	A	Pts
Guiseley	30	24	4	2	78	25	76
North Shields	30	23	2	5	75	29	71
Spennymoor Utd	30	19	4	7	55	29	61
N Ferriby Utd	30	14	8	8	55	42	50
Brigg Town	30	13	8	9	40	40	47
Maltby United	30	13	7	10	44	46	46
Harrogate R A	30	12	9	9	49	40	45
Ossett Town	30	10	10	10	42	38	40
Armthorpe W	30	10	6	14	52	55	36
Winterton Rangers	30	9	9	12	49	65	36
Thackley	30	9	7	14	43	46	34
Sutton Town	30	9	6	15	53	60	33
Belper Town	30	7	10	13	37	52	31
Ossett Albion	30	3	12	15	34	51	21
Denaby United	30	5	6	19	33	81	21
Pontefract Col	30	4	4	22	34	74	16

SCORELINE COMBINATION

Premier Division	P	W	D	L	F	A	Pts
WM Police	40	22	14	4	84	41	80
Solihull B	40	24	6	10	74	35	78
Evesham	40	21	11	8	83	46	74
Sandwell B	40	20	14	6	63	31	74
Stratford Town	40	19	12	9	81	43	69
Northfield	40	18	13	9	63	37	67
Stapenhill	40	18	12	10	61	50	66
Coleshill	40	18	11	11	57	42	65
Highgate	40	18	11	11	48	35	65
Hinckley	40	18	9	13	56	47	63
Walsall W	40	17	8	15	53	48	59
Boldmere	40	14	11	15	51	56	53
Kings Heath	40	14	7	19	47	66	49
Bloxwich T	40	11	11	18	64	73	44
Bolehall	40	12	5	23	41	79	41
Mile Oak	40	9	10	21	40	73	37
Chelmsley	40	9	9	22	43	77	36
Princes End	40	10	6	24	34	71	36
Polesworth	40	5	12	23	39	86	27
Kings Norton	40	4	8	28	32	80	20

Division One	P	W	D	L	F	A	Pts
Alcester Town	28	20	4	4	85	28	64
Wilmcote	28	19	3	6	47	20	60
Pershore	28	17	6	5	63	20	57
Studley Bkl	28	16	8	4	56	27	56
Stapenhill	28	12	7	9	58	57	43
Wellsbo	28	11	7	10	57	52	40
Dudley SP	28	11	5	12	42	45	38
Handrahan	28	10	7	11	43	52	37
Triplex	28	9	8	11	34	41	35
Southam	28	9	7	12	39	48	34
Kings Heath	28	7	7	14	41	54	28
WN Fire Services	28	8	4	16	37	64	28
West Heath	28	6	5	17	39	65	23
Upton	28	5	7	16	31	57	23
Wythall	28	5	5	18	28	70	20

GREENE KING SPARTAN

Premier Division	P	W	D	L	F	A	Pts
Walthamstow Penn	36	24	9	3	77	30	81
Barkingside	36	24	8	4	77	32	80
Northwood	36	23	9	4	85	33	78
Cheshunt	36	20	7	9	56	38	67
Cor Casuals *	36	22	3	11	78	40	66
Harringey Boro'	36	18	8	10	67	44	62
Brimsdown Rovers	36	18	6	12	54	47	60
Hanwell Town	36	15	7	14	58	56	52
Waltham Abbey *	36	14	8	14	49	47	47
Amersham Town	36	13	6	17	62	67	45
Southgate Ath	36	13	6	17	55	67	45
Brook House	36	12	8	16	52	60	44
Beaconsfield Utd	36	12	6	18	48	65	42
Beckton Utd	36	12	5	19	61	71	41
Croydon Ath	36	12	3	21	60	76	39
Hillingdon Boro'	36	8	7	21	47	73	31
N Greenford Utd	36	7	7	22	44	76	28
Eltham Town	36	7	5	24	39	93	26
Thamesmead Town	36	6	6	24	43	97	24

KEY CONSULTANTS SOUTH MIDLANDS

Premier Division	P	W	D	L	F	A	Pts
Thame United	38	25	5	8	76	28	80
Wolverton AFC	38	24	8	6	98	51	80
Biggleswade T	38	22	9	7	77	43	75
Leighton Town	38	22	8	8	77	38	74
Shillington	38	21	10	7	77	40	73
Letchworth GC	38	19	10	9	65	45	67
Harpenden T	38	19	8	11	64	53	65
Wingate	38	18	8	12	71	62	62
Hoddesdon T	38	16	8	14	74	60	56
Electrolux	38	13	16	9	50	38	55
Totternhoe	38	13	12	13	74	64	51
Welwyn G C	38	13	9	16	51	57	48
Langford	38	13	8	17	45	54	47
Pirton	38	12	9	17	56	54	45
The 61 FC	38	11	5	22	54	84	38
Pitstone & Iv	38	10	3	25	43	77	33
New Bradwell	38	9	6	23	42	87	33
Brache Sparta	38	8	7	23	37	84	31
M K Borough	38	7	7	24	40	84	28
Winslow Utd	38	3	8	27	27	95	17

UNIJET SUSSEX LEAGUE

Division One	P	W	D	L	F	A	Pts
Littlehampton T	34	24	5	5	89	30	77
Peacehaven & Tel	34	24	5	5	70	31	77
Langney Sports	34	20	7	7	85	44	67
Wick	34	18	5	11	61	49	59
Burgess Hill Town	34	17	7	10	66	43	58
Three Bridges	34	15	9	10	65	47	54
Arundel	34	14	12	8	54	46	54
Oakwood	34	14	5	15	53	60	47
Whitehawk	34	12	9	13	39	36	45
Shoreham	34	11	7	16	53	77	40
Ringmer	34	9	10	15	51	66	37
Hailsham Town	34	10	6	18	55	75	36
Haywards Heath T	34	9	8	17	52	61	35
Bexhill Town	34	8	8	18	46	77	32
Eastbourne Town	34	7	7	20	32	54	28
Seaford Town	34	5	8	21	34	79	23
Selsey	34	3	3	28	28	105	12

Division Two	P	W	D	L	F	A	Pts
Newhaven	30	20	4	6	60	30	64
Chichester City	30	18	8	4	56	24	62
Horsham YMCA	30	17	7	6	45	23	58
Redhill	30	15	8	7	53	38	53
Portfield	30	14	7	9	60	38	49
Worthing United	30	14	6	10	53	42	48
Lancing	30	14	6	10	39	33	48
Broadbridge Heath	30	14	4	12	57	47	46
Bosham	30	12	6	12	50	53	42
Stamco	30	11	5	14	42	37	38
Little Common Alb	30	10	7	13	39	53	37
Midhurst & Eastbo'	30	8	7	15	40	58	31
Crowborough Ath	30	5	10	15	35	61	25
Saltdean United	30	5	9	16	31	60	24
Sidley United	30	5	8	17	42	70	23
Franklands Vill	30	4	6	20	22	57	18

DAN AIR COMB COUNTIES

Premier Division	P	W	D	L	F	A	Pts
Farnham Town	32	24	4	4	88	29	76
Chipstead	32	24	2	6	87	27	74
Malden Town	32	22	6	4	74	33	73
Merstham	32	19	6	7	67	41	63
Ashford Tn (Middx)	32	15	9	8	57	38	54
Farleigh Rovers	32	15	7	10	65	50	52
Bedfont	32	15	4	13	46	44	49
Ash United	32	13	8	11	45	43	47
Frimley Green	32	12	5	15	53	64	41
Cobham	32	11	6	15	46	51	39
Westfield	32	11	5	16	60	63	38
Steyning Town	32	10	6	16	47	56	36
Godalming Town	32	9	7	16	35	47	34
Hartley Wintney	32	8	5	19	29	64	29
Cranleigh	32	7	6	19	36	69	27
Horley Town	32	7	4	21	37	85	25
Sandhurst Town	32	1	8	23	22	90	11

ESSEX SENIOR LEAGUE

Senior Section	P	W	D	L	F	A	Pts
Southend Manor	28	20	4	4	52	20	64
Brentwood	28	18	6	4	66	30	60
Burnham Ramblers	28	17	8	3	57	30	59
Sawbridgenorth T	28	15	5	8	47	26	50
Bowers United	28	14	7	7	50	32	49
Stambridge	28	13	5	10	50	38	44
Ford United	28	13	4	11	47	33	43
East Thurrock Utd	28	11	9	8	46	38	42
Canvey Island	28	9	7	12	34	47	34
Stansted	28	7	8	13	40	42	29
Eton Manor	28	6	9	13	35	45	27
Hullbridge Sports	28	5	8	15	16	38	23
Maldon Town	28	6	5	17	27	57	23
East Ham Utd	28	5	4	19	35	95	19
Woodford Town	28	5	3	20	33	64	18

WEBSTERS CENTRAL MIDLANDS LEAGUE

Supreme Division	P	W	D	L	F	A	Pts
Hucknall Town	32	23	6	3	79	30	75
Heanor Town	32	21	4	7	70	33	67
Lincoln United	32	20	6	6	70	25	66
Arnold Town *	32	18	11	3	59	22	64
Nettleham	32	15	6	11	43	40	51
Harworth CI	32	13	9	10	47	36	48
Sheffield Aurora	32	13	8	11	71	47	47
Rossington Main	32	11	9	12	43	45	42
Boston	32	12	6	14	50	65	42
Louth United	32	11	8	13	47	53	41
Oakham United	32	9	10	13	40	46	37
Borrowash Vic	32	11	1	20	46	66	34
Gainsboro' Town	32	8	6	18	36	66	30
Priory (Eastwood)	32	6	11	15	37	58	29
Melton Town	32	7	8	17	49	81	29
Wombwell Town	32	7	6	19	37	75	38
Blidworth	32	6	7	19	40	76	25
* 1 point deducted							

Premier Division	P	W	D	L	F	A	Pts
Mickleover R B L	34	25	3	6	104	42	78
Highfield Rangers	34	23	7	4	71	31	76
Blackwell W M	34	22	6	6	69	38	72
Glapwell	34	20	8	6	82	43	68
Shirebrook Coll	34	17	9	8	68	42	60
Bulwell Utd	34	14	9	11	65	56	51
Derby Rolls Royce	34	14	7	13	64	55	49
Lincoln Moorlands	34	13	7	14	54	62	46
Radford	34	12	5	17	37	56	41
Brailsford	34	12	4	18	51	81	40
Rossington	34	9	12	13	48	51	39
Long Eaton United	34	11	6	17	41	72	39
Kilburn W M	34	11	4	19	39	57	37
West Hallam	34	11	4	19	42	64	37
Stanton	34	8	9	17	39	48	33
Slack & Parr	34	7	10	17	45	76	31
Newhall United	34	8	6	20	53	74	30
Kimberley Town	34	7	8	19	38	62	29

ROGER SMITHS NOTTS ALLIANCE

Premier Division	P	W	D	L	F	A	Pts
Rainworth MW	30	23	5	2	76	21	51
Dunkirk	30	18	8	4	84	36	44
Worthington Sim	30	17	4	9	62	54	38
Pelican	30	16	5	9	65	39	37
GPT Plessey	30	16	4	10	68	47	36
Clipstone Welfare	30	15	4	11	51	53	34
Ruddington	30	13	5	12	40	46	31
Notts Police	30	10	9	11	44	45	29
Basford United	30	13	2	15	70	50	28
Hucknall Rolls R	30	12	4	14	45	50	28
Greenwood M'dows	30	9	8	13	46	58	26
Cotgrave C W	30	10	5	15	55	66	25
John Player	30	9	5	16	36	58	23
Clifton All Whites	30	8	6	16	39	63	22
Southwell City	30	5	5	20	26	73	15
City Sherwood H	30	4	5	21	33	81	13

EVERARD LEICS SENIOR

Premier Division	P	W	D	L	F	A	Pts
Lutterworth Town	30	17	6	7	60	30	57
Anstey Nomads	30	16	9	5	67	38	57
Oadby Town	30	16	8	6	53	33	56
Syston St Peters	30	15	10	5	56	36	55
Pedigree Petfoods	30	16	5	9	51	40	53
Barlestone St Giles	30	14	7	9	49	37	49
Holwell Sports	30	12	5	13	68	43	41
Newfoundpool	30	11	7	13	38	42	39
Friar Lane OB	30	11	6	13	39	43	39
Birstall United	30	10	8	12	51	47	38
St Andrews S C	30	10	6	14	37	45	36
N'boro & L'thorpe	30	9	7	14	39	54	34
Barwell Athletic *	30	10	7	13	48	65	34
Hillcroft	30	7	6	17	26	42	27
Rolls Royce	30	6	8	16	35	54	26
Thringstone	30	5	5	20	25	93	20

ALLIANCE & CONFERENCE RECORDS 1979-91

SEASONS OF MEMBERSHIP AND FINAL POSITIONS

Club	79/80	80/1	81/2	82/3	83/4	84/5	85/6	86/7	87/8	88/9	89/90	90/91
Altrincham	1	1	11	12	3	5	4	5	14	14	16	3
AP Leamington	18	16	22	-	-	-	-	-	-	-	-	-
Aylesbury United	-	-	-	-	-	-	-	-	20	-	-	-
Bangor City	9	20	-	13	21	-	-	-	-	-	-	-
Barnet	17	17	18	15	9	15	14	2	2	8	2	1
Barrow	14	9	8	21	-	18	21	-	-	-	14	10
Bath City	16	6	12	10	6	4	12	10	20	-	-	20
Boston United	4	8	10	5	17	17	13	6	16	3	18	18
Cheltenham Town	-	-	-	-	-	-	11	11	13	15	11	16
Chorley	-	-	-	-	-	-	-	-	-	17	20	-
Colchester United	-	-	-	-	-	-	-	-	-	-	-	2
Dagenham	-	-	5	14	18	19	19	15	22	-	-	-
Darlington	-	-	-	-	-	-	-	-	-	-	1	-
Dartford	-	-	21	-	-	3	21	-	-	-	-	-
Enfield	-	-	2	1	14	7	1	4	12	13	22	-
Farnborough Town	-	-	-	-	-	-	-	-	-	-	21	-
Fisher Athletic	-	-	-	-	-	-	-	-	15	18	19	22
Frickley Athletic	-	10	15	16	12	11	2	21	-	-	-	-
Gateshead	-	-	-	-	16	21	-	22	-	-	-	17
Gravesend & Northfleet	5	15	20	-	-	-	-	-	-	-	-	-
Kettering Town	7	2	19	19	19	12	9	16	3	2	5	4
Kidderminster Harriers	-	-	-	-	10	8	3	12	7	5	13	13
Lincoln City	-	-	-	-	-	-	-	-	1	-	-	-
Macclesfield Town	-	-	-	-	-	-	-	-	11	7	4	7
Maidstone United	6	7	16	2	1	13	17	3	9	1	-	-
Merthyr Tydfil	-	-	-	-	-	-	-	-	-	-	9	9
Newport County	-	-	-	-	-	-	-	-	-	Exp	-	-
Northwich Victoria	8	4	6	8	7	9	16	17	17	10	15	12
Nuneaton Borough	10	18	-	11	2	2	18	18	-	-	-	-
Redditch United	20	-	-	-	-	-	-	-	-	-	-	-
Runcorn	-	-	1	4	5	14	6	8	4	6	3	8
Scarborough	11	3	7	9	13	6	15	1	-	-	-	-
Slough Town	-	-	-	-	-	-	-	-	-	-	-	19
Stafford Rangers	19	11	14	22	-	-	7	13	6	19	17	15
Sutton United	-	-	-	-	-	-	-	7	8	12	8	21
Telford United	13	13	3	6	11	10	8	9	5	16	12	6
Trowbridge Town	-	-	17	18	22	-	-	-	-	-	-	-
Wealdstone	15	19	-	3	4	1	10	19	21	-	-	-
Welling United	-	-	-	-	-	-	-	20	19	11	6	11
Weymouth	2	5	9	7	15	16	5	14	10	21	-	-
Worcester City	3	12	4	17	8	20	-	-	-	-	-	-
Wycombe Wanderers	-	-	-	-	-	-	20	-	18	4	10	5
Yeovil Town	12	14	13	20	20	22	-	-	-	9	7	14

Exp = Newport County were expelled from the League midway through the season.

DID YOU KNOW?

Altrincham, Barnet, Boston United, Kettering Town, Northwich Victoria and Telford United are the only clubs to have been members of the league throughout its 12 year history.

AP Leamington and Barnet are the only teams to have played a league game on plastic. The teams met at Loftus Road, Queens Park Rangers, on January 17 1982 because Barnet's Underhill ground was unavailable.

AP Leamington lost 22 of their first 26 games at the beginning of the 1981/82 season.

Barnet did not score a goal in eight league games between March 29 and April 26 1980.

Barrow's prolific scorer Colin Cowperthwaite holds the honour of the fastest goal scored in the league's history. He struck after only 3½ seconds against Kettering Town on December 8 1979.

Barrow, Darlington, Lincoln City, Merthyr Tydfil, Newport County and Northwich Victoria have all been members of the Football League.

Bath City recorded 11 clean sheets in 15 games between December 6 1980 and March 7 1981. This included runs of six and five games in a row without letting a goal in.

Darlington, Lincoln City, Maidstone United and Scarborough have all been promoted to the Football League after winning the league title.

Nicky Evans of **Kettering Town, Barnet and Wycombe Wanderers**, has scored goals in all twelve league seasons.

Kidderminster Harriers' striker Kim Casey scored in 12 consecutive games between August 18 and October 4 1984. He scored 18 times.

Nuneaton Borough's Paul Culpin scored in 13 out of 14 games between March 2 and May 4 1985. He scored 23 times.

Trowbridge Town scored only three times in fourteen games between April 10 and September 11 1982. This run was extended to five goals in 17 games up to October 9.

Yeovil Town lost 12 of their first 13 games at the beginning of the 1984/85 season.

The league's 1000th game was played on January 26 1982. Games played that day were Runcorn v Enfield and Gravesend v Barnet.

The 5000th game was the 124th of the 1990/91 season.

The 1000th win and loss was recorded on October 18 1982 when Nuneaton beat Altrincham 3-1.

The 2500th win and loss was the seventh of eight results recorded on January 31 1987.

The 1000th draw was recorded on February 18 1984. It was the third draw of four played on that day.

The 2500th draw was played on April 25 1990 when Farnborough and Wycombe drew 1-1.

The 1000th goal was the second one scored in ten games on August 23 1980.

The 5000th goal was scored during September 1984.

Paul Taylor of Dagenham scored the league's 10,000th goal, against Wealdstone on April 11 1987.

Left
Colin Cowperthwaite, Barrow's record goalscorer who had registered 116 Conference goals for the club by the end of the 1990-91 season.

Right
Nicky Evans, in Wycombe Wanderers colours, but who joined Barnet having scored in the Alliance/Gola League/Conference competition in every one of its twelve years.

HONOURS LIST

ALLIANCE PREMIER LEAGUE

	Champions	Runners-up	3rd	4th
1980	Altrincham	Weymouth	Worcester City	Boston United
1981	Altrincham	Kettering Town	Scarborough	Northwich Victoria
1982	Runcorn	Enfield	Telford United	Worcester City
1983	Enfield	Maidstone United	Wealdstone	Runcorn
1984	Maidstone United	Nuneaton Borough	Altrincham	Wealdstone

GOLA LEAGUE

	Champions	Runners-up	3rd	4th
1985	Wealdstone	Nuneaton Borough	Dartford	Bath City
1986	Enfield	Frickley Athletic	Kidderminster H	Altrincham

GM VAUXHALL CONFERENCE

	Champions	Runners-up	3rd	4th
1987	Scarborough	Barnet	Maidstone U	Enfield
1988	Lincoln City	Barnet	Kettering T	Runcorn
1989	Maidstone United	Kettering Town	Boston United	Wycombe W
1990	Darlington	Barnet	Runcorn	Macclesfield Town
1991	Barnet	Colchester United	Altrincham	Kettering Town

LEAGUE CUP FINALS

Scores and attendances are aggregates of two legs.

1980	Northwich Victoria 2-2 Altrincham (6178)
	Northwich won on pens.
1981	Altrincham 3-2 Kettering Town (3892)
1982	Weymouth 6-4 Enfield (2792)
1983	Runcorn 3-3 Scarborough (2618)
	Runcorn won on away goals.
1984	Scarborough 2-1 Barnet (2129)
1985	Runcorn 3-0 Maidstone United (1439)
1986	Stafford Rangers 3-1 Barnet (2407)
1987-1989	No competition
1990	Yeovil Town 4-1 Kidderminster Harriers (2618)
1991	Sutton United 6-1 Barrow (2357)

CHALLENGE SHIELD

Champions v League Cup winners

1980	Altrincham 0-1 Northwich Victoria (1784)
1981	Altrincham 4-2 Kettering Town (1150) #
1982	Runcorn 4-0 Weymouth (756)
	Runcorn won on pens.
1983	Enfield 4-1 Runcorn (660)
1984	Maidstone Utd 3-1 Scarborough (643)
1985	Wealdstone 2-2 Runcorn (529)
1986	Enfield 0-1 Stafford Rangers (403)

Champions v FA Trophy winners

1987	Scarborough 1-2 Kidderminster Harriers (1104)
1988	Lincoln City 3-1 Enfield (1257)
1989	Maidstone Utd 2-0 Telford United (504)
1990	Darlington 4-0 Barrow (2104)
	(played at Barrow)

Altrincham had won both competitions so Kettering as runners-up were invited to participate.

SUCCESSFUL ALLIANCE CLUBS IN FA TROPHY

	Winners	Runners-up	Semi-Finalists
1982	Enfield (2)	Altrincham (11)	Northwich Victoria (6)
1983	Telford United (6)	Northwich Victoria (8)	Dagenham (14)
1984	Northwich Victoria (7)	Bangor City (21)	-
1985	Wealdstone (1)	Boston United (17)	Enfield (7) / Kettering (12)
1986	Altrincham (4)	Runcorn (6)	-
1987	Kidderminster Harriers (12)	-	-
1988	Enfield (12)	Telford United (5)	-
1989	Telford United (16)	Macclesfield Town (7)	-
1990	Barrow (14)	-	Stafford Rangers (17)
1991	Wycombe Wanderers (5)	Kidderminster Harriers (13)	Altrincham (3)

Final League positions in brackets)

SEQUENCES & RECORDS
1979-1991

RECORDS

Games without defeat	28 Altrincham (90/1)
Games without a win	26 AP Leamington (81/2)
Consecutive victories	9 Altrincham (84/5)
Consecutive draws	5 Nuneaton Borough (84/5), Scarborough (86/7) & Cheltenham Town (87/8)
Consecutive defeats	12 Dagenham (87/8)

HOME & AWAY WINS & DEFEATS

	Home	Away
Without defeat	35 Nuneaton (82-85)	16 Scarborough (86/7)
Without a win	14 AP Leamington (80-82)	23 Stafford Rangers (79-81)
Consecutive wins	10 Runcorn (89/90)	13 Scarborough (86/7)
Consecutive draws	5 Cheltenham (87/8) & Stafford Rangers (90/1)	5 Gravesend (79/80), Stafford (80/1) & Northwich (87/8)
Consecutive defeats	7 AP Leamington (80-82)	11 Redditch (79/80) & Dartford (85/6)

STARTS TO SEASON

Longest unbeaten starts to a season
15 – Kettering Town (90/91)
13 – Darlington (89/90)
12 – Wealdstone (82/3)
11 – Wealdstone (83/4)

Longest start to a season without a win
26 – AP Leamington (81/2)
17 – Gateshead (84/5)
16 – Trowbridge Town (82/3)
14 – Redditch United (79/80)
13 – Barnet (81/2) & Barrow (85/6)

Longest winning start to a season

5 – Runcorn (83/4), Weymouth (87/8)
4 – Boston Utd (84/5 & 88/9), Kettering (88/9), Darlington (89/90)

Longest losing start to a season
11 – AP Leamington (81/2)
8 – Yeovil Town (84/5)
4 – Trowbridge, Kidderminster & Bangor (83/4), Newport (88/9)

Longest drawing start to a season
4 – Weymouth (79/80)
3 – Boston (82/3), Cheltenham & Sutton (87/8), Yeovil (88/9), Merthyr (89/90)

WINS

Biggest home wins	Runcorn 9-0 Enfield (3.3.90), Altrincham 9-2 Merthyr Tydfil (16.2.91) Sutton United 8-0 Kettering Town (14.10.86), Barnet 8-1 Fisher A (16.10.90)
Biggest away wins	Gateshead 0-9 Sutton U (22.9.90) Wycombe Wanderers 0-7 Barnet (15.9.87) Boston United 0-6 Runcorn (28.9.88) Wealdstone 0-6 Barnet (19.3.88)
Highest aggregates	11 Altrincham 7-4 Nuneaton Borough (9.11.85) 11 Altrincham 9-2 Merthyr Tydfil (16.2.91)

FIRSTS

To win 100 games	Altrincham (28.8.82) v Trowbridge Town
To score 100 goals	Altrincham (1.11.80) 1st goal in 4-3 win v Scarborough
To score 500 goals	Altrincham (8.10.86) 2nd goal in 2-2 draw v Scarborough
To lose 100 games	Yeovil Town (27.8.87) v Worcester City
To concede 100 goals	Leamington (6.12.80) 2nd goal in 2-2 v Frickley
To concede 500 goals	Boston (4.3.87) Only goal in 2-1 win v Kettering
To draw 100 games	Scarborough (7.2.87) v Maidstone United

Statistics compiled by Steven Penny (AFS member)

TOTAL LEAGUE RECORDS 1979-91

			Home					Away					Total					
	Ssn	Pld	W	D	L	F	A	W	D	L	F	A	W	D	L	F	A	Pts
Altrincham	12	452	129	49	48	416	219	70	64	92	285	325	199	113	140	701	544	623
AP Leamington	3	118	12	19	28	65	97	9	13	37	54	137	21	32	65	119	234	78
Aylesbury United	1	40	7	4	9	27	30	2	5	13	16	41	9	9	22	43	71	36
Bangor City	4	160	29	25	26	114	113	15	20	45	87	160	44	45	71	201	273	150
Barnet	12	452	110	50	66	380	263	73	51	102	276	343	183	101	168	656	606	601
Barrow	8	286	64	37	42	207	169	21	40	82	134	269	85	77	124	341	438	292
Bath City	10	370	81	51	53	273	207	54	44	87	205	295	135	95	140	478	502	444
Boston United	12	452	122	51	53	439	297	61	52	113	266	410	183	103	166	705	707	589
Cheltenham Town	6	208	46	32	26	188	135	25	35	44	122	169	71	67	70	310	304	267
Chorley	2	82	15	9	17	52	58	11	3	27	47	80	26	12	44	99	138	90
Colchester United	1	-	-	-	-	-	-	-	-	-	-	-	-	-	-	-	-	-
Dagenham	7	294	53	38	56	199	206	34	32	81	175	288	87	70	137	374	494	307
Darlington	1	42	13	6	2	43	12	13	3	5	33	13	26	9	7	76	25	87
Dartford	3	126	21	18	24	87	83	14	13	36	68	116	35	31	60	155	199	122
Enfield	9	376	97	38	53	371	238	72	42	74	301	303	169	80	127	672	541	553
Farnborough Town	2	42	7	5	9	33	30	3	7	11	27	43	10	12	20	60	73	42
Fisher Athletic	4	124	23	12	27	93	89	13	19	30	75	115	36	31	57	168	204	139
Frickley Athletic	7	290	78	31	36	273	178	30	38	77	159	280	108	69	113	432	458	337
Gateshead	4	126	15	22	26	88	117	12	16	35	70	133	27	38	61	158	250	106
Gravesend & Nthflt	3	118	27	14	18	96	70	13	14	32	52	98	40	28	50	148	168	118
Kettering Town	12	452	115	52	59	394	262	58	65	103	280	385	173	117	162	674	647	572
Kidderminster H	8	292	65	39	42	280	223	61	24	61	236	248	126	63	103	516	471	414
Lincoln City	1	42	16	4	1	53	13	8	6	7	33	35	24	10	8	86	48	82
Macclesfield Town	4	124	30	16	16	102	69	22	18	22	81	91	52	34	38	183	160	190
Maidstone United	10	410	111	53	41	410	207	68	60	77	274	285	179	113	118	684	492	589
Merthyr Tydfil	2	42	9	9	3	41	30	7	5	9	26	33	16	14	12	67	63	62
Northwich Victoria	12	452	106	59	61	342	236	56	65	105	245	356	162	124	166	587	592	552
Nuneaton Borough	7	286	70	41	32	253	162	34	38	71	172	246	104	79	103	425	408	333
Redditch United	1	38	4	5	10	18	29	1	3	15	8	40	5	8	25	26	69	18
Runcorn	10	376	113	47	28	377	180	66	57	65	245	266	179	104	93	622	446	613
Scarborough	8	328	81	55	28	263	154	55	46	63	208	239	136	101	91	471	393	450
Slough Town	1	-	-	-	-	-	-	-	-	-	-	-	-	-	-	-	-	-
Stafford Rangers	10	368	72	53	59	255	219	38	54	92	227	324	110	107	151	482	543	410
Sutton United	5	166	45	19	19	178	99	21	31	31	112	124	66	50	50	290	223	248
Telford United	12	452	117	53	56	372	253	68	60	98	270	358	185	113	154	642	611	606
Trowbridge Town	3	126	20	16	27	72	87	9	9	45	55	142	29	25	72	127	229	109
Wealdstone	8	328	67	55	42	258	196	46	44	74	186	247	113	99	116	444	443	387
Welling United	4	166	35	20	28	135	102	18	20	45	83	150	53	40	73	218	252	199
Weymouth	10	410	106	49	50	355	232	58	53	94	248	321	164	102	144	603	553	524
Worcester City	6	244	60	32	30	208	154	33	26	63	139	222	93	58	93	347	376	288
Wycombe Wdrs	5	166	35	24	24	138	127	23	23	37	99	141	58	47	61	237	268	214
Yeovil Town	9	326	67	41	55	259	229	35	35	93	195	336	102	76	148	454	565	342
Expunged Record																		
Newport County	¾	29	3	3	7	18	26	1	4	11	13	36	4	7	18	31	62	19

RECORDS

	Total	Home	Away
Most wins:	28 Runcorn (81/2)	17 Runcorn (81/2), Maidstone (83/3)	15 Scarborough (86/7)
Most draws:	20 Cheltenham (87/8)	11 Cheltenham (87/8), Wealdstone (87/8)	12 Weymouth (84/5)
Most defeats:	31 Dagenham (87/8)	14 Trowbridge (83/4), Dagenham (87/8)	17 on six occasions
Most goals for:	103 Barnet (90/1)	57 Enfield (82/3), Barnet (87/8)	53 Barnet (90/1)*
Most against:	105 AP Leamington (81/2)	46 Dagenham (87/8)	63 Yeovil (82/3)
Least wins:	4 AP Leamington (81/2)	1 AP Leamington (81/2)	1 on nine occasions
Least draws:	3 Barnet (82/3)	1 on five occasions	0 Barnet (82/3), Kidderminster (86/7)
Least defeats:	5 Runcorn (81/2), Enfield (85/6), Scarborough (86/7)	0 Altrincham (79/80), Nuneaton (84/5)	3 on seven occasions
Least goals for:	26 Redditch (79/80)	15 Trowbridge (83/4)	8 Redditch (79/80)
Least against:	25 Darlington (89/90)	8 Bath (80/1)	13 Darlington (89/90)

Most points: 93 Runcorn (81/2)

Least points: 18 [23*] Redditch (79/80); 19 [22*] Trowbridge; 21 Dagenham (87/8)

[*] denotes point total if three points for a win was used.

Notes: 1979/80 & 80/1 = 2 points for a win.
81/2, 82/3 & 86/7 to date = 3 points for a win.
83/4 - 85/6 = 3 points away win, 2 points home win.

79/80 & 80/1 = 38 games played.
81/2 - 87/8 & 89/91 = 42 games.
88/9 = 40 games.

LOWEST ATTENDANCES

Altrincham	332 v Sutton United *Apr 5 1989*	Lincoln City	1995 v Cheltenham *Oct 31 1987*
AP Leamington	204 v Scarborough *Apr 14 1983*	Macclesfield Town	555 v Yeovil Town *Apr 22 1991*
Aylesbury Utd	742 v Welling Utd *Apr 4 1989*	Maidstone United	506 v Chorley *Oct 15 1988*
Bangor City	154 v Maidstone U *Apr 25 1981*	Merthyr Tydfil	427 v Stafford *Feb 23 1991*
Barnet	291 v Wealdstone *May 6 1985*	Newport County	943 v Maidstone U *Oct 1 1988*
Barrow	281 v Weymouth *May 7 1983*	Northwich Victoria	367 v Dagenham *May 3 1986*
Bath City	277 v Telford Utd *Apr 27 1987*	Nuneaton Borough	369 v Weymouth *Feb 1 1986*
Boston Utd	602 v Bath City *Apr 20 1983*	Redditch United	150 v Maidstone U *Dec 29 1979*
Cheltenham Town	602 v Welling Utd *Apr 24 1991*	Runcorn	309 v Enfield *May 2 1985*
Chorley	437 v Boston Utd *Nov 25 1989*	Scarborough	443 v Northwich V *Feb 29 1984*
Colchester United	1958 v Northwich V *Sep 1 1990*	Slough Town	613 v Gateshead *Feb 23 1991*
Dagenham	368 v Kiddermin'r *Mar 28 1987*	Stafford Rangers	546 v Boston Utd *Nov 30 1982*
Darlington	2616 v Kiddermin'r *Aug 26 1989*	Sutton United	445 v Frickley Ath *Mar 29 1987*
Dartford	349 v Barrow *Mar 16 1985*	Telford United	561 v Bangor City *Nov 1 1980*
Enfield	335 v Yeovil Town *Mar 24 1984*	Trowbridge Town	204 v Bangor City *Apr 29 1984*
Farnborough Town	535 v Chorley *Dec 16 1989*	Wealdstone	304 v Stafford Rgrs *May 1 1986*
Fisher Athletic	175 v Boston Utd *Dec 15 1990*	Welling United	450 v Runcorn *Dec 13 1986*
Frickley Athletic	207 v Barrow *Mar 5 1983*	Weymouth	342 v Macclesfield *May 3 1989*
Gateshead	121 v Trowbridge *Dec 10 1983*	Worcester	615 v Dagenham *Apr 27 1982*
Gravesend & N'fleet	660 v Northwich V *Apr 28 1989*	Wycombe Wandrs	540 v Bath City *Feb 26 1991*
Kettering Town	532 v Cheltenham *Apr 30 1986*	Yeovil Town	716 v Barnet *Mar 28 1984*
Kidderminster Harrs	414 v Altrincham *Oct 15 1983*		

ALLIANCE & CONFERENCE RECORDS

ATTENDANCES OF MORE THAN 4000

9432	Lincoln City v Wycombe Wandrs *May 2 1988*	4481	Barnet v Enfield *Dec 26 1989*
7542	Lincoln City v Boston United *Apr 4 1988*	4450	Kettering Town v Welling Utd *Apr 1 1989*
7221	Colchester United v Altrincham *Apr 20 1991*	4402	Lincoln City v Stafford Rangers *Apr 30 1988*
5880	Barnet v Darlington *Mar 31 1990*	4377	Kettering T v Kidderminster *Mar 25 1989*
5822	Boston Utd v Lincoln City *Dec 26 1987*	4297	Darlington v Wycombe Wandrs *Apr 14 1990*
5640	Scarborough v Weymouth *May 2 1987*	4283	Fisher Athletic v Barnet *May 4 1991*
5525	Darlington v Cheltenham Town *Apr 28 1990*	4247	Barnet v Enfield *Jan 2 1989*
5143	Barnet v Runcorn *Apr 30 1988*	4244	Barrow v Darlington *Jan 1 1990*
5020	Kettering Town v Colchester *Apr 17 1991*	4239	Wycombe W v Kidderminster *Feb 18 1989*
4892	Lincoln City v Maidstone Utd *Apr 27 1988*	4237	Yeovil Town v Telford United *May 5 1990*
4890	Wycombe Wanderers v Kettering *Apr 8 1989*	4159	Lincoln City v Wealdstone *Apr 16 1988*
4872	Yeovil Town v Weymouth *Dec 26 1979*	4135	Kettering Town v Lincoln City *Apr 23 1988*
4741	Darlington v Barrow *Dec 26 1989*	4130	Barnet v Enfield *Dec 26 1986*
4624	Lincoln City v Barnet *Oct 28 1987*	4121	Lincoln City v Kidderminster H *Dec 28 1987*
4546	Darlington v Macclesfield Town *Apr 3 1990*	4105	Barnet v Enfield *Dec 26 1987*

CLUB RECORDS

	Biggest win	Heaviest defeat	Highest attendance
Altrincham	9-2 v Merthyr (90/1)	2-7 v Maidstone (88/9)	3000 v Barnet (90/1)
AP Leamington	5-0 v Telford (79/80)	0-7 v Bath (81/2)	968 v Northwich (79/80)
Aylesbury United	4-1 v Weymouth (88/9)	0-5 v Welling, Runcorn (88/9)	2406 v Wycombe (88/9)
Bangor City	5-1 v Redditch (79/80A), Barrow (82/3A)	1-6 v Maidstone (82/3)	1500 v Altrincham (79/80)
Barnet	8-1 v Fisher (90/91)	0-6 v Wealdstone (82/3)	5880 v Darlington (89/90)
Barrow	6-0 v Frickley (83/4)	0-6 v Bath (85/6)	4244 v Darlington (89/90)
Bath City	7-0 v AP Leamington (81/2)	0-6 v Maidstone (79/80)	1840 v Yeovil (79/80)
Boston United	6-0 v Maidstone (81/2), Gateshead (86/7)	1-7 v Frickley (83/4)	5822 v Lincoln (87/8)
Cheltenham Town	6-1 v Dagenham (86/7)	0-5 v Runcorn (85/6), Altrincham (89/90)	2622 v Darlington (89/90)
Chorley	4-0 v Northwich (88/9A), Welling (89/90), Telford (89/90A)	0-5 v Barnet (89/90)	1881 v Darlington (89/90)
Colchester United	4-0 v Northwich (90/1)	0-3 v Merthyr (90/1)	7221 v Altrincham (90/1)
Dagenham	6-2 v Trowbridge (83/4)	0-6 v Altrincham (87/8)	1243 v Enfield (82/3)
Darlington	6-1 v Boston (89/90)	2-3 v Kidderminster (89/90)	5525 v Cheltenham (89/90)
Dartford	5-0 v Yeovil (81/2)	0-5 v Runcorn (85/6)	1182 v Gravesend (81/2)
Enfield	6-0 v Worcester (84/5)	0-9 v Runcorn (89/90)	2240 v Barnet (88/9)
Farnborough Town	4-0 v Cheltenham (89/90)	0-4 v Cheltenham (89/90)	1925 v Wycombe (89/90)
Fisher Athletic	5-1 v Dagenham (87/8H&A)	1-8 v Barnet (90/1)	4283 v Barnet (90/1)
Frickley Athletic	7-1 v Boston (83/4)	1-7 v Telford (81/2)	988 v Altrincham (84/5)
Gateshead	5-1 v Barrow, Telford (90/1)	0-9 v Sutton (90/1H)	972 v Barnet (90/1)
Gravesend & Northfleet	5-1 v Barrow (79/80)	0-5 v Scarborough (81/2)	2051 v Dartford (81/2)
Kettering Town	6-1 v Frickley (80/1), Bath (84/5A)	0-8 v Sutton (86/7)	5020 v Colchester (90/1)
Kidderminster Harriers	8-2 v Wycombe (85/6)	0-5 v Maidstone (86/7)	2841 v Macclesfield (88/9)
Lincoln City	5-0 v Altrincham (87/8)	1-4 v Sutton, Runcorn (87/8)	9432 v Wycombe (87/8)

Macclesfield Town	5-0 v Northwich (87/8)	0-5 v Wycombe (87/8)	3143 v Darlington (89/90)
Maidstone United	6-0 v Bath (79/80), Scarborough (82/3), Trowbridge (82/3), Telford (83/4)	0-6 v Boston (81/2)	2861 v Kettering (88/9)
Merthyr Tydfil	7-0 v Fisher (90/1)	2-9 v Altrincham (90/1)	3253 v Darlington (89/90)
Newport County	4-0 v Weymouth (88/9)	1-7 v Barnet (88/9H)	1871 v Kettering (88/9)
Northwich Victoria	6-0 v Boston (87/8)	1-6 v Barrow, Maidstone (81/2)	2530 v Altrincham (80/1)
Nuneaton Borough	5-0 v Bath (82/3), Yeovil (84/5)	0-6 v Wealdstone (86/7)	1970 v Kettering (79/80)
Redditch United	4-1 v Wealdstone (79/80)	0-6 v Weymouth (79/80)	936 v Worcester (79/80)
Runcorn	9-0 v Enfield (89/90)	1-6 v Bath (90/1)	1682 v Enfield (81/2)
Scarborough	6-1 v Bath (79/80), AP Leamington (81/2)	0-6 v Maidstone (82/3)	5640 v Weymouth (86/7)
Slough Town	3-0 v Barrow (90/1)	2-7 v Yeovil (90/1)	3394 v Wycombe (90/1)
Stafford Rangers	5-0 v Welling (87/8A)	1-6 v Wycombe (88/9)	2658 v Altrincham (90/1)
Sutton United	9-0 v Gateshead (90/1A)	2-6 v Barnet (87/8)	1496 v Colchester (90/1)
Telford United	7-1 v Frickley (81/2)	0-6 v Maidstone (83/4)	2824 v Barnet (87/8)
Trowbridge Town	3-0 v Maidstone (81/2)	0-6 v Maidstone (82/3), Wealdstone (83/4)	1967 v Bath (83/4)
Wealdstone	6-0 v Barnet (82/3), Trowbridge (83/4), Nuneaton (86/7)	0-7 v Barnet (84/5)	1725 v Enfield (82/3)
Welling United	6-0 v Boston (89/90), Gateshead (90/1)	0-5 v Stafford (87/8H)	2621 v Darlington (89/90)
Weymouth	6-0 v Redditch (79/80)	0-5 v Boston (85/6), Welling (86/7)	3500 v Lincoln (87/8)
Worcester City	4-0 v Bath (79/80A), Barnet (80/1), Barrow (81/2) Yeovil (83/4)	0-6 v Enfield (84/5)	2405 v Weymouth (79/80)
Wycombe Wanderers	6-1 v Stafford (88/9), Fisher (89/90)	0-7 v Barnet (87/8H)	4890 v Kettering (88/9)
Yeovil Town	7-2 v Slough (90/1)	1-7 v Altrincham (81/2)	4872 v Weymouth (79/80)

Abbreviations: H = Home, A = Away
Unless stated otherwise, all record wins are at home, defeats away.
Results are not necessarily most goals scored/conceded, e.g. a 5-0 win counts as greater than 7-3, etc.
Where a team has lost by a similar number of goals, the higher score is shown, e.g. 6-1 rather than 5-0.
All records compiled and researched by Steven Penny (AFS member).

ALL TIME LEADING SCORERS 1980-91

	80	81	82	83	84	85	86	87	88	89	90	91	Total
				Bangor		Runcorn						Barnet	
Mark Carter				9	17	12	23	30	22	23	19	18/1	174
		Kettering			Barnet					Wycombe		Barnet	
Nicky Evans*	13	24	11	6	8	13	20	22	22	5/3	4	7/9	167
			Kettering		Nuneaton			Kettering		Barnet			
Frank Murphy*			21	22	11/5	21	15	4	13	14	9	4	139
			AP Leam				Kidderminster					Cheltenham	
Kim Casey			11				36	38	17	3	16	14	135
					Yeovil	Weymouth			Maidstone	Yeovil	Alty Runcorn		
Mick Doherty					14	4/13	25	15	6/4	7/0	18		106
			Trowbridge			Kidderminster							
Paul Davies**			8	0		19	21	15	23	19	0	6	111
	Barrow												
Colin Cowperthwaite	12	15	16	15		13	15				12	18	116
		Worcester				Kidderminster						Chelt/Stafford	
Mick Tuohy		8	18	14	8	11	12	8	7	10	1	0/7	104
	Telford	Northwich	Scarboro'	Telford					Alty Runcorn				
Colin Williams	2/3	25	26	11	11	4	10	4	0/0				96
		Boston									Alty		
Chris Cook		1	0	6	17	8	13	23	6	15	3/0	3	95
				Nuneaton								Barnet (loan)	
Paul Culpin				13	41	36						2	92
				Wealdstone									
Mark Graves				23	30	15	10	12					90
		Stafford							Macclesfield				
Steve Burr*		2	14	12					18	21	16	11	94
					Telford		Runcorn		Stafford		Telford	Altrincham	
Ken McKenna					8	18	23	5		4	12	22	92

* Also scored one versus Newport 1988-89, since expunged   ** Scored two versus Newport

FOUR OR MORE GOALS IN A GAME

Colin **Cowperthwaite** (Barrow) 4 v Kettering away Dec 8 1979

Graham **Smith** (Northwich) 5 v Barrow Dec 26 1979

Tom **Paterson** (Weymouth) 4 v Bangor City Apr 4 1980

Colin **Williams** (Northwich) 4 v Gravesend Oct 10 1980

Nicky **Evans** (Kettering) 4 v Nuneaton Borough away Apr 18 1981

Barry **Whitbread** (Altrincham) 4 v Runcorn Sep 8 1981

Damien **Richardson** (Gravesend) 4 v AP Leamington Feb 6 1982

John **Rogers** (Altrincham) 5 v Worcester City Apr 5 1982

John **Bartley** (Maidstone Utd) 4 v Scarborough May 7 1983

Paul **Culpin** (Nuneaton Borough) 5 v Barrow Dec 14 1985

Steve **Skeete** (Runcorn) 4 v Kidderminster Nov 27 1985

Dave **Singleton** (Bath City) 4 v Barrow Dec 14 1985

Chris **Townsend** (Cheltenham Town) 4 v Nuneaton Borough Apr 19 1986, (Bath City) 4 v Northwich Vic Apr 16 1991

Paul **McKinnon** (Sutton Utd) 4 v Kettering Town Oct 14 1986

Nicky **Evans** (Barnet) 4 v Wycombe Wanderers away Sep 15 1987

Nicky **Francis** (Enfield) 5 v Wycombe Wanderers away Oct 10 1987

Lenny **Dennis** (Sutton Utd) 4 v Welling Utd away Jan 2 1988

Mark **Boyland** (Cheltenham Town) 4 v Chorley away Mar 11 1989

Mick **Doherty** (Runcorn) 5 v Enfield Mar 3 1990

Hughie **Mann** (Fisher Athletic) 4 v Merthyr Tydfil May 5 1990

Ian **Benbow** (Kettering) 4 v Telford Apr 6 1991

Gary **Bull** (Barnet) 4 v Slough Town Aug 21 1990, 4 v Fisher Athletic Oct 16 1990

Chris **Burton** (Cheltenham) 4 v Boston Utd May 1 1991

Mark **Carter** (Runcorn) 4 v Kidderminster Sep 15 1990

Chris **Cook** (Boston United) 4 v Lowestoft Town Sep 15 1990

Malcolm **O'Connor** (Northwich Vic) 4 v Cheltenham Town May 4 1991

Mark **West** (Wycombe Wanderers) 4 v Kettering Nov 3 1990, 4 v Sutton Utd Dec 15 1990

Left

Mark Carter has scored more goals (174) in the Conference than any other striker. He was transferred to Barnet in their promotion season having spent most of his career with Runcorn.

Photo: W Leigh

STAR NAMES TO APPEAR WITH LEAGUE CLUBS

ALTRINCHAM – **Alex Stepney** (Man Utd & England), **Roger Kenyon** (Everton)

BARNET – **Martin Chivers** (Spurs & England), **Steve Whitworth** (Leicester & England), **Mark Lawrenson** (Liverpool & Eire)

BARROW – **Jim Pearson** (Everton & Newcastle), **vic Halom** (Sunderland)

CHELTENHAM – **Andy Gray** (Everton, Aston Villa & Scotland)

CHORLEY – **Frank Worthington** (Leicester, Leeds & England)

DARLINGTON – **Frank Gray** (Leeds, Nottm Forest & Scotland)

ENFIELD – **Jimmy Neighbour** (Spurs)

FISHER ATHLETIC – **Malcolm Allison** (Manager) (West Ham, Man City)

GATESHEAD – **Terry Hibbitt** (Leeds, Newcastle & Birmingham), **Pop Robson** (Newcastle, West Ham & Sunderland), **Jim Pearson** (Everton & Newcastle)

KETTERING – **Steve Daley** (Wolves, Man City), **Dennis Mortimer** (Coventry & Aston Villa)

KIDDERMINSTER – **Jim Arnold** (Everton)

MACCLESFIELD – **Derek Parlane** (Rangers, Leeds, Man City & Scotland)

MAIDSTONE UTD – **Peter Taylor** (Crystal Palace, Spurs & England)

NEWPORT COUNTY – **John Mahoney** (Manager) (Stoke & Wales)

NORTHWICH – **Brian Hall** (Liverpool), **Gordon Hill** (Man Utd & England), **Alan Kennedy** (Newcastle, Liverpool & England), **Stuart Pearson** (Manager) (Man Utd & England), **Peter Barnes** (Man C, Leeds & England)

NUNEATON – **Jon Samuels** (Arsenal & Leicester), **Jimmy Holmes** (Coventry & Spurs)

SCARBOROUGH – **Peter Springett** (Sheffield Wednesday), **Colin Appleton** (Manager) (Leicester)

STAFFORD – **Gordon Hill** (Man Utd & England)

TELFORD – **Gordon Banks** (Manager) (Leicester, Stoke & England), **Gerry Daly** (Derby & Eire)

TROWBRIDGE – **Alan Birchenall** (Sheffield Utd & Leicester), **George Armstrong** (Arsenal)

WORCESTER – **Willie Carr** (Coventry, Wolves & Scotland), **Phil Parkes** (Wolves)

WYCOMBE – **Martin O'Neill** (Manager) (Nottm Forest & N Ireland)

FA CUP ACHIEVEMENTS

BEST PROGRESS

Fifth Round – Telford United (1984/85)

HIGHEST AWAY ATTENDANCES

47 402 – Everton v Telford United (84/5)
37 170 – Liverpool v Altrincham (80/1)
23 073 – Norwich City v Sutton United (88/9)
21 488 – Derby County v Telford United (83/4)

HIGHEST HOME ATTENDANCES

9058 – Bath City v Bristol City (86/7) *
9003 – Darlington v Cambridge United (89/90)
8124 – Telford United v Darlington (84/5)
8000 – Sutton United v Coventry City (88/9)
7844 – Altrincham v Orient (79/80)
* (played at Ashton Gate, Bristol)

Above
A moment to remember. Matthew Hanlon scores the winning goal for Sutton United against First Division Coventry City. Just note how many Sutton players were in the area!
Right
To play at Anfield is exciting enough. But to score in the FA Cup against Liverpool must be unbelievable! Graham Heathcote slots home a penalty in 1981 for Altrincham.   Photo: John Rooney

FOOTBALL LEAGUE CLUBS BEATEN BY APL MEMBERS

1979/80
Altrincham bt Crewe Alex (4)
Altrincham bt Rotherham Utd (3)
1980/81
Altrincham bt Scunthorpe (4)
1981/82
Altrincham bt Sheffield Utd (4)
Enfield bt Wimbledon (3)
Altrincham bt York City (4)
1982/83
Boston Utd bt Crewe Alex (4)
Altrincham bt Rochdale (4)
Telford Utd bt Wigan Ath (3)
Northwich Vic bt Chester (4)
Worcester City bt Wrexham (3)
Weymouth bt Cardiff City (3)
1983/84
Telford Utd bt Stockport (4)
Maidstone Utd bt Exeter (3)
Worcester City bt Aldershot (4)
Telford Utd bt Northampton (4)
Telford Utd bt Rochdale (4)
( ) = Division
Clubs with most 'scalps' – Altrincham & Telford Utd, 10 each
Most 'scalped' club Crewe Alexandra 4

1984/85
Northwich Vic bt Crewe Alex (4)
Altrincham bt Blackpool (4)
Telford Utd bt Lincoln City (3)
Dagenham bt Swindon Town (4)
Enfield bt Exeter City (4)
Telford Utd bt Preston NE (3)
Dagenham bt Peterborough Utd (4)
Telford Utd bt Bradford City (3)
Telford Utd bt Darlington (4)
1985/86
Telford Utd bt Stockport (4)
Wycombe Wdrs bt Colchester (4)
Dagenham bt Cambridge Utd (4)
Frickley Ath bt Hartlepool (4)
Altrincham bt Blackpool (3)
Altrincham bt Birmingham City (1)
1986/87
Telford Utd bt Burnley (4)
Maidstone Utd bt Cambridge (4)

1987/88
Lincoln City bt Crewe Alex (4)
Runcorn bt Chester City (3)
Macclesfield Town bt Carlisle (4)
Sutton Utd bt Aldershot (3)
Sutton Utd bt Peterborough (4)
Macclesfield Town bt Rotherham (3)
1988/89
Altrincham bt Lincoln City (4)
Runcorn bt Wrexham (4)
Enfield bt Leyton Orient (4)
Kettering Town bt Bristol Rovers (3)
Sutton Utd bt Coventry City (1)
Kettering Town bt Halifax Town (4)
1989/90
Darlington bt Halifax Town (4)
1990/91
Colchester Utd bt Reading (3)
Barnet bt Northampton Town (4)

WHERE THEY WERE IN 1979

Football League Division 3 – Colchester United

Football League Division 4 – Darlington, Lincoln City, Newport County

Alliance Premier – Altrincham, AP Leamington, Bangor City, Barnet, Barrow, Bath City, Boston United, Gravesend, Kettering Town, Maidstone United, Northwich Victoria, Nuneaton Borough, Redditch United, Scarborough, Stafford Rangers, Telford United, Wealdstone, Weymouth, Worcester City, Yeovil Town.

Northern Premier – Frickley Athletic, Gateshead, Macclesfield, Runcorn.

Southern League Southern Division – Aylesbury United, Dartford

Southern League Midland Division – Cheltenham Town, Kidderminster Harriers, Merthyr Tydfil, Trowbridge Town

Isthmian League Premier Division – Dagenham, Enfield, Slough Town, Sutton United, Wycombe Wanderers

Isthmian League Division 1 – Farnborough Town

Cheshire County – Chorley, Witton Albion

Spartan – Fisher Athletic

Athenian – Welling United

No Such Club: Redbridge Forest (amalgamation of other clubs)

WHERE THEY ARE NOW

Football League Division 3 – Darlington

Football League Division 4 – Barnet, Lincoln City, Maidstone United, Scarborough

Football Conference – Altrincham, Barrow, Bath City, Boston, Cheltenham Town, Colchester United, Farnborough Town, Gateshead, Kettering Town, Kidderminster Harriers, Macclesfield, Merthyr Tydfil, Northwich Victoria, Redbridge Forest, Runcorn, Slough Town, Stafford Rangers, Telford United, Welling United, Witton Albion, Wycombe Wanderers, Yeovil Town

Northern Premier – Bangor City, Chorley, Frickley Athletic

Southern League Premier Division – Dartford, Fisher Athletic, Gravesend, Trowbridge, Wealdstone, Worcester City

Southern League Southern Division – Weymouth

Southern League Midland Division – Nuneaton Borough, Redditch United

Isthmian League Premier Division – Aylesbury United, Dagenham, Enfield, Sutton United

Defunct – AP Leamington, Newport County

(AP Leamington's final season, 1987/88, was spent in the Midland Combination. Newport spent their last season, 1988/89, in the Conference.)

The last Newport County team photo.

SEMI-PROFESSIONAL INTERNATIONALS

INTRODUCTION

After the demise of the 'amateur' in 1974 there were no real representative honours available to 95% of English footballers.

Office Cleaning Services (OCS) did sponsor a very popular inter-league knock out tournament in 1976, in which the senior leagues in the country played each other. Very strong representative sides were fielded and in the first tournament The Southern League beat The Northern Premier League at Yeovil and in the second year The Cheshire County League beat The Southern League to cause quite a surprise at the time. Looking back at the calibre of John Williams' squad (Micky Roberts, George Oghani, Steve Joel, etc) perhaps it wasn't such a shock.

In the following year The Alliance Premier League was formed and claimed a bye to the final. As this was not acceptable to the other leagues and of course the cream of the players were in the Alliance, the purpose of the competition – to give representative football to the best non-league players and perhaps lead the way to semi-pro internationals – was no longer viable. The competition was withdrawn but it had led the way to a new series of Internationals as the Football Association invited Scotland, Italy and Holland to join them in an end of season four nations tournament.

Semi-Professional Internationals were introduced and have flourished ever since. The tournament was played through twice, in eight seasons, with all four countries acting as hosts twice and now regular internationals are played against Wales and Italy.

There is no doubt that this International level does deserve more attention. The England squad are a wonderful example to their level of the game and it is sad that more effort isn't made to give them more varied opposition and perhaps a new end of season tournament.

Skipper David Howell and Gary Simpson lead out the England Semi-Professional team against Eire in Cork in 1990.

ENGLISH SEMI-PROFESSIONAL INTERNATIONALS

Date	Opponents	Score	Players	Substitutes	Venue
31.5.79	Scotland	5-1	Arnold *Stafford* Thompson *Yeovil* Davison *Altrincham* Adamson (2p) 3 *Boston* Peake *Nuneaton* Jennings *Enfield* O'Keefe *Mossley* Phillips *Nuneaton* Mutrie 1 *B Spartans* Houghton *B Spartans* Whitbread 1 *Runcorn*	Simmonite *Boston* Watson *Wealdstone*	Stafford Rangers
3.6.79	Holland	1-0	Arnold *Stafford* Thompson *Yeovil* Davison *Altrincham* Adamson *Boston* Peake *Nuneaton* Jennings *Enfield* O'Keefe 1 *Mossley* Phillips *Nuneaton* Mutrie 1 *B Spartans* Watson *Wealdstone* Whitbread *Runcorn*	Simmonite *Boston*	Stafford Rangers
3.6.80	Italy	2-0	Clarke *B Spartans* Simmonite *Boston* Davison *Altrincham* Jennings *Enfield* Adamson *Boston* Mutrie *B Spartans* Watson *Wealdstone* Whitbread *Altrincham* Smith 1 *Mossley* Hill 1 *Maidstone* Hayman *Northwich V*	Merrick *Weymouth*	Veenendaal, Holland
5.6.80	Scotland	2-4	Parker *Yeovil* Simmonite *Boston* Davison *Altrincham* Jennings *Enfield* Merrick *Weymouth* Adamson *Boston* Mutrie 1 *B Spartans* Watson *Wealdstone* Smith *Mossley* Hill 1 *Maidstone* Hayman *Northwich V*	Phillips *Kettering* Whitbread *Altrincham* Clarke *B Spartans*	Veenendaal
7.6.80	Holland	2-1	Clarke *B Spartans* Stockley *Nuneaton* Hill *Maidstone* Jennings *Enfield* Simmonite *Boston* Phillips *Kettering* Adamson *Boston* Watson 1 *Wealdstone* Denham *Northwich V* Mutrie *B Spartans* Whitbread 1 *Altrincham*	Smith *Mossley*	Veenendaal, Holland
9.6.81	Holland	2-0	Clarke *B Spartans* Thompson *Maidstone* Davison 1p *Altrincham* Barrett *Enfield* Jennings *Enfield* Sellers *Scarborough* Finnigan *Weymouth* Watson *Scarborough* Howard *Altrincham* Williams 1 *Scarborough* Rogers *Altrincham*	Ovard *Maidstone*	Lucca, Italy
11.6.81	Scotland	0-0	Clarke *B Spartans* Thompson *Maidstone* Davison *Altrincham* Barrett *Enfield* Jennings *Enfield* Sellers *Scarborough* Finnigan *Weymouth* Watson *Scarborough* Howard *Altrincham* Williams *Scarborough* Rogers *Altrincham*	Johnson *Altrincham* Ovard *Maidstone*	Empoli, Italy
13.6.81	Italy	1-1	Clarke *B Spartans* Thompson *Maidstone* Davison 1p *Altrincham* Barrett *Enfield* Jennings *Enfield* Sellers *Scarborough* Watson *Scarborough* Johnson *Altrincham* Howard *Altrincham* Whitbread *Altrincham* Rogers *Altrincham*	Ovard *Maidstone*	Montecatini, Italy
27.4.82	Gibraltar	3-2	Phillips *Barnet* Barrett *Enfield* Davison *Altrincham* Jennings *Enfield* Waite *Enfield* Sellers *Scarborough* Srephens 1 *Sutton* Johnson *Altrincham* Ashford *Enfield* Howard *Altrincham* Rogers *Altrincham*	Smith *Alvechurch*	Gibraltar FA
1.6.82	Italy	0-0	Clarke *B Spartans* Thompson *Maidstone* Davison *Altrincham* Jennings *Enfield* Barrett *Enfield* Johnson *Altrincham* Watson *Scarborough* Stephens *Sutton* Howard *Altrincham* Williams *Scarborough* Smith *Alvechurch*	Rogers *Altrincham*	Pitlodrie, Aberdeen

Left

It's England's Trophy and captain Tony Jennings (in Dutch shirt), who was later to act as Team Manager for the side, receives the cup from Chairman of the FA's Representative Committee, Barney Mulrenan.

Below

The first Four Nations Tournament was played at Stafford and Northwich. In this photo the Dutch keeper saves from Eamonn O'Keefe and Les Mutrie (right) during England's 1-0 win in the Final at Marston Road.

Above   *One of the fastest players to wear an England shirt was Alan Cordice. He is seen here scoring with his head during one of England's greatest displays – their 6-0 thrashing of Holland at Scarborough in 1983.* Photo: Mike Joss
Top   *Those who saw England's displays in Scarborough in 1983 were convinced the quality of play surpassed anything they had seen before at non-league level. Victories over the Italians (2-0), Holland (6-0) and Scotland (2-1) gave them the championship and all credit to all concerned for the enjoyment this team gave.*

Date	Opponents	Score	Players	Substitutes	Venue
3.6.82	Holland	1-0	Clarke *B Spartans* Thompson *Maidstone* Davison *Altrincham* Jennings *Enfield* Barrett *Enfield* Johnson *Altrincham* Watson *Scarborough* Stephens *Sutton* Howard *Altrincham* Ashford 1 *Enfield* Smith *Alvechurch*	Sellers *Scarborough*	Pitlodrie, Aberdeen
5.6.82	Scotland	1-1	Clarke *B Spartans* Thompson *Maidstone* Davison *Altrincham* Jennings *Enfield* Barrett *Enfield* Sellers *Scarborough* Watson *Scarborough* Johnson 1 *Altrincham* Howard *Altrincham* Rogers *Altrincham* Ashford *Enfield*	Stephens *Sutton*	Pitlodrie, Aberdeen
31.5.83	Italy	2-0	Richardson *Maidstone* Thompson *Maidstone* Davison *Altrincham* Robinson *B Spartans* Barrett *Enfield* Sellers 1 *Scarborough* Watson *Maidstone* Johnson *Altrincham* Cordice 1 *Wealdstone* Williams *Telford* Ashford *Enfield*		Scarborough
2.6.83	Holland	6-0	Clarke *B Spartans* Thompson *Maidstone* Davison 1p *Altrincham* Robinson *B Spartans* Barrett *Enfield* Sellers *Scarborough* Watson 1 *Maidstone* Johnson 1 *Altrincham* Cordice 1 *Wealdstone* Williams 1 *Telford* Ashford 1 *Enfield*	Ironton *Enfield* Derbyshire *Mossley*	Scarborough
4.6.83	Scotland	2-1	Clarke *B Spartans* Thompson *Maidstone* Davison 1p *Altrincham* Robinson *B Spartans* Barrett *Enfield* Sellers *Scarborough* Watson *Maidstone* Johnson *Altrincham* Cordice *Wealdstone* Williams 1 *Telford* Ashford *Enfield*	Derbyshire *Mossley* Ward *Northwich V*	Scarborough
27.3.84	Wales	1-2	Richardson *Maidstone* Thompson *Maidstone* Robinson *B Spartans* Newson *Maidstone* Davison *Altrincham* Smith 1 *Runcorn* Morley *Nuneaton* Ironton *Enfield* Cordice *Wealdstone* Culpin *Nuneaton* Ashford *Enfield*	Barrett *Enfield* Watson *Maidstone*	Newton, Wales
5.6.84	Holland	3-3	Clarke *B Spartans* Thompson *Maidstone* Barrett 1 *Enfield* Newson *Maidstone* Davison 1p *Altrincham* Watson Maidstone Morley *Nuneaton* Taylor *Maidstone* Johnson 1 *Altrincham* Williams *Telford* Ashford *Enfield*		Parma AC SpA, Italy
7.6.84	Scotland	2-0	Clarke *B Spartans* Thompson *Maidstone* Barrett *Enfield* Newson *Maidstone* Davison *Altrincham* Watson *Maidstone* Morley *Nuneaton* Taylor *Maidstone* Johnson 1 *Altrincham* Williams 1 *Telford* Ashford 1 *Enfield*	Cordice *Wealdstone* Joseph *Telford*	Modena AC SpA, Italy
9.6.84	Italy	0-1	Clarke *B Spartans* Thompson *Maidstone* Robinson *B Spartans* Newson *Maidstone* Davison *Altrincham* Watson *Maidstone* Morley *Nuneaton* Taylor *Maidstone* Johnson *Altrincham* Williams *Telford* Ashford 1 *Enfield*	Cordice *Wealdstone* Pearce *Harrow*	AC Reggiana SpA, Italy
26.3.85	Wales	1-0	Charlton *Telford* Robinson 1 *B Spartans* Glover *Maidstone* Turner *Telford* Newton *Burton* Joseph *Telford* Morley *Nuneaton* Ashford *Enfield* Mell *Burton* Hooley *Frickley*	Pape *Harrow* Culpin *Nuneaton* Smithers *Nuneaton*	Telford
11.6.85	Italy	2-2	Charlton *Telford* Constantine *Altrincham* Barrett 1 *Enfield* Glover *Maidstone* Davison *Altrincham* Johnson *Altrincham* Joseph *Telford* Smithers *Nuneaton* Cordice *Wealdstone* Williams *Telford* Culpin 1 *Nuneaton*	Ashford *Enfield*	Houten, Holland

SEMI-PROFESSIONAL INTERNATIONALS

Date	Opponents	Score	Players	Substitutes	Venue
13.6.85	Holland	3-0	Pape *Harrow* Constantine *Altrincham* Barrett *Enfield* Glover *Maidstone* Davison *Altrincham* Newton *Burton* Joseph *Telford* Johnson *Altrincham* Cordice *Wealdstone* Williams *Telford* Culpin 3 *Nuneaton*	Howell *Enfield*	Vieuten, Holland
15.6.85	Scotland	1-3	Pape *Harrow* Constantine *Altrincham* Barrett *Enfield* Glover *Maidstone* Davison *Altrincham* Newton *Burton* Joseph *Telford* Johnson *Altrincham* Cordice *Wealdstone* Williams 1 *Telford* Culpin *Nuneaton*	Howell *Enfield* Morley *Nuneaton* Weymouth	Harderwijk, Holland
18.3.86	Wales	1-3	Richardson *Maidstone* Constantine *Wilton* Davison *Altrincham* Howell *Enfield* Wilcox *Frickley* Stephens *Sutton* Walker *B Spartans* Smithers *Nuneaton* Wilson *Frickley* Davies 1 *Kidderminster* Casey *Kidderminster*	Johnson *Altrincham* Joseph *Telford* Doherty *Weymouth* Pape *Enfield*	Merthyr Tydfil
24.5.86	Eire	2-1	Pape *Enfield* Shirtliff *Frickley* Davison *Altrincham* Howell *Enfield* Wilcox *Frickley* Stephens *Sutton* Walker *B Spartans* Johnson 1 *Altrincham* Ashford *Enfield* Richards *Enfield* Casey 1 *Kidderminster*	Simpson *Stafford* Buchanan *B Spartans* Pape *Enfield*	Kidderminster
26.5.86	Eire	2-1	Richardson *Maidstone* Shirtliff *Frickley* Davison *Altrincham* Howell *Enfield* Wilcox 1 *Frickley* Johnson *Altrincham* Clayton *Burton* Simpson *Stafford* Ashford *Enfield* Buchanan *B Spartans* Agana 1 *Weymouth*	Stephens *Sutton* Walker *B Spartans* Casey *Kidderminster*	Nuneaton Borough
17.3.87	Wales	2-2	Pape *Enfield* Shirtliff *Frickley* Thompson *Scarborough* Brazier *Kidderminster* Howell *Enfield* Jones *Weymouth* Margettison *Barnet* Joseph *Telford* Casey 1 *Kidderminster* Carter *Runcorn* Davies *Kidderminster*	Ashford 1 *Wycombe*	Gloucester City
18.5.87	Italy	1-2	Pape *Enfield* Shirtliff *Frickley* Howell 1 *Enfield* Cuddy *Altrincham* Thompson *Scarborough* Ashford *Wycombe* Farrelly *Altrincham* Simpson *Stafford* Casey *Kidderminster* Carter *Runcorn* Davies *Kidderminster*	Abbott *Welling* Joseph *Telford*	Dunfermline
20.5.87	Holland	4-0	Pape *Enfield* Shirtliff *Frickley* Howell *Enfield* Cuddy *Altrincham* Thompson *Scarborough* Ashford *Wycombe* Farrelly *Altrincham* Simpson *Stafford* Joseph *Telford* Carter 4 *Runcorn* Davies *Kidderminster*	Golley *Sutton* Humphries *Barnet*	Kircaldy
23.5.87	Scotland	2-1	Pape *Enfield* Cuddy *Altrincham* Howell 1 *Enfield* Golley *Sutton* Thompson *Scarborough* Ashford *Wycombe* Simpson *Stafford* Farrelly *Altrincham* Joseph *Telford* Carter 1 *Runcorn* Davies *Kidderminster*	Abbott *Welling* Walker *B Spartans*	Dunfermline
25.2.88	Wales	2-0	Pape *Enfield* Shirtliff *Frickley* Teale *Weymouth* Howell *Enfield* Densmore *Runcorn* Joseph *Telford* Golley *Sutton* Codnor *Barnet* Davies *Kidderminster* Carter 2 *Runcorn* Butler *Maidstone*	Brooks *Cheltenham* Norris *Telford* McKenna *Boston*	Rhyl

Date	Opponents	Score	Players	Substitutes	Venue
29.1.89	Italy	1-1	Pape *Enfield* Shirtliff *Boston* Gridlet *Hendon* Howell *Enfield* Densmore *Runcorn* Lake *Macclesfield* Bancroft *Kidderminster* Joseph *Telford* Golley *Maidstone* Carter 1 *Runcorn* Butler *Maidstone*	Davies *Kidderminster* Lee *Telford* Shearer *Cheltenham* Beeney *Maidstone*	La Spezia
21.3.89	Wales	2-0	Pape *Enfield* Shirtliff *Boston* Gridlet *Hendon* Howell *Enfield* Watts *Leytonstone* Joseph *Telford* Golley *Maidstone* Rogers *Sutton* Bancroft *Kidderminster* Carter 1 *Runcorn* Butler *Maidstone*	Cook *Kettering*	Kidder-minster
25.2.90	Italy	0-2	McKenna *Boston* Shirtliff *Boston* Howell *Enfield* Skivington *Barrow* Watts *Redbridge* Hessenthaler *Dartford* Rogers *Sutton* Joseph *Kidderminster* Simpson *Altrincham* Furlong *Enfield* Carter *Runcorn*	Pape *Enfield* Hone *Welling* Conner *Dartford* Bancroft *Kidderminster* Cook *Kettering*	Salerno
6.3.90	Wales	0-0	Pape *Enfield* Shirtliff *Boston* Bancroft *Kidderminster* Howell *Enfield* Skivington *Barrow* Gridelet *Barnet* Askey *Macclesfield* Hanlon *Macclesfield* Furlong *Enfield* Ashford *Redbridge* Simpson *Altrincham*	McKenna *Boston* Watts *Redbridge* Rogers *Sutton* Ekoku *Sutton* Brooks *Cheltenham*	Merthyr Tydfil
25.5.90	Eire	2-1	McKenna *Boston* Shirtliff *Boston* Bancroft *Kidderminster* Watts *Redbridge* Howell *Enfield* Gridelet *Barnet* Brooks *Cheltenham* Clarke *Barnet* Carter 2 (1p) *Runcorn* Ashford *Redbridge* Simpson *Altrincham*	Rogers *Sutton* Furlong *Enfield* Joseph *Kidderminster*	Dublin
27.5.90	Eire	3-0	Pape *Enfield* Shirtliff *Boston* Rogers *Sutton* Watts *Redbridge* Howell *Enfield* Gridelet *Barnet* Joseph *Kidderminster* Furlong 1 *Enfield* Carter 1 *Runcorn* Ashford 1 *Redbridge* Simpson *Altrincham*	McKenna *Boston* Bancroft *Kidderminster* Brooks *Cheltenham* Clarke *Barnet* Skivington *Barrow*	Cork
5.3.91	Italy	0-0	McKenna *Boston* Lee *Witton* Watts *Redbridge* Skivington *Barrow* Nicol *Kettering* Conner *Redbridge* Lowe *Barnet* Rogers *Sutton* Carter *Barnet* Furlong *Enfield* Showler *Altrincham*	Ashford *Redbridge* Willis *Barnet*	Kettering
17.5.91	Wales	1-2	McKenna *Boston* Lee *Witton* Bancroft *Kettering* Skivington *Barrow* Nicol *Kettering* Conner *Redbridge* Lowe *Barnet* Rogers *Sutton* West *Wycombe* Todd *Berwick* Furlong *Enfield*	Showler *Altrincham* Humphreys *Kidderminster* Carter *Barnet*	Stafford

SEMI-PROFESSIONAL INTERNATIONALS

ENGLAND SEMI-PROFESSIONAL INTERNATIONAL CAPS 1979-1991

Gary Abbot (Welling) 87 v I(Sub) S(Sub) (2)
David Adamson (Boston Utd) 79 v SH, 80 v ISH (5)
Tony Agana (Weymouth) 86 v RI (1)
Jim Arnold (Stafford Rangers) 79 v SH (2)
Noel Ashford (Enfield & Redbridge For) 82 v GHS, 83 v IHS, 84 v WHSI, 85 v WI(Sub), 86 v Rep Ireland, RI, 87 v W(Sub) IHS, 90 v WRI(2), 91 v I(Sub) (22)
John Askey (Macclesfield) 90 v W (1)
Paul Bancroft (Kidderminster & Kettering T) 89 v IW, 90 v IWRI(2) 91 v W (7)
Keith Barrett (Enfield) 81 v HSI, 82 v GIHS, 83 v IHS, 84 v W(Sub) HS, 85 v IHS, 91 v Italy (17)
Mark Beeney (Maidstone) 89 v I(Sub) (1)
Colin Brazier (Kidderminster) 87 v W (1)
Steve Brooks (Cheltenham) 88 v W(Sub), 90 v W (3)
David Buchanan (Blyth) 86 v RI(Sub) RI (2)
Steve Butler (Maidstone) 88 v W, 89 v IW (3)
Mark Carter (Runcorn & Barnet) 87 v WIHS, 88 v W, 89 v IW, 90 v IRI(2), 91 v I, W(Sub) (11)
Kim Casey (Kidderminster) 86 v WRI, RI(Sub), 87 v WI (5)
Kevin Charlton (Telford) 85 v WI (2)
Andrew Clarke (Barnet) 90 v RI(2), (2)
David Clarke (Blyth Spartans) 80 v IS(Sub) H, 81 v HSI, 82 v IHS, 83 v HS, 84 v HSI (14)
Gary Clayton (Burton) 86 v RI (1)
Robert Codner (Barnet) 88 v W (1)
Steve Conner (Dartford & Redbridge F) 90 v I, 91 v I, W (3)
David Constantine (Altrincham) 85 v IHS, 86 v W (4)
Robbie Cooke (Kettering) 89 v W(Sub), 90 v I (2)
Alan Cordice (Wealdstone) 83 v IHS, 84 v WS(Sub), I(Sub), 85 v IHS (9)
Paul Cuddy (Altrincham) 87 v IHS (3)
Paul Culpin (Nuneaton) 84 v W, 85 v W(Sub) IHS (5)
Paul Davies (Kidderminster) 86 v W, 87 v WIS, 88 v W, 89 v W (6)
John Davison (Altrincham) 79 v SH, 80 v IS, 81 v HSI, 82 v GIHS, 83 v IHS, 84 v WHIS, 85 v IHS, 86 v WRI, RI (24)
John Denham (Northwich Victoria) 80 v H (1)
Peter Densmore (Runcorn) 88 v W, 89 v I (2)
Phil Derbyshire (Mossley) 83 v H(Sub) S(Sub) (2)
Mick Doherty (Weymouth) 86 v W(Sub) (1)
Mick Farrelly (Altrincham) 87 v IHS (3)
Trevor Finnegan (Weymouth) 81 v HS (2)
Paul Furlong (Enfield) 90 v IIR(2), 91 v I, W (5)
John Glover (Maidstone Utd) 85 v WIHS (4)
Mark Golley (Sutton) 87 v H(Sub) S, 88 v W, 89 v IW (5)
Phil Gridlet (Hendon & Barnet) 89 v IW, 90 v WIR(2) (5)
Steve Hancock (Macclesfield) 90 v W (1)
Steve Hanlon (Macclesfield T) 90 v W (1)
Andy Hessenthaler (Dartford) 90 v I (1)
Kenny Hill (Maidstone Utd) 80 v ISH (3)
Mark Hone (Welling) 90 v I (1)
Gary Hooley (Frickley) 85 v W (1)
Keith Houghton (Blyth Spartans) 79 v S (1)
Barry Howard (Altrincham) 81 v HSI, 82 v GIHS (7)

David Howell (Enfield) 85 v H(Sub) S(Sub), 86 v WRI, 87 v WIHS, 88 v W, 89 v IW, 90 v IWRI(2) (15)
Delwyn Humphreys (Kidderminster) 91 v W(Sub) (1)
Steve Humphries (Barnet) 87 v H(Sub) (1)
Nicky Ironton (Enfield) 83 v H(Sub), 84 v W (2)
Tony Jennings (Enfield) 79 v SH, 80 v ISH, 81 v HSI, 82 v GIHS (12)
Jeff Johnson (Altrincham) 81 v SI, 82 v GIHS, 83 v IHS, 84 v HSI, 85 v IHS, 86 v W(Sub) RI(2) (17)
Tom Jones (Weymouth) 87 v W (1)
Antone Joseph (Telford Utd & Kidderminster) 84 v S(Sub), 85 v WIHS, 86 v W(Sub), 87 v WI(Sub) H, 88 v W, 89 v IW, 90 v IR(2) (14)
Mike Lake (Macclesfield) 89 v I (1)
Andy Lee (Telford) 89 v I(Sub), 91 v I, W (3)
Kenny Lowe (Barnet) 91 v I, W (2)
John McKenna (Boston Utd) 88 v W(Sub), 90 v IR(2), 91 v I, W (6)
Paul Mayman (Northwich Vic) 80 v IS (2)
Stewart Mell (Burton) 85 v W (1)
Neil Merrick (Weymouth) 80 v I(Sub) S (2)
Trevor Morley (Nuneaton Bor) 84 v WHSI, 85 v WS(Sub) (6)
Les Mutrie (Blyth Spartans) 79 v SH, 80 v ISH (5)
Mark Newson (Maidstone U) 84 v WHSI, 85 v W (5)
Doug Newton (Burton) 85 v WHS (3)
Paul Nicol (Kettering) 91 v I, W (2)
Steve Norris (Telford) 88 v W(Sub) (1)
Eamon O'Keefe (Mossley) 79 v SH (2)

John Davison, the most capped England International skippered the side from left back and also scored 5 penalties.

234

Frank Ovard (Maidstone) 81 v H(Sub) S(Sub) I(Sub) (3)

Andy Pape (Harrow & Enfield) 85 v W(Sub) HS, 86 v W(Sub) RI, 87 v WIHS, 88 v W, 89 v IW, 90 v IWE (15)

Brian Parker (Yeovil Town) 80 v S (1)

Trevor Peake (Nuneaton Bor) 79 v SH (2)

David Pearce (Harrow Bor) 84 v I(Sub) (1)

Brendan Phillips (Nuneaton B, Kettering) 79 v SH, 80 v S(Sub) H (4)

Gary Philips (Barnet) 82 v G (1)

Carl Richards (Enfield) 86 v RI (1)

Derek Richardson (Maidstone U) 83 v I, 84 v W, 86 v RI (4)

Peter Robinson (Blyth S) 84 v IHS, 84 v WI, 85 v W (6)

John Rogers (Altrincham) 81 v HSI, 82 v I(Sub) S (5)

Paul Rogers (Sutton) 89 v W, 90 v IR(2) 91 v W (5)

Neil Sellars (Scarborough) 81 v HSI, 82 v GH(Sub) S, 83 v IHS (5)

Peter Shearer (Cheltenham) 89 v I(Sub) (1)

Paul Shirtliff (Frickley & Boston) 86 v RI(2), 87 v WIH, 88 v W, 89 v IW, 90 v IWRI(2) (12)

Paul Showler (Altrincham) 91 v I, W(Sub) (2)

Gordon Simmonite (Boston Utd) 79 v S(Sub) H(Sub), 80 v ISH (5)

Gary Simpson (Stafford) 86 v RI(2), 87 v IHS, 90 v IWRI(2) (9)

Glenn Skivington (Barnet & Barrow) 90 v IWRI, 91 v I, W (5)

Alan Smith (Alvechurch) 82 v GIS (3)

Ian Smith (Mossley) 80 v ISH(Sub) (3)

Ossie Smith (Runcorn) 84 v W (1)

Tim Smithers (Nuneaton) 85 v W(Sub) I, 86 v W (3)

Mickey Stephens (Sutton Utd) 82 v GS(Sub), 86 v WIRI(Sub) (5)

Bob Stockley (Nuneaton Bor) 80 v H (1)

Peter Taylor (Maidstone) 84 v HSI (3)

Shaun Teale (Weymouth) 88 v W (1)

Brian Thompson (Yeovil & Maidstone) 79 v SH, 81 v HSI, 82 v IHS, 83 v IHS, 84 v WHSI (Gibraltar)

Kevin Todd (Berwick) 91 v W (1)

Tony Turner (Telford) 85 v W (1)

David Waite (Enfield) 82 v G (1)

Paul Walker (Blyth) 86 v WRI(Sub), 87 v S(Sub) (4)

Mark Ward (Northwich Victoria) 83 v S(Sub) (1)

John Watson (Wealdstone, Scarborough & Maidstone) 79 v S(Sub) H, 80 v ISH, 81 v HSI, 82 v IHS, 83 v IHS, 84 v W(Sub) HSI (18)

Paul Watts (Redbridge Forest) 89 v W, 90 v IR(2), 91 v I (5)

Mark West (Wycombe) 91 v W (1)

Barry Whitbread (Runcorn & Altrincham) 79 v SH, 80 v ISH, 81 v I (6)

Russ Wilcox (Frickley) 86 v WRI (2)

Colin Williams (Scarborough & Telford) 81 v HS, 82 v IHS (12)

Roger Willis (Barnet) 91 v I(Sub) (1)

Paul Wilson (Frickley) 86 v W (1)

Key: G=Gibraltar, H = Holland, I = Italy, RI = Eire, S = Scotland, W = Wales.

John Watson, another England captain who was a competitive mid field player.

Colin Williams, a classy striker who scored five goals in twelve games.

ENGLAND GOALSCORERS

Player	Clubs	Goals	Player	Clubs	Goals
Mark Carter	Runcorn	12	Barry Whitbread	Altrincham	2
Noel Ashford	Enfield, Wycombe	6	Tony Agana	Weymouth	1
John Davison	Altrincham, Runcorn	5 *	Paul Davies	Kidderminster	1
Colin Williams	Telford, Scarborough	5	Eamon O'Keefe	Mossley	1
Paul Culpin	Nuneaton	4	Peter Robinson	Blyth	1
Jeff Johnson	Altrincham	4	Neil Sellers	Scarborough	1
David Adamson	Boston	3 *	Ian Smith	Mossley	1
Keith Barrett	Enfield, Wycombe	2	Ossie Smith	Runcorn	1
Kim Casey	Kidderminster	2	Mickey Stephens	Sutton	1
Alan Cordice	Wealdstone	2	Russ Wilcox	Frickley	1
Kenny Hill	Maidstone	2			1 **
David Howell	Enfield	2	Paul Rogers	Sutton	1
Les Mutrie	Blyth	2			
John Watson	Wealdstone, Scarborough, Maidstone	2	* All penalties ** Own goal		

Mark Carter, England's record goalscorer who has totalled twelve in eleven games.

TRANSFERS

INTRODUCTION

The success of Barnet under the inspirational managership of Barry Fry has opened up a new world for senior semi-professional clubs. They now realise that many of the best players within their ranks are worth a lot of money to the right Football League Club and what's more, the Football League Clubs have learned that they usually get their money's worth when recruiting from non-league football. Andrew Clarke had trials with Manchester United and Arsenal, as many other clubs tried to make up their minds about Barnet's flying winger. Barry Fry held firm for the 'right price' and in the end it was Wimbledon who probably picked up a potential million pounds profit when they signed Andrew for £250,000. He had been playing in a London business league just two seasons ago and his discovery was as startling as that of Andy Hunt, who had joined Kettering Town from local football and found himself following such names as Stubbins, Milburn, Macdonald, Mirandinha and Quinn in the No. 9 shirt at Newcastle United within half a season.

Even the domestic transfers have reached £40,000 between Conference clubs and it was understandable that Barnet should be happy to splash out themselves, considering the wonderful income generated by some quite brilliant salesmanship – who can possibly follow Barry Fry?

TRANSFERS BETWEEN NON-LEAGUE AND LEAGUE CLUBS – £20,000 AND ABOVE

Fee	Player	From	To	Date
£250,000 + Int.	Andrew Clarke	Barnet	Wimbledon	1991
£175,000	Phil Gridelet	Barnet	Barnsley	1990
£150,000	Andy Hunt	Kettering	Newcastle United	1988
£125,000	Robert Codner	Barnet	Brighton	1988
£125,000	Nicky Bissett	Barnet	Brighton	1988
£100,000	Peter Guthrie	Weymouth	Tottenham	1988
£100,000 + Apps.	Stan Collymore	Stafford Rangers	Crystal Palace	1991
£80,000	Ian Woan	Runcorn	Nottingham Forest	1989
£75,000*	Iain Dowrie	Hendon	Luton	1988
£60,000	Cohen Griffith	Kettering	Cardiff City	1989
£60,000	Darren Carr	Burton Albion	Crystal Palace	1990
£60,000	Mike Lake	Macclesfield	Sheffield United	1989
£60,000	Paul Harding	Barnet	Notts County	1990
£60,000	Peter Guthrie	Tottenham Hotspur	Barnet	1989
£57,000**	Jason Dodd	Bath City	Southampton	1989
£52,000	Richard Hill	Nuneaton	Northampton	1985
£50,000	Neil Morton	Northwich	Chester City	1990
£50,000 + Int + Apps	Shaun Teale	Weymouth	AFC Bournemouth	1989
£50,000	Paul Culpin	Nuneaton	Coventry City	1985
£46,000	Steve Norris	Telford United	Scarborough	1988
£43,000	David Leworthy	Fareham	Tottenham Hotspur	1984
£40,000	Brett Angell	Cheltenham	Derby County	1988
£40,000***	John Goodman	Bromley	Millwall	1990
£35,000 + Apps	Andy Comyn	Alvechurch	Aston Villa	1989
£35,000	Trevor Senior	Dorchester	Portsmouth	1981
£35,000	Tony Agana	Weymouth	Watford	1987
£30,000	Keith Scott	Lincoln City	Wycombe	1991
£30,000	Steve Cotterill	Burton Albion	Wimbledon	1989
£30,000	Garry Birtles	Long Eaton Utd	Nottingham Forest	1976
£30,000	John Gassle	Burton Albion	Wimbledon	1989
£30,000	Paul Holsgrove	Wokingham	Luton	1991
£27,750	Trevor Peake	Nuneaton	Lincoln	1979
£27,000	John Barton	Worcester City	Everton	1978
£25,000	David Wiffill	Bath City	Manchester City	1980

Kettering Town's Cohen Griffith blasts past Darlington keeper Mark Prudhoe only for the ball to be handled on the line – he was sold to Cardiff City for £60,000 in 1989.

Fee	Player	From	To	Date
£25,000	Eamon O'Keefe	Mossley	Everton	1979
£25,000****	Mick Bodley	Northampton	Barnet	1990
£25,000 + Apps	Gary Piggott	Dudley Town	WBA	1991
£25,000	John Muir	Dudley Town	Doncaster Rovers	1990
£25,000	Richard Brown	Kettering	Blackburn	1990
£25,000	Chris Burns	Cheltenham	Portsmouth	1991
£25,000	Stuart Pearce	Wealdstone	Coventry	1983
£25,000	David Regis	Barnet	Notts County	1990
£25,000	Don Page	Runcorn	Wigan Ath	1989
£25,000	Mark Harris	Wokingham	Crystal Palace	1988
£21,275	John Cockerill	Stafford	Grimsby	1988
£20,000 + Apps	Andy McFarland	Cradley Town	Portsmouth	1991
£20,000	Tony Cunningham	Stourbridge	Lincoln City	1979
£20,000	Liburd Henry	Redbridge Forest	Watford	1990
£20,000	Andy Williams	Sutton Coldfield	Coventry	1985
£20,000	Neil Parsley	Witton Albion	Leeds	1988
£20,000	Trevor Morley	Nuneaton	Northampton	1985
£20,000	Eric Young	Slough	Brighton	1982
£20,000	Kerry Dixon	Dunstable	Reading	1980
£20,000	Gary Crosby	Grantham	Nottingham F	1987
£20,000	Kevin Wilson	Banbury	Derby	1979
£20,000	Tim Smithers	Nuneaton	Oxford Utd	1980

* Total amount received includes cut of transfer to West Ham 1991
** Total includes amount for playing for England under-21s
*** Transferred without actually playing for Bromley after summer move from Leyton-Wingate
**** Total includes £5,000 clause in transfer upon promotion to Football League
+ Apps   Fee increases according to number of appearances made
+ Int   Fee increases if international honours are won

Tony Agana (right) joined Watford from Weymouth for £35,000 in 1987

Photo: Dorset News

NON LEAGUE OLD BOYS XI

(Selected from players who enjoyed outstanding form in 1990-91)

TIM CLARK
(Halesowen Town to Coventry City)

JASON DODD
(Bath City to
Southampton)

NICKY BISSETT
(Barnet to Brighton)

TREVOR PEAKE
(Nuneaton to
Coventry City)

STUART PEARCE
(Wealdstone to
Coventry City. Now
Nottingham Forest)

PAUL HARDING
(Barnet to Notts
County)

ROBERT CODNER
(Barnet to Brighton)

GARY CROSBY
(Grantham to
Nottingham Forest)

IAN WOAN
(Runcorn to
Nottingham Forest)

TREVOR MORLEY
(Nuneaton to
Northampton. Now
West Ham United)

STEVE NORRIS
(Telford United to
Scarborough. Now
Halifax)

Two Bargains!

Above left *Mark Ward – Northwich Victoria to Oldham Athletic to West Ham United to Manchester City.*
Above right *Alan Smith – Alvechurch to Leicester City to Arsenal (and England).*   Photo: Bob Thomas
Below *Paul Gridelet and Andrew Clarke – £425,000 for Barnet.*   Photo: Eric Marsh

TRANSFERS BETWEEN NON-LEAGUE CLUBS – (£10,000 AND ABOVE)

Fee	Player	From	To	Date
£40,000	Gary Abbott	Barnet	Enfield	1988
£40,000	Mark Carter	Runcorn	Barnet	1991
£40,000	Kenny Lowe	Barrow	Barnet	1991
£35,000*	Ken Charlery	Fisher	Maidstone	1988
£32,000	Micky Evans	Barnet	Wycombe	1989
£27,500*	David Arter & Jeff Ross (combined fee)	Ashford	Hythe Town	1991
£25,000	Brendan Hackett & Steve Fergusson (combined fee)	Worcester	Gloucester	1991
£25,000	Kim Casey	Kidderminster	Cheltenham	1990
£25,000	Nicky Evans	Wycombe	Barnet	1991
£25,000	Duncan Horton	Welling	Barnet	1991
£25,000	Paul Harding	Enfield	Barnet	1989
£20,000	Noel Ashford	Barnet	Maidstone	1988
£20,000	Gary Donnellan	Yeovil	Enfield	1989
£20,000	Andy Lee	Telford	Colne Dynamoes	1990
£20,000	Edwin Stein	Dagenham	Barnet	1982
£17,500	Gary Jones	Grantham	Kettering	1989
£17,000	Anton Joseph	Telford	Kidderminster	1989
£16,000*	Mark Golley	Sutton Utd	Maidstone	1988
£15,000	Mark Doherty	Yeovil	Runcorn	1989
£15,000	Joe Jackson	Worcester	Yeovil	1990
£15,000	Joe Jackson	Yeovil	Dover	1991
£15,000	Dave Tomlinson	Boston Utd	Barnet	1990
£15,000	Tony Lynch	Wealdstone	Barnet	1990
£15,000	Jeff Sherwood	Yeovil	Gloucester	1991
£15,000	Dave Hadley	Moor Green	Kidderminster	1991
£15,000	Shaun Teale	Northwich	Weymouth	1987
£15,000	Phil Gridelet	Hendon	Barnet	1989
£15,000	Tony Rodwell	Runcorn	Colne Dynamoes	1989
£15,000	Jeff Meacham	Weymouth	Bath	1987
£15,000	Glyn Creaser	Barnet	Wycombe	1988
£15,000	Noel Ashford	Wycombe	Barnet	1987
£15,000	Kevin Durham	Wycombe	Barnet	1990
£15,000	Gary Abbott	Welling	Barnet	1987
£13,500	Colin Sowerby	Dartford	Redbridge F	1991
£13,000	Peter Conning	Weymouth	Yeovil	1988
£13,000	Paul Wilson	Boston Utd	Yeovil	1989
£12,500	Paul Shirtliff	Frickley	Boston Utd	1988
£12,000	Paul Bancroft	Burton Albion	Kidderminster	1987
£12,000	Paul Bancroft	Kidderminster	Kettering	1990
£12,000	Paul Richardson	Kettering	Barnet	1990
£12,000	Chris Townsend	Dorchester	Bath	1991
£12,000	Steve Butterworth	VS Rugby	Stafford	1991
£12,000	Derek Payne	Hayes	Barnet	1989
£11,000	Alan Kurila	Stafford	Kidderminster	1990
£10,000	Les Lawrence	Kettering	Aylesbury Utd	1988
£10,000	David Kitchen	Goole	Stafford	1989
£10,000	Martin Hardy	Worksop	Boston Utd	1989
£10,000	Dave Sansom	Barnet	Chesham Utd	1988
£10,000	Steve McNeilis	Northwich	Colne Dynamoes	1988
£10,000	Sean Norman	Wycombe	Wealdstone	1988
£10,000	Sean Norman	Wealdstone	Chesham Utd	1989
£10,000	Mark Whitehouse	Burton Albion	Kidderminster	1989
£10,000	Graham Westley	Barnet	Wycombe	1987
£10,000	Chris Townsend	Gloucester	Dorchester	1990
£10,000	Frank Murphy	Kettering	Barnet	1988
£10,000	Jeff Meacham	Bath	Trowbridge	1988
£10,000	Joe Connor	Hyde Utd	Witton Albion	1990
£10,000	Glenn Beech	Boston Utd	Kettering	1988

Kettering Town's Paul Bancroft (left) who has figured in two £12,000 transfers between non-league clubs, challenges Eddie McGoldrick who left Nuneaton Borough for Northampton Town before joining Crystal Palace.
Photo: Mick Cheney

At a time when arguments are raging about the influence of television and sponsors on our national sports, it may be good to reflect on the impact of the initial sponsorship of our regional Football Leagues in Britain.

I was lucky to be in the right place at the right time when, as a non-smoking public relations man for Carerras Rothmans, I was able to approach the Marketing Director with an idea for sponsoring local football leagues.

As the company policy at the time was to promote the Rothmans name at grass roots level, the idea of linking the company name with the town football teams in four leagues certainly appealed. So, first the Hellenic and then the Isthmian, Northern and Western Leagues added the name of Rothmans to their titles and the company had 'built-in' publicity through the local newspapers in over 100 towns. As the 'mentions' in one north eastern Sunday newspaper totalled ten on the back page alone, this was a major break-through for the press and publicity departments of many national companies who had spent hundreds of thousands on flashy sponsorships in which nobody cared a jot for the sponsors' efforts.

In semi-professional football, if an individual or a company invests time, money or care with your club or your league, than all concerned make an effort to repay them for their support. There is a genuine feeling of concern, and member clubs and league officials do all they can to ensure that the sponsors' efforts are appreciated.

This was certainly the case in the Rothmans experiment and I

The Rothmans touring party, selected from their sponsored leagues (four players each) who played four matches in the Canary Islands in 1969. Back row, left to right: Tommy Holden (Willington), Ronnie Dicks (Welton Rovers), Dave Lesbirel (Vale Recreation, Guernsey), Fred Hissett (Tow Law Town), Geoff Hurst (guest), Colin Shepherd (Moreton Town), Alan Hurford (Bridgwater Town), Rory Crick (First Tower, Jersey), Joe Scott (Falmouth Town), Rod Oland (Newbury Town), Dave Colyer (Sutton United), Bobby Green (Tooting & Mitchum), Mal Harkins (Dagenham). Front row: Alan Shoulder (Bishop Auckland), Bob Perrot (Glastonbury, with mascot), John Cooper (Leatherhead), Stan Bradley (Northern League), Ingram Whittingham (Isthmian League), Tony Williams, Norman Matthews (Hellenic League), Les Phillips (Western League), Jimmy Kelman (Hungerford Town, Team Manager), Mick Pugh (Moreton Town, Physio), Brian Faulkes (Hungerford Town).

Mentioned in Despatches … An illustration of how the sponsorship of competitions builds brand awareness among the readers of the sports pages.

EVENING Despatch | Sports Extra

DARLINGTON, SATURDAY, SEPTEMBER 25, 1976

ROTHMANS KNOCKOUT CUP FINAL

BLYTH KEEPER SAVES PENALTY

WHITBY took this afternoon's Rothman's Knockout Cup final at Spennymoor to Blyth, and should have opened the scoring, but missed a penalty.

Whitby, who had already beaten Blyth 5-2 in the league at Croft Park earlier this season were without Webb and Hempton. Blyth were without Ronnie Young, who is not eligible, and Alan Gauden, who is serving a club suspension.

Whitby: Coleby, Shepherd, Dillworth, Gibson, Stonehouse, Storey Linacre, Burluraux, McFadden, Poskett, Readman. Sub.: Bloor.

Blyth : Morgan, Waterson, Harrison, Dixon, Scott, Tones, Pink, Smith, Slane Dagless, Leeming. Sub.: Murray.

Whitby attacked from the kick off and Morgan had to race out to rob Readman of a possible scoring chance.

In Blyth's first attack Smith combined well with Pink, but Stonehouse was on hand to clear the danger. Early play, however, was being dictated by Whitby and a smart pass from Gibson found Poskett, but the Whitby inside left fired wide.

Keeping up a relentless barrage, Whitby, well led by Gibson forced attack after attack, but despite some good approach work were finding it difficult to penetrate the Blyth defence.

Readman had a hard ground shot saved at the second attempt by Morgan then the same player headed just wide.

RUGBY

Mowden's superiority on show

Mowden Park v Acklam

MOWDEN Park went into the lead when John MASON, the full back, came up to join his threequarters in a concerted attack on the visitors's line and took the defenders by surprise to score a well deserved try.

John Widdall converted the try and later kicked a penalty. Acklam got back in the game when Hoyle charged down a 25 yard drop out and started a break which led to Derek ROWLANDS scoring a try. **Half-time: Mowden Park 9, Acklam 4.**

Mowden's back row were having an impressive game and the home forwards were superior in the line-outs but both sides missed a number of penalties, probably because of the attrocious conditions.

Arthur Clark, Skol Northern League Chairman and Lawrie McWilliams, Free Trade Director, North East signing the new three year sponsorship agreement worth £170,000 between the League and Joshua Tetley & Son Ltd. at the League's Annual Dinner in May 1987 when the announcement was made.

know it is the same as far as the quite brilliant Vauxhall sponsorship of the Conference of the nineties.

I couldn't believe my luck as I had a good budget with which I could spend all my time thinking of ways in which Rothmans could promote themselves and at the same time help non-league football. We published monthly magazines, launched the Rothmans National Cup in which clubs from these four leagues (and indeed the Channel Islands) could play each other and even had the pleasure of organizing two tours

to the Canary Islands.

In return, all clubs offered to sell the Rothmans brands of cigarettes and some even opted for selling *only* the sponsor's brands. This sponsorship was an amazing success, and at about £8 per club per week for regular brand awareness and actual sales opportunities, it was a dream that continued beautifully until we entered the Common Market. Rothmans then had to invest all their spare money in an effort to keep the prices of their king size cigarettes down to compete with their rivals, and sponsorship fin-

ished overnight.

The principle of sponsorship is now with us for ever. It was the lively brain of Jimmy Hill who masterminded the sponsored awards (for goals and fair play) in the initial deal and it was his idea to introduce three points for a win. This was such a success that it didn't take long for the Football League to adopt the idea.

Rewards for goals and fair play were scorned by many, but with member clubs concentrating on the elimination of dissent and retaliation, the Isthmian clubs enjoyed their best FA Cup seasons for years and Blyth Spartans swept all before them without conceding a single caution. It was quite clear that disciplined sides won the honours, many friends and the respect of referees.

Since the Rothmans pioneering days, most leagues have acquired sponsors, and with the ever increasing popularity of the game at this level with more media coverage, the backers are certainly getting their money's worth. Live games on television, big matches 'piped' into clubrooms, and generally bigger at-tendances, all make the proposition more attractive.

During the depressing recession of the early nineties, it was good to see the positive attitude of DIADORA, an Italian sportswear company, with Seb Coe as Chairman, who took over the massive sponsorship of the Isthmian League in the most flamboyant style. I'm sure the wonderful FA Cup exploits of Woking did the Isthmian cause no harm at all!

The secret of good sponsorship is for the company to appoint someone within the company public relations depart-ment to liaise with the league officials. That person needs to be given the time to concentrate on the job and he or she should be someone who cares for the game as well as their parent company.

The appointment of 'Scott & Jones' as the promotions company to link with Alan Mackay's office at Vauxhall has probably proved the perfect method of gaining full advantage for the sponsor while giving football a truly prestigious sponsorship.

Tony Williams

Rothmans sponsored inter-league representative matches between 'their' four leagues. Here the Rothmans Isthmian League XI line up before playing the Rothmans Hellenic League at Loakes Park, Wycombe. Back row, left to right: Alan Phillips (Hendon), David Reid (Leatherhead), Howard Kettleborough (Hitchin Town), Peter Harris (Oxford City), Terry Reardon (Wycombe Wanderers), Alan Evans (Oxford City), Ray Eaton (Enfield). Front row: Tony Horseman (Wycombe Wanderers), Tony Jennings (Enfield), Larry Pritchard (Wycombe Wanderers), Chris Kelly (Leatherhead), Paul Giggle (Hitchin Town). Photo: Robert Mead

THE MEDIA DISCOVERS NON-LEAGUE FOOTBALL

The official link between the Alliance Premier League and the Fourth Division of the Football League in 1987 saw the acceptance of all the hard work that had been put in to create the non-league 'pyramid' of football.

The Football Association and the Alliance Premier Football League (now the Conference) had set the scene in which the Football League could hardly refuse to acknowledge the ready-made pyramid on which their Fourth Division would fit very nicely.

At the same time as this monumental step was about to be taken, a huge band of enthusiasts (groundhoppers) were 'collecting' football grounds by touring the country watching football at all levels, adding to the considerable number of loyal fans already supporting their own clubs every week. The non-league family was really growing – and the media don't miss much.

The Daily Telegraph had always found room for a Friday and Saturday non-league column plus a Monday review.

The Times and the Independent gave excellent features on Fridays and gradually the Sunday papers realised that a massive section of their readership was involved with football outside 'the 92'.

The Non-League Annual which started as a pocket book in 1978-79 has now developed into the FA Non-League Club Directory*. The 1992 edition will have 1008 pages and will feature every level of the huge 'pyramid' structure. The book is now a best-seller with W H Smith's every year and is the best-selling team sports annual at Sportspages, the sports bookshop in Charing Cross Road, London. Additional books such as 'The FA Non-League Football Grounds of Great Britain'* and 'The Non-League Footballer's Who's Who'* have also been very popular, and the game outside the Football League is also very well served by an excellent selection of magazines.

Indeed this level of the game enjoys the prestigious sponsorship of the Mail on Sunday whose awards are greatly appreciated and whose coverage is excellent.

Semi-professional clubs also enjoyed superb coverage in the FA Cup, in particular the 1990-91 competition, in which a number of live games were televised by the BBC and BSB, while Conference games were piped live into many clubs and pubs throughout the country.

SOME NON-LEAGUE FOOTBALL MAGAZINES

FOOTBALL FOCUS
A monthly mixture of news and photos with interesting articles.

PYRAMID FOOTBALL
A really newsy round-up of all that is happening in the leagues that make up the pyramid. (£7.50 for five issues per season. Tony Incenzo, P O Box 553, London N2 8LJ)

BUREAU OF NON-LEAGUE FOOTBALL
Full league tables and cup results on a monthly basis. (£1.00. Mike Ford, 173 Leytonstone Road, London E15)

NON LEAGUE TRAVELLER
Just what the groundhopper needs to give him all the weekly fixtures. (£29 for 36 issues)

THE COMMERCIAL MANAGER
A monthly which aims to help the club fund raisers. (£2.00)
(for details of these two contact Gary Harding 0775 821182)

THE NON-LEAGUE FOOTBALL MAGAZINE
A national monthly covering all non-league football, published by Burlington Publishing (10 Sheet Street, Windsor, Berkshire)

TEAM TALK
Produced by the Football Directories Team, this is also a national non-league monthly featuring the whole pyramid within its 68 pages. (£2 from Football Directories, North Curry, Taunton, Somerset, TA3 6DV (0823) 490684)

The Magazine for Non-League Fans By Non-League Fans

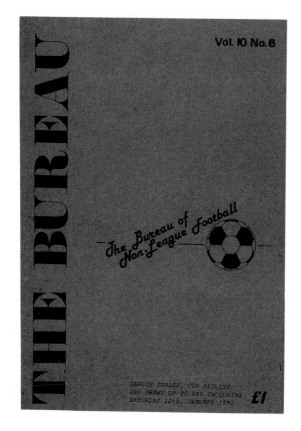

Vol. 10 No. 6

The Bureau of Non-League Football

LEAGUE TABLES, CUP RESULTS
AND DRAWS UP TO AND INCLUDING
SATURDAY 12th. JANUARY 1991

£1

Vol 4 — **NON LEAGUE TRAVELLER** — No. 14

Even transfers in and out of Non-League clubs became 'news' as players commanded large fees and leading Conference players were signed by First Division clubs.

The final example of just how the non-league game has been accepted must surely be seen in this book. Could you imagine Guinness Publishing bothering with a book like this ten years ago?

Times have certainly changed for the better, but we still have a way to go – just try selling adverts for a National Non-League Football magazine!

Tony Williams

* These three publications can be ordered from Football Directories, North Curry, Taunton, Somerset, TA3 6DV (0823 490684)

£1.40

non-league FOOTBALL

Vol. 3   No.1   SEPTEMBER 1991

BARNET DO IT AT LAST!
The Bees full Non-League Record

FA VASE
Guiseley show their style in classic Final

FA TROPHY
West makes his mark

NEWCOMERS
The Northern League joins the Pyramid

The COMMERCIAL MANAGER

The Football Club management magazine

Issue 3   ISSN 0962 — 886X   £2

CHESHAM UTD FC

A 'PREMIER' CLUB

FIRST ISSUE · AUGUST 1991 · £2.

TEAM TALK

Featuring Conference to County league football

F.A. TROPHY · CUP · VASE

THE NON-LEAGUE
FOOTBALL
MONTHLY

EXCLUSIVE
F.A. CUP
DRAW

F.A. TROPHY
+ VASE

CONFERENCE +
BEAZER, H.F.S.
DIADORA +
FEEDER LEAGUES

EDITOR:
TONY WILLIAMS

CLUB OF THE MONTH:- WOKING

9 770963 049002

THE FUTURE

Well, you've reached the end of our first Non-League Football Fact Book. As it has only 256 pages, it has obviously been impossible to include a completely comprehensive coverage of all that has happened in the development of the game outside the Football League, but I do hope you have enjoyed our choice of features.

The game is withstanding a power struggle between the Football Association, who look after the needs of all levels of the game, and the Football League, whose interests only really lie with their own 93 clubs.

At the time of writing, the outcome is in the balance, but a Premier Division of super clubs may well lead to an increase in clubs featured in the remainder of the Football League, so maybe we will see another structural change to the senior levels of the non-league 'pyramid' and there will be new talking points for future fact books.

What stands out within football is a really sincere caring for our national winter sport. Thousands of players, club and league officials, and of course the administrators at the Football Association have brought the game to its present position – one based on a very secure and well-planned 'pyramid'. Improvements will of course be made and changes will be proposed and sometimes introduced. Indeed, a look ahead to see the structure in 25 years time would be fascinating.

One thing is certain and that is that progress will be well-logged in the ever-improving library of non-league publications, and hopefully you will see a lot more non-league football on television.

It gives me a great sense of satisfaction to see this level of the game being enthused over by a growing audience. I have been thrilled with the enthusiasm of Guinness Publishing who decided that non-league football was ready for a book in their very popular sporting series of fact books.

If this book has introduced you to a new level of the game that you hadn't realised existed, then I hope you will keep up to date by following its progress through the publications we have listed. I will be happy to help in any way I can should you contact me through Football Directories and if you haven't already been, why not look in at your local non-league clubs – I'm sure you will be well received and pleasantly surprised.

There's no better picture with which to leave you! The spirit, sportsmanship and entertainment shown at Wembley when Gresley Rovers met Guiseley in the 1990-91 FA Vase Final (4-4 after extra time), was an inspiration to all lucky enough to be there. Managers Frank Norwood (Gresley Rovers, left) and Gordon Raynor show us what the game is all about. Full marks too to photographer Paul Dennis who caught this special moment.

Page numbers in *italics* refer to illustrations

The Author's thanks go to Paul Marsh (FA Cup statistics), Steve Penney (Conference statistics), Philip Pike (historical league and club features), Colin Startup (statistics), Steve Whitney (transfers), James Wright (club records and general help) and everyone at Football Directories, plus all the photographers and special thanks to typesetter John Dowell.

Tony Williams